edition 3

WW

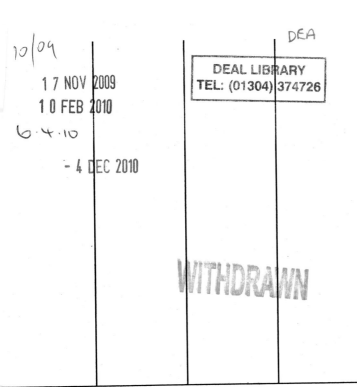

Bradt T
The Glo

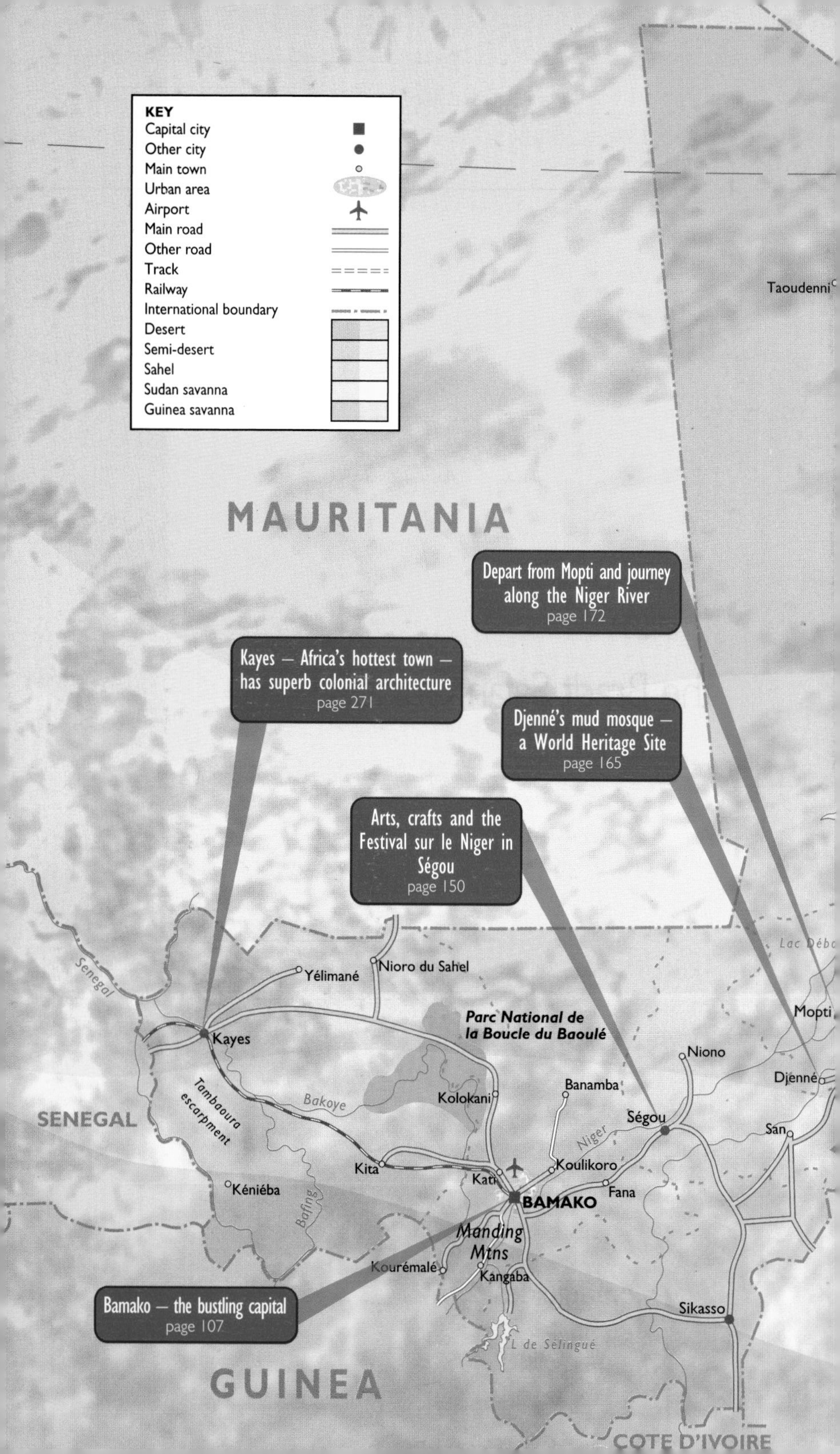
KEY
Capital city
Other city
Main town
Urban area
Airport
Main road
Other road
Track
Railway
International boundary
Desert
Semi-desert
Sahel
Sudan savanna
Guinea savanna
Taoudenni
MAURITANIA
Depart from Mopti and journey along the Niger River page 172
Kayes – Africa's hottest town – has superb colonial architecture page 271
Djenné's mud mosque – a World Heritage Site page 165
Arts, crafts and the Festival sur le Niger in Ségou page 150
Senegal
Yélimané
Nioro du Sahel
Lac Débo
Parc National de la Boucle du Baoulé
Kayes
Mopti
Niono
Djenné
Banamba
Tambaoura escarpment
Bakoye
Kolokani
SENEGAL
Ségou
Niger
San
Kita
Koulikoro
Kati
Kéniéba
Fana
BAMAKO
Bafing
Manding Mtns
Kourémalé
Kangaba
Bamako – the bustling capital page 107
Sikasso
L de Sélingué
GUINEA
COTE D'IVOIRE

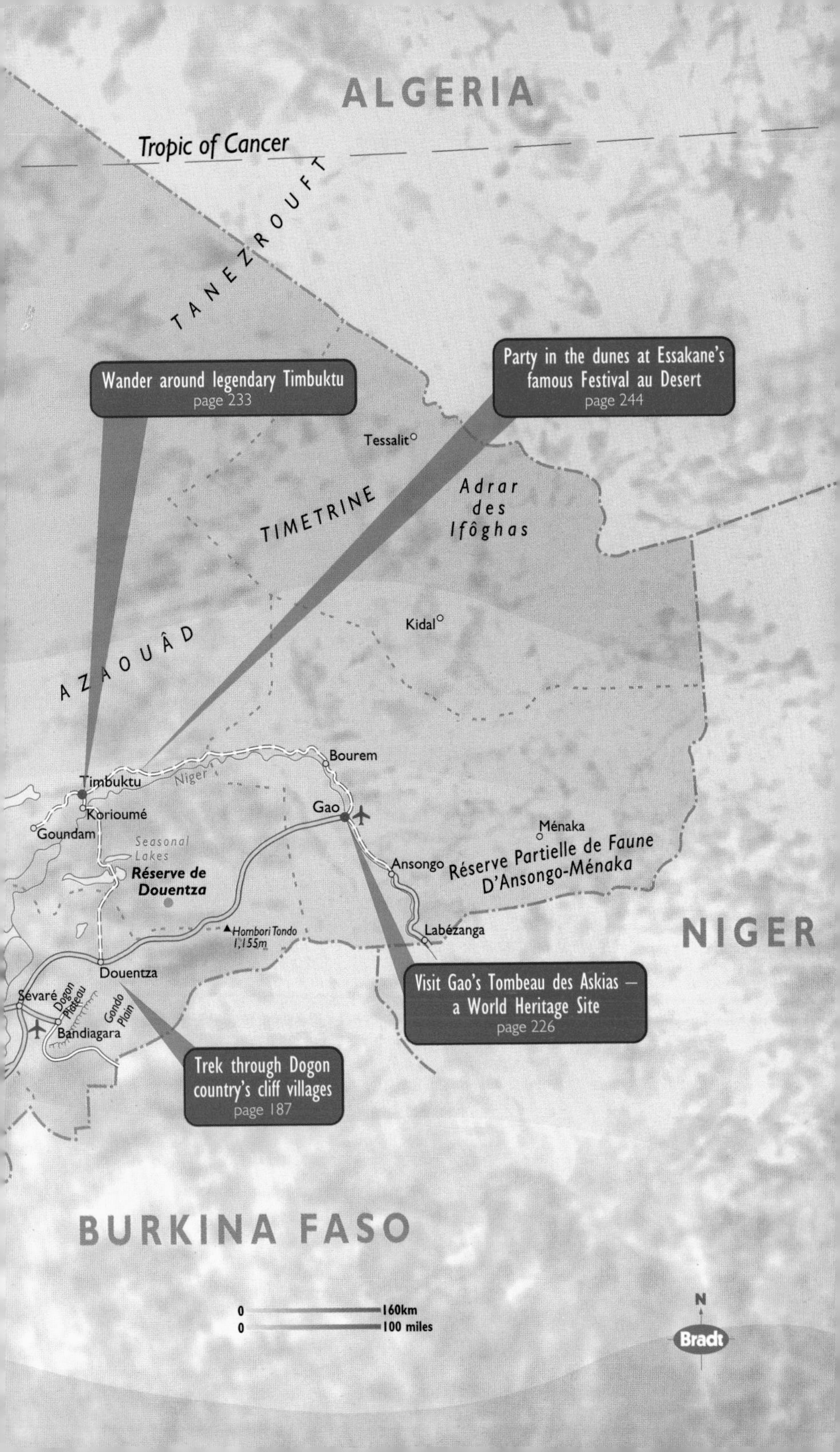

ALGERIA
Tropic of Cancer
TANEZROUFT
Wander around legendary Timbuktu
page 233
Party in the dunes at Essakane's famous Festival au Desert
page 244
Tessalit
Adrar des Ifôghas
TIMETRINE
Kidal
AZAOUÂD
Bourem
Niger
Timbuktu
Korioumé
Goundam
Gao
Ménaka
Seasonal Lakes
Réserve de Douentza
Ansongo
Réserve Partielle de Faune D'Ansongo-Ménaka
Hombori Tondo 1,155m
Labézanga
NIGER
Douentza
Sévaré
Dogon Plateau
Gondo Plain
Bandiagara
Visit Gao's Tombeau des Askias – a World Heritage Site
page 226
Trek through Dogon country's cliff villages
page 187
BURKINA FASO
0 160km
0 100 miles
N
Bradt

Mali Don't miss...

Trekking in Dogon Country
(JA) page 187

World-famous mud architecture
Djenne's mud mosque – a World Heritage Site – and its Monday market (SP) page 165

Desert festivals
The world-famous Festival au Desert
(JA) page 86

Journey on the Niger River
(SP) page 174

Camel rides through the desert with a Tuareg guide
(JA) page 249

Festival au Desert pages 244–5

above Not your usual crowd: a group of Tuareg and their camels take in the tunes (JA)

below Malian musicians take to the stage (JA)

above Local boy escapes from the midday heat under one of the muslin tents (JA)

above right Crowds listen whilst resting on raised dunes (JA)

below right A tour member finds his own inspiration (JA)

below Impromptu performance from a local group – they're using calabashes as drums (JA)

left **Sunset on Timbuktu's famous mud mosque** (SP) page 246

below **Aerial view of Timbuktu in the top left-hand corner you can make out the circular garden allotments** (P/TIPS) page 246

AUTHOR

Ross Velton (e *rvelton@yahoo.com*) has authored or co-authored over ten travel books on destinations ranging from Haiti to Walt Disney World, by way of Cap d'Agde, the world's largest nudist resort. In addition to his work for Bradt Travel Guides, Ross is an author for Rough Guides and a contributor to magazines and newspapers, including *The Times* and *The Independent*. He currently lives in Montreal, Canada.

UPDATER

Suzanne Porter (*www.suzanneporter.com*) first travelled to Mali in 2001 to make a film on the as then unknown Tuareg musicians, Tinariwen. Her research documenting the hero guitarists' rise to fame and fortune saw her travelling extensively across the Sahara over the following six years. During this time Suzanne became the proud owner of a battered 4x4 and a mild-tempered camel called Sarah. As a photographer, Suzanne has promoted the work of a number of international NGOs in west Africa, as well as writing travel features for magazines such as *Wanderlust* and *Travel Africa*. Her photos, film and educational workshops on the lives of the nomadic Tuareg were displayed at the British Museum as part of a week-long exhibition, *Secrets of the Sahara*.

CONTRIBUTOR

Gill Harvey has two main passions in life: writing and Africa. Research for Bradt, novels set in ancient Egypt, regular travel articles in *The Independent* and retellings of African myths are just some of the ways she's been tugging them together over recent years.

FEEDBACK REQUEST

Every effort has been made to ensure that the details contained within this book are as accurate and up to date as possible. Inevitably, however, things move on. Any information regarding such changes, or relating to your experiences in Mali – good or bad – would be very gratefully received. Such feedback is invaluable when compiling further editions. Send your comments to Bradt Travel Guides Ltd, 23 High Street, Chalfont St Peter, Bucks SL9 9QE, England; e info@bradtguides.com.

PUBLISHER'S FOREWORD

Hilary Bradt

The first Bradt travel guide was written in 1974 by George and Hilary Bradt on a river barge floating down a tributary of the Amazon. In the 1980s and '90s the focus shifted away from hiking to broader-based guides covering new destinations – usually the first to be published about these places. In the 21st century Bradt continues to publish such ground-breaking guides, as well as others to established holiday destinations, incorporating in-depth information on culture and natural history alongside the nuts and bolts of where to stay and what to see.

Bradt authors support responsible travel, and provide advice not only on minimum impact but also on how to give something back through local charities. In this way a true synergy is achieved between the traveller and local communities.

* * *

Several years ago I received a laconic postcard from a friend in West Africa: 'Timbuktu hasn't changed much since I last saw it.' A comment on any other town would have been unremarkable, but Timbuktu has an almost mythical quality – it's hard to believe that it really exists. The same could be said for much of Mali: the Dogon villages, the Djenné mosque and the River Niger. However, the third edition of Ross Velton's ever-popular guidebook – updated by Suzanne Porter, with invaluable contributions from Gill Harvey, Jolijn Geels and backpacker John Kupiec – brings all these places very much to life.

Third edition September 2009 First published 2000

Bradt Travel Guides Ltd, 23 High Street, Chalfont St Peter, Bucks SL9 9QE, England
www.bradtguides.com

Published in the USA by The Globe Pequot Press Inc, 246 Goose Lane,
PO Box 480, Guilford, Connecticut 06475-0480

British Library Cataloguing in Publication Data

A catalogue record for this book is available from the British Library
ISBN-13: 978 1 84162 218 7

Photographs Ariadne Van Zandbergen (AVZ), Chuck Young/TIPS (CY/TIPS), Photononstop/TIPS (P/TIPS), Jenny Acheson (JA), Jon Arnold Images Ltd/Alamy (JAI/Alamy), Suzanne Porter (SP)
Front cover Masked ceremonial dancers, Sangha, Dogon Country (JAI/Alamy)
Back cover Decorated camel, Festival au Desert (JA), Local man, Festival au Desert (JA)
Title page Mali nomad (SP), Local tea (JA), Masked dancer, Tereli (SP)
Maps Malcolm Barnes

Typeset from the author's disk by Wakewing
Printed and bound in India by Nutech Print Services

Acknowledgements

FROM ROSS I have depended on the support of many people to write this book. One of my greatest debts of gratitude is to Odile, François and Martin Gil, Maverick, Jingle, Mr Sidibé and the others, whose welcome was always warm and unconditional. Thanks to Colette Martin-Chave for making the introductions and Fanny Couquaux for her moral support during a difficult time.

Various people in Mali were kind enough to give me their time and the benefit of their experience. Thanks to Maureen and Tore Rose, Martine Latraye, Oumar Balla Touré, David Rawson, Aminata Dramane Traoré, Violet Diallo and Dr Téréba Togola in Bamako; Amadou Camara in Djenné; Jean-Pierre Dougnon in Mopti; Lassana Cissé, Seydou Ouattara and Domo Guindo in Bandiagara; Daniel Thera and Gadioula Dolo in Sanga; Mamadou Baga Samaké in Douentza; Sister Anne-Marie Saloman in Gossi; Ali Ouls Sidi in Timbuktu; Mamadou Lamine Diakité in Kabara; Mamadou Bréma Keita in Sikasso; and the Coopérative des Transporteurs Routiers de Kayes in Kayes.

I also greatly appreciate the practical assistance provided by the Office Malien du Tourisme et de l'Hôtellerie (OMATHO), Air Afrique, Air Mali and Club Direct.

When travellers are on the road exploring unfamiliar places, they are ultimately dependent on the help and generosity of the local people. I thank everyone in Mali for their advice, friendship and hospitality.

Moral support was provided, as always, by my mother and father.

FROM SUZANNE Of all the staff at OMATHO, I am especially grateful to Aliou Diarra in Kayes, M Maiga in Gao, Etienne in Sikasso, Oumar Balla Touré and Mamadou Koné in Bamako, Moctar Bâ in Mopti and Sane Chirfi Alpha in Timbuktu. I would also like to thank Aliou Touré, the President of l'Association des Hôteliers et Restaurateurs et l'Espace de Loisir for looking after me so well in Kayes.

A huge thank you to Paul Bondsfield and Fran Hughes at Explore and Anneli Elasla at Royal Air Maroc for getting me to Mali and Karen Crabbs of Toguna Travel, for going above and beyond all expectations in her assistance. To Mohamed Almahmoud in Timbuktu, Mamatal Ag Dahmane, Ainhoa Barrio, Sophie Sarin at Djenné-Djeno, Samer Asmar at l'Auberge in Segou, Alous and Khalis in Timbuktu and Dao Dolo in Sangha, heartfelt thanks for your help and support on the ground, as well as to Miranda Dodd from Sahara Passion in Timbuktu, Ian Merkel, Siaka at Hotel Splendide in Sevare, and Thierno Nassar in Mopti for the invaluable information and updates. Dany at La Chaumiere in Bamako, the owners of Hotel Tata in Sikasso, Motel Sevare and Le Repos du Dogon in Sevare and Hotel Medine in Kayes; your hospitality and generosity were very much appreciated. And for the readers who took the time to write in to share their experiences: Philip Hanes, Helen MacKintosh, Axel Santo-Passo, Chris Clayman, Joumana El-Khoury, Brooks Goddard, Jutta at Mankante, Gunnar Wegner, Eliza Reid, David and Janet Carr and Marion Wahl.

Thanks to Melissa Mullan in Bamako for some great insider's extras; to Miranda Dodd in Timbuktu for hospitality and help with locations and maps; and Sue Adams for her boxed text on kola nuts.

Thank you to the intrepid John Kupiec from the USA for his unique accounts of adventures off the beaten track and the team at Bradt Travel Guides, for their co-operation and understanding, particularly Adrian Phillips and my editor Emma Thomson.

And finally, thank you to the numerous Malians for providing various kinds of assistance during my many visits. To Manny Ansar for encouraging and organising my first trip to the desert and the hospitality of the Tuareg and to Egmar ag Jaffar for giving me my camel Sarah – but please let me bring her home to Marrakech!

ABOUT THIS BOOK

I hope that I have followed the many Bradt authors before me who have given their readers well-balanced and thought-provoking background information to the country they are about to visit. I also hope that I have produced a practical and user-friendly guide that will save you time and perhaps a little money. I have written it for travellers who are serious about exploring this country independently, using public transport and finding their own places to stay and things to do. This guide is not simply a listing of all the hotels and restaurants in Mali, nor is it by any means comprehensive. I have tried to point you in the right direction by giving you a few ideas and supplying what I think is useful information. The actual exploring and discovering is up to you.

The guide itself divides Mali into regions, which are then divided into towns and other places of interest. When I travel, I find that one of the most time-consuming and frustrating things can be finding out how to get from A to B. With this in mind, I have tried to make the *Getting there and away* section for each town as detailed and specific as possible. Where there is no map, I hope that my directions are clear and simple. Accommodation is another important consideration when travelling. At the very least, it should be safe and preferably clean. Since the first-time visitor has no way of knowing whether or not this is the case, I have placed a strong emphasis on the *Where to stay* sections.

PRICES One of the biggest drawbacks of a guidebook is how quickly it dates. This is especially true where prices are concerned. It may be that by the time you visit Mali few of the prices are as quoted in this guide. Nonetheless, I have chosen to be as specific as possible about the price of things. Even if they are not spot-on when you arrive, they will give you a good idea of how to plan your holiday budget.

SPELLINGS You can virtually guarantee that for every place name, ethnic group, culinary speciality or important historical figure there will be an alternative spelling. In some cases – Timbuktu, for example – more than one other version exists. This is hardly surprising in a country where French is the official language and over 30 other indigenous languages are spoken. All spellings in this book are randomly chosen. In many cases I have opted for the French spelling of a word, although sometimes – Timbuktu is, once again, a good example – other spellings are more easily recognisable to the English-speaker. In no case, however, do I expect you to confuse one name or word for an entirely different and unconnected one.

DEDICATION

Dedicated to the remarkable women of Mali.

Contents

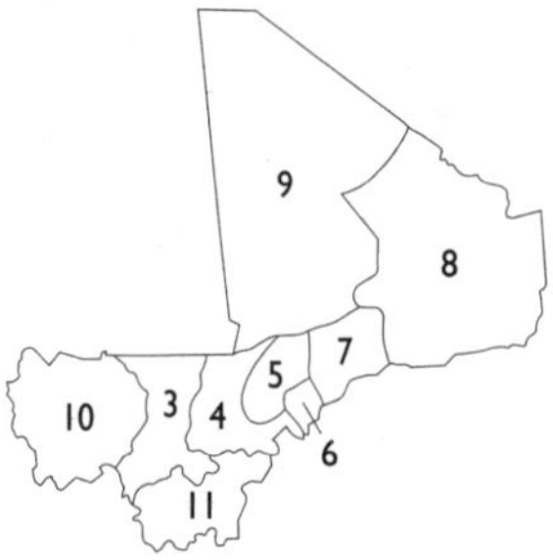

LIST OF MAPS

Introduction

A brick had been thrown through a window of the Malian Consulate in Paris when I arrived to collect my visa on a bitterly cold December morning. Despite the chilling wind which had effectively refrigerated the building, the gaping hole in the glass had been left uncovered, while the consular staff, the lucky ones wearing heavy anoraks over their boubous, sat round a table drinking tea and discussing how best to solve the problem. 'Fools,' I thought.

Two months later on a dusty street in Bamako, a young lad stood accused of stealing a taxi driver's transistor radio. An expectant crowd had gathered as accuser and accused squared off to exchange threats, counter-threats, insults, evil looks and, at the critical moment of the confrontation, saliva. At this point a fistfight seemed to be the natural and inevitable progression; how could either side back down now after such an insult? But both sides did back down. Chairs were called for, a team of self-appointed mediators sprang from the crowd of onlookers, and the protagonists sat down to discuss their problem rather than fight it out.

I remembered the staff at the consulate in Paris and realised that I had been wrong to criticise their inaction. Now, having spent some time in Mali, I understood that they had been taking action – not in the Parisian way, but in the Malian way. For this is a country with its own, unique, dynamic. Like the great river which winds its way through Mali's vast Sahelian and Saharan landscapes, the pace of life is slow and forceful. Newly arrived travellers still in the Western groove may find this frustrating at first, but give it a while and the charm and sense of humour of these mild-mannered people will win you over.

The tourist attractions in Mali speak for themselves and need no introduction. Grim stories about uncomfortable bus journeys in searing heat and annoying guides, which are hardly original in west Africa, might put you off visiting Mali – and buying this book! So I have opened on safe ground by introducing some of the most gentle and welcoming people in Africa. The rest is for you to discover.

Part One

GENERAL INFORMATION

MALI AT A GLANCE

Location Western Africa, southwest of Algeria
Area 1,240,190km² (the second-largest country in west Africa and five times as large as Great Britain)
Population 12,666,987 (July 2009 estimate)
Main languages French and Bambara
Ethnic groups Mande 50% (Bambara, Malinké, Soninké), Peul 17%, Voltaic 12%, Tuareg and Moor 10%, Songhai 6%, other 5%
Religion Muslim 90%, indigenous beliefs 9% Christian 1%
Capital Bamako; population 1,264,000 (2009)
Other main towns Ségou (population 102,200), Mopti (115,500), Sikasso (127,900), Kayes (88,100), Gao (57,978)
Principal tourist attractions Dogon country, River Niger, Sahara Desert, Timbuktu
Climate Hot and dry; semi-tropical in the extreme south
Time GMT
Money CFA franc; CFA1=100 centimes
Exchange rate £1=CFA753; US$1=CFA477; €1=CFA656 (June 2009)
Measures Metric system
International telephone code +223
Electricity 220V 2-pin round European plug
Political system Republic
Head of state (President) Amadou Toumani Touré (since June 2002)
Head of government (Prime Minister) Modibo Sidibé (since 28 September 2007)
Territorial divisions Eight regions: Kayes (First Region), Koulikoro (Second Region), Sikasso (Third Region), Ségou (Fourth Region), Mopti (Fifth Region), Gao (Sixth Region), Tombouctou (Seventh Region – French spelling) and Kidal (Eighth Region), which are divided into *cercles* and subdivided into *arrondissements*. Bamako is governed by the autonomous District of Bamako.
GDP US$8.776 billion (estimated at official exchange rate of 2008)
GDP per capita US$1,200 (estimate 2008)
Foreign debt US$2.8 billion (2002)
Average wage US$2–3 per day (2007)
Average life expectancy 50.35 years
National flag Three equal vertical bands of green, yellow and red
Public holidays 1 January (New Year's Day); 20 January (Armed Forces' Day); *9 March, Mawloud (Prophet's Birthday); *10 April (Easter Monday); 26 March (Day of Democracy); 1 May (Labour Day); 25 May (Africa Day); 22 September (Independence Day); *21 September, Korité (End of Ramadan); *28 November, Tabaski (Feast of the Sacrifice); 25 December (Christmas Day).
* indicates variable dates

Reference: Economist Intelligence Unit, Encyclopaedia Britannica, IMF, UNDP and CIA's World Fact Book

1

Background Information

'Where are you going on holiday this year?'
'Mali'
'Wow, Bali. That should be nice.'
'No, Mali.'
'Where's that?'
'In west Africa. It's where you'll find Timbuktu.'
'Is that the capital?'
'No, that's...hmm...that's...well, that's not Timbuktu.'

GEOGRAPHY

Despite being generally flat, Mali is better known for its highland areas of sandstone mountains and plateaux limited by steep escarpments. The most famous is the Dogon Plateau which rises eastwards from the Niger Valley and ends abruptly in cliffs known as the Bandiagara Escarpment. These cliffs run southwest to northeast, cutting a 200km swathe through central Mali and reaching heights of about 350m. Continuing east, some of the country's most dramatic landscape – including unusual rock formations and Mali's highest point, Hombori Tondo (1,155m) – is found in the Hombori Mountains. Other highland areas tend to be extensions of larger mountain ranges to the south and east. For instance, the Manding Mountains are an extension of the Fouta Djallon Highlands in Guinea and stretch from the Guinean border to within a few kilometres east of Bamako, while the series of small, broken hills in the region of Sikasso are the remnants of the Guinea Highlands to the south. The Bambouk Mountains reach their westward limit below the town of Kayes, where the Tambaoura Escarpment runs parallel to the Senegalese border. In the desert, the heavily eroded sandstone plateau called Adrar des Ifôghas is part of the Hoggar mountain system and has a valley called Tîlemsi running along its western edge for some 275km.

The rest of Mali is flat – sometimes very flat. Put a tennis ball on the Tanezrouft, a vast plain of bare rock stretching across the Malian and Algerian Sahara, and often it will be the only object visible on the horizon. South of the Tanezrouft and north of Timbuktu the Azaouâd and Timétrine are sandy plains which are drier than the Sahel, but not as arid as the desert. In contrast to the north, much of central Mali is covered by the fertile floodplains of the River Niger.

RIVERS The River Niger rises in the Fouta Djallon Highlands in Guinea and flows for 4,200km through four west African countries before emptying into the Gulf of Guinea on the Nigerian coast. The river traverses Mali for about 1,700km, literally bringing life to a country with no coastline and a negligible amount of rainfall. All along its banks fruit and vegetables are grown, in certain areas rice is cultivated, and the 20,000km^2 Niger Inland Delta is the largest reservoir of freshwater fish in west

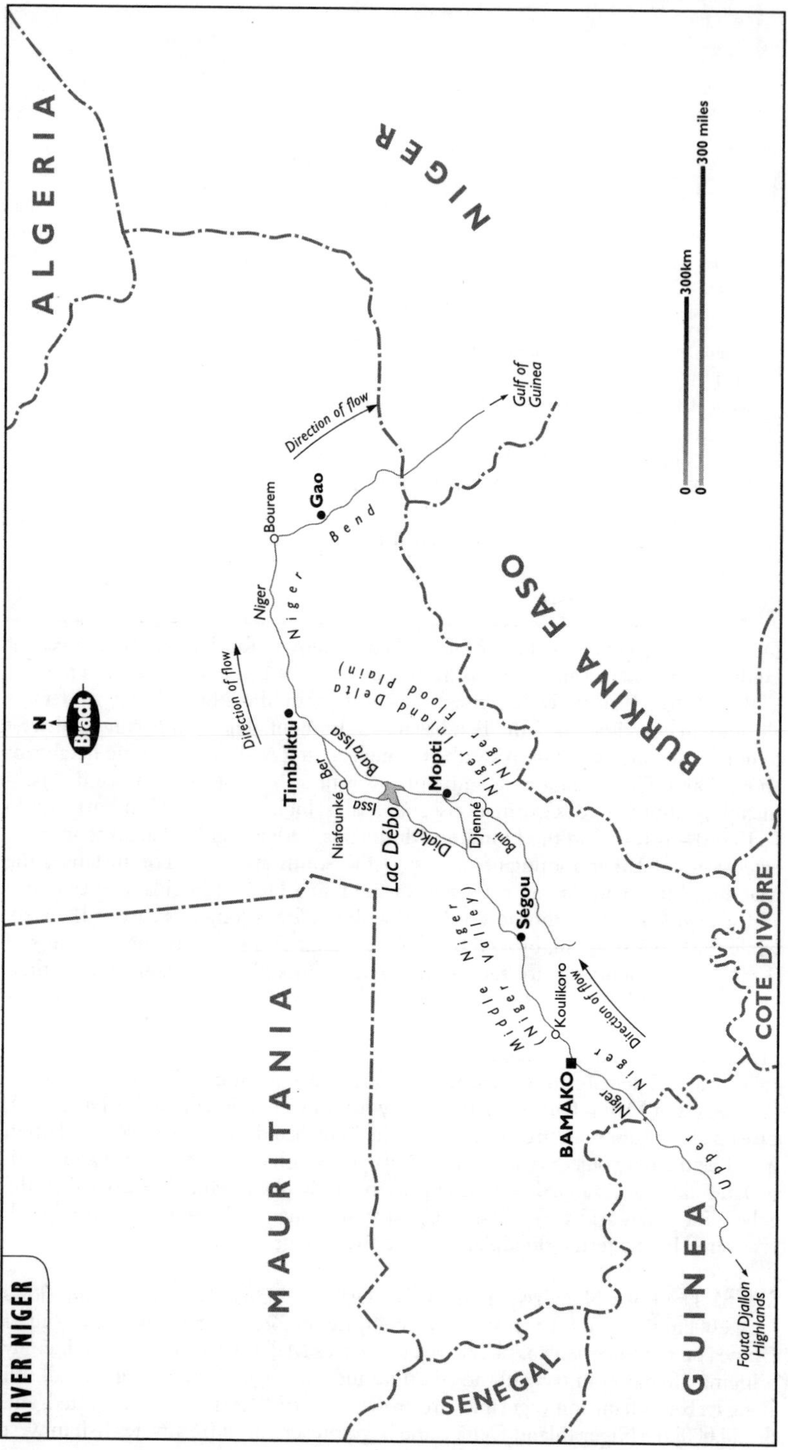
RIVER NIGER
ALGERIA
NIGER
MAURITANIA
BURKINA FASO
COTE D'IVOIRE
GUINEA
SENEGAL
Gao
Bourem
Niger Bend
Direction of flow
Gulf of Guinea
Niger
Direction of flow
Timbuktu
Issa Ber
Bara Issa
Niafounké
Lac Débo
Mopti
Diaka
Djenné
Bani
Niger Inland Delta (Flood plain)
Ségou
Middle Niger (Niger Valley)
Koulikoro
Direction of flow
BAMAKO
Niger
Upper Niger
Fouta Djallon Highlands
N
0 300km
0 300 miles

Africa. The river also provides a vital means of communication, linking remote desert towns such as Timbuktu to the rest of the country. Perhaps this is why the name 'Niger' is derived from the Berber word, *gber-n-igheren*, meaning 'river of rivers'. Other names for the Niger, depending on whom you ask, include: *Djoliba* (Bambara), *Mayo* (Peul) and *Issa Ber* (Songhay). Entering Mali near the town of Kangaba, the Niger flows northeast across the Manding Mountains and passes Bamako before spreading out in a wide valley just beyond the town of Koulikoro. Continuing northeast, after Ségou the Niger forms a vast inland delta of channels, streams and lakes – the combined effect of the extremely flat land and the river's almost non-existent descent. The Niger then receives its main tributary, the river Bani, at Mopti. Beyond Timbuktu, the river's course changes from a northeasterly to an easterly direction and then bends dramatically to the southeast at the town of Bourem. It continues to flow in this direction and passes Gao on its way to the Niger border at Labézanga. The River Niger is navigable for larger craft during its high-water period between about July and January. The upper Niger is the first to rise (July–October), then the inland delta (September–November) and finally the Niger Bend (December–January).

Mali's other great river, the River Senegal, is formed by the confluence of the rivers Bafing and Bakoye at the town of Bafoulabé. It flows in a northwesterly direction for 900km, following the border between Senegal and Mauritania before emptying into the Atlantic Ocean at the Senegalese town of St-Louis. The river is at its highest between about July and October.

SAHARA, SAHEL AND SAVANNA The majority of the surface area of Mali is taken up by desert and semi-arid land known as the Sahel, while in the southern areas there are subtropical savanna grasslands.

The Sahara is the world's largest desert. Roughly speaking, it extends from the Atlantic Ocean to the Red Sea and the Mediterranean Sea to the River Niger, occupying a total area of some 7,000,000km^2. The Malian Sahara extends north from the latitude of the Niger Bend and is characterised by extensive plains and *ergs* or shifting 'seas' of sand which make up about 28% of the total area of the Sahara. This is one of the hottest regions in the world and, despite the presence of a small nomadic population, one of the most inhospitable. The Sahel occupies an area between the Niger Bend and a line linking the towns of Bandiagara and Kayes – although recent desertification (see page 12) has blurred this boundary. The Sahel is a transitional zone of semi-arid desert and thorny scrub: hot and dry – the well-watered floodplain of the River Niger notwithstanding – and susceptible to periods of drought. The further south of the Bandiagara–Kayes line you go, the less Sahelian the landscape becomes. These are Mali's savanna lands, where the climate is more humid, the landscape greener and one or two things can actually grow.

CLIMATE *with Lyn Mair*

Hot, dry and dusty are the three words that accurately sum up the weather for most of Mali for most of the year. This weather pattern is governed by the Inter-Tropical Convergence Zone, (ITCZ), which affects the weather of the entire tropical zone of Africa. The ICTZ, a low-pressure zone, oscillates north and south annually following the sun but lagging behind by about five weeks. Warm and moist winds from the Atlantic are drawn into the low-pressure area when the ICTZ lies over the Tropic of Cancer around the northern summer solstice. Mali receives its rainfall from this wind between June and October, the rainy season. The southwestern part of the country has an annual rainfall of over 1,000mm accompanied by high temperatures and humidity. The effect of this weather system diminishes eastwards, and the further east, the less precipitation (rainfall) there is. Timbuktu has an average annual rainfall of only 200mm. During this period Mali is at its greenest; the rivers are high, the lakes full and the country as lush as it ever is.

During the months of November to June, the dry season, when the ICTZ moves south, the first wind to blow is the alize from the northeast. From December to February this wind brings a relatively cool spell, dropping temperatures to around a comfortable 25°C. For this reason the traditional tourist season is between these months – in other words, the European winter. From about February to June the hot, dry, dusty harmattan blows in from the east, drawing in the dust of the Sahara, raising temperatures, eliminating humidity and turning much of the country into a dust bowl. Indeed, dust is a major inconvenience when travelling in Mali. The Sahara generates an estimated 300 million tonnes of dust a year (60% of the total global production), and much of it is blanketed across west Africa by the harmattan. Bear this in mind when you choose your travel dates as dust can cause health problems, irritate contact-lens wearers and reduce the quality of photographs.

Temperatures in Bamako are usually at their coolest in August (21–31°C). The same is generally true for everywhere else in the country. The town of Kayes is considered to be the hottest in Africa, with temperatures occasionally rising to a sticky 50°C. The desert can be unbearable during the hotter months, although during the cooler months temperatures at night can fall dramatically (5°C is not unheard of in Timbuktu). Meanwhile, the coolest part of the country is in the south, in the region of Sikasso, where the maximum temperatures rarely exceed the high 30s.

NATURAL HISTORY *with Lyn Mair*

FLORA So much of Mali's natural vegetation has been lost to agriculture of one sort or another, but odd patches of woodland and some fine old trees can still be found here and there. Much of the grassland is fast vanishing to the herds of grazing cattle and goats. Increased desertification is also playing a role in this respect.

In the extensive desert regions of northern Mali, the true Sahara, plant life is extremely sparse, if not non-existent, except around oases. However, as one approaches the Sahel with its scant rainfall, scrubby bushes and tough, hardy drought-resistant palms and trees can be seen.

Many plants growing in such harsh conditions develop clever mechanisms to prevent loss of water and to retain whatever small amount comes along. Leaves are generally very small and will sometimes turn the thin edge to face the sun to avoid excess moisture loss; fine hairs act as an insulating layer as they cover the leaf surface.

Most of the trees do not have common names but I will mention a few that can be found in specific areas.

The **Doum palm**, *Hyphaene thebaica*, the only palm with a branching trunk, is common around Djenné and other dry areas. The long straight trunks are often used in the construction of mud buildings, and can be seen poking out of the walls.

Within the **Caesalpiniaceae** family, *Bauhinia rufescens*, with its tiny bilobed leaves and blackish twisted seed pods that remain on the tree for ages, is commonly seen in the Bandiagara region. Both Alexandrian and Italian senna, *Cassia senna* and *C. italica*, are to be found in the Timbuktu region. The Alexandrian senna is an undershrub with zigzag branchlets and upright spikes of bright yellow flowers.

Within the **Mimosaceae** family, **acacias**, with tiny leaves and thorns or prickles to protect them against browsing animals, are one of the most widespread plant families found in the Sahelian region. *Acacia senegal*, found around Timbuktu, is a small tree up to 7m tall, with a grey fissured bole, yellow peeling twigs and fragrant spikes of fluffy cream flowers.

In the Bandiagara region you may notice *Acacia pennata*, a scrambling and prickly shrub with little balls of white flowers.

Albizia species are also part of this family and the tallish, flat-crowned tree is distinctive and widespread. Like the other mimosas the leaves are composed of many tiny leaflets. *A. chevalieri* with its crimson flowers can be seen around Djenné.

Still with the Mimosaceae, there is a historically interesting tree that belongs to this family named after Mungo Park, the great 18th-century explorer. One of the most common savanna trees in Mali is the locust bean *Parkia biglobosa*; it has a spreading crown with orangey-red flowers, and animals love the nutritious seeds that look like little balls on the end of a string.

There is also the karité tree with many names; it produces karité or shea butter. The old name *Butyospermum paradoxum parkii* has been changed to *Vitellaria paradoxa* (see box, page 8).

Bombacaceae family members are usually very large and distinctive trees with showy flowers. One of the most characteristic trees of the drier areas is the **baobab**, *Adansonia digitata*; the name comes from the Arabic *bu-hibab*, meaning 'the fruit with many seeds'. The huge wide trunk is a purplish coppery colour with branches, usually bare of leaves, haphazardly reaching up to the sky. In optimum conditions the girth can reach monstrous proportions of up to 28m in circumference, although it will only grow to between 15m and 18m in height, making it a tree of squat proportions. It is very soft and fibrous and quite useless for furniture-making. The bark is pounded to make rope and coarse fabric for floor mats. The large white waxy flowers, which turn brown when they drop, are thought to be pollinated by bats.

The velvety-looking seed pods are at least 12cm long and the seeds are embedded in white powdery pulp containing large quantities of tartaric acid. They are refreshing to suck and make a palatable drink, and when dry they make lovely baby rattles. It is said that many of the larger baobabs have reached an incredibly old age. Original carbon dating estimated that the oldest tree was about 3,000 years old. More recent estimates put some of the older trees at a mere 800 years. Whatever, they do live for a very long time, which is perhaps why baobabs are thought to be tightly connected to the spirit world, and there are many folkloric tales throughout Africa about the importance of these strange and magnificent trees. In fact, as you travel through the drier areas you may find most of the natural vegetation removed except for a baobab standing as a lone representative of what was once a more wooded region.

Still within the general family is the red silk cotton, *Bombax ceiba*, also known as *Bombax malabaricum*. This is a tree native to tropical Asia, which has been extensively grown all over the drier parts of west Africa. It is a lovely tree with big red to orange flowers, which appear when there are no leaves; it reaches a height of about 15m and is found in the Koulikoro district.

One of the most spectacular trees in all of western Africa is the silk cotton or kapok tree, *Ceiba pentandra* (*fromager* in French), which can be found in the slightly moister regions of Guinea savanna in the southern part of Mali. This magnificent tree can reach lofty heights of over 60m and has enormous sprawling buttress roots for extra support. The young trees have sharp prickles on the trunk, which diminish with age; the large flowers are white and appear on the leafless branches. The elliptical fruits are full of silken floss, which blows on the wind.

Another distinctive family is the **Papilonaceae** or pea family, and included in this group are the 75 species and 200 subspecies of **indigofera** or indigo plants. They are mostly low, shrubby little trees or bushes with red or pink pea-shaped

KARITÉ BUTTER

Lyn Mair

Karité butter, also known as shea butter, is produced from the karité tree. It was formerly known as *Butyospermum paradoxum parkii* but with the latest taxonomical divisions it is now called *Vitellaria paradoxa*. The trees can be seen growing along the road between Bamako and Ségou and are especially common around the small village of Zantiguila. Karité trees have a dense crown of dark-green foliage and if it looks as though the trees have been trimmed in a neat line 1.5m from the ground, this is in fact the goat- and cattle-browse line, as the animals like eating the leaves. The trees produce dark-brown, oil-rich nuts, which are gathered and processed by women and children. In fact this is often an important part of a woman's livelihood.

The nuts are stored in pits to preserve them and to prevent animals from eating them. When a sufficient amount has accumulated, a fire is lit at the base of a mud oven and the nuts are placed on top where they slowly roast. These ovens or kilns are often seen along the roadsides. Then the process of extracting the oil begins as the nuts are pounded with a little water and placed in enormous cauldrons and cooked over an open fire. They have to be stirred and watched carefully to prevent burning. The dark chocolatey-looking mixture soon begins to ooze a rich oil, which is ladled out and re-boiled to remove impurities. When cool it is a soft creamy colour and has the consistency of butter, and is known as either karité (pronounced 'karitee'), or shea butter.

In many of the markets butter-balls the size of small tennis balls are piled up in enamel basins for sale, but the majority of the butter is collected and exported to France to be used in the cosmetic industry in lotions and soap. Locally, the karité butter is used for cooking, as well as being used as a skin cream and for keeping the Fulani girls' hair smooth and supple, especially attractive when decorated with those lovely flat amber beads. There is a soap factory in Koulikoro, and the luxurious soap produced there can be found in some upmarket shops in Bamako.

flowers, and they grow in the sub-arid zones. Indigo dye, which comes from the *Indigofera tinctoria* species, is used extensively in the Bandiagara region and in Djenné, where cloth is woven and made into clothes and blankets. In the same large family are the lovely **erythrina** trees, sometimes known as lucky bean or coral trees. There are many species of this tall tree of the drier savanna, the two most common being *E. vogelii* and *E. senegalensis*. In November and December the scarlet cones of flowers make a strong contrast to the generally brown countryside between Bamako and Ségou, in the patches of dry deciduous forest. The trees are in flower when there are no leaves present and later in the season the twisted seed pods are full of small, shiny, hard, red and black beans. The trees grow rapidly from cuttings and are very important in folkloric beliefs and traditions.

The **Moraceae**, or fig and mulberry, family contains large numbers of fruiting trees, the figs in particular. There are over 60 **ficus** species in west Africa and it is sometimes very difficult to separate them. They are usually large and sprawling with dark green, leathery leaves and a pale, smooth bark. The flowers form directly on the bark and therefore the fruits hang on the trunk of the tree. They are much loved by birds and insects, and often the figs, which are edible, are infested with worms and wasps – extra bird food. There are some amazing ficus species on the banks of the Bani River at the Djenné crossing; how they survive with so many exposed roots is a mystery. *Ficus platyphylla* can be found between Mopti and Djenné; the bark is rusty or pinkish and the figs are often pink-tinged. *F. abutifolia* is a smaller tree of up to 7m and can be found on the rocky hillsides of the Bandiagara Escarpment.

F. sycamorus is a savanna tree with a very large spreading crown growing near rivers. It has a pale yellow bark with yellowish to red figs.

The **Meliaceae** family harbours some of Africa's finest hardwoods and the west African mahogany, *Khaya senegalensis*, falls into this group. It is a beautiful tree up to 30m tall, with a wide dense crown of shining foliage. An avenue of them lines the Bani River outside the Kanaga Hotel in Mopti.

The arboretum behind the museum in Bamako has a wide selection of trees from all over the country. Sadly the names have worn off most of the labels, but you might be able to guess some of the trees, and it is a great place for a spot of birding as most of the trees are old and well established.

On the road between Bamako and Ségou, stands of trees can be seen in close proximity to the villages. These are fast-growing exotic trees from Asia, **Gmelina** species, and were planted as a source of firewood by the first president after independence.

FAUNA

Mammals With encroaching desertification, increasing herds of cattle and goats, and ever-expanding agriculture, the wildlife of Mali is not doing too well. There are parks and reserves, but hunting is still permitted in certain areas of them. Yet, looking at the folklore of Mali, it is not hard to realise that in years gone by there must have been a fairly rich wildlife here.

There may still be a few **chimpanzees** in the southernmost forests while several species of monkey inhabit the Parc National de la Boucle du Baoulé.

Common or golden **jackals** favour the drier regions and can even be found in the vicinity of villages. Jackals are very important in the divination rituals of the Dogon people and they are fairly common in the Bandiagara region; side-striped jackals are more commonly found in wetter areas.

What are left of Mali's **lions** take refuge in the extreme western *cercle* of Kéniéba around the river Falémé. **Cheetahs** are extremely rare.

The **elephants** of the Gourma region are justifiably famous. Constituting one of the last remaining Sahelian herds, each year it is estimated that between 360 and 630 elephants undergo a seasonal migration of some 800km (round trip) as they walk north from Burkina Faso in search of water and return south from the lakes and ponds of Gourma after the first rains in June. A visit to the Réserve de Douentza – where most of the elephants are concentrated – is as close as you'll get to a safari in Mali (see *Chapter* 7, *Gourma*, page 215).

Hippos can still be found in certain parts of the Niger, particularly between Gao and Ansongo. Arguably the most dangerous of all African animals, they claim many lives, so it is important to watch out and to give them a wide berth between dusk and dawn when they leave the safety of the water to consume vast quantities of grass.

Antelope are becoming more scarce. In the drier Sahelian zone, the Dorcas gazelle is very patchily distributed. In slightly moister areas the red-fronted gazelle, a subspecies of Thomson's gazelle, may be found in suitable habitats.

Termites Evidence of these amazing little creatures can be seen in many patches of uncleared land. Termites have the most sophisticated systems in place for living, reproducing, feeding themselves and keeping cool! The alates or flying ants that hatch out just after the rain provide food for innumerable birds, animals and even people. The termite mounds are often found in association with specific trees and other plants, and many creatures use the empty holes as homes: snakes, lizards, mongooses, porcupines and even warthogs. After a heavy downpour of rain, the mounds can be worn down to resemble giant mushrooms. Eugene Marais wrote most eloquently about the *Soul of the White Ant* and Joan and Alan Root made a stunning documentary film, *Termites: Castles of Clay*.

Fish Although Mali is so far inland, many people depend on fish for their protein intake. The great rivers, the Niger and Bani, have an abundant supply of edible and delicious fish but, with the ever-increasing population, it remains to be seen how long the fishing industry can be sustained.

The choice fish is the *capitaine* (see box *The capitaine's table*, page 83), which can be found in many restaurants and which makes very good eating.

Birds While Mali is not the region to rush to on a specific birding trip, because of its lack of infrastructure as well as its huge size and inhospitable climate, there are some interesting and important birds among the 655 species recorded here. Mali boasts one endemic bird – the Mali firefinch, see page 12.

There are six important areas for birding:

- Adrar des Ifôghas on the Algerian border
- Lac Faguibine north of the Niger Delta
- Central Niger Delta
- Bandiagara Escarpment
- Boucle du Baoulé National Park, north of Bamako
- Mandigues Mountains, west of Bamako

Many birds that breed in Europe in the northern summer will migrate to or from more southerly parts of Africa and will stop over in Mali or may even spend the northern winter there. The waterways of the great rivers host huge numbers of Palearctic passage migrants at the end of the European summer, and again as they return to the northern hemisphere to breed in spring, as well as all the resident birds. During the southern winter, some species of birds will migrate internally within Africa and spend time in Mali before returning south to breed in the austral spring.

Large concentrations of **waterbirds** move in response to conducive conditions, and sometimes enormous flocks of white-faced whistling duck, *Dendrocygna viduata*, congregate in the Central Niger Delta together with visitors from Europe, including numerous northern pintail, *Anas acuta*, garganey, *A. querquedula*, and Northern Shoveler, *A. clypeata*. Hundreds of black kites, *Milvus migrans*, can be seen swirling around the built-up towns on the banks of rivers, brazenly scavenging whatever they can find to eat. Passage migrant raptors, harriers and buzzards also pass over the Sahelian and savanna regions.

The African endemic **Egyptian plover**, *Pluvialis aegyptius*, is a smart little bird that can be seen on the banks of the Bani River around the ferry crossing to Djenné, as well as on the sand banks at the Bani/Niger confluence at Mopti. Its striking grey, black and buff colouring is distinctive.

Another African endemic, the beautiful and small **grey pratincole**, *Glareola cinerea*, is an intra-African migrant and can occasionally be seen in small flocks on large sand banks on quieter parts of the large rivers. Some heron, egret and ibis species are part of the birdlife diversity around the waterways and together with the astonishing array of wading birds, inland gulls and terns make any visit to the rivers worthwhile. Gull-billed terns, *Gelochelidon nilotica*, whiskered terns, *Chlidonias hybridus*, and white-winged terns, *C. leucopterus*, can be seen hawking for insects over the water.

Bee-eaters are amongst the most colourful birds you are likely to see in Mali. The red-throated bee-eater, *Merops bulocki*, and the white-throated bee-eater, *Merops albicollis*, favour grasslands, whereas the little green bee-eater, *Merops*

ACCESSIBLE PLACES TO LOOK FOR BIRDS

Philip Briggs

If you are in Bamako, go to the arboretum at the back of the museum in Avenue de la Liberté. Here you will find tall mature trees and all sorts of birds from woodpeckers to warblers. There is a fitness track in the arboretum so you are likely to be in the company of plenty of joggers. Many of the trees are labelled, but most of the writing has worn off so you are none the wiser about the identification of the trees. Another good, accessible birding spot is the otherwise dismal zoo in Bamako: the lush woodland between the cages is full of avian life, most vociferously and visibly flocks of cackling Western plantain-eaters.

When in Timbuktu, look for blue-naped mousebirds, *Urocolius macrourus*, in the courtyard of the Djingareiber Mosque.

The Bandiagara Escarpment is really good for birding as there are several habitat types, including cliff faces, some small rivers, grassland and even some woodland. Stop near any bit of natural habitat and you are likely to find something of interest. Yellow-billed shrikes, *Corvinella corvine*, abound, and you are likely to hear the ringing calls of the yellow-crowned gonolek, *Laniarius barbarus* (old name Barbary shrike). Pitch-black, fork-tailed drongos, *Dicrurus modestus*, are always seen.

While Djenné cannot be described as a birding spot, the gardens around the Campement de Djenné are replete with indigo birds, sunbirds, weavers and even the occasional Kulikoro firefinch.

If you are seriously into birdwatching, *Birds of Western Africa*, a Helm identification guide by Nick Borrow and Ron Demey, is indispensable, although it is rather a heavy book to carry around.

orientalis, is often found in the drier Sahel. **Rollers**, too, are very colourful birds with deep blue and turquoise markings. Both the Abyssinian roller, *Coracias abyssinicus*, and the blue-bellied roller, *C. cyanogaster*, are often observed perching on power lines waiting to pounce on insects.

Barbets are chunky, medium-sized and often brightly coloured fruit-eating birds that are generally found in forests, but the yellow-breasted barbet, *Trachyphonus margaritatus*, frequents the dry acacia savanna and desert edge, and can be found in the Niger Inland Delta.

Larks and **sparrow larks**, typical of the dry, arid belt, are usually cryptically coloured and difficult to spot, though the male sparrow larks have bold black-and-white head markings and a black belly. Migrating and resident **swallows** and **martins** can be seen throughout Mali at certain times of the year. Look out for Preuss's cliff swallow, *Hirundo preusi*, along cliff faces near rivers, especially along the Bandiagara Escarpment. **Wheatear** and **wagtail** species migrate through Mali, but the boldly marked African pied wagtail, *Motacilla aguimp*, is resident in southern Mali, and Heuglin's wheatear, *Oenanthe heuglini*, is the only resident or intra-African migrant wheatear in Mali. It has buffy, rufous underparts and frequents degraded savanna, burnt ground and farmland.

One of the most widespread birds in Mali is the **common bulbul**, *Pycnonotus barbatus*, found in every locality, cheerfully and noisily making its presence known. The **tawny flanked prinia**, *Prinia subflava*, a small and vociferous bird, is also widespread, but if you are on the banks of the Niger between Gao and Tillabéri, check the prinias carefully as you may see the very rare **river prinia**, *Prinia fluviatilis*. Another very noisy little bird, common throughout Africa, is the **grey-backed cameroptera**, *Cameroptera brachyura*, which skulks in any vegetation.

The **cricket warbler**, *Spiloptila clamans* (old name scaly-fronted warbler), is a gorgeous little bird with a streaky head and black-and-white markings on the wings. Look out for small parties of them in the dry scrubby vegetation around Djenné-Djeno.

Only two **sunbirds** are likely to be seen in the dry Sahelian zones: the pygmy sunbird, *Hedydipna platura*, has a bright yellow belly with long tail streamers and the beautiful sunbird, *Cinnyris pulchellus*, is iridescent green with a red breast bordered with yellow, and long, dark tail streamers. The males are brightly coloured and only maintain the brilliant plumage in the breeding season while the females are much duller at all times. **Sparrows** are represented by the rather dull northern grey-headed sparrow, *Passer griseus*, and the brilliant, tiny Sudan golden sparrow, *Passer luteus*, which lives up to its name.

White-billed buffalo weavers, *Bubalornis albirostris*, build huge, scruffy, communal nests and forage mostly on dry open ground, whereas the **village weaver**, *Ploceus cuculatus*, constructs a very tidy woven nest that can be seen in dense colonies near villages with trees.

The only endemic bird to Mali is the **Kulikoro firefinch**, *Lagonostica virata* (old name Mali firefinch). Its taxonomic status is debatable; in some instances it is variously considered a species of either Jameson's firefinch or blue-billed firefinch. This very small, mostly red bird is found in rocky, grassy areas between Mopti and Bamako.

ENVIRONMENTAL CONCERNS The widespread famine in the countries of the Sahel in the late 1960s and early 1970s was, like the Vietnam War, a televised event. The global community was shocked by what it saw and promised to take action. Momentum gathered, until finally in 1977 the United Nations Conference on Desertification (UNCOD) was convened in Nairobi, Kenya. Drought, it was decided, was not the sole cause of the Sahel's problems; desertification was also a major contributing factor. It was now official: Mali's chief environmental concern was 'the encroaching Sahara'.

In an African context, desertification is often defined in terms of the Sahara and its gradual southern advance. 'The Sahara continues to creep forward,' announces one commentator, 'claiming an area the size of New York State every decade'. The encroachment of sand dunes can be locally significant – in Timbuktu, for example, where desert sands have destroyed vegetation, the water supply and many historical structures in the city. In response to the threat of the encroachment, Timbuktu was inscribed on the World Heritage List in Danger in 1990 and UNESCO established a conservation programme to safeguard the city. This was subsequently removed in 2005 when it was deemed sufficient progress in management and conservation had taken place. Yet Mali is not really being swallowed by the desert. I prefer the less emotive and more scientific definition of desertification given by UNCOD: 'the diminution or destruction of the biological potential of the land that can lead ultimately to desert-like conditions.' This is what is happening in Mali. In a nutshell, soil erosion is the main problem. This, in turn, is the result of a number of largely man-made causes.

Deforestation is arguably public enemy number one. Fuel wood is the leading energy source in Mali, providing more than 90% of the country's energy needs, with Bamako alone requiring about 400,000 tonnes of wood a year to keep going. At one time, fuel wood was always gathered from dead wood on farms and common lands, but, due to the rapidly increasing human population, live trees are now being felled to meet the demand. Population pressures also contribute to the problem of overgrazing, which destroys vegetation cover and tramples soil surfaces. In recent years periods of drought have forced nomadic herders such as the Tuareg, who have traditionally inhabited the edges of the desert, to move south to the outskirts of Sahelian towns. The subsequent concentration of grazing has also led to land degradation. Elsewhere, overcultivation, overirrigation, inadequate drainage and the inappropriate use of agricultural machinery have further damaged the soil. Once stripped of its plant cover by deforestation, overgrazing, or any of the other means mentioned above, the topsoil has no protection from wind erosion, and each year, as the harmattan and other desert winds blow across the Sahel, they take a piece of Mali's environmental future with them.

Despite recurring droughts, flooding also remains a continuous threat. The latest, in August 2007, affected more than 42,000 people in Mali. The worst flood-affected regions were Kayes, Koulikoro, Ségou, Mopti, Sikasso and Gao. As well as houses collapsing, roads were damaged, bridges washed away and crops and livestock destroyed. In addition, floods exposed the population to serious health risks such as water-borne diseases, malaria and malnutrition.

HISTORY

It is only really in the past 40 years that we have been able to talk about the history of Mali, the nation state. Previously, this land in the middle of the western Sudan had been the stomping ground of some of Africa's greatest empires and kingdoms, heroes and villains. Ask a Malian today about the history of his or her country and you will be regaled with stories of Soundiata Keita, Kankan Moussa and the great Mali Empire – a name the country adopted when it won its independence in 1960. The fact that this empire, along with others such as Ghana and Songhay, actually spread across the modern-day boundaries of several west African states does nothing to diminish the feeling that this is *Mali's* history and every Malian is very proud of it.

EARLY TIMES The earliest discoveries of the existence of man were made in east Africa at Olduvai Gorge (Tanzania), Lake Turkana (Kenya) and the river Omo (Ethiopia). These finds have been attributed to a period known as the Early Stone Age, dating back over two million years. This was a time when man was beginning to dominate animals through the use of rudimentary tools and weapons chipped out of stone, although his physical appearance was still some way between primates and modern man. There is scant evidence of Early Stone Age people in west Africa, and even less in Mali itself.

About 30,000 years ago, man's body had adopted the form recognisable in all races of mankind today. He had become clever at making tools and gradually shifted from hunting and gathering to actually producing food – in other words, farming.

Agriculture began in Africa about 7,000 years ago in the Late Stone Age or Neolithic period. At this time, the Sahara was covered with grass and trees and, according to early rock paintings and engravings, supported elephant, hippopotamus and giraffe populations – animals which could not possibly survive there nowadays. Later drawings, such as those found in the Adrar des Ifôghas in the northeastern corner of Mali, depict domesticated animals and men hunting, farming and cattle-rearing. Further evidence of a rich and fertile Sahara supporting a dense human population was found to the west of the Adrar at the oasis of Asselar, where the fossilised remains of a man dating back to the Neolithic period were unearthed. However, the Sahara was gradually drying out and the grass was disappearing, forcing the farmers and pastoralists to migrate southwards into moister savanna areas such as the Niger Inland Delta.

The arrival of the Iron Age in west Africa between about 500BC and 400BC was of immense significance. Iron tools made agriculture more efficient and, consequently, food was more abundant. Mere survival became less of a day-to-day concern, giving people the opportunity to indulge in other activities. Craftsmen,

traders, clerics and rulers emerged from the crowd, societies developed, and the foundations were laid for the economic, political and cultural changes which were to take place in the region during the first millennium. The knowledge of iron-smelting was probably imported to west Africa by the Phoenicians of Carthage (in modern-day Tunisia) across the trade routes of the Sahara.

TRANS-SAHARAN TRADE The earliest trade route used by the Phoenicians and Berber traders from north Africa was via Ghat (in modern-day Libya), crossing the Hoggar Mountains and following the River Niger down to Gao. A western route, meanwhile, linked southern Morocco to the Upper Niger. Initially, horse-drawn carts were used to transport goods across the Sahara between north and west Africa. However, by about the beginning of the Christian era, camels had been introduced to Africa, making trans-Saharan trade more practical and profitable (camels could travel further with less water and carry greater loads). It is at around this time that gold became the main commodity of trans-Saharan trade. Originating in the forests of west Africa, gold was carried in great quantities across the desert to north Africa, where it formed the basis of the Arabic monetary system. Ivory, ostrich feathers and leather also interested the Arabs and, in time, slaves were to become as popular. Meanwhile, salt from mines in the Sahara was in great demand in west Africa, as were horses, and metals such as copper. Trans-Saharan trade could not have developed into the big business it had become by the end of the first millennium without the presence of a dominant power in the western Sudan able to ensure the stability and security of the region so that trade could prosper.

THE GHANA EMPIRE The kingdom of Ouagadou was probably founded some time during AD400 by the Soninké, who lived in the northern part of the lands dominated by the Mande peoples of the western Sudan. However, the first accounts of this kingdom were provided by Arab geographers and chroniclers in the 11th century when Ouagadou had developed into a fully fledged political state covering much of what is now northwestern Mali (and parts of southern Mauritania) and known to the Arabs as the Ghana Empire. The trans-Saharan trade in gold was the impetus for Ghana's ascendancy and the reason why it dominated the region until the 12th century. Control of the gold fields of Bambouk and Buré was the key to Ghana's economic prosperity, which was derived primarily from taxes on all gold passing through the empire on its way to north Africa. The Arab chronicler, El Bekri, writing in 1067–68, describes Ghana's ancient capital, Koumbi Saleh (in modern-day southern Mauritania), as two towns several kilometres apart: one for the king and his court and another for visiting Arab traders. The rulers of Ghana were essentially animist, believing that natural objects possess souls, but they were also receptive to Islam. This had the dual advantage of enabling them to command the respect and allegiance of subjects who followed the ancestral religion, while at the same time not alienating Muslim merchants and thus jeopardising trade. The result by the middle of the 11th century was an empire in which rulers exercised a degree of central authority over a network of smaller states hitherto unseen in the western Sudan, and a climate in which the gold trade could – and did – thrive.

In the early 11th century, just as the Ghana Empire was at its zenith, a group of Islamic reformers known as the Almoravids was formed in the western Sahara. Before too long, this group split in two and the southern faction, led by Abu Bakr Ibn 'Umar, turned its attentions towards the infidels of Ghana. Almoravid raids disrupted trade from 1062 onwards, and in 1076 the Almoravids conquered the Ghana Empire. A Muslim king was installed and many Soninké were converted to Islam. Those who resisted conversion fled to the fringes of the empire and formed separate states, the most important of which was Sosso to the southeast of Ghana. In 1087, Abu Bakr Ibn 'Umar was killed trying to suppress a revolt, and a short time afterwards Ghana regained its independence. The old empire, however, was in terminal decline and had been replaced by Sosso and other newly formed states as the region's true power brokers. In the 12th century, Sosso successfully invaded Ghana, definitively ending the hegemony of the first great empire in the western Sudan. Another was soon to follow.

THE MALI EMPIRE Around 1230, a young man named Soundiata Keita became the ruler of a small Malinké state in the Manding Mountains called Mali, which at this time was a vassal of Sosso, whose leader, Soumangourou Kanté, frequently used force to compel Malinké allegiance. After the failure of his brother to repel Sosso aggression, expectations were high when Soundiata took over. His early years certainly suggested that here was a legend in the making. A witch-doctor had predicted that Soundiata's mother, an extraordinarily ugly princess named Sogolan, would give birth to the greatest king in the world – a prophesy which seemed ludicrous when she produced a boy with paralysis in both legs. However, when he was nine years old Soundiata miraculously gained the use of his legs and he quickly developed into a prodigiously strong young man, who excelled in the arts of hunting and witchcraft. Soundiata's legendary status was secured in 1235 when he confronted and defeated Kanté at Kirina (near modern-day Koulikoro) and assumed the title Mansa or King of Kings. Having conquered Sosso, Soundiata set about transforming Mali from an alliance of independent Malinké chiefs into an empire, and, by the time he died in 1255, Mali encompassed most of the western part of modern-day Mali, including the all-important gold field at Buré. The empire's apogee, however, was still to come.

The Niger Inland Delta, Timbuktu and Gao were all conquered between 1285 and 1300, and during the reign of Kankan Moussa (1317–37) the Mali Empire extended from the Atlantic Ocean in the west to Gao in the east and from the desert town of Tadmekka (or Tadamat) in the north to the Fouta Djallon Highlands in the south. Kankan (or Mansa) Moussa was, along with Soundiata, Mali's most colourful and successful ruler. Islam had been established as the court religion after years of contact with Muslim traders from the north and Kankan was keen to display the magnitude of his own faith. In May 1324, he set off on a pilgrimage to Mecca with an entourage of over 60,000 – each one carrying a bar of gold. He stopped off in Cairo and visited the sultan, giving away so much gold in the city that the Egyptian money market crashed. Although it would take another ten years for the price of gold to recover, Kankan's visit had instantly put Mali on the map and his pilgrimage helped to foster political, cultural and intellectual links between the western Sudan and the Arab world. Trans-Saharan trade, meanwhile, continued to prosper in the secure and stable conditions provided by Mali's strong rulers, who received tribute from the many different clans stretching across the empire. In the second half of the 14th century, however, a series of weak rulers encouraged internal power struggles which, in turn, damaged the strong leadership upon which Mali's success had been based. Revolts broke out far from the Malinké heartland in the centre and west of the empire, and by the end of the 14th century Mali had started to decline.

THE SONGHAY EMPIRE The most rebellious part of the Mali Empire was in the Sahelian and desert regions in the east. As Mali gradually lost control of these outlying provinces, a small vassal state along the banks of the Niger called Songhay grew in strength and began to fill the power vacuum. Songhay also benefited from a general west-to-east shift in the focus of trans-Saharan trade. The Akan gold fields (in modern-day northern Ghana) began to supersede Bambouk and Buré, while Timbuktu and Gao (the Songhay capital) became important trading posts between the gold fields in the south and the salt mines of Téghaza in the north.

The first of Songhay's two ruling dynasties, the Sonni dynasty, was responsible for transforming this small chiefdom into the western Sudan's leading power for the next 100 years or so. Sonni Ali Ber (1465–92), a great warrior and ruthless leader, greatly expanded Songhay territory and enhanced its political hegemony, capturing Timbuktu in 1468 and freeing Songhay from Mali rule. Sonni Ali Ber's son, who succeeded his father in 1492, was overthrown by a lieutenant in Ber's army named Mohamed Touré. Touré took the title 'Askia', marking the end of the Sonni dynasty. Askia Mohamed (or Askia the Great) was also a great warrior, but, unlike Sonni Ali Ber, he was a devout – and practising – Muslim. He went on a pilgrimage to Mecca in 1496 and under his rule Islamic learning and scholarship flourished at Timbuktu. Askia Mohamed was himself overthrown in 1529 by his son, Askia Daoud, and for the next 50 years or so the Songhay Empire was at its zenith, stretching from the headwaters of the River Senegal in the west to what is now Niger and Nigeria in the east, and controlling the lucrative gold trade which passed through Djenné and Timbuktu. However, just as internal power struggles had weakened the Mali Empire at the end of the 14th century, when Askia Daoud died in 1583 dynastic rivalries brought to an end years of strong leadership and made the Songhay Empire vulnerable to external threats.

THE MOROCCANS Ahmed el Mansur, the Sultan of Morocco, had been waiting for an opportunity to invade Songhay and take control of the gold trade. Internal

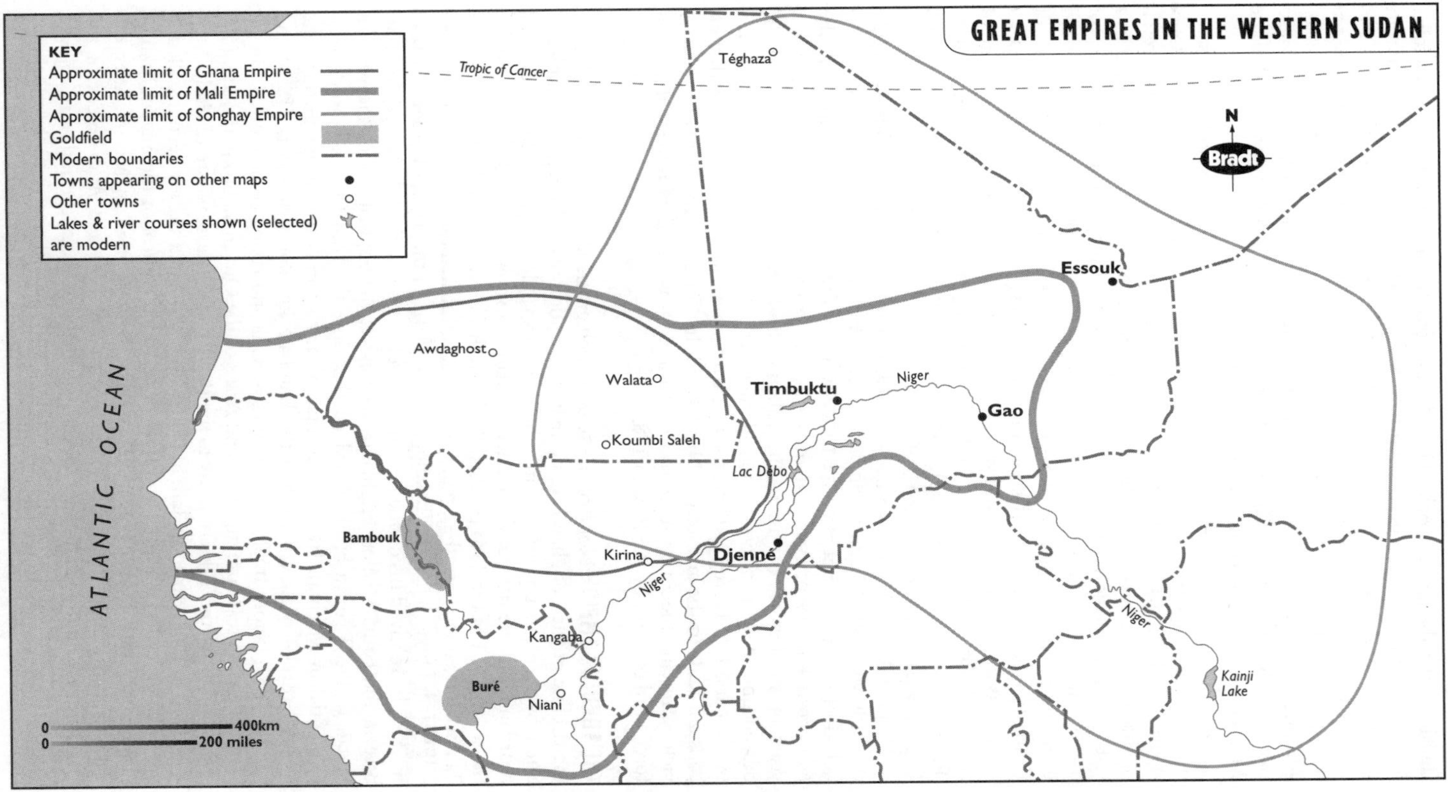
GREAT EMPIRES IN THE WESTERN SUDAN
KEY
Approximate limit of Ghana Empire
Approximate limit of Mali Empire
Approximate limit of Songhay Empire
Goldfield
Modern boundaries
Towns appearing on other maps
Other towns
Lakes & river courses shown (selected) are modern
N
Bradt
Tropic of Cancer
Téghaza
Essouk
Awdaghost
Walata
Koumbi Saleh
Timbuktu
Niger
Gao
Lac Débo
Bambouk
Kirina
Djenné
Niger
Kangaba
Buré
Niani
Niger
Kainji Lake
ATLANTIC OCEAN
0 400km
0 200 miles

divisions after the death of Askia Daoud presented this opportunity, and in October 1590 he sent a force of 4,000 men armed with muskets, gunpowder and mortars across the Sahara to confront 40,000 Songhay warriors, with spears and bows and arrows, north of Gao along the banks of the River Niger. The two armies met at Tondibi in 1591 and the Songhay fled when they heard the sound of the muskets. Although military engagements between the two sides would continue for the next two years, Songhay was finished as a major power and the torch was passed to the Moroccans, who now controlled Djenné and Timbuktu.

The Moroccans, however, never managed to dominate the region in the same way that the empires of Mali, Songhay and, to a lesser extent, Ghana had done. Apart from having a strong presence in Timbuktu and around the central stretch of the River Niger, much of the rest of the former Songhay lands remained in a state of anarchy, allowing new states to develop and marking the emergence of Tuareg influence in the region. Among the new states to appear during this period were the Bambara kingdom of Ségou (see page 141); the Bambara kingdom of Kaarta (see page 271); a Peul kingdom which emerged in the Niger Inland Delta as early as the 15th century and was eventually replaced by the theocratic state of Amadou Sekou (see page 165); the Kénédougou kingdom (see page 253); Samory Touré's domains (see page 255); and several smaller states, such as Khasso and Logo in western Mali (see page 269).

Meanwhile, the Moroccans had established Timbuktu as their headquarters. In the early years after the invasion *pashas* were sent directly from Fez to govern on behalf of the sultan, but after 1604 they were locally elected and, along with the Moroccan soldiery or Arma, gradually became a law unto themselves. Seventy years or so after the invasion, the sultan's authority had disappeared and the descendants of the invaders – who had intermarried with Africans – governed their own affairs. The Tuareg had become the Arma's most immediate threat, with their constant raids in the area of the Niger Bend. In 1737, the Tuareg won a decisive victory, forcing the Arma to retreat to Timbuktu, where they remained a major force until overrun by the Peul in 1883.

THE TUKULOR EMPIRE None of the states which emerged in the vacuum left after the decline of the Songhay Empire managed to dominate the region completely. Some were more powerful than others and expanded beyond their traditional heartland, but the days of the western Sudan's great empires had passed. During the second half of the 19th century, the Tukulor Empire created by El Hadj Omar Tall became, along with the French, the most influential force in the region.

El Hadj Omar Tall was a Tukulor Muslim cleric of the Tijaniya order of Islam. In 1852, he received his divine revelation and launched a jihad (holy war) from his base in the Fouta Djallon Highlands to convert the populations of the western Sudan to the Tijaniya brotherhood (at this time the rival Quadiriya order was influential in Macina). By 1862, El Hadj Omar's forces had swept through the western part of Mali, conquering the Bambara kingdoms of Kaarta (1854) and Ségou (1862) before finally overcoming Macina and taking control of its capital, Hamdallaye. In response, the Peul and Arabs of the Quadiriya brotherhood joined forces and drove the Tukulor army to the Bandiagara Plateau, where El Hadj Omar was killed in 1864. Amadou Tall, El Hadj Omar's son, had already been installed as the Tukulor leader at Ségou, and now he assumed control of the Ségou Tukulor Empire. Meanwhile, his cousin, Tijani Tall, became head of Macina after the Tukulor had gained the upper hand against the Peul and Arab forces of the Quadiriya brotherhood. Amadou never managed to exercise the authority enjoyed by his father and was constantly contending with internal rivals and the rebellious Bambara, who had never accepted Tukulor control of their lands. Thus deprived of the allegiance of much of his empire, Amadou was no match for the French when they finally arrived at Ségou in 1890.

THE FRENCH Prior to 1890, the French had tried to regulate their relations with the Ségou Tukulor Empire – the most powerful of the indigenous African states in Mali during the second half of the 19th century – through treaties and trade agreements. After the abolition of slavery, French commercial interests in the area were concentrated on gum arabic (a resin found in some acacia trees and used for fixing textile dyes and starching clothes). To protect this trade, forts were built along the River Senegal and agreements were discussed with Amadou Tall so that the trade based in and around Senegal could be linked to that in Algeria via Tukulor lands in Mali. This was all part of a policy inspired by the French governor in Senegal in the 1850s and '60s, Louis Léon César Faidherbe, to extend French influence in Africa from the Atlantic Ocean to the Red Sea. Amadou Tall was in no doubt as to the long-term French objective in the western Sudan and stubbornly refused to co-operate, stalling negotiations despite the ultimate inevitability of the French conquest. Finally, in 1887, Amadou signed the Treaty of Gouri, which made the Ségou Tukulor Empire a French protectorate and allowed traders access to the River Niger. It was now only a matter of time before the French annexed the Tukulor lands in Mali and joined them to what had become known as French West Africa. To this end, Lieutenant-Colonel Louis Archinard led a series of military campaigns in the late 1880s and early 1890s. In 1890, he entered Ségou, forcing Amadou Tall to flee to Nigeria where he died in 1898; in 1893, Macina, Bandiagara and Timbuktu fell to the French; the Kénédougou kingdom in the south was conquered when the French entered Sikasso in 1898; and Samory Touré was captured in the same year and exiled to Gabon. By the turn of the century, all of what is now Mali was under French control.

The French adhered to the time-honoured recipe for successful government in the western Sudan by adopting a highly centralised system of administration. The territory was divided into *cercles*, each one headed by a French commandant who reported to the governor of the colony, who, in turn, reported to the governor-general of French West Africa in Dakar. The name of the colony which, after independence, became known as Mali changed several times during the period of colonial rule.

Before the French conquests further east, the western part of Mali was renamed Upper Senegal in September 1880, with Kayes as its capital. In August 1890, French Sudan was created, comprising territory which would later be reapportioned to Senegal, Guinea, Côte d'Ivoire and Dahomey. In October 1899, Upper Senegal and Middle Niger came into existence, surviving for a short while before the colony was renamed Senegambia and Niger in 1902. During these changes, from 1890 to 1904, the eastern part of Mali was divided into three military districts. In October 1904, Upper Senegal and Niger replaced Senegambia and Niger, and four years later the capital was transferred from Kayes to Bamako. The three military districts were incorporated into the colony and Niger and Upper Volta (later Burkina Faso) were created in 1911 and 1919 respectively, from territory formerly belonging to Upper Senegal and Niger. In December 1920, the name 'French Sudan' was restored, and would remain until the dissolution of the federation of French West Africa in October 1958.

The nature of colonial rule in French West Africa was initially dominated by a policy of 'assimilation' – educating Africans so that they could absorb French culture – but this was later abandoned for an approach based on 'association', encouraging Africans to associate their culture with French culture so that they could evolve towards the European idea of civilised society.

DISCOVERING MALI

Pride of place in tourist brochures, pamphlets and websites about Mali is often reserved for Timbuktu and the River Niger. These two attractions remain as potent today in enticing travellers to Mali as they were hundreds of years ago when explorers dreamed of reaching a city where the streets were said to be paved with gold and discovering the source and flow of a river which many thought was the main tributary of the Nile.

During the 11th century, various Arab geographers and chroniclers were writing about the ancient Ghana Empire and its capital at Koumbi Saleh. One of the earliest accounts of Koumbi – and the important trading centre of Awdaghust (in modern-day Mauritania) – was provided by the Mesopotamian traveller, **Ibn Hawkal**, who wrote in his travelogue, *On the Shape of the Earth*, about a land of fabulous wealth and a great river which flowed to the east and, therefore, was surely the upper course of the Nile. The famous Moroccan explorer, **Ibn Battuta**, was another early pioneer of travel to Mali. In 1325, after 25 years spent exploring Arabia, Persia, India, China, Sumatra and Africa, he crossed the Sahara with a camel caravan and arrived in Timbuktu, where he wrote a detailed record of the city's early growth.

These forays into Mali by early explorers and their written accounts of a land of untold riches, as well as stories heard at trading posts on the west coast of Africa about a mysterious river and a fabled city of gold, had caught the imagination of the Europeans. In 1788, a group of English gentlemen formed the Association for Promoting the Discovery of the Interior Parts of Africa, which became known as the Africa Association; two of its main priorities were to discover the source and flow of the River Niger and the city of Timbuktu.

After two abortive attempts, the Africa Association sent **Daniel Houghton**, a bankrupt Irishman who needed a job, to west Africa with instructions 'to ascertain the course and, if possible, the rise and termination of that mysterious river'. Houghton set off up the river Gambia in July 1790, only to be robbed and left to die by Muslim tribesmen in what is now eastern Senegal. Although he never reached Mali and the River Niger, his last letter spoke of a navigable river flowing eastward through a country where opportunities for trade in gold, ivory and slaves were great. This information was enough to persuade the Africa Association to fund another expedition, led this time by a Scottish doctor from Foulshiels, near Selkirk, with a passion for travel and a desire to break out of his humdrum life in the Borders.

Mungo Park's first expedition started as inauspiciously as Houghton's failed attempt to discover the Niger five years earlier. He set off up the river Gambia in December 1795, reaching Ségou in July 1796 after having been deserted by his companions and robbed and tortured by local Muslim kings. His reward was to be the first European to set eyes on the River Niger, 'glittering to the morning sun, as broad as the Thames at Westminster, and flowing slowly to the eastward'. Park wanted to continue down the Niger to Timbuktu, but only got as far as Sansanding before sickness forced him to

INDEPENDENCE Open opposition to colonial rule came primarily from the Tuareg in the east, the Bambara in the Bélédougou region north of Bamako, and a Muslim sect known as the Hamallists (after its leader, Shaykh Mohamed al Tishiti Hamallah) in the west of the country. Otherwise, political opposition came from the African elite, who, by the late 1930s, had organised themselves into a number of voluntary organisations. These were not political parties, but rather cultural and sporting associations where the elite could meet with French approval, providing a forum within which politics – and eventual independence – could be discussed.

Around the same time, in 1937, trade unions started to be formed, one of the first being the teachers' union founded by Mamadou Konaté. It is important to

abandon the journey. His second expedition, sponsored by the British government, was on a much grander scale than the first. A force of 40 Europeans set off in May 1805, but by the time it reached Bamako in August 1805 dysentery and malaria had reduced its number to seven. At Sansanding, the King of Ségou gave Park two canoes, which were joined together to make a raft, *His Majesty's Schooner Joliba* (*joliba* being the Bambara word for the River Niger). Park's team – four soldiers, three servants and a new guide by the name of Fatouma – left Sansanding in November 1805. Five years later the British government tracked down Fatouma, who explained what had happened to Park and his friends. They had continued down the Niger, passing Kabara (where they were refused permission to visit Timbuktu) and Gao before entering the small Hausa state of Yauri (in modern-day Nigeria) in March or April 1806. They received a hostile reception from the local king, who attacked the raft, forcing Park and his men to jump into the river where they eventually drowned in the Bussa rapids.

While Park's travels had taught Europeans much about the River Niger, Timbuktu was still a mystery; the race was now on to be the first European to visit the fabled city. **Major Alexander Gordon Laing** was another Scotsman, who had been stationed in Sierra Leone as a member of the British army. In July 1825, he led an expedition across the Sahara, ostensibly to discover the source of the River Niger. He joined a camel caravan heading south and, after a close encounter with the Tuareg in the desert, became the first European to set foot in Timbuktu on 18 August 1826. He stayed in the city for about six weeks before joining another caravan heading north. Two days out of Timbuktu he was stopped by the Tuareg and killed with a spear through the heart. Meanwhile, the French Geographical Society had offered a 10,000-franc reward to the first European who could travel to Timbuktu.

One of the contenders was **René Caillié**, the son of a poor Parisian baker. Fearing the hostile reception that he would receive as a Christian in an Islamic land, Caillié spent nine months living with a Muslim tribe on the banks of the River Senegal in preparation for his trip. He learnt Arabic and studied the Koran so that he would be able to pass himself off as a Muslim. This tactic paid dividends as he travelled through Mali in 1828, visiting Djenné in March and arriving at Timbuktu by boat in April. The following month he joined a caravan heading north and travelled safely through Tuareg country, thus becoming the first European to visit Timbuktu and return home to tell the tale.

Of the explorers who followed Laing and Caillié to Timbuktu, **Heinrich Barth** was the most noteworthy. A German by nationality, Barth was employed by the British government and is best known for his five-year expedition across the Sahara to Lake Chad. In September 1853, he arrived at Timbuktu, having travelled overland from Say (in modern-day Niger) disguised as a Tuareg. The houses in Timbuktu where Laing, Caillié and Barth stayed – along with those of later explorers who reached the city – can still be seen today.

note that neither the voluntary organisations nor the trade unions united people along ideological or ethnic lines. The former simply facilitated communication between the elite, while the latter facilitated communication between the elite leaders and urban masses where social and economic concerns were paramount.

The formation of political parties in Mali can be dated to August 1945, when Africans were invited to participate in elections for the First Constituent Assembly of the Fourth Republic as part of a French policy to expand local involvement in the government of its overseas colonies. In response to the election of the pro-colonial candidate, Fily Dabo Sissoko, a number of political parties were formed. The Parti Progressiste Soudanais (PPS) was created by Sissoko's supporters and backed by the colonial administration, while the Union Soudanaise (US) led by Mamadou Konaté was affiliated with the Pan-African Rassemblement Démocratique Africain (RDA), which, in turn, was affiliated with the French Communist Party. By the time of National Assembly elections in 1956, universal suffrage had been introduced and the overwhelming popularity of the US-RDA was reflected in the election result.

Following its defeat, the PPS joined the US-RDA, whose leader, Mamadou Konaté, was now established as the country's leading political figure. Then, in the same year as his party's election victory, Konaté died of liver cancer. The co-founder of the Union Soudanaise, Modibo Keita, took over as head of the party – and would eventually be the man to lead his country to independence.

In October 1958, the federation of French West Africa was dissolved and replaced by the French Community, within which states could enjoy either political autonomy or complete independence from France as they saw fit. Only Guinea opted for immediate independence. Modibo Keita, who was now the leader of the Sudanese Republic (the new name for French Sudan), entered into talks with Léopold Sédar Senghor, the Senegalese leader, to unite their two countries in an independent federation.

These talks eventually led to the creation of the Mali Federation, which declared its independence from France on 20 June 1960 with Keita as its president. This unlikely alliance was to last just over three months. After independence, the thorny issue of presidential elections had to be addressed. This highlighted and exacerbated major policy differences between the two countries over vital issues such as the Federation's relationship with France and the command of the armed forces. Tension mounted, forces on both sides were mobilised, the border was closed and Modibo Keita returned to Bamako in a sealed train from Dakar where he had been campaigning for the elections. On 22 September 1960, the US-RDA declared the independence of the Republic of Mali.

Modibo Keita Modibo Keita had enjoyed a long association with the French communists and the first years of Mali's history as an independent state were to follow Marxist lines: a one-party state with a state-run economy modelled on the Soviet Union. One of Keita's first – and most drastic – actions was to withdraw Mali from the West African Monetary Union in July 1962 and introduce a national, unconvertible currency called the Mali franc. This move upset Mali's regional merchants (numerous in a landlocked country with seven international borders), whose trade was badly hit by the introduction of an unconvertible currency. The riots which followed provided Keita with the ideal opportunity to strengthen his grip on power, and once the army had restored order several of the president's potential opponents, including Fily Dabo Sissoko, were rounded up, charged with treason and attempting a coup and sent to the desert prison in Kidal. In 1964, Sissoko and other prisoners were killed by a Tuareg ambush – although many believe that the government had ordered their deaths. The Keita regime was similarly uncompromising when it ruthlessly put down an armed revolt by the Tuareg (supported by Algeria and Morocco) in northeastern Mali in 1963.

Meanwhile, Keita's economic policies were not having their desired effect. The unconvertible currency was largely responsible for the country's lack of hard currency, a scarcity of consumer products and, ultimately, food shortages. Eventually, in 1967, Keita was forced to swallow his pride and sign monetary accords with France which provided for a 50% devaluation of the Mali franc. The radicals in the party were outraged by this loss of dignity and demanded some tough national policies to restore the authority of the regime. Keita responded by announcing a cultural revolution. The Comité National de Défense de la

Révolution assumed control of the government and had the objective of restoring Mali's Marxist policies and philosophy. The Popular Militia fulfilled the same role as the Red Guard in Mao's China, rooting out corruption and purifying the party using tactics based on harassment, intimidation and torture. They soon became hated by the people and resented by the army, whose younger officers were not spared their harassment. The military opposition rather than a great groundswell of popular dissent proved to be the catalyst for the coup d'état which would topple the Keita regime in 1968. On 19 November 1968, while Keita was attending a conference in Mopti, there were rumours in the capital that the president was preparing to arrest a number of army officers on his return. Rather than test the truth of these rumours, the army, led by a young lieutenant named Moussa Traoré, carried out a bloodless and successful coup. Keita was arrested on his way back to Bamako, bringing to an end independent Mali's First Republic.

Moussa Traoré In the aftermath of the coup a provisional government, the Comité Militaire de Libération Nationale (CMLN), was established with the stated intention of solving the country's economic ills before returning it to civilian rule. The sensitive issue of the former government's socialist philosophy was not criticised by the new regime, which realised that many urban dwellers had benefited from secure employment during the Keita years and would not react well if they felt that their livelihoods were now under threat. Captain Yoro Diakité was placed at the head of the provisional government, although the real power lay in the hands of one of Diakité's inferior officers at military school, Lieutenant Moussa Traoré.

Moussa Traoré had always been a military man. Born in the region of Kayes, he received his military training in France before returning to Mali in 1960 and becoming an instructor at a military school in Kati. On 19 November 1968, he led the group of 14 other officers in the coup d'état which toppled the Keita regime, and afterwards he was charged with the responsibility of returning the country to civilian rule. Not surprisingly, perhaps, Mali remained under military government for the next 11 years.

In the same way that Keita had used his first years as president to strengthen his grip on power, Traoré used the early 1970s to consolidate his own position and that of the CMLN. In April 1971, Yoro Diakité, Traoré's greatest political threat, was expelled from the CMLN on charges of conspiring to overthrow the government; he died two years later in prison.

In the same year as Diakité's expulsion Traoré was promoted to colonel, and in June 1974 a referendum result gave overwhelming support to a new constitution which gave the CMLN a further five years to prepare the country for civilian rule. Arguably, Traoré's greatest challenge in the early 1970s – a period during which greater individual freedom and the encouragement of private enterprise had brought about a short-term economic improvement – was drought in the Sahel between 1970 and 1974. International criticism of the Malian government's apathetic response to the plight of the nomadic Tuareg and Maure people most affected by the drought was widespread and vocal, and external pressure finally forced Traoré to establish refugee centres in the north – but not before a good deal of the assistance intended for the refugees had been embezzled by the elite in Bamako.

Internal pressure, meanwhile, came mainly from Keita's supporters and trade unionists active under the Keita regime (Keita himself had died suddenly of lung cancer in May 1977 after having been moved from prison in Kidal to Bamako – although many believe that he was murdered by lethal injection). As the transition to civilian rule drew nearer, military hard-liners in the CMLN became increasingly anxious. In 1976, a political party, the Union Démocratique du Peuple Malien (UDPM), was formed in preparation for the transition, and the following year

Traoré was elected as its secretary-general. Several members of the CMLN, along with many other army officers, attempted to bolster the military status quo by planning a coup d'état in 1978. The plot was discovered, the culprits were removed from the CMLN, and Traoré was left virtually unopposed by the time general elections were held on 19 June 1979. All of the UDPM candidates were elected to the new National Assembly and the CMLN was disbanded, although the military still dominated the government, and Traoré took over as president of Mali's new civilian government.

The second half of the Traoré regime was characterised by growing economic hardship and increasingly outspoken opposition. The short-term economic improvements brought about after the Keita years were, by the beginning of the 1980s, negated by an inflated bureaucracy and widespread government corruption. Pressure from external organisations such as the IMF and World Bank forced Traoré to make economic reforms. Mali abandoned the Mali franc and was readmitted to the West African Monetary Union in 1984 and privatisation programmes and a (half-hearted) war against corruption and embezzlement were initiated. To make matters worse, low levels of rainfall in 1984 caused drought across most of the country. Human rights and civil liberties were also pushed onto the agenda when President Mitterrand linked foreign aid to democratisation in 1990. Until now, protests against the Traoré regime had been due largely to economic grievances brought about by the government's austerity measures (its failure to pay employees was a common gripe). By mid 1990, however, pro-democracy movements were starting to form. At the beginning of 1991, students, trade unionists and other pro-democracy campaigners took to the streets, and for the next three months protests were more or less ongoing. Finally, between 22 and 24 March, Traoré used military force to suppress a demonstration in Bamako, killing 106 protestors and injuring many more. A day later, on the night of 25 March, Traoré was overthrown in a coup d'état led by Lieutenant-Colonel Amadou Toumani Touré.

Amadou Toumani Touré The strength and momentum of the pro-democracy movement dispelled any thoughts that Touré and his supporters might have had of replacing the Traoré regime with yet another military government. Threatened with continued violent protests and the suspension of Western aid if democracy was not restored, the Comité de Transition Pour le Salut du Peuple (CTSP) was established in March 1991 to prepare for the transition to a democratically elected civilian government. In the meantime, Touré served as the country's third president.

Other than the call for democracy, the most pressing political issue inherited by the provisional government was a **Tuareg revolt** which had broken out in the north in 1990. Economic difficulties in Algeria and Libya had resulted in the repatriation of thousands of Malian Tuareg, who had taken refuge in these countries during the 1970–74 drought. In the late 1980s they returned to Mali, many of the younger men now possessing military skills and arms provided by the Libyans. Tuareg and Maure groups began attacking the Malian army along the Malian–Mauritanian border in early 1990, organising themselves into various freedom movements calling for the independence of the Azaouâd, a large area of desert north of Timbuktu. A peace accord was negotiated by President Traoré at the Algerian town of Tamanrasset in January 1991 which, amongst other concessions, included the creation of the autonomous region of Kidal, but attacks by Tuareg splinter groups continued despite the accord. President Touré worked hard to bring the revolt to an end, involving other countries such as Algeria, Mauritania and France in the peace negotiations. Finally, the National Pact was signed in April 1992 between the government and the Mouvement des Fronts Unis de l'Azaouâd

(MFUA), an umbrella organisation containing four smaller groups all fighting for the independence of the Azaouâd. However, although the National Pact would eventually provide the basis for a lasting peace, violence and banditry continued throughout 1992 and 1993. In response, sedentary populations in the north started to group themselves into ethnically based self-defence militias to combat the Tuareg threat and protect their own interests. The most important of these militias was the Songhay-dominated Ganda Koy (Masters of the Land), which enjoyed the sympathy of the Malian army. At this stage, the situation could have escalated into a full-scale civil war. However, dialogue continued, and by 1995 all sides were working to find a peaceful solution. A process of disarmament was gradually set in motion, while at the same time the Tuareg – and other ethnic groups in the north – started to be integrated into the civilian and military arms of the government, according to the provisions of the 1992 National Pact. The end of the revolt was celebrated by the symbolic burning of weapons in the Flame of Peace at Timbuktu on 27 March 1996 (see page 248).

Alpha Oumar Konaré The Tuareg problem was still far from being resolved when presidential elections were held in April 1992 and Alpha Oumar Konaré became the country's first democratically elected president in over 30 years. Meanwhile, the outgoing President Touré had won widespread popularity and respect for handing over power to a civilian government and for his efforts in resolving the Tuareg problem. Konaré himself was formerly a teacher, with degrees in history and archaeology; his party, the Alliance pour la Démocratie au Mali (ADEMA), was born out of the pro-democracy forces which had toppled the Traoré regime.

The problems facing Konaré at the start of his presidency were nothing new: a bloated bureaucracy, protests by civil servants, trade unionists and students for better pay, conditions and guaranteed state employment after graduation, a large foreign debt and a weak private sector. There was also the spectre of Moussa Traoré to deal with. The former dictator's trial began in November 1992, and in February 1993 he was condemned to death for his role in the deaths of the 106 protesters in Bamako nearly two years earlier. Konaré commuted this sentence to life imprisonment in November 1997, but a second trial – this time for embezzlement – resulted in a second death sentence in January 1999. As a last gesture, only days before stepping down from his presidential seat in June 2002, Konaré pardoned and liberated Traoré, which was very much in line with general opinion.

The Association des Elèves et des Etudiants du Mali (AEEM) had become the most powerful and intransigent of the student interest groups which were demanding increased grants and improved conditions, and rioting in 1993 and 1994 brought down Konaré's first two prime ministers, Younoussi Touré and Abdoulaye Sékou Sow (a 50% devaluation of the CFA franc in January 1994 also contributed to Sow's departure). In February 1994, Ibrahim Boubacar Keita was appointed to the post and quickly gained a reputation as a 'hawk', arresting all of the AEEM's leaders and initiating rigorous post-devaluation austerity measures.

Presidential and legislative elections in 1997 secured Konaré a second five-year presidential term and confirmed the ADEMA as Mali's dominant political party. However, these elections were poorly organised and widely boycotted by opposition parties, marking the beginning of a political stalemate between the ADEMA and the radical opposition, who organised themselves into the Collectif des Partis de l'Opposition (COPPO) in November 1997 and boycotted subsequent municipal elections in June 1998 and May and June 1999.

Despite Konaré's internal problems – which were relatively trivial in the greater scheme of African politics – his government enjoyed a significant amount of goodwill from Western countries. Konaré proved to be a generally co-operative leader, who made an effort to reform the economy and was, after all, one of Africa's very few democratically elected rulers.

ATT: soldier for democracy During the 2002 presidential elections, Mali showed the world that it understood the meaning of democracy. For one, Konaré never disputed the constitutionally determined limit of two full terms; he stepped down peacefully in May 2002. In the meantime, no fewer than 24 candidates had stepped forward as presidential candidates – one of whom was a woman. Eventually the field narrowed down to two candidates: Soumaïla Cissé – member of the ruling ADEMA Party and considered favourite – and a surprising opposition candidate, former transitional president General Amadou Toumani Touré. The latter, affectionately called 'ATT' by the Malians, had spent the ten years of Konaré's presidency working as a benefactor in the humanitarian sector, and he was highly appreciated for his integrity. His return to politics came as a surprise, especially since ATT refused to side with any political party, although there were many to choose from. When it came down to the last poll, most of the opposition candidates, support groups and even incumbent president Konaré – despite belonging to the ADEMA Party – supported ATT. The popular outsider, whose lack of personal ambition had gained him the other nickname of 'soldier for democracy', won 68% of the votes.

ATT started his term with powerful promises; he pledged to improve the economy and to promote social housing, education and jobs for the young. At the same time he moved carefully, leaving most of Konaré's government intact and aiming to unite the Malians in a politically stable environment. It was ATT's decision to implement strict IMF-supported reforming programmes that caused a first ripple in the calm waters of the political system. Two years down the road with ATT, the Malian economy was performing surprisingly well, despite difficult circumstances. And even though unemployment was still soaring, about 35,000 jobs for the young had actually been created, while the housing programme was also yielding success with new residential areas popping up around Bamako and other towns.

Outsiders claimed that ATT would soon lose the popularity he had gained during Konaré's presidency But they were to be proved wrong, as ATT continued to enjoy the support of the majority of Malians.

Internationally, in September 2003, he earned a high standing for the Malian contribution to the liberation of 14 European hostages who had been held captive by terrorists in Algeria.

However, ATT may have started his term with rising figures but they soon plummeted to where they came from. Despite his reform programme, putting an emphasis on improving the economy, the conditions were not favourable. With an economy largely based on agriculture, one season of drought can make all the difference and, in that respect, 2003 was not a good year. A second cause was the ongoing crisis in Côte d'Ivoire. With no access to the economically important port of Abidjan and no obvious alternative, international trade was hit hard. To a certain degree it could be said that the optimistic 2002 figures were also positively affected by a one-off event: the Coupe Africaine des Nations in 2002.

The IMF, meanwhile, continued to praise and support Mali's achievements. Despite renewed clashes between the Malian army and Tuareg rebels in the northern part of the desert, in April 2007, ATT was re-elected, winning 71.2% of the vote. His opponent, Ibrahim Boubacar Keita, took 19.2%.

As President Bush remarked upon meeting ATT in February 2008: 'I was touched by the president's concern about the life of the average citizen in Mali.' The next election will be held in April 2012. Despite his popularity he will not be voted back in as presidents in Mali can stay in office for only two terms.

ECONOMY

Mali is among the poorest countries in the world with 65% of its land area, desert or semi-desert and with a highly unequal distribution of income. The economy is heavily based on agriculture, which accounts for 45% of the country's GDP and occupies the lives of more than 80% of the population. Most people are engaged in subsistence agriculture, cultivating millet, sorghum, rice, corn (maize) and, to a lesser extent, potatoes, yams and cassava, to meet their own needs. Until the mid 1960s Mali was self-sufficient in these crops, but a combination of restrictive agricultural policies and drought made the country increasingly dependent on food imports and handouts. A return to food self-sufficiency was made a government priority in the 1970s and, thanks to agricultural reforms and adequate rainfall, the production of subsistence crops gradually recovered during the late 1980s and, by 1990, food self-sufficiency had been restored. The main export crops are cotton, rice, groundnuts and, to a lesser extent, sugarcane, tobacco and tea. The most productive agricultural area is along the banks of the River Niger between Bamako and Mopti and extends south into the region of Sikasso. The Office du Niger (see page 142), where most of the country's rice is produced, is in the region of Ségou. Livestock is also of great commercial importance: 10% of the population is nomadic, and, with the exception of Nigeria, no other country in west Africa raises as many goats, sheep and cattle. Mali is also one of west Africa's largest producers of fish. Because Mali is dependent on the agricultural sector, its economy is vulnerable to environmental shocks. In 2004/05 swarms of locusts invaded the regions of Timbuktu, Gao and Kayes and had a catastrophic effect on food production as well as agricultural exports and rural incomes. Droughts and flooding also remain a continual threat.

The service sector provides 39% of GDP. The country's officials have reported revenue generated by tourism increased from just over US$154 million in 2001 to more than US$262 million in 2007, with the number of visitors arriving at Senou, Bamako's international airport, estimated at 221,328 in 2007 compared with 94,300 in 2001. Mali is home to four World Heritage Sites, which are among the most visited destinations in the country: Timbuktu, Djenné, the cliffs of Bandiagara in the Dogon region and the Tomb of Askia. In addition, Mali's musicians and the new wave of cultural festivals are certainly making people more aware of Mali than they might otherwise have been. The government has made it a priority to develop tourism, especially ecotourism and cultural tourism.

Industry is considerably less important than agriculture to Mali's economy, accounting for only 17% of the country's GDP. Food processing and the refining of agricultural products such as cotton and sugarcane are probably the most important industrial concerns. Mining is also growing in importance, although it remains marginal. Gold accounts for about 80% of mining activity (the largest mine is at Sadiola in the region of Kayes), while other resources such as salt (at Taoudenni), marble and kaolin (at Bafoulabé), and limestone (at Diamou) are exploited in relatively small quantities. Although iron ore is also widespread, it is not exploited due to Mali's limited infrastructure. Meanwhile, the construction of dams at Markala, Sotuba, Sélingué, Félou and Manantali has led to an increase in the role played by hydro-electric power.

Malian trade is dominated by the export of cotton and gold, which together account for 89% of the country's export revenue; livestock, dried and smoked fish and groundnuts are the other main exports. Much of this trade is with neighbouring west African countries, as well as Italy and Thailand. However, despite being the largest producer of cotton in west Africa (west Africa itself is the third-largest cotton producer in the world), Mali has always suffered large trade deficits as it imports food, textiles, machinery and petrol, mainly from Côte d'Ivoire and France.

MALI AFTER CAN2002 In 2002, Mali hosted the pan-African soccer tournament called the Coupe Africaine des Nations (CAN2002), or African Cup of Nations. In preparation for the arrival of the continent's finest soccer teams and thousands of supporters, new stadiums were built in Bamako, Ségou, Mopti, Sikasso and Kayes. However, building the sportsgrounds where the Malian Eagles would defend the honour of their country was only the beginning. More facilities were needed to accommodate all the participants and visitors, and obviously Mali wanted to look its best in every possible way, so the five cities that hosted CAN2002 have largely benefited from the soccer tournament. All five towns have a Village CAN, which – like the Olympic village – served as a secluded shelter in the vicinity of the soccer stadium, where participants could relax or prepare for the next game undisturbed. After the tournament, the soccer players left and Malian citizens moved into these newly built villages, which now serve as residential areas for the better off or hotels (Sevare). Also, in these towns the structure and quality of the road system has been greatly improved. Ségou, for example, used to have only one paved road before 2002, but that has changed dramatically. Even some airports have seen considerable improvements, with extended runways or a new terminal building. In Kayes, the airport has been rebuilt altogether. Then there were existing projects which were simply speeded up because of the international attention Mali would get from the tournament. Some monuments were hastily finished and inaugurated, and new out-of-centre bus stations were built so that access to public transport would become easier and the traffic situation within the towns would improve.

While these changes are long-lasting, CAN2002 boosted the economy for only a short period of time, but then life returned to normal. In combination with the negative impact from the crisis in Côte d'Ivoire and the inadequate rainfall in 2003, it was the last straw for some. Many people of enterprise, who had seized the opportunity to set up a business in advantageous economic circumstances, are now struggling to stay afloat, while some of the new hotels and restaurants that mushroomed during CAN2002 have already had to close down.

PEOPLE

The many ethnic groups in what is now Mali have all played their part in the country's history, and as such they share a strong Malian identity which, with the exception of the Tuareg, generally takes precedence over their ethnic one. Indeed, although the potential for ethnic rivalries and violence in Mali is great, apart from the Tuareg problem (see page 24) and occasional disputes between sedentary and nomadic people (see page 65) – problems which are ultimately solved by peaceful negotiation – the people get on remarkably well together. This ethnic harmony is often attributed to Mali's most precious asset: social capital. This concept is almost the opposite of financial capital and cannot be neatly defined in terms of GNP, GDP or national debt. Instead, social capital relates to cultural, spiritual and human values, where interaction between people is more important than individual wealth. In this way, we can talk about 'rich countries with poor people' and 'poor countries with rich people'; Mali falls into the latter category. Due in part to strong historical ties, but also because of the harsh environment and difficult living conditions, relationships between different sets of neighbours in Mali are based on mutual respect and interdependence. There is a strong sense of both family and community, which transcends clan and ethnic affiliations and, despite depressing economic statistics, makes Mali one of the world's richest countries in human terms.

A crude distinction can be made between ethnic groups where agriculture is the main occupation and those people who are primarily pastoralists. The sedentary people can be divided into three sub-groups: Manding (including Bambara, Malinké, Dioula and Kassonké), Sudanese (including Songhay, Soninké and Dogon) and Voltaic (including Sénufo, Minianka, Bobo and Mossi). The main nomadic people are the Tuareg and Maures. Meanwhile, the Peul – one of Mali's largest ethnic groups – are nomadic cattle herders in some parts and sedentary farmers in others. To confuse matters further, the Bozo and Somono are neither agriculturists nor pastoralists, but fishermen.

The **Bambara** constitute about 30% of the country's population and dominate socio-political life. As was the case during the time of the old Bambara kingdoms of Ségou and Kaarta (see pages 141 and 271 respectively), the modern-day Bambara population stretches from Nioro du Sahel in the west to Nara in the east and extends south towards the Côte d'Ivoire border. The other principal Manding people, the **Malinké**, are the descendants of the Mali Empire whose heartland still lies between Bamako and the Guinean border. The **Songhay** live along the Niger Bend, the **Dogon** on the Dogon Plateau and along the Bandiagara Escarpment, while the **Sénufo** and other Voltaic people are found in the southern part of the country.

Arguably, the two proudest ethnic groups – and the ones most easily identifiable for visitors – are the Peul and the Tuareg. The **Peul** are Mali's second-largest minority and are found all over the country – but especially in and around the Niger Inland Delta. Noted for their ornate jewellery, the Peul are also physically distinct from other tribes, being tall, thin, light-skinned and often possessing Caucasian rather than Negroid facial features. As descendants of the Berbers, the **Tuareg** of northern Mali are also lighter-skinned than the majority of their compatriots and are referred to as 'whites' by them; the Tuareg, however, call themselves 'Tamasheq', after the language they speak. Spread across five different African countries – Algeria, Libya, Mali, Niger and Burkina Faso – there might be as many as 500,000 Tuareg in Mali itself. Until the disruptive influences of the droughts of the 1970s and '80s, Tuareg society was highly organised and run along feudal lines. Women had – and still have – an important role in the decision-making process, while, historically, black captives have been used as slaves – one of the reasons, perhaps, for the animosity between Mali's Negro majority and the Tuareg (for more about this animosity and its effects, see page 24).

WOMEN IN MALI

Behind every beard you can see the point of a plait

Manding proverb

Not having the space to launch into an in-depth analysis of the position of women in west African society, I must restrict myself to one or two subjective comments about the remarkable women of Mali. I am on safe ground when I say that Mali's women bear the brunt of the daily workload. Apart from during the wet season when the men tend the fields, the division of labour between the sexes in the country's rural areas seems to be grossly disproportionate. In addition to their childbearing and rearing responsibilities, the daily chores of an average Malian woman might include collecting wood and water, pounding millet, carrying produce to market and selling it. Meanwhile, the men try to earn a living the best way they can, but jobs are in short supply and their days are often spent sitting in the shade, watching and waiting for something to happen. I might be selling the men short, but the capacity, resolve and unflagging good humour of the women are self-evident.

The fact that women are overworked in Mali – as in most other west African societies – is a result of poverty rather than their social status (before the invention of electricity, running water and washing machines, Western women were overworked). Actually, the position of women in Malian families and society as a whole is, in the words of Amadou Hampaté Bâ (see page 41), 'almost divine'. They symbolise peace and harmony, communal decisions are never taken without prior consultation with the mothers of the families and, while children can disobey their fathers, a mother's word is final.

The traditional, symbolic importance of Mali's women is gradually being given political recognition. For example, in September 1997 the new government contained six female ministers, which was apparently a record in Africa. Moreover, in urban areas women are starting to be employed in non-manual jobs as secretaries, clerks and health workers, even if their salaries are often given to husbands and fathers. In rural areas, however, traditional gender roles remain largely intact and women continue to act as the country's 'engine-room'.

LANGUAGE

French is the official language of Mali and is spoken and understood – at least by someone – almost everywhere you go. This can act as either a blessing or a hindrance to travellers. On the one hand, Western visitors are more likely to be able to get by in French than in any of the other indigenous African languages spoken in Mali. Conversely, travellers who don't speak any French at all will be at a disadvantage because French is spoken as an *alternative* to English rather than in conjunction with English. Therefore, brush up on your French before coming to Mali – and don't expect people to speak or even understand English.

There are over 30 other spoken languages in Mali. The lingua franca of trade and administration is Bambara or Bamana, with about 80% of the population speaking either Bamana (standard Bambara) or a Bambara dialect such as Dyangirte, Kalongo, Masasi, Nyamasa or Somono. Of the other significant languages, the most widely spoken are Fulfulde (Peul) – the lingua franca of the Niger Inland Delta – Malinké, Soninké, Songhay and Tamasheq (Tuareg).

See *Appendix 1* for a list of useful expressions and words in French, Bambara and Tamasheq.

RELIGION

Islam is the dominant religion in Mali, and even the smallest villages possess a mosque. However, although most people are devout and practising Muslims – in other words, they pray regularly and observe Ramadan and other Islamic holidays – Mali is not a slave to its religion and is by no means a 'dry' state (a state where alcohol is prohibited). The infidel visitor should accept and respect religious practices – buses stopping mid journey so that passengers can pray to Allah at the correct time of day is one which directly affects travellers – but should not be restricted, embarrassed or otherwise inconvenienced by the Malian brand of Islam (not that it is any of our business!).

Islam arrived in west Africa during the first millennium, having been brought across the Sahara by traders from north Africa. Subsequent conversions – either voluntary or imposed by jihads – have continued throughout the second millennium, and today about 90% of Malians are Muslim. The majority of these belong to one of the two main Sufi brotherhoods: the Quadiriya (originating in Baghdad in the 11th century and brought to west Africa in the 15th century) and the Tijaniya (founded in Fez in the 18th century and popularised by the Tukulor cleric, El Hadj Omar Tall, in the 19th century). While other smaller – and invariably radical – brotherhoods such as the Hamallists (see page 20) and the Wahabiya have come and gone during the course of the 20th century, attracting clearly defined sections of society with a particular point to make, the Quadiriya and Tijaniya have remained the principal groups, the former being strong in the eastern part of the country and the latter popular in the centre and the west.

Before Islam began to filter across the Sahara, the people of the western Sudan were animist. Today, animism is still practised by the Bambara, Malinké, Bobo, Songhay, Sénufo, Dogon and other ethnic groups. One of the many consequences of this religious diversity is a bewildering number of names for God, including Maa (Bambara), Irké (Songhay), Koulouikière (Sénufo) and Amma (Dogon). It should be mentioned, however, that while animism still exists, Islam is gaining a foothold among animists and conversion rates are high.

Although Christianity has also made its mark in Mali, with converts amongst the Bobo and Dogon, for example, it remains a relatively minor religion. This might not seem the case given that most sizeable towns possess a Mission Catholique and, in a more restricted area, some form of Protestant representation. These missions, however, are far more important for their social and economic influence than their doctrinal clout.

CULTURE

MUSIC Mali is a country full of music and musicians. You will hear it in the street and on buses; in the desert and on the river – just about everywhere. In fact, it's when there's no music that you notice its silence.

The following list by no means covers all of Mali's diverse musical talent – it just about scratches the surface. But it's a good starting point to sample some of the variety of different styles. The increasingly popular music festivals popping up in different regions across Mali are great opportunities to catch a number of artists all in one place. You'll also find music venues in every town and village, from 1,600-seater stadiums to the more small and intimate *espaces culturels*. Performances tend to happen at weekends. If you're interested in buying music, then the **Centre Culturel Français (CCF)** (☎ *2022 40 19*) or **Mali K7** in Quinzambougou (☎ *2021 75 08*) both sell non-pirate CDs in Bamako for CFA1,600. This is often cheaper than those you see being sold on the street and at least you know that some money is going to the artist. They also have a great website – www.mali-music.com – with biographies in English and some downloadable clips. All major towns have at least one radio station. They are fascinating places to look around and will often have an archive of cassettes that they can copy for you for a small fee.

Traditional music The Mande people of Mali, Guinea, Senegal and The Gambia have a rich musical heritage. In Mali this tradition can be traced back to the days of Soundiata Keita and the Mali Empire, where *griots* or *jalis* (also spelt *dyeli*) sang the praises of the kings and noblemen to whom they were attached. Nowadays, *jalis* sing the praises of their *jatiguis*, the wealthy politicians and businessmen who support them with money and gifts, while still performing old songs about Soundiata and other notable figures of Mali's past. In Mande society, *jalis* form a caste rather like the minstrels of medieval Europe – not high on the social scale, but respected for their skills as entertainers. They are praise singers and the traditional keepers of oral tradition, which is often conveyed through song and dance. There are two basic styles of Mande music in Mali: the Malinké and Bambara styles. The former is noted for its medium tempo, attractive melodies and engaging vocals, while the latter has a slower tempo with starker and more haunting melodies and vocals. Wassoulou music, which has become popular in recent years, has a lot in common with the Bambara style.

In traditional Mande music, the men are the musicians, while the women or *jalimusolu* are the singers – and the stars. In the years after independence several praise singers established their reputations. Fanta Sacko was one of the first, with her light, rhythmic melodies and trend-setting songs about love. Her most famous and only recorded song was 'Jarabi', which appeared in the *Anthology of Malian Music* produced by the Ministry of Information in 1970. She was never paid for this work and retired in the mid 1980s following an overdose of mercury-based skin bleach (many *jalimusolu* associate a pale skin with fame and fortune). Fanta Damba started recording in the 1960s and, unlike Sacko, had a degree of international success, being the first *jalimuso* (singular of *jalimusolu*) to tour Europe. The Ségou-born Damba sang in the Bambara style and was noted for her stark, powerful voice. She retired in 1985. The late Siry Mory Diabaté was another highly respected *jalimuso* of the earlier generation. More moralistic than praising, she was popular during the Modibo Keita years, but fell out of favour when she failed to sing songs in praise of Moussa Traoré. Many of the newer generation of *jalimusolu* – those who rose to prominence during the 1980s – have now become international stars. Ami Koita broke onto the scene with her 1988 album *Tata Sira* and has subsequently established herself as one of Mali's most successful musical exports. Tata Bambo Kouyaté and Kandia Kouyaté both sing for one of the richest men in Mali, Baba Cissoko, whose hotel lies half-finished on the banks of the River Niger in Bamako. Tata Bambo's most famous song, sung in her characteristically hot, gritty and passionate voice, is *Hommage à Baba Cissoko*, while Kandia's first international release, *Kita Kan*, was in 1999, after years spent as one of Mali's top *jalimusolu*.

There are three traditional instruments in Mande music in Mali. The *kora*, a cross between a harp and a lute, is arguably the most recognisable, with its 21 strings (in Senegal and The Gambia there can be up to 25) and large gourd or calabash resonator. Although many of the greatest *kora* players are Gambian or Senegalese in origin, Mali boasts some of its finest exponents in Sidiki Diabaté, his son, Toumani Diabaté, and Batourou Sékou Kouyaté. The *ngoni* is a cross between a guitar and a lute and a forerunner to the banjo. It has three to five strings and, despite being a notoriously difficult instrument to master, is extremely popular in Mali. Tidiane Koné, founder of the Rail Band (see page 33), is one of the country's finest *ngoni* players. The *balafon* is an 18–21-key xylophone with a gourd resonator and is often played by two people – one performing the basic tune while the other improvises. Keletigui Diabaté is arguably Mali's seminal *balafon* player. There are three traditional Mande drums: the *tama* (popular in Senegal and The Gambia), the *doundoun* (a large, double-headed drum played with a stick) and the *djembe* (single-headed, goblet-shaped, high-pitched and played with the hands). If you understand French, the website www.djembe.com will tell you everything you ever wanted to know about the *djembe* and its greatest exponents. Non-traditional instruments such as the saxophone, trombone and horn have also been introduced, and the electric guitar has become the instrument *par excellence* of modern Mande music. Mali's great guitarists include the late Ali Farka Touré, Bassoumana Cissoko, Zani Diabaté, Baboucar Traoré, and Tinariwen (see *Solo artists,* pages 33–9).

Dance bands The development of Malian music and the international reputation enjoyed by some of its stars today are thanks largely to the dance bands and state-sponsored orchestras which flourished after independence.

Before independence, orchestras in towns such as Kita and Ségou played music strongly influenced by jazz and by Latin and Afro-Cuban sounds. This trend continued after independence, when a number of state-subsidised, regional orchestras and Mali's first national electric dance band, the Orchestre National, were formed. Keletigui Diabaté, the *balafon* virtuoso, was head of the Orchestre National, and under his influence traditional Mande material began to be introduced into the repertoire of the modern electric band – although Cuban dance music remained the biggest influence on Malian music during the 1960s. At the end of the decade Mali's new leader, Moussa Traoré, was keen to promote a return to a more indigenous style of music and several new bands, incorporating traditional Mande music with the popular jazz and Afro-Cuban sounds, were formed. Among the first were Super Biton de Ségou, Super Djata and Kené Star of Sikasso. Meanwhile, National Badema became the official state orchestra, using a mixture of traditional and modern electric instruments.

However, the two dominant Malian bands of the 1970s were the Rail Band – formed in 1970, state-sponsored and playing largely Mande songs at their permanent venue in Bamako, the Buffet Hotel de la Gare – and Les Ambassadeurs, formed in 1971, privately funded and playing many foreign-style pop songs, rumbas, foxtrots and Cuban dance numbers. These two bands were to be the training ground for a number of Mali's biggest stars, including Salif Keita (see page 38) and the Guinean-born Mory Kanté. Sadly, by the end of the 1970s, Mali's big bands were in decline. Their best singers had left to pursue solo careers and their funding had been adversely affected by government austerity measures. Although the Rail Band (renamed the Super Rail Band) and Les Ambassadeurs (renamed the Ambassadeurs Internationaux) survived longer than most – indeed, the Super Rail Band is still playing today – Mali's big-band era had petered out by the beginning of the 1980s.

By the late 1980s, the Mande praise singers faced stiff competition from practitioners of the Wassoulou style of music from southern Mali. Unlike other Mande musicians, the singers of Wassoulou (over 90% of whom are women) are not *jalimusolu* and do not sing songs in praise of patrons. Instead, their subjects are life, love, jealousy, tradition and the position of women in modern-day Malian society. The most successful contemporary Wassoulou singers are Nahawa Doumbia, Sali Sidibé and Oumou Sangaré, whose 1989 release of *Moussoulou* (Women) sold over 200,000 copies.

SOLO ARTISTS *with Suzanne Porter*

Abdoulaye 'Djoss' Diabaté Diabaté was born in Kela to a *jali* family and raised in the heart of the Mande tradition. At 18, he'd already developed into a remarkable singer and guitarist and left his village to join Tenetemba Jazz in Bamako. In 1975, he moved to Abidjan, the capital of Côte d'Ivoire where he formed a 12-piece band called Super Mande, joined by some of Mali's greatest stars such as Salif Keita and Ousmane Kouyate. His style was a mix of *balafon*, percussion, drums, electric guitars and a horn section. Ever respectful of tradition and a great collector of historical Malian tales, Abdoulaye was an unforgettable presence on stage. This *griot*'s performances were full of fun and entertainment. The band became one of the leading ensembles and, in 1978, Super Mande released their first recording *Wahabia-Ke Daschi.* The album, however, was banned from airplay as the title song criticised some *marabouts* or religious leaders. In the early 1990s, Abdoulaye was enlisted as the star singer in the celebrated Ballets Koteba and in the mid 1990s, toured the world with Les Go de Koteba. In 2002, he was noted for his remarkable performance on the Smithsonian Folkways compilation *Badenya, Manden Jaliya in New York City.* He has since collaborated with jazzmen Don Byron, Peter Apfelbaum and guitarist-journalist Banning Eyre and, in 2005, released his own album *Haklima*.

Afel Bocoum (*www.contrejour.com/artists/afelbocoum*) Bocoum was born in Niafunké in 1955. This small town on the banks of the River Niger was also home to his mentor, the late Ali Farka Touré, to whom he affectionately referred as *tonton*, or 'uncle'. He began his career aged 13 as a member of Ali's group ASCO. Little did he know they were to work together for the next 30 years; his haunting vocals and acoustic guitar complementing Ali's electric guitar and deeper, throaty voice. Afel's first solo performance was in 1968 at a musical competition in Mopti but it wasn't until the early 1980s that he formed his group Alkibar (meaning 'messenger of the great river'). In 1987, he won a scholarship to a government agricultural school and began working as a development worker. This allowed him to travel within Mali. His lyrics, written in Songhay, Peul, Tamasheq and Bambara, were a commentary on contemporary society: 'parents, do not force your daughters to marry; a home will never flourish without true love' (*Mali woymoyo*). His first solo album, *Alkibar*, was recorded in 1999 in a derelict school near Niafunké. In 2002, Afel collaborated with Damon Albarn (of Blur and Gorillaz fame) on the popular *Mali Music* album, a project that arose after Albarn visited Mali with Oxfam to work with local musicians. The year 2006 saw the release of Afel's latest album, *Niger*, the same year as he featured on what was to be Ali Farka's last album, *Savane*.

Ali Farka Touré Touré was born in 1939, his mother's tenth child and the first to survive infancy. He was given the nickname 'Farka' (donkey) in commemoration of his dead siblings and his own stubborn refusal to die. In 1946, the family moved to the Sahelian town of Niafunké. Although his family were of noble lineage far removed from the caste of musicians, Touré was drawn to music at an early age and started to play the *monocorde* (traditional single-string guitar) for fun. He took the decision to make music his life when he saw a performance by the great Guinean guitarist, Keita Fodeba, in 1956. After this, Touré made the transition from the traditional guitar to the Western instrument in no time at all. He made his name in the regional orchestras and troupes which thrived in the post-independence climate of cultural awareness and promotion. In 1968, he made his first trip outside Africa to represent Mali at an international festival of the arts in Sofia, Bulgaria. It was here that he bought his first guitar. In the same year he heard the music of the Mississippi blues man, John Lee Hooker, for the first time. He was struck by the similarity of Hooker's music to his own. 'I thought he was Malian because of what I heard,' said Touré, who has been dubbed 'the John Lee Hooker of Africa' by European critics.

Touré's international career began in 1975 when, on the advice of a journalist friend, he sent a number of recordings of his radio broadcasts to a record company in Paris. In a matter of months the first Ali Farka Touré album was released. His most acclaimed work was produced in collaboration with the UK record label, World Circuit; titles such as *Ali Farka Touré* (1987), *The River* (1987), *The Source* (1989), the Grammy award-winning *Talking Timbuktu* (1994) with Ry Cooder, and *Niafounké* (1999), which was recorded in his home town. In 2003, he took part in the documentary *Feel Like Going Home* directed by Martin Scorsese, but in 2004 Ali was appointed Mayor of Niafunké and chose to retire from music as his full-time career. In 2005, *In the Heart of the Moon*, a duet with Toumani Diabaté, was released, winning a Grammy, making Ali the only African to have received two such prestigious honours. Sadly, Ali would not see the release of *Savane*, the third album from the Mande hotel trilogy. He died on 7 March 2006 at the age of 66. Yet his name lives on through his son, Vieux Farka Touré and the Fondation Ali Farka Touré who have set up an international festival in his honour. See www.fondationalifarkatoure.org.

Amadou and Mariam Bagayoko (*www.amadou-mariam.com*) This duo met in 1977, when they were both studying braille at the Institute for the Blind in Bamako. Mariam had grown up singing at weddings while Amadou launched his musical career as a guitarist for the legendary Les Ambassadeurs. They started performing together in the Institute's orchestra and in 1980, the year they played their first official concert as a duo, they married. However, frustrated by the lack of musical opportunities in Mali, in 1986 they moved to Abidjan, Côte d'Ivoire, where they recorded a number of cassettes: *1990–1995: Le Meilleur des Années Maliennes* and a special box set *1990–1995: L'intégrale des Années Maliennes*, which are now available on CD. The cassettes made them stars in Mali and caught the attention of a French producer who persuaded them to move to Paris, where they recorded three albums between 1998 and 2002: *Sou Ni Tilé*, *Ge ni Mousso* and *Wati*. In 2004, they teamed up with Manu Chao of 'Clandestino' fame, who produced *Dimanche à Bamako*. It was highly successful and reached far wider than the specialist world music audience, winning them Les Victoires de la Musique award and a nomination for the Prix Constantin. In Britain they've appeared on *Later with Jools Holland* and been nominated for both a MOBO and the BBC Radio 3 Awards for World Music. Their new album, *Welcome to Mali*, was released in November 2008.

Bassékou Kouyaté Kouyaté was a double winner of the BBC Radio 3 Awards for World Music in 2008 and is one of the true masters of the *ngoni*. He was born in the small village of Garana, 40 miles from Ségou, and when he was 12, his *griot* grandfather taught him to play the *ngoni*. He formed part of the Symmetric Trio with Toumani Diabaté on the *kora* and Kélétigui Diabaté on the *balafon*. His collaboration with Taj Mahal and Toumani Diabaté on *Kulanjan* in 1989 highlighted the *ngoni*'s role as the ancestor of the banjo and the relationship between pentatonic music (a musical scale with five pitches per octave), from the region of Ségou, and American blues. Kouyaté was one of the main musicians on the late Ali Farka Touré's album, *Savane*, recorded in 2006. He's also played with Ali's son, Vieux Farka Touré, Dee Dee Bridgewater and Youssou N'Dour. Yet it's only since the release of his album, *Segu Blue* (2007), that he's received the praise so long overdue. The songs on *Segu Blue*, almost entirely acoustic, are largely adapted from the traditional *griot* repertoire. Having played on so many other people's albums, Kouyaté called in a few favours, most notably electric guitarist Lobi Traoré and the voice of Kasse Mady. For many though the real discovery is his wife, Amy Sacko, known as the 'Tina Turner of Mali'. This must, however, be for her looks more than her voice, which for the most part is light and soft-textured.

Boubacar Traoré Traoré is one of the best-known 'African Blues' singers, songwriters and guitarists. He was nicknamed 'KarKar', 'the one who dribbles too much', in Bambara, a reference to his soccer skills. He started composing at an early age, influenced by American blues and *kassonké*, the traditional music style from his region. He taught himself to play guitar, and developed a unique style, blending American blues with Arab and pentatonic structures. His songs were immensely popular; he was a bit of a superstar in post-independence Mali. In the 1960s, people woke every morning to hear him on the radio with hits such as 'KarKar Madison' or 'Mali Twist'. However, he made no recordings, which meant no royalties, and as his popularity faded in the 1970s, earning a living took priority over music. After a 20-year absence, KarKar was invited to perform on Malian TV and people couldn't believe their eyes. Two years later, his wife, Pierrette, tragically died, and heartbroken, he left for France to work in construction, to support his six children. A record producer, discovering a tape of one of his radio performances, tracked him down and brought him to England where he finally signed a record deal. His first album, *Mariama*, was released in 1990. Since then he's enjoyed great popularity, touring Europe and even being the subject of a film, *Je chanterai pour toi*, released on DVD in 2005, the same year he released his latest CD, *Kongo Magni*.

Djelimady Tounkara Tounkara is one of the foremost guitarists of Mali. Though not one of the founder members of the Super Rail Band, he joined them as a youngster at the end of 1972. As a Tounkara, Djelimady was born into a family of *griots* in the town of Kita, east of the Malian capital. He grew up surrounded by traditional music and, as a boy, played the *dejmbe* and *ngoni*. In the 1960s, he moved to Bamako, planning to work as a tailor. But music proved a stronger calling and he was soon playing guitar in a large, government-sponsored neighbourhood band. He became recognised as an artist capable of evoking the three major traditional instruments, *ngoni*, *balafon* and *kora* on guitar. Impressed by his skills, he was chosen to join the Orchestre National as a rhythm guitarist. The band's solo guitarist in those days was Keletigui Diabaté, one of the best *balafon* players in west Africa today. By 1972, Salif Keita had co-founded the Rail Band, but when he left to form Les Ambassadeurs, Mory Kante moved in to take Salif's place, leaving a convenient slot for Djelimady on lead guitar. He became the star arranger for the Rail Band during its glory years. He continued to work in more traditional contexts, backing the great *griot* singers of Mali on recordings, in concerts and at wedding and baptism ceremonies. His album *Bajourou* is an acoustic trio with another *griot* guitarist, Bouba Sacko, and singer Lafia Diabaté. *Sigui*, released in Europe in 2001, is rich in exploration of Tounkara's past, winning him a BBC Radio 3 Award for World Music. His last album, *Solon Kono*, was released in 2006.

Habib Koité (*www.contrejour.com/artists/habibkoite*) Koité was born in 1958, to a noble line of traditional performers, otherwise known as Khassonké *griots*. With 17 brothers and sisters, his passion for music was inherited from his grandfather, who played the *djeli n'goni*, a traditional four-stringed instrument associated with the hunters of the Wassoulou region. His unique style of guitar developed while accompanying his *griot* mother at weddings and other celebrations. He'd planned to become an engineer but his uncle, spotting his musical talent, insisted he enrol at Bamako's National Institute of Arts. He studied music for four years and graduated top of the class. During his studies, he was lucky enough to play with artists such as Toumani Diabaté and Kélétigui Diabaté (who later went on to join Koité's talented band, Bamada). After earning some money, winning first prize at the Voxpole Festival in Perpignan in 1991, Koité was able to record his first song, 'Cigarette Abana' (No more Cigarettes). It was a hit throughout west Africa and won him the prestigious Radio France International (RFI) Discoveries prize. He embarked on his first tour outside Africa and, in 1994, released his debut album, *Muso Ko*. Internationally, Koité became one of Mali's most successful musicians, producing three more albums: *Ma Ya* (1999), *Baro* (2001) and *Fôly!*, a double CD of live material (2003).

Issa Bagayogo (*www.issabagayogo.com)* Bagayogo was born in southern Mali in 1961. From an early age, he seemed set to work on his father's farm, with his 14 brothers and sisters. But he was drawn to music. He started singing and playing the *daro*, a rustic iron bell, rung behind farm workers to drive them along. Becoming a bit of a local celebrity, in 1991 he tried his luck in the capital, Bamako, where he produced two cassettes, playing *the kamele n'goni* (a six-stringed instrument similar to a banjo). After, he returned home to train as a bus driver. The cassettes earned him no money and, disillusioned, he turned to drink until eventually his wife left him. Things weren't looking good for Issa. After some time, he returned to the studio in Bamako, where he met a French engineer and the guitarist Foamed Koné, from Ali Farka Touré's band. They began mixing traditional music with a techno beat in what was to become known as Afro-techno and earning Issa the nickname 'Techno-Issa'. Their first CD, *Sya* (1999), was a huge success, enabling him to quit his job as a bus driver. The trio went on to record a second album, *Timbuktu* (2002), an international hit and Issa's last album, *Tassoumakan* (2004), was his third release on the label Six Degree Records.

Kasse Mady Diabaté (*www.mali-music.com/Cat/CatK/KasseMadyDiabate.htm*) Diabaté was one of many musicians who played with Salif Keita, before establishing himself as a solo artist in his own right. Though as a singer Kasse Mady is in the same league as Salif, he's never achieved the same kind of international success. He was born in Kela, Mali, in 1949, to one of the biggest families of *griots*. He started singing with Super Mande, helping them win the 1973 Biennale Festival, before joining Las Maravillas de Mali, a group that had just returned from eight years in Cuba. In the mid 1970s, they changed their name to National Badema du Mali but within ten years, their big-band style was no longer in demand. In 1983, Kasse Mady decided to go solo. He joined the steady stream of west African musicians, trying their luck in Paris. Here, he recorded two solo albums, *Fode* (1989), a hugely successful electric dance album, followed a year later by *Kela Tradition*, an acoustic album of Kela *jeli* songs. His natural tenor voice can be heard on *Songhai II*, recorded in 1994 with Spanish flamenco group Ketama and *kora* player, Toumani Diabaté. But by 1998 he was struggling in Paris and returned to Mali where a revival of traditional acoustic music was well underway. In 1999, he appeared as a guest on Taj Mahal's album *Kulanjan*. Its success paved the way for the making of his strongly autobiographical album, *Kassi Kasse*, recorded in his home town of Kela and released in 2003.

Oumou Sangare Sangare or 'Sangare kono' (the songbird), as Mali's great diva describes herself, is inspired by the music and traditions of the Wassoulou region. Her music features strong hypnotic dance rhythms and lyrics talking about general aspects of life in contemporary Mali. She was born in 1968 and raised in Bamako in a very poor family. When she was only two years old, her father took a second wife, emigrating to Côte d'Ivoire, leaving her and her pregnant mother behind. By the age of five, she was well known for her talents as a singer and at 16, went on tour with the percussion group Djoliba. She recorded her debut album *Moussoulou* (women) in 1990. It took west Africa by storm, launching one of the world's most 'astounding female voices' and propelling her to stardom at just 21. Her powerful songs spoke of life in her country, particularly the problems faced by women. She had a mission to improve their subservient position within society. The success of *Moussoulou* attracted the attention of Nick Gold of World Circuit who signed her to the label. Two albums followed: *Ko Sira* (1993) and *Worotan* (1996), with extensive touring, winning her the reputation as one of Africa's most original and striking female singers. At 6ft tall she's beautiful, gutsy and stylish. In 2003, she was appointed ambassador for the Food and Agriculture Organization (FAO) of the UN, giving her a position to challenge a wider range of issues on a global scale. See www.worldcircuit.co.uk.

Rokia Traoré (*www.rokiatraore.net*) Traoré is an award-winning singer and songwriter, who plays her own guitar. She was born in 1974 in Kolokani in the northwest of the Koulikoro region. With a diplomatic father, she travelled widely as a child, exposing her to many influences. Noble families such as her own were often forbidden from singing, this being reserved for the lower *griot* caste.

However, as part of the Bambara ethnic group, the restriction was not so strictly observed and from childhood she would sing at weddings and other celebrations. She started performing publicly as a university student in Bamako. In 1997, she met Ali Farka Touré who gave her guidance, and in the same year she won the RFI African Discoveries prize, previously awarded to Habib Koité. In 1998, she recorded her first album, *Mouneïssa*. It sold 40,000 copies across Europe and was highly acclaimed for its fresh treatment and combinations of Malian music traditions, such as her use of *ngoni* and *balafon*. In 2000, she was joined on her second album, *Wanita*, by Boubacar Traoré, Coco Mbassi and Toumani Diabaté playing *kora*. Written and arranged by herself, her lyrics covered issues including respect, traditions and relationships. In 2003, *Bowmboi* was released, winning the BBC Radio 3 Awards for World Music, for which she'd been nominated three times. Her latest album, *Tchamantché* (2008), manages to sound contemporary yet still distinctively African. The songs are mainly written in Bambara, with two in French and one in English.

Salif Keita (*www.salifkeita.artistes.universalmusic.fr;* French only) Keita is the biggest name in Malian music. His rise to fame is remarkable, not least because he broke down barriers of caste and attitude, which would normally have barred the way to a career as a musician. Firstly, he was not born into the caste of *jalis*, but was instead of a higher lineage considered 'above' singing and playing musical instruments. Secondly, as an albino he had to contend with discrimination and fear – Keita trained as a schoolteacher, but bad eyesight and the fact that his appearance frightened the children prevented him from teaching for a living. So he turned to music and was asked to join the Rail Band when it was formed in 1970. He left in 1972 when the Guinean musician Mory Kanté supplanted him as lead singer, which led him to join rival group Les Ambassadeurs. Keita remained with Les Ambassadeurs until 1982 when a dispute with another of the group's leading musicians, Kanté Manfila, persuaded him to leave and move to Paris. In 1987, *Soro* was released, putting Keita and Mande music firmly on the world map and becoming one of the biggest-selling African records ever. In 1991, with the help of Carlos Santana, Wayne Shorter and a number of other musicians from Mali and France, his album *Amen* made Keita the first African bandleader to win a Grammy nomination. Following the release of his 2002 album *Mouffou*, *M'bmeba* – released in October 2005 – was a return to his roots and the only one of his albums that he recorded in Mali.

Tinariwen (*www.tinariwen.com*) Tinariwen are legendary Tuareg guitarists from the deserts of northern Mali. Between the rebellion of 1960 and the drought of 1970–73, thousands of Tuareg youths fled the desert as part of the *ishoumar,* the name given to the unemployed moving between Mali, Algeria and Libya with no official papers. Amongst them were the founder members of the group. They met in a military training camp in Libya, set up by Colonel Gaddafi. There, they wrote and recorded songs, containing messages of unity and a need for change. The cassettes were smuggled illegally back home to the Tuareg camps. With no hospitals, schools, water or electricity in the Malian desert, they'd felt abandoned by their government. When the Tuareg rebellion of 1990 started, within each troop was a musician, encouraging the fighters during moments of ceasefire. Ibrahim, the lead singer, became known as a great fighter, riding into battle with his Kalashnikov and a guitar. The Malian army couldn't understand how it was so well organised; the words of Tinariwen's songs were credited with keeping the nomads informed. With the peace treaty signed and Tinariwen local heroes, they were keen to hit the international stage and tell the world of the Tuareg problems. The

Festival in the Desert in 2001 launched them to fame and they haven't looked back since. After the success of their first two albums, *Radio Tisdas Sessions* (2001) and *Amassakoul* (2004), *Aman Iman* (2007) hit the top of the World Music Charts in the UK, France, Germany, Sweden and Japan. Their extensive touring schedule has included support for the Rolling Stones and Robert Plant of Led Zeppelin fame and two live appearances on *Later with Jools Holland*. In 2005, they won a BBC Radio 3 Award for World Music.

Toumani Diabaté Diabaté is the man we can thank for bringing the *kora* to audiences around the world. He was born in Bamako in 1965 to a long tradition of *kora* players, most notably his father, Sidiki Diabaté who, in 1970, was the first to record a *kora* album. Toumani began playing when he was five, at a time when the government was encouraging regional ensembles to represent local traditions. He was recruited to the ensemble from Koulikoro, making his public debut at the age of 13, to great local acclaim. In 1984, he accompanied the grand diva, Kandia Kouyaté, the most powerful female *griot* in Mali and in 1986, visited the UK for the first time with another Malian singer, Ousmane Sacko. He ended up staying for seven months during which time he recorded his first album, *Kaira*, (taking a single afternoon with no retakes). In 1988, Toumani joined the Spanish flamenco group, Ketama, to release *Songhai I* and *Songhai II*. His openness to experiment continued, producing *Kulanjan* with American blues musician Taj Mahal; *MALIcool* with American jazz trombonist, Roswell Rudd, and playing on Bjork's album, *Volta*. In 2003, he was awarded the Tamani d'Or, for the best *kora* player in the world, and in 2004 was the first black African to be awarded the UNESCO prize, Zyriab des Virtuoses, at the Mawazine Festival, organised by the Moroccan king. The first of a trilogy of albums recorded at the Mandé Hotel in 2004 in Bamako, *In the Heart of the Moon*, with the late Ali Farka Touré, won the 2006 Grammy for best traditional world music album. See www.worldcircuit.co.uk.

Other well-known Malian artists that you might want to consider listening to are Baba Sissoko, Fanta Damba, Ami Koita, Idrissa Soumaoro, Ousmane Sacko, Kandia Kouyaté, Neba Solo's (real name Souleymane Traoré), Lobi Traoré, Tartit, Haira Arby and many more...

CINEMA Despite the prevalence of kung-fu movies in cinemas all over the country, Malian film-making enjoys one of the finest reputations in Africa. The following are names of note.

Adama Drabo Drabo's film career began as a hobby. For ten years he was a schoolteacher in a Malian village and in his spare time he painted and wrote plays. In 1979, he joined the CNPC and worked as assistant director to Cheikh Oumar Sissoko on *Nyamanton* in 1986 and *Finzan* in 1989. In 1991, he produced his first full-length film, *Ta Dona* (Au feu!), which was nominated for the Gold Lion prize at Locarno and featured at FESPACO.

Abderrahmane Sissako Strictly speaking Sissako is from Mauritania, but his father is Malian. Two of his best-known films are set in Mali: *La vie sur terre* (Life on Earth), 1998, is set in Sokolo in the region of Ségou. The recipient of wide international acclaim, *La vie sur terre* is about the director's return to the town where his father still lives – and his subsequent readjustment to the pace and rhythms of African life (Sissako himself lives in Paris). Nothing much happens during the film, but the images and tableaux of day-to-day life in the Sahel are enchanting and beautiful. If you cannot get to Sokolo – and towns like it – yourself, this film is the next best thing. *Bamako* (2007, distributed on DVD by Artificial Eye) following a trial set in the courtyard of a home in Bamako, earned Sissako the Jury Special Prize at the Carthage Film Festival in 2006 and the Best Francophone Prize at the Lumière Awards in 2007.

Cheikh Oumar Sissoko Sissoko was born in San in 1945. After graduating in African history and sociology from Paris University, he studied film at the Ecole National Louis Lumière. He then returned to Mali to work at the Centre National De Production (CNPC) in Bamako for which he made several short films including *Secheresse et Exode rural*. His film *Guimba, the Tyrant* won the l'Etalon de Yennenga at FESPACO 1995 and Special Jury Prize at the Locarno International Film Festival in 1996. In 2002, Sissoko became the Minister of Culture for Mali.

Souleymane Cissé Born in Bamako in 1940, Cissé is one of the leading figures of contemporary African cinema. Raised in a Muslim family, he was passionate about cinema from an early age. It was his first job as assistant projectionist on a documentary about the arrest of Patrice Lumumba that fuelled his desire to make a film of his own and he was accepted on a scholarship to the Moscow School of Cinema and Television. He returned to Mali in 1969 and produced his first medium-length film, *Cinq Jours d'une Vie* (Five Days in a Life), in 1972. His films are noted for their realism: Cissé prefers to use non-professional actors who come from the same socio-cultural background as the characters they portray, and he focuses on social themes emphasising the customs, problems and aspirations of his society. Cissé's films are invariably acknowledged at film festivals around the world, and in 1987 *Yeelen* (The Light) won the Jury's Prize at the Cannes Film Festival. Other Cissé films to look out for include *Den Muso* (The Young Girl), *Baara* (Work) and *Finyé* (The Wind), which depicts student opposition to the Moussa Traoré regime and was, at the time (1983), the most popular black African film ever shown on French movie screens.

Other notable Malian film-makers, some of whom also received their training in the Soviet Union, include Djibril Kouyate, Kalifa Dienta, Assane Kouyate and the former professional footballer, Mahamadou Cissé.

A very important date in African Cinema is FESPACO, the highly regarded Pan African Film and TV Festival, which takes place in Ouagadougou, Burkina Faso in February, every other year. Founded in 1969, it's the largest event of its kind in Africa with screenings and competitions of exclusively African films. The most recent festival took place from 28 February to 7 March 2009. See *www.fespaco.bf/index_en.html* for more information.

Anyone wishing to make a film or documentary in Mali should obtain a film permit from the CNCM (Centre National de la Cinématographie du Mali) in Bamako, found behind the Hotel L'Amitié (☎ *2021 77 62*). A permit costs CFA500,000, half of which is refundable on the production of a VHS of the edited film. You will need the permit if bringing lots of filming equipment through the airport and it's also worth it to avoid any hassle from authorities who are likely to approach you otherwise, every time you point the camera. This applies mainly to urban areas. Once you're in rural Mali, you should be fine.

PHOTOGRAPHY Photography in Mali took a long time to be recognised as a profession and a form of art. But it now is, thanks in part to the success of internationally renowned Malian photographer Malick Sidibé. Sidibé was Bamako's first photojournalist, most noted for his black-and-white studies of popular culture on the streets of 1960s' Bamako. His intimate shots show exuberant young Africans intoxicated with Western styles in music and fashion and capture the spirit of the city as Mali made the transition from colony to independent country. In the 1970s, he turned towards studio portraiture and his legendary studio, Studio Malick, is still thriving. He continues to photograph, more recently for French fashion magazines such as *Vogue*, *Elle* and *Cosmopolitan*. Sidibé received the Hasselblad Award for photography and the Venice Biennale's Golden Lion lifetime achievement award in 2007. His 2001–2003 exhibition *You look beautiful like that: The Portrait of Photographs of Seydou Keïta and Malick Sidibé* was on show at the National Portrait Gallery in London.

A portrait of this great photographer can be seen in Cosima Spender's BBC documentary *Dolce Vita Africana*, a journey through Malian history inspired by his iconic images. See *Appendix 2* for more details.

Other Malian photographers include Alioune Ba, Mohamed Camara and Seydou Keïta.

The biggest photography festival in Africa, Rencontres Africaines de la Photographie, is held every other year in November in Bamako. Started in 1994, more than 150 contemporary photographers from Mali and other African countries compete for prizes in a series of exhibitions held over the course of a month in cultural centres across Bamako, including the Bibliothèque National in ACI 2000 and the 3,000m^2 industrial wasteland at Quartier Orange. In April 2008, the Association des Photographes et Cameramen du Mali (APCM) organised their first week-long exhibition in Commune III on the theme 'A glimpse of my community'. It will be continued every year, alternating between the different communes.

At other times of the year, Chab Touré hosts exhibitions of local and international photographers at Chab Gallery in the Bamakocoura *quartier* of Bamako (see *Chapter 3*, *Entertainment and nightlife*, page 128). Also, festivals such as the Festival sur le Niger in Ségou will often include exhibitions and private views.

ART Mali is full of artisans who you will come across hawking their wares in every town, village and deserted corner of the desert. However, some of Mali's internationally exhibited artists to look out for are Abdoulaye Konaté (painter), Aly Guindo Dolo (*bogolan* – the traditional art of dyeing Malian fabric with fermented mud), Keita Kader (painter, *bogolan*), Bourama Diakite (painter, *bogolan*), Brehima Kone (painter), Souleymane Ouologuem (painter) and the sculptors Abdoulaye Traoré and Amahigueré Dolo. More evidence that Mali is taking its arts scene very seriously is the first ever exhibition of a world-famous artist, when the French painter Claude Viallat puts his work on show at the Quartier Orange in Bamako in 2009 before moving to the Musée National as part of a larger exhibition to coincide with the Football World Cup in South Africa in 2010.

LITERATURE The greatest storytellers in Mali are the *griots* or *jalis*, the keepers of oral history and tradition, who speak or sing their stories – but never write them down. This led the famous historian, diplomat and writer, **Amadou Hampaté Bâ** (1901–91), who devoted much of his life to translating oral tradition and attempting to put it down on paper, to invent the phrase: *Quand un vieillard meurt, c'est une bibliothèque qui brûle* ('When an old man dies, it is as if a library burns down'). This has not prevented many authors writing about Mali and giving their own versions of what went on in days gone by. (Almost all of the literature is in French rather than Bambara and other indigenous languages.) The most famous novel written by a Malian is *Le devoir de violence* (Bound to Violence) by Yambo Ouologuem. Covering the centuries since the Mali Empire, Ouologuem describes in every detail the crimes of violence and debauchery committed, not by Europeans and other foreign invaders as is the normal position of many African novelists, but by the Africans themselves. *Le devoir de violence* won the coveted French literary award, the Prix Renaudot, in 1968, but subsequent studies of the book have revealed close similarities between some of its passages and those of other works written by different authors – including Graham Greene's *It's a Battlefield*. Published a few years earlier, another well-known book, *Les bouts de bois de dieu* (God's Bits of Wood) by Ousmane Sembene, presented the railwaymen of the Dakar–Bamako railway in the more conventional role of good and virtuous Africans struggling to preserve and protect their culture from the onslaught of Western imperialism.

The other eminent writers of Mali are a mixture of novelists, poets, historians, anthropologists, politicians, etc. There is Maryse Condé, for instance, whose historical novel *Segu* (1987) is about the social forces and conflicts at work during the apogee of the Bambara kingdom of Ségou, which is considered to be in the same league as Ouologuem and Sembene's efforts. There is also Massa Makan Diabaté, with his satirical tales about daily life in the small village of Kouta; Moussa Konaté, the highly regarded author of *Le prix de l'âme* (1981); and the politician-poet, Fily Dabo Sissoko, with his *Poèmes d'Afrique noire* (1963). Malian literature might not be as famous as the country's music, but it is certainly worth a look (there are English translations of *Le devoir de violence*, *Les bouts de bois de dieu* and *Segu*).

2

Practical Information

WHEN TO VISIT

The most comfortable time to visit Mali is between October and March, after the rainy season (which lasts from June to September) and before the heat which becomes unbearable from April to June particularly as you travel further north. The daytime temperatures during this period are relatively cool, averaging around 25°C. Temperatures can drop sharply at night – especially in the desert and during December and January – to just a few degrees above freezing. The majority of Mali's festivals take place between January and February.

HIGHLIGHTS AND SUGGESTED ITINERARIES

HIGHLIGHTS

- The music scene in the capital of Bamako
- The mud mosque at Djenné
- A boat trip on the River Niger
- Trekking in the Dogon Country
- The Festival in the Desert or one of Mali's cultural festivals
- An adventure on camel back and a night under the stars in a Tuareg camp

SUGGESTED ITINERARY As there are no direct flights from the UK and travelling times are long and flights expensive, Mali is unfortunately not the first choice destination for a weekend break. It's possible, but the more time you can spend in the country, the more rewarding your visit will be as you absorb the diversity of the different tribes and their culture.

Long weekend A four-day trip is just enough time to visit one of the music festivals, such as the Festival au Desert, held between January and February every year. Spend the first night in the capital city of Bamako so you can see Mali's famous artists in one of the lively music venues, before catching an early morning flight to Timbuktu. A 4x4 will whisk you the 60km to Essakane, the festival site, nestled amongst glistening white sand dunes, where you can spend three wondrous days listening to some of the Tuareg's finest musicians under the stars. Alternatively, the Festival sur le Niger – set along the banks of the river in Ségou – is easy to reach, just three hours drive from the capital, and also has an exceptional musical line-up.

One week Visit Djenné, home of the stunning mud mosque and wander around the Monday market. Then drive a short distance to the busy harbour town of Mopti to rent a small pole-operated wooden canoe for a tour of the harbour before watching the sun setting over the River Niger with a juice at the Bissap Café. Leave early for the Dogon country and a two–three day trek, exploring the myths and legends of the villages nestling in the *falaise*. The arty, colonial town of Ségou, is a good place to sample the local 'capitaine' dish and enjoy a night on the tiles at the Alphabet Bar. Just time for some pottery shopping before heading back to Bamako for a tour of the capital and then fly home.

Two weeks Catch a motorised *pinasse* for the three day journey along the River Niger to Timbuktu, camping along the river banks or in small villages such as quaint Niafunké, home of the late, great Ali Farka Touré. Arriving at the mythical city of Timbuktu, explore the labyrinth of streets containing mud mosques and the houses of ancient explorers and discover the secrets contained within the ancient manuscripts. Then take a camel ride into the desert and stay in a traditional Tuareg camp or visit the remote town of Arouane, being reclaimed by the desert. Just time for a couple of days tracking the desert elephants of Gourma or some rock-climbing at the Main de Fatma in Hombori on the way back to Bamako.

A month or more... All of the above. Then take the train from Bamako to Kayes to visit the old colonial buildings and enjoy the slow pace of life in this laidback town, or the lush vegetation and waterfalls of humid Sikasso. Take the COMONAV ferry – or the 'big boat' as it's known locally – all the way to Gao and explore the remote Northern Desert region around Tessalit and Kidal. Or join one of the camel caravans from Timbuktu for the three-week journey to the salt mines of Taoudenni.

TOURIST INFORMATION

L'OMATHO AND THE MISSION CULTURELLE Formal tourist offices are a rarity in Mali. The Office Malien du Tourisme et de l'Hôtellerie (or OMATHO) is a governmental institution working under the Ministère de l'Artisanat et du Tourisme. Its objectives include charting and streamlining potential tourist destinations and events, promoting and increasing tourism in Mali, and implementing compulsory training for professional guides. The OMATHO also seeks to improve the quality of various services, such as dispensing information to visitors: it is a kind of tourist office, one could say, and is sometimes even signposted as such. Although staff are very friendly and ready to help, in real terms it is mainly a place to pick up some brochures and not much else.

Having said that, you may encounter the *chef* or a member of staff who is passionate about his profession, and find yourself discussing local history and culture in depth – at times even in English! In short: the OMATHO has not yet come to full bloom, but can no longer be ignored, so give it a try. Apart from the main office in Bamako (*Rue Mohamed V, BP 191;* ☎ *2022 56 73;* **f** *2022 55 41;* **e** *omatho@le-mali.com; www.le-mali.com*), there are representations in Kayes, Sikasso, Ségou, Mopti, Timbuktu, Gao and Kidal. A regional office in Bamako represents Bamako and Koulikoro.

Look for the Mission Culturelle at Djenné, Bandiagara and Timbuktu. Established to protect, restore and promote Mali's World Heritage Sites, the tasks of the Mission Culturelle sometimes overlap with those of a conventional tourist office. However, although all three offices are run by leading authorities on the history of Djenné, Dogon country and Timbuktu, they should not be treated as tourist offices. Ask them for advice and recommendations by all means; but also understand – and take an interest in – their struggle to protect the country's patrimony from a multitude of sins (see box *Responsible tourism in Dogon country*, page 194, for more about these 'sins').

GUIDES The OMATHO and the Mission Culturelle are working together to improve the quality of the tourist guides in Mali. This is just as well, because as things stand there is very little regulation. The result has been a proliferation of *petits guides* – young men and boys who may know how to get from A to B, but are not necessarily able to explain what A and B mean.

Lack of knowledge, although disappointing for inquisitive tourists and potentially damaging from a cultural point of view (see box *Responsible tourism in Dogon country*, page 194), can be forgivable, provided that guides are friendly and obviously trying their best. In this case, you are paying for their company rather than expertise. However, in too many towns – Bamako, Mopti and Djenné are amongst the worst – good nature has been replaced by an uncharacteristically aggressive streak. Some blame this on drug addiction, the alienating effects of unemployment and other social ills but, whatever the cause, the effect on the visitor – especially in a small place such as Djenné where there is no escaping the guides – is tiring and frustrating.

The Minister of Culture is aware of the problem; trying to solve it, however, is another matter. In 2005, the OMATHO introduced an exam for guides to get certified and receive their badge or *carte professionnelle*, which you should ask to see. However, there are many good guides who have not been able to get their badge. The OMATHO does not hold yearly certification exams – in fact, the last one was in 2005!

TOUR OPERATORS

The list below represents a small fraction of the travel agencies and tour operators around at the moment. They are all well established and most tend to specialise in independent travel – some offering tailor-made tours to Mali. In many cases these agencies also sell travel insurance and have health clinics for vaccinations and other medical advice.

UK

Cox and Kings 6th Floor, 30 Millbank, London SW1P 4EE; ☎ 020 7873 5000; e sales@coxandkings.co.uk; www.coxandkings.co.uk. Have been organising trips to Mali since 2003.

Dragoman Overland Camp Green, Debenham, Stowmarket, Suffolk IP14 6LA; ☎ 01728 861133; e info@dragoman.co.uk; www.dragoman.com

Exodus Grange Mills, Weir Rd, London SW12 0NE; ☎ 0845 863 9600; e sales@exodus.co.uk; www.exodus.co.uk

Explore Worldwide Nelson Hse, 55 Victoria Rd, Farnborough, Hants GU14 7PA; ☎ 0845 013 1537; f 01252 760001; e hello@explore.co.uk; www.explore.co.uk

Fulani Travel 14 Fron Whion Dolgellau, Gwynedd LL40 1SL; ☎ 01341 421969; e info@fulanitravel.co.uk; www.fulanitravel.co.uk

Imaginative Traveller 1 Betts Av, Martlesham Heath, Suffolk IP5 3RH; ☎ 0845 077 8802; e online@imtrav.net; www.imaginative-traveller.com

Intrepid 6 Upper St, Islington, London N1 0NU; ☎ 0203 147 7777; e ask@intrepidtravel.com; www.intrepidtravel.com

Peregrine 1st Floor, 8 Clerewater Pl, Lower Way, Thatcham, Berks RG19 3RF; ☎ 0844 736 0170; e sales@peregrineadventures.co.uk; www.peregrineadventures.co.uk

Songlines Music Travel ☎ 020 8505 2582; e songlines@thegroupscompany.com; www.songlines.co.uk/musictravel. 2 to 3 musical tours a year in Jan, Feb & Nov.

STA Travel 6 Wrights Lane, London W8 6TA; ☎ 0871 230 0040; e enquiries@statravel.co.uk; www.statravel.co.uk. STA has 12 branches in London and 30 or so around the country and at different university cities.

Steppes Travel 51 Castle St, Cirencester, Glos GL7 1QD; ☎ 01285 880980; f 01285 885888. Tailor-made holidays.

Tim Best Travel 4 Cromwell Pl, London SW7 2JE; ☎ 020 7591 0300; f 020 7591 0301; e info@timbesttravel.com; www.timbesttravel.com

US

Adventure Center ☎ +1 800 228 8747; e it@adventurecenter.com; www.adventurecenter.com

Adventure Travel Company ☎ +1 800 467 4595; e sanfrancisco@atcadventure.com; www.atcadventure.com

Mountain Travel–Sobek 1266 66th St, Emeryville, CA 94608; ☎ +1 800 687 6235; e info@mtsobek.com; www.mtsobek.com
Palace Travel 5301 Chestnut St, Philadelphia, PA 19139; ☎ +1 800 683 7731 or +1 215 471 8555; www.palacetravel.com/
Spector Travel of Boston 581 Boylston St, Boston, MA 02116; ☎ +1 617 351 0111; e africa@spectortravel.com; www.spectortravel.com
Turtle Tours PO Box 1147, Carefree, AZ 85377; ☎ +1 480 488 3688; e turtletours@earthlink.net; www.turtletours.com
Wilderness Travel 1102 Ninth St, Berkeley, CA 94710; ☎ +1 800 368 2794; www.wildernesstravel.com

IN MALI Tour operators in Mali – and there is no shortage of them – fulfil a number of functions. The larger ones, most of which are based in Bamako, sell airline tickets, arrange vehicle hire and offer a number of *circuits* or tours in Mali and neighbouring countries. Others specialise in certain regions (Dogon country, the desert, etc) and may be based outside Bamako. As far as the tours in Mali are concerned, the majority of tour operators are sent groups of tourists by travel agencies acting as their partners in Europe. Independent travellers are quite welcome to turn up and book a tour, but it is often expensive, especially if you are not travelling in a group yourself. There are, however, advantages to taking a tour. Provided that you choose a reputable operator, you should be guaranteed a decent guide who knows what he's talking about. Transportation problems are also negated by 4x4 vehicles and, for river trips, comfortable *pinasses* (for further information, see page 74). The downside, of course, is the expense and the minimal contact with the realities of Malian life.

Almost all tour operators organise trips to places such as Ségou, Djenné, Mopti, Dogon country and Timbuktu (by river or road). Gao is a good place to join organised trips into the desert, but, unfortunately, Mali's national parks and reserves do not interest tour operators eager to cash in on the country's better-known attractions. *Chapter 3* contains a list of the major tour operators in Bamako – all of them reputable enough, but perhaps lacking the personal touch found at some of the out-of-town options. If you want to avoid the larger agencies in Bamako, try the meticulous **Tara Africa Tours** (see page 115), a Dutch–Dogon partnership that provides tailor-made tours throughout the country. For obvious reasons, Tara Africa Tours is particularly good for trips to Dogon country. Another agency that combines expertise with a personal touch is **Toguna Adventure Tours** (see page 115). **Affala Voyages** (see page 232) in Kidal is a solid choice for ventures deep into the desert. The agency is run by the same respectable Tuareg who used to be the president of the committee which organises Takoubelt – the Tuareg festival in the Kidal region (see page 91). Be persistent; at times Affala Voyages is difficult to contact. Tour operators are listed separately under the relevant town.

RED TAPE

ENTRY REQUIREMENTS In general, the following documents are required to enter Mali:

- A passport with at least six months' validity remaining
- A visa
- An International Certificate of Vaccination or Revaccination against Yellow Fever

Visas Unless you are a national of a selection of north and west African countries, or the Principalities of Monaco and Andorra, you will need a visa to visit Mali. Visas are issued without much fuss in countries with Malian representation; the problem is finding these countries. There is currently no embassy or consulate in London, so residents of the UK are obliged to send their passports to either Paris or Brussels. The Consulat Général du Mali in France is quick and efficient at issuing visas. Write to them – or the Centre d'Information et de Documentation at the embassy in Paris – for an application form, and return it with two photographs, €30, your passport and, most importantly, a stamped addressed envelope (or addressed envelope plus international reply coupons). The visa itself takes four days to issue, but you must allow at least another ten days while your application is held up in the post.

Visas at the consulate in Brussels take three working days to issue. Although you can send in your passport by post, the consulate will not post it back to you; you must either collect it in person or use a courier service such as DHL or APS. Alternatively, you could pay a visa service to do the work – which will be expensive, because they must also deal with consulates abroad. For example, Travcour (☎ *020 7223 5295;* e *info@travcour.com; www.travcour.com*) will send your application to the embassy in Belgium for you for £70. This pays for the courier and service charge only. If you want them to apply on your behalf, it's an extra £35.

Another option is to stop in Paris *en route* to Mali and submit your application in person (see *The Paris option*, page 48). The visa issued permits a single entry and is valid for one month after the date of arrival. If you intend to leave Mali and return at a later date, you must obtain a new visa.

For American citizens, the application procedure is similar and the visa issued is valid for three months. The Malian Embassy in Washington asks for five working days to process applications and charges US$80 for a three-month visa plus postage. Visit their website for more details (see page 49).

If obtaining a visa before travelling to Mali is not an option, there is always the possibility of getting a *visa d'entrée* at Bamako Sénou International Airport. This visa costs CFA15,000 and is valid for five days only, so you will have to have the visa validated and extended within a matter of days. Do check with your airline to make sure you can board the plane without a visa. Because of a communication breakdown somewhere along the line, Air France requests passengers to show a Malian visa at check-in and often will not allow people to fly without one. If you're travelling with an agency, they should be able to send you a letter addressed to Air France, informing them that it's possible to obtain a visa upon arrival at Bamako. With this letter, you shouldn't be refused boarding. Alternatively, with a fax or scan of the photo page in your passport and CFA15,000 the agency should be able to get a *visa d'entrée* on your behalf and send it to you. At the airport, the *visa d'entrée* is payable in local currency only, but you should be able to change euros or US dollars at the exchange office before going through customs. If the exchange office happens to be closed – which does occur – officials will refer you to unofficial ways to obtain the necessary CFAs. At some border posts – like Diboli at the Senegalese border – a *visa d'entrée* may be issued under the same conditions.

When you are travelling overland, you may be able to get a visa in one of the neighbouring countries. In Dakar (Senegal) a visa costs CFA23,000 and takes 24 hours to issue. In Ouagadougou (Burkina Faso) a visa (single-entry, one-month validity) costs less and takes only 15 minutes to issue. For more details of embassies and consulates see page 48.

Once you are in Mali, visa extensions can be obtained at the Direction Générale de la Police Nationale in Bamako in ACI 2000. If you have a *visa d'entrée* this is free, otherwise stamps for each additional month cost CFA5,000, regardless of whether or not you intend to be in Mali for the whole month. Extending your visa in Bamako can usually be done on the same day if you hand your passport in before 10.00. Otherwise, it's 24 hours and requires two photographs. Compared with many other countries in west Africa, the Malians are not big on bureaucracy, so, provided that your papers are in order, red tape should not be too much of a problem.

There have been reports, though, about the Direction Générale de la Police Nationale in Bamako being foul-tempered at times. If you have the choice, get your visa extended in Mopti instead. Service is much quicker and always friendly, so the whole procedure should take no more than the time it takes to fill out the necessary forms, and stamp and sign your passport. In Mopti you need two photographs, and wherever you get your visa extension, remember that one empty page in your passport is required.

The Paris option Whether by choice or necessity, stopping in Paris *en route* to Mali has a number of advantages and is worth considering.

Firstly, flights to Bamako from Paris are cheaper and more numerous than from other European capitals. There is also a Malian Consulate in Paris (nearest metro: Chemin Vert) which issues visas quickly and efficiently; and at the embassy (nearest metro: Vaneau) the Centre d'Information et de Documentation (🕘 *09.00–13.00 & 14.00–17.00 Mon–Fri*) has a lot of relevant reading material, including telephone directories and Malian newspapers. Other information and travel aids, such as the excellent map of Mali produced by the Institut Géographique National de France and numerous books about the country and its attractions, are also more readily available in Paris than, for example, London or New York. Finally, if you need any last-minute vaccinations or medical advice, the Dispensaire Edison (nearest metro: Place d'Italie) is run by the Mairie de Paris (Paris Town Council) and is cheaper than the private clinics – although the service is slower (see page 55).

E EMBASSIES AND CONSULATES

The extent of Mali's representation abroad is not vast. The more important embassies and consulates are as follows:

ABROAD

Belgium 487 Av Molière, 1060 Brussels; ☎ 02 345 7432; f 02 344 5700; e ambassade.mali@skynet.be; 🕘 09.00–12.00 Mon–Fri

Burkina Faso 2569 Av Bassawarga, Ouagadougou; ☎ 5038 1922; f 5038 1921

Canada 50 Goulburn Av, Ottawa, Ontario K1N 8C8; ☎ 613 232 1501; f 613 232 7429; e ambassadedumali@rogers.com; www.ambamalicanada.org

Côte d'Ivoire Maison du Mali, 46 Bd Lagunaire, 01 BP 2746, Abidjan; ☎ 20 32 31 47; f 20 21 55 14; e ambamalirci@yahoo.fr

France *Paris* Embassy: 89 Rue du Cherche Midi, 75006 Paris; ☎ 01 45 48 58 43; f 01 45 48 55 34; Consulate: 43 Rue Chemin Vert, 75011 Paris; ☎ 01 48 07 85 85; *Marseille* Consulate: 47 Rue de la Paix, 13001 Marseille; ☎ 01 91 33 76 30; www.consulat-mali-france.org

Ghana Agostino Neto Rd, Hse No 8, Airport Residential Area, Accra, BP GP 1121; ☎ 21 775 160; f 21 774 339

Guinea Coleach Corniche, BP 299, Conakry; ☎ 461 418/443 303; f 463 703

Germany Basteistrasse 86, D-53713 Bonn; ☎ 0228 35 70 48; f 0228 36 19 22; Kurfurstendamm, 7210709 Berlin; ☎ 030 319 98 83; fax: 030 319 98 49; e ambmali@01019freenet.de

Italy (Consulate) Via Antonia Bosio 2, 00161 Rome; ☎ 06 44 25 4068; f 06 44 25 4029; e amb.malirome@tiscalinet.it

Japan 3-12-9, Kamiosaki, Shinagawa-ku, Tokyo; ☎ 00 81 35 44 76 881; e info@ambamali-jp.org; www.ambamali-jp.org; 🕘 10.00–16.00 Mon–Fri.

Mauritania BP 184, Nouakchott; ☎ 525 4078/81; f 525 4083

Morocco 58 Cité OLM Ext-Streissi II, Rabat; ☎ 00212 7759125/ 00212 7759121; f 00212 775474; 🕘 09.00–15.00

Niger Bd de la Liberté, BP 10115, Niamey; ☎ 75 42 90/75 41 88; f 73 33 46; e consmali@intnet.net; www.gsi-niger.com/consulat-mali

Senegal 48 St Maginot, BP 478, Dakar; ☎ 824 62 50/52, 823 48 94

Switzerland (Consulate) St Jakobs-Strasse 30, case postale, CH-4002, Basel; ☎ 061 295 38 88; **f** 061 295 38 89; **e** office@maliconsulat.ch; www.maliconsulat.ch
Togo (Consulate) Quartier Ablogame, Rue de la Paix, BP 821, Lomé; ☎ 213 458
US *Washington DC* 2130 K St NW, Washington, DC 20008; ☎ 202 332 2249; **f** 202 332 6603; *New York* tel; 212 794 1311/737 4150; **f** 212 472 3778; **e** info@maliembassy.usa.org; www.maliembassy.us (useful general info)

IN MALI

Belgium (Consulate) Hippodrome, Route de Koulikoro (opposite the Dutch Embassy); BP 187; ☎ 2022 39 75; fax: 2022 98 81; **e** bamako@diplobel.be; www.diplomatie.be/bamako; ⏲ 08.00–12.30 & 14.00–17.00 Mon–Fri, 08.00–12.00 Sat.
Burkina Faso ACI 2000, near the Police Nationale; ☎ 2021 31 71; **f** 2021 92 66; **e** ambfaso@datatech.toolnet.org
Canada Immeuble Semega, Route de Koulikoro, Commune II, opposite the Luna Parc; ☎ 2021 22 36; **f** 2021 43 62; **e** bmako@international.gc.ca; www.mali.gc.ca; ⏲ 07.30–16.00 Mon–Fri.
Côte d'Ivoire Pl Patrice Lumumba, Immeuble Tam Voyages, opposite Air France, BP 3644; ☎ 2021 22 89; **f** 2022 13 76
Denmark Immeuble UATT, Quartier du Fleuve; ☎ 2023 03 73; **f** 2023 01 94; **e** bkoamb@um.dk; www.bamako.um.dk/da
France Sq Patrice Lumumba, BP 17; ☎ 2497 57 57; **f** 2497 57 09; **e** ambassade@france-mali.org.ml
Germany Badalabougou Est, Rue 14, Av de l'OUA (1 block after the Pont des Martyrs), BP 100; ☎ 2022 32 99; **f** 2022 96 50; **e** allemagne.presse@afribone.net.ml; www.bamako.diplo.de
Ghana ACI 2000, near Hotel Bouna; ☎ 2029 60 83; **f** 2029 60 84
Guinea Immeuble Saïbou Maïga, Quartier du Fleuve, BP 118; ☎ 2022 29 75/2021 08 06
Italy Quinzambougou, BP 2386; ☎ 2021 73 10
Mauritania Hippodrome (just before the Fort premises to the left); ☎ 2021 48 15
Netherlands Hippodrome, Route de Koulikoro, BP 2220; ☎ 2021 56 11; **f** 2021 36 17; **e** bam@minbuza.nl
Niger Represented by Côte d'Ivoire in Mali
Norway (Consulate) Badalabougou Est; ☎ 2022 38 84; **f** 2022 62 74
Senegal Hippodrome, BP 42; ☎ 2021 82 74; **f** 2021 82 73
Spain (Vice-consulate) Rue Lyantey, BP 1823; ☎/**f** 2024 64 52
South Africa Diarra Bldg, Hamdallaye, ACI 2000; ☎ 2029 29 25; **f** 2029 29 26; **e** bamako@foreign.gov.za; www.saemali.info
Sweden Immeuble Babemba; ☎ 2022 32 40; **f** 2022 45 66; **e** anders.ostman@sida.se
Switzerland (Consulate) Route de Sotuba, BP 2386; ☎ 2024 45 49; fax: 2021 32 05; **e** coop.suisse@afribone.net.ml
UK (British Embassy Liaison Office – BELO – located in the Canadian Embassy) Hippodrome, Route de Koulikoro, BP 2069; ☎ (emergency) 2021 34 12, (consular) **m** 7640 08 08; **f** 2021 83 77; **e** belo@afribone.net.ml
USA Rue 243, Porte 297, ACI 2000; ☎ 2070 23 00; (consular direct) **m** 7600 79 79; www.mali.usembassy.gov

GETTING THERE AND AWAY

BY AIR

From Europe There are no direct flights to Mali from the UK. However, Royal Air Maroc operates flights via Casablanca, Ethiopian Airlines via Addis Ababa and Air France via Paris. Paris is the main European gateway for flights to Bamako: Air France has daily direct flights to the capital of Mali, but their flights are amongst the more expensive ones. There are, however, less pricey options to choose from.

Since December 1995, a French organisation called Point Afrique (see *Airline offices in Bamako*, page 51) has been operating flights between Paris, Lyon and Marseille (in the south of France) to Bamako, Mopti and Gao. Their ethos is to provide access to the more isolated parts of west Africa – they also fly to Burkina Faso, Mauritania, Niger, Algeria and Senegal – and, although you have to get to Lyon or Paris first, there is no cheaper way of travelling to Mali from Europe. Most flights, with the exception of Bamako, operate during the high season only (October to April). Air Mali – previously known as Compagnie Aérienne du Mali (CAM) (*www.camaero.com*) – also have reatively inexpensive flights from Paris to

Bamako. It is well worth checking out their website, as they sometimes have special offers. Obviously these flights do fill up rather quickly. **Nouvelles Frontières** (*www.nouvelles-frontieres.fr*) is a website that searches a number of different airlines flying out of Paris.

Without exception, choosing another airline implies flying via another African country – often one of Mali's neighbouring countries. Also listed below are most airline companies operating regular services to and from Bamako, with flights to and from west African capitals like Ouagadougou, Nouakchott, Cotonou, Accra, Dakar and Niamey. As a matter of fact, you could even opt for a flight to one of these destinations, then travel to Mali overland. Depending on where in Mali you would like to start your trip, this may well be an easy way to cut down your expenses.

From North America Residents of the USA, like their British counterparts, will have to make at least one connection before arriving in Mali. This could be in Europe (Paris or Marseille) or several destinations in Africa, depending on your choice of airline (see *Airline offices in Bamako*, below).

From Africa Several of the airlines mentioned below are regional carriers, flying to Bamako from around Africa. Air Mali goes to various countries in the region, including Brazzaville in Congo, and Cotonou in Benin. South African Airways has flights from South Africa to Abidjan or Accra. The other companies, their names incorporating the country they are based in, operate at least between Bamako and their respective capitals – but more often than not their flight schedule includes more African destinations. In short, continental air travel to and from Mali is not a problem.

Arriving at Bamako-Sénou International Airport Arriving in a new country is exciting and, at the same time, a little daunting. After a long, tiring flight, the last thing you want to do is grapple with awkward immigration officials and persistent taxi drivers. Fortunately, Bamako-Sénou Airport (☎ *2020 27 01;* **m** *7600 70 71*) is as informal and relaxed as a west African airport can be.

Planes stop a short distance from the terminal buildings. Walk across the tarmac, enter the terminal, change some money and buy a temporary visa if applicable, complete a simple landing card, get your passport stamped, show your Yellow Fever Certificate to a man in a white coat, and collect your baggage – all of which should not take more than 30 minutes. Remember to retain your boarding pass with the luggage barcode or number; you have to present it on leaving the terminal to prove that your luggage is really yours. Porters are available – and sometimes even hard to avoid – and taxis will be waiting outside in the car park.

If you are arriving from Paris, you can buy some CFA at the bureau de change in the departure lounge at Charles de Gaulle Airport. It is a good idea to have some local currency before you arrive, just in case the exchange office at Bamako-Sénou is closed.

(See *Chapter* 3, *Getting there and away*, page 109, for information about other facilities available at Bamako-Sénou Airport, as well as transportation from the airport to Bamako.)

Airport tax The international departure tax should be included in your air fare. The airport tax for domestic flights is CFA2,750, payable before checking in.

Airline offices in Bamako

Afriqiyah Airways Av de la Marne, Hôtel de l'Amitié; ☎ 2021 39 63; www.afriqiyah.aero

Air Algérie Av Modibo Keita, Centre Commercial No 324; ☎ 2022 31 59; **f** 2022 84 05.

Air Burkina Av de la Marne, Hôtel de l'Amitié; ☎ 2021 01 78; e airburkinabko@afribone.net.ml; www.air-burkina.com
Air France Hamdalaye, ACI 2000; ☎ 2070 03 30; f 2022 47 34; www.airfrance.com; ⏲ 08.00–12.15 & 14.00–17.00 Mon–Fri, 09.00–12.00 Sat
Air Ivoire Ex Immeuble USAID Av de l'Iser; ☎ 2023 95 58/59; f 2023 95 75; e airivoirebko@airivoire.com; www.airivoire.com
Air Mali Immeuble Tomota, Av Cheick Zayed; ☎ 2022 24 24/26 26; f 2022 71 11; e resacam@cam-mali.org; www.camaero.com
Air Sénégal 555 Av Modibo Keita; ☎ 2023 98 11/2/3/5; f 2023 98 16; e bamako@airsenegalinternational.sn; www.air-senegal-international.com
Ethiopian Airlines Sq Patrice Lumumba; ☎ 2022 22 08; f 2022 60 36; e bkoam@ethiopianairlines.com; www.ethiopianairlines.com
Ghana Airways GH Sq Patrice Lumumba, Immeuble SCIF, BP 932; ☎ 2021 31 50; www.fly-ghana.com
Kenyan Airways Immeuble le Babemba (Ground Floor); ☎ 2022 12 35; f 2022 94 50; e info@kenya-airways.co.ml; www.kenya-airways.com
Mali Air Express (MAE) Av de la Nation; ☎ 223 14 65; e sae@cefib.com; www.malipages.com/mae/
Mauritania Airways c/o Tunis Air, Av de la Marne, Hôtel de l'Amitié; ☎ 2021 86 42/43/04; f 2021 86 17; www.fly-mauritaniaairways.com
Point Afrique BIE France Le Village, 07 700 Bidon; ☎ +33 (0)4 75 97 20 40; f +33 (0)4 75 97 20 50; e contact@point-afrique.com; Immeuble Ex UsAid, Quartier du Fleuve; ☎ 4490 07 35 or 2023 54 70; f 2023 57 76; e bamako@point-afrique.com; www.point-afrique.com
Royal Air Maroc Av de la Marne, Hôtel de l'Amitié; ☎ 2021 61 05; f 2021 43 02; e rambko@afribone.net.ml; www.royalairmaroc.com
Tunis Air Av de la Marne, Hôtel de l'Amitié; ☎ 2021 86 42/43; f 2021 86 17; e tunisairbko@ikatelnet.net; www.tunisair.com

BY RIVER The River Niger rises in Guinea and flows through Mali before bending south towards Niger. The country's other great waterway, the River Senegal, starts in the eastern region of Kayes and flows along the border between Senegal and Mauritania. Therefore, in theory, it is possible to travel to Mali by river from four neighbouring countries. In practice, however, it is rarely done. All international river travel is a question of finding a boat going in your direction, fixing an acceptable price and hoping that the river is navigable. Travelling to and from Mali by this means is for real adventurers, and the River Senegal might be more practicable than the Niger (see *Chapter 11*, *Getting there and away*, page 273).

BY TRAIN The Dakar–Bamako railway was completed in 1923 and, although it has certainly seen better days, it remains of great economic importance and one of the favourite ways for travellers to get to Mali. 'Favourite' is perhaps an ill-chosen word, for the overcrowded and habitually late Dakar–Bamako train is no *Orient Express*. There is now only a single train still running, and all pretence at a timetable has been abandoned. The train takes roughly a week to complete the round trip. Go to Dakar station (or others along the route) to find out when it's next expected, and if they say 'tomorrow', don't hold your breath… Even so, it does provide a link between the two capitals that ensures its continued popularity for the foreseeable future.

In 2003, all services operating between Dakar and Bamako were reportedly cancelled, owing to the condition of the track and a couple of derailments every year. Operation of the railway was handed over to a Canadian company and in 2005, a weekly express was reinstated. Trains were timetabled to leave Bamako on a Wednesday, arriving in Dakar the following day. In reality, they were only running every eight–nine days and though scheduled as a 24-hour journey, were regularly arriving more than 12 hours late. New locomotives and carriages were due in 2007 and service was expected to be faster and much improved. However, by early 2008 they had not yet arrived and, at the time of writing, the new timetable was not available. For the latest information, contact the station in Bamako (☎ *2022 58 16*) or Dakar (☎ *+221 849 46 46*) or see www.seat61.com/Senegal.htm.

BY ROAD With Mali being a landlocked country with seven different international borders, many of its visitors arrive by road. As far as independent travellers are concerned, the routes to and from Senegal and Burkina Faso are arguably the most popular. The bus leaving daily from Senegal to Kayes is the locals' preferred mode of transport; tickets are the same price as a second-class ticket on the train (CFA25,000), and the journey takes one day as opposed to two or three.

Public transport is also available from Burkina to several Malian towns, including Bamako, Ségou, Mopti and Sikasso and to Niger (from Gao). Fewer people choose to travel to Guinea and the war-torn countries of this corner of west Africa, although *bâchées* (for further information, see page 78) do run from Bamako to the Guinean border and from Sikasso to Côte d'Ivoire. The desert routes to Mauritania and Algeria are not served by public transport, although *locations* and *camions* (see page 79 for an explanation of these terms) can be found. A steady stream of tourists with their own 4x4 vehicles cross into Mali from Mauritania, but, owing to the security situation in Algeria and Tuareg banditry in the desert, the so-called Route de Tanezrouft is seldom used. The road linking Mali to Burkina Faso is paved and in a generally good state; elsewhere, there are only tracks.

(For more information about road travel between Mali and neighbouring countries, see the *Getting there and away* sections for the relevant towns.)

Border crossings The most commonly used border crossings between Mali and its neighbours are as follows:

- **Algeria** Via Gao and Tessalit (which is not actually on the border itself, but the last settlement before you cross into Algeria)
- **Burkina Faso** Via Koutiala and Kouri (although a substantial number of visitors with their own vehicles go via Bankass and Koro, stopping in Dogon country *en route*)
- **Côte d'Ivoire** Via Sikasso and Zégoua
- **Guinea** Kourémalé (about 100km from Bamako)
- **Mauritania** Via Nioro du Sahel or, more rarely, Nara
- **Niger** Via Gao, Ansongo and Labézanga
- **Senegal** Via Kayes and Diboli

HEALTH *with Dr Felicity Nicholson*

People new to exotic travel often worry about tropical diseases, but it is accidents that are most likely to carry you off. Road accidents are very common in many parts of Mali so be aware and do what you can to reduce risks: try to travel during daylight hours, always wear a seatbelt and refuse to be driven by anyone who has been drinking. Listen to local advice about areas where violent crime is rife too.

PREPARATIONS Preparations to ensure a healthy trip to Mali require checks on your immunisation status: it is wise to be up to date on tetanus, polio and diphtheria (now given as an all-in-one vaccine, Revaxis, that lasts for ten years), and hepatitis A. Immunisations against meningococcus and rabies may also be recommended. Proof of vaccination against yellow fever is needed for entry into Mali regardless of where you are coming from. The World Health Organization (WHO) recommends that this vaccine should be taken for Mali by those over nine months of age, although proof of vaccination is only officially required for those over one year of age. If the vaccine is not suitable for you then obtain an exemption certificate from your GP or a travel clinic. Immunisation against cholera may be recommended for people who are living and working in more rural areas. The vaccine comprises two doses that need to be taken at least one week apart and at least one week before entering the country.

Hepatitis A vaccine (Havrix Monodose or Avaxim) comprises two injections given about a year apart. The course costs about £100, but may be available on the NHS; it protects for 25 years and can be administered even close to the time of departure. Hepatitis B vaccination should be considered for longer trips (two months or more) or for those working with children or in situations where contact with blood is likely. Three injections are needed for the best protection and can be given over a three-week period if time is short for those aged 16 or over. Longer schedules give more sustained protection and are therefore preferred if time allows. Hepatitis A vaccine can also be given as a combination with hepatitis B as 'Twinrix', though two doses are needed at least seven days apart to be effective for the hepatitis A component, and three doses are needed for the hepatitis B. This rapid schedule can only be used for those aged 18 or over.

The newer injectable typhoid vaccines (eg: Typhim Vi) last for three years and are about 85% effective. Oral capsules (Vivotif) are currently available in the US (and soon in the UK); if four capsules are taken over seven days it will last for five years. They should be encouraged unless the traveller is leaving within a few days for a trip of a week or less, when the vaccine would not be effective in time. Meningitis vaccine containing strains A, C, W and Y, is recommended for all travellers especially for trips of more than four weeks (see *Meningitis*, page 61). Vaccinations for rabies are ideally advised for everyone, but are especially important for travellers visiting more remote areas, especially if you are more than 24 hours from medical help and definitely if you will be working with animals (see *Rabies*, page 61).

Experts differ over whether a BCG vaccination against tuberculosis (TB) is useful in adults: discuss this with your travel clinic.

In addition to the various vaccinations recommended above, it is important that travellers should be properly protected against malaria. For detailed advice, see page 54.

Ideally you should visit your own doctor or a specialist travel clinic (see page 55) to discuss your requirements, if possible at least eight weeks before you plan to travel.

Protection from the sun Give some thought to packing suncream. The incidence of skin cancer is rocketing as Caucasians are travelling more and spending more time exposing themselves to the sun. Keep out of the sun during the middle of the day and, if you must expose yourself to the sun, build up gradually from 20 minutes per day. Be especially careful of exposure in the middle of the day and of sun reflected off water, and wear a T-shirt and lots of waterproof suncream (at least SPF15) when swimming. Sun exposure ages the skin, makes people prematurely wrinkly, and increases the risk of skin cancer. Cover up with long, loose clothes and wear a hat when you can. The glare and the dust can be hard on the eyes, too, so bring UV-protecting sunglasses and, perhaps, a soothing eyebath.

Respiratory problems Mali is a dusty country at the best of times. When the desert winds start to blow, especially during the harmattan months, dust particles are swept off the ground and into the atmosphere, where it becomes impossible not to breathe them in. Long-term exposure to dust can cause serious respiratory problems, especially if it enters the lungs. Even relatively brief stays in this sort of environment can be uncomfortable, and respiratory infections such as colds and bronchitis are common. The discomfort is most pronounced in the desert regions, which, of course, is why the Tuareg, Songhay and other people of the desert wear turbans. Consider following their example. Note also that dust and wind are a lethal combination for contact-lens wearers.

Malaria Along with road accidents, malaria poses the single biggest serious threat to the health of travellers in most parts of tropical Africa, Mali included. It is unwise to travel in malarial parts of Africa whilst pregnant or with children: the risk of malaria in many parts is considerable and these travellers are likely to succumb rapidly to the disease. The risk of malaria above 1,800m is low.

Malaria in Mali The risk of malaria in Mali is high in all parts of the country all the year round. The risk is greatest in the savanna regions of the south and decreases as you travel north through the Sahel towards the desert.

Malaria prevention There is not yet a vaccine against malaria that gives enough protection to be useful for travellers, but there are other ways to avoid it. Since most of Africa is very high risk for malaria, travellers must plan their malaria protection properly. Seek current advice on the best antimalarials to take: usually mefloquine, Malarone or doxycycline. If mefloquine (Lariam) is suggested, start this two-and-a-half weeks (three doses) before departure to check that it suits you; stop it immediately if it seems to cause depression or anxiety, visual or hearing disturbances, severe headaches, fits or changes in heart rhythm. Side effects such as nightmares or dizziness are not medical reasons for stopping unless they are sufficiently debilitating or annoying. Anyone who has been treated for depression or psychiatric problems, has diabetes controlled by oral therapy or who is epileptic (or who has suffered fits in the past) or has a close blood relative who is epileptic, should probably avoid mefloquine.

In the past doctors were nervous about prescribing mefloquine to pregnant women, but experience has shown that it is relatively safe and certainly safer than the risk of malaria. That said, there are other issues, so if you are travelling to Mali whilst pregnant, seek expert advice before departure.

Malarone (proguanil and atovaquone) is as effective as mefloquine. It has the advantage of having few side effects and need only be continued for one week after returning. However, it is expensive and because of this tends to be reserved for shorter trips. Malarone may not be suitable for everybody, so advice should be taken from a doctor. The licence in the UK has been extended for up to three months' use and a paediatric form of tablet is also available, prescribed on a weight basis.

Another alternative is the antibiotic doxycycline (100mg daily). Like Malarone it can be started one day before arrival. Unlike mefloquine, it may also be used in travellers with epilepsy, although certain antiepileptic medication may make it less effective. In perhaps 1–3% of people there is the possibility of allergic skin reactions developing in sunlight; the drug should be stopped if this happens. Women using the oral contraceptive should use an additional method of protection for the first four weeks when using doxycycline. It is also unsuitable in pregnancy or for children under 12 years.

Chloroquine and proguanil are no longer considered to be effective enough for Mali but may be considered as a last resort if nothing else is deemed suitable.

All tablets should be taken with or after the evening meal, washed down with plenty of fluid and, with the exception of Malarone (see above), continued for four weeks after leaving.

Despite all these precautions, it is important to be aware that no antimalarial drug is 100% protective, although those on prophylactics who are unlucky enough to catch malaria are less likely to get rapidly into serious trouble. In addition to taking antimalarials, it is therefore important to avoid mosquito bites between dusk and dawn (see box *Avoiding insect bites*, page 62).

There is unfortunately the occasional traveller who prefers to 'acquire resistance' to malaria rather than take preventive tablets, or who takes homeopathic prophylactics thinking these are effective against killer disease. Homeopathy theory dictates treating like with like so there is no place for prophylaxis or immunisation in a well person; bona fide homoeopathists do not advocate it. Travellers to Africa cannot acquire any effective resistance to malaria, and those who don't make use of prophylactic drugs risk their life in a manner that is both foolish and unnecessary.

Malaria diagnosis and treatment Even those who take their malaria tablets meticulously and do everything possible to avoid mosquito bites may contract a strain of malaria that is resistant to prophylactic drugs. Untreated malaria is likely to be fatal, but even strains resistant to prophylaxis respond well to prompt treatment. Because of this, your immediate priority upon displaying possible malaria symptoms – including a rapid rise in temperature (over 38°C), and any combination of a headache, flu-like aches and pains, a general sense of disorientation, and possibly even nausea and diarrhoea – is to establish whether you have malaria, ideally by visiting a clinic.

Diagnosing malaria is not easy, which is why consulting a doctor is sensible: there are other dangerous causes of fever in Africa, which require different treatments. Even if you test negative, it would be wise to stay within reach of a laboratory until the symptoms clear up, and to test again after a day or two if they don't. It's worth noting that if you have a fever and the malaria test is negative, you may have typhoid or paratyphoid, which should also receive immediate treatment.

Travellers to remote parts of Mali would be wise to carry a course of treatment to cure malaria, and a rapid test kit. With malaria, it is normal enough to go from feeling healthy to having a high fever in the space of a few hours (and it is possible to die from falciparum malaria within 24 hours of the first symptoms). In such circumstances, assume that you have malaria and act accordingly – whatever risks are attached to taking an unnecessary cure are outweighed by the dangers of untreated malaria. Experts differ on the costs and benefits of self-treatment, but agree that it leads to overtreatment and to many people taking drugs they do not need; yet treatment may save your life. There is also some division about the best treatment for malaria, but either Malarone or Coarthemeter are the current treatments of choice. Discuss your trip with a specialist either at home or in Mali.

Water sterilisation You can fall ill from drinking contaminated water so try to drink from safe sources, eg: bottled water where available. If you are away from shops such as halfway up a mountain and your bottled water runs out, make tea, pour the remaining boiled water into a clean container and use it for drinking. Alternatively, water should be passed through a good bacteriological filter or purified with iodine or the less-effective chlorine tablets (eg: Puritabs).

TRAVEL CLINICS AND HEALTH INFORMATION A full list of current travel clinic websites worldwide is available on www.istm.org/. For other journey preparation information, consult www.nathnac.org/ds/map_world.aspx. Information about various medications may be found on www.netdoctor.co.uk/travel.

UK

Berkeley Travel Clinic 32 Berkeley St, London W1J 8EL (Near Green Park tube station); ☎ 020 7629 6233; ⏲ 10.00–18.00 Mon–Fri; 10.00–15.00 Sat.

Cambridge Travel Clinic 41 Hills Rd, Cambridge CB2 1NT; ☎ 01223 367362; f 01223 368021; e enquiries@travelcliniccambridge.co.uk;

www.travelcliniccambridge.co.uk; ⌚ 10.00–16.00 Mon, Tue & Sat, 12.00–19.00 Wed & Thu, 11.00–18.00 Fri.

Edinburgh Travel Health Clinic 14 East Preston St, Newington, Edinburgh EH8 9QA; ☎ 0131 667 1030; www.edinburghtravelhealthclinic.co.uk; ⌚ 09.00–19.00 Mon–Wed, 09.00–18.00 Thu & Fri. Travel vaccinations and advice on all aspects of malaria prevention. All current UK prescribed anti-malaria tablets in stock.

Fleet Street Travel Clinic 29 Fleet St, London EC4Y 1AA; ☎ 020 7353 5678; www.fleetstreetclinic.com; ⌚ 08.45–17.30 Mon–Fri. Injections, travel products & latest advice.

Hospital For Tropical Diseases Travel Clinic Mortimer Market Centre, 2nd Flr, Capper St (off Tottenham Ct Rd), London WC1E 6AU; ☎ 020 7388 9600; www.thehtd.org; ⌚ 09.00–16.00. Offers consultations & advice, & is able to provide all necessary drugs & vaccines for travellers. Runs a healthline (☎ *020 7950 7799*) For country-specific information & health hazards. also stocks nets, water purification equipment & personal protection measures. Travellers who have returned from the tropics & are unwell, with fever or bloody diarrhoea, can attend the walk-in emergency clinic at the hospital without an appointment.

MASTA (Medical Advisory Service for Travellers Abroad), at the London School of Hygiene & Tropical Medicine, Keppel St, London WC1 7HT; ☎ 09068 224100 www.masta-travel-health.com; enquiries@masta.org. This is a premium-line number, charged at 60p per min. For a fee, they will provide an individually tailored health brief, with up-to-date information on how to stay healthy, inoculations & what to take.

MASTA Pre-Travel Clinics ☎ 01276 685040. Call or check www.masta-travel-health.com/travel-clinic.aspx for the nearest; there are currently 30 in Britain. They also sell malaria prophylaxis, memory cards, treatment kits, bednets, net treatment kits, etc.

NHS travel website www.fitfortravel.nhs.uk. Provides country-by-country advice on immunisation & malaria prevention, plus details of recent developments, & a list of relevant health organisations.

Nomad travel stores Flapship Store: 3–4 Wellington Terrace, Turnpike Lane, London N8 0PX; ☎ 020 8889 7014; f 020 8889 9528; e turnpike@nomadtravel.co.uk; www.nomadtravel.co.uk. Walk in or appointments ⌚ 09.15–17.00 every day with late night Thu. 6 stores in total country wide: 3 in London, Bristol, Southampton, Manchester. As well as dispensing health advice, Nomad stocks mosquito nets & other anti-bug devices, & an excellent range of adventure travel gear.

Interhealth Travel Clinic 111 Westminster Bridge Rd, London, SE1 7HR; ☎ 020 7902 9000; e info@interhealth.org.uk www.interhealth.org.uk; ⌚ 08.30–17.30 Mon–Fri. Competitively priced, one-stop travel health service by appointment only.

Trailfinders Immunisation Centre 194 Kensington High St, London W8 7RG; ☎ 020 7938 3999; www.trailfinders.com/travelessentials/travelclinic.htm; ⌚ 09.00–17.00 Mon, Tue, Wed & Fri, 09.00–18.00 Thu, 10.00–17.15 Sat. No appointment necessary.

Travelpharm The Travelpharm website (*www.travelpharm.com*) offers up-to-date guidance on travel-related health & has a range of medications available through their online mini-pharmacy.

Irish Republic

Tropical Medical Bureau Grafton St Medical Centre, Grafton Bdgs, 34 Grafton St, Dublin 2; ☎ 1 671 9200. Has a useful website specific to tropical destinations: www.tmb.ie.

USA

Centers For Disease Control 1600 Clifton Rd, Atlanta, Ga 30333; ☎ (800) 232 4636 Or (800) 232 6348; e cdcinfo@cdc.gov; www.cdc.gov/travel. The central source of travel information in the USA. Each summer they publish the invaluable *Health information for international travel*.

IAMAT (International Association for Medical Assistance to Travelers): 1623 Military Rd, #279 Niagara Falls, NY 14304-1745; ☎ 716 754 4883; e info@iamat.org; www.iamat.org. A non-profit organisation with free membership that provides lists of English-speaking doctors abroad.

Canada

IAMAT (International Association for Medical Assistance to Travellers) Suite 1, 1287 St Clair Av W, Toronto, Ontario M6E 1B8; ☎ 416 652 0137; www.iamat.org

TMVC Suite 314, 1030 W Georgia St, Vancouver, BC V6E 2Y3; ☎ 905 648 1112; e info@tmvc.com; www.tmvc.com. One-stop medical clinic for all your international travel medicine & vaccination needs.

Australia, New Zealand, Thailand

TMVC (Travel Doctors Group) ☎ 1300 65 88 44; www.tmvc.com.au. 22 clinics in Australia, New Zealand & Thailand, including: *Auckland* Canterbury Arcade, 170 Queen St, Auckland; ☎ 9 373 3531; *Brisbane* 75a Astor Terrace, Spring Hill, Brisbane, QLD 4000; (07) 3815 6900; brisbane@traveldoctor.com.au; *Melbourne* Dr Sonny Lau, 393 Little Bourke St, 2nd Floor, Melbourne, Vic 3000; ☎ (03) 9935 8100; melbourne@traveldoctor.Com.Au; *Sydney* Dr Mandy Hu, Dymocks Building, 7th Flr, 428 George St, Sydney, Nsw 2000; ☎ 2 9221 7133; f 2 9221 8401

IAMAT Po Box 5049, Christchurch 5, New Zealand; www.iamat.org

South Africa

SAA-Netcare Travel Clinics e travelinfo@netcare.co.za www.travelclinic.co.za. 12 clinics throughout South Africa.

TMVC NHC Health Centre, Cnr Beyers Naude & Waugh Northcliff; ☎ 0 11 214 9030; traveldoctor@wtmconline.com; www.traveldoctor.co.za. Consult the website for details of clinics.

Switzerland

IAMAT 57 Chemin Des Voirets, 1212 Grand-Lancy, Geneva; e info@iamat.org; www.iamat.org

PERSONAL FIRST-AID KIT A minimal kit contains:

- A good drying antiseptic, eg: iodine or potassium permanganate (don't take antiseptic cream)
- A few small dressings (Band-Aids)
- Suncream
- Insect repellent; antimalarial tablets; impregnated bed-net or permethrin spray
- Aspirin or paracetamol
- Antifungal cream (eg: Canesten)
- Ciprofloxacin or norfloxacin, for severe diarrhoea
- Tinidazole for giardia or amoebic dysentery (see box on page 60 for regime)
- Antibiotic eye drops, for sore, 'gritty', stuck-together eyes (conjunctivitis)
- A pair of fine-pointed tweezers (to remove hairy caterpillar hairs, thorns, splinters, coral, etc)
- Alcohol-based hand rub or bar of soap in plastic box
- Condoms or femidoms
- Malaria diagnostic kits (5) and a digital thermometer (for those going to remote areas)

COMMON MEDICAL PROBLEMS

Travellers' diarrhoea Travelling in Mali carries a fairly high risk of getting a dose of travellers' diarrhoea; perhaps half of all visitors will suffer and the newer you are to exotic travel, the more likely you will be to succumb. By taking precautions against travellers' diarrhoea you will also avoid typhoid, paratyphoid, cholera, hepatitis, dysentery, worms, etc. Travellers' diarrhoea and the other faecal-oral diseases come from getting other people's faeces in your mouth. This most often happens from cooks not washing their hands after a trip to the toilet, but even if the restaurant cook does not understand basic hygiene you will be safe if your food has been properly cooked and arrives piping hot. The most important prevention strategy is to wash your hands before eating anything. You can pick up salmonella and shigella from toilet door handles and possibly bank notes. The maxim to remind you what you can safely eat is:

PEEL IT, BOIL IT, COOK IT OR FORGET IT

LONG-HAUL FLIGHTS, CLOTS AND DVT

Dr Felicity Nicholson

Any prolonged immobility, including travel by land or air, can result in deep-vein thrombosis (DVT) with the risk of embolus to the lungs. Certain factors can increase the risk and these include:

- Having a previous clot or a close relative with a history
- People over 40, with increased risk in over 80s
- Recent major operation or varicose-veins surgery
- Cancer
- Stroke
- Heart disease
- Obesity
- Pregnancy
- Hormone therapy
- Heavy smokers
- Severe varicose veins
- People who are tall (over 6ft/1.8m) or short (under 5ft/1.5m)

A deep-vein thrombosis causes painful swelling and redness of the calf or sometimes the thigh. It is only dangerous if a clot travels to the lungs (pulmonary embolus). Symptoms of a pulmonary embolus (PE) – which commonly start three to ten days after a long flight – include chest pain, shortness of breath, and sometimes coughing up small amounts of blood. Anyone who thinks that they might have a DVT needs to see a doctor immediately.

PREVENTION OF DVT

- Keep mobile before and during the flight; move around every couple of hours
- Drink plenty of fluids during the flight
- Avoid taking sleeping pills and excessive tea, coffee and alcohol
- Consider wearing flight socks or support stockings (see www.legshealth.com)

If you think you are at increased risk of a clot, ask your doctor if it is safe to travel.

This means that fruit you have washed and peeled yourself, and hot foods, should be safe but raw foods, cold cooked foods, salads, fruit salads which have been prepared by others, ice cream and ice are all risky, and foods kept lukewarm in hotel buffets are often dangerous. That said, plenty of travellers and expatriates enjoy fruit and vegetables, so do keep a sense of perspective: food served in a fairly decent hotel in a large town or a place regularly frequented by expatriates is likely to be safe. If you are struck, see the box on page 60 for treatment.

Eye problems Bacterial conjunctivitis (pink eye) is a common infection in Africa; people who wear contact lenses are most open to this irritating problem. The eyes feel sore and gritty and they will often be stuck together in the mornings. They will need treatment with antibiotic drops or ointment. Lesser eye irritation should settle with bathing in salt water and keeping the eyes shaded. If an insect flies into your eye, extract it with great care, ensuring you do not crush or damage it, otherwise you may get a nastily inflamed eye from toxins secreted by the creature. Small elongated red-and-black blister beetles carry warning colouration to tell you not to crush them anywhere against your skin.

Prickly heat A fine pimply rash on the trunk is likely to be heat rash; cool showers, dabbing dry, and talc will help. Treat the problem by slowing down to a relaxed schedule, wearing only loose, baggy, 100% cotton clothes and sleeping naked under a fan; if it's bad you may need to check into an air-conditioned hotel room for a while.

Skin infections Any mosquito bite or small nick in the skin gives an opportunity for bacteria to foil the body's usually excellent defences; it will surprise many travellers how quickly skin infections start in warm humid climates and it is essential to clean and cover even the slightest wound. Creams are not as effective as a good drying antiseptic such as dilute iodine, potassium permanganate (a few crystals in half a cup of water), or crystal (or gentian) violet. One of these should be available in most towns. If the wound starts to throb, or becomes red and the redness starts to spread, or the wound oozes, and especially if you develop a fever, antibiotics will probably be needed: flucloxacillin (250mg four times a day) or cloxacillin (500mg four times a day). For those allergic to penicillin, erythromycin (500mg twice a day) for five days should help. See a doctor if the symptoms do not start to improve within 48 hours.

Fungal infections also get a hold easily in hot, moist climates so wear 100% cotton socks and underwear and shower frequently. An itchy rash in the groin or flaking between the toes is likely to be a fungal infection. This needs treatment with an antifungal cream such as Canesten (clotrimazole); if this is not available try Whitfield's ointment (compound benzoic acid ointment) or crystal violet (although this will turn you purple!).

Other insect-borne diseases Malaria is by no means the only insect-borne disease to which the traveller may succumb. Others include sleeping sickness and river blindness (see the box on page 62). Dengue fever is becoming more common in Mali and there are many other similar arboviruses. These mosquito-borne diseases may mimic malaria but there is no prophylactic medication against them. The mosquitoes that carry dengue fever viruses bite during the daytime, so it is worth applying repellent if you see any mosquitoes around. Symptoms include strong headaches, rashes and excruciating joint and muscle pains and high fever. Viral fevers usually last about a week or so and are not usually fatal. Complete rest and paracetamol are the usual treatment; plenty of fluids also help. Some patients are given an intravenous drip to keep them from dehydrating. It is especially important to protect yourself if you have had dengue fever before, since a second infection with a different strain can result in the potentially fatal dengue haemorrhagic fever.

Bilharzia or schistosomiasis *with thanks to Dr Vaughan Southgate of the Natural History Museum, London, and Dr Dick Stockley, The Surgery, Kampala*

Bilharzia or schistosomiasis is a disease that commonly afflicts the rural poor of the tropics. Two types exist in sub-Saharan Africa – *Schistosoma mansoni* and *Schistosoma haematobium*. The disease is an unpleasant problem that is worth avoiding, although it can be treated if you do get it. This parasite is common in almost all water sources in Mali, even places advertised as 'bilharzia free'. The most risky shores will be close to places where infected people use water and wash clothes, and in Mali this will be along the banks of the rivers Niger and Senegal.

It is easier to understand how to diagnose it, treat it and prevent it if you know a little about the life cycle. Contaminated faeces are washed into the lake, the eggs hatch and the larva infects certain species of snail. The snails then produce about 10,000 cercariae a day for the rest of their lives. The parasites can digest their way through your skin when you wade, or bathe in infested fresh water.

TREATING TRAVELLERS' DIARRHOEA

Dr Jane Wilson-Howarth

It is dehydration that makes you feel awful during a bout of diarrhoea and the most important part of treatment is drinking lots of clear fluids. Sachets of oral rehydration salts give the perfect biochemical mix to replace all that is pouring out of your bottom but other recipes taste nicer. Any diluted mixture of sugar and salt in water will do you good: try Coke or orange squash with a three-finger pinch of salt added to each glass (if you are salt-depleted you won't taste the salt). Otherwise make a solution of a four-finger scoop of sugar with a three-finger pinch of salt in a 500ml glass. Or add eight level teaspoons of sugar (18g) and one level teaspoon of salt (3g) to one litre (five cups) of safe water. A squeeze of lemon or orange juice improves the taste and adds potassium, which is also lost in diarrhoea. Drink two large glasses after every bowel action, and more if you are thirsty. These solutions are still absorbed well if you are vomiting, but you will need to take sips at a time. If you are not eating you need to drink three litres a day plus the amount of whatever is pouring into the toilet. If you feel like eating, take a bland, high carbohydrate diet. Heavy greasy foods will probably give you cramps.

If the diarrhoea is bad, or you are passing blood or slime, or you have a fever, you will probably need antibiotics in addition to fluid replacement. A dose of norfloxacin or ciprofloxacin repeated twice a day until better may be appropriate (if you are planning to take an antibiotic with you, note that both norfloxacin and ciprofloxacin are available only on prescription in the UK). If the diarrhoea is greasy and bulky and is accompanied by sulphurous (eggy) burps, one likely cause is giardia. This is best treated with tinidazole (four x 500mg in one dose, repeated seven days later if symptoms persist).

Winds disperse the snails and cercariae. The snails in particular can drift a long way, especially on windblown weed, so nowhere is really safe. However, deep water and running water are safer, while shallow water presents the greatest risk. The cercariae penetrate intact skin, and find their way to the liver. There male and female meet and spend the rest of their lives in permanent copulation. No wonder you feel tired! Most finish up in the wall of the lower bowel, but others can get lost and can cause damage to many different organs. *Schistosoma haematobium* goes mostly to the bladder.

Although the adults do not cause any harm in themselves, after about four to six weeks they start to lay eggs, which cause an intense but usually ineffective immune reaction, including fever, cough, abdominal pain, and a fleeting, itching rash called 'safari itch'. The absence of early symptoms does not necessarily mean there is no infection. Later symptoms can be more localised and more severe, but the general symptoms settle down fairly quickly and eventually you are just tired. 'Tired all the time' is one of the most common symptoms among expats in Africa, and bilharzia, giardia, amoeba and intestinal yeast are the most common culprits.

Although bilharzia is difficult to diagnose, it can be tested at specialist travel clinics. Ideally tests need to be done at least six weeks after likely exposure and will determine whether you need treatment. Fortunately it is easy to treat at present.

Avoiding bilharzia If you are bathing, swimming, paddling or wading in fresh water which you think may carry a bilharzia risk, try to get out of the water within ten minutes.

- Avoid bathing or paddling on shores within 200m of villages or places where people use the water a great deal, especially reedy shores or where there is lots of water weed

- Dry off thoroughly with a towel; rub vigorously
- If your bathing water comes from a risky source, try to ensure that the water is taken from the lake in the early morning and stored snail-free, otherwise it should be filtered or Dettol or Cresol added
- Bathing early in the morning is safer than bathing in the last half of the day
- Cover yourself with DEET insect repellent before swimming: it may offer some protection

HIV/AIDS The risks of sexually transmitted infection are extremely high in Mali, whether you sleep with fellow travellers or locals. About 80% of HIV infections in British heterosexuals are acquired abroad. If you must indulge, use condoms or femidoms, which help reduce the risk of transmission. If you notice any genital ulcers or discharge, get treatment promptly since ulcers increase the risk of acquiring HIV. If you do have unprotected sex, visit a clinic as soon as possible; this should be within 24 hours, or no later than 72 hours, for post-exposure prophylaxis.

Meningitis This is a particularly nasty disease as it can kill within hours of the first symptoms appearing. The telltale symptoms are a combination of a blinding headache (light sensitivity), a blotchy rash and a high fever. Immunisation protects against the most serious bacterial form of meningitis and the tetravalent vaccine ACWY is recommended for Mali by British travel clinics.

Although other forms of meningitis exist (usually viral), there are no vaccines for these. Local papers normally report localised outbreaks. A severe headache and fever should make you run to a doctor immediately. There are also other causes of headache and fever; one of which is typhoid, which occurs in travellers to Mali. Seek medical help if you are ill for more than a few days.

Rabies Rabies is carried by all mammals (beware the village dogs and small monkeys that are used to being fed in the parks) and is passed on to man through a bite, scratch or a lick of an open wound. You must always assume any animal is rabid, and seek medical help as soon as possible. Meanwhile scrub the wound with soap under a running tap or while pouring water from a jug. Find a reasonably clear-looking source of water (but at this stage the quality of the water is not important), then pour on a strong iodine or alcohol solution of gin, whisky or rum. This helps stop the rabies virus entering the body and will guard against wound infections, including tetanus.

Pre-exposure vaccinations for rabies is ideally advised for everyone, but is particularly important if you intend to have contact with animals and/or are likely to be more than 24 hours away from medical help. Ideally three doses should be taken over a minimum of 21 days, though even taking one or two doses of vaccine is better than none at all. Contrary to popular belief, these vaccinations are relatively painless.

If you are bitten, scratched or licked over an open wound by a sick animal, then post-exposure prophylaxis should be given as soon as possible, though it is never too late to seek help, as the incubation period for rabies can be very long. Those who have not been immunised will need a full course of injections. The vast majority of travel health advisors including WHO recommend rabies immunoglobulin (RIG), but this product is expensive (around US$800) and may be hard to come by – another reason why pre-exposure vaccination should be encouraged.

Tell the doctor if you have had pre-exposure vaccine, as this should change the treatment you receive. And remember that, if you do contract rabies, mortality is 100% and death from rabies is probably one of the worst ways to go.

AVOIDING INSECT BITES

As the sun is going down, don long clothes and apply repellent on any exposed flesh. Pack a DEET-based insect repellent (roll-ons or sticks are the least messy preparations for travelling). You also need either a permethrin-impregnated bed-net or a permethrin spray so that you can 'treat' bed-nets in hotels. Permethrin treatment makes even very tatty nets protective and prevents mosquitoes from biting through the impregnated net when you roll against it; it also deters other biters. Otherwise retire to an air-conditioned room or burn mosquito coils or sleep under a fan. Coils and fans reduce rather than eliminate bites. Travel clinics usually sell a good range of nets, treatment kits and repellents.

Mosquitoes and many other insects are attracted to light. If you are camping, never put a lamp near the opening of your tent, or you will have a swarm of biters waiting to join you when you retire. In hotel rooms, be aware that the longer your light is on, the greater the number of insects will be sharing your accommodation.

Aside from avoiding mosquito bites between dusk and dawn, which will protect you from elephantiasis and a range of nasty insect-borne viruses as well as malaria (see page 59), it is important to take precautions against other insect bites. During the day it is wise to wear long, loose (preferably 100% cotton) clothes if you are pushing through scrubby country; this will keep off ticks and also tsetse and day-biting *Aedes* mosquitoes which may spread viral fevers, including yellow fever.

Tsetse flies hurt when they bite and it is said that they are attracted to the colour blue; locals will advise on where they are a problem and where they transmit sleeping sickness.

Minute pestilential biting blackflies spread river blindness in some parts of Africa between 190°N and 170°S; the disease is caught close to fast-flowing rivers since flies breed there and the larvae live in rapids. The flies bite during the day but long trousers tucked into socks will help keep them off. Citronella-based natural repellents (eg: Mosi-guard) do not work against them.

Tumbu flies or *putsi*, often called mango flies in Mali, are a problem where the climate is hot and humid. The adult fly lays her eggs on the soil or on drying laundry and when the eggs come into contact with human flesh (when you put on clothes or lie on a bed) they hatch and bury themselves under the skin. Here they form a crop of 'boils' each with a maggot inside. Smear a little Vaseline over the hole, and they will push their noses out to breathe. It may be possible to squeeze them out but it depends if they are ready to do so as the larvae have spines that help them to hold on.

In *putsi* areas either dry your clothes and sheets within a screened house, or dry them in direct sunshine until they are crisp, or iron them.

Jiggers or sandfleas are another flesh-feaster, which can be best avoided by wearing shoes. They latch on if you walk barefoot in contaminated places, and set up home under the skin of the foot, usually at the side of a toenail where they cause a painful, boil-like swelling. They need picking out by a local expert.

Tickbite fever African ticks are not the rampant disease transmitters they are in the Americas, but they may spread tickbite fever and a few dangerous rarities in Mali. Tickbite fever is a flu-like illness that can easily be treated with doxycycline, but as there can be some serious complications it is important to visit a doctor.

Ticks should ideally be removed as soon as possible, as leaving them on the body increases the chance of infection. They should be removed with special tick tweezers that can be bought in good travel shops. Failing that you can use your fingernails: grasp the tick as close to your body as possible and pull steadily and firmly away at right angles to your skin. The tick will then come away complete, as long as you do not jerk or twist. If possible douse the wound with alcohol (any spirit will do) or iodine. Irritants (eg: Olbas oil) or lit cigarettes are to be discouraged since they can cause the ticks to regurgitate and therefore increase the risk of disease. It is best to get a travelling companion to check you for ticks; if you are travelling with small children, remember to check their heads, and particularly behind the ears.

Spreading redness around the bite and/or fever and/or aching joints after a tick bite imply that you have an infection that requires antibiotic treatment, so seek advice.

Snakebite Snakes rarely attack unless provoked, and bites in travellers are unusual. You are less likely to get bitten if you wear stout shoes and long trousers when in the bush. Most snakes are harmless and even venomous species will dispense venom in only about half of their bites. If bitten, then, you are unlikely to have received venom; keeping this fact in mind may help you to stay calm. Many so-called first-aid techniques do more harm than good: cutting into the wound is harmful; tourniquets are dangerous; suction and electrical inactivation devices do not work. The only treatment is antivenom. In case of a bite that you fear may have been from a venomous snake:

- Try to keep calm – it is likely that no venom has been dispensed
- Prevent movement of the bitten limb by applying a splint
- Keep the bitten limb BELOW heart height to slow the spread of any venom
- If you have a crêpe bandage, wrap it around the whole limb (eg: all the way from the toes to the thigh), as tight as you would for a sprained ankle or a muscle pull
- Evacuate to a hospital that has antivenom

And remember:

- NEVER give aspirin; you may take paracetamol, which is safe
- NEVER cut or suck the wound
- DO NOT apply ice packs
- DO NOT apply potassium permanganate

If the offending snake can be captured without risk of someone else being bitten, take this to show the doctor – but beware since even a decapitated head is able to bite.

HOSPITALS, DOCTORS AND PHARMACIES IN MALI There are two large hospitals in Bamako and one in each of the country's regional centres which deal with emergency cases. Otherwise, doctors, pharmacies and your own medical kit will normally suffice to treat most travellers' maladies. Although the quality of the medical care should be of the same standard in clinics and hospitals alike, private clinics are generally better equipped for care and comfort than general hospitals. English-speaking doctors are available in Bamako, and you should contact the American Embassy or the embassy or consulate of your country for recommendations. In case of a serious medical situation, the African Trans Services or ATS (☎ *2022 44 35/78 92*) in Immeuble Babemba can offer assistance. Outside the capital, however, you might have to get by in French. Traditional medicine is very popular in Mali. Apart from the dubious cures derived from the diverse range of west African fauna sold behind the main mosque in Bamako (see page 136), traditional medicine also includes herbal remedies which have proved so effective that the hospitals in Bamako have departments dedicated to researching this form of medicine.

Meanwhile, pharmacies in Mali are generally well equipped and normally stock most of the component parts of a good medical kit. They can be found all over the country. (For further information on health see pages 52–63.)

TRAVEL INSURANCE With a bit of luck, money spent on travel insurance will be money down the drain. This, of course, is not much of an incentive to buy it in the first place, but you should never leave home without it.

Buying travel insurance is really no different to buying a pair of shoes: shop around and opt for the policy which best fits your needs. Avoid being pressured into buying the comprehensive insurance offered by most travel agents when you purchase your ticket. Compensation of £2,000 for the inconvenience of being hijacked might sound impressive, but do you really need it?

Some degree of health cover is obviously essential. Most policies offer at least £1 million in emergency medical expenses and repatriation to your home country – which should be sufficient to cover most disasters. Note that in most cases the first £50 or so of any claim is payable by the policy holder.

Your most difficult decision will probably be whether or not to insure your baggage and personal belongings. This really bumps up the cost of travel insurance, so calculate if the amount of cover offered would reimburse the amount you stand to lose. It rarely does, in which case you would be better off saving your money – or leaving your camera at home. If you have other personal or household policies, they may cover some belongings: check the small print.

The standard travel policy covers you for a single trip and is priced according to your destination and the length of your stay. Most travel insurance companies these days also offer 'multi-trip' policies designed for travellers who make a number of journeys during the year. The premium is often very good value, but the length of each trip abroad is normally restricted to about four weeks. Most of the travel agencies specialising in independent travel (see page 70) also sell travel insurance, which is tailored to the needs of the independent traveller and often slightly cheaper than the norm. You can also buy your insurance quickly, cheaply and painlessly over the telephone. In the UK I particularly like the friendly and efficient service provided by **Club Direct** (☎ *0800 083 2466; www.clubdirect.com*), which has several policies to suit various needs. You pay by credit card and your policy schedule is dispatched within a couple of days. **Columbus Direct** (☎ *0845 330 8518;www.columbusdirect.co.uk*) is one of several other companies working along the same lines.

SAFETY

Following the end of the Tuareg rebellion in 1995, Mali enjoyed a period of political stability until 2006, when trouble in the northern parts of the desert flared up again. The government responded by striking a new deal with the help of Algerian mediators, promising to speed up development in the northern regions while the rebel groups agreed to drop their demands for autonomy. One faction of the Tuareg group refused to sign and in August 2007 clashes reignited between rebels and the Malian army around Kidal and the Niger border, with a number of deaths and hostages taken. In July 2008, another ceasefire agreement was reached, bringing an end to the conflict. Hopefully this is the last of the trouble and the population can now go about rebuilding their lives. These attacks were in no way targeted at tourists but it is not recommended to travel to the desert, north or east of Gao until the situation is clear.

In addition, expensive 4x4 vehicles are particular targets for good old-fashioned Tuareg banditry; victims have included both politicians and the French military and in January 2008, four Italians were robbed in Araouane, 150 miles north of Timbuktu. Another reason not to head north at the current time is because of a group calling themselves al-Qaeda in the Maghreb who, according to security experts in the US, have crossed the border from Algeria and are running mobile training grounds for Islamic militants from other north African countries.

If you're travelling to the Festival in the Desert in Essakane, however, there is no need to worry. It is such an important event for the Malian government that security along the 60km between Timbuktu and Essakane and at the festival itself is very strong. It may not be wise, however, to travel after dark. All other festivals in the region of Kidal have been cancelled at the present time.

National and local authorities are very much aware of the impact insecurity has had on the lives of the northern communities and the devastating affect on tourism. The problem is being addressed at different levels. Authorities in towns that could be labelled as gateways to the desert – like Timbuktu and Gao – ask tourists who intend to travel further north with their own vehicles to take safety precautions: seek local advice and register before heading out to remote destinations. Travellers using public transport are at less risk than those with their own transport. To keep up to date with the current situation in the north check http://africa.reuters.com/nbc/ML.

A decade ago, the areas around Nioro du Sahel and Nara along the Mauritanian border were sensitive because of conflict between sedentary farmers (largely Bambara and Soninké) and nomadic cattle-herders (Peul). These days, the situation is a lot calmer.

Elsewhere, travelling in Mali is as safe as it can be in Africa. Common-sense precautions, such as watching your belongings – particularly at bus and railway stations – and avoiding dodgy areas at night, should be taken as a matter of course. Confidence-tricksters operate in Mali, as anywhere else in the world, but incidents involving violence are rare. There is a strong police presence all over the country, all traffic passes security checkpoints when entering and leaving major towns and you are never very far from a *commissariat de police* – for what it's worth!

Emergency telephone numbers are 15 for health services, 17 for the police and 18 for the fire brigade.

WOMEN TRAVELLERS *with Janice Booth*

When attention becomes intrusive, it can help if you are wearing a wedding ring and have photos of 'your' husband and children, even if they are someone else's. A good reason to give for not being with them is that you have to travel in connection with your job – biology, zoology, geography, or whatever. (But not journalism – that's risky.)

Pay attention to local etiquette, and to speaking, dressing and moving reasonably decorously. Look at how the local women dress, and try not to expose parts of yourself that they keep covered. Think about body language. Direct eye contact with a man may be seen as a 'come-on'; sunglasses are helpful in this context.

Don't be afraid to explain clearly – but pleasantly rather than as a put-down – that you aren't in the market for whatever distractions are on offer. Remember that you are probably as much of a novelty to the local people as they are to you, and the fact that you are travelling abroad alone gives them the message that you are free and adventurous. But don't imagine that a Lothario lurks under every bush: many approaches stem from genuine friendliness or curiosity, and a brush-off in such cases doesn't do much for the image of travellers in general.

Take sensible precautions against theft and attack – try to cover all the risks before you encounter them – and then relax and enjoy your trip. You'll meet far more kindness than villainy.

NOTES FOR DISABLED TRAVELLERS

Gordon Rattray (www.able-travel.com)

Despite Mali's best-known highlights involving towering escarpments and vast deserts, travellers with mobility problems should not be put off. More time researching the trip and thought towards logistics may be necessary, but it will be surprising just how much is possible.

PLANNING AND BOOKING I know of no operators running specialised trips to Mali for disabled people, but most travel companies will listen to your needs and try to create an itinerary suitable for you. For the more independent traveller, it is possible to limit potential surprises by contacting local operators and accommodation by email in advance.

ACCOMMODATION Few establishments, except perhaps the large international hotels in Bamako, have made any considerations for wheelchair users. Despite this, if you are prepared to accept help, you will find that Malians will be happy to oblige. Many places have ground floor rooms and if you can cope with a standard bathroom then accommodation should not be impossible to find.

TRANSPORT

By air An aisle chair is not guaranteed at Bamako airport and assistance may not be as experienced or highly trained as you are used to. However, if you explain fully how you like to be helped, you should have few problems.

By bus and train There is no effective legislation in Mali to facilitate disabled travellers' journeys by public transport; therefore, if you cannot walk at all then both of these options are going to be difficult. You will need to ask for help from fellow passengers to lift you to your seat, it will often be crowded and it is unlikely that there will be an accessible toilet.

By car Distances are great and roads are often bumpy, so if you are prone to skin damage you need to take extra care. Place your own pressure-relieving cushion on top of (or instead of) the original car seat and if necessary, pad around knees and elbows.

BLACK TRAVELLERS IN MALI *with Bola Fatimilehin*

As a black woman travelling in Mali, I had many exhilarating and thought-provoking adventures. The red dust, which for me is a mark of true African soil, will be forever ingrained on my mind – thanks to long arduous bus journeys taken in 40°C heat with windows shut tight.

Visiting out-of-the-way places brought me into contact with genuinely warm and friendly people. Most memorably, when travelling along the escarpment where the Dogon people live, the chief of one of the villages took a particular shine to me and my white partner. It emerged that the Dogon creation story involves twins, one of whom is black, the other white; under the influence of millet beer, we had become mythology in the flesh.

Often in Mali, local people would assume I knew far more about what was going on than I actually did. This had definite advantages in that I could pay less for things and avoid insincere banter aimed at parting me from my money. On one occasion, I was even bribed to keep my mouth shut by a guide! He had secured a week's work with a single American tourist for about ten times the amount I was paying. He did not want to lose his prime fee so gave me a brass necklace as 'hush money'.

If you're not sticking to the main roads, you will need to use a 4x4 vehicle, which will be higher than a normal car, possibly making transfers more difficult. Drivers/guides are normally happy to help, but are not trained in this skill, so you must thoroughly explain your needs and always stay in control of the situation.

HEALTH AND INSURANCE Doctors will know about 'everyday' illnesses, but you must understand and be able to explain your own particular medical requirements. Malian hospitals and pharmacies are often basic, so it is wise to take as much essential medication and equipment as possible with you, and it is advisable to pack this in your hand luggage during flights in case your main luggage gets lost. Mali can be hot; if this is a problem for you then try to book accommodation and vehicles with fans or air-conditioning, and a useful cooling aid is a plant-spray bottle.

Travel insurance can be purchased from Age Concern (*0800 169 2700; www.ageconcern.org.uk*), who have no upper age limit, and Free Spirit (*0845 230 5000; www.free-spirit.com*), who cater for people with pre-existing medical conditions. Most insurance companies will insure disabled travellers, but it is essential that they are made aware of your disability.

SECURITY Although the vast majority of people will only want to help you, it is worth remembering that, as a disabled person, you are more vulnerable. Stay aware of who is around you and where your bags are, especially during car transfers and similar.

TIPS AND ADVICE As well as the following online sources of information, Bradt Travel Guides' new title *Africa: Safaris for People with Limited Mobility* provides a plethora of information, some of which will apply equally well to Mali.

www.able-travel.com This is my website with both worldwide and country-specific information.
www.globalaccessnews.com A searchable database of disability travel information.
www.rollingrains.com A searchable website concentrating on disability and travel.

Finally, a word of advice: pull wheelchairs backwards through soft sand!

For the black traveller, feelings of isolation may come as a surprise. In general, the most common image of 'the tourist' is of a white person – black tourists are still considered a rarity. Local black men and women were often bemused and suspicious of me, assuming I was there for some sort of economic gain. It is understandable that both Malians and white tourists – for similar and different reasons – do not have a ready image of the black person as a tourist. However, the isolation which may descend as a result of this dubious privilege can be overcome by creating opportunities to talk to people. Getting my hair done was one way of meeting and talking to women in Mali – rusty and rudimentary though my French is! The quality of hair braiding was incredibly high and, at only CFA300 (about US$2), excellent value for money. The other tactic I found very useful was to show people photographs of family and friends at home. This worked well, both to stimulate conversation and to allay some suspicion, as Malians are always interested in family connections.

Travelling on a budget meant sleeping in cheap hotels – but at the risk of being mistaken for a prostitute. Staying in more expensive hotels might have avoided this situation, but my budget would not allow for it. Bamako felt like a relatively safe city and there were advantages in staying at the centre of things: being able to mingle with the market traders, street sellers, beggars, bus touts and ordinary citizens, and generally absorb *l'ambience*.

WHAT TO TAKE

The golden rule is to travel light. By definition, independent travel involves using public transport, finding your own accommodation and being on the move a good deal of the time. A heavy and cumbersome bag – or bags – will metaphorically and literally drag you down. Moreover, quite apart from the hassle and discomfort, there are sound financial reasons for keeping your baggage to a minimum, as bus companies, *bâchées* and *pinasses* invariably charge extra for large bags and backpacks. So, bearing this golden rule in mind, what should you take?

BAGGAGE Backpacks have become synonymous with independent travellers – and not without good reason. As long as it is well packed and worn properly, even a heavy backpack can be carried for hours with little discomfort. Meanwhile, your hands are left free to consult this guide! Try to centre most of the pack's weight on the hip belt and minimise the pressure on your shoulders – otherwise it will drag you down.

Durability is also important in a country where luggage is rarely handled with care. These days, most backpackers opt for internal frames which tend to be better for active travel and keep the load closer to your own centre of gravity. However, for hiking in hot weather – in Dogon country, for example – and carrying large loads, you might consider an external frame, which is stronger and allows air to circulate between your body and back. The purchase of a new backpack can eat up a lot of your holiday money, so make sure that you choose one to last. Check the material, the stitching, the zips and the straps before you hand over your hard-earned cash.

You could, of course, elect to carry your worldly possessions in something other than a backpack – a suitcase, for example. A good compromise is a small, black attaché case with one compartment for clothes and another for notebooks, etc This type of bag can actually be more convenient to carry than a bulky backpack, slipping nicely between legs on crowded *bâchées* and fitting easily into aircraft overhead lockers. Choose your bag for its practical suitability, but also think whether it could benefit you psychologically. If your bag doesn't make you feel conspicuous, it's likely to have positive a knock-on effect when it comes to interacting and communicating with the local people.

CLOTHING Selecting your wardrobe for a trip to a hot country such as Mali should be an exercise in common sense. Cool, light clothing is good for the days – white, however, is not the most practical given that the red dust of Bamako clings to everything. Trousers and a long-sleeved shirt will help fend off mosquitoes in the evenings. A comfortable pair of shoes is obviously very important, especially if you're trekking in the Dogon. Although the desert sand around Timbuktu may look inviting for your toes, beware of prickly little burs known as *cram cram*, which attach themselves painfully to your skin. Closed shoes may be more practical than sandals (but do remember to check them for scorpions!) You can buy a hat once you're there.

You won't need lots of clothes. A 'wash and wear' approach works well in Mali, where everything dries quickly in the sun. Laundry soap or washing powder (in conveniently sized sachets) are dirt cheap and widely available across the country. Alternatively, put a little extra into the economy and get your washing done by local women. Note, though, that it's considered bad form to give them your underwear, as everything is washed by hand.

Don't forget that during the cool season it can be very cold – even freezing – in the desert areas at night. Hotels are often quite stingy when it comes to providing blankets, so consider bringing a sleeping bag if you plan to spend a lot of time in the desert between about November and February. A lightweight silk sleeping bag is always handy to climb into, given the state of the sheets in some of Mali's cheaper hotels. Turbans can also be a good investment in the desert, where even the slightest wind kicks up the sand – which gets everywhere. Accordingly, **contact lenses** are not recommended – not just in the desert, but all over this dusty country. Note that if you do bring them, cleaning fluids and replacements are almost impossible to find in Mali.

MAPS Thanks to the recent – and continuous – roadworks all over the country, you would be lucky to find a map that matches reality. However, a good map was produced in 2005 by the Institut Géographique National de France (IGN): it is one of the few to deal with the country on its own, and is widely available (scale 1:2,000,000). A new (2007) Mali map by ITMB Publishing (*www.itmb.com*) shows a huge number of smaller villages rather than the overall road system. It doesn't appear to be highly accurate, with erroneous degrees of latitude and plenty of inaccurate place names. In the 2004 edition (scale 1:2,400,000), the source of the information was clearly a lot older than that. Nevertheless, the map may prove to be useful for hikers and cyclists. At the Institut Géographique du Mali (or IGM: Mali's counterpart of the IGN) in Sogoniko Fasso Kanu (*2020 28 40; www.igm-mali.org*) in Bamako, more updated road maps are available. At the time of writing, the latest version dated from November 2002 (scale 1:3,500,000). It shows little detail, but is fairly adequate where the condition of the main roads is concerned. The map can be printed out while you wait and costs CFA8,500. Detailed Ordnance Survey maps are also available at the IGN. The Ministère de l'Environnement, opposite the National Museum (*2022 24 98*) can provide you with updated maps of the national parks. Mali is also included on the various regional maps of west Africa, which are good if you are planning to visit other countries in the area. In the UK, a good source of maps is Stanfords in Long Acre, London (*020 7836 1321; www.stanfords.co.uk*).

$ MONEY

Mali, along with six other French-speaking countries in west Africa, is a member of the West African Monetary Union. There is a central bank, the Banque Centrale des États de l'Afrique de l'Ouest (BCEAO), with its headquarters in Dakar, Senegal, and the member states share a common currency, the CFA (Communauté Financière Africaine) franc. Mali was admitted to this union in 1984, at which time the CFA franc (here abbreviated as CFA, although you may also see CFAF and CFAFr) replaced the Malian franc.

The exchange rate is fixed at CFA655.957 (often rounded up to CFA656) for €1. Other currencies are bought and sold, although the fluctuating rates are usually less advantageous; at the time of going to press US$1 is worth about CFA477 while £1 buys you around CFA753 (June 2009). The CFA franc comes in new notes of 10,000, 5,000, 2,000 and 1,000. Old coins are of CFA250, 100, 50, 25, 10 and 5 denominations, while there are new coins of CFA500 and 200.

A word of caution: some older editions of notes lost their value in the first half of 2004. Care should be taken to avoid becoming the dumping ground for the worthless notes that were not returned to the bank in time. Familiarise yourself with the notes that were handed out to you by the bank and look out for posters at the bank with images of the notes concerned.

NECESSITIES AND LUXURIES

Many of the items mentioned below as 'necessities' are downright patronising and as obvious as your nose. Treat this section as a checklist, ticking off the items you should not leave home without (the 'necessities') and pondering whether or not to take one or two articles to make your life more comfortable (the 'luxuries'). You should be able to buy most of the 'luxuries' you've forgotten, once you're in Mali.

NECESSITIES

- Passport
- Airline ticket
- Insurance policy
- Photocopies of passport, airline ticket and insurance policy
- Travellers' cheques and credit card
- Money belt to store the above. You should always wear it underneath your clothing.
- First-aid kit (see page 57)
- Spare glasses (avoid contact lenses if possible; see page 58)
- Dust-cleaning kit for digital cameras

LUXURIES

- Penknife
- Torch (flashlight) and batteries (power cuts are common)
- Lipsalve to protect against chapped lips caused by the sun and wind
- Map – detailed and recent (see page 69)
- Calculator for currency conversion
- Camera with some spare film
- Sunglasses
- Binoculars for wildlife/birdwatching

A 'mozzie tent' (available for about £30 in the UK – or just take the inner section of a simple dome tent) – lightweight, with a base and poles, can be put up quickly on rooftops where there's nowhere to hang a net. A mattress on the roof/terrace costs only about CFA2,500 across Mali, so you can quickly make your money back on room fees.

Ideally, you should carry the majority of your money as cash and the rest as travellers' cheques, along with a Visa card for emergencies. ATMs are available in most – but not all – cities nowadays, allowing you to withdraw local currency using your Visa card or, to a lesser extent, MasterCard. However, only in the more expensive establishments is Visa occasionally accepted as a means of payment, normally with a hefty commission. American Express can be used at the AMEX office in Bamako and in top-end hotels and restaurants only.

EXCHANGING MONEY There have been many problems with stolen or counterfeit travellers' cheques, and as a result many banks no longer deal with them. Those that still do charge two commissions: one payable to the government and another to the bank and it involves a long and arduous procedure with a mountain of paperwork. As with Visa cards, planning when and where to exchange travellers' cheques for local currency is crucial. Travellers' cheques in euros are more widely accepted than cheques in US dollars. Other currencies are not recommended. Note that banks will ask to see the receipt, and that a hefty commission charge is incurred. As a result, it is probably easier to carry most of your money in cash. The preferred foreign currency in Mali is, for obvious reasons, the euro. Euro notes are easily exchanged for CFA all over the country, and preferably travellers should carry at least some of their money in this way. Smaller notes, such as €10 and €20, will permit you to change only as much as you need at any one time. However, notes less than €10 can be difficult to change, even in banks in the north where they want larger denominations. US dollars come only second in popularity with banks, but are still widely accepted at a fluctuating rate.

Always have a good supply of cash in small denominations, so that you can avoid buying more CFA than you need at any one time. Bring other currencies only if you have no alternative and when you do not mind changing a significant quantity at once because you are limited to the banks that will accept your currency.

There is a black market, especially in Bamako. However, the usual warnings apply: changing money or travellers' cheques on the black market is illegal, the rates vary and may or may not be beneficial (but are sometimes negotiable), and there is always the risk of running into the wrong person at the wrong time, which could be both nasty and costly.

BANKING Banking hours in Mali vary according to the bank and its location. Generally speaking, they are open until the early afternoon (not usually later than 15.00) from Mondays to Thursdays, while on Fridays they are normally closed by midday. Some banks are open on Saturday mornings, and a few branches of certain banks open on Sunday mornings as well. Do not count on it, though, and plan ahead when and where to exchange cash or travellers' cheques.

Mali's national bank is the Banque Centrale des États de l'Afrique de l'Ouest (BCEAO). Other main banks include: Banque de Développement du Mali (BDM); Banque Internationale pour le Mali (BIM); Banque Nationale de Développement Agricole (BNDA); Banque of Africa (BOA); and Banque de l'Habitat du Mali (BHM).

In general, the BIM and BHM are of little use to travellers, as they do not deal with foreign currency (though the BHM sometimes exchanges euros). The more useful banks are the BDM and BNDA, since they are widely represented all over Mali and usually accept Visa cards (BDM) or cash and travellers' cheques (BNDA). Many banks – and post offices – have a Western Union office for international money transfers. Many Western Union branches usually have longer opening hours than banks, and are often also open on Saturdays and Sundays. Practical though they are in case of a precarious cash flow situation, their services do not come cheap.

BUDGETING

Travel in Mali is not as cheap as you may expect, especially compared with other African countries. However, there's something to suit everyone's pocket and you'll probably find that the lower your budget, the more integration you'll have with the locals and the richer your cultural experience – such as travelling in local buses or shared taxis and eating at local food stalls. Hotels in the capital, Bamako, and major cities are more expensive and those on a budget will not get much for their money. The further out of towns and cities you get, the cheaper things become though standards are more basic. Accommodation for example, may consist of a mattress on the roof, a bed in a dorm or a mattress in the sand. Private car hire is expensive and a luxury reserved for those on a larger budget and you'll find that all prices are inflated during festival season (see page 86) when accommodation may also be scarce.

The following guide lists daily budgets for one person, based on two people sharing accommodation.

SAMPLE PRICES

1.5 litre bottle of mineral water	CFA400–500 (shop) CFA750–1,500 (restaurant/ hotel)
Coffee in local restaurant	CFA200
Small beer	CFA500
Large beer	CFA1,000
Main dish in local restaurant	CFA1,000
Main dish in tourist restaurant	CFA3,500
Litre of fuel	CFA500 diesel/CFA 550 petrol
Taxi ride in Bamako	CFA1,500

PENNY-PINCHING You can get by on a budget of less than CFA10,000 per day if you're happy taking public transport, eating local food from stalls, and sleeping on a mattress on a roof or taking a bed in a dorm room. This would also leave you with a few extra CFA for museum entrances and a cold beer or two.

MODEST For around CFA20,000 a day you can stay in basic but decent accommodation and eat well in cafés and restaurants. This would also allow for paying for a local guide for a trek through the Dogon or an excursion on camel back in the desert, plus entrance to one of the traditional festivals or celebrations. But you'd still be taking public transport to get around.

COMFORTABLE A budget of CFA40,000 per day would cover a good mid-range room and a substantial meal in a tourist-standard restaurant, with extra for taxis to get around or for activities such as trekking elephants in Gourma, or taking the COMONAV boat along the river Niger. It would also leave a little left over for some basic souvenir shopping for pottery, a *cheche* or a small wood carving. It would also be possible to hire a 4x4 with driver if sharing between four or five people.

LUXURIOUS For CFA80,000 per day, you can afford to hire a 4x4 with a driver split between two people, stay in the best hotels in town (though in Bamako, allow for extra) and partakein all activities to a high standard. It can also cover the entrance ticket to the rather expensive music festivals such as the Festival au Desert or Festival sur le Niger, the odd internal flight and some high quality *bogolan* or chunky Tuareg silver jewellery.

A ROYAL SPLURGE On a budget of CFA120,000 plus, the sky's the limit. Unlimited internal flights, chauffeur driven 4x4, staying in the best 5★ accommodation in Bamako, VIP tent at the Festival au Desert, a camel caravan expedition to the salt mines of Taoudenni, or chartering a motorised *pinasse* along the River Niger.

GETTING AROUND

✈ **BY AIR** Given the immense size of Mali, the isolation of some of its main towns, and the shortcomings of ground transportation, getting around by air is an option worth considering. From the tourist's point of view, flying to places such as Timbuktu, Gao and Kayes will save time and avoid arduous journeys. On the other hand, flying is a rather sterile and unrewarding experience which minimises contact with the realities of life in one of the world's poorest countries. Therefore, fly to save time – not to see Mali. The two domestic airlines are **Mali Air Express (MAE)** (☎ *2023 14 65;*

www.malipages.com/mae/) and **Air Mali** (previously known as Compagnie du Mali, CAM) (*www.camaero.com*). So far they seem to be reliable and predictable.

Mali Air Express (MAE)

Day	Destination	Departs	Arrives
Monday	BKO–Kayes	07.00	08.10
	Kayes–BKO	13.35	14.40
Tuesday	BKO–Kayes	07.00	08.10
	Kayes–BKO	08.40	09.50
	BKO–Mopti	07.00	08.15
	Mopti–Timbuktu	08.50	10.05
Wednesday	Timbuktu–Mopti	08.00	08.50
	Mopti–BKO	09.20	10.35
Thursday	BKO–Kayes	07.00	08.10
	Kayes–BKO	13.35	14.40
Friday	No flights	—	—
Saturday	BKO–Kayes	07.00	08.10
	Kayes–BKO	08.40	09.50
	BKO–Mopti	07.00	08.15
	Mopti–Timbuktu	08.50	10.05
Sunday	Timbuktu–Mopti	08.00	08.50
	Mopti–BKO	09.20	10.35

Also flies from Bamako to Yélimané Monday and Thursday, returning the same day and via Nioro on Thursday

One-way fares	*CFA*		
BKO–Kayes	69,000	BKO–Timbuktu	97,600
BKO–Mopti	60,500	Mopti–Timbuktu	65,000

Air Mali/CAM

Day	Destination	Departs	Arrives
Monday	BKO–Kayes	07.15	08.25
	Kayes–BKO	08.50	10.00
Tuesday	No flights	—	—
Wednesday	BKO–Mopti	07.15	08.30
	Mopti–Timbuktu	09.00	09.45
Thursday	Timbuktu–Mopti	08.00	08.45
	Mopti–BKO	09.15	10.30
	BKO–Kayes	11.00	12.10
Friday	BKO–Mopti	07.15	08.30
	Mopti–Timbuktu	09.00	09.45
	Timbuktu–Mopti	10.15	11.00
	Mopti–BKO	11.30	12.45
Saturday	BKO–Mopti	07.15	08.30
	Mopti–Timbuktu	09.00	09.45
Sunday	Timbuktu–Mopti	08.00	08.45
	Mopti–BKO	09.15	10.30
	BKO–Kayes	15.30	16.40
	Kayes–BKO	17.10	18.20

Fares are similar to MAE. NB: all MAE and Air Mali/CAM fares exclude CFA2,750 airport tax.

BY RIVER Quite apart from its romantic past and dramatic presence today, the River Niger is a vital means of communication, especially for the isolated towns of the Niger Inland Delta and the Sahara. Travelling along the Niger can be slow and uncomfortable, but is rarely dull or forgettable.

When the level of the water is high enough – roughly from the end of July to the end of December – the River Niger can be navigated by large diesel ferries run by **COMANAV** (*Compagnie Malienne de Navigation;* ☎ *2126 20 94*) between Koulikoro, 57km from Bamako, and Gao. The total voyage takes just under a week, although most passengers get on and off at various ports *en route*, including Ségou, Mopti and Kabara (for Timbuktu). There are currently three COMANAV boats in service: the *Kankou Moussa*, the *Général Soumaré* and the *Tombouctou*. The *Kankou Moussa* is the largest of the three, although the *Tombouctou* is in the best condition (though this is all relative). There are five classes in total: the *cabines de luxe* have twin or double beds, air conditioning, a bathroom and are on the upper deck; first-class cabins have two beds (usually bunks) and a basin, and are on the upper or middle deck; second-class cabins sleeping four people are on the middle deck; third-class cabins with bunk beds for at least 12 people are on the lower deck; while fourth class is the lower deck or upper deck. On the last named – a popular option with backpackers – you rub shoulders (and everything else) with a host of local families; the lower deck is a hive of activity shared by female fruit-and-vegetable traders, the boat's cooks, mini-stores that sell basics such as teabags and cigarettes,

ALONG THE RIVER NIGER

Peter Udell

My journey along the Niger ended in chaos at 3 o'clock on a Sunday morning, after two days and – almost – three nights on board an old, steel-built river steamer. Its sailors shouted raucously to each other as it docked at Korioumé, the nearest port to Timbuktu. The passengers surged in disarray down the gangplank, carrying, dragging and pushing their possessions.

The journey had begun in similar chaos at 8 o'clock on the previous Thursday evening, just a few hours after I'd booked my berth in a first-class cabin for two, rather than in a cabin for four or more, at a quayside office in the river port of Mopti. Crowds of men and women – some carrying their babies on their backs – struggled on board. They climbed up the gangplank with baskets of fruit and vegetables, with bulging sacks, with pots and pans and food for the journey. They settled down on the open decks where they lived, cooked, ate and slept.

There had, too, been chaos at each of the larger villages where the steamer made its scheduled stops. As we approached them, villagers dressed brightly in all the colours of the rainbow – and more besides – appeared as if from nowhere. Women from the villages came to sell their chickens and fish, sometimes piled in baskets on their heads. Women from the steamer rushed ashore to sell their fruit and vegetables. Some of us passengers followed, and were surrounded by the smiles and greetings of the instant crowd.

A different chaos came at the many more unscheduled stops our steamer made; with a huge barge strapped to its side – and, I was disconcerted to discover, filled with petrol – it ran aground again and again. Sometimes it was pushed into the riverbank by strong winds. At others it ran onto mud banks where the Niger had, by the very last days of November, become too shallow. Whatever the cause, the crew made frantic and often ineffective attempts to refloat it.

But for most of my time on board, what was most memorable – and extraordinarily enjoyable – was the calm and peace. The fish market smells and flies of Mopti were forgotten. The extreme dry midday heat of Timbuktu was still to come.

At our leisurely meals we – the tiny band of first-class passengers who included two

vast mounds of cargo (everything from motorbikes to sacks of rice and watermelons) and, of course, livestock.

Do not delude yourself with phrases like *cabines de luxe*; these characterisations are merely meant to describe the level of luxury – or the lack of it – as compared with the other classes. There are communal showers and toilets for those not in luxury cabins. Deluxe, first- and second-class fares include three meals a day in allocated dining rooms; those in lower classes fend for themselves, but this is hardly a problem with so much trading going on, both on board and *en route*. The *luxe*/first-class restaurant also has a bar, where anyone can buy chilled drinks (including bottled water and beer); those in lower classes can pay for a meal if they wish. Fares range from very expensive to dirt cheap, depending on the level of comfort required. The quality of food varies between the classes. The following is a selection of prices in CFA to some of the more popular ports for tourists:

	Deluxe	**1st class**	**2nd class**	**3rd class**	**4th class**
Koulikoro–Gao	287,915	152,637	109,079	64,090	14,506
Koulikoro–Ségou	43,984	25,816	17,139	10,127	2,706
Koulikoro–Kabara	199,728	106,680	75,804	44,554	10,315
Koulikoro–Mopti	114,381	62,165	43,475	25,659	6,124
Mopti–Gao	179,290	95,952	67,919	39,910	9,322
Mopti–Kabara	90,915	49,110	39,910	20,535	5,021

nurses and an airline pilot from Luxembourg, and a Greek artist with his Italian wife – talked at length in a mixture of French, German and English. Over river fish and sometimes meat, and rice with almost everything – in no way *haute cuisine* but perfectly edible – we spoke about the adventures we'd already had in Burkina Faso, Senegal, Mali, and about the goal that had by chance brought us all together: Timbuktu.

Between meals, sitting for hours on the steamer's windswept top deck or leaning on the rail outside our tiny bunk-bed cabins and along from our showers and lavatories – primitive but mostly in working order! – we watched the world pass slowly by.

Although it was sailing downstream, the steamer moved only at a snail's pace past the long, narrow wooden boats of the river's fishermen. It slid past their little villages, each a line of huts with mud walls and thatched roofs and water lapping almost up to their doors. It slid past thick reedbeds that stretched as far as the eye could see, an enormous expanse of dry green framed by the pale grey blue of the sky and by the darker grey blue of the Niger. It slid past the half-desert of the Sahel. Past dark green trees, low and scattered. Past scrubland whose bushes and grasses seemed at best only partly living, and which were in danger of being overwhelmed by the sand. Past near desert where the pale sand was interrupted only by occasional plants.

But most dramatic, memorable and magnificent were the sunrises and sunsets. Before dawn, the sky in the east and the high, thin clouds were set on fire, until the sun burst up from behind the horizon and the flaming orange faded away.

At dusk, the sky behind us, and the waters of the Niger with it, became orange again, until the stars, so brilliant and so close, filled the sky and, from being part of the magic of a Mali sunset, I became part of the magic of an African night.

These nightfalls on the Niger were, quite simply, unforgettable – as unforgettable as the next when, from a Tuareg camp on the very edge of the desert that I'd reached on camelback, I watched the sun setting behind the sand dunes and, soon after, the stars beginning to appear over the Sahara and over the crumbling walls and decaying buildings of the legendary city of Timbuktu.

The beginning and end of the season – when navigation is restricted – are characterised by a limited service between Mopti and Kabara only. Roughly between mid-August and late November, a regular departure schedule becomes operational for journeys from Koulikoro to Gao. Though departure times are more or less respected at the start of the trip, the COMANAV boats rarely cover the distance without delays. There is one weekly departure on Tuesdays, with the three boats alternating. The *Tombouctou* and the *Général Soumaré* go all the way to Gao in five to six days, returning on Mondays. The *Kankou Moussa*, meanwhile, arrives at its final destination, Kabara, after four to five days, returning to Koulikoro on Sundays.

Tombouctou/Général Soumaré
Depart: Koulikoro Tuesday 22.00
Arrive: Mopti Thursday 15.00
Arrive: Kabara Saturday 07.00
Arrive: Gao Sunday 00.00

Depart: Gao Monday 20.00
Arrive: Timbuktu Wednesday 18.00
Arrive: Mopti Friday 16.00
Arrive: Koulikoro Sunday 00.00

Kankou Moussa
Depart: Koulikoro Tuesday 22.00
Arrive: Kabara Saturday afternoon
Depart: Kabara Sunday 14.00
Arrive: Koulikoro Thursday late afternoon/night

When the river is too low for the COMANAV steamers, travel is still possible – although extremely unpredictable – by *pinasse* and pirogue (dugout canoe). Roughly speaking, a *pinasse* is a large pirogue with a motor used to transport goods and people along the river. Even though there is space for passengers on *pinasses* transporting goods, it is often severely restricted – which is tolerable during the day but uncomfortable at night. By contrast, the smaller – and much more expensive – *pinasses* run by tour operators (primarily to Timbuktu) have mattresses, tents and other creature comforts. The *Getting there and away* sections for towns along the river have more information about this form of travel. Note, however, that much depends on the level of the water at the time, and most voyages will take longer than you think. The rivers Senegal and Bani are also navigable, although they are less travelled than the Niger.

BY TRAIN For years, it was a policy decision not to build a road between Bamako and Kayes for fear that it would compete with the railway, which links these two towns and passes through other regional centres such as Kati, Kita and Bafoulabé. Daily trains used to be hopelessly overcrowded and overworked. However, in recent years the road system in the region of Kayes has been significantly improved, and for the first time in history road transport can now compete with the railway for efficiency and comfort.

Many Malians now prefer to travel by road, resulting in the decline of the number of people travelling by rail. The railway track is now mainly used for freight transport, and there are only three passenger trains running in either direction. One of them is the famous Bamako–Dakar express. The railway has been privatised since October 2003, changing its name from Chemin de Fer du Mali (CFM) to Trans Rail SA. Even though the heyday of the famous railway may be over, the new Canadian owners intend to upgrade the track, locomotives and carriages over time and keep the trains running.

All trains have first and second class, and are usually in a poor condition. In first class, seats are reserved and the carriages are slightly more spacious, although by no means luxurious, with sagging seats and torn upholstery. In second class, seats are claimed on a first-come-first-served basis (despite what your ticket might say) and the carriages are a lot more crowded. Two trains have a luxury class with couchettes and a bit more space. Only the Bamako–Dakar express has a restaurant carriage where you may get basic meals and a chilled drink at best. Seats in the restaurant are often taken by jolly drinkers for the duration of the journey. At every stop, vendors will sell some food, fruit and chilled – but untreated – water.

When travelling by train in Mali, bear in mind the following advice:

- Always try to buy your ticket the day before you intend to travel.
- Although delays are habitual, turn up at the station at the scheduled time of departure.
- Beware of theft, especially during the rush to board the train and during stops along the way. Once on the train, lock big luggage and keep your hand luggage with you. Be aware when putting money away; someone may be watching.
- If you're delayed, you have to wait on the platform. There is no electricity and the cockroach-filled platforms are not a nice place to be after dark.

The Bamako–Dakar express service is now a single train that does the round trip in about a week – so allow roughly three days for the journey. It should take about four hours to get to Kita and 15 to Kayes, but delays are so regular that the timetable has been abandoned. Go to Bamako station to see when a train is next expected. Fares for the express are as follows:

Bamako to:	**Couchette**	**1st class**	**2nd class**
Kita	CFA12,370	CFA6,370	CFA4,600
Kayes	CFA22,190	CFA16,190	CFA11,480
Dakar	CFA53,145	CFA34,620	CFA25,480

There are currently only two other trains that run to Kayes. One is the weekday train, which leaves Bamako on Mondays and Wednesdays at 07.15 and returns the following morning, ie: on Tuesdays and Thursdays. The other train is the weekend service, which leaves Bamako at 19.30 on a Friday night and returns on Saturday. It is slightly more expensive and has couchettes, though these are hardly necessary for Kita. Fares are as follows:

Bamako to:	**Couchette**	**1st class**	**2nd class**
Kita weekday	n/a	CFA4,625	CFA2,855
Kita weekend	CFA11,730	CFA5,795	CFA5,175
Kayes weekday	n/a	CFA11,670	CFA6,970
Kayes weekend	CFA18,775	CFA12,840	CFA9,285

For more information ✆ 2022 58 16.

Theoretically it is still possible to have your vehicle transported by train. With the construction of the paved road linking Bamako to Kayes, the need for this service is no longer obvious. Nevertheless, for a handsome sum of money cars can still be hoisted on and off freight trains (not passenger trains) in Dakar, Kayes and Korofina – the last being the freight train station in Bamako, along the Route de Sotuba.

BY ROAD Although the proportion of *goudron* or tarred road in Mali is not as high as in neighbouring countries such as Senegal, Côte d'Ivoire and Burkina Faso, most of the main tourist attractions (with the notable exception of

Timbuktu) are on – or not far from – the principal highway, which stretches for over 1,000km from Bamako to Gao on the edge of the Sahara. The country's other main road does a loop in the southern region, linking the capital to Sikasso and Abidjan, Mali's closest port. Until only a few years ago, apart from one or two other stretches of paved road, that was it; the rest of the country had to make do with dusty, sandy tracks. Financed by both the Malian government and foreign funds, however, ambitious plans have been put into effect, turning existing road maps into historical documents. And more road construction works are in progress.

The biggest achievement so far must be the construction of a paved road linking Bamako to Kayes, opening up a region that was almost totally bereft of good roads – and even of good tracks. But the smooth tar to Bandiagarahas also turned an expedition to this major stepping stone to Dogon country into almost a picnic.

The improved *piste* to Timbuktu, meanwhile, certainly reduces the time needed to drive from Douentza to Korioumé – the ferry across the Niger at 19km from Timbuktu – but the going is still tough. However, with all that has been achieved in just a few years, one may even be tempted to believe that the rumours of a Bamako–Timbuktu highway may materialise one day. Indeed, road construction workers from various European countries have moved in already, taking on the challenge to improve the section from Timbuktu to Goundam and Niafunké for a start. By no means does all this mean that the whole of Mali has been – or will be – opened up; it has just become somewhat easier to reach the more inaccessible parts of the country in a fairly comfortable way.

By hired car Having a 4x4 vehicle at your disposal is a definite luxury, permitting you to forget the hassles of public transport and navigate the more difficult tracks to out-of-the-way places. It saves time and is the most comfortable way to see Mali by land. However, for all this you pay a small fortune. A 4x4 with driver – and you should not consider anything else unless you are sticking to the paved roads – never costs under CFA50,000 a day, and quite often considerably more. This price, of course, does not include petrol and the driver's meals and accommodation. The larger hotels and most tour operators can arrange car hire. Be wary of individuals offering a similar service for considerably less money, as there is usually a catch.

By bus, bâchée and bush taxi For travel along the main highways and tracks where 4x4 is not absolutely essential, a combination of bus, *bâchée* and bush taxi is at the traveller's disposal. You will find them at certain departure points and bus yards or – in French – *gares routières*.

There are several bus companies in Mali. Some run along the Bamako–Gao highway, whereas others serve the region of Sikasso. Examples of the former include Bani Transport, Somatra, Binké Transport and Diakité Transport, while Kénédougou Voyages and Somatrie are examples of the latter. These buses leave at fixed times and stop only at the larger towns. Buy your ticket from the company's representative (often sitting at a desk beside the bus). Some buses are advertised as air conditioned. Whether they are or not remains a mystery as they never seem to turn it on. The first 30kg of baggage is included in the price of your ticket. Any extra is charged at CFA50 per kg. They will try to get you to pay anyway, but stand your ground. Your name will be put on a list and you wait for it to be announced before boarding. It's best to get there early, so your name's further up the list, otherwise you'll be last on the bus, and probably stuck at the back, three people away from the window. It all seems rather chaotic, but in fact seats are rarely overbooked. Whether or not the bus departs on time, however, is another matter. Once you finally get going, there are endless stops along the way for pickups and drop-offs and to let on the many vendors selling snacks and cold water.

Bâchées and bush taxis (*taxi brousse* in French) ply the routes along the paved highways and also serve the smaller towns and villages. A *bâchée* can be anything from a small van or minibus to a Peugeot 504 or 505 converted into something resembling a pick-up truck. Bush taxis, meanwhile, are these same Peugeots, kept in their original state, but which are used to carry at least twice their intended load. Travelling by *bâchée* and bush taxi, therefore, is not particularly comfortable, especially if the road is dusty and the weather hot. However, prices are charged per place and one trick to make the journey slightly easier is to buy two seats. This type of transport invariably leaves when there are enough passengers to justify the trip – which means that if you are the first to buy your ticket, be prepared to wait several hours before the others are sold. The net result is that travel is often as slow as it is uncomfortable and, although the road might be in a good state, going just a few kilometres can take a big chunk out of your day.

Some roads – in the desert and the region of Kayes, for instance – are too rough for buses, *bâchées* and bush taxis. In these cases, the traveller must either look for a ride on a *camion* (the French word meaning 'lorry' or 'truck') or find a *location* (from the French word meaning 'hire'). A *location* is often a Land Rover – preferred for their renowned resilience – with enough space in the back for about 16 people. They are most common in Timbuktu and other desert towns where a 4x4 is necessary. The price of a *location* or a *camion* is usually fixed, but is sometimes a matter for discussion between the passenger and driver.

Hitchhiking If – or when – the buses and *bâchées* start to get you down, hitchhiking is a feasible option. Along the main highway, especially between Bamako and Mopti, there is a fair amount of NGO and tourist traffic – your best bets for free rides. The section of the highway between Mopti and Gao is considerably quieter, while on some other routes – in the desert, for example – there can be nothing at all. The best place to wait for rides is at the police checkpoints a few kilometres out of the towns. Tell the police where you want to go and they will sometimes stop vehicles on your behalf.

ON FOOT Though Bamako is best seen by walking the streets, some attractions and hotels are quite far from the centre. The capital has an extensive system of organised transport, which makes travelling around the city easy and efficient. Bamako is famous for its green minibuses and *bâchées*, known as *sotramas* and *dou dourenis* respectively. They are cheap and plentiful, with often less than a minute between vehicles plying the same routes. Taxis for private hire are called *locations* (not to be confused with the *locations* mentioned above), while shared taxis provide the same service, but pick up and drop off passengers along the way.

Mali's other towns are easily covered on foot, and sometimes the only alternative is the relatively expensive *location* or private taxi. Some expansive towns, on the other hand, may have a limited system of public transport, using the same, easily recognisable green *sotramas* and *bâchées*, and yellow taxis.

ACCOMMODATION

Trying to categorise hotels in Mali is a dangerous business; and labelling accommodation 'expensive', 'moderate' or 'budget' according to its price is

ECO HOTELS COME TO MALI

Suzanne Porter

The Malian government has prioritised the development of its tourism industry, especially in the areas of eco and cultural tourism. Realising the potential of this niche market, they have committed to the advancement of the industry and a number of projects are underway.

In the meantime, a couple of private projects have already paved the way. Teriya Bugu (see page 154), situated halfway between Bamako and the Dogon country on the banks of the Bani River, was Mali's first foray into eco and ethical tourism. It was born in the mid 1960s after a friendship flourished between a visiting missionary, Father Bernard Vespieren, and a Bambara fisherman, Lamine Samake. Together they set up a number of projects for the disadvantaged local population through the creation of their NGO, the Association for Rural Development (AEDR) and Mali Aqua Viva. The projects were based around a hotel built in a large park surrounded by eucalyptus, mango and frangipani trees, with local birds and wild animals including monkeys, cayman and gazelles. The belief behind the project was that tourism wasn't just a one-way thing but demanded respect for the local environment and even more so for the population of the host country, through communication and understanding between the two. The nearby village was home to 500 people and they encouraged the inhabitants and those from the surrounding villages to get involved in the tourist activities by providing guided visits, for which they got paid. Profits from the hotel were used by AEDR to finance the development of local schools, clinics, youth centres and rural activities.

Father Vespieren was also a pioneer in solar energy in west Africa and installed a number of solar panels to run water pumps for irrigation and a solar water system to heat water. Sadly he has now passed away, but his memory lives on as the project continues to operate. On the hotel premises, there is a research centre for the use of renewable energy. A new programme has just been started for using vegetable oil as biofuel, as well as research into 'Transpaille', a technology which produces methane through the fermentation of animal faeces and dried vegetal compost.

The hotel itself is an ideal place to discover African culture, the problems of the population and the future of their development. The hotel offers everything you can wish for in terms of accommodation: spacious rooms, a bar, swimming pool, zoo and pedalos, plus guided tours to the villages. There's a well-equipped farm, employing over 50 families that supplies the restaurant with fresh products such as fish, eggs, honey, fruit and vegetables.

A tribute to the life's work of Father Vespieren (*www.tb-mali.com/e-father-bernard-verspieren.html*) can be seen at the free museum on the site between Ségou and San, see page 154.

Another project to have recently opened is Campement Tenéré, on the main *piste* from Douentza and 30km from the embarkation point for the ferry to Timbuktu. It was opened in December 2007 by local Tuareg, Abdou Salam whose father before him had a *campement* with a few rooms. When he died, the village begged the sons to start it up again. They agreed, but on condition that all of the village would participate and that the profits would be redistributed amongst those bringing something either physical or financial to the project. So far the profits have funded a maize mill and water supply and contributed to educating a villager through medical school, who will look after them until they have enough money to set up a hospital. One of the brothers runs a 'responsible' tourism agency called Tadaada, which also helps fund these projects. The *campement* forms part of the Eco Tuareg Museum, showing all aspects of traditional Tuareg life, still being practised in the community. For more details see *Chapter 9*, *Tiboraghene*, page 250.

often misleading. Just because you pay CFA15,000 for a room – a price I consider to be above average – does not necessarily mean that you will end up with good or even moderate accommodation. Travellers often complain that you pay a lot for a little in Mali and, on the whole, I agree. This is why I have tried to avoid pigeon-holing hotels, preferring to give an opinion as to whether or not I think they are good value for money.

Luxury hotels, as Westerners understand the term, are rare in Mali. There are, however, many comfortable hotels designed for tourists or people visiting the country on business, most of which are found in Bamako. Outside Bamako, several 'boutique' hotels have opened up offering stylish accommodation for tourists at a reasonable price. If you pay more than CFA30,000 for a place to stay, you can normally expect all mod-cons: air conditioning, television, telephone, en-suite toilet and sometimes even a bath. The frills disappear as you start to economise, and you should not take it for granted that a CFA15,000 room, for example, has luxuries such as air conditioning and an en-suite toilet. Once you're out of Bamako, many hotels under this price will have only cold water, though they will normally heat it up if you ask. The cheapest places in Mali are around CFA2,500, which buys you a mud box or a place on the roof under the stars.

If a town does not have a hotel, it will often have a *campement*. Although at many you can bring your own tent and pitch it in the garden, most people stay in the functional – but not luxurious – rooms. However, you can stumble across a *campement* which is every bit as good as, if not better than, an expensive hotel. This will not be the case, however, in Dogon country, where *campements* are now available in most of the popular villages. Almost without exception, these places are very basic and without running water; but at the same time, very welcoming and often quite charming.

If you arrive in a town where there seems to be nowhere to stay, what are your options? In places where there is a *Mission Catholique* (Catholic mission), you might be able to stay in accommodation reserved for visiting clerics and their families. In fact, in Bamako the religious missions have become favourites with backpackers and other budget travellers.

Maison de passage is an ambiguous French expression which can embrace many types of lodgings, but typically refers to the ad hoc accommodation one finds in family homes, restaurants, bars and NGO houses. For these opportunities, however, you have to ask around and be willing to make friends. Always offer to pay. Occasionally you may find a *chambre de passage* with an hourly rate. Although theoretically these could be used to freshen up and rest for a while, more often than not these rooms are a cover for prostitution.

HOTEL PRICE CODES

Accommodation listings are laid out in decreasing price order, under the following categories: Luxury, Upmarket, Mid-range, Budget, and Shoestring. The following key (also on the inside front cover) gives an indication of prices. Prices are based on a double room per night.

$$$$$	CFA58,195+
$$$$	CFA29,107–58,195
$$$	CFA14,560–29,107
$$	CFA7,283–14,560
$	<CFA7,283

TAXES There is a tourist tax on hotel rooms of CFA500 per night. This may be included in the total price or added on to the basic room rate. The prices quoted in this book usually include the tourist tax.

TRADITIONAL DISHES

'Do you have any Malian specialities?'
'Yes, rice.'

The manager of the Hotel Lac Débo in Bamako was neither overstating nor underselling his nation's cuisine. Alimentation in Mali is heavily based on cereals – not only rice, but also millet, sorghum, *fonio* and, to a lesser extent, maize. Couscous in Mali is made from millet rather than wheat, as is common in north Africa, while *tô* is moist, millet-or maize-based dough with a consistency similar to plasticine. *Fonio* is a variety of millet with very fine grains. *Fonio* is another cereal altogether, with very fine grains; when seen growing in the fields it looks rather like hay, unlike the tall stands of sorghum and millet.

As well as cereals, Malians fill up on root crops – you will find both cassava and sweet potatoes, the former often minced and mashed to create a surprisingly light dish called *atieké*. Yams are becoming popular too. The terms can get confusing; note that *manioc* is French for cassava, and *patates* are sweet potatoes, not potatoes (which are *pommes de terre*).

For breakfast, Malians often eat *bouillie* – a sweet, soothing milk-and-cereal concoction not unlike runny rice pudding. You'll be lucky to find this, though, as it's mostly made and eaten in the home. Try transport hubs, where you may also find *galettes de mil* – millet or sorghum patties fried in little round moulds, and the more common *beignets* (doughnut-like balls). Once the morning's over, traditional dishes can be found in many restaurants as well as on the street (see box *Eating on the Street* page 84). It's common for smaller restaurants to rotate a menu, serving a different dish each day alongside 'international' options.

The sauce is what makes – or breaks! – a traditional Malian meal. *Sauce arachide* (peanut sauce) is one of the most typical. Served with rice, the base is made from a peanut butter-like paste which is dissolved in water and cooked with oil, a few tomatoes and onions. Results can vary, but it is usually pretty tasty and rarely inedible. The same is not necessarily true for *gumbo*, a thick, green sauce made with okra pods, which is commonly served with *tô*. Popular in Dogon country, the colour and consistency of this meal – which should be eaten with your fingers – may be as significant as its musty taste in deterring a second try. On the other hand, you might love it. Experiment! Another staple of the Malian diet is *sauce de feuilles* (leaf sauce), which comes in various guises and can be made with cassava, sweet potato or baobab leaves. *Saga-saga* is one local term for this, as is *fakahoye* from the Songhay region (although according to some, this is a herb sauce with lamb). The Songhay also serve *algafta*, a sort of Scotch egg, while the Tuareg speciality is *alabadja* – white rice mixed with minced meat and soaked in a butter sauce and traditionally served at weddings. These regional dishes – and others like them – might be available in one or two

RESTAURANT PRICE CODES

Restaurant listings are laid out in decreasing price order, under the following categories: Upmarket, Above average, Mid-range, Cheap and cheerful, and Rock bottom. The following key (also on the inside front cover) gives an indication of prices. Prices are based on the cost of a main meal per person.

$$$$$	CFA10,923+
$$$$	CFA7,282–10,923
$$$	CFA4,367–7,282
$$	CFA2,183–4,367
$	CFA728–2,183

THE CAPITAINE'S TABLE

Order fish at a Malian restaurant and it will most likely be *capitaine*. However, this is just the first step, for then you must decide how you want your *capitaine* prepared. You might like to have it fried in breadcrumbs as *croquette de capitaine* or, provided that a banana is added to the dish, *capitaine à la bamakoise*. Grilled or barbecued is another option, with a simple *brochette de capitaine* consisting of huge chunks of fish speared onto a skewer and cooked over an open fire being a popular choice. A variety of sauces await the more discriminating palate. *Capitaine au beurre blanc* and *capitaine à la sauce moutarde* should both be self-explanatory: butter- and mustard-based sauces respectively. *Capitaine à l'Africaine* is the more ambiguous name for a tomato sauce, while *capitaine à la sauce aurore* or 'daybreak sauce' is a tomato sauce with a splash of crème fraîche. For something even more exotic, try *capitaine papillot* (the French verb *papilloter* means 'to twinkle'), which involves cooking the fish in vegetable soup before wrapping it in aluminium foil and roasting it on a fire.

restaurants specialising in African cuisine, but are by no means as widespread as *sauce arachide* or *sauce de feuilles*.

Traditional eating may appear to be a good way forward for vegetarians, but beware: many of the sauces, if not sporting obvious chunks of meat (often found in *sauce arachide*), contain at the very least fish paste. Think of the mounds of dried fish at Mopti; sauces are where it ends up. But it's always worth asking, because as with traditional dishes the world over, recipes vary.

INTERNATIONAL CUISINE 'International cuisine' can mean different things depending on where you are in the country. In Bamako there are restaurants serving food from all over the world: French, Italian, Chinese, Indian, Lebanese, etc. In other towns, however, where restaurants tend to be less sophisticated, 'international cuisine' may involve no more than a pile of spaghetti and a scrawny chicken leg. In Bamako there are also several excellent *pâtisseries* serving cakes, pastries and croissants. The French influence is equally apparent in the quality of the bread, which, although it varies from town to town, is consistently high. In Timbuktu the bread is baked in distinctive clay furnaces and has a sandy texture. Finally, a wide range of imported food products is available in the larger supermarkets in Bamako. These are mainly from France and are expensive.

FRUIT AND VEGETABLES It stands to reason that exotic fruit and vegetables do not exactly thrive in a dry, landlocked country such as Mali. Having said this, however, a surprising range of produce grows along the banks of the River Niger, and the Malians have become adept at getting the most out of semi-arid land. Moreover, thanks to the railway and paved road linking the remote western and eastern parts of the country to Bamako and the fertile south, fruit and vegetables are available almost everywhere – although in places such as Timbuktu the choice is often limited to sour oranges and withering tomatoes.

The fruit on offer is either grown locally or imported from nearby Côte d'Ivoire. The aforementioned oranges are widely available, while bananas, papayas, pineapples and mangoes are found in many of the larger markets. The mangoes are grown in Sikasso and deserve special mention – if only for their remarkable size.

Many of the riverside gardens produce potatoes, onions, carrots, tomatoes, cucumbers, aubergines, beetroots, cauliflowers and lettuce. If you don't see vegetables in their own right in a Malian dish, it is possible that they have been used to make the accompanying sauce.

EATING ON THE STREET

Gill Harvey

Spot a woman sitting behind a table laden with bowls, and you've spotted Malian street food. The problem for the uninitiated is that many of the bowls are covered. Be brave: sit yourself down on the little wooden bench and take a few minutes to see what she's got. There's often an astonishing array of carbs – any combination of rice, *riz au gras*, spaghetti, macaroni, *fonio*, *tô*, chips, *aloro* (fried plantain), *atieké* (minced cassava) and, especially in Bamako or at transport hubs, bread. There's often the option of *haricots*, too – a big vat of tasty beans that are surprisingly good with spaghetti or slapped into a sandwich. Then there are the sauces: *sauce arachide* is popular, along with other stews of chicken, beef, fish or the excellent meatballs known as *boulettes* (sometimes called '*surprises*' because there's a boiled egg inside). If rice or *tô* are on offer, there's likely to be a traditional green sauce to go with them – *saga-saga*, *gumbo* or *fakohoye* – especially at lunchtime.

Add to all this fresh fried fish, sizzling brochettes and salads, and the choice is wide indeed. All along the Niger, you can be sure that the fish is fresh, and there's plenty of choice; you'll find everything from hunks of *capitaine* to *tinani*, the little fish that look like whitebait and are similarly eaten whole. Ask for salad and the woman will prepare it on the spot – fresh lettuce, tomatoes, onions and cucumber, chopped and tossed with vinegar, oil and salt (specify *un peu* if you don't want your salad drowned, and watch out for Maggi sauce and meat fat!). You'll get a boiled egg on top if you're lucky.

The fun of street stalls is that you can mix and match your dishes, and this is hungry backpackers' heaven: eat as much as you like and you'll still come away with change from CFA1,000. Locals determine quantity by giving a price – CFA100–200 will get you a portion of most things, so if you want just a taster, say 'à 50 francs, pour goûter,' and she'll get the idea.

The same does not quite apply when it comes to grilled meat. Stalls selling goat, beef and mutton proliferate the further east you go, and are almost always the preserve of men. Choose your scrawny but tasty cut and he'll chop it up and serve it in brown cement-bag paper with a liberal sprinkling of salt. This is luxury street food – a packetful will set you back about CFA1,000. It's also where to head if you're feeling adventurous; stomach, liver, heart and other unidentified body parts all find their way onto the grills. Good luck!

DRINKS The globally ubiquitous soft drinks such as Coca-Cola, Fanta and Sprite are widely available in Mali. The local brand, D'jino, comes in several flavours and, despite being described as 'juice', is as fizzy and sweet as its foreign counterparts. Freshly squeezed juices are neither as common nor as exotic as you might expect. Orange juice is probably the most widespread, although other flavours such as lime and pineapple are not unheard of. Cold milk sold in sachets is also popular. Bottled water can be found all over the country, Diago and Tombouctou being two of several brands. Tap water is treated with chlorine in all the major towns, and many travellers drink it without a problem; others choose not to risk it. Another option is the treated water sold in 33cl or 50cl plastic sachets – either blue or clear with blue writing declaring it *eau potable* (drinking water). These are a much cheaper alternative to bottled water and are even available free (chilled!) on Gana Transport buses. Water in unlabelled polythene bags is sometimes seen, the origins of which may be dubious. Note that Dogon villages still rely on wells and pumps; water from the latter is usually clean, but well water is always a dodgy prospect. Rather than carry or buy endless mineral water, consider carrying water purification tablets.

AFRICA'S CAFFEINE FIX

Sue Adams

A cattle herder with a conical hat standing in the crush of a masked dance celebration in Dogon country in Mali offered me a small slice of a large nut. Without thinking I popped it in my mouth and chewed. My resulting shudder and grimace made him roar with laughter. Soon all his friends were grinning at me as I swallowed my gift. Unknowingly I had tasted my first kola nut.

In west Africa being given a kola nut is like taking tea with a Tuareg. You must accept or it will be considered rude. As with the Indian peace pipe it is offered as a sign of friendship and respect. But don't expect it to be pleasurable: 'interesting' might be a better word. It has a bitter taste and is only for chewing. You are meant to spit, and not swallow, so my reaction to my cattle herder's gift was doubly funny.

Since ancient times the kola nut has been used all over west Africa as a quick fix energy boost. Some people describe it as the 'poor man's friend' for its high caffeine content. A poor diet and intense heat make labouring in west Africa very hard. The caffeine in kola nuts can give you the little bit of extra energy and strength you need to get through your hard day. A Dogon guide told me that the old men in the villages use it when they are feeling very tired but I noticed that young modern west Africans in the bigger cities shun it. Maybe they have found more Western versions of high energy supplements.

However, this special nut also has huge social significance in west Africa. It is offered at any social occasion and, when visiting a village chief or an important person, you should take a gift of kola nuts. It is quite normal to offer some kola nut to the people around you even though you don't know them – as I found to my detriment.

In some areas a prospective husband is expected to deliver a handful of nuts to his bride's parents. If accepted it means he is approved as the husband and is now expected to bring a huge basket of nuts for the family. It is also used as a sign of peace at the end of a conflict. A kola nut is broken in half and a piece given to each party as a signal that there is resolution and goodwill. But make sure that your nut is white, a symbol of peace, as the red ones are a sign of bloodshed and war.

Traditionally the West Africans also use the kola nut for its health benefits. It is believed to aid the stomach and improve digestion, be good as an antidepressant and stop vomiting and diarrhoea. Its high caffeine content can also help with relieving migraines as well as acting as an appetite suppressant.

Although the Coca-Cola recipe is considered secret, the original one is known to have contained kola nut – hence the 'cola' name. Kola was used to make a whole range of cola soft drinks but nowadays drinks are mostly made with artificial flavourings. Recently the kola nut has become quite popular in alternative medicine in the West and 'Blow', the energy drink that caused a furore in the UK in 2007, contains kola nut extract.

The Kola tree (*Cola acuminata*) is indigenous to the moister areas of west Africa and can grow up to 18 metres. It looks rather like a chestnut with glossy oval pointed leaves. The pod is large and contains a number of kola nuts nestled together. Each nut is about the size of a chestnut and can be red or white. When sold in the markets they are usually kept moist and the fresher the better as they lose their caffeine content with age. Nigeria is the biggest producer of kola nuts and, although some is exported, the bulk of the crop is consumed in west Africa.

So if you are travelling in this part of the world and you want to greet a chief, make a friend, stay up late or need a bit of energy, then kola nuts are the currency. But be careful that you are not asking for someone's hand in marriage and don't swallow!

One of the most thirst-quenching of the local specialities on offer is *djablani*, sold on virtually every street corner in the country. Often flavoured with *bissap* (the red variety of *djablani*), made from hibiscus, ginger, or the fruit of the baobab tree, these small polythene bagfuls of juice are boiled before being frozen and are therefore generally safe to drink. Moreover, at CFA50 a time, there is no cheaper way to take the edge off your thirst. Served mainly in restaurants and homes, *jijimbere* and *crème de miel* are two other popular drinks: the former is made with water, crushed ginger, lemon juice, sugar and mint leaves, while the latter contains ginger, lemon and honey and slightly resembles a milkshake. Tea (*attiya*) is an institution across the country. It is green tea rather than black, served sweet and strong after an elaborate pouring ritual that ensures plenty of foam. The teapots are filled three times; according to the Tuareg, the first cup is said to be *fort comme la mort* ('strong as death'), the second is *doux comme la vie* ('mild as life') and the third is *sucré comme l'amour* ('sweet as love').

It's very unusual to be charged for *attiya*, unless you specifically ask for it. When offered a glass, drink it fairly quickly (Malians tend to make lots of slurping noises through the foam), then hand the glass back so that it can be washed and filled for someone else.

Despite Mali being an Islamic country, alcohol is not prohibited. *Une petite* or *une grande* of the locally produced Castel (NB: not Castle) used to be the main choice when it came to bottled beer, but Flag has made it over from Senegal and is making a big bid for the market, judging by the number of buntings and signs now on show. *Bière de mil* (millet beer) – *dolo* (the Dogon name), *tchapulo* (the Bambara name) – is the preferred tipple of the country's rural population. Mali also produces whisky, sold in sachets in selected bars around the country, and imported beer, wine and spirits are available in the larger supermarkets in Bamako.

PUBLIC HOLIDAYS

Being a country where Islam and Christianity dominate, Mali's public holidays are largely based on these two religions. The dates for the various Islamic holidays (Ramadan, Tabaski, Maouloud, etc) vary from year to year, so check a current diary. The other public holidays in Mali are:

1 January	New Year's Day
20 January	Army Day
26 March	Martyrs' Day
March/April	Easter
1 May	Labour Day
25 May	Africa Day
22 September	Independence Day
25 December	Christmas Day

FESTIVALS *with Suzanne Porter*

Throughout Mali and throughout the year there are numerous festivals and celebrations. The majority are based on traditional or religious festivities but visitors are welcome. Communities are being urged to open up these events to the public and some have in fact been designed or reshaped for the benefit of tourists. But, don't go there expecting them to be like Western festivals such as Glastonbury, as you'll only be disappointed. The chaos and uncertainty are all part of the charm. Most festivals take place in the cooler months between October and March. Obviously, certain events are strictly seasonal by nature, but some festivals have indeed been rescheduled to facilitate access to a wider public and take advantage of the tourist season. Even though there is a growing tendency to invite the public to participate, some rituals and festivities are sacred and intended for a select group of the population only. Your only chance of attending such a ceremony or festivity is by personal invitation.

Some of the more popular festivals and celebrations – all open to the public – are listed below. The list by no means covers everything. More and more are popping up every year, and at the same time, some may fall by the wayside. It's always advisable to check with the OMATHO (the Office Malien du Tourisme et de l'Hôtellerie; see page 44) where you're going to be, to see if you'll be lucky enough to catch a local celebration while you're there.

NATIONAL

La Fête de Tabaski (Eid al-Adha)/The Festival of the Sacrifice (*Held annually at the end of Hajj, on the 10th of Dhu'l-Hijja, the last month of the Islamic calendar*) A religious festival celebrated by Muslims all over Mali in honour of Abraham's dedication to God, in his willingness to sacrifice his own son. At the last minute, God replaced him with a sheep. The *fête* starts in the morning with prayer before each family returns home to sacrifice their own ram. The festivities last for three days of visiting friends, asking forgiveness and sharing large quantities of meat. It's a real family occasion but if you're lucky enough to be invited to join in, particularly in the more remote communities, you will be guaranteed a memorable experience.

REGIONAL

Bamako region For more details on festivals in this region, contact the OMATHO in Bamako (*☎ 2022 56 73;* **e** *omathoo@yahoo.fr*).

Festival des Masques de Koulouba (*No fixed date*) A popular Bambara celebration during which traditional masks are exhibited in the villages of Koulouba and Sogonafing.

Festival de Percussion de Bamako (Festip) (*Contact 'Domba' at the Maison des Jeunes; ☎ 2022 23 20;* **m** *6678 40 89; held, since 2004, annually in February*) More than a dozen African groups from Guinea, Niger, Mali, Senegal, Guinea-Bissau, Burkina Faso and Côte d'Ivoire join musicians from Europe at this European Union-supported international festival of percussion.

Festival International du Manden (Fesmanden) 'Bogna ma Segui' (**e** *fesmanden@gmail.com; www.fesmanden.org; held, since: 2008, annually in February*) A celebration of the Manden culture taking place in Kangaba in the region of Koulikoro, 100km south of Bamako and 50km from the Guinean border. A three-day festival with exhibitions of traditional Manden musical instruments, a market with arts and crafts and traditional medicine and in the evening, theatre performances and folk demonstrations revealing the mysteries and magic of the hunters through the telling of local legends around the fire, underneath the baobab tree.

Les Paris-Bamako (**e** *info@les-paris-bamako.com; www.les-paris-bamako.com; held, since 2005, annually in April*) Over the duration of a week, Amadou and Mariam, the famous blind musicians from Mali, work and rehearse with other African and international artists. Some amazing collaborations materialise and it all culminates in a concert on the last night at the Institut des Jeunes Aveugles in Faladie. Neneh Cherry, Manu Chau and Yuri Buenaventura from Colombia, plus African artists

Keziah Jones, Toumani Diabaté and Daby Touré have all joined the couple in the past. There are also film showings and photography exhibitions. The festival contributes towards several projects for the Institute for the Young Blind of Bamako such as the training of specialist teachers and the purchase and installation of solar panels and pedagogical equipment.

Festival du Ouagadou (*Biennial; held since 2007 in April*) This festival is held on different sites but mainly opposite the old prison on the main square in the heart of Nara, 380km northeast of Bamako in the Koulikoro region. No fewer than 10,000 people take part in the opening ceremony, launching the three-day festivities with folk displays from Falou, Goumbou and Mourdiah on horses and camels, masked dance, traditional fighting by young warriors armed with rifles and all before the evening's cultural and artistic entertainment has even begun.

Festival International des Cauris (Fescauri) (*2029 61 88; e koryconsult@gmail.com; www.koryconsult.com; held annually, since 2007, in late October/early November*) Held in the rural commune of Siby, 45km from Bamako, this event is based around the Cauris, a small sea snail, otherwise known as the money cowry. In early civilisation the shell was used as a form of currency, an ornament or a mythical object. The festival held on the town's football pitch has performances from traditional hunters as well as musicians from Mali and other African countries. There's storytelling, fashion shows, art exhibitions and the chance to visit local tourist sites.

Rencontres de la Photographie Africaine (*www.culturesfrance.com/evenement/Les-expositions-des-septiemes-Rencontres-de-Bamako/ev646.html; biennial; held since 1994 in November*) A month-long festival of exhibitions and competitions originally created to promote the work of African photographers. It takes place in a number of venues across Bamako including the 'Maison Photo' room at the Bibliothèque National in ACI 2000 and the Quartier Orange in the industrial district (sponsored by the well-known mobile-phone company). In the past, it has helped promote the work of respected Malian photographers Seydou Keita and Malick Sidibé.

Festival des Chasseurs (*Contact Mr Sangaré at the Palais de la Culture; 2022 33 70; held every three years, since 2001, between November and January*) 700 hunters from Gambia, Guinea, Niger, Senegal and Mali gather at the Palais de la Culture in Bamako for three days to exchange their knowledge and know-how in demonstrations and ceremonies, open to the public. Healers and soothsayers offer their services to visitors in the palace gardens and there's a portrait exhibition of hunters and hunting. Also takes place in Yanfolila and Ségou at the same time.

Ségou region For more details on festivals in this region, contact the OMATHO in Ségou (*2132 24 94*).

Festival sur le Niger (*2132 18 04; e info@festivalsegou.org; www.festivalsegou.org; held, since 2005, annually at end of January/beginning of February*) A town-based festival held over four days with all the action focused on the quayside. Every year has a different theme: 2008 was *'Environmental solutions'*. It's the festival for world music lovers with an impressive lineup of Mali's top musicians: Salif Keita, Habib Koité, Bassékou Kouyaté and Abdoulaye Diabaté, amongst others, performing on a stage over the river. Also pirogue races, art exhibitions, traditional dance and puppet shows, storytelling and crafts. The little town of Ségou is buzzing so it is advisable to book accommodation early. (For more details see box on page 150.)

Festival des Masques et Marionettes de Markala or Fesmamas (*Held annually on a 'favourable' date according to the lunar calendar, normally the first week in March*) The *Théâtre des Marionettes* is one of the largest of its kind in Mali. It is grafted onto two traditional rituals during which the gods are invoked or thanked for a successful harvest. The Festival of Masks and Puppets usually takes the form of dances in human or animal costumes endowed with some historic or symbolic meaning. For this occasion, however, the masks and puppets provide a profane but spectacular display. Malian and international groups take part in competitive and vivid choreographies, staged in two quarters of Markala. These festivals also take place in other Bozo areas.

Sankémon An animist ritual involving sacrifices, incantations and 'collective fishing' in the Mare de San. (See also page 157.)

Mopti region For more details on any of these events, contact the OMATHO in Mopti (*2143 05 06;* e *officetourismemopti@yahoo.fr*).

Festival Diamwari of Mopti (m *6672 62 72; www.festivalculturelmopti.org; held annually, since 2008, during January/February*) Following the success of the first staging of this festival, the organisers decided to make it an annual event. Held at the point where the Bani and the Niger rivers cross, the festival plays homage to the river, the origin of the posterity of the city. Over three days, discover the rich arts and culture of Mopti, or the 'Venice of Mali', as they like to call it. There are pirogue races, traditional dance from all over Mali (including the masked dance from the Dogon), visits to famous sites, artisans' market, art exhibitions and musical performances. In 2008, Habib Koité and Mariam and Amadou were amongst those who performed.

Crépissage de la Mosquée (*Held annually, usually in April*) The ends of wood sticking out of the façade of Djenné's famous mosque do actually serve a purpose. Each year before the start of the rainy season and at a time decided by the water level, the people of Djenné volunteer to resurface the mosque with a new layer of *banco* by hand. Huge quantities of *banco* are hauled up to the Djennenké, whose feet seek support on the wooden protrusions; traditionally it's the women who carry water to the masons working on the mosque. It starts at 03.00 and the whole town takes part. Not so much a festival but a huge event all the same.

Diafarabé (*Held annually, since 1818, on a Saturday in November/December*) A day of celebration of *transhumance* (nomadism). The exact timing of this event, 122km from Mopti, is decided at a local level and typically isn't known until about three days beforehand. As the grasslands of the northern Sahel dry out, the semi-nomadic Peul return with their cattle to the River Niger. New pastures await on the other side, but the cattle have to swim across. Diafarabé is the scene of the biggest and most important crossing. It starts at around 09.00 with approximately 20,000 cattle making it across. Families stay reunited for a few days only, before the herders move on, which makes this short gathering both exuberant and emotional. Typically only 15–20 tourists are there every year.

Sofara (*Held annually exactly one week after Diafarabé on a Saturday*) Some 35km from Djenné, around the same amount of cattle as at Diafarabé cross the river of approximately the same width.

NB: The cattle crossings continue every Saturday in various locations, along the River Niger until the first weekend in April. However, they don't involve as many cattle as at Diafarabé or Sofara and the rivers themselves are noticeably narrower and less interesting.

Dogon country

Festival de Festifa (*Contact the Association pour la Promotion duTourisme au Mali;* m *7913 94 34;* e *aptm2003@yahoo.fr; held annually at the end of November*) A new cultural festival organised in the centre of Sangha, taking place over four days, and planned to commence in 2010. Live the rhythms of the Dogon country. Sample their local knowledge with a range of cultural activities; Dogon rites, tales and legends and music and dance performances.

Festival Culturel et Artistique de Bandiagara (*Contact the Mission Culturelle de Bandiagara or* e *chevalblancmali@yahoo.fr or noegui-nouh@yahoo.fr; biennial but may become annual, held since 2006 at the end of December*) Events, held over five days, start at 15.00, behind the bus station in the centre of town. There's *bogolan* (see page 93) and indigo dyeing demonstrations, an artisan market, African meals and even a hairdresser. Music and the masked dance take place, as well as hunters from Bandiagara and a fighting competition accompanied by the sound of the *balafon*, *djembe* and *calabash*. From 20.30 at the cultural centre, the evening's entertainment starts with concerts and cultural themed evenings such as the election of Miss Festival and Mr Rap. Entrance CFA4,000 for adult non-residents, CFA2,000 per child.

Festival des Danses des Masques (*Held annually towards the end of December or the beginning of January*) This festival is held in a different village every year, along the *falaise* de Bandiagara (see page 197). Various groups of masked dancers from all over Dogon country compete for the honour of being the best group of all. Like a performance for tourists in any village, these dances are grafted onto their sacred counterparts, but without the ritual denotation. However, it's the element of competition that makes all the difference, as all dancers give it their best shot to impress the international audience and their kinsmen alike. This gathering offers a spectacular opportunity to see a whole variety of costumes, masks and dances. Entrance fee CFA4,000, which buys you the right to take pictures.

Sigui (*Held every 60 years*) A religious celebration of initiation and atonement in the region of Sangha. The signal for the commencement is the appearance of a glimmer of red light in the east. The next one should be in 2027.

Gourma region

Traversé des troupeaux du Gourma (*Held when the water level of the Niger starts dropping*) In the Gourma area troops will also swim across the river. As in Diafarabé, this event goes hand in hand with frolic festivities.

Timbuktu region

Festival au Desert, Essakane (*www.festival-au-desert.org; held annually, since 2001, at the beginning of January*) In the white-sand dunes of Essakane, 65km from Timbuktu. A phenomenal achievement by the Tuareg organisers and in 2008, 1,200 tourists made it there. Yet what started as a festival to raise awareness of the Tuareg culture and celebrate peace in the desert has now become a showcase with many non-Tuareg elements creeping in. Over three days, activities include forum discussions, a fashion show, poetry, an arts and crafts market and camel racing at dusk to traditional *tindé* drums. At night the spectacle commences with music from Tuareg groups as well as from other parts of Mali, Africa and the rest of the world. There are restaurants, bars and even a nightclub on site. Entrance €120 for the three days. The festival charter a plane from Bamako every year, leaving on Thursday, taking 45 minutes and costing €150 one-way; add an extra €75 for a 4x4 from the airport to Essakane return. (For more information see *Timbuktu*, pages 244–5.) .

Ali Farka Touré International Festival (*Contact Fondation Ali Farka Touré, Hamdallaye ACI 2000, pres de l'Hotel Bouna, Bamako;* **m** *7903 39 08;* **e** *faft_faft@yahoo.fr; www.fondationalifarkatoure.org; held annually since 2008 in November*) This festival was created in honour of the late, great musician by the Ali Farka Touré Foundation. Held in the quaint riverside town of Niafunké, Ali's home town and the place where he recorded the album of the same name. In 2008, the lineup included Toumani Diabaté, Vieux Farka Touré, Afel Bocoum, Bassekou Kouyaté, Oumou Sangaré and Baaba Maal from Senegal. During the day there are pirogue rides and workshops with artists.

Gao and Kidal regions You may find that some of the festivals in this region have been cancelled for the time being, owing to insecurity. However, with peace agreements in place, things will hopefully be back to normal soon. For the latest updates see the websites below or consult the local OMATHO (*www.visitgaomali.com*).

Takoubelt: the 'Saharan Nights of Essouk' (*www.keltinariwen.org, or www.kidal.info/FETE/Essouk; held annually since 1997 in January*) From the 1960s onwards, Tuareg rebellion and droughts prevented traditional gatherings. It was not until 1997 that the first Takoubelt (which means 'gathering' in Tamasheq, the Tuareg language) was held again in the region of Kidal. The second took place in 2000, and from then on it became a yearly event, attracting not only Tuareg – from as far away as Mauritania and Niger – but also growing numbers of other visitors. In 2004, the festival moved to Essouk, where it was to stay. There's almost exclusively Tuareg music, dance and poetry, camel racing, a beauty contest, forum discussions about current issues and excursions to nearby historical sites. Accommodation is in beautifully decorated traditional tents on a sandy ridge in the shape of a crescent.

Tamadacht: Festival d'Andéramboukane (*www.visitgaomali.com; biennial in February*) The Tamadacht Festival is a celebration of Tuareg arts and culture, with many participants – including other ethnic groups such as the Woodabe – from both Mali and Niger. The location is Andéramboukane, a speck on the map situated about 400km east of Gao, on the border between the two countries and next to a small but attractive lake. Its basic principles are similar to those of the Kidal festival. It's an authentic festival with traditional Tuareg activities, such as camel racing and sand hockey as well as musical performances. Highly recommended, if you can make it there.

La Fête du Chameau (*www.feteduchameau.net; held annually since 2007 at the end of December/beginning of January*) A festival to honour everything that is the dromedary, during three days of camel racing (both long distance and the sprint) and parades, to the beat of the traditional *tindé* drum. Other Tuareg activities include sand hockey and even the donkeys get a turn, with their own race. It's located in the very north of the Malian desert in Terist, close to the oasis of Tessalit, and 280km from the town of Kidal. As the birthplace of Ibrahim and other members of the group Tinariwen, you can expect good music and it's pretty likely they'll be performing there themselves.

Kayes region For more details on any of these events, contact the OMATHO in Kayes (☎ *2152 35 98*).

Festival of Kayes – Médine (*www.festival-kayes-medine.com; held annually since 2005 in mid-February*) For a long time Kayes was isolated from the rest of Mali. Now accessible by road from Bamako and Senegal, in celebration both countries have joined together for an inter-state festival of sound and light. It takes place over three days in Kayes and Médine in Mali and Tambacounda in Senegal. Each day there's visits to traditional sites such as the waterfalls of Gouina. And at night, artists perform traditional music and dance. .

Festival de Gouina; 'the waterfalls that sing' (m *7644 01 49; held annually since 2004 in February*) Held at the impressive waterfall 50km from Kayes, the objective of this festival is to safeguard the ecosystem and promote the region of Kayes as a tourist destination. A three-day picnic with traditional Malinké, Khassonké and Peul dance and musicians such as Ousmane Sacko and Souleymane Sissoko from Bamako. You can arrive by train, bus, or fly the 650km from Bamako.

Sikasso region

Koumantou Festival of Traditional Music and Dances (e *adakom@yahoo.fr; held biennially since 2006 between March and May*) Koumantou is the capital of a rural commune in the Cercle of Bougouni, 140km from Sikasso and located near the Ivorian border. The festival is organised by the Association for the Development of the Commune of Koumantou (ADAKOM) and held on three sites (Koumantou, Kola and Niable) over three days. It was created as an opportunity to meet the villagers in an exchange of cultures and bustles with traditional singing, dance and music, celebrating instruments such as the *balafon*, *wassamba*, *bari* and the traditional flute. There are visits to sites and monuments and the nights are for storytelling and public forums.

Le Festival des Chasseurs, Yanfolila (*Held every three years since 2001 between November and January*) Nearly 700 hunters from Burkina Faso, Gambia, Guinea, Niger, Senegal and Mali meet to exchange their know-how and knowledge during three days. The powerful healers and soothsayers offer their services to visitors while the Hunting Museum displays an exhibition on hunting 'from yesterday until today'. It also takes place at the same time at the Palais de la Culture in Bamako and in Ségou.

'Triangle du Balafon' (*Held annually any time between April and November*) The *balafon* has been present for centuries in a number of aspects of social life in Mali, Guinea, Burkina Faso and Senegal. This festival, taking place over four days, is a meeting of experts from all of these countries exploring and exchanging their different rhythms. The objective is to strengthen the unity and peace between the border populations. Musical performances continue until the early hours.

Other small festivals in the Sikasso region include the **Festival des Danses des Masques de Konna**, a masked dance held every year in April/May, concentrated around going down some stairs; **Semaine touristique and culturelle de Woroni**, a Senoufo festival held in March, and the **Danse des Masques de Koury**. For more details, contact the OMATHO office in Sikasso (☎ *2162 18 05*).

SHOPPING

A guidebook probably goes too far when it starts telling you what to buy when you visit Mali. Many of your souvenirs will – and should – be spontaneous purchases made at the market. In provincial towns and villages the main market usually takes place on a certain day of the week; in Bamako it is a daily event. Haggle for the best deal, but always pay a fair price.

Mali is well known for its arts and crafts, which vary from region to region. Woodcarvings and *bogolans* are two of the most popular souvenirs. The former are sold all over Dogon country, along with wooden masks and enough jewellery to sink the *Titanic* (see box *Responsible tourism in Dogon country*, page 194, for advice on souvenir-hunting there). *Bogolans* can be blankets, or items of clothing, decorated with a dye made from mud, tree bark and various other ingredients, and are of particularly good quality in Mopti, Ségou, and some Dogon villages like Endé. Pottery, meanwhile, is a speciality in Ségou, and Tuareg metalwork – especially daggers and swords – is certainly worth a look. The standard of basketwork and leatherwork in Mali can be quite high; musical instruments, such as *djembes*, *koras* and *balafons* (see page 32), are original – and often expensive – souvenirs; and few people leave without having invested in some form of headwear – be it a turban (5m is a good length), a pointed Peul hat, or a rather comical (to our eyes at least) Dogon bonnet.

MEDIA AND COMMUNICATIONS

POST Most towns in Mali have a post office. They are normally open from about 08.00 to 16.00 Monday to Friday, sometimes interrupted by a lunch-break, and from 08.00 to 12.00 on Saturday morning, although precise opening times differ from town to town. Sending mail is generally safe and reliable. Letters and postcards to France seem to arrive quickest, whereas post to elsewhere in Europe and the Americas takes longer. The price of postage for a postcard/letter under 100g is CFA500 to France, to the rest of Europe and to the USA, Canada, Australia, etc.

As for receiving mail, the larger offices around the country have poste restante facilities. An alternative is to have your post, faxes and emails sent to the **American Express Travel Service (AMEX)** in Bamako (*Av Kasse Keita, Immeuble Babemba, BP 2917;* ☎ *2022 44 35/78 92;* **f** *2022 94 50;* **e** *agence@ats.com.ml*) (AMEX share an office with the travel agency Afric Trans Services.) Whether using poste restante or AMEX, ask your correspondent to write your surname clearly in capital letters and to underline it to avoid your letter being filed under the wrong name.

TELEPHONE (*The international dialling code for Mali is +223*). Much of the 'action' of the Malian film *La vie sur terre* (see page 39) takes place at the post office around the one telephone in Sokolo. At one point in the film, the phlegmatic telephone operator states that *la communication est une question de chance* (communication is a matter of luck). This still applies to certain towns (like Djenné and Kidal) and in remoter areas, where sometimes there is a dialling tone, sometimes not. However, with a growing demand for a reliable network for both telephone and access to the internet, times are a-changing. The existing network is improving as installations are being upgraded.

The Société des télécommunications du Mali (Sotelma) is responsible for Mali's landline network, as well as the public telephone boxes in the major towns throughout the country. You can buy telephone cards to use in these boxes. However, although they work out slightly cheaper than calling from a *cabine téléphonique*, they are not as reliable. *Cabines téléphoniques* are privately run call shops which sometimes also have fax and photocopy machines. The cost of your call depends on the number of units used. A short local call normally consumes one unit, which is priced at around CFA150, whereas a ten-minute call I made from Sévaré to Bamako needed 85 units or CFA12,750! International calls are even more expensive.

As opposed to an estimated 82,500 landline telephone users in 2006, 1.5 million are mobile users. The two major mobile network providers are Malitel and Orange. Although there is little variation between them, Orange has a better

PHOTOGRAPHIC TIPS

Ariadne Van Zandbergen

EQUIPMENT Although with some thought and an eye for composition you can take reasonable photos with a 'point and shoot' camera, you need an SLR camera with one or more lenses if you are at all serious about photography. The most important component in a digital SLR is the sensor. There are two types of sensor: DX and FX. The FX is a full size sensor identical to the old film size (36mm). The DX sensor is half size and produces less quality. Your choice of lenses will be determined whether you have a DX or FX sensor in your camera as the DX sensor introduces a 0.5x multiplication to the focal length. So a 300mm lens becomes in effect a 450mm lens. FX ('full frame') sensors are the future, so I will further refer to focal lengths appropriate to the FX sensor.

Always buy the best lens you can afford. Fixed fast lenses are ideal, but very costly. Zoom lenses are easier to change composition without changing lenses the whole time. If you carry only one lens a 24–70mm or similar zoom should be ideal. For a second lens, a lightweight 80–200mm or 70–300mm or similar will be excellent for candid shots and varying your composition. Wildlife photography will be very frustrating if you don't have at least a 300mm lens. For a small loss of quality, teleconverters are a cheap and compact way to increase magnification: a 300 lens with a 1.4x converter becomes 420mm, and with a 2x it becomes 600mm. NB 1.4x and 2x teleconverters reduce the speed of your lens by 1.4 and 2 stops respectively.

The resolution of digital cameras is improving the whole time. For ordinary prints a 6-megapixel camera is fine. For better results and the possibility to enlarge images and for professional reproduction, higher resolution is available up to 21 megapixels.

It is important to have enough memory space when photographing on your holiday. The number of pictures you can fit on a card depends on the quality you choose. You should calculate how many pictures you can fit on a card and either take enough cards or take a storage drive onto which you can download the cards' content. You can obviously take a laptop which gives the advantage that you can see your pictures properly at the end of each day and edit and delete rejects. If you don't want the extra bulk and weight you can buy a storage device which can read memory cards. These drives come in different capacities.

Keep in mind that digital camera batteries, computers and other storage devices need charging. Make sure you have all the chargers, cables, converters with you. Most hotels/lodges have charging points, but it will be best to enquire about this in advance. When camping you might have to rely on charging from the car battery.

coverage in the north around Timbuktu and Kidal. Receiving range is approximately 30km around most major towns. SIM cards are available in Bamako from CFA3,000, and scratchcards to feed your credit are widely available all over the country. Note that mobile calls are fairly expensive.

EMAIL AND INTERNET As in most countries in the world, the internet is very popular. All bigger towns have cybercafés where the public have access to the internet and email services. The charge varies from CFA500 to CFA1,000 per hour. See the *Practical information* sections of *Chapters 3* to *11*.

MEDIA The press in Mali is in French. *L'Essor*, founded in 1949, is the oldest and the best newspaper, with plenty of national coverage as well as international news and sports stories. *Les Echos* and *Nouvel Horizon* are other daily newspapers, while *L'Observateur*, *Le Républican* and *L'Indépendant*, amongst several others, are published weekly. In general, English-language newspapers and magazines are hard to find. If you do come across them, they will probably be in Bamako and something like the *International Herald Tribune*, *Time* or *Newsweek*.

DUST AND HEAT Dust and heat are often a problem. Keep your equipment in a sealed bag, and avoid exposing equipment to the sun when possible. Digital cameras are prone to collecting dust particles on the sensor which results in spots on the image. The dirt mostly enters the camera when changing lenses, so you should be careful when doing this. To some extent photos can be 'cleaned' up afterwards in Photoshop, but this is time-consuming. You can have your camera sensor professionally cleaned, or you can do this yourself with special brushes and swabs made for this purpose, but note that touching the sensor might cause damage and should only be done with the greatest care.

LIGHT The most striking outdoor photographs are often taken during the hour or two of 'golden light' after dawn and before sunset. Shooting in low light may enforce the use of very low shutter speeds, in which case a tripod/beanbag will be required to avoid camera shake. The most advanced digital SLRs have very little loss of quality on higher ISO settings, which allows you to shoot at lower light conditions. It is still recommended not to increase the ISO unless necessary.

With careful handling, side lighting and back lighting can produce stunning effects, especially in soft light and at sunrise or sunset. Generally, however, it is best to shoot with the sun behind you. When photographing animals or people in the harsh midday sun, images taken in light but even shade are likely to look nicer than those taken in direct sunlight or patchy shade, since the latter conditions create too much contrast.

PROTOCOL In some countries, it is unacceptable to photograph local people without permission, and many people will refuse to pose or will ask for a donation. In such circumstances, don't try to sneak photographs as you might get yourself into trouble. Even the most willing subject will often pose stiffly when a camera is pointed at them; relax them by making a joke, and take a few shots in quick succession to improve the odds of capturing a natural pose.

Ariadne Van Zandbergen is a professional travel and wildlife photographer specialised in Africa. She runs 'The Africa Image Library'. For photo requests, visit www.africaimagelibrary.co.za or contact her direct at e *ariadne@hixnet.co.za*

Malian television is restricted to one channel which plays a lot of music and shows Brazilian soap operas dubbed into French. Many hotels, however, have a selection of channels beamed in by satellite from France. Any town worth its salt seems to have its own radio station; and if you have a short-wave radio, try tuning in to the BBC World Service (MHz 17.83 – 15.40 – 11.76 – 9.605) or Voice of America (MHz 21.49 – 15.60 – 9.525 – 6.035). (Note that these frequencies are subject to change.)

CULTURAL ETIQUETTE

RESEARCH Before travelling to Timbuktu, the French explorer René Caillié (see page 21) prepared for his trip by spending nine months studying the Koran and learning Arabic with a Muslim tribe on the banks of the River Senegal. Caillié knew that Christians were not welcome at that time in the fabled city, so he had to pass himself off as a Muslim. These days a trip to Mali requires less meticulous preparation, but Caillié's spirit of research is no bad thing to emulate.

It pays dividends to know something about the country you are about to visit. Not only does research whet the appetite before departure, it can also help to break

A NOTE ABOUT TELEPHONE NUMBERS

On 1 November 2008, all Mali telephone numbers, including mobiles, changed from seven to eight digits. All the numbers in this guide have been updated accordingly, but the (rather complicated) conversions have been set out below should you need them.

SOTELMA LANDLINES Put simply, the initial **2** now changes to **20** in Bamako and **21** outside Bamako. For example:

- Bamako numbers that used to start with 220, 221, 222, 223, 224, 228, 229 and 279 have changed to 2020, 2021, 2022, 2023, 2024, 2028, 2029 and 2079.
- Koulikoro used to be 225, 226, 227; now 2125, 2126, 2127
- Ségou was 23, now 213
- Mopti was 24, now 214
- Kayes was 25, now 215
- Sikasso was 26, now 216
- Gao was 28, now 218
- Timbuktu was 29, now 219

ORANGE LANDLINES These are few and far between, but used to start with 42, 43 and 49. Place an additional **4** in front of these.

MALITEL MOBILES Place a **6** in front of the following prefixes:

- 65, 66, 67, 68, 69
- 55, 56, 57, 58, 59
- 95, 96, 97, 98, 99

A **6** also goes in front of Malitel helpline numbers, eg: **6 700**, **6 777**

ORANGE MOBILES Place a **7** in front of the following prefixes:

- 30, 31, 32, 33, 34
- 40, 41
- 44, 45, 46, 47, 48
- 50, 51, 52, 53, 54
- 60, 61, 62, 63, 64
- 85, 86, 87, 88, 89
- 90, 91, 92, 93, 94

A **7** also goes in front of Orange helpline numbers, eg: **7 400**, **7 401**

the ice and establish contact with the local people if you know something – anything! – about their country and way of life. I hope that the background sections of this book are informative and interesting. In *Appendix 2* I have suggested some further reading and a selection of websites to visit, so that you can become an 'armchair expert' before hitting the road and seeing it all for yourself. If you are from the UK, consider contacting **Friends of Mali** (e *info@friendsofmali-uk.org; www.friendsofmali-uk.org*), a London-based organisation that seeks to promote Mali and the Malian culture through a variety of activities such as talks, concerts and film showings. Caillié never had it so good!

WHAT TO WEAR As a predominantly Muslim country, it is recommended that you dress respectfully, particularly in the north and remote villages, less exposed to tourism. Women should cover their shoulders and wear trousers or a skirt that reaches below the knee (this does not however apply to the Dogon country – if you're trekking there, pretty much anything goes). You may want to consider getting traditional clothes made by a local tailor. It takes from two days up to a week during holiday time and you will have to buy the material and deliver it to the tailor. For women, a *voile* is very handy in the desert. It's a long piece of material that wraps around the body like a veil. *Voiles* can be found in the market in a variety of bright colours for CFA3,000 upwards. Not only is a *voile* a practical item of clothing to protect against the heat and dust, but it also forms a handy 'tent', when nature calls and there's not a tree in sight. You may have to enlist the help of a female nomad to show you how to wear it.

TIPPING It is customary to tip in Mali – a standard 10% in cafés and restaurants. Drivers and guides should also be rewarded for good work. With the average wage being US$2–3 per day, it will be greatly appreciated.

TRAVELLING POSITIVELY

'Responsible tourism' is a wonderful expression. It defines all of our obligations as tourists without really describing any. The ambiguity of the word 'responsible' is perfect. Picking up your rubbish and taking off your shoes before entering a mosque is, of course, responsible behaviour; but so is speaking a little of the local language and paying a fair price for things at the market. Responsible tourism means more than just obeying rules of social etiquette and being on your best behaviour. You must be proactive as well as reactive. In a nutshell, try to *give something back* to the country you are visiting. Speaking a little French, Bambara, or any of the other local languages – even just 'hello' and 'thank you' – is respectful and demonstrates a willingness to adapt to the local culture, which might in turn help you to make some friends. Remember that Mali is a developing country where life can be hard and very little is taken for granted. Think twice before haggling for an hour over the price of a T-shirt or a bunch of bananas. Paying a tourist price is not necessarily a bad thing if it is for the benefit of the local economy – in other words, the street vendors and hawkers in the market, who are normally the last to see the financial rewards of mass tourism. Most travellers are in the privileged position of being able to give something back directly to the people because we are in constant contact with them. Our ultimate responsibility, then, is to make sure that this opportunity is not wasted.

CULTURAL SENSITIVITY In addition to the above, ask before you take photographs of people and places of worship, and refrain from overusing energy resources such as water and electricity – so precious in Mali. Less obvious, but equally important, try to not wash in lakes or rivers (regardless of local practices) or getting too close to the wildlife, both of which act to the detriment of the natural world. Pollution of the environment by waste – polythene bags mainly – is a sensitive issue too, as there is no elaborate waste-disposal system worth mentioning. Survival International (see below) suggests the following:

- All human waste should be buried and toilet paper burned or buried.
- Rubbish should be disposed of as follows: paper should be burnt, biodegradable waste should be buried, and containers given away.

- Rather than using plastic bags for shopping, use longer lasting bags.
- It is better to buy drinks in returnable glass bottles than in cans or plastic bottles.

The need for low-impact tourism is arguably at its greatest when tribal peoples are involved (see box *Responsible Tourism in Dogon Country*, page 194). Visiting communities with alien cultures and where there has been only minimal contact with the outside world is a minefield for tourists, and blunders – often quite unintentional – are easily made (for example, apparently innocuous diseases such as colds and influenza might prove to be killers amongst people with no immunity).

Survival International 6 Charterhouse Bldgs, London EC1M 7ET; ☎ 020 7687 8700; **f** 020 7687 8701; **e** survival@gn.apc.org; www.survival-international.org. This worldwide organisation has its headquarters in London and supports tribal peoples. In its own words, Survival 'stands for their (tribal people's) right to decide their own future and helps them protect their lives, lands and human rights'. It is currently campaigning on behalf of the Tuareg.

Tourism Concern Stapleton Hse, 277–281 Holloway Rd, London N7 8HN; ☎ 020 7133 3330; **f** 020 7133 3331; **e** info@tourismconcern.org.uk; www.tourismconcern.org.uk. Another London-based charity devoted to promoting responsible tourism throughout the world.

INTERNATIONAL CHARITIES AND NGOS Many of the largest international charities and NGOs (non-governmental organisations), along with high-profile United Nations organisations such as UNESCO and UNICEF, are currently active in Mali. The main British NGOs with offices in Mali are as follows:

ACORD BP 1969, Rue Nelson Mandela, Hippodrome, Bamako; ☎ 2021 09 48; **f** 2021 82 16
Action on Disability and Development ☎ 2023 91 50; www.add.org.uk
Christian Aid ☎ 2021 59 49; www.christian-aid.org.uk
Handicap International Trokorobougou Sema, Rue 306, Porte 1045, Bamako; ☎ 2023 27 14; **e** hiansdir@afribone.net.ml; www.handicap-international.org.uk
International Service Rue 539, Porte 380, Hamdallaye ACI 2000; ☎ 2029 24 05; **f** 2029 77 65; www.internationalservice.org.uk
Islamic Relief UK ☎ 2021 44 41; www.islamic-relief.org.uk
Oxfam Hippodrome, St 228, No 1213, Bamako; ☎ 2021 24 24; www.oxfam.org.uk
PLAN International Rue 22, Badalabougou Est, Face au Fleuve, BP 1598, Bamako; ☎ 2023 05 83; www.plan-international.org
Sight Savers ACI 2000, pres de l'Hotel Residence KOME BP: E 1844, Bamako; ☎ 2029 31 55; www.sightsavers.org
SOS Sahel c/o Madame Ballo, Sahel ECO, ACI 2000, Rue 402, 03 BP 259, Bamako; ☎ 2029 30 04; **e** saheleco@afribonemali.net; www.sahel.org.uk
SPANA BP E 3940, Rue 77, Porte 54, Badalabougou, Bamako; ☎ 2022 26 44; **f** 2022 41 88; **e** spana@cefib.com; www.spana.org
WaterAid ACI 2000, Hamdallaye, Bamako; ☎ 2029 54 50; **f** 2029 54 51; **e** info@wateraid-mali.org; www.wateraid.org

There is obviously not enough space here to describe each of these charities' work in great detail. Suffice it to say that most of them are concerned with basic needs, such as improving health care and ensuring that the population is properly nourished, while some have additional, more clearly defined tasks. **WaterAid**, for example, have been working for ten years to provide water, sanitation and hygiene support to communities in five out of Mali's eight regions. Although the means employed to provide these basic needs may vary, it seems to be universally agreed that sustainable development is every bit as important as giving handouts. For instance, most international NGOs in Mali operate credit schemes in conjunction with local partners. These schemes are normally aimed at the country's indefatigable women (see page 29), who borrow – and repay – money to invest in

FOREIGN AID: EVERY LITTLE HELPS

Jolijn Geels

The Malian economy is IMF-controlled to a large degree. Despite the negative impact of the economic crises in neighbouring countries like Côte d'Ivoire, the structural adjustment programme implemented by the IMF is considered to be beneficial overall. Nevertheless, according to statistics, the gross domestic product (GDP) per capita rose to an 'astonishing' US$900 before plummeting again to no more than a few hundred US dollars: a telltale figure. In the real world, this means that, while some Malians have it all, over 60% of the Malian population still lives below the poverty line, the majority in rural areas. Illiteracy is very common, since schools may be few and far between, and many parents cannot afford the expense of education anyway. By the same token, access to medical facilities is sometimes extremely limited – again, especially in rural areas. The statistics for infant mortality and HIV are shocking, while outbreaks of cholera claim most victims amongst the poorest of all. Indeed, Mali is rated one of the poorest countries in the world, and is heavily dependent on foreign aid. Some widely known international charities and NGOs are represented in Mali, and often very visibly so, with signposts and 4x4s adorned with their logos. Apart from these giants in foreign aid, numerous anonymous benefactors are devoted to supporting well-demarcated projects.

One example – both touching and impressive – is that of the Dutch architect Joop van Stigt and his wife Gonny van Stigt-Amesz. In the 1960s, Joop was invited to participate in the extensive expedition led by Herman Haan to study the Tellem – and so he travelled to the Dogon country for the first time. He was impressed, shocked and inspired by all that he saw, and returned on several occasions. The restoration of a number of *ginnas* and *binous* (see page 193), and the construction of two dams in 1988, were only the initial impetus of a long chain of projects with which he became involved. On his visits to the Dogon country, Monsieur Joop – as he became known – always provided some soccer balls for local schools. One day, the response of one of the teachers must have hit him like a bombshell: 'You are a professor and an architect, you teach at a university. Instead of giving us soccer balls, you should build us a new school.'

It marked a turning point. In 1995, the first school – fully equipped and with ablution blocks, solar panels and a well – was built, and Monsieur Joop has not stopped building since. In 1996, during a serious drought and famine, he financed the purchase and transport of 530 sacks of wheat to feed several villages. Until then, all of the funds for the dams, the school and the food support had been drawn from the van Stigt's personal accounts, but in 1998, Mr Joop and Gonny set up a foundation to meet the growing demand for schools and wells. Donations came trickling in only after a number of years, but by now the couple were fully dedicated and unstoppable. The foundation has completed the construction of many schools – with a total of 50 classrooms – more dams, a library and a hospital, and the installation of tens of solar-powered pumps and wells. The latest project-in-progress is the construction of a school for technical education in Mopti.

Mr Joop recently turned 70, but he and his wife still regularly visit Dogon country to initiate, support and follow up the various projects. When visiting the part of the *falaise* that is described in *Chapter 6*, page 207, you will pass schools built by Mr Joop in Kani Kombolé and Amani. In Sanga, you could actually meet the couple in the Hotel Campement La Guina if they happen to be there on one of their many visits. Should you like to know more about the foundation, contact Joop and Gonny van Stigt by email (see *Charities and NGOs*, page 100). Newsletters in Dutch, French and English are available and a website is under construction. Donations are welcome, of course, as every little helps.

making food products, arts and crafts and other small businesses. These modest money-making projects generally prosper, enabling the women to care properly for their children and giving them a degree of independence and self-esteem.

In the words of a Malian woman who took part in one of the more successful schemes sponsored by the American charity, **Freedom from Hunger** (*2024 39 78; e ffh@malinet.ml*): 'With the three loans I have taken out, I have been able to triple my production of *bogolan* (mudcloth) and triple my earnings. When I had the capital to buy a lot of materials at once, I increased my production. Now when buyers come, I have a selection to show them and sometimes I can sell everything at once.'

Sponsoring a child through **PLAN International** is another variation on the development theme. You make an annual donation and follow it up with letters and gifts to your 'adopted' child. In return, you receive regular progress reports and letters from the child's guardians, which gives you the opportunity to see at first hand the difference that your contribution is making to someone's life and that of their community. Incidentally, PLAN's one-millionth sponsored child was a nine-year-old girl from Mali. The work of **SPANA** (Society for the Protection of Animals Abroad) is focused on improving the plight of Mali's donkeys, especially the unfortunate animals working in Bamako pulling the city's rubbish carts. SPANA's small veterinary team treats wounds caused by ill-fitting harnesses and saddles, which, in extreme cases, can cause a trauma known as fistulous withers. Concentrating on animals in a country where the human population is confronted with so many problems might seem irrelevant. In reality, however, the interdependence between man and donkey in Mali is so great that the fortunes of one are often inextricably linked to the well-being of the other.

LOCAL CHARITIES AND NGOS Making a donation to a local charity is one of the more obvious ways in which you can give something back to the country you are visiting. There are more than 600 national charities and NGOs in Mali and most are listed in the *Annuaire des ONGs*, a directory of NGOs currently active in the country. You should be able to get hold of a copy at the headquarters of most international development agencies in Bamako, or the **Comité de Coordination des Actions des ONG**. There will obviously be one or two bad apples in the barrel – the NGO privilege of having a duty-free vehicle is open to abuse by unscrupulous opportunists – but the majority are worthwhile and deserving of your support. On your travels you are bound to come across good causes which merit a small donation or help in some other form. In the meantime, here are three of my own discoveries:

AGVF (Association des Groupements Villageois Féminins) BP 37, Bandiagara (see the map on page 198). This is one of many national organisations devoted to the promotion of women. In this case, the focus is on rural women in the *cercle* of Bandiagara. As with many international NGOs, there is a strong emphasis on credit schemes which allow women to develop their own small businesses &, in turn, a degree of self-sufficiency & independence. General education in matters such as family planning & the protection of the environment is also promoted. The AGVF office is conveniently located in the centre of Bandiagara & it is no hassle to pop in & find out more about the work they do. They should also be able to give you the addresses of other women's organisations around the country – or at least in the region of Mopti.

Les amis de Gossi or La Retraite Gossi s/c Mission Catholique, BP 32, Gao. Sister Anne-Marie Saloman is in her 12th year at Gossi. She has run the local hospital since it opened in 1992, continuing her work during the dangerous & unpredictable years of the Tuareg rebellion. Well known in these parts, Anne-Marie is a woman of the cloth by vocation, who began her medical studies at the age of 45. The hospital on the edge of Gossi was originally established for Tuareg nomads displaced during the war. Nowadays, it treats all-comers – between 70 & 100 patients a day – for a variety of diseases, including tuberculosis, cholera & AIDS. All types of donations are welcome, although money (to pay salaries & purchase medication) is by far the most useful form of assistance. If you are intending to visit Gossi – to see the elephants, for example – be sure to say hello to Sister Anne-Marie.

JOLIBA TRUST

Helen MacKintosh

Working at the heart of Mali's Dogon country, Joliba is a small, highly effective NGO with an impressively ethical ethos. It operates with total community involvement and spends 95% of *all* monies raised on the ground. Field staff are all from the area including the impressive director, Apomi Saye, and a small team of midwives and teachers, foresters and environmental experts, accountants and engineers. Joliba's key aims are to help improve the environment and promote long-term food security. They also focus on women through micro-credit and midwifery training schemes.

The system is that, if a village wishes to take part in any project, they have to apply for funds, be prepared to work and prove they're well organised. So, for example, to be successful with an environmental application – which might include building dykes on the plateau to stop the torrential annual rains washing away topsoil and leaving the land infertile; or working to hold back the dunes which are rolling in from the south, threatening the iconic villages of the cliff face and the fertile valley at their foot; or planting thousands of trees as windbreaks, shade, fruit, compost and firewood in the plains – a village must sign up to all the labour involved. In return workers will be helped with training and supplies. Joliba also tries to keep a store of grain which they can use for various purposes. For instance, they can use the grain as 'food for work' and they also trade it, pound for pound, for unhatched locust eggs which are unearthed by the villagers and which can then be destroyed without recourse to chemical sprays. The original Joliba project, a micro-credit scheme where women apply for funds, which they must pay back with interest, is still going strong. To participate, villages send two women to be trained over a year in both literacy and accounts so that they can then administer their village's local scheme. After five years, if all goes well, the village will be given back all the interest they have paid which will become the basis of their own enterprise fund. What started out as a loan of under £100 some 20 years ago has now grown into a revolving credit scheme of £300,000. Training is also a cornerstone of the midwifery scheme. To participate, villages send two of their traditional *sage-femmes* to be taught by hospital-qualified midwives. Nearly 1,000 have qualified as birth attendants and, equipped with a kit (bowl, soap, antiseptic, etc), a new understanding of the role of diet in pregnancy and the ability to identify when foetal or maternal distress means a pregnant woman must be taken, however difficult, to a clinic, infant mortality has dropped dramatically. The midwives are also working with communities to make villagers aware of the dire consequences of female genital mutilation. It's a slow process which challenges a practice that has been around for thousands of years, but it is beginning to succeed.

Joliba (*8 Nattadon Rd, Chagford, Devon TQ13 8BE;* ☎ *01647 432018;* **e** *jolibatrust@hotmail.com; www.jolibatrust.org.uk*) has operated in the Dogon country since 1984. It became a registered UK charity in 1996 and is a registered Malian NGO, Joliba Ediouko.

Tin Hinan An association originally set up in Burkina Faso to bring aid to the northern Malian refugees fleeing the Tuareg rebellion. Today, it works to promote the rights of nomadic women everywhere & has over 500 members in Mali, Niger & Burkina Faso. Their main objective is to reinforce the worth of nomadic women & improve the possibilities available to them by providing education for young girls, literacy for adult women & training in traditional artisanal techniques, such as needlework, dyeing, carpet making & tanning, amongst other things. You can always find Saouda, the Tuareg creator of the association, in a tent at the Festival in the Desert selling *voiles*, jewellery & other artisanal items made by the ladies during training courses. Otherwise you can contact the Bamako office (*BP E 1648;* **m** *7602 47 87;* **e** *tinhinbf@yahoo.fr*)

STUFF YOUR RUCKSACK – AND MAKE A DIFFERENCE

www.stuffyourrucksack.com is a website set up by TV's Kate Humble which enables travellers to give direct help to small charities, schools or other organisations in the country they are visiting. Maybe a local school needs books, a map or pencils, or an orphanage needs children's clothes or toys – all things that can easily be 'stuffed in a rucksack' before departure. The charities get exactly what they need and travellers have the chance to meet local people and see how and where their gifts will be used.

The website describes organisations that need your help and lists the items they most need. Check what's needed in Mali, contact the organisation to say you're coming and bring not only the much-needed goods but an extra dimension to your travels and the knowledge that in a small way you have made a difference.

BACK AT HOME When Mali is not being confused with Bali, it is synonymous with poverty and drought. Simply by talking about the many other, positive aspects of the country will help to dispel preconceived – and often erroneous – stereotypes. You might also consider joining groups through which you can continue to contribute to the country you have just visited such as the **Mali Development Group**, a volunteer-based group working to develop contact and exchange between Mali and the UK and to support development and understanding between the two cultures. Along with Survival and Tourism Concern, there are many other international charities, environmental organisations and conservation projects worth investigating. Below is a list of some of the charities and NGOs with programmes in Mali. For others, you can contact Andy Benson, who runs a small virtual network of these called the Mali Interest Group (e *info@penandy.co.uk*). There are, of course, many more from all over the world, especially France, Germany and Scandinavia.

Charities and NGOs

UK

ACORD Development Hse, 56–64 Leonard St, London EC2A 4LT; t 020 7065 0850; f 020 7065 0851; www.acordinternational.org

Action on Disability and Development Vallis Hse, 57 Vallis Rd, Frome, Somerset BA11 3EG; t 01373 473064; f 01373 452075; www.add.org.uk

CARE UK 10–13 Rushworth St, London SE1 0RB; www.careinternational.org.uk

Christian Aid 35 Lower Marsh, London SE1 7RL; t 020 7620 4444; www.christian-aid.org.uk

Handicap International 32–36 Loman St, London SE1 0EH; t 0870 774 3737; e hi-uk@hi-uk.org; www.handicap-international.org.uk

Islamic Relief 19 Rea St South, Birmingham B5 6LB; t 0121 622 0654; www.islamic-relief.org.uk

Joliba Trust 108 Egerton Rd, Bristol BS7 8HP; t 0117 989 2599; e jolibatrust@hotmail.com; www.jolibatrust.org.uk

Mali Development Group 50 Friars St, Sudbury, Suffolk CO10 2AG; e john.hedge1@virgin.net; www.malidg.org.uk

Médecins du Monde 1 Canada Sq, London E14 4JB; t 020 7516 9103; www.medecinsdumonde.org.uk

Oxfam Oxfam Hse, John Smith Drive, Cowley, Oxford OX4 2JY; t 0300 200 1300; e oxfam@oxfam.org.uk; www.oxfam.org.uk

Plan International 5–6 Underhill St, London NW1 7HS; t 020 7482 9777; f 020 7482 9778; www.plan-uk.org

Sightsavers Grosvenor Hall, Bolnore Rd, Haywards Heath, West Sussex RH16 4BX; t 01444 446600; www.sightsavers.org

SOS Sahel The Old Music Hall, 106–108 Cowley Rd, Oxford OX4 1JE; t 01865 403305; www.sahel.org.uk

SPANA 14 John St, London WC1N 2EB; t 020 7831 3999; f 020 7831 5999; e hg@spana.org; www.spana.org

WaterAid 47–49 Durham St, London SE11 5JD; t 0845 6000 433; e wateraid@wateraid.org; www.wateraid.org/uk

US

CARE US 151 Ellis St NE, Atlanta, GA 30303; ☎ 1 800 521 2273 ext 999; e info@care.org; www.care.org

Freedom From Hunger 1644 DaVinci Court, Davis, CA 95618; ☎ 1 530 758 6200 ext 1042; f 1 530 758 6241; e info@freefromhunger.org; www.freefromhunger.org

Peace Corps 1111 20th St NW, Washington DC, 20526; ☎ 1 800 424 8580; www.peacecorps.gov

Plan International US 155 Plan Way, Warwick, RI 02886; ☎ 1 800 556 7918; f 401 738 5608; www.planusa.org

Save The Children US 54, Wilton Rd, Westport, CT 06880; ☎ 1 203 221 4000; f 1 203 227 5667; e info@savechildren.org; www.savethechildren.org

Netherlands

Stichting Dogon Onderwijs (Dogon Education Foundation; see box, page 99) Herengracht 408, 1017BX Amsterdam; e info@dogononderwijs.nl; www.dogononderwijs

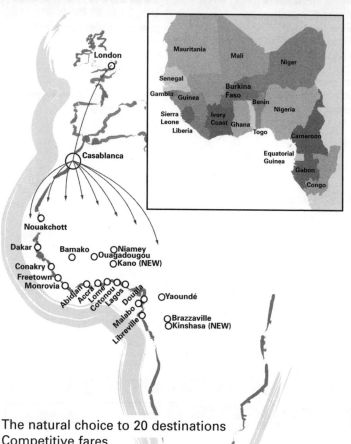

Part Two

THE GUIDE

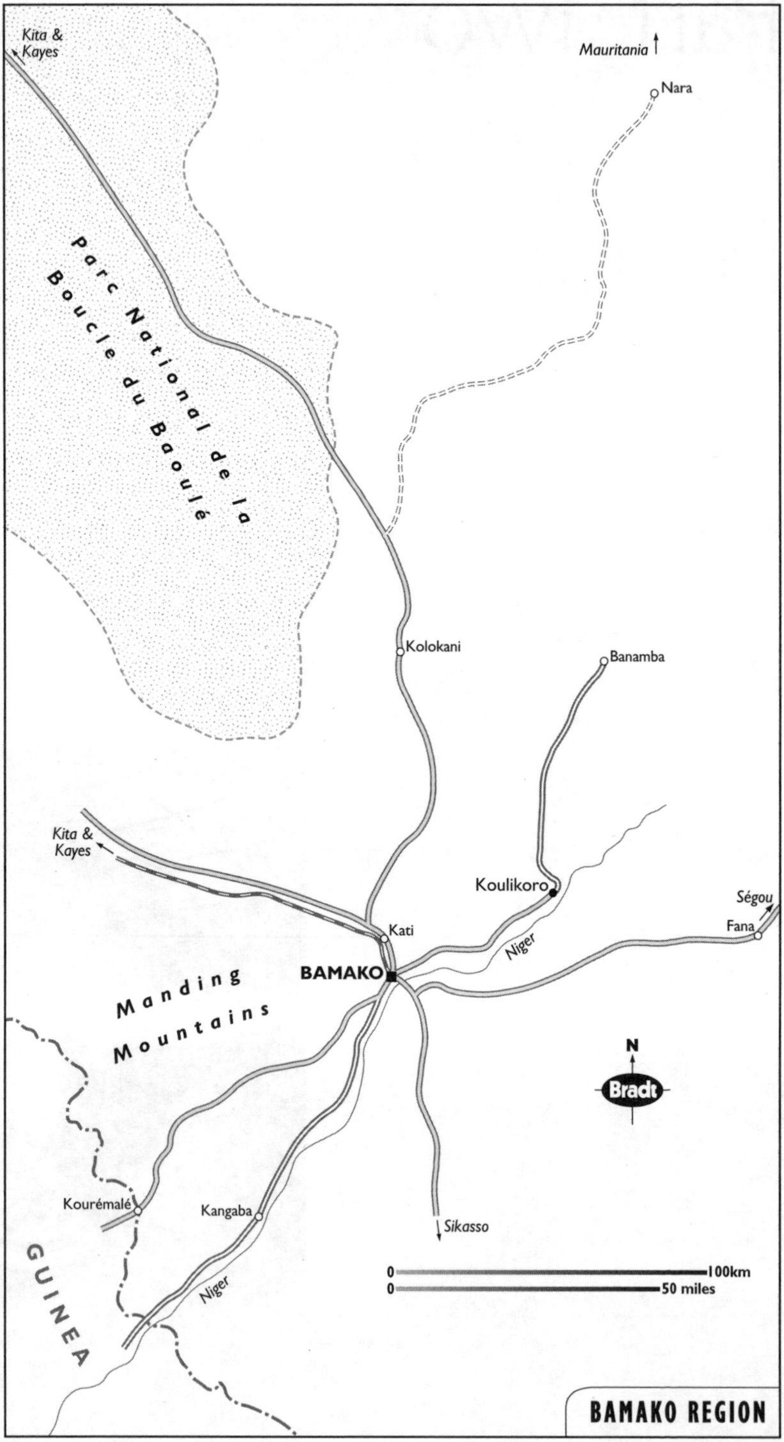
Kita & Kayes
Mauritania
Nara
Parc National de la Boucle du Baoulé
Kolokani
Banamba
Kita & Kayes
Koulikoro
Ségou
Fana
Kati
Niger
BAMAKO
Manding Mountains
N
Bradt
Kourémalé
Kangaba
Sikasso
GUINEA
Niger
0
100km
0
50 miles
BAMAKO REGION

3

Bamako

Far too many guidebooks delight in describing Bamako, Mali's capital, as 'the most African of all African cities'. Should we take this to mean that Bamako is the dirtiest and overcrowded place on the continent – for these are certainly characteristics shared by many African cities – or a city of mud houses without a single skyscraper in sight? It is, of course, neither one nor the other – but a bit of both: a rather typical African city, in fact, facing the same contemporary problems as most other metropolises in the developing world.

Overcrowding is one of these problems. In a country with a population of over 12 million, around one million live in Bamako. In recent years the perimeters of the city have expanded eastwards, westwards and, most dramatically, south of the River Niger, so that now Bamako occupies an area of $40km^2$. However, there are not enough jobs and the urban infrastructure is inadequate to support these growing numbers. This is the Bamako of littered streets and impossible traffic jams; an oppressive city of noise, pollution, dust and unbearable heat. Fortunately, however, there is more to this place than meets the eye. You need to stay a while before you start to feel it, but Bamako's true heartbeat has more to do with the gentle ebb and flow of the river than rush-hour traffic and its chorus of beeping horns. For this is a relaxed city – and can also be a relaxing city. People are busy, but not so busy that they no longer want to communicate with one another. Simple things, such as smiling at passers-by, throw-away *bonjours* and *ça vas*, and shaking hands are still important in Bamako. Could we say the same thing for London, Paris and New York – or, for that matter, Dakar, Abidjan and Lagos? In this way, I suppose, Bamako has remained typically African.

HISTORY

The general consensus is that Bamako was founded some time during the 16th century. Precise details of the town's creation, however, are contested by the conflicting oral traditions upon which the hapless historian has no choice but to rely. The most common version of events is that Niakaté, a hunter from Lamidou near Nioro du Sahel in the Kaarta region, travelled down to the Niger Valley to look for new hunting grounds, and met another hunter, Samalé Bamba, who granted him an area of land upon which Niakaté founded Bamako. Niakaté was gradually shortened to Niaré – the town's first ruling dynasty – after which Bamako's first quarter, Niaréla, was named. This tidy explanation of Bamako's beginnings is disrupted by the Malian historian, Dominique Traoré, who claims that, before Niakaté arrived, another hunter, this time from the town of Kong in northeastern Côte d'Ivoire, had already established the town on the banks of the river. Bamba Sanogo, having killed an elephant while hunting, sought and was granted permission from the local Bambara ruler to create a town in the place where the elephant had fallen. It was initially called Bamba Kong after its founder and his town of origin, but was later shortened to Bamako, meaning 'the posterity of Bamba'. If all this seems a little too dry, you might prefer the story according to which Bamako owes its name to the crocodile-infested stretch of river beside which it was created – *bama* meaning 'crocodile' and *ko* meaning 'river'. These are just some of the stories explaining the origins of Bamako. There are variations on each theme and probably several other versions of events.

Whatever you choose to believe, by the time Mungo Park (see page 20) arrived in 1805, Bamako was a small trading centre of about 6,000 people – most of them Bozo fishermen. Between then and 1883, however, when the town was captured for the French by Lieutenant-Colonel Borgnis-Désbordes, its population had dwindled to under 1,000.

The coming of the railway proved to be the making of Bamako. Work was started in 1904 on a line between Bamako and the western town of Kayes which, along with the former's better location, was the main reason why the capital of Upper Senegal and Niger was moved from Kayes to Bamako in 1908. When the railway reached Dakar and the Atlantic coast in 1923, Bamako also replaced Kayes as the country's commercial centre – a title it has never renounced.

ORIENTATION

In all likelihood, your first arrival in Bamako will be by air, road or train. Bamako-Sénou International Airport is about 15km south of the city near the village of Sénou on the road to Sikasso; the main bus station or *gare routière* is in the quarter of Sogoniko, 5km south of the River Niger; and the railway station is in the downtown area.

METROPOLITAN BAMAKO Tourist brochures avoid describing Bamako as a 'dust bowl', although during the dry season dust and bluish clouds of exhaust fumes seem to hang over the capital like a vindictive blanket. This is because Bamako lies in a depression, with the foothills of the Manding Mountains rising to nearly 500m in the north, the smaller hills of Badalabougou and Magnambougou in the south, and the River Niger flowing through the middle.

Originally, Bamako was confined to a modest area on the left bank of the Niger – that is to say, north of the river. Nowadays, the city has sprawled to the east, west and, most notably, south of the river. The District of Bamako consists of six *communes* which stretch as far south as the airport, but do not include the administrative district of Koulouba and Point G in the north. Each *commune* is divided into several *quartiers* or quarters.

From the visitor's point of view, the oldest quarters (those in Communes II and III) are the most interesting. Commune II consists of the following quarters: Bozolo, Niaréla, Bagadadji, Quinzambougou, Cité du Niger, Zone Industrielle, Médina Koura, Missira and Hippodrome. This is arguably the oldest part of Bamako, characterised these days by foreign embassies and consulates, hotels, restaurants and nightclubs. Commune III, meanwhile, is essentially what I have treated as downtown Bamako.

Most of Bamako's recent development has taken place south of the river, where largely residential neighbourhoods have almost doubled the size of the city. Two bridges link the northern and southern parts of town. Pont des Martyrs – also known as *ancien pont* (old bridge) – serves traffic coming from the heart of downtown and is always crowded. For this reason, a new bridge – Pont du Roi Fahd – was built by the Saudis half a kilometre or so east of the old one to divert traffic away from the centre, thus improving access to Bamako and the airport.

There are two main roads leading out of Bamako. Cross Pont des Martyrs and continue along the same road for several kilometres – passing the *gare routière* after about 5km – and you reach the main highway for towns in the east and south of the country. Back in the downtown area, Avenue Al Quds becomes Route de Koulikoro after a few kilometres – the trunk road to the port of Koulikoro. Another short stretch of paved road leads up to Koulouba and on to the nearby town of Kati, after which it becomes a track and continues as such in the direction of Kayes.

DOWNTOWN BAMAKO For the purposes of this chapter, downtown Bamako includes the quarters of Commune III – Centre Commercial, Dravéla, Bamako Koura and Quartier du Fleuve – as well as the western edges of Bozola and Bagadadji. In more visual terms, the heart of Bamako lies more or less between the minarets of the Grande Mosquée (great mosque) in the north and the giant buildings of the Hotel de l'Amitié and the Banque Centrale des États de l'Afrique de l'Ouest (BCEAO) in the south. These three landmarks, visible from almost anywhere in the city, should be your main points of reference.

That's about as much help as Bamako is prepared to give the first-time visitor, as the roads, traffic circulation and street signs are all totally user-unfriendly. Start off by grasping the basics, and then add to your knowledge as you become accustomed to the layout of the capital. The main thoroughfare is Boulevard du Peuple, which runs from south to north through the heart of Bamako. It is crowded, dirty and chaotic, but hard to avoid. Avenue du Fleuve – renamed Avenue Modibo Keita, but still widely known by its old name – is for the north-to-south cross-town traffic. Both of these roads emanate from Square Lumumba, where several airline offices and the French Embassy can be found. Most of the main tourist attractions, however, are in the northern part of the downtown area, as is Bamako's railway station and Le Grand Hotel. One other road you should try to remember is Avenue de la Liberté, which continues north when Avenue du Fleuve stops more or less at the railway track. Avenue de la Liberté winds up to Koulouba and Point G, passing the National Museum and the zoo *en route*.

GETTING THERE AND AWAY

BY AIR For international arrivals and departures see *Chapter 2, Getting there and away*, page 49. Similarly, for the schedule and fares for domestic flights to some of Mali's provincial towns, see page 73. Note that these schedules are liable to change.

Bamako-Sénou International Airport Bamako-Sénou International Airport (☎ *2020 27 01; information on flights:* m *7600 70 71*) is small, informal and occasionally chaotic – but it works. Airport facilities are limited to an exchange office which opens at erratic hours, public telephones, one or two gift shops, a small bookshop, an upstairs restaurant overlooking the runway, and an information kiosk which dispenses airport information only. Outside, across the car park, is the restaurant Cordon Bleu – basic, but convenient to have a drink and a bite while waiting.

The airport is several kilometres from Bamako. There is no inexpensive method of public transport shuttling between the airport and Bamako, but it's not such a long walk from the airport to the road going into Bamako where it is possible to take a *sotrama* into town. However, if you arrive in the evening or at night, as many international flights do, the *sotramas* will have stopped running. So, unless you manage to get a ride on one of the airport buses provided by the bigger hotels, taking a taxi is probably going to be your best, if not only, bet. Try to find other

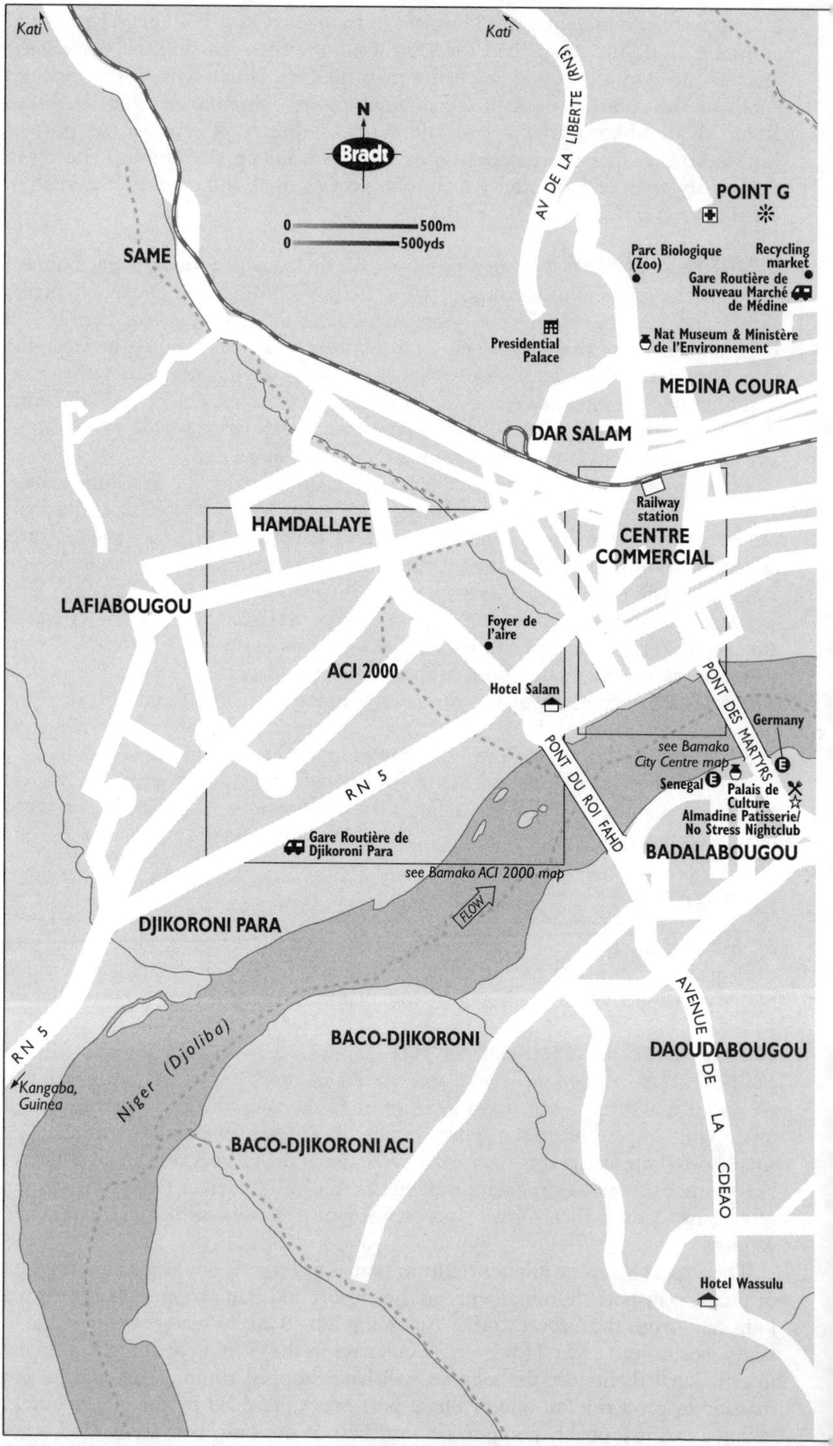
Kati
Kati
AV DE LA LIBERTE (RN3)
N
Bradt
0 500m
0 500yds
POINT G
SAME
Parc Biologique (Zoo)
Recycling market
Gare Routière de Nouveau Marché de Médine
Presidential Palace
Nat Museum & Ministère de l'Environnement
MEDINA COURA
DAR SALAM
Railway station
HAMDALLAYE
CENTRE COMMERCIAL
LAFIABOUGOU
Foyer de l'aire
ACI 2000
Hotel Salam
PONT DES MARTYRS
Germany
PONT DU ROI FAHD
see Bamako City Centre map
Senegal
Palais de Culture
Almadine Patisserie/ No Stress Nightclub
RN 5
Gare Routière de Djikoroni Para
BADALABOUGOU
see Bamako ACI 2000 map
FLOW
DJIKORONI PARA
AVENUE DE LA CDEAO
RN 5
Niger (Djoliba)
BACO-DJIKORONI
DAOUDABOUGOU
Kangaba, Guinea
BACO-DJIKORONI ACI
Hotel Wassulu

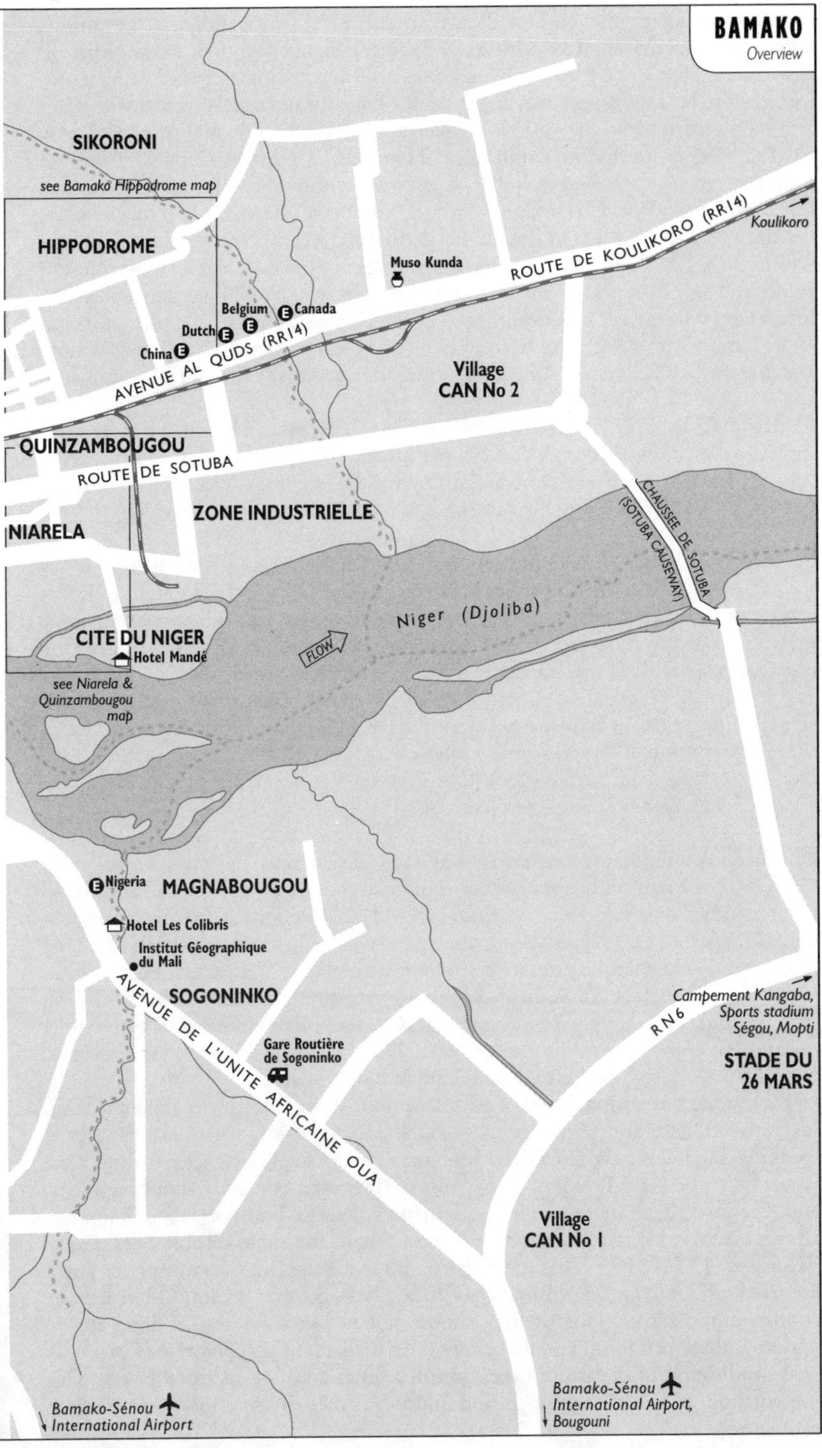
BAMAKO
Overview
SIKORONI
see Bamako Hippodrome map
HIPPODROME
ROUTE DE KOULIKORO (RR14)
Koulikoro
Muso Kunda
Belgium
Canada
Dutch
China
AVENUE AL QUDS (RR14)
Village
CAN No 2
QUINZAMBOUGOU
ROUTE DE SOTUBA
ZONE INDUSTRIELLE
NIARELA
CHAUSSEE DE SOTUBA
(SOTUBA CAUSEWAY)
Niger (Djoliba)
FLOW
CITE DU NIGER
Hotel Mandé
see Niarela & Quinzambougou map
Nigeria
MAGNABOUGOU
Hotel Les Colibris
Institut Géographique du Mali
SOGONINKO
AVENUE DE L'UNITE AFRICAINE OUA
Gare Routière de Sogoninko
RN6
Campement Kangaba, Sports stadium Ségou, Mopti
STADE DU 26 MARS
Village
CAN No 1
Bamako-Sénou International Airport
Bamako-Sénou International Airport, Bougouni

travellers to share the cost, and note that, at the instigation of the airport authorities, taxi drivers have reluctantly fixed and signposted their rates. Although this reduces the space for outrageous fares and negotiation tremendously, it also turns out to be a semi-legal way to inflate the fares for unsuspecting tourists. Rates are fixed according to the various *communes*, exceeding CFA6,000 (per ride) only for the two most distant communes. However, a separate signpost fixes the uniform rate for the bigger hotels – all well within the CFA6,000 zone – at CFA7,500, for no obvious reason. Until the authorities have handled this scheme, the only way around it is to double-check that the hotel of your choice is indeed within the CFA6,000 range (see *Orientation*, page 108), then have the exact amount ready, and stay firm while your driver argues why you should pay more than the local client who got off just around the corner. Be slightly aware of guides and taxis at the airport who sometimes attempt to direct weary passengers, particularly those arriving on the 02.30 Royal Air Maroc flight, to hotels that pay them a commission.

BY RIVER COMANAV (☎ *2026 20 94/2022 38 02*) occupies a building not far from the railway station. Although you can get information and buy tickets here, boats actually leave from Koulikoro, 57km downriver (see page 138). COMANAV's fares and timetable are listed in *Chapter* 2, *Getting around*, pages 75 and 76.

BY TRAIN See page 77 for an indication of times and fares or ☎ 2022 58 16. Always try to buy your ticket the morning before you intend to travel. The train to Kayes can be overcrowded, which means that the station platform fills up very quickly prior to departure. Take care of your belongings whilst you are waiting to board the train, and especially *as* you board the train. Two attempts were made on my camera in the space of 30 seconds, as I joined hundreds of other passengers in the massive scramble for seats. In retrospect, I should have waited until the rush was over so that I could more effectively survey whose hands were where. This is fine if you have a reserved seat, but less appealing if you are in a carriage where places are allocated on a first-come-first-served basis.

BY ROAD Although the occasional bus still leaves from the city centre, since CAN2002 virtually all bus stations or significant bus stops have been banished to the outskirts. Some smaller buses and a handful of exceptions aside, this means that departure points for different destinations and companies are very much clustered into several *gares routières*, even more so than beforehand. The main one by a head is the **Gare Routière de Sogoninko**, about 5km south of the river in the district of Sogoninko. A couple of kilometres past the bus station you come to a monument known as the 'Tour d'Afrique'. Here the road splits: turn left for Ségou, Mopti and Gao, right for Sikasso and Côte d'Ivoire.

Back at the bus station, buses of all descriptions serve most towns along the main highways in these directions – roughly to the east and south of Bamako. Generally speaking, big buses have fixed departure times, while smaller vehicles tend to leave when full. The Gare Routière de Sogoninko, however, is mainly about big buses, and there are plenty to choose from: Somatra/Balanzan Transport, Bani Transport, Binké, Gana and Bittar Transport to name a few of the more reliable ones. **Gana Transport** (☎ *2021 99 30*) has some air-conditioned buses for the same price. These are used randomly and it's a matter of luck if you get one or not. Often the air-conditioning isn't working or they choose not to put it on and as there are no windows that open it can end up being hotter than a non air-conditioned bus.

An indication of departure times, journey times and fares is listed below. This information is liable to change and journey times are no more than rough estimates.

Ségou Hourly, 4hrs, CFA3,000
Niono 08.00, 10.00, 12.00 & 16.00 daily, 5hrs, CFA3,500
Massina 10.00 Mon, Wed, Fri & Sat, 5hrs, CFA4,000
San 08.00, 10.00, 15.00 & 18.00 daily, 6hrs, CFA6,500
Djenné Carrefour 08.00, 10.00, 15.00 & 18.00 daily, 8hrs, CFA7,000
Mopti 08.00, 10.00, 15.00 & 18.00 daily, 10hrs, CFA8,000
Hombori 08.00, 10.00 & 16.00 Mon, Thu & Sat, 14hrs, CFA13,000
Gao 08.00, 10.00 & 16.00 Mon, Thu & Sat, 18hrs, CFA16,000
(Bani Transport via Douentza (CFA10,000) leaves daily 07.00)
Sikasso 08.00, 10.00, 12.00, 14.00 & 17.00 daily, 5hrs, CFA3,500 or CFA5,000 (note that some buses travel via Bougouni, others via Ségou & Koutiala)
Bougouni 12.00 & 17.00 daily, 3hrs, CFA2,300
Bobo-Dioulasso (Burkina Faso) 08.00 daily, 9hrs, CFA10,500
Ouagadougou (Burkina Faso) 08.00 daily, 14hrs, CFA17,500

YT Transport (m *6678 02 37*) has buses leaving for Bouaké for CFA12,000 and Abidjan (Côte d'Ivoire) for CFA25,000. It's best to contact them for a timetable. Alternatively, travel to Sikasso first to find onward transport to Côte d'Ivoire.

Bear in mind that if you want to go to Djenné or Bobo-Dioulasso, for example, you can always do the trip in stages.

A motley collection of vehicles (buses of all sizes, and *camions*) depart from the **Gare Routière de Ngolonina**, not far from Niaréla. It is located within walking distance to the east of the Hotel l'Amitié, and is chaotic in a pleasant sort of way. Although there seem to be official departure times, nobody was quite sure where to get these. However, these are the fares for destinations – to the four winds of the compass – in clockwise order:

Ségou CFA2,500
Niono CFA4,000
Djenné Mostly on Sun to meet the Mon market, CFA7,000
Koro (via Somodougou) CFA10,500
Sikasso (via Koutiala) CFA5,500 (CFA4,500); (via Bougouni) CFA4,000 (CFA2,000)
Kouri (bordering Burkina Faso) CFA6,500
Zégoua (bordering Côte d'Ivoire) CFA6,500
Kita CFA3,000
Diéma CFA5,500 (trucks) or CFA11,000
Nioro du Sahel CFA13,750
Kolokani CFA3,100
Nara CFA6,500
Koulikoro 10.00 & 17.00, 1½hrs, CFA1,000

Several times a week Sangue Transport operate buses leaving for Timbuktu for CFA17,000.

The **Gare Routière du Nouveau Marché de Médine** – not far from Stade Modibo Keita – is the place to look for transport to the west and north of Bamako, and for the occasional *camion* to Timbuktu. Apart from *bâchées* and minibuses to Kati (CFA300) and Koulikoro (CFA900), Gana, Bani and Jema are amongst many bus companies that service the following:

Banamba 11.00 daily, 2hrs, CFA2,000
Nioro du Sahel 07.30 Mon & Thu, 6hrs, CFA10,000
Kayes Gana Transport 05.30, 06.00, 07.00 & 07.30 daily, 7hrs, CFA10,000
Kita 08.00 & 14.00 daily, 3hrs, CFA2,500
Dakar 08.00 Tue & Sun, 06.00 Sat, 2 days, CFA25,000
Diéma Everyday 06.00, CFA6,000
Yélimané 07.00 Mon & Thu, CFA12,500

Mandé Transport leaves daily for Kita at 10.00 and 16.00 for CFA2,500, and Nioro du Sahel and Touroungoumbé on Saturday afternoon at 14.00 for CFA6,500 or CFA10,000, depending on the type of vehicle

Faguibine Transport has one weekly departure for Niafounké and Tonka on Thursdays (to return on Sundays) for CFA11,000 and CFA12,000.

Bani Transport and Bram leave for Diré at 16.00 on Thursday and Friday for CFA13,000. The odd one out is Somatra, leaving for Bandiagara on Wednesday and Saturday for CFA7,000.

The bus station for the Manding Mountains and Guinea is the **Gare Routière de Djikoroni Para** in the far western quarter of Djikoroni. To get there from downtown, take a *sotrama* from the Monument de l'Indépendance, or a *location*, which should not cost more than CFA1,500.

Vehicles vary from smaller buses to bush taxis, with a few comfortable buses running to Kourémalé on the Guinean border. However, it's hard to imagine why anyone would want to go to Kourémalé without crossing into Guinea, and changing transport makes little sense – there's a long no-man's-land between the border posts. Apart from the buses, which allegedly leave for Kourémalé at 14.00 and 17.00 every day, transport leaves only when full.

Siby About 1hr, CFA1,000
Kourémalé 2–3hrs, CFA2,500
Kankan (Guinea) 4–5hrs, CFA10,000
Conakry (Guinea) 16–17hrs, CFA20,000
Kangaba 2–3hrs, CFA2000

For more transport to Kangaba (Manding Mountains) and Koulikoro, Gana du Nord have a departure point between the National Museum and the Stade Modibo Keita. The only public transport to leave from behind the Grand Mosque and the unpaved nearby streets are some *grands cars* with daily departures at 16.00 for Mopti (CFA6,000), and sometimes *petits cars* to Nara and Niono.

A slightly unusual way to reach Bamako is by joining the **Budapest to Bamako rally** (*www.budapestbamako.org*). Now in its fourth year, it leaves from Budapest every January or, two days later, from Murcia in Spain. In 2008 over 400 people joined the rally, choosing between the less demanding 'touring' or more challenging 'racing' routes. The event's charitable objective, Adopt-A-Village, assigns each team an African village, to which they must deliver medicine, toys, school supplies and clothing or Help-A-School bringing education supplies to a school in Bamako.

GETTING AROUND

Bamako is a sprawling city. Although most of the main attractions are within walking distance of each other in the downtown area, many other facilities, such as hotels and restaurants, are some way from the centre. This means that at some point you might contemplate using public transport to get around.

The yellow taxis in Bamako are generally shared. They will take you where you want, picking up and dropping off passengers along the way. The standard fare for a journey around town (eg: downtown to Hippodrome) is CFA1,000, going up to CFA1,500 to cross the river or get to a *gare routière*; rush-hour or late-night fares may be more. They tend to be per person, so may go up if you prefer to be taken from A to B without stopping for other passengers. In that case you should specify that you want a *location*.

Minibuses and converted Peugeot 504s and 505s – all painted bright green – represent the cut and thrust of Bamako's public transport. The standard fare is CFA100–150 and they go virtually everywhere. The minibuses are known locally as *sotramas*, after the Société de Transport Malienne, the first company to operate them. The smaller vehicles – often Peugeot estates converted into something resembling a pick-up truck – are called *dou dourenis*, which is Bambara for '25 francs', their original fare.

Three of the main departure points for *sotramas* and *dou dourenis* are Square Lumumba (for destinations south of the river, including the *gare routière*), at the intersection of Boulevard du Peuple and Avenue Al Quds (for Hippodrome and Route de Koulikoro) and Rue Baba Diarra in front of the railway station (for various destinations in all directions).

NB From Monday to Friday the Pont des Martyrs is closed in one direction during rush hours. From 06.00 to 09.00 it is open only to traffic going into town, while from 16.00 to 19.30 outgoing traffic can make use of the bridge. All transport in the opposite direction has to make the detour using the other bridge.

TOURIST INFORMATION

TOURIST OFFICE The main **Office Malien du Tourisme et de l'Hôtellerie** (*2022 56 73;* e *omathoo@yahoo.fr*) is on Rue Mohamed V near Square Lumumba. They have several, dated leaflets on the country's main tourist attractions (Bamako, Mopti, Djenné, etc), but not a great deal else. They can help plan itineraries and give advice and some of the staff speak good English. A new office – the Bureau Régional du Tourisme – representing the OMATHO for Bamako and Koulikoro opened in February 2004; it is located in ACI 2000 near the Hotel Résidence Bouna.

TOUR OPERATORS AND TOUR GUIDES

Balanzan Tours BP E 4453; 2028 00 20; f 2028 69 36; e info@balanzantours.com; www.balanzantours.com
Cheche Tours BP E 3318; m 6673 43 00; f 2028 75 44; e info@chechetours.com; www.chechetours.com
Continent Tours 2022 70 89; f 2022 70 92; e mali@continenttours.com; www.continenttours.com
Dougou Dougou Travel Rue 530, Porte 100, Quinzambougou, BP E 2495; 2021 66 71; e info@grp-montecristo.com; www.grp-montecristo.com
Mali-Aventours BP E 1433; m 0621 15 44 99; e info@mali-aventours.com; www.mali-aventours.com
Mamadou Tapily PO Box 1916, Bamako; e mamadoutapily@yahoo.fr. Recommended by Bradt reader, Sue Adams, Mamadou has been working as a guide for 15 years, speaks English, French & Spanish. 'We found him knowledgeable, willing to share his information yet unobtrusive in group situations &, best of all, exceptionally organised & flexible' she comments.
Point Afrique Le Village, 07700 Bidon; +33 (0)4 75 97 20 40; f +33 (0)4 75 97 20 50; e contact@point-afrique.com; Immeuble Ex UsAid, Quartier du Fleuve; m 4490 07 35; 2023 54 70; f 2023 57 76; e bamako@point-afrique.com; www.point-afrique.com
Riverside Rue 12, Porte 291, Badalabougou Est; 2022 19 31; e contact@riverside-mali.com; www.riverside-mali.com
Saga Tours Magnambougou Rural, Secteur 2, Porte 43-AT-1; 2020 27 08; m 6673 16 31; e sagatours@sagatours.com www.sagatours.com
Sahara Passion ACI Baco Sud Golf; m 7648 05 14; e spassion@bluewin.ch; www.saharapassion.com
Tara Africa Tours BP E 5661; /f 2028 70 91; e tara@afribone.net.ml; www.tara-africatours.com
Toguna Adventure Tours BP E 5096, ACI 2000, Hamdallaye; /f 2029 53 66/69; e togunaadventure@afribone.net.ml; www.geocities.com/toguna_adventure_tours
Touareg Tours BP E 3962; /f 2220 03 71/ 2610 32 13 / 2674 18 18; e info@touaregtours.com; www.touaregtours.com. Owned by a Luxembourgish lady and her Touareg husband. English-speaking guides must be booked in advance.

WHERE TO STAY

Accommodation in Bamako is not cheap. Apart from one or two notable and often unappealing exceptions, rooms for under CFA15,000 are hard to find. The cheapest – and the most expensive – accommodation is in the centre of town. Elsewhere, mid-range and expensive hotels mingle with the foreign embassies in Niaréla and Hippodrome, while other options exist south of the river in districts such as Badalabougou.

DOWNTOWN

Luxury $$$$$

Hotel Salam (124 rooms) 2022 12 00; e salamcom@azalaihotels.com; www.azalaihotels.com. This nice-looking hotel exceeds both of the other 5-star options & offers all that one could wish for in terms of service, glamour & luxury. There is a lovely garden with a pool & tennis courts & a plush, popular bar, Pacha.

The restaurant is excellent. B/fast extra at a hefty CFA7,500. Free transfer from the airport.

Laico El Farouk (90 rooms) Bd 22 Octobre, Quartier du Fleuve; 2023 18 30; e reservation.bamako@laicohotels.com; www.laicohotels.com. On the banks of the River Niger, with the same Libyan owners as L'Amitié, this fairly new hotel is high quality & more intimate than the other. All rooms have views of the river & there is a decent pool though traffic passes nearby on the Pont des Martyrs, has a great view! The bright & airy, modern restaurant offers decent but rather expensive food. All AC rooms are equipped with TV, fridge & free high-speed internet.

Laico Hotel L'Amitié (191 rooms) Av de la Marne; 2021 43 21; e resa.lamitie@laicohotels.com; www.laicohotels.com. Along with the mosque & the BCEAO building, this hotel dominates the Bamako skyline, although on closer inspection it is no more attractive than a high-rise block on a gloomy London housing estate. In return, you get to enjoy a room with a view of the hotel's golf course & the River Niger. There is also a heart-shaped swimming pool, a casino & a lobby, with boutiques & a motley collection of tour operators, car-rental agencies & moneychangers. Recently renovated in contemporary design, as is often the case with African 5-star hotels, the atmosphere is rather sterile & service sometimes lacking.

Upmarket $$$$

Hotel Mirabeau (48 rooms) Rue 311, Quartier du Fleuve; 2023 53 18; e mirabeau@cefib.com; www.mirabeau.50webs.com. At the lower end of the upmarket hotels, all of the self-contained rooms in this quiet & clean hotel have baths for relaxing in after a dusty day in the city. Bright & airy with free Wi-Fi & satellite TV. There's a decent-sized swimming pool & a bar, shop & even a cash machine that takes Visa. B/fast extra at CFA5,000.

Le Grand Hotel (92 rooms) 2022 24 92; e azalaigrandhotel@azalaihotels.com; www.azalaihotels.com. The 4-star alternative owned by the same group as the Hotel Salam. With a more personal atmosphere, catering especially for people visiting Bamako on business, it's comfortable with friendly staff & similar facilities (swimming pool, tennis courts, shops, etc), while all rooms are completely renovated & have direct access to the internet.

Mid-range $$$ The rest of the options in the centre of town are some way down the scale in terms of price and comfort.

Hotel Lac Débo (14 rooms) 2022 96 35. Friendly, very central & relatively cheap. The building, which is more than 50 years old, is quite beautiful despite its lack of maintenance, & the rooms, although suffering from the same neglect, are OK.

Hotel Yamey (20 rooms) 211 Rue 311, Quartier du Fleuve; 2023 86 88; e hotelyamey@orangemali.net. Situated on the same shady street as the Mirabeau, away from the crowds & not far from the river. The AC rooms with en-suite bathroom are clean & reasonably priced. But they can fill up quickly – often with Italian tourists. Free Wi-Fi.

Budget $$

Auberge Lafia Rue 367, Bamako Coura, behind a photo studio near the Centre Culturel Français; 7623 41 29. This hotel benefits from a quiet yet very central location close to the city's main attractions. The plain rooms with fans are kept pretty clean. *Dorm beds are also available at CFA4,000.*

Hotel Buffet de la Gare 2023 19 10/2028 73 73. A dapper establishment during colonial times & the long-time home of the famous Super Rail Band (see page 33), romantics might be drawn here but should be sufficiently put off by the dingy, showerless overpriced rooms. The hotel is located opposite the train station, not the safest area of town.

Shoestring $ Some budget accommodation in town is provided by the religious missions. A word of warning, however, before you approach them looking for a bed for the night: remember that these rooms are intended for visiting clerics andtheir parents, and tourists will only be put up if space permits. You should neither demand a room as of right nor overstay your welcome.

Carrefour des Jeunes Opposite the Musée de Bamako, Av Kasse Keita; 2022 43 11. This is a lively place selling beer that often has practising drummers or dancers. Basic rooms come with or without fan.

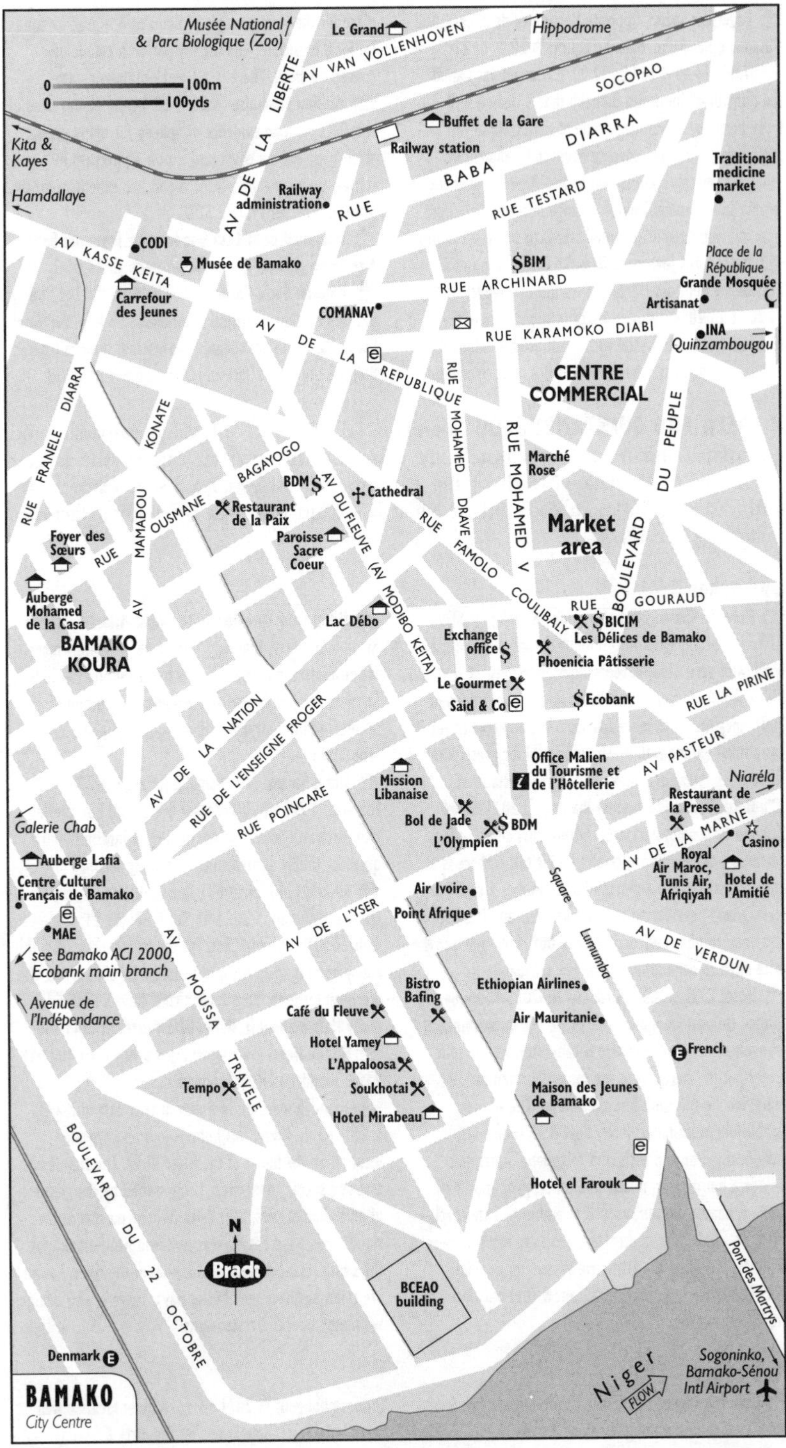
Musée National & Parc Biologique (Zoo)
Le Grand
Hippodrome
AV VAN VOLLENHOVEN
0 100m
0 100yds
SOCOPAO
AV DE LA LIBERTE
Buffet de la Gare
Railway station
Kita & Kayes
DIARRA
BABA
RUE
Traditional medicine market
Hamdallaye
Railway administration
RUE TESTARD
CODI
AV KASSE KEITA
Musée de Bamako
BIM
Place de la République
Grande Mosquée
Carrefour des Jeunes
RUE ARCHINARD
Artisanat
COMANAV
RUE KARAMOKO DIABI
INA
Quinzambougou
AV DE LA REPUBLIQUE
CENTRE COMMERCIAL
RUE MOHAMED DRAVE
RUE MOHAMED V
BOULEVARD DU PEUPLE
RUE FRANELE DIARRA
KONATE
Marché Rose
BAGAYOGO
BDM
AV DU FLEUVE (AV MODIBO KEITA)
Cathedral
RUE OUSMANE
Restaurant de la Paix
RUE FAMOLO COULIBALY
Market area
Foyer des Sœurs
AV MAMADOU
Paroisse Sacre Coeur
Auberge Mohamed de la Casa
RUE GOURAUD
Lac Débo
BICIM
Les Délices de Bamako
BAMAKO KOURA
Exchange office
Phoenicia Pâtisserie
Le Gourmet
Said & Co
Ecobank
RUE LA PIRINE
AV DE LA NATION
RUE DE L'ENSEIGNE FROGER
Office Malien du Tourisme et de l'Hôtellerie
AV PASTEUR
Mission Libanaise
Niaréla
RUE POINCARE
Restaurant de la Presse
Galerie Chab
Bol de Jade
BDM
L'Olympien
AV DE LA MARNE
Casino
Auberge Lafia
Royal Air Maroc, Tunis Air, Afriqiyah
Hotel de l'Amitié
Centre Culturel Français de Bamako
Air Ivoire
Square Lumumba
Point Afrique
MAE
AV DE L'YSER
AV DE VERDUN
see Bamako ACI 2000, Ecobank main branch
AV MOUSSA TRAVELE
Bistro Bafing
Ethiopian Airlines
Avenue de l'Indépendance
Café du Fleuve
Air Mauritanie
Hotel Yamey
French
L'Appaloosa
Tempo
Soukhotai
Maison des Jeunes de Bamako
Hotel Mirabeau
BOULEVARD DU 22 OCTOBRE
Hotel el Farouk
N
Bradt
BCEAO building
Pont des Martrys
Denmark
Sogoninko, Bamako-Sénou Intl Airport
Niger
FLOW
BAMAKO
City Centre

Foyer des Soeurs Opposite Mohanmed de la Casa, Rue Ousamane Bagayoko, Bamako Coura; 2022 77 61; 07.00–13.00 & 16.00–22.00. A tranquil oasis amid the clamour of downtown Bamako that is clean & well looked after by a charming group of sisters. Note: you must arrive within the opening hours to be allowed in; otherwise the courtyard is kept locked. There is no check-in on a Sun morning. There is a range of accommodation, from individual rooms (often all taken) to single-sex dorms.

Maison des Jeunes de Bamako Off Sq Lumumba next to the Pont des Martyrs, Quartier du Fleuve; 2022 23 20; e maisjeunes@yahoo.fr. The nearest Mali has to a youth hostel with small private rooms & dorms or camping in the garden. It is a popular meeting place for the young people of Bamako & a practice area for local musicians who usually put on a couple of concerts a week. There is a 1-week maximum stay.

Mission Libanaise 2023 50 94. In serious need of some TLC with no evidence of upkeep for many years. What used to be a courtyard is now a junkyard for lorries. Dirty, uncomfortable rooms are expensive for the price. *Dorm beds CFA2,500.*

Mohamed de la Casa Opposite the Foyer des Soeurs. A real backpackers' place. *Dorm beds CFA4,000.*

Paroisse Sacré Coeur Av Modibo Keita; 2022 58 42. Opposite the cathedral a few blocks up from the Hotel Lac Debo, rooms are cheap, have internal showers (shared toilet) & are safe. B/fast inc. *Dorm beds CFA5,000.*

NIARÉLA AND QUINZAMBOUGOU Niaréla is a district full of foreign embassies and consulates and most of its hotels are a stone's throw from one of the largest embassies in Bamako. North of the Russian Embassy, at least seven hotels are within about 200m of each other. Most hotels in this area offer great facilities including free Wi-Fi.

Upmarket $$$$

Hotel Le Campagnard (20 rooms) Niaréla; 2021 92 96; e lecampagnard@afribone.net.ml. A comfortable hotel, with very clean AC rooms, mosquito nets, TV & fridge. Ask for a room on the third floor; newly added in 2007, they are much more spacious. The adjacent annex has a small garden with a swimming pool for guests' use. There is a popular but smoky bar & great restaurant.

Hotel Dafina (25 rooms) Niaréla; 2021 03 04. Situated on a quiet backstreet within easy reach of local amenities, the rooms are clean, if a bit tatty. There is a limited restaurant & American bar as well as a pool bar, serving cold beer during the summer months. The pool is also open to non-residents for CFA2,000. Free internet & price open to negotiation in the low season.

Hotel Le Rabelais (45 rooms) No 2005 Route de Sotuba, Quinzambougou; 2021 52 98; e touraine@orangemali.net. Full of charm & character. As one tour leader put it: 'there's been the same doorman for 10 years, but he still can't find the rooms.' The whole establishment is immaculately kept & all rooms are individually designed with TV & telephone. Amenities include a hairdresser, nurse, pharmacy, gym, mud bath, sauna & beauty parlour, as well as a library. Late check-out is available. Non-guests have access to most of these facilities, including the attractive swimming pool for CFA3,500. There's a great restaurant & cosy bar. Internet inc. B/fast not inc.

Hotel Safir (previously Le Grand Atlas) Behind the Russian Embassy, Niaréla; 2021 48 17. Caters more for businessmen than tourists & has a slightly sterile feel. Comfortable but typical of the uninspiring brand of accommodation for which Bamako has gained a reputation.

Hotel Sarama (12 rooms, 5 suites) Rue 220, Niaréla; 2021 05 63. Rather overpriced but offering many extras – like a swimming pool & internet – in a quiet, tastefully decorated & welcoming setting.

Le Loft (24 rooms) 687 Rue Achkabad, Quinzambougou; 2021 66 90; f 221 49 21; e leloft@orangemali.net. For the true connoisseur, this classy hotel is small & sophisticated with ornate rooms & a central location. Pure French chic; there's nothing really Malian about it. Buffet b/fast extra at CFA3,500

Mandé Hotel (50 rooms) Cité du Niger; 2021 19 93; e mandehotel@afribonemali.net; www.mandehotel.com. In a new district east of Niaréla called Cité du Niger, this hotel enjoys an unrivalled location on the banks of the River Niger. The Mandé has a strong soccer connection, being owned by the greatest of all Malian players, Salif Keita. When you stay at the Mandé, you swap easy access to downtown Bamako for the peace, tranquillity & mosquitoes of the river. Rooms are clean but have seen better days. There is also a large swimming pool & 2 restaurants.

Mid-range $$$

Auberge Toguna (8 rooms) A little further east from Hotel La Chaumière along Route de Sotuba, Porte 2239, Quinzambougou; 2021 16 93. A quiet location well away from hectic downtown. Yet the dirty &

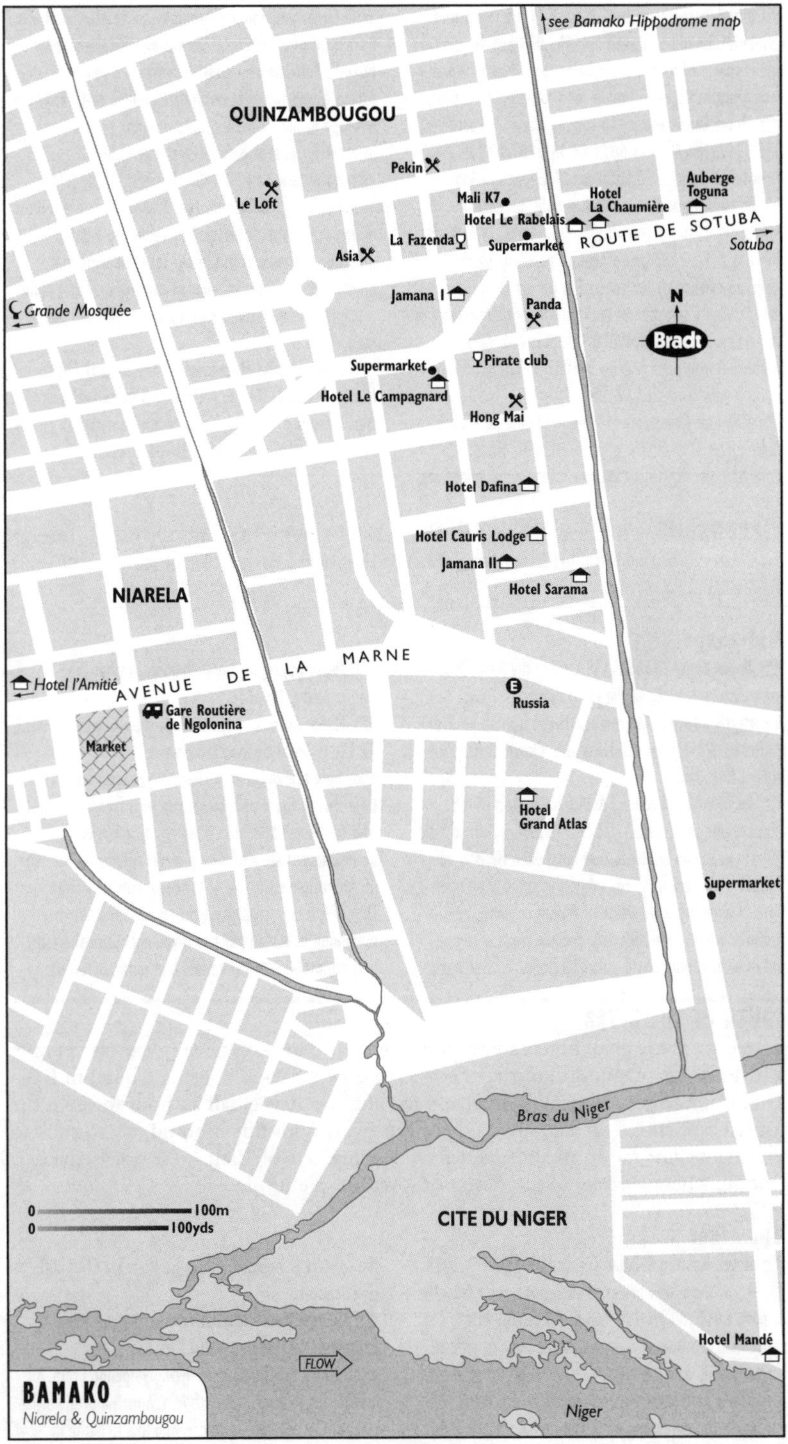
see Bamako Hippodrome map
QUINZAMBOUGOU
Pekin
Le Loft
Mali K7
Hotel La Chaumière
Auberge Toguna
Hotel Le Rabelais
La Fazenda
Supermarket
ROUTE DE SOTUBA
Sotuba
Asia
Jamana I
Panda
Grande Mosquée
N
Bradt
Supermarket
Pirate club
Hotel Le Campagnard
Hong Mai
Hotel Dafina
Hotel Cauris Lodge
Jamana II
Hotel Sarama
NIARELA
AVENUE DE LA MARNE
Hotel l'Amitié
Gare Routière de Ngolonina
Russia
Market
Hotel Grand Atlas
Supermarket
Bras du Niger
0 100m
0 100yds
CITE DU NIGER
Hotel Mandé
FLOW
Niger
BAMAKO
Niarela & Quinzambougou

characterless rooms with AC & small TV are overpriced. Camping should be allowed for CFA5,000 but there have been reports of some people being turned away. No restaurant but they will make food to order. B/fast inc.

Hotel Cauris Lodge (10 rooms) Rue 461, Porte 29, BPE 3217, Niaréla; m 6679 14 38/7903 70 13; e hotelcaurislodge@gmail.com. A lovely, low-key French owned guest house with simple, spacious AC rooms, well maintained with mosquito nets, TV & Wi-Fi. There is a small swimming pool in the shady garden reserved exclusively for guests & a bar under a thatched roof serving a selection of cocktails. Airport transfers can be arranged for CFA10,000. B/fast of bread, cakes, yoghurt & fruit juice is extra at CFA2,500. A good choice. *Rooms with fans CFA12,500.*

Hotel La Chaumière (14 rooms) Route de Sotuba, Porte 2029, Quinzambougou; 2021 76 60; e lachaumiere@cefib.com; www.hotellachaumiere.net. With large, well-equipped rooms, this quieter hotel will have a bit of a hard time competing with the more buzzing Rabelais next door. However it is reasonably priced & well suited to business travellers with TV, phone & fridge in the rooms & gym, swimming pool & free internet for guests. B/fast extra at CFA2,500.

Hotel Jamana I BP 1686, Niarela; 2021 34 56; e hojamana@cefib.com. The very friendly receptionist makes up for the rather gloomy corridors & badly maintained rooms of this hotel. Yet the bathrooms function & there is a minibar in each room. There is no restaurant though they're happy to recommend one of many close by. B/fast inc.

Hotel Jamana II (previously the Dakan) (28 rooms) Niaréla; 2021 91 96. A cheaper & better-value option than Jamana I. It also has a pleasant garden with plenty of shade, where camping is allowed. B/fast inc.

HIPPODROME Hippodrome is another district with its fair share of foreign embassies, consulates and hotels, although it is best known for its restaurants, bars and clubs.

Mid-range $$$

Damu Lodge (5 rooms) Just along the Av Al Quds from L'Express, after all the plant nurseries. Quiet, clean & perfectly adequate AC rooms. There's a small pool, plus a kitchen & fridge for residents' use. *Dorm beds (fan only) CFA8,000.*

Le Djenné (28 rooms) About 200m west of the Hippodrome in Missira; 2021 30 32. A *maison d'hôte* (guesthouse) run by the former outspoken Minister of Culture and Tourism. Predictably, this small & pleasant hotel is a veritable showcase of Malian culture. The rooms, each of them different, are like small museums, full of local handicrafts & colourful *bogolans* (see page 93). You're paying for hotel character rather than comfort here. No pool.

Tamana (36 rooms) Rue 216, Hippodrome; 2021 37 15; e hoteltamana@ikaso.net; www.hoteltamana.com. A charming guesthouse, this time east of the Hippodrome, run by a French couple who try, with some success, to create a family atmosphere. They also have a travel agency on site. The AC rooms are attractive – Art Deco with an African twist. There is a tropical garden with restaurant & fair-sized swimming pool. You pay less if you choose to share the immaculately clean communal bathroom. B/fast inc.

SOUTH OF THE RIVER

There are some great hotels south of the river in Bamako's newer districts yet only a handful are practical in terms of access to downtown. Choosing a hotel in Bako Djikoroni, for example, will involve travelling for maybe half an hour to reach the tourist attractions on the other side of the river. With this in mind, try to stick to the places not far from the main road leading out of Bamako towards the *gare routière*, where *sotramas* to the centre of town are plentiful.

Upmarket $$$$

Hotel Wassulu Kalaban Coura, Pl Sogolon; 2028 76 74. For those who prefer to stray not too far from the airport, this hotel provides comfort & quality in a convenient location. It is owned by the famous *vedette* singer Oumou Sangaré (see page 37), & on Sat when she is not on a tour, she treats her guests to concerts in the garden by the swimming pool. The rooms are pricey but the concert is included, otherwise there's a CFA5,000 cover charge.

Olympe Hotel International (130 rooms) Voie Express de L'Aéroport; 2023 46 63; e olympehotel@yahoo.fr; www.olympehotel.com. An uninspiring 4-star hotel, with AC rooms & a presidential suite at CFA150,000, for those who like to bathe in luxury. 2 swimming pools including 1 for children & an international restaurant. B/fast inc.

Villa Soudan (10 rooms) West Badalabougou; 2022 88 46; e reservation@villasoudan.com; www.villasoudan.com. In a peaceful neighbourhood on the road to the Palais de la Culture, this newly opened villa has a great location overlooking the river. There is a good-size swimming pool in the garden & all AC rooms have a terrace facing the river: perfect for b/fast which is inc.

Mid-range $$$

Auberge Djamilla (8 rooms) No 19, St 108, Badalabougou Sema 1, past the Palais de la Culture & after the Lycée Tieny Konaté; m 7948 56 36; e aubergedjamilla@yahoo.fr. Chez Fanny & Nico is a good choice if you like smaller & more intimate places. Double rooms have fans or AC or you can sleep in a 20-bed Libyan tent with mosquito net for CFA3,500. For overlanders there is parking for 6 vehicles & a charge of CFA2,500 including access to the bathrooms, kitchen & salon. Wi-Fi CFA2,000/day. The large garden around the building keeps it cool and has lots of quiet corners. B/fast not inc.

Hotel L'Aquarius (13 rooms) Just after Pont du Roi Fahd, Torokorobougou; 2028 18 31. Another option within a reasonable distance of downtown. B/fast inc.

Hotel Les Colibris (57 rooms) Av de L'Oua, Route de Magnambougou; 2022 6637; e contact@hotelcolibris.com; www.hotelcolibris.com. Opposite the Saudi Arabian Embassy, 10mins from the airport & 5mins from the city centre, this is a cosy, quiet & good-value hotel. Prices for AC bungalows range from CFA20,000 to CFA30,000 & all of them are well above average in terms of quality & comfort. Satellite TV & free Wi-Fi.

Hotel Séguéré (10 rooms, 1 dorm) Commune 5, No 9, corner of St 307 & 313 (the 2nd house after the South Point NGO) Torokorobougou; 2028 69 08; e seguere@seguere.com; www.seguere.com. A relaxed French-run guesthouse catering for all budgets but targeted mainly towards visiting NGOs. All rooms have a fan & mosquito net with free Wi-Fi & an honesty fridge for drinks. There is a pool for guests & great food. They also use Kofi (m *7614 96 44*), one of the friendliest & most reliable taxi drivers in Bamako. If you arrive at night, the guardian will show you to your room. B/fast inc. *Dorms CFA6,000.*

Budget $$

Tounga Bed & Breakfast (4 rooms) Badalabougou-est, next to the river, close to the German Embassy; 2023 24 72; e info@toungatours.com; www.toungatours.com. Run by a Belgian/Malian couple who also have a travel agency by the same name that supports local humanitarian projects. The town centre is within easy reach by foot across the Pont des Martyrs. Simple rooms with fans & communal bathrooms in a spacious garden. B/fast is CFA2,000, with real coffee.

Shoestring $

Mission Catholique 'Paroisse' Rue 100, Badalabougou. Also a religious mission, and the same reservations apply here as they do to the missions in the downtown area (see page 116). Walk across Pont des Martyrs, turn right at the second set of traffic lights, & the mission is near the police station of the 4th *arrondissement*.

ACI 2000

The newly developed administrative district just west of Bamako has some well-located accommodation particularly suited to business travellers.

Luxury $$$$$

Radisson SAS Hotel (73 rooms); 429 00 00; e reservation.bamako@radissonsas.com; www.bamako.radissonsas.com. Newly opened in mid 2008 with undoubtedly the best rooms in Bamako. Clean & modern with impeccable service & all the luxuries you'd expect from 5-star accommodation; swimming pool, fitness centre, sauna & steam room, free high-speed internet, restaurants serving international cuisine & an impressive buffet b/fast. There is a bar with live music.

Upmarket $$$$

Azalai Nord Sud (58 rooms); 2029 69 00; e azalainordsud@azalaihotels.com; www.azalaihotels.com. 3-star lower-end business accommodation with standard facilities such as a bar, restaurant, swimming pool & superb bookshop. Free parking or free transfer from the airport. B/fast extra at CFA5,500.

ZONE INDUSTRIELLE

Budget $$

Djembe Hotel (2 rooms, sleeping 12 people) Near the entrance to CMDT (cotton factory) Rue 942, Porte 184; m 7923 75 40; e rootsyrecords@yahoo.com; www.rootsyrecords.com. Situated in an area just south of Route Sotuba & east of Cité du Niger, this is not a hotel in the classic sense, but more of a 'home' where people can study music & dance. American Jeremy Chevrier, the founder of Rootsy Records, has been studying *djembe* for 15 years & can put you in touch with well-known teachers (CFA5,000/hr) & provide a space where you can make as much noise as you like (until 22.00!). His Malian wife Tewah provides delicious meals which are all included in the price. Free Wi-Fi.

OUTSKIRTS OF BAMAKO

Mid-range $$$

Campement Kangaba (10 rooms) 10km from the city centre on the road to Ségou; m 7640 30 37; e campement@kangaba.com; www.kangaba.com. Continue for 2km after the new stadium, where you'll see a big sign by the side of the road, saying 'Campement Kangaba'. Turn left & approx 4km down a dirt road there's a little slice of paradise. Located in the 'bush', next to beautiful hills, this charming *campement* is sprawled over 6ha of land. It is run by 2 French guys, 1 of whom speaks English. Activities include *djembe* making, wood sculpting, *bogolan* dyeing, carpentry & African dance lessons. And if that doesn't keep you busy, there is a swimming pool, badminton & volleyball courts, horseriding, bicycle rental & canoes. Accommodation is in 1 of 7 individual round AC huts or you can camp or sleep in a 20-person tent for CFA3,500. The 2 well-stocked bars & dancefloor are made for the musical performances every Sat & a great restaurant serves a choice of *plat du jour* at CFA5,000 or *menu complet* at CFA8,000. Bread is baked on the premises. Though a way out of town, a taxi to the centre costs just CFA5,000. B/fast extra at CFA1,500.

WHERE TO EAT

Most restaurants in Bamako serve international cuisine of varying standards. There are some very good French restaurants and some very bad ones. Chinese, Thai, Moroccan, Indian and Lebanese food is also available, and some of the town's *pâtisseries* are excellent. African food, meanwhile, is a hit-and-miss affair. In addition to the places mentioned below, bear in mind that almost all of the hotels have restaurants or are willing to prepare you a meal if you give them enough notice.

DOWNTOWN

Above average $$$$

Hotel L'Amitié Av de la Marne; 2021 43 21; 12.00–15.00 & 18.30–23.00. Of the hotel's 2 restaurants, the Table du Chef has a very good reputation for gourmet French cuisine whilst the Djoliba serves a Sun lunch buffet by the pool. Both are expensive.

Le Grand Hotel 2022 24 92. Restaurant Azalaï, at Le Grand, serves a similar, cheaper buffet lunch to the Djoliba at the l'Amitié, but the poolside ambience is less agreeable.

Mid-range $$$

Appaloosa Restaurant Rue 311, Quartier du Fleuve; 2022 16 14. The interior is designed like an American ranch, though the new Lebanese owners have spared the waiting staff from dressing up as cowboys. Serves simple & nicely prepared Spanish & Lebanese food; the Malian beef is particularly tender. The bar (see page 129) is a popular meeting place & is open late at w/ends.

Le Café du Fleuve Quartier du Fleuve, Rue 311, Porter 211; m 7918 91 43; 12.00–late daily. African décor & live music on the w/end. The *salade du chevre chaud* wouldn't be out of place in any Parisian restaurant, otherwise the usual meat & side dishes. Be warned: only order the potent dessert, Coupe Colonel, if you're staying at the Hotel Yamey next door, as it has almost half a litre of vodka in it. Free Wi-Fi.

Restaurant L'Olympien Just off Sq Lumumba near the BDM bank; 2023 87 93; 12.00–23.00 non-stop. A popular expat hangout. This is by virtue of the excellent bar & selection of French wines as much as the cooking, most of which is *provençal* (the restaurant is

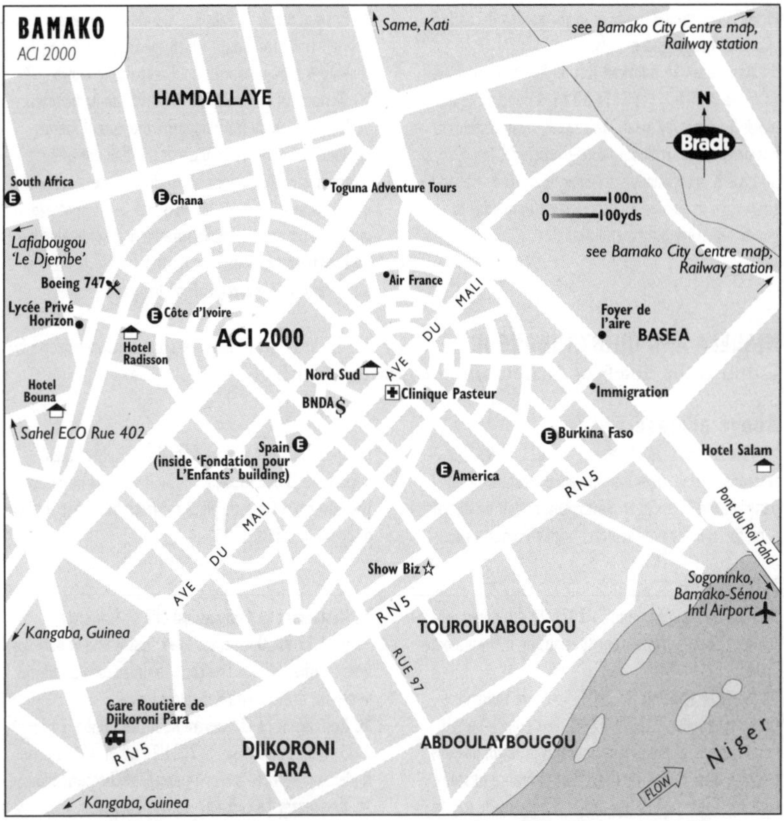

named after Marseille's soccer team, Olympique Marseille) Plats du jour like *escalope du veau gratinée* or reasonable pizzas can also be home-delivered.

✕ **Restaurant Soukhotai** Rue 311, along the river next to the bar L'Appaloosa, Quartier du Fleuve; ☎ 2022 24 48. An authentic Thai restaurant owned by a Belgian expat & his Thai wife; the restaurant is extremely popular with the local crowd & serves tasty dishes unrivalled in the capital.

Cheap and cheerful $$

✕ **Le Casino** At the casino, next to the Hotel de l'Amitié; ☎ 2021 85 54. Once considered by expats to be the best restaurant in Bamako until it was replaced by a bar playing live music & serving snacks. Good spot for lunch though.

✕ **Patio du Centre Culturel Français** Bd de l'Indépendance, around the side of the CCF itself; ⌚ 11.00–01.00 Mon–Sat, from 17.00 Sun. Very popular with expats & the music/cultural crowd, especially before & after the many events at the CCF. Nicely prepared *capitaine*/beef brochettes, good salads (the lentil & smoked ham is very tasty), enormous hamburgers, plus Castel on tap & drinkable wine by the glass.

✕ **Restaurant Bol de Jade** Rue 310, Porte 172, Quartier du Fleuve; ☎ 2022 63 03; ⌚ 20.00–midnight. Serving Vietnamese food under the supervision of Madame Cat since the 1960s. Her son, meanwhile, prepares the Oriental food at the Hotel Débo in Sevaré (see page 183).

Rock bottom $ In the downtown area of Bamako the choice of restaurants is probably better at the cheaper and considerably less pretentious end of the market.

✕ **Bistro Bafing** On the next street up from the Hotel Yamey, Quartier du Fleuve; m 6672 07 81. An inexpensive bar/restaurant on a quiet street with friendly service, ice-cold beers & daily specials including local dishes. Served inside or in the garden decorated with wall hangings & murals.

✕ **Restaurant Le Gourmet** Just off Rue Mohamed V & near the OMATHO; m 6676 30 65. A good place for lunch & take-away meals. This small, clean restaurant has daily menus including *sauce arachide*, *fonio*, *tô*, *riz au gras* & occasionally something specifically Malian like *saga-saga* or *fakoye*. Get there close to midday to guarantee everything is still available.

✕ **Restaurant de la Paix** Rue Ousmane Bagayogo. Another small restaurant which specialises in Senegalese cooking & is popular with the backpacking crowd.

✕ **Restaurant La Presse** ORTM (Office de Radiodiffusion et de Télévision du Mali) opposite the Hotel L'Amitié; ⊕ lunchtime. The restaurant at the Mali television centre is vaguely reminiscent of the BBC canteen. Service is surly & food is simple but you may get to spot a local celebrity. Go early to make sure there is something left.

✕ **Restaurant le Tempo** Av Moussa Travele. Serves the usual variety of cheap meals on the patio.

NIARÉLA AND QUINZAMBOUGOU Some of the best restaurants in Bamako are to be found at the hotels of Niaréla and the quarters nearby.

Above average $$$$

✕ **Mandé Hotel** Cité du Niger; ☎ 2021 19 93. The 2 restaurants here enjoy an unrivalled location on the banks of the River Niger. Restaurant Le Toît de Bamako is on the top floor of the hotel, with a French menu, European prices & a more formal atmosphere than Restaurant Le Pilotis, which is built on stilts in the river. The latter is a fantastic place to watch fishermen in their pirogues at b/fast.

Mid-range $$$

✕ **Asia** Quinzambougou; ☎ 2021 22 48. Reputably the best Chinese restaurant specialising in Vietnamese dishes.

✕ **Hotel Le Rabelais** No 2005, Route de Sotuba, Quinzambougou; ☎ 2021 52 98. This French-owned hotel has one of the best restaurants in town, possibly because their Malian chef was sent to France to study cooking. Some superb fish dishes & homemade ice cream. Good food but not cheap.

✕ **Pirate Club** Opposite Le Campagnard; ☎ 2133 43 33; ⊕ 12.00–15.00 & 18.00–02.00 daily. Owned by local tour operator, Cheche Tours, the Pirate is one of a popular breed of trendy bars/restaurants in Bamako with international dishes including pork. Live music; rock, blues, jazz & African 5 nights a week.

✕ **Restaurant Le Campagnard** BPE 486, Niarela; ☎ 2021 92 96. Open since 1991, this is one of Bamako's finest. Dishes include French specialities such as prawns in cognac or beef with Roquefort sauce.

✕ **Restaurant La Chaumière** Route de Sotuba, Porte 2029, Quinzambougou; ☎ 2021 76 60. A refined menu & pleasant service. Serves an excellent chocolate mousse.

✕ **Restaurant Le Loft** 687 Rue Achkhabad, Quinzambougou, just to the north of Route du Sotuba; ☎ 2021 66 90. A sophisticated restaurant specialising in the *cuisine du Périgord*, which includes duck & fowl *à la Française* as well as Italian & Asian dishes.

Cheap and cheerful $$

There are two other Chinese restaurants which may appeal to those on a tighter budget.

✕ **Panda Bar Restaurant** Rue 461, Porte 372; ☎ 2021 33 15. Authentic food from a Chinese chef who has been cooking at the Panda for more than 10 years.

✕ **Restaurant Hong Mai** Niaréla; m 7940 59 45; ⊕ 12.00–15.00 & 19.00–23.00 Tue–Sun. Serves Vietnamese dishes with home delivery.

Rock bottom $

✕ **Bar Restaurant La Fazenda** Near the Rabelais, Route de Sotuba, Quinzambougou; m 7916 11 28. More like a beer garden but also serves typical Malian & Ivoirian dishes such as *foutou*, pigeon & braised chicken with chips & fried banana. A large beer costs CFA800.

HIPPODROME Avenue Al Quds is just another busy, oppressive road in Bamako until you reach the turning for the Hippodrome, after which it becomes a hotspot for some of the most popular places to eat in the capital.

Mid-range $$$

✕ **Bla Bla Bar** Route 235; m 6674 82 64. One of the trendiest eating/drinking spots in Bamako & a good place to start your evening. Food is served on the terrace or a small AC room inside; you can order meals & simple snacks; brochettes, pizza & a selection of beers. Listen to good music & sit back & watch the beautiful people.

✕ **La Rose des Sables** Route de Koulikoro, next to the Chinese Embassy; ☎ 2021 04 04; ⏲ 12.00–15.00 & 18.00–23.00 daily. A smart new Moroccan restaurant serving authentic dishes such as pigeon pastilla & lamb tagine with preserved lemons. Worth making an effort for a special night out.

✕ **Le Relais** Route de Kouilkoro; ☎ 2021 02 29; e resa@relaiscampa.com.ml. An Italian restaurant with a wood-fired pizza oven, serving the best pasta in town & excellent fish dishes. The bright lighting destroys the ambience but the food more than makes up for it.

✕ **Montécristo Restaurant** Rue 249; ☎ 2021 66 71. Further along Al Quds – which becomes Route de Koulikoro – past the Canadian Embassy. Owned by the local travel agency Dougoudougou with a gourmet French restaurant on the ground floor, more typical of the Niaréla area than the Hippodrome & has a nightclub above.

✕ **Restaurant Akwaba** (meaning 'welcome' in some Ghanaian & Ivoirian languages) Left just past L'Express down Rue 235; ☎ 2021 06 45. Try to dine here in the evenings on Sat, when there should be some live music. Otherwise, this is a pleasant place to eat & is another favourite of the expat crowd.

✕ **Restaurant Le San Toro** Corner of Av Al Quds & the Hippodrome rd; ☎ 2021 30 82. Like Le Djenné (see page 120), this restaurant is run by the former Minister of Culture and Tourism. The style of the hotel is mirrored by the restaurant, with its arts & crafts shop, Malian décor, garden, superb live *kora* music & a menu featuring many excellent national dishes. A real favourite. No alcohol is served here, but the mixed fresh juices are great.

Cheap and cheerful $$

✕ **Pili Pili** Rue 259, Porte 501; ⏲ 10.00 until dawn daily. The pleasant courtyard is tranquil at lunchtime, livelier later. There are African variations on otherwise standard meat, poultry or fish dishes, which can be served with the usual sides or *aloko* (plantain) or *atieke* (minced cassava). The homemade juices (*bissap*, *gingembre*) are good.

✕ **Pizzeria da Guido** Rue 250, Porte 920, Carrée d'Affanga; m 7632 77 88; ⏲ for dinner daily except Thu. Not far from the Bla Bla, this small, lively restaurant is run by a couple of Italian brothers serving what is rumoured to be the best pizza in town.

✕ **Restaurant Piano** Av Al Quds, past the duo of Lebanese places (see next entry) but before the Canadian Embassy. A Chinese restaurant where the evenings are enhanced with live piano music.

Le Relax (☎ *2021 79 18*) and **L'Express** (☎ *2021 02 24*), both further along Avenue Al Quds, past the two large supermarkets, are virtual carbon copies of each other. These Lebanese-owned restaurants with *pâtisseries* serve burgers-and-fries type food, spiced up by the odd *kafta* and kebab dish. Le Relax is perhaps the more popular, especially with travellers, and is open until late for the custom brought in by the nightclub next door.

TOWARDS KOULIKORO Continuing along Route de Koulikoro, there are several places worth a mention:

Mid-range $$$

✕ **Le Diplomat** Route de Koulikoro, before Savana if you are coming from the Hipppodrome. An outdoor restaurant/bar with live music on Sat nights. Simple, well-cooked food with good-sized portions; chicken or *brochette de capitaine* with chips. A small beer is CFA1,000.

✕ **Restaurant Gwa Kunda** Nearby, at Muso Kunda (see page 136). Has a good a selection of Malian dishes. There are daily menus & the staff are both friendly & knowledgeable about the food they serve – something you cannot always take for granted.

Cheap and cheerful $$

✕ **Le Savana** Route de Koulikoro, Korofino Nord; m 7631 41 56/6671 08 24; ⏲ 18.00–02.00 Tue–Sun. A very popular bar/restaurant with dining in a pleasant, large outdoor courtyard & live music on Wed/Thu. Reasonably priced dishes such as pizza & carp.

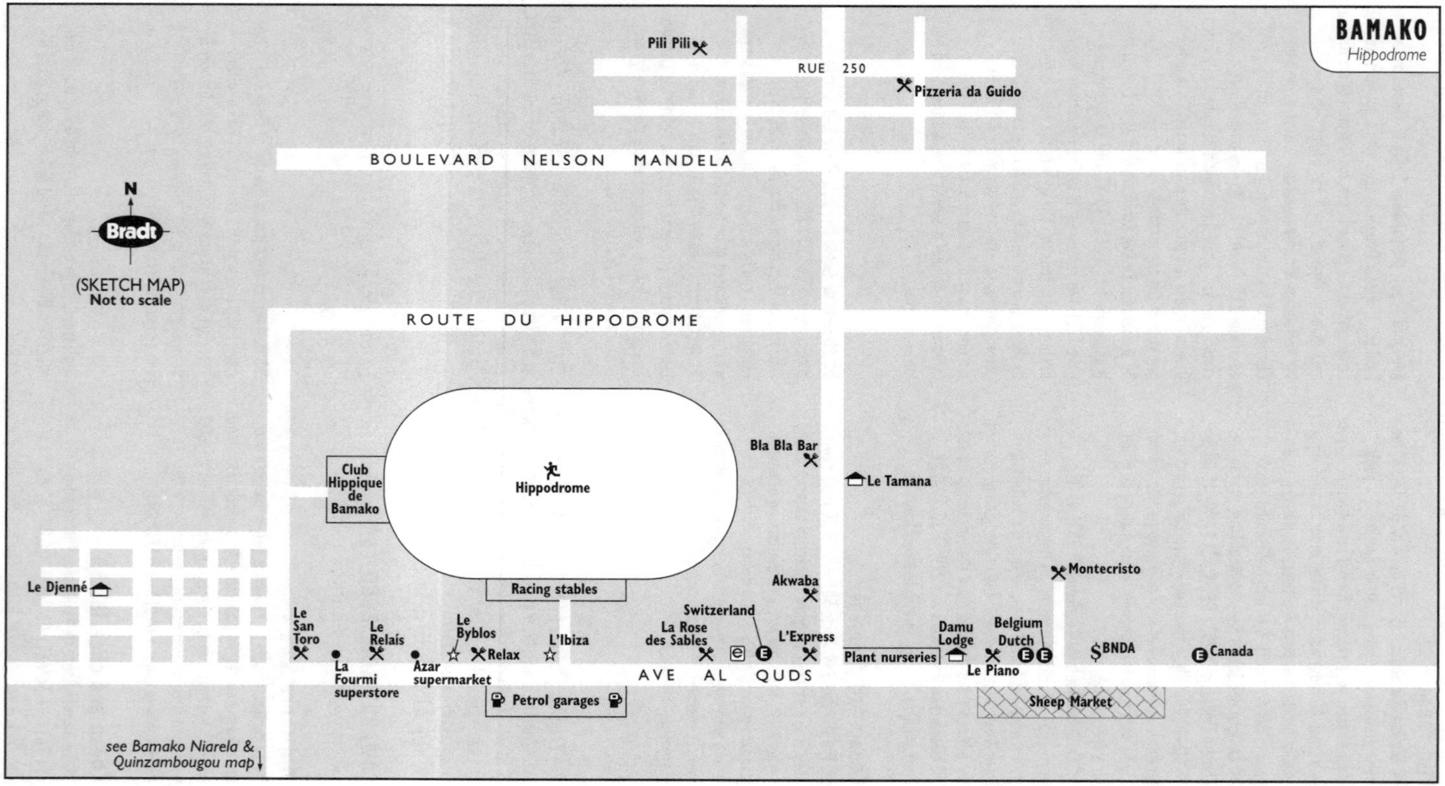
BAMAKO
Hippodrome
Pili Pili
RUE 250
Pizzeria da Guido
BOULEVARD NELSON MANDELA
N
Bradt
(SKETCH MAP)
Not to scale
ROUTE DU HIPPODROME
Club Hippique de Bamako
Hippodrome
Bla Bla Bar
Le Tamana
Le Djenné
Racing stables
Montecristo
Akwaba
Switzerland
Le San Toro
Le Relais
Le Byblos
Relax
L'Ibiza
La Rose des Sables
L'Express
Damu Lodge
Belgium
Dutch
BNDA
Canada
Plant nurseries
Le Piano
La Fourmi superstore
Azar supermarket
AVE AL QUDS
Petrol garages
Sheep Market
see Bamako Niarela & Quinzambougou map

SOUTH OF THE RIVER

Mid-range $$$

Restaurant Pâtisserie Amandine Along Av de l'OUA not far from the Pont des Martyrs. Although there have been reports recently of standards dropping, this used to be the best *pâtisserie* in town. An excellent choice of pastries & tasty food (like pizzas, salads & *capitaine* dishes) as well as banana splits. A popular place for *toubabous* (white people) to hang out.

Restaurant Wassulu Route Aéroport, Pl Sogolon; 2028 73 73. A decent choice of meals at sensible prices with live music & the possibility of a performance by Oumou Sangaré on Sat nights.

Cheap and cheerful $$

Pâtisserie de l'Étoile Just past the Gare Routière de Sogoninko. Quite acceptable if you have to wait a few hours for a bus.

Restaurant le Kandjo At Hotel Colibris. In a garden next to the hotel serving very reasonably priced meals.

Rock bottom $

Alassane Restaurant Badalabougou; m 7872 10 21. Very reasonably priced specialities from Mali, Senegal & even Cameroon.

ACI 2000

Rock bottom $

Le Boeing 747 Walking distance from the Radisson Hotel in ACI 2000, Hamdallaye; m 7922 11 63/6581 58 15. A new & inexpensive local restaurant in Bamako serving tasty African dishes from Mali & Senegal.

ZONE INDUSTRIELLE

Rock bottom $

Café Bagami A few blocks south of the Route de Sotuba across from Mali Lait, next to the slaughterhouse; 2021 37 05; e bagami@groupeami.com; daily from early morning until late, with 24hr take-out window. Bagami is the closest thing to a European café that you will find in Mali. Tasty pastries, good sandwiches & salads & coffee are served in modern surroundings. Has WiFi & a computer with free internet access.

WEST OF THE CENTRE

Mid-range $$$

Eden Village Sébénikoro; 2023 83 71. Located in a scenic setting on the banks of the Niger, Eden Village serves standard fare such as brochettes & sandwiches, but its appeal is its quiet garden setting. It also has one of the largest pools in Bamako open to visitors (free if ordering the *menu du jour*, otherwise CFA2,000). There are a few AC rooms with TV at CFA25,000 in the courtyard. To get there, take any public transport heading toward Siby or Guinea & ask to be dropped at Sébénikoro-Eden Village, just after a small roundabout. From the main road it's a short walk down a dirt road to the river.

ENTERTAINMENT AND NIGHTLIFE

MUSIC AND THE ARTS The state of the arts in Mali has never been better. Malian music enjoys worldwide acclaim, its cinema is starting to receive international recognition, and in recent years Bamako has hosted an African festival of theatre, the Paris-Bamako Music Festival, and the biennial photography festival, Rencontres Africaines de la Photographie, see page 88).

Centre Culturel Français de Bamako (CCF) (*Bd de l'Indépendance; 2022 40 19; www.ccfbko.org.ml; 11.00–01.00 Mon–Sat, from 17.00 Sun*) The best place to go to sample some of Mali's art and culture. Regular concerts – not just by Malian performers, but musicians and dance troupes from all over Africa and the world –

are staged in the evenings in the CCF's large theatre, where Malian favourites, such as Oumou Sangaré, Baba Salah and Amy Koita (see page 32), rub shoulders with drummers from Burundi and Canadian jazz bands. Ticket prices range from free to CFA10,000 and you should pick up a monthly programme of events or check the website to see what's going on. There is a good patio café-restaurant on the grounds where you can eat and have a beer whilst reading books and magazines.

Quartier Orange (*Zone Industrielle, Route de Sotuba Bamako*) This exhibition centre in the industrial zone, sponsored by the mobile-phone company Orange, was the first to host an exhibition by a world-famous artist in Mali. Claude Viallat showed in February 2009. It is also one of the venues for the international photography festival, Rencontres Africaines de la Photographie (for further information, see page 88), that takes place in autumn every other year, as well as exhibitions organised by CCF.

Galerie Chab (*178 Rue Fancélé Diarra, opposite ADEMA (the head office of a political party), not far from CCF; m 7915 49 37; ⌚ 09.00–12.00 & 16.00–19.00 daily during exhibitions except Mon*) The only photography gallery in the capital, owned by photography expert Chab Touré who hosts fabulous exhibitions of well-known African and international photographers. Phone to check current exhibitions.

Musée National (*Route de Koulouba towards Point G; ☎ 2022 34 86; admission CFA500*) The museum has weekly concerts and other events on Thursday afternoons at 16.30, and sometimes on Friday mornings. Every day except Monday, at 10.00 and 14.00, films about the history and culture of Mali are screened. They will also be hosting a large exhibition in January 2010 to coincide with the Football World Cup in South Africa, featuring French painter Claude Viallat along with artists from other African countries and France and Spain .

The Palais de la Culture Amadou Hampaté Ba (*Badalabougou SEMA; ☎ 2022 33 70; www.palaiscultureahb.net*) The current *palais*, constructed in 1996, was named after the famed Malian novelist and national hero Amadou Hampaté Ba. An imposing, pink building on the banks of the river to the right of the Pont des Martyrs, it is arguably the most important artistic venue for the cultural heritage of Mali. The concert hall, in 3ha of pleasant garden, holds most of the big performances of the capital – Amadou and Mariam, Abdoulaye Diabaté, etc. It is home to the National Theatre Company, the National Ballet, the National Orchestra and the National Institute of the Arts, with rehearsals most mornings from about 10.00. If you ask nicely, you should be allowed to watch. For those interested in learning *djembe*, you can take lessons from members of the national ballet: Madu Fané (*m 7647 30 05*) and Boubacar Diabaté, who speaks English (*m 7649 52 78*).

It is a non-profit-making, state-funded structure and a lot of events are free, especially during celebrations such as Pan African Women's Day. Otherwise concerts and other events range from CFA2,000 to CFA3,500 and will always start late.

Institut National des Arts (INA) (*Bd du Peuple, close to the Grand Mosque*) During the day, lively theatre classes and workshops take place in rooms around the edge of a large shaded courtyard. A small bar is open every day, except Sunday. A good place to pass a few hours in the centre of town.

Maison des Jeunes Behind the Pyramid de Souvenir. A popular meeting place for young people in the capital with a number of cultural activities going on, such as concerts, art and music lessons. *Bogolan* teaching is one of the most popular programmes and a regular workshop is held in the garden of the *maison*, under the shade of the mango trees, taught by well-known artist, Kader Keita.

Bamako is a town of music and musicians. As well as the larger venues listed above, some of Mali's best-loved musicians join Amadou and Mariam at the **Paris-Bamako Festival** held every year at the **Institut des Jeunes Aveugles** (the school for the blind) in Faladie (see page 87, or visit *www.les-paris-bamako.com*).

There are many smaller music venues where you can catch live performances. Even the best live music clubs rarely charge admission of more than CFA2,500–5,000.

LIVE MUSIC

☆ **Akwaba** Left just past L'Express, Rue 235, Hippodrome; ☎ 2021 06 45. Live music on Sat. Listen while you dine.

☆ **Carrefour des Jeunes** Next to the Pl de la Liberté, Av Kasse Keita; ☎ 2022 43 11. Another cultural centre showcasing young, local talent. You can catch evening rehearsals of traditional dance & music & from time to time they have concerts. Handy for finding out what's going on in town from the numerous flyers & posters. Also possible to learn *djembe*, *balafon* & African dance.

☆ **Cheval Blanc** Torokorobougou, south of the river. Not the most salubrious of open-air clubs, under a well-worn thatch roof with plastic chairs, but serves cold beers & has a Fri night lineup of local emerging talent.

☆ **Djembe** Lafiabougou; ⏲ every night. A fun venue, with a great atmosphere, where *griots* or praise singers take it in turns to sing with the band & you may catch some famous musicians who go there for a jamming session. Everyone is up & dancing & there are some impressive synchronised routines. The best bands are on Fri/Sat. Inexpensive alcohol is served in the dimly lit interior.

☆ **Espace Bouna** Rue 360, ACI 2000; ☎ 2029 54 68. A large open-air beer garden that charges CFA3,000 if someone famous is playing. Previous artists have included Habib Koité, Toumani Diabaté & the Super Rail Band.

☆ **Exodus** Next to Nightclub Ibiza, Hippodrome; m 7514 55 28. A restaurant/bar/dancing cultural centre in a small garden with a Congolese percussion group performing on a Sat night.

☆ **Hogon** Off Av Kasse Keita, N'Tomikorobougou neighbourhood. Unfortunately Toumani Diabaté's bar, & the best music venue on Fri nights, closed at the end of 2008 so the owner could build a mosque on the land. He may well have relocated, so ask around.

☆ **Mouffou** Kalabankoro Bada. Salif Keita's club. If he's in town, he's billed to play here Thu–Sat. But there's no guarantee, as he doesn't always show up.

☆ **Parc des Princes** Faladié, not far from the Tour d'Afrique; entry around CFA 2,000 inc a drink, depending on the night & who's playing. While a bit out of town, Parc des Princes is a good bet for live music, with performances every night except Sun (when a DJ spins tunes). Music tends to start after 22.30; smaller bands are the general rule, but from time to time bigger performers pop in. Dark, filled with run-down couches & with a great atmosphere, this is very much a Malian nightspot popular with locals.

☆ **Savana** Korofino Nord; m 7631 41 56. On Wed nights, Djibee 5, a popular local singer-guitarist, draws a young, fashionable crowd with an assorted mix of international & African tunes.

☆ **Wassulu Hotel** Route de l'Aéroport, south of Bamako; ☎ 2028 76 74. Malian diva Oumou Sangaré's club where she plays on a Sat night if she's in town. CFA5,000 entrance or free if you're a guest at the hotel.

BARS The best nightlife experience you can hope to have in Bamako is getting invited to a wedding or any other local celebration. Your hotel should be able to help you and the friendliness and hospitality of Malians means this is fairly easy to arrange.

Otherwise, there are a number of trendy restaurants/bars, open until 02.00, some of which will also have live music.

Downtown

🍸 **Appaloosa** Rue 311, Quartier du Fleuve, next door to Sukhotai; ☎ 2022 15 14. Long-legged blondes serve behind the well-stocked bar with a huge variety of alcohol; some local beers plus a substantial cocktail menu. Very crowded at weekends & a good meeting place, before going to the clubs. Wed is karaoke night.

Niaréla

🍸 **Pirate Club** ☎ 2133 43 33; 🕘 18.00–02.00 daily. The Pirate has live music 5 nights a week. Choose from several bars; the interior one with AC has kitsch 1970s' furniture, big leather chairs & a large flat-screen TV while the exterior one is in the style of a Swiss chalet. Beer is reasonable at CFA1,000 & *shisha* pipes are available.

Hippodrome

🍸 **Bla Bla Bar** Route 235; m 6674 82 64. Where the beautiful people go. Sit back on the large fanned terrace or the small AC room inside & watch wealthy Malians with their girlfriends rub shoulders with music stars, Rastas or volunteers. There is a large choice of cocktails & wine & good music to get you going for the rest of the night.

🍸 **Montecristo** Route de Koulikoro, Rue 249; ☎ 2021 66 71. Upmarket establishment owned by Dougou Dougou Travel (see page 115), with a gourmet restaurant on the ground floor and nightclub above.

🍸 **Terrasse** 🕘 from 19.00 daily. Nice décor & laidback atmosphere but a bit of a pulling joint. Live music at weekends & the best place to go for salsa on Thu.

At the other extreme, there are plenty of local bars to be found in every *quartier*; not only are they cheaper, but they're great places to soak up the atmosphere and have a truly authentic experience.

🍸 **Foyer del Aire** At the next roundabout southwest of the Pl de la Nation (taking a left at this roundabout brings you to the Pont de Roi), you'll find 2 bars next to each other in the same building. It's CFA650 for a large beer in one building & CFA750 in the one next door, which not only has fans, but also the colder of the 2 beers. On the grounds are also a canteen, food/tea stall, a thatched-roof circular performance area for live music & a couple of the same for sitting and drinking.

NIGHTCLUBS Bamako is a city that comes alive after dark and on weekends it's a party town. Clubs get going around midnight and don't close until dawn. Nightclubs in Bamako fall into two categories: expensive Western-style discotheques playing international music for a largely expat crowd (cover charge around CFA5,000; often includes the first drink); and Malian nightclubs. The latter – playing mostly African music – are not hard to find in Bamako. Albeit many of the streets do not have names, taxi drivers usually know how to find the hotspots. Try **Le Tempo** (*Quartier du Fleuve;* ☎ *2022 88 00*), or **Le Metropolis** (*Route de Sotuba*), which is arguably the most popular. For Western-style music try:

☆ **Bla Bla Club & Privilege** Badalabougou. Best on Fri/Sat nights.

☆ **Le Byblos** Next to Le Relax on Route de Koulikoro (see page 125); ☎ 2021 79 19; 🕘 00.30–dawn. The best nightclub in town with queues to prove it, even though the new & brighter L'Ibiza lies half empty next door. Even on Sat nights when this place is invariably packed, there is an easy-going, seductive atmosphere. A word of warning, though: gorgeous Malian ladies, dressed to kill & with a smile to match, who approach men – particularly older men – asking to dance, are not necessarily doing it for the pleasure of their company. International hits & local classics guarantee a busy dancefloor.

☆ **L'Ibiza** Down the road at L'Express; ☎ 2021 73 25. Lebanese-run, this new & mega-glitzy nightclub has the best sound system in town. It's stylish but expensive & as yet has not taken off like Le Byblos.

☆ **Le Spot** Route de Koulikoro in Korofina. Its dancefloor also remains uncluttered while Le Byblos enjoys the lion's share of the expat market.

☆ **No Stress** Badalabougou, just above Amandine restaurant near the Pont de Martyrs; m 7851 61 61; entry CFA5,000, small beer CFA2,000. This is the newest, hottest nightclub in Bamako, playing a mix of West African *coupé décalé*, American hip-hop & European techno long into the night. Doors open around midnight, but the place doesn't really get going until 12.30 or 01.00. The largely Malian crowd will be dressed to impress, but as long as you avoid shorts & flip-flops, you'll be fine.

☆ **Platinium** Immeuble Babemba, Av Kasse Keita. A popular nightspot.

☆ **Polo** Korofina, just past Le Diplomat and Savannah; m 6672 82 85; entry CFA5,000; open from midnight. Another newer nightclub, this place draws a local crowd & is less flashy than its bigger competitors Byblos & No Stress.

☆ **Show Biz** 2 blocks from the American Embassy next to SNG, ACI 2000; m 7610 86 16. A new, smaller night club that is inexpensive but still trendy.

OTHER NIGHTLIFE The one casino in town is operated by Hotel de l'Amitié on the Avenue de la Marne.

The best and biggest cinema in Bamako is the fairly new Babemba in Oulafabougou Bolibana, on the corner of Avenue Kasse Keita and the Boulevard de l'Indépendance. You can see top-of-the-bill films that have been released in the US just a few months earlier (CFA2,000) and usually there is one African selection as well. Two films are shown every evening except Mondays (*2023 95 77 for information on their weekly programme*). French – and sometimes Malian – films are screened at the Centre Culturel Français on Sundays. The production company, Kora Films, is in the process of constructing a projection room in Magnambougou (*202 Rue 372; 2020 05 43; e korafilms@hotmail.com for up-to-date information*). If you're into senseless karate films, Cinema Vox, almost opposite the cathedral, is going to be your best bet.

For information on the various cultural events in Bamako, pick up the monthly programme from the Centre Culturel Français and the monthly edition of *Le Dourouni*, an interesting booklet aimed at expats. It is distributed rather randomly and they are sometimes hard to find. Try the Centre Culturel Français, the embassies, the bigger hotels or the CODI (see page 113). L'ORTM (Office de Radiodiffusion et de Télévision du Mali) also advertises events on the television and radio.

SHOPPING

Several large supermarkets in Bamako service the needs of the city's expat community. Most of the produce, therefore, is imported from France and is very expensive. Opened in February 2004, the **Azar Libre Service** (*Av de l'OUA, Badalabougou Est; 2021 42 92; 08.00–13.00 & 15.30–20.00 Mon–Sat, 09.00–13.00 Sun*) is easily the best supermarket in town. This is *the* place to spend a fortune on camembert and Italian salami, vintage wines and energy drinks, crunchy muesli and chilled hazelnut chocolate bars. **La Fourmi** (*2021 61 67*) and a smaller Azar branch, both on Avenue Al Quds between Restaurant Le San Toro and Le Relax, are lesser gods but nonetheless well stocked. In Niaréla, underneath the Hotel Le Campagnard, Le Metro is convenient if you are staying at one of the many hotels in this part of town.

ACTIVITIES

The sporting options for visitors to Bamako are somewhat limited. There are **tennis courts** at the big hotels: l'Amitié, Salam, Grand and the Carrefour des Jeunes. You can also rent a court at the Tennis Club in Dravela (*2022 35 89; CFA2,000–4,500/hr*). There are large **swimming pools** at l'Amitié, Le Grand, the Mandé Hotel, Hotel Les Colibris and Le Rabelais, to name a few, charging non-guests between CFA2,000 and CFA5,000 for the day. For golf lovers there is a nine-hole, par-three **golf course** behind l'Amitié, where a round of golf, including club rental and a caddy, will cost about CFA15,000 (there's no charge if you are staying at the hotel).

Bamako's **horseriding club** (*Club Hippique de Bamako; 2021 06 04*) is next to the dry, dusty Hippodrome, but is membership only; short-term membership is possible if you're around for a few weeks. Of more interest to tourists are the racing stables, also at the Hippodrome (turn left at the Ibiza on Avenue Al Quds). They house about 100 horses and from late November through to July, **horse racing** takes place on a Sunday. Gates open at 16.30 and entry is only CFA500 – a spectacle of thundering hooves and dust seems guaranteed. At other times, you can hire out retired racers, with or without a guide depending on your experience, for CFA5,000–6,000 an hour.

To see **professional football matches**, go to the Stade Omnisport at the foot of the hill leading up to Point G, and the Stade du 26 Mars along the road to Ségou.

OTHER PRACTICALITIES

HEALTHCARE There are two main hospitals in Bamako. **Hôpital Gabriel Touré** (☎ *2022 27 12*) on Avenue Van Vollenhoven near Le Grand Hotel is the more central, while **Hôpital du Point G** (☎ *2022 50 02*) is on a hill overlooking the city.

Although these hospitals are adequate for outpatient treatment and analysis, they are not places where you will find a lot of comfort and compassion. In case you should be admitted, a private hospital like **Clinique Pasteur** is the better option.

Pharmacies are thick on the ground and normally stock the main creams, pills and lotions. Contact-lens fluid, however, is almost impossible to find, and you'll be wasting your time in a pharmacy. If you are in desperate need, contact the eye hospital behind Hôpital Gabriel Touré or any other eye specialist. One optician (☎ *2023 62 08*) near the Hotel Mirabeau has fluid for hard contact lenses only.

Each *arrondissement* in Bamako has a police station, so you will rarely be very far from the law. The **Direction Générale de la Police Nationale** – where you should go for visa extensions (see *Chapter 2, Red tape and immigration*, pages 45–6) – is just off Avenue Kwamé N'Krumah in the quarter of ACI 2000, not far from the Pont du Roi Fahd.

MEDIA AND COMMUNICATIONS The post office (⏲ *07.30–17.30 Mon–Fri, 08.00–12.30 Sat*) occupies an impressive building on Rue Karamoko Diabi. All services, including poste restante, are available. Making telephone calls – local, national or international – is a simple procedure from the numerous *cabines téléphoniques* around Bamako, many of which also have fax and photocopy machines. Alternatively, use your Sotelma card in the public phone boxes. There are a number of Orange and Malitel branches selling mobile phones and SIM cards. The main branches, meanwhile, are in Hamdallaye just past the Centre Culturelle Islamique for Orange, and on Avenue Kasse Keita behind the Musée de Bamako for Malitel.

Within the past few years, Bamako has seen a true proliferation in the number of establishments with internet access. In some areas whole clusters of cybercafés seem to happily coexist, although at the same time some may suddenly abandon business while new ones keep popping up. A few addresses are marked on the map (see page 117). A particularly reliable one with fast connection is Said & Co, one block from the OMATHO (CFA500/hr). Without any doubt you will stumble upon plenty of others.

If you are expecting to receive mail at the American Express office in Bamako, you can find it at the travel agency called Afric Trans Service in Immeuble Babemba, at the corner of Avenue Kasse Keita and the Boulevard de l'Indépendance.

The best library in Bamako is at the **Centre Culturel Français** (*the following opening hours apply for the library only:* ⏲ *09.30–13.00 &14.30–17.30 Tue/Wed & Fri, 13.00–17.30 Thu, 09.30–17.00 Sat, closed 13.00–14.30*). They have books on Mali, as well as a wide selection of newspapers and magazines – all in French. A small stand with books and maps on Mali is in the open-air bar area. For newspapers and magazines in English, go to the **Centre Culturel Americain** (*located inside the new American Embassy in ACI 2000; ☎ 2023 65 85; ⏲ 08.30–16.30 Mon & Wed, 13.30–16.30 Thu, 08.30–11.00 Fri*). Do not expect to find books about Mali, as the centre is mainly focused on providing information on the United States to Malians. The **Centre d'Orientation et de Documentation et d'Information** or **CODI** (☎ *2023 68 13*) is located on Avenue Kasse Keita, behind the Musée de Bamako. Theoretically, this is where you can learn just about everything you ever wanted to know about Bamako's past and present. Access to the information, though, depends very much on who is around to help you. However, the notice boards, with a selection of articles and useful addresses, are always there, and so is the reading table with a selection of newspapers in French. The old historian at Bibliothèque Bakary (*Kamian Rue 98, Porte 9, Korofina Sud;* ☎ *2024 48 22*) is a wonderful place to visit with his collection to peruse at your leisure.

There's a bookshop, **Librairie Donko-Ba** (*Bibliothèque Nationale, Hamdallaye;* ☎ *2029 20 67;* e *livresbah@yahoo.fr*). Other good bookshops can be found at the Hotel Nord Sud and Hotel Salam. Ankakalan Bookstore in Niaréla sells books in French, and also maps. The area between the Mission Libanaise and Avenue de la Nation is littered with book stalls that sell a colourful amalgam of both new and secondhand books. Almost everything here, however, is in French. You can usually pick up a recent copy of *Time* or *Newsweek* from the magazine vendors around Square Lumumba. Haggle over the price.

For fairly up-to-date and detailed maps, contact the **Institut Géographique du Mali or IGM** (☎ *2020 28 40*) at nearby Hotel Les Colibris in Badalabougou Est. You can pick and choose from many maps and have a copy printed out while you wait. The **MAE** office (☎ *2023 14 65*) – for domestic flights, see pages 72–3 – is on Avenue de la Nation near the Centre Culturel Français. The **Air Mali** office (☎ *2022 24 24*) – for more domestic flights – is on Avenue Cheick Zayed in Hamdallaye.

A place very important in Malian music is **Mali K7** in Quinzambougou (☎ *2021 7508; www.mali-music.com;* ⏲ *08.00–19.00 Mon–Fri, though best to go early in the morning*). Mali K7 is associated with the late Ali Farka Touré, selling legal CDs for CFA1,600, which is the same price, if not cheaper, than the pirate copies sold on the streets. Buying direct from them at least means you know that some money is going to the musicians. They also have the recording studio opposite, Studio Bogolan, where most of Mali's stars have recorded. CDs can be bought for the same price at the CCF.

MONEY There are two BDM banks on Avenue du Fleuve, on the corner of Square Lumumba and opposite the cathedral, to change euros, US dollars and sometimes other currencies, and for Visa cash advances. The BIM branches near the railway station and the Centre Culturel Français have a Western Union office (as do many other banks), but do not deal with foreign currency. The main branch of Ecobank near the Monument de l'Indépendance also changes cash and travellers' cheques (euros and US dollars). The Bank of Africa, on Avenue de la Marne next to Hotel de l'Amitié, changes both cash and travellers' cheques in most currencies. The BHM bank on Avenue Kwamé N'Krumah, opposite the Direction Générale de la Police Nationale, changes euros only. Beware of the hefty 5% commission on travellers' cheques and Visa transactions.

Every day new cash dispensing machines are being installed in Bamako by the banks. They all take Visa cards and some of them take MasterCard, but those accepting the latter are more difficult to find. During busy periods, such as holidays and weekends, you may have to try a few before you find one with cash in it:

Downtown

$ BICIM Bd du Peuple & Hotel de L'Amitié, Av de la Marne
$ BDM Atlantic Bank & Ecobank at their main branches in Quartier du Fleuve
$ Bank of Africa At the main branch in Bozola next to the Grand Hotel

Hippodrome

$ BICIM Next to Le Byblos Nightclub

South of the river

$ BCIM Azar Libre Service Supermarket & Atlantic Bank at the Amandine Restaurant, in Badalabougou
$ BNDA Faladjé
$ BDM Sogoniko

ACI 2000

$ BNDA Main branch

Towards Koulikoro

$ BDM Korofina Nord

There are a number of exchange offices – one of them is marked on the map (see page 117) – where you can change cash at the official exchange rate, but travellers' cheques are exchanged at an adverse rate. They are so keen to change your money, that if you take their number, you can often get them to come to you and actually negotiate for a better deal. The same applies for exchanging cash or even travellers' cheques on the black market, but beware of conmen who may end up having it all, while you are left empty handed.

WHAT TO SEE

VIEWS OF BAMAKO Before doing anything else, go to **Hotel de l'Amitié**, take the lift to the 14th and top floor, and enjoy the semi-panoramic view of the northern part of Bamako, dominated by the twin minarets of the Grande Mosquée and the foothills of the Manding Mountains. While you are up here, ask to have a look at the rooms, each of which has a balcony with unobstructed views of the River Niger. This is the quickest, simplest and cheapest way to see Bamako.

For truly panoramic views, go up into the hills overlooking the city. After the zoo, Avenue de la Liberté starts to wind up to **Koulouba**, the hill on top of which perches the Presidential Palace, government ministries and several decaying colonial houses. Before you reach the top, signposts indicate a *piste touristique* – one for Koulouba and another for **Point G**, the hill next to Koulouba where Bamako's largest hospital is situated. These *pistes*, or tracks, wind around the sides of each of these hills, affording spectacular views of Bamako and, when the dust is not too thick in the air, the River Niger and beyond. There are also some **grottoes** at the foot of Point G, with rock paintings depicting hunting scenes, men, tools and animals, which date back to perhaps as early as the Palaeolithic period some three million years ago.

THE RIVER NIGER The River Niger is not at its most picturesque as it flows past Bamako, but it is a focal point of activity and as such is interesting to see. Although nowadays two proper bridges link the left and right banks of the river – **Pont des Martyrs** and **Pont du Roi Fahd** or the 'old' and 'new' bridges respectively – at one time the only way for vehicles to cross the Niger was by the **Chaussée de Sotuba** (Sotuba Causeway). Situated about 8km east of the centre of Bamako, this causeway is cut into rocks which line the riverbed and are submerged, along with the road itself, when the water is high. A couple of kilometres upstream, the **Barrage des Aigrettes** is a dam dedicated to providing the capital with hydro-electric power.

Mention of the River Niger often conjures up images of women washing clothes and children splashing about in its murky waters. This type of activity seems to be most popular on the right bank or south of the river next to Pont des Martyrs. On the same side, between the old and new bridges, **flower and vegetable gardens** are common. These are found all along the river (even in desert towns such as Gao), but in Bamako they seem to be greener and more colourful than elsewhere, and the number and variety of plants and vegetables grown is greater. Bougainvillea, poinciana, mango trees and Chinese trees with their distinctive yellow flowers are grown (and sold) in the gardens close to the British Consulate, while potatoes, onions, carrots, tomatoes, cucumbers, aubergines, beetroot, cauliflower, lettuce and other vegetables are cultivated in the small plots of land beside the river. Back on the left bank opposite the BCEAO building, women can be seen pounding and sifting *fonio*, one of Mali's staple foods (see page 82).

MUSÉE NATIONAL (*Route de Koulouba; ☎ 2022 34 86; www.mnm-mali.org; ⏲ 09.00–18.00 Tue–Sun; admission CFA2,500*) Reopened to the public in 2003 after some major renovations, Mali's national museum – situated just before the zoo – must be one of the most well-presented and informative museums in west Africa. The permanent exhibits include artefacts from almost every era of Malian history, accompanied by good written descriptions – for now only in French. Another permanent exhibition is an excellent display of a whole array of textiles, highlighting historical facts as well as details about the different materials and techniques used to make them. In addition, there is a temporary display dedicated to contemporary shows and performances. Guided tours in French are available for CFA3,000 per person. From Tuesday to Friday, films are scheduled to be shown at 10.00 and 14.00 about the history and cultures of Mali. The programme is regularly available from the Centre Culturel Français. The admission fee for the films only is CFA500, but for visitors to the museum access to the auditorium is included in the admission fee. Also on the premises is a shop selling pricey books about Malian – and African – culture, and souvenirs. Enquire about the concerts and events, scheduled for every Thursday afternoon at 17.00. These events generally attract a good number of visitors, many of them expats. The museum has a bright, modern, air-conditioned café (**$$**) on the grounds serving reasonable meals such as couscous or *capitaine* with rice and vegetables and a selection of teas and coffee.

MUSÉE DE BAMAKO (*Av de la Liberté; ⏲ 09.00–18.00 Tue–Sun; admission CFA500*) When compared with the mature National Museum, the Musée de Bamako (see *Bamako City Centre* map) is the younger stepsister that still has to get over her teething troubles. As the museum was inaugurated only in December 2003, it is forgivable that it may not yet be apparent to the public what the museum is about. Two small rooms with pictures and some artefacts are dedicated to Mali's colonial era, with the emphasis on the evolution of Bamako. Another room shows a number of ethnic artefacts, as well as reviews on saltmining and the life and culture of the Maures. To add to the confusion, the first floor is all about contemporary Malian art, with a mishmash of textiles and paintings of extremely diverse quality. It doesn't matter; this is a museum in the making and there is always the attractive garden – with some colourful, life-size animal sculptures – to be enjoyed. Services of a guide can be hired for CFA500.

MUSO KUNDA (MUSÉE DE LA FEMME) (*Route de Koulikoro;* ☎ *2024 06 73;* 🕘 *09.00–18.00 Tue–Sun; admission free*) Muso Kunda (see *Bamako Overview* map), dedicated to the women of Mali, was opened by its founder, Adame Ba Konaré, the spouse of the former president, on 8 March 1998 – International Women's Day (*muso kunda* means 'from the woman's side'). The very existence of a place like this in a country where the women do so much (see page 29) is perhaps more significant than its rather questionable merits as a museum with interesting things to see. Apart from a few statues, masks and photographs, the main exhibit is a glass cabinet full of mannequins dressed in colourful regional costumes. The museum shop sells handicrafts made by women, and there is a good restaurant serving some of the best African food in Bamako.

PARC BIOLOGIQUE (🕘 *07.00–18.30 daily; admission CFA500*) As Avenue de la Liberté winds up to Koulouba and Point G, it passes Bamako's zoo. The selection of animals is limited and, while their living conditions are certainly not ideal, they could be worse. The gazelles and warthogs seem to have the best of it, wandering about in relatively large, open spaces, while the caged animals – the monkeys, birds, etc – are worst off. A camel, a crocodile and a couple of mangy lions are the other main attractions. There is a restaurant which has cold drinks and a small menu.

ARBORETUM Turn right just before you reach the Parc Biologique for the Arboretum, a park used by many of Bamako's keep-fit enthusiasts. This is quite a nice spot for a stroll, away from the dust and noise of the centre; and if you are contemplating a visit to Mali's largest national park, the Office du Parc National de la Boucle du Baoulé is situated here. (See also page 285.)

GRANDE MOSQUÉE (*Rue Karamdro Didbi*) The Grande Mosquée (see *Bamako City Centre* map) was built by the Saudis in a style more in keeping with Mecca than Mali. Although this is not the most attractive mosque in the country, it is not as strict as others about admitting foreigners. You should not, of course, assume that you can enter as and when you like, but rather seek the necessary authorisation and then observe the appropriate etiquette once inside.

CATHEDRAL The sandstone cathedral is on Avenue du Fleuve. Services are in the evening at 18.00, which is when you should turn up if you want to have a peek inside; at most other times it is shut. Every Sunday morning at 10.00 it is possible to attend mass, which is French-spoken in the cathedral, and English-spoken in the courtyard at the mission across the street.

MARKETS Bamako's original Grand Marché (main market), affectionately known as the *Marché rose* (pink market), burned down in 1993. A new one, built in neo-Sudanese style, bears a striking resemblance to the original. The area, bounded by Rue Mohamed V to the west and Boulevard du Peuple to the east, is also almost entirely given over to commerce. It takes time and patience to walk around these streets and, while everything is probably available if you look for it, a monotonous procession of imitation brand-name clothing, shoes, bags, pots and pans is the reward for your efforts.

Behind the mosque in the Place de la République, a market specialising in **traditional medicine** has a morbid fascination. It is ultimately very sad to see animal skins, skulls of monkeys, crocodiles, warthogs and hyenas, dried chameleons and snakes and various other animals or parts of animals being sold to cure maladies or bring good luck, but it can be fascinating to see the sick and superstitious hand over a month's wages for these cures and charms, never doubting that they will work. Be warned that if you want to take photographs of the *marabouts* (witchdoctors) and their medicines, there will, in all likelihood, be a fee.

An interesting but noisy place to visit is the **recycling market** in the Marché de Médine (see *Bamako Overview* map). A group of NGOs founded a place where all the blacksmiths could work together and make as much noise as they liked in an area where they wouldn't disturb the neighbours. Wander around and see used cars and empty cans having the life battered out of them and transformed into objects for sale.

EXCURSIONS FROM BAMAKO

THE MANDING MOUNTAINS The Manding Mountains are an extension of the Fouta Djallon Highlands and stretch from the Guinean border to about 50km west of Bamako. Made up of eroded sandstone cliffs and well watered by various affluents of the country's two great rivers, the Senegal and the Niger, this is an area of striking rock formations, waterfalls and a fair amount of birdlife in the mountains and around the rivers and streams – although serious birders will prefer the Niger Inland Delta (see page 159). Furthermore, as the original home of the Malinké, whose Mali Empire was to become one of the greatest in the history of west Africa, the Manding Mountains are of considerable historical interest.

Access is obviously easiest with your own vehicle – although it's not impossible by public transport. The bus station for the Manding Mountains is the Gare Routière de Djikoroni Para (see *Chapter 2, Getting there and away*, page 114). Gare Routière de Djikoroni Para is in the far western quarter of Djikoroni. Some of the most interesting things to see are along Route de Guinea, which leads to the border town of Kourémalé. For example, there is an archaeological site at **Woyowayanko**, where there was a battle between the forces of the last west African emperor, Samory Touré (see page 255), and the French colonialists; and at **Kourounkorokalé** there are ancient grottoes and rock paintings.

SIBY The village of Siby, located 45km southwest of Bamako in Manding territory, makes a perfect day trip from the capital. It's located in a scenic area, with cliffs and rock formations to one side; Saturday is market day, when the main street is packed with people selling fruit, vegetables and the usual household items. At **La Maison de Karité** you can watch how shea butter is made, and proceeds from sales of the fair-trade butter go to a local women's collective. The **Centre Culturel Bougou Saba** arranges exchanges between local and international artists and musicians and organises local cultural events such as concerts and films. They also have a few huts available for visitors for CFA5,000, if they are not occupied by visiting artists.

The main highlights of Siby are outside the village. The natural **rock arch of Kamandjan** overlooks the village 4km south of town, and offers a beautiful view of the cliffs and plain below. A bit further, 16km down a bumpy road, is **Dièdié Waterfall**, which falls into a natural pool that is safe for swimming – but note that it is not worth visiting at the height of the dry season. You can camp on the rocks around the waterfall or in the beautiful surrounding countryside. Visiting the natural areas around Siby attracts a CFA1,000 per person visitor tax, which should be paid either to the Tourist Bureau or the *Coopérative des moniteurs d'escalade de Siby*. You will be given a receipt; the money goes to support the local community and promote tourism.

The professional, knowledgeable and friendly **Co-opérative des moniteurs d'escalade de Siby** (m *7925 66 61 or 7540 21 74;* e *coopérativesiby2004@yahoo.fr*), arranges rock-climbing and repelling trips and can organise visits to all the natural attractions in the area. Guided visits of the village cost CFA3,000 per person, to the arch CFA4,000 and the waterfall CFA5,000, all including tourist tax. Half a day's climbing costs CFA4,000 including guide, equipment and tourist tax; a full day's climbing up to the arch costs CFA8,000. Repelling and traversing excursions cost CFA6,500.

Getting there and away Transport to Siby leaves from the *gare routière* in Djikorono Para and takes about an hour (CFA1,000).

Where to stay

Campement Kuru Ninba Just at the entrance to town arriving from Bamako; m 7901 25 47. Has basic huts for CFA3,000pppn. Meals can be arranged on request.

The Hotel Kamadjan 2028 79 34/7612 90 59; e keitaconsult@yahoo.fr; www.hotelkamadjansiby.net. Located just beside the turn-off to the arch and waterfall, Kamadjan houses the *Coopérative des moniteurs*. They can also arrange visits to many of the area's attractions. An on-site restaurant offers basic, but filling Malian meals. Basic huts with mosquito net cost CFA3,000 pppn, trpls CFA7,500; huts with living room are CFA10,000.

KANGABA At the foot of the Manding Mountains, some 96km from Bamako, Kangaba is the spiritual home of the Manding people – a term used to cover a number of west African ethnic groups, including the Malinké and Bambara. It was here in 1235 that the Manding rulers signed a pact creating the Mali Empire in a clearing known as **Kouroukan-Fouga** at the town's northern entrance. However, it is the *casse sacré* (sacred house) of the Manding people, **Kamablo**, for which the town is famous. Only the *griots* (see *Chapter 1, Traditional music*, page 31) know exactly what is inside: fetishes belonging to the ancestors of the Mali Empire are most likely; ancient Islamic manuscripts from Mecca are a possibility; and, according to legend, the Kamablo also contains a sacred rock from Mecca. Every seven years, the all-knowing *griots* perform a ritual ceremony whereby the thatched roof of the sacred house is lifted on to the ground, with the help of magic verse, so that it can be cleaned and repaired.

Note that there are two roads to Guinea: one goes through the Manding Mountains, while the other runs parallel to the river. Kangaba is along the second of these two routes. (For transport, see *Chapter 2, Getting there and away*.)

KATI Kati is an important market town a few kilometres north of Bamako. The town is sprawling, unattractive and not much of a sight in itself. However, 10km further down the road in the direction of Kita, in a large, open space known as Darale, one of the largest cattle markets in the country takes place on Saturday mornings. Do not confuse this with the meat, fruit and vegetable market at Kati which takes place on Sundays.

The simplest way to get to Kati is by waiting for a *bâchée* or taxi on Avenue de la Liberté (next to the Musée National is a good place to stand). On Saturdays you should have no problem finding transport to and from Darale.

KOULIKORO

In 1977, Koulikoro became the second region of Mali. Geographically, it includes the areas of the former Bamako region such as Kangaba and Nara near the Mauritanian border, but not the city of Bamako itself. Its administrative centre is the town of Koulikoro, 57km east of the capital and, after Mopti, the country's most important river port. Indeed, the river is what brings most visitors to Koulikoro, for it is from here that the COMANAV boats leave for their weekly voyages downstream to Gao. Otherwise, Koulikoro is an industrial town dominated by Mali's largest factory, Huicoma, which processes cotton, oil and Koulikoro's famous soap. This town is more aesthetically pleasing than Mali's other factory towns, such as Koutiala and Bougouni and, as well as the river and its sandy beaches, there are some attractive colonial buildings – particularly the Commissariat de Cercle and the railway station – and a fair amount of greenery and hills to the north of the river. Indeed, the road between Bamako and Koulikoro is a good place for birdwatching. Look out for Egyptian plover, grey patincole, rock-loving cisticola and the endemic Mali firefinch.

Koulikoro sprawls over several kilometres and three distinct villages, which is important to know for transport purposes. The first *gare routière* that you reach is in Souban, some distance from Koulikoro proper (though Souban has the best hotel – see below). About 3km later comes Koulikoro Gare, the commercial and administrative centre where you should get out for COMANAV, while another 2–3km further on is Koulikoro Ba, where the descendants of the town's original inhabitants live. Minibuses and *bâchées* continue as far as the market in Koulikoro Ba; buses seem to stop at the *gare routière* in Souban. Local minibuses ply the route between the three villages, and you can hop on or off anywhere, so getting back to Souban is easy. Trains, meanwhile, carry goods but not passengers between Bamako and Koulikoro.

GETTING THERE AND AWAY

By river The COMANAV building (☎ *2126 20 95*) is on the bank of the river in Koulikoro Gare and is clearly signposted on the main road. When coming from Bamako, start looking out for it once the road has veered left past a series of factories. From August through to about the end of November, the voyage to Gao or Kabara starts every week on Tuesday evenings at about 22.00. The scheduled return from Gao is two weeks later on Sundays, while the boat from Kabara returns on Thursdays (see page 221 for more information and fares).

By road Gana du Nord has a departure point for Koulikoro between the National Museum and the Stade Modibo Keita, where buses leave at 10.00 and 17.00, take about 1.5 hours and cost CFA1,000. Minibuses and *bâchées* leave from the nearby Gare Routière du Nouveau Marché de Médine and also charge CFA1,000.

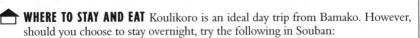

WHERE TO STAY AND EAT

Koulikoro is an ideal day trip from Bamako. However, should you choose to stay overnight, try the following in Souban:

Auberge du Niger (8 rooms) Pretty thatched place close to the river, signposted on the right on the road to Koulikoro Gare. It has 6 AC rooms with TV & 2 with fans. A nice rooftop bar/restaurant & pool. $$$

Club Le Patronat Sign on the left opposite the one for the Auberge. A local drinking den/brothel with a somewhat alarming zebra-print theme. It serves food, has some reasonable AC rooms & a couple with fans (condoms supplied…). $$

However, with the main reason to stay in Koulikoro being to catch the ferry, the most convenient accommodation is:

Maison du Jumelage Located 300m before you reach the COMANAV sign in Koulikoro Gare. Simple rooms with fan contain 3 or 4 beds. Meals can be provided if ordered in advance, or head to the Favelas bar just up the road for the standard fare of brochettes, chicken, salads & cold beer. $

Centre d'Accueil At the far end of Koulikoro Ba, Centre d'Accueil has gloomy, grubby, overpriced rooms though the big grounds with chairs beneath the mango trees are pleasant enough & it serves decent *capitaine* & cold beer. It's a long walk beyond the gare routière, though – too far to be practical. $

OTHER PRACTICALITIES

Koulikoro has basic facilities, including a post office and a bank (BDM and Western Union). Internet access is available at Cyber à la

Bibliothèque in the same grounds as the Maison du Jumelage. There is also a regional OMATHO office (☎ *2126 27 78*).

KOLOKANI AND NARA

Few travellers choose to go all the way to Nara, but remote and little-known places seem to have an irresistible appeal to the adventurous John Kupiec. He provided the following information.

Travelling from Bamako to Kolokani, just past the village of Tiorobougou, is the turning to Lac Ouénia (sometimes spelt Lac Wanga). From there, John walked the 17km towards the lake: 'You will come to a wide open space. On your left, look for a slanted, tin-covered corrugated roof. This is a chapel, part of a fenced compound and other buildings owned by the Catholic Mission.' Walk around the compound to find the lake, which John describes as 'a peaceful swimming place, tree-lined and with a few birds'.

Transport to Kolokani (CFA2,500 from Bamako) is best found on market day, which is Wednesday. There are two mosques in the market area.

Market day in Nara (CFA6,500 from Bamako) is usually on Friday and there is a mud-built mosque here. On the road leading to the market there are two places to stay: the Novotel and a *campement*.

4

Ségou

For many travellers starting their trip in Bamako, the region of Ségou will be their first taste of provincial Mali or, as the expatriate community like to say, *la brousse* ('the bush'). This is a gentle introduction, for Ségou is one of the country's richest regions and the countryside, whilst not exactly lush, is considerably more hospitable than the Sahelian and desert areas, which begin in earnest further north and east. Much of the greenery in this area is provided by the *balanzan* or shea-tree, which is typical of the region and is the symbol of its principal town, Ségou.

HISTORY

THE BAMBARA KINGDOM OF SÉGOU Much of the history of the region of Ségou is tied up with the history of the Bambara kingdom of Ségou and its two great dynasties: Coulibaly and Diarra. Before the first of these ruling families took control, however, the Bambara people, who had arrived in the region some time during the 16th century, lived in small districts under the control of the ruling Soninké aristocracy.

This remained the case until 1712, when all of the villages of the Niger Valley from Niamina (about 80km west of Ségou) to Sansanding were grouped together under the leadership of the first of the Bambara rulers of Ségou, Mamary or Biton Coulibaly, who established his court at Ségoukoro (see page 151). Biton was able to challenge and conquer the Soninké – and then gradually expand his kingdom – with the help of an extremely loyal army known as the *ton djon*. Rival Bambara clans were suppressed without mercy, and one – the Massassi – fled northwest to Kaarta, where they created a second Bambara kingdom (see page 271). By the time Biton died in 1755, a powerful kingdom under strong autocratic rule had been created to fill the void left by the decline of the Mali and Songhay empires. However, while the *ton djon* had given their allegiance to Biton, they were reluctant to accept the authority inherited by his sons, and for the next ten – generally anarchic – years the kingdom was ruled by a succession of *ton djon* chiefs, thus marking the end of the Coulibaly dynasty.

In 1766, N'Golo Diarra – a *ton djon* leader and husband of one of Biton's daughters – came to power, establishing the Diarra dynasty and restoring stability to the kingdom. N'Golo was a great warrior and an intelligent organiser, and under his leadership the Bambara kingdom continued to expand, stretching from the desert in the north to Tengréla (Côte d'Ivoire) in the south, and from Kouroussa (Guinea) in the west to Lake Débo in the east. When N'Golo died in 1787, the Diarra dynasty was continued by his sons – first Nianankoro (1787–92), then Monzon (1792–1808) – and then by a succession of Monzon's sons, beginning with Da Monzon (1808–27). Despite enjoying great military victories and presiding over a renaissance of Bambara culture, Da Monzon and the seven brothers that were to succeed him as *fama* (king) of Ségou found it increasingly

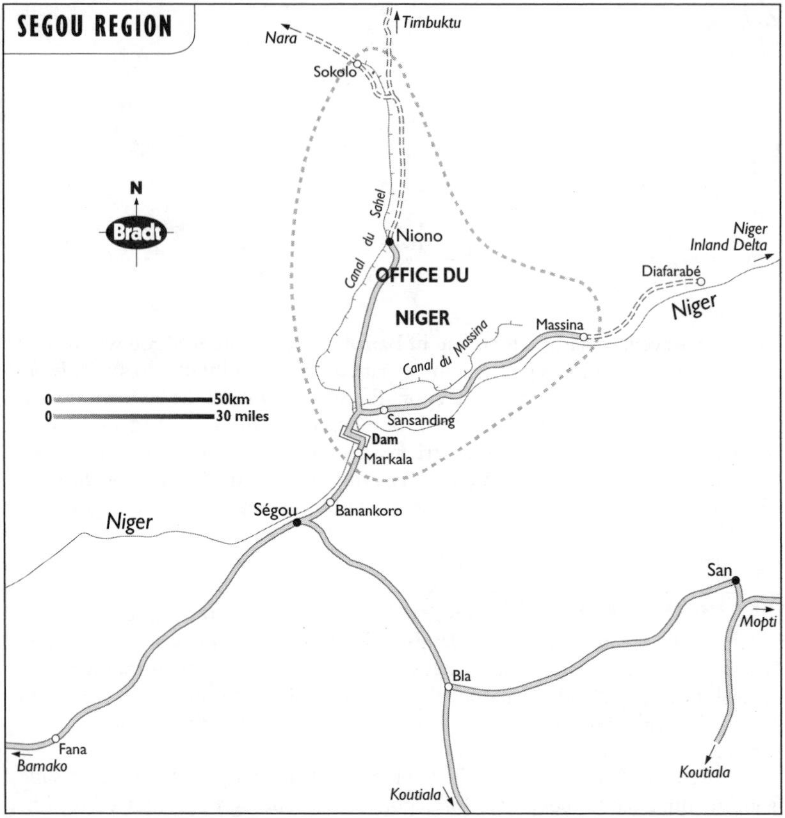

difficult to rule effectively. The kingdom had grown too large and unwieldy, making distant wars difficult and expensive to wage. There were also new enemies to fight, such as the theocratic Peul Empire of Macina to the east (see page 172) and the Tukulors from the Fouta Djallon led by El Hadj Omar Tall (see page 18).

The declining Bambara kingdom finally fell to El Hadj Omar at the Battle of Wéta on 11 March 1861, and Ségoukoro became the capital of the Ségou Tukulor Empire – part of a much larger Tukulor Empire founded in 1852. El Hadj Omar died in 1864 while fighting in Macina, leaving his son, Amadou, in charge. However, although the town of Ségou and its surroundings were under effective Tukulor control, elsewhere the Bambara remained unconquered and in rebellious mood right up until April 1890 when French colonial troops, led by Colonel Louis Archinard, took control of the region.

OFFICE DU NIGER The Office du Niger is the great legacy of colonialism in the region of Ségou. The vision of its first director-general, the French engineer Emile Bélime, was to turn deserts into farms by irrigating nearly one million hectares of a zone northeast of Ségou known as the *delta mort* (dead delta), which was once supposed to have been a major arm of the River Niger. After an initial experiment with irrigation in the form of the Sotuba Dam (completed in 1929), the Office du Niger was created in 1932 as a semi-autonomous government agency dedicated to the production of cotton and rice through extensive irrigation. To this end, a massive dam was built at Markala (see page 152) and two canals were dug to bring water to the *delta mort*. This construction work was performed by forced labour, as was the subsequent cultivation of the land. However, when forced labour in French West Africa was abolished in 1946, Office du Niger managers could no longer compel construction crews or farmers to work. Therefore, by 1946, a scheme originally intended to provide French industries with raw materials was only producing cotton for the domestic market. By 1960, a mere 60,000 of a possible 960,000ha of the *delta mort* had been irrigated; and in 1970 the Office du Niger formally abandoned its commitment to cotton, concentrating instead on the cultivation of rice and sugarcane. Two sugar refineries have been established, while experimental rice-cultivation is taking place under the supervision of Chinese experts. Only just over 10% of the total capacity of the Office du Niger has been cultivated over the last few years, as farmers complain that the levy they have to pay for the use of the land – which is owned by the Office du Niger – makes it hardly worth their while. These days, the Office du Niger continues to operate, but faces the combined problems of rising production costs and an outdated infrastructure.

SÉGOU TOWN

Ségou is the first main stop on the highway to Gao, 235km east of Bamako on the banks of the River Niger. After independence in 1960, Ségou became the capital of the country's fourth region and was widely recognised as Mali's second city. It was – and still is – a town of great economic potential, being the headquarters of the Office du Niger and several other important national industries such as Comatex (Compagnie Malienne de Textiles) and Ségou Lait (milk). However, this economic importance should not fool you into thinking that Ségou is an industrial blackspot full of factories, foul smells and smoke – because it is not. Instead, spending time here can be more pleasant than in some of Mali's other larger towns and, while it does not quite deserve the label 'tranquil', Ségou is certainly one of the least stressful places on the tourist circuit in the eastern part of the country. There is no one outstanding attraction at Ségou – like the port at Mopti or mosque at Djenné – but rather a little bit of everything: the River Niger, historical villages, colonial architecture, arts and crafts, etc. Since playing host to the annual Festival sur le Niger at the end of January, it has developed a thriving contemporary arts scene attracting artists to set up workshops and studios and hold exhibitions. The influx of visitors from the festival has boosted the town's social scene with cool new restaurants, bars and cafés opening up and an active local music scene. This makes Ségou a somewhat subtle and understated tourist town – which is precisely why it is worth visiting.

Trees – many of them *balanzans* – line either side of the main highway on the approach to Ségou from Bamako. According to legend, the town was built on a forest of *balanzans* by N'Golo Diarra, who himself used to sit under a great shea-tree (or *balanzan*) during his time as a customs officer before becoming king. The name of the town comes from Sikoro, which means 'at the foot of a *balanzan*'.

ORIENTATION Like many other towns in Mali, orientation in Ségou is a question of familiarising yourself with different quarters rather than street names, which are, in any case, largely non-existent. Visitors will spend most of their time in places like Office du Niger (where much of the colonial architecture is found), Balankoro and Sokalakono (the old quarters), and Centre Commercial (with the market and main hotels). The main drag is the highway from Bamako. The left bank of the River Niger and town centre are due north, while most of the residential quarters begin on the other side of the road. Although Ségou itself is not large, many of the interesting things to see are a few kilometres away. For example, Ségoukoro is

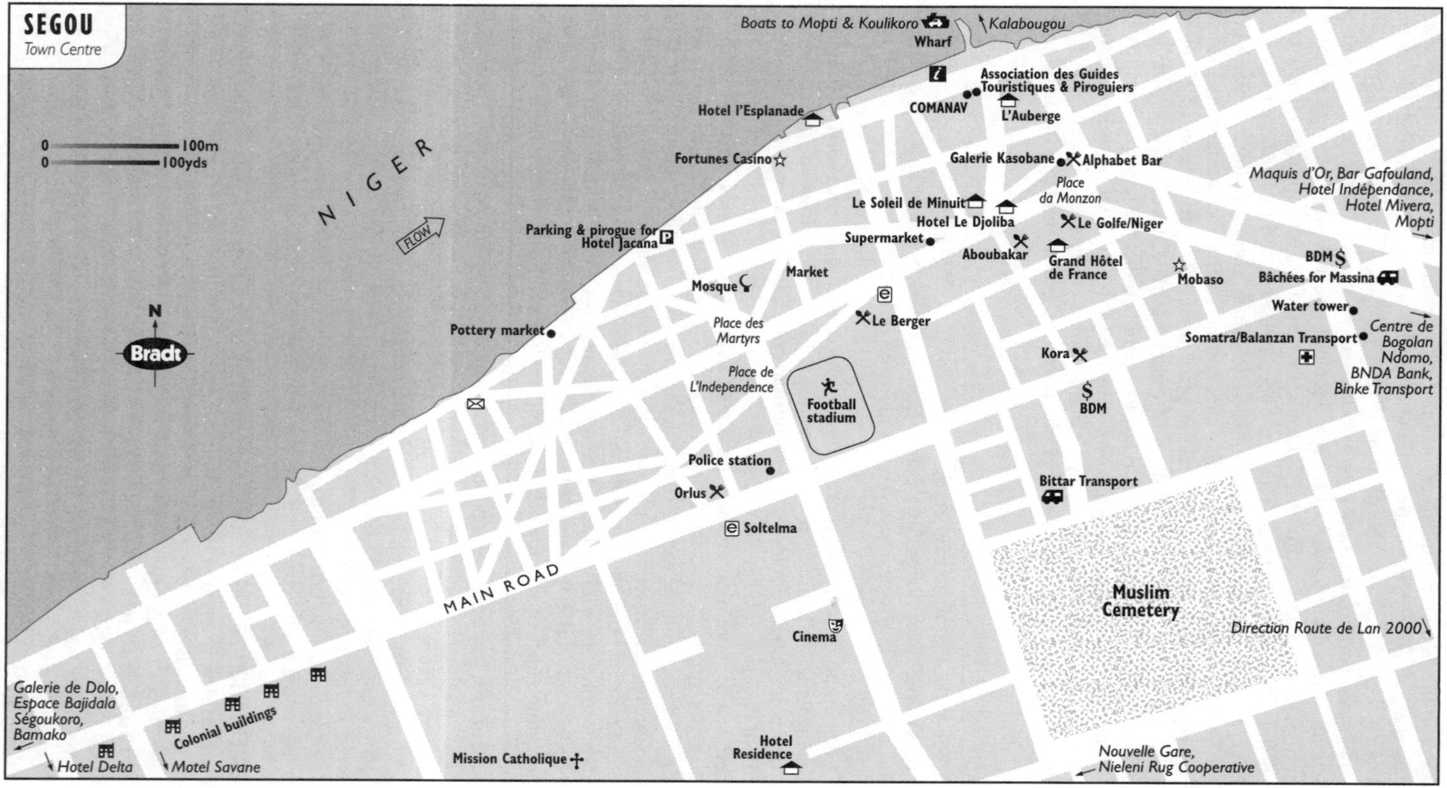
SEGOU
Town Centre
0 100m
0 100yds
N
Bradt
NIGER
FLOW
Boats to Mopti & Koulikoro
Wharf
Kalabougou
Association des Guides Touristiques & Piroguiers
COMANAV
L'Auberge
Hotel l'Esplanade
Fortunes Casino
Galerie Kasobane
Alphabet Bar
Place da Monzon
Maquis d'Or, Bar Gafouland, Hotel Indépendance, Hotel Mivera, Mopti
Le Soleil de Minuit
Hotel Le Djoliba
Le Golfe/Niger
Parking & pirogue for Hotel Jacana
Supermarket
Aboubakar
Grand Hôtel de France
Mobaso
BDM
Bâchées for Massina
Market
Mosque
Le Berger
Water tower
Pottery market
Place des Martyrs
Somatra/Balanzan Transport
Centre de Bogolan Ndomo, BNDA Bank, Binke Transport
Kora
Place de L'Independence
Football stadium
BDM
Police station
Bittar Transport
Orlus
Soltelma
MAIN ROAD
Muslim Cemetery
Cinema
Direction Route de Lan 2000
Galerie de Dolo, Espace Bajidala Ségoukoro, Bamako
Colonial buildings
Hotel Delta
Motel Savane
Mission Catholique
Hotel Residence
Nouvelle Gare, Nieleni Rug Cooperative

10km along the road to Bamako, and Kalabougou and other villages are on the right bank of the river.

GETTING THERE AND AWAY

By river The COMANAV building (☎ *2132 02 04*) is by the wharf near Hotel L'Auberge. Boats stop at Ségou on Wednesdays for Mopti, Timbuktu and Gao, and on certain Wednesdays or Saturdays for Koulikoro. (See *Chapter 2, Getting there and away* for more information and fares.) *Pinasses* ply the section of river between Ségou and Mopti, although the existence of a good road link makes the river of secondary importance as far as trade is concerned.

By road There are a number of different bus companies providing transport to and from Ségou leaving from different *gares routières* in and around town. All companies regularly service Bamako, leaving daily between 05.00 and 18.00 (3–4 hours; CFA3,000).

Somatra Balanzan leaves from the water tower at the hospital roundabout. As well as Bamako, buses leave daily for Mopti at 09.00 and around noon (6 hours; CFA5,500), Bandiagara at 21.00 on Wednesdays and Saturdays (9 hours; CFA5,000), Sikasso daily at 09.00 and Bobo Dioulasso daily at 12.30 (CFA7,500).

Bittar Transport (☎ *2132 18 54*) is the closest bus station to town situated between the hospital roundabout and the stadium. It has the most regular departures of all companies to Bamako but also departs for Sikasso at 10.00, Mopti at 11.00, 14.00 and 20.00 (6 hours; CFA5,500), Niono at 11.00, 14.00 and 19.00 (2 hours), Ouagadougou daily at 11.00 and Lomé every Saturday at 11.00.

Many of the smaller bus companies run from the *nouvelle gare*, which can be found 2km further out of town from l'Avenue de l'An 2000. Bani Transport has daily services to Bamako at 10.00, 12.30, 19.00 and 22.30 (CFA3,000), Mopti at 10.00 and 11.30, Gao at 12.00 and 15.00 and Bobo Dioulasso at 11.30. Diarra Transport has services to Bamako and Koutiala daily while Coulibaly Transport, SOGEBAF, Gana Transport and STV all depart from here.

Binké (☎ *2132 18 53*) has a station on the Rue l'An 2000 to the west of the Commisseriat of the 2nd district. Buses leave for Bamako, Mopti at 11.00 and 18.00 (6 hours; CFA5,500), Gao on Mondays and Thursdays at 08.00, (11 hours; CFA13,000), Koutiala daily at 17.00 (2–3 hours; CFA3,000) and international departures to Cotonou, on Saturday (45 hours; CFA27,500) and Niamey on Tuesday at 10.00.

TSR (m *7508 98 23*) leaves from the Boulevard de l'Indépendance before the hospital roundabout. Buses leave daily for Bamako, Mopti, Sikasso and Timbuktu at 22.00 (15 hours) Ouagadougou, Cotonou and Lomé every Wednesday and Saturday at 12.00.

Along with those larger companies, smaller 17–25-seat buses with destinations like Niono, Massina, San, Bla and Djenné (the last only on Saturdays and Sundays) leave when full from the Marché de Sougou and from the unpaved roads across the street from the Somatra/Balanzan bus yard and water tower.

TOURIST INFORMATION At the port on the quayside you will find a tourist office, offering little except a few handy leaflets. Just across from the tourist office is the museum (*admission free*). Tucked away behind the Marché Sougou is the **Office Malien du Tourisme et de l'Hôtellerie** or OMATHO (☎ *2132 24 94*) (see also page 115). The *chef de bureau* will gladly inform you about guides, festivals in the region and local history and should you run into any trouble with guides or piroguiers, he should be able to sort it out. However, as long as you use a guide carrying an official badge, you should be fine. The **Association des Guides**

TOUBAB, GIVE ME A PEN! *Jolijn Geels*

Imagine you are driving in your car on the highway, it is rush hour, and all of a sudden you get caught in slow-moving traffic: who is driving in front of that lengthy chain of cars? Who caused the traffic jam?

Now think of Mali – or Africa for that matter – and think of the chains of children sticking out empty hands, asking for pens and sweets and money and what not. Who was the first tourist who came up with the brilliant idea to teach these kids to do so?

Of course that is not how it happened; no one person is responsible for a traffic jam during rush hour, and no one tourist can be singled out and accused of turning children into beggars. However, in a country where lengthy greetings are commonplace, children are somehow allowed to get down to business straight away, with phrases like: '*Toubab*, give me a pen!' or '*Ça va? Vous avez un bonbon?*' This attitude evolved over time and it is not going to go away just like that. Unless perhaps – one can always dream – all visiting Westerners change their behaviour and start preaching new ways for children to get a gift: earn it! Do something in return and do not naturally expect foreigners to carry bags full of pens! Such a new approach would take a while to sink in, but educating people has worked before. Have some former poachers not become rangers in countries where wildlife needed protecting? Did we ourselves (read: Westerners) not need a lot of time to understand the importance of recycling waste or wearing seatbelts in a car, to name a few examples? So, theoretically, changing attitudes is possible.

Some kids – some adults, too – have become quite cunning at coaxing gifts and donations from tourists. In Ségou, for example, young boys regularly approach tourists with a convincing story of their new soccer team which is in desperate need of soccer balls, shirts and such. Could you please help the team? Any donation given is not likely to be invested in the team, though, so be cautious and try to check out similar schemes before handing over your money.

Although all of the above sounds rather discouraging, there is nothing wrong with giving as such. On the contrary: in a country like Mali, where there is no system of social security, the unfortunate, the crippled and the blind sometimes have no other

Touristiques and Piroguiers of Ségou (m *7616 29 57;* e *agtps@voila.fr; www.guidesegou.skyblog.com*) has an office next to COMONAV. They can give you a flyer with various prices for services, provide official guides or pirogues and organise visits around the region. There is a useful website with practical information on Ségou (*www.tourisme-segou.com*).

WHERE TO STAY

Mid-range $$$

Espace Bajidala Rue 529 Ségou Koura, at the exit of the Administrative Quarter; 2132 34 37; m 7631 97 99; e bajidala@aol.com; www.bajidala.com. If you don't mind being a little out of town & are a lover of art, then this is the place for you. A beautiful *banco* building with a view of the river, 2.5km from the town centre in the direction of Bamako. A well-organised gallery exhibits west African artists in peaceful gardens where they grow their own vegetables. Rooms are furnished with contemporary art & built using local materials. All AC with private bathrooms & hot water. You can eat *en famille* with the French owners for CFA5,000. Poets, writers & storytellers are welcome. Wi-Fi available.

Hotel L'Auberge (28 rooms, 2 suites) 2132 01 45; e hotelauberge@cefib.com; www.promali.org/aub-ind. This superbly located hotel is a firm favourite & run with efficiency by a couple of Lebanese brothers. All rooms are invariably clean & sometimes quite large. The hotel has a swimming pool, which is well hidden behind trees in the garden where meals are taken, so don't miss out on this small & rare luxury. AC, minibar & free Wi-Fi. Visa is accepted (not MasterCard) but there is a 6% charge. They can also change euros at a good rate. *Some cheaper rooms with fan for CFA15,000.*

Hotel D' Joliba (26 rooms) Centreville; 2132 15 72; e zarth@afribone.net.ml; www.segou-hotel-

option but to beg for food and money. As one of the pillars of Islam, giving alms is actually a matter of course. The young boys who are attending Koran-school are even dependent for food on begging; they roam the streets – a bucket or tin container in their hand – and recite Koran verses, hoping for something to fill their stomachs. In the Malian society, both these pupils and the unfortunate are genuine beggars with little choice. They rely on handouts from Malians and visitors alike: a coin, some food, or even fresh leftovers. Did you know that when you are eating out, it is totally acceptable to have your leftovers passed on to the needy? Ask for a doggy-bag (and remember that dogs in Europe or the US may well be better off than the poorest people in Mali) or empty your plate in the bucket or tin of a pupil. Although it may feel strange at first, this makes more sense than putting a pen or a sweet in the hand of an endearing nipper.

If you wish to contribute directly while you are travelling, the best way to go is through a local authority or an organised channel like a charity. A box of pens, exercise books and all the educational necessities you can think of will be of use for schools, while a women's association or a children's home will always highly appreciate a gift of clothes and substantial amounts of rice, flour, sugar, cooking oil and soap (see box on page 102). If you wish to donate something to a clinic, do not automatically assume that the leftovers from your medical kit are what is needed. In any case, local clinics should never be seen as a dumping ground for anything that is past the 'best before' date. Many clinics and hospitals, however, will gladly accept a gift of money – often they keep a record of donations – and will use it to purchase whatever meets the particular needs of the institution.

As for the chain of kids demanding a gift: I tend to ignore them most of the time, but occasionally – when I am in the right mood – I give them time and attention instead of sweets. That is hardly ever disappointing. Children may seem greedy when they take their chances as you are skimming past their lives, but spend some time with them and curiosity supersedes.

djoliba.com. Centrally located with comfortable & tastefully decorated rooms centred around a pleasant courtyard. Lovely 1st floor patio overlooking the street so you can watch comings & goings while eating dinner. Run by a German family who have been Malian residents since 2001. The bathrooms are spotless & if the AC rooms are too pricey a mattress & mosquito net on the terrace costs CFA4,000. TV & Wi-Fi. B/fast extra at CFA2,000.

Hotel l'Esplanade (40 rooms) Quartier commercial; 2132 01 27; e hotel.esplanade@hotmail.com; www.malipages.com/esplanade. Most rooms are en suite with a fan or AC, TV, fridge & phone. Some rooms have river views. There's a great bar-restaurant located on the riverbank which is perfect for sundowners. No pool yet but scheduled for 2009. B/fast inc. *Budget rooms CFA10,000.*

Hotel Indépendance (29 rooms, 4 suites) Quartier Pélenguana; 2132 04 62; e hotelindependance@cefib.com; www.promali.org/aub-ind. Located some way from the centre on the road to Mopti, you can't miss it thanks to the life-size giraffe in the garden. Same owners as L'Auberge & same prices. Wi-Fi & swimming pool.

Hotel Le Jacana Over the Niger from Ségou; m 6671 10 90/6672 00 53; e infos@mali-safaris.com; www.mali-safaris.com. A little piece of paradise on the banks of the river. Access via pirogue free to residents – there's an office on the riverside just along from Hotel L'Esplanade. The boat trip takes 15–20mins. Accommodation is in pretty, self-contained thatched huts with *bogolan*-style curtains & hot water. 9 have AC, 7 have fan, all have double beds & there is 1 family hut with an extra double bunk at no extra cost. The sitting area/restaurant is a lovely thatched affair overlooking the river. A 3-course dinner is CFA7,500. Pirogue trips, etc, can be arranged. Great spot for birding.

Motel Savane Quartier Administrative, 2km from the centre, off the Bamako road; 2132 09 74; e savane@motelsavane.com; www.motelsavane.com.The friendly service at this Dutch/Malian-run hotel coupled with its quiet location in the old colonial district close to the river may make it worth the walk into town. If not, a taxi driver can always take you there for CFA500. Accommodation is in thatched huts. Self-contained rooms are well maintained, comfortable & clean with TV & either AC or fan. Alternatively, you can camp or take a bed in the dorm. Bikes are available to hire for CFA1,500/day. Hot water available. *Dorm beds CFA3,000.*

Budget $$

Galerie de Dolo (2 rooms) m 7608 71 72. Adjoining Espace Bajidala in Ségou Koura, the Malian sculptor Amahigueré Dolo is building 2 simple rooms above his studio with great views over the river that he will rent out as an artists' residence or guesthouse. A taxi driver will know how to get there. Prices have not yet been set but are expected to be more towards the budget end of the scale

Hotel Delta (14 AC, 4 fan rooms) 2132 02 72. Just after the turning for the Hotel Savana, this hotel (also known as Campement de l'Office du Niger) is set in spacious grounds typical of the Office du Niger *quartier*. There are perfectly adequate AC rooms with TV, but the little white huts with fan are nicer & cheaper. This is a good place to camp if you have your own vehicle (CFA3,000–3,500) – there's a nice spot under the trees.

Hotel Residence Down the road that faces the police station & on the left; 2132 22 20; m 7649 43 16; e residencesegou@yahoo.fr; http://residence.segou.net. Formerly the Kaarta, now fully renovated. The spotless (if rather functional) rooms vary in size rather than facilities – all have AC & TV. Possibly the best value close to town. B/fast extra at CFA1,000.

Le Soleil de Minuit (5 rooms) At the top of the road leading to the wharf; m 7614 04 32. A few simple rooms above this popular restaurant in the centre of town. Self contained & very clean, some toilets even have seats – a rarity in budget priced hotels. Hot water & fans. *Camping or sleeping on the terrace CFA 4,000.*

Motel Mivera (15 rooms) 2132 03 31. Also a fair hike from town, at the crossroads for Mopti-Niono. There is nothing wrong with this hotel except that it is too far from the centre to be practical for those without their own transport.

Shoestring $

Grand Hotel de France (18 rooms) Centre commerciale; 2132 03 15. Centrally located, friendly & good value. Rooms have a fan & mosquito net but are in a pretty bad state. However, there is free transport to the bus station – not that it is very far to walk. If you are lucky, you might meet the 'Grand Griot', the big, jovial owner who occasionally gives music concerts in the hotel courtyard.

Maquis D'Or Hamdallay. More of a bar than a guesthouse, you get what you pay for here – very cheap & very basic rooms, normally rented by the hour. There is a sign on the main road indicating its location.

Mission Catholique (3 AC, 24 fan rooms & 5 dorms with 8 beds) 2132 04 17. This place is set up for travellers. The compound is designed like cloisters with many different types of rooms. Some have internal bathrooms. Situated in a quiet neighbourhood where you can find local bars & millet beer.

WHERE TO EAT Outside the hotels, most of which have restaurants serving the usual range of international cuisine, there are several good restaurants in town.

Mid-range $$$

Alphabet Bar Rue 17, Porte 172; m 6676 20 97; e baru_oumar@yahoo.fr; 12.00–15.00 & 18.00–02.00 Mon–Sat. African cuisine with a European/Asian twist, or as the amiable owner, Oumar, likes to describe it, 'world' cooking. *Capitaine*, chicken, etc all creatively presented as you eat in the courtyard amongst the trees. Everything in the restaurant is made locally except the glasses & the forks. Even the plates are Ségou pottery. There is an art gallery for exhibitions & music from regional groups, normally at the weekend.

Hotel L'Auberge 06.30–22.00. Of all the hotel restaurants, this is the most pleasant. The food is well prepared & there are some Lebanese dishes on the menu, but the real draw is the lush garden, which is cool during the day & peaceful in the evenings. There is also a wood-fired pizza oven & great chocolate mousse.

Hotel l'Esplanade 11.00–15.00 & 18.00–22.00. The hotel restaurant was taken on by the Italian chefs from Pizza la Guindo in Bamako. Serves great pasta & other Italian food such as pizza, antipasti, bruchetta, gnocchi, etc. You can eat on the banks of the Niger, as long as the 2 caged crocodiles (who have been there for 15 years) don't put you off your food. Don't forget the mozzie spray.

Cheap and cheerful $$

✕ **Hotel Le Djoliba** ⌚ 11.30–14.30 & 18.30–22.00. On Sat evenings, enjoy some live music while you wait for your pizza to be baked in the furnace on the 1st-floor terrace. Other dishes are created according to the local market & seasons. *Capitaine*, pasta, meat, salads, etc.

✕ **Kora Restaurant** ☎ 2132 09 50; ⌚ 08.00–01.00 Mon–Thu, 08.00–03.00 Fri–Sat. A mixed European & African menu served in a beautiful courtyard, often with live music on a Fri/Sat night. Typical fish, chicken & meat dishes.. A very agreeable atmosphere in which to have dinner.

✕ **Restaurant Le Soleil de Minuit** ☎ 2132 15 05; ⌚ 06.30–midnight. Plenty of tasty *capitaine* dishes (see box *The capitaine's table*, page 83). A great terrace for a drink & some people-watching during the day, especially during the Festival sur le Niger. In the evening there is often local music.

Rock bottom $

✕ **Le Berger** ⌚ 07.30–midnight. Near the market, this place has friendly staff & is good for salads, breakfasts & the standard rice, fish & meat dishes.

✕ **Restaurant Le Golfe** (also known as **Le Niger**) by the roundabout in Pl Da Monzon; m 6682 42 99; ⌚ 07.30–midnight. A cheaper restaurant with a more Malian feel; *hamburgers à cheval* (a beef hamburger with an egg on top) & good breakfasts.

✕ **Restaurant Orlus** Opposite Sotelma's cybercafé; ⌚ 07.30–midnight. A small restaurant serving cheap, tasty meals.

An enterprising young ex-chef from Hotel D'Joliba by the name of Aboubakar has set up a little open-air bar-restaurant down a side street towards the Grand Hotel de France. The food is great and so is his attitude. He serves an omelette breakfast for CFA1,000, a different Malian dish each lunchtime and a greater choice at night. Excellent pizzas are CFA3,000. There are one or two other restaurants in Ségou around the bus yards and on the road to Mopti, but these are probably only worth a visit if you happen to be passing. The market and various small grocery stores sell basic foodstuffs and bottled water. There is a supermarket, Chez Tony, just across from Soleil de Minuit.

ENTERTAINMENT AND NIGHTLIFE Just off the main road, Ségou's cinema specialises in violent Indian and Oriental films and pornography (⌚ *once a month; entrance CFA300*). If you are in Mali during the football season, matches are played at the weekends on real grass at the smart stadium in the centre of town.

For a sunset drink, the Hotel l'Esplanade is the place to go for aperitifs in the bar beside the river. The popular garden or the air-conditioned bar at the entrance of Hotel L'Auberge is a good alternative, serving sprits and Grand Castel (CFA1,200).

Many of Ségou's bars and restaurants have live music, especially at the weekends. You can choose from the following, though it's best to check with venues as timetables change:

☆ **Alphabet Bar** Sat/Sun & during the festival (see below)
☆ **Bar Gafou Land** Pelengana, 500m opposite the Hotel Indépendance; Fri/Sat or on demand
☆ **Bar Java** Just north of the Mission Catholique; Thu–Sun
☆ **Kora** Fri/Sat night
☆ **Mabaso Garden** Mon–Wed
☆ **Restaurant du Golfe/Niger** 19.00–23.00 Tue & Fri
☆ **Soleil de Minuit** During the festival & on demand

Balafon performances can also be arranged at your hotel, if not offered already.

For those up for a late-night drink, the **Alphabet Bar** (⌚ *until 02.00*) is the place to go. It is the owner, Oumar, who makes this place. Born in Mali but raised in Côte d'Ivoire, he returned when the war started to set up the bar. It's smart and trendy with lots of style and a real locals' hangout. You know you've made it if he asks you to sign the bar. You could find a quiet night with chilled conversation and Oumar spinning his favourite tunes or stumble across a crazy one with dancing on the bar and salsa-ing across the courtyard.

LE FESTIVAL SUR LE NIGER

Suzanne Porter

The Festival sur le Niger takes place at the end of January. It's a town-based festival, close to amenities and due to its proximity many locals make the short three-hour journey from Bamako to enjoy three days of festivities.

Most of the action is concentrated around the waterfront. During the day there are numerous activities including puppet shows, traditional music, artisans' market, storytelling, and racing in traditional dug-out canoes. It's a very cultural town so apart from music you also find art exhibitions and private photography viewings. At night, the stagelights reflect on the river.

Though just as chaotic as it's desert rival, the Festival in Ségou is better funded and the line up of Malian musicians is impressive – a must for World music fans. In 2008 Habib Koité, Salif Keita, Abdoulaye Diabaté and Bassekou Kouyate all performed.

Most restaurants also have live performances and the packed bars and clubs stay open until dawn. Tickets cost €100 for the three days. See the Festival website for more details: www.festivalsegou.org.

The **Mobaso Nightclub**, on the road linking Place Da Monzon to the main highway, is only open at weekends when there is sometimes live music on Friday, Saturday and Sunday. During the festival every night is packed, otherwise it's Saturday night that's party night.

There is also a **Fortunes Casino** down on the waterfront by the Hotel l'Esplanade.

SHOPPING With the cotton-producing Office du Niger within a stone's throw, it is no wonder that various cotton-processing businesses have been established in Ségou. Two eye-catching *galeries* opposite the Hotel l'Auberge show some fine examples of *bogolans* that were manufactured in their respective workshops, both of which can be visited. The **Soroble Centre** is in the Sokalakono quarter next to the Collège Moderne; the other one is just out of town past the Carrefour Markala. Impossible to overlook, the workshop of artist Doumbia at **Centre de Textile Ndomo** is built in the same style as his associated Galérie Kasobané.

The **Club des Mères de Bougoufiè** (*Rue 210, no 579, not far off Av Biton Coulibaly;* ☎ *2132 16 33*) is their more idealistic counterpart. What started as a programme to combat illiteracy gradually evolved into an association of women joining forces to improve their standard of living. Most of their activities include the processing of cotton fabric in some form or another, and their products (*bogolans*, clothes, soft toys and more) are sold directly from the workshop. These Mères de Bougoufiè are a jolly bunch of women who welcome visitors.

The **Nieleni rug** women's co-operative was established in 1923. Heavy hand-knotted wool rugs with Malian designs are made and it is open to tourists who can watch the women in action.

If you take a trip to **Galerie de Dolo** in Ségou Koura village you may be lucky to find the Malian sculptor Amahigueré Dolo at work and see some of his finished exhibits. Phone ahead to check he's home (m *7608 71 72*). In the same area, there is also a female artisans' workshop boutique.

OTHER PRACTICALITIES Most of Ségou's public buildings are along the main highway. The notable exception is the post office, which is rather out of the way by the river at the western end of town. To send postcards and small letters, the postbox at the Hotel l'Auberge is perhaps more convenient; they also sell stamps. There are three banks. BDM has a Western Union branch and does Visa cash advances. BNDA (at Carrefour Markala, the crossroads for Niono) is supposed to take cash and travellers' cheques in euros and US dollars but it is not always possible. BHM takes no foreign currency at all. The best place to change euros and US dollars is at the Hotel L'Auberge. There are several internet cafés in the centre of town charging CFA400 for half an hour but the connections are slow. Sotelma, Sotelma's internet (CFA1,000 per hour) and the police station are all close to each other on the main highway. The hospital is opposite the Somatra/Balanzan bus yard.

WHAT TO SEE Ségou's main attractions are a short distance from the town itself (see *Excursions from Ségou* below).

Since Ségou was the headquarters of the Office du Niger, the French spent a lot of time there during the colonial occupation. Today, government ministries occupy most of the **colonial buildings** along the main road in the western part of town. Nearby, at the Mission Catholique, there is a large church, while in the side streets behind the church you can watch millet beer being made. Ask for directions when you arrive at the church. In the same vicinity (ie: south of the main highway), there is a large **Muslim cemetery** where piles of stones define each grave.

If you arrive in Ségou on a Monday, check out the market. Although the port is not the hive of activity it is at Mopti, for example, a walk along the **River Niger** is a good way to while away the time. Working your way west from the port, you'll see a **pottery market**, **vegetable gardens** and **pirogue-makers**. In the evening – perhaps after dinner at the Hotel L'Auberge – walk down to the **wharf** and enjoy the stars and the silence.

EXCURSIONS FROM SÉGOU

SÉGOUKORO Today, Ségoukoro (old Ségou) is a small village 10km from Ségou along the road to Bamako. In the 18th century, it was from here that the Bambara kings ruled a kingdom which stretched for thousands of kilometres across west Africa. The tomb of the founder of this kingdom, Biton Coulibaly (1712–55), is still in the village, along with three mosques, one built by Coulibaly for his Islamic mother, Ba Sounou Sacko – the king himself was animist. Guides will routinely show you the tomb and mosques, but also take time to explore the village itself – the Sudanese architecture, granaries and activity down by the river.

There are two ways to get to Ségoukoro: by river or by road. Pirogues can be arranged through **Savane Tours** in the administrative quarter (*t 2132 18 04; e savane@savanetours.com; www.savanetours.com*); or with the guides outside the Hotel L'Auberge for about CFA25,000. *Bâchées* do not venture out of Ségou, so you must take a taxi or walk to Ségoukoro. Guides, it seems, are obligatory. Upon arrival, you will be taken to the chief – a descendant of King Coulibaly – who levies a CFA2,500 tax to visit the village. This permits you to ask him questions about the village and take photographs.

The government has embarked on a programme of restoration and development in Ségoukoro aimed at emulating the achievements of Songo in Dogon country (see page 207). In addition to the renovation of the village's historical monuments, there are plans to open places for tourists to spend the night and promote arts and crafts in the area.

KALABOUGOU Kalabougou is on the other side of the river about 45 minutes by pirogue from Ségou, roughly northeast as the crow flies. This village produces much of the pottery for which Ségou is renowned. During the week, women are preoccupied with moulding and shaping the pottery, while at the weekends the furnaces are lit. Men traditionally forge iron, although they do not seem to work as regularly as the women.

Privately arranged pirogues to Kalabougou cost around CFA20,000 – a little more if a guide is included. Find the village chief when you arrive and introduce yourself; be prepared to pay a visitors' tax.

BOZO FISHING VILLAGE The village on the other side of the river visible from the wharf at Ségou is a small settlement of Bozo fishermen. This is a shorter excursion and, unlike at Ségoukoro and Kalabougou, there is a public pirogue costing CFA150 which leaves when full from beside the wharf.

BETWEEN SEGOU AND NIONO

Much of the land between Ségou and Niono is Office du Niger country, and the paved road between these two towns is testament to the area's economic importance. It also facilitates relatively quick and easy travel in the central part of the region. Continuing north from Niono, however, is rather more arduous.

BANANKORO Banankoro was the village administered by Da Monzon before he became the Bambara ruler in 1808: now it is his final resting place. Apart from the king's tomb, Banankoro is no more spectacular or pretty than other villages around Ségou.

As the first settlement on the road to Niono, the best way to get to Banankoro is by taking a bus bound for Niono. The village is about 9km from Ségou. As always, introduce yourself to the village chief before wandering about.

MARKALA AND MASSINA About 40km from Ségou, a bridge crosses the River Niger at the town of Markala. This bridge and a 2,600m-long dam, the **Barrage de Markala**, were constructed between 1933 and 1949 as the central nervous system of the Office du Niger's hydrologic machinery. The idea was to raise the level of the water in the Niger to such a point that it would overflow into two manmade canals with raised dykes along their banks, thus irrigating, but not flooding, the *delta mort*. One of these canals, the **Canal du Sahel**, branches off towards Niono in the north, while the other, the **Canal du Massina**, passes Sansanding and continues eastward in the direction of Massina.

This impressive dam is not the only reason to visit Markala. The **Festival des Masques et des Marionnettes (Fesmamas)** takes place in March and is one of the largest of its kind in Mali. Invented by the Bozo and traditionally performed by groups of young people, the *Théâtre des Marionnettes* usually takes the form of dances in human or animal costumes endowed with some historic or symbolic meaning. Although the dancing at Markala is well reputed, these festivals also take place in other Bozo areas.

There is accommodation at Markala. Try the **Centre d'Accueil 'Le Cacao'** (☎ *2134 20 43*) or **Hotel Campement Emile Bélime** just before the bridge.

Since the road is now tarred all the way, **Massina** is easily accessible by public transport (see *Chapter 2, Getting there and away*). It is also possible, though, to travel to and from Massina by pirogue on the River Niger. On Independence Day (22 September), Massina stages masked dances and *concours de pirogues* (pirogue races) take place on the river. For more information on this event, contact the OMATHO office in Ségou. A *campement* provides basic accommodation in Massina.

While sailing to Mopti by pirogue – count on two days – you pass **Diafarabé**, which is the scene of the most important cattle crossing in Mali. It is said that hippos reside along this stretch of the river.

For more information on both Fesmamas in Markala and the cattle crossing in Diafarabé, see *Chapter 2*, *Festivals*, pages 88–9.

NIONO

The paved road becomes increasingly pot-hole-ridden as it approaches its terminus at Niono. Beyond here, there are only sandy tracks across the Sahel.

The town of Niono is well worth a visit. The bulk of the Office du Niger's rice cultivation takes place here, which makes it one of the most important economic centres in the region and, as a result, not an obvious port of call for tourists. However, there is a famous mosque and a canal in town, although descriptions of Niono as 'the Malian Venice' should be taken with a shovelful of salt.

GETTING THERE AND AWAY Some bus companies have regular services linking Bamako and Niono (CFA3,500). Bittar Transport, for example, leaves daily at 08.00, 10.00, 12.00 and 16.00 from the *gare routière* in Sogoninko, Bamako (see *Chapter 3*, *Getting there and away*). It is quite feasible – and perhaps preferable – to visit Niono as a day trip from Ségou. The journey takes about two hours and costs CFA1,500.

All buses leave Niono from the small yard which serves as the town's *gare routière*. As well as returning to Ségou, you might also be able to travel to Timbuktu from Niono via Léré, Niafounké and Goundam. No-one in town will commit themselves to stating a precise time, but vehicles seem to make the journey once a week when there is sufficient demand. The route north of Niono is a track, so journey times are subject to wide fluctuations according to the season and the condition of the road.

WHERE TO STAY AND EAT

Hotel Niono and Centre d'Accueil 1km from the mosque along the road leading out of town, opposite the police station; 2135 21 58. Perfectly acceptable for a short stay. The simplest rooms have fans & mosquito nets. You pay a little more for AC. There is also a restaurant & bar – which is fortunate given the lack of similar facilities in town. $

CEFE About 3km from the Hotel Niono not far off the road to Molodo. Dorm beds cost CFA2,500, while private rooms & food are also available. $

OTHER PRACTICALITIES Between the mosque and *campement* are a post office, two banks and the aforementioned police station.

WHAT TO SEE Use the bus yard as your main point of reference. Turn right out of the main entrance, walk along the paved road until you reach the Total service station, and on your left is Niono's main attraction, the **Mosquée du Vendredi** (Friday Mosque). In 1983, this structure won first prize in an international Islamic architecture competition, and it remains one of the most noteworthy mosques in Mali today. You should not enter without permission, but the building's design allows you to peer inside without actually going in. The **Canal du Sahel** is behind the bus yard. On the other side of this long stretch of water – which is the most pleasant place for a walk – are the **rice paddies** of the Office du Niger. 'I started to walk along the canal from Niono to Sokolo. It was a beautiful day and by walking on the dyke itself I was able to view the rice fields and activities on the other side; the canal itself; the road to my right, along with villages and mosques; and the layout of compounds of the villages and the people inside them.' (John Kupiec).

About 50km further north the canal peters out and the Sahel begins in earnest. This is where **Sokolo**, the town made famous by the film *La vie sur terre* (see page 39), is situated.

BETWEEN SÉGOU AND SAN

One-and-a-half hours from Ségou, you'll reach one of Mali's first eco hotels, the **Teriya Bugu**, or the 'hut of friendship' as it's known in the Bamanan language (*2132 00 30;* **m** *6669 96 86;* **e** *info@tb-mali.com; www.tb-mali.com; dorm beds CFA5,000; $$$*). Situated on the banks of the River Bani, surrounded by more than 200,000 eucalyptus, frangipani, and coconut trees, the 20 spacious, en-suite rooms with either air-conditioning or ceiling fan, provide water warmed by solar energy while the restaurant serves food made from fresh farm produce. There's a large swimming pool to relax in or you can take a tour of the area with a local guide. Profits from the hotel support the neighbouring villages, providing employment, schools and clinics. To get there, either land your private jet on the approved runway (not so eco!) or for simpler folk, turn off the tar road after Bla and the camp is 30km along a rough track. For more details see box page 80.

SAN

There is little else in the region to detain the visitor for very long. The main highway continues southeast from Ségou for about 80km to the town of **Bla**, which is one of the larger settlements in the region and a crossroads for traffic continuing south towards Koutiala and east towards Mopti (213km). If you're looking to eat or drink, it is hit or miss whether you'll find anything in Bla. There can be times when the fridges are bare and even finding a warm Coke in town is mission impossible. This region is of mixed religion so do not be surprised to see the odd pig wandering around and if you're lucky enough to find food, it could well be pork.

A further 111km from Bla along the road to Mopti, San is possibly worth a short visit. Few tourists stop here for more than lunch, which makes it relatively free from the tourist-induced hassles of nearby Djenné, Mopti and, to a lesser extent, Ségou. On the other hand, San is not as attractive as its more illustrious neighbours and there is less to see and do. With many buildings under construction, the outskirts of San lack any sort of grace, and sadly the whole town is littered with waste and plastic bags. However, the centre of town is pleasantly lively, especially on market day (Monday).

GETTING THERE AND AWAY All big bus companies running between Bamako and Mopti stop at San at their respective bus yards; and there are many. However, buses are usually full since San is not a major destination. Certain companies, like Bittar Transport, sometimes reserve a number of seats to be filled by passengers leaving from San. As they are sold on a first-come-first-served basis, you may be in for a long wait, even though buses will be passing through at regular intervals.

Reporting time for Bittar buses to Ségou (CFA2,500) and Bamako (CFA5,000) are 10.00, 13.00 and 18.00, while the times for Mopti (CFA2,500) are 14.00, 16.30, 22.00 and 01.00. A regular Bittar service to Koutiala (CFA2,500) and Sikasso (CFA5,000) leaves from Restaurant Bon Coin. Like Bittar, Bani Transport also has buses driving all the way to Gao (CFA8,500), scheduled to leave at 14.00 and 17.00. You can catch the Djenné bus as it returns from Bamako on Tuesdays and Fridays (CFA2,500).

Bâchées and small buses with the same destinations leave when full from the bus yard in the centre of town next to the *campement*. For direct transport to Bobo-Dioulasso (CFA5,000), check with Satime at the same bus yard. On certain days of the week, especially on Monday which is market day at both ends, you may find *bâchées* going directly to Djenné. Alternatively, take a *bâchée* bound for Mopti and get off at Carrefour Djenné, from where you should be able to find an ongoing *bâchée*.

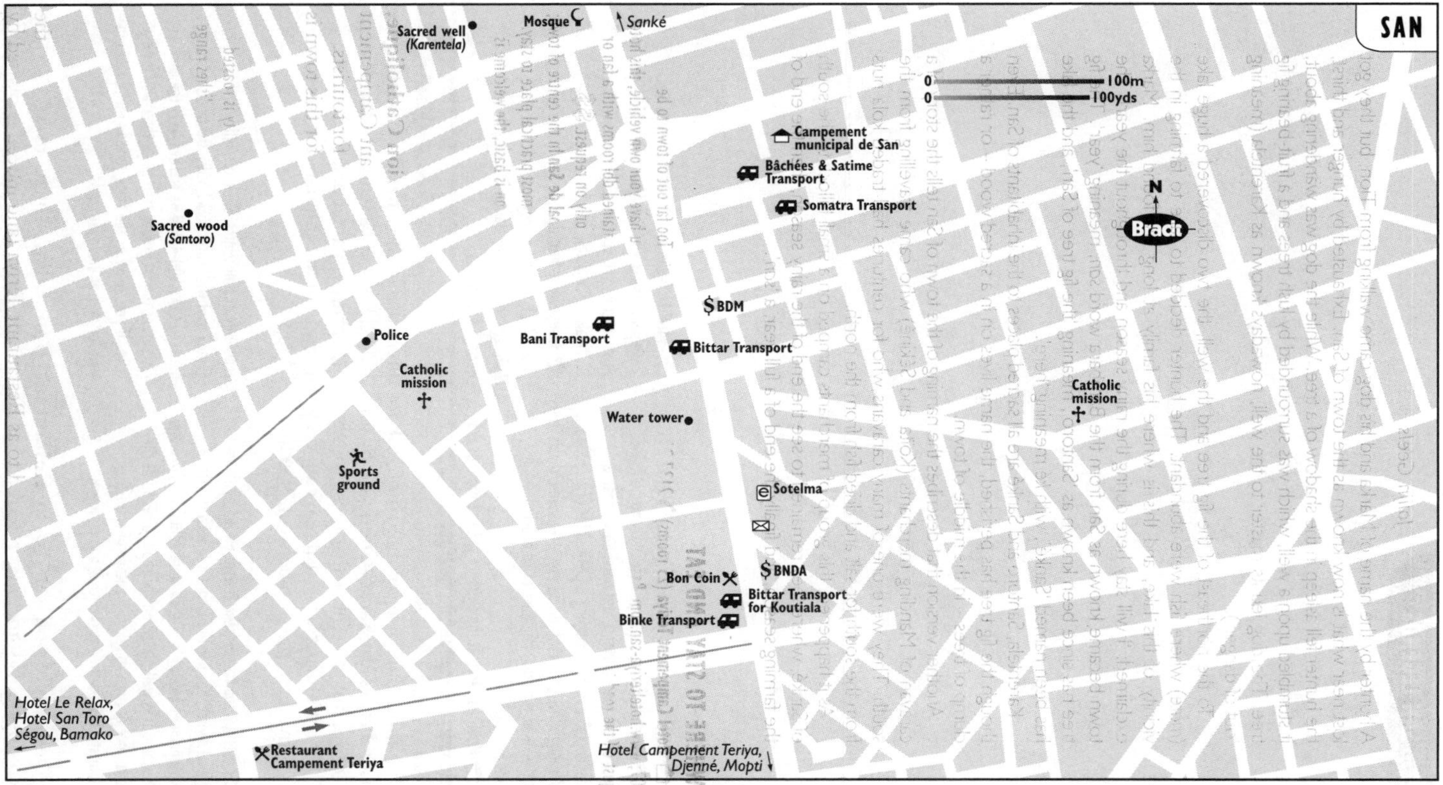
SAN
0 100m
0 100yds
N
Sacred well
(Karentela)
Mosque
Sanké
Sacred wood
(Santoro)
Campement municipal de San
Bâchées & Satime Transport
Somatra Transport
$BDM
Bani Transport
Bittar Transport
Police
Catholic mission
Water tower
Catholic mission
Sports ground
Sotelma
$BNDA
Bon Coin
Bittar Transport for Koutiala
Binke Transport
Hotel Le Relax,
Hotel San Toro
Ségou, Bamako
Restaurant Campement Teriya
Hotel Campement Teriya,
Djenné, Mopti

SAN LEGENDS

Jolijn Geels

A hunter by the name of Marka and his dog came walking from Tion, but they got lost near what is now known as the town of San. Exhausted by hunger and thirst, the hunter fell asleep in the shadow of a tree. While the dog was wandering about, it stumbled upon a well, which was surrounded by lush trees and a fruit-bearing fig tree. The dog led its master to the well, nowadays known as Karentela (meaning 'out of danger').

To the northeast of the fig tree and the well, the two discovered a huge lake (*mare*) where fish were abundant. The hunter decided to take to farming in the vicinity of this lake, and this is where his family at long last found him. Marka exclaimed: 'I will stay here during the rainy season and throughout the year!' The town became known as San from the Bambara word *san*, meaning 'year'. The fig tree has since been known as 'Santoro', meaning 'the fig tree of San', and the lake has been named 'Sanké', with *ké* meaning 'here'.

Karentela, Santoro and Sanké are all sacred places to the inhabitants of San. Even though the fig tree has perished, the name lives on in a sacred wood – or rather a clump of trees – in the middle of town.

Another version that describes the naming of the town of San tells the story of a caravan of Manding merchants (Koïta and Sékiné) who came travelling from the south. They were one of many caravans who for centuries had traded kola nuts from the south for salt and dried fish from the north.

As it happened, this group of merchants camped on a small hillock to the south of Sanké, where they remained to see the end of the rainy season, then the end of the farming season, and finally the end of a full year, a '*san*'.

WHERE TO STAY AND EAT

Hotel Campement Teriya (25 rooms) 2137 21 07; www.hotelteriya-san.com. Recently renovated and just off the road to Mopti, this hotel offers clean & comfortable rooms. Camping is allowed for CFA2,500pp. Although the restaurant has an extensive menu, meals other than the usual fare have to be ordered well in advance. $$$

Hotel San Toro At the entrance to San from Bamako, this smart newly opened hotel has AC rooms. $$$

Hotel Le Relax Too far out of town to be convenient, unless you have your own vehicle, this hotel offers spacious self-contained dbl rooms with a fan or AC. Meals are available only on request. $$

Campement Municipal de San In the centre of town; 2137 21 15. This is the most practical place to stay. Although the accommodation is basic, the welcome is warm & friendly. $

For more budget accommodation, ask for directions to the **Mission Catholique, Les Frères du Sacré-Coeur de San** (*2137 21 85*) at Restaurant Campement Teriya, but remember that these rooms are not primarily intended for tourists.

Most tourists who visit San stop only long enough to eat lunch, for this town is a convenient pit-stop between Bamako and Mopti.

Restaurant Campement Teriya (owned by the same jovial owner, but not to be confused with the Hotel Campement Teriya) 06.00–midnight. This 90-seater restaurant is well placed on the road to Ségou at the entrance of town to take advantage of transiting tourists. It has efficient service & a good menu, especially at lunchtimes. Their speciality is roasted guinea fowl with chips (CFA2,500). Other dishes range between CFA3,500-4,000 Be warned, it is the only restaurant tourist groups stop at on their way through town. If you arrive at the same time as them, you can wait for over an hour for food. $$

Alternatively you can go to **Restaurant Bon Coin**, which, to add to the confusion, is sometimes referred to as Restaurant Teriya (and indeed is owned by the same person). The chicken and some other dishes are cooked in the same kitchen as Restaurant Campement Teriya and brought over. They are basic but very tasty and around lunchtime buses often stop here.

Anywhere else, restaurants are of the soup kitchen variety.

OTHER PRACTICALITIES The post office and BNDA bank are both near Restaurant Bon Coin. The BDM bank in the centre of town does not change foreign currency, but it has a Western Union branch. In the not-too-distant future, you may find internet connections at the Restaurant Campement Teriya.

WHAT TO SEE A sacred well, a sacred wood and a sacred lake (see box *San legends* opposite) are there to be seen to this day, though the well is now walled in. Ask the family across the road for the key. Suffice it to say that these are the main attractions in an otherwise rather ordinary town.

However, if you happen to be here in the seventh lunar month of the year, the Sankémon is a festival of celebration which takes place by the sacred lake and involves offerings, incantations and a lot of fishing.

The traders at the market in Bamako specialising in traditional medicine (see page 136) speak of a *marabout* in San who can prepare an irresistible love potion which, once administered, will induce its taker to fall in love with the first person she or he sees. Despite my best efforts, however, I failed to find him.

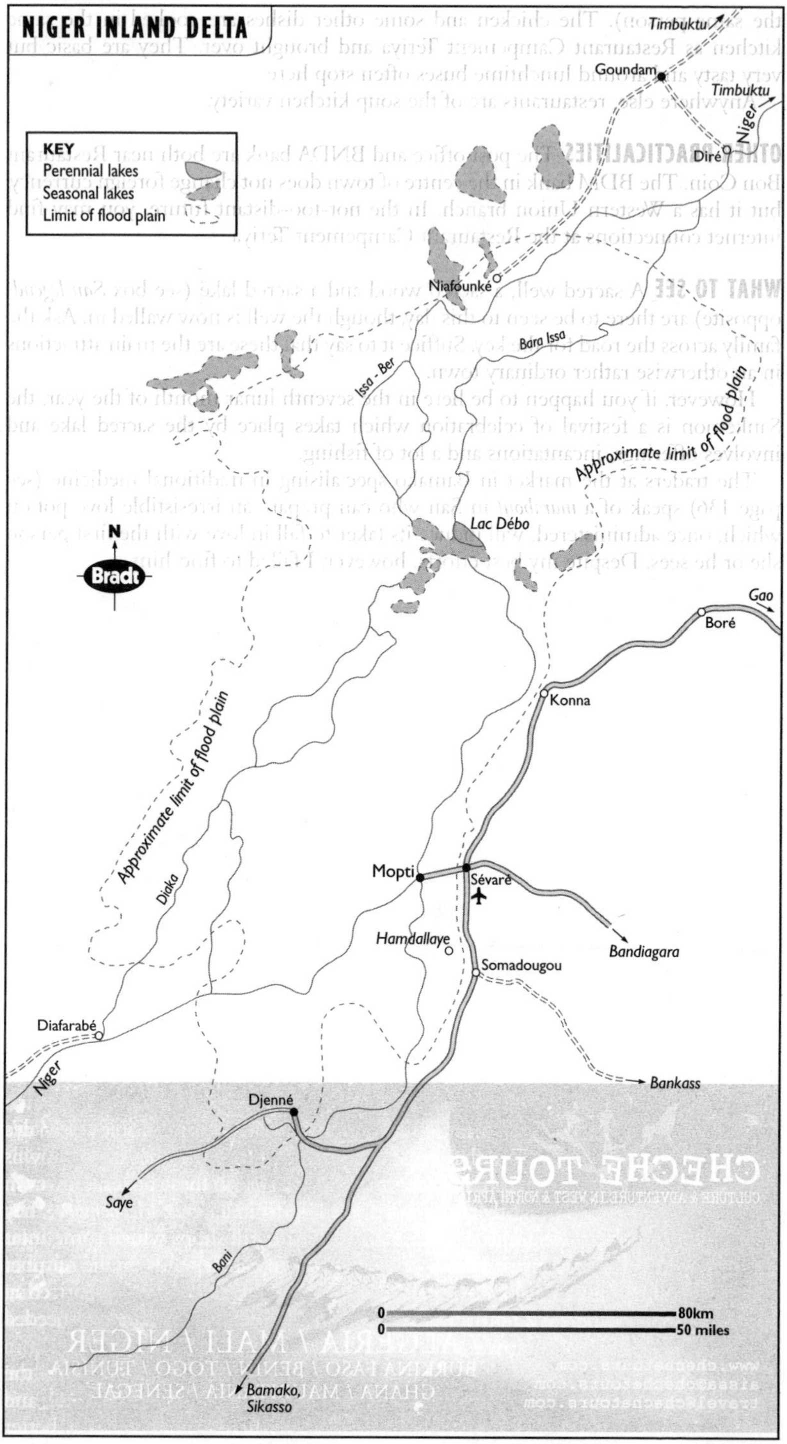
NIGER INLAND DELTA
KEY
Perennial lakes
Seasonal lakes
Limit of flood plain
Timbuktu
Goundam
Timbuktu
Niger
Diré
Niafounké
Bara Issa
Issa - Ber
Approximate limit of flood plain
Lac Débo
N
Bradt
Gao
Boré
Konna
Approximate limit of flood plain
Diaka
Mopti
Sévaré
Hamdallaye
Somadougou
Bandiagara
Diafarabé
Niger
Bankass
Djenné
Saye
Bani
0
80km
0
50 miles
Bamako,
Sikasso

5

The Niger Inland Delta

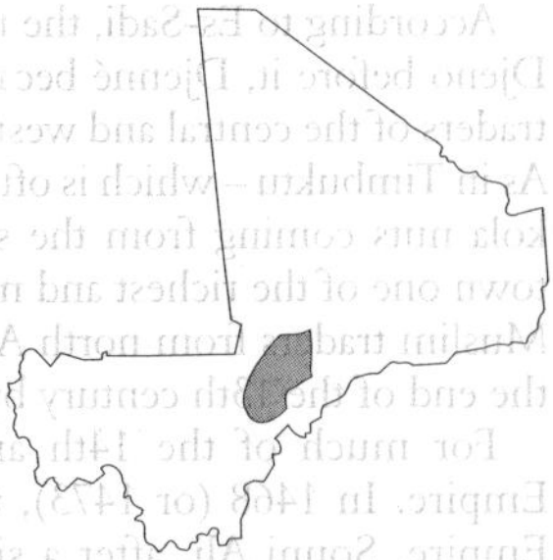

As the River Niger continues to flow in a northeasterly direction through the region of Ségou and into the region of Mopti – which also includes Dogon country and part of Gourma (see *Chapters 6* and 7) – it forms a vast inland delta. Beyond the region's principal town, Mopti, the river splits into two main channels – the Issa-Ber and the Bara Issa – which, along with a network of smaller branches, spread out across a large, flat plain, flooding it during the rainy season and creating shallow lakes. The Niger floodplain stretches almost to the edge of the desert before the Issa-Ber and the Bara Issa are reunited and the River Niger flows past Timbuktu.

Most visitors come to see the towns of Mopti and Djenné, both of which are accessible by road and river: the main Bamako–Gao highway runs along the southeastern edge of the inland delta before veering eastwards after the town of Konna; the River Niger receives its main tributary, the river Bani, at Mopti, and Djenné is on the banks of the Bani at the southern edge of the floodplain. This is also the best place in Mali for birdwatching. Between November and March the numerous lakes and ponds of the floodplain are full of wintering Palaearctic waterfowl and shorebirds, as well as plenty of African species.

DJENNÉ

Historians allege that Djenné's best days are behind it. Competing at one time with Timbuktu as the western Sudan's pre-eminent centre of trans-Saharan trade and Islamic scholarship, nowadays Djenné is a moderately important agricultural town situated on an island in the Niger Inland Delta, with a population of around 10,000 people and a lively market on Mondays. However, perhaps Djenné's best days are yet to come – as Mali's pre-eminent tourist attraction. With its famous World Heritage mosque and unique architecture, Djenné is already a firm fixture on the tourist circuit – a fact demonstrated by the emergence of hotels and restaurants to cater for the town's growing number of visitors. Unfortunately, the guides have also latched on to Djenné's potential and, perhaps because the town itself is so small, are omnipresent and, at times, aggressive. This is the downside of a visit to Djenné. On the other hand, you will not find a more beautiful or well-preserved town in Mali. Physically, at least, not much has changed here in the past few centuries, and walking around, particularly at the end of the day when the setting sun casts mysterious shadows and shafts of light on the mud-brick skyline and winding alleys, is absolutely enchanting.

HISTORY Much of the historical information about modern-day Djenné is contained in the *Tarikh es-Sudan*, a 17th-century chronicle of the western Sudan written by the Islamic scholar, Es-Sadi. (For details about Djenné's ancient predecessor, Djenné-Djeno, see page 170.)

According to Es-Sadi, the town was founded in the 13th century. Like Djenné-Djeno before it, Djenné became an important commercial centre, frequented by traders of the central and western Sudan and those of the Guinea's tropical forests. As in Timbuktu – which is often described as Djenné's 'twin city' – gold, slaves and kola nuts coming from the south were exchanged for Saharan salt, making the town one of the richest and most cosmopolitan in Africa. Indeed, the influence of Muslim traders from north Africa contributed to Djenné's conversion to Islam at the end of the 13th century by its 26th ruler, Koy Kounboro.

For much of the 14th and 15th centuries, Djenné was part of the Mali Empire. In 1468 (or 1473), the city was captured by the ruler of the Songhay Empire, Sonni Ali, after a siege which, according to Es-Sadi, lasted for seven years, seven months and seven days. Djenné's best years were those spent under the stability and security of Mali and Songhay rule – a time when trade flourished and the city developed into a centre of Islamic scholarship. When the Moroccans took over in 1591, however, Djenné started its gradual and irreversible decline. The Moroccan period of control in the western Sudan was characterised by instability and anarchy (see page 16) which, along with the general shift of trade routes towards the coast where the Europeans had landed during the 16th century, had a detrimental effect on trans-Saharan trade – the key to Djenné's fortune. The arrival of Sékou Amadou in 1819 and his attempts to reform the practice of Islam in Djenné did nothing to restore stability, and the period of Tukulor control from 1862 to 1893 was equally unsuccessful. In fact, for nearly 300 years Djenné had been successively occupied and exploited by regimes lacking the authority and legitimacy of the Mali and Songhay empires, so that in April 1893, when Colonel Archinard marched into the town without opposition, he found only the remnants of one of the most important centres of trade and culture in Africa. The French preferred Mopti as the region's commercial centre, leaving Djenné to continue life as an agricultural town with a glorious past.

GETTING THERE AND AWAY

By river It is possible to travel from Djenné to Mopti along the river Bani. Departure points vary according to the level of the water: when it is high enough, pirogues sometimes leave from the riverbank beside the town itself; however, the more common departure point is a stretch of water a few kilometres away, where vehicles arriving at and leaving Djenné are carried across the river by a ferry. The OMATHO are trying to regulate these fares. The listed price to hire a motorised *pinasse* for the 12-hour journey to Mopti is CFA200,000. A pole-powered pirogue costs CFA70,000 for the 60-hour journey. If you want to stretch the duration of the trip, camping on the riverbank is a wonderful way to experience the desolation of the Delta. Do bring a tent or mosquito net and plenty of repellent, for the absence of people is amply made up for by the presence of mosquitoes.

By road Buses and *bâchées* leave from the marketplace. The volume of traffic to and from Djenné is dictated by the town's Monday market.

On Monday and Thursday mornings there is a new-ish bus that goes to Bamako via San (CFA2,500) and Ségou (CFA5,000), returning from Bamako on Tuesdays and Fridays. The driver's name is Sidi (m *7604 27 93*). He can tell you if there are seats and what time it leaves. Otherwise there is always a way to get to or to leave Djenné. You can hire someone with a motorbike to take you to the Carrefour Djenné (the turn-off for Djenné on the main highway) about 30km from town along a paved road. If you go in the morning you should be able to catch one of the

POLLUTION IN DJENNÉ

Jolijn Geels

Although you have every reason to wander around at leisure and admire the beautiful *banco* buildings in Djenné, you may find yourself watching where to put your feet much of the time. Many of the narrow streets are marred by open gutters, and in the rainy season one has to be really agile to avoid the wet and slippery ooze; in Djenné you should wear wellies rather than sandals. However, the danger can also come from above, from the pipes sticking out of the façades. Beware of sudden showers of waste water! As they routinely manoeuvre around the gutters, the Djennenké (as the local people are called) do not seem to find it too bothersome that their town is scarred and dirty. Do not be fooled by appearances, though; it hasn't always been like this and the Djennenké do not like it any more than visitors do.

In fact, less than a few decades ago, the gutters weren't even there. The Djennenké used to use the river Bani to bathe in, to do the laundry, clean cooking pots, and so on. Only a limited amount of water, mostly from wells and used for drinking and cooking, found its way to the many households. Then – financed through foreign aid – numerous pumps, water pipes and taps were installed throughout Djenné. As more and more families benefited from this luxurious novelty, the problem of waste water gradually grew out of proportion. This consequence had simply been overlooked. Narrow trenches have been dug to funnel off the murky water, and when the channels get clogged – as is often the case – the black, slimy substance is scooped out and deposited along the edges; not a pretty sight, and most of all, a serious health hazard. More foreign aid had to be found in order to address this problem. Two quarters of Djenné have had specially designed cesspools with filter systems installed. It was thought that by 2004 all individual households would have received their own installation, but the project is still ongoing.

What about the other kind of pollution, ie: the waste and plastic littering the big market square and the streets? With no money to set up a sophisticated waste-disposal programme, the government is trying to encourage the people to act themselves. This results in occasional and isolated cleaning frenzies, with groups of volunteers – mostly women – sweeping, picking up and burning rubbish. Others are taking bigger steps to improve the problem: local *bogolan* producer and clothes manufacturer, Malimali (*contact Hôtel Djenné Djenno for more details:* **m** *6660 01 17; http://hoteldjennedjenno.com/10/*) pays Talibe boys 50 francs to pick up plastic bags. The collected bags are then either used to make paving bricks (in a scheme established by the Aga Khan Foundation) or weaved to make other items sold in the hotel shop.

big buses – Bani preferably – passing on their way between Mopti and Bamako. If space permits, they'll pick up passengers. The price should be CFA7,000–8,000 and it takes about seven hours. Buses to Sikasso (CFA7,000) and Koutiala (CFA5,000) leave only in the morning. At other times, the only regular service is to Mopti (2 hours; CFA2,000). The price of baggage is not included in the ticket and they will try to get CFA500 per bag. *Bâchées* are waiting at the Carrefour Djenné to ferry people into town for CFA1,250. A *taxe touristique* of CFA1,000 is payable. Retain your ticket for the duration of your stay in Djenné.

When you are driving your own vehicle, note that the ferry crossing costs CFA3,000 for a car, if it's before 18.00, and CFA500 for a motorbike. Since at some point you will be leaving Djenné again, most likely by the same way, these rates include the return trip. A new road (exiting Djenné at the western end) is under construction though. Eventually, this road will link Djenné directly to Ségou,

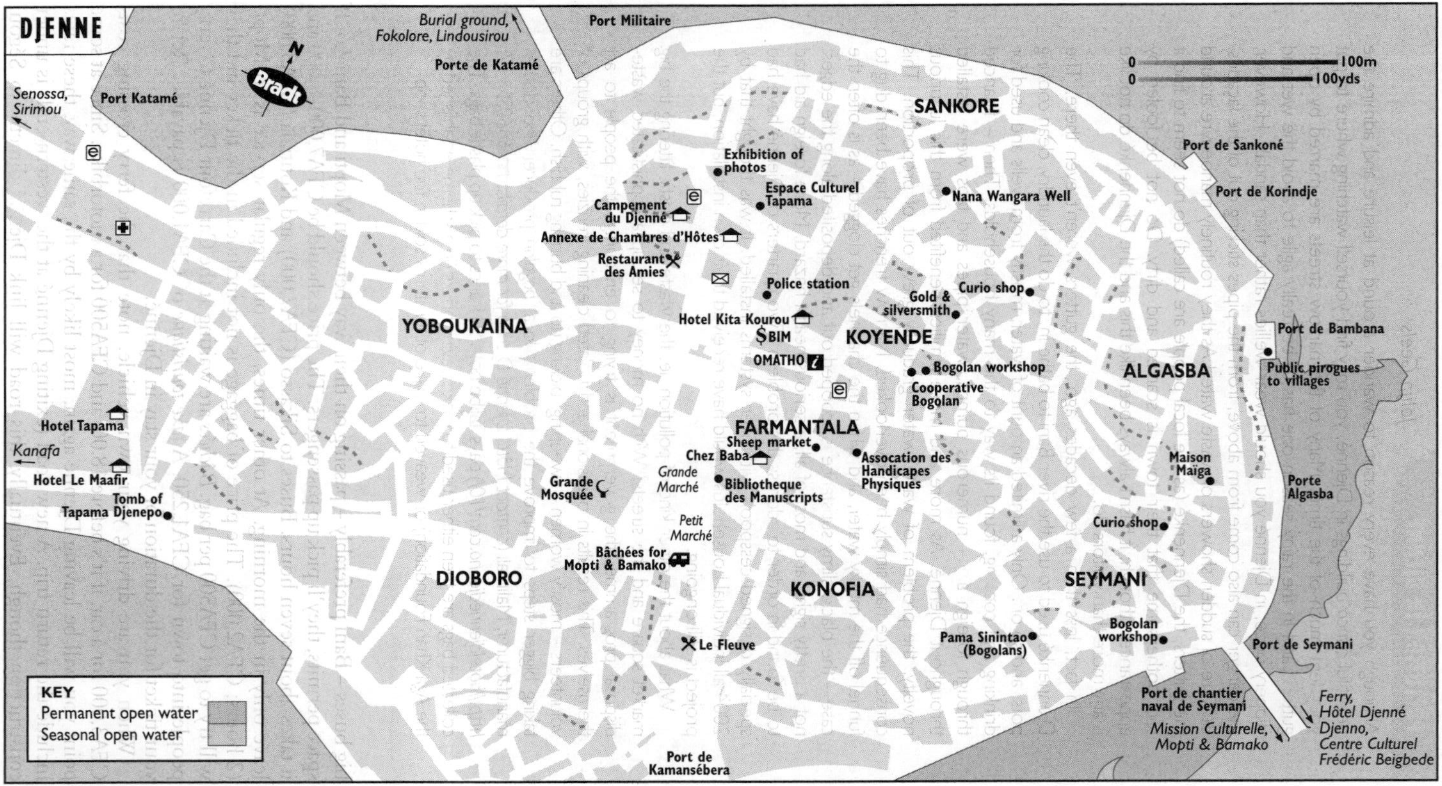
DJENNE
Burial ground, Fokolore, Lindousirou
Port Militaire
Porte de Katamé
Senossa, Sirimou
Port Katamé
Bradt
N
0 100m
0 100yds
SANKORE
Port de Sankoné
Port de Korindje
Exhibition of photos
Espace Culturel Tapama
Nana Wangara Well
Campement du Djenné
Annexe de Chambres d'Hôtes
Restaurant des Amies
Police station
Curio shop
Gold & silversmith
Hotel Kita Kourou
BIM
OMATHO
YOBOUKAINA
KOYENDE
Port de Bambana
Bogolan workshop
Cooperative Bogolan
ALGASBA
Public pirogues to villages
Hotel Tapama
Kanafa
Hotel Le Maafir
Tomb of Tapama Djenepo
FARMANTALA
Sheep market
Chez Baba
Assocation des Handicapes Physiques
Grande Marché
Bibliotheque des Manuscripts
Grande Mosquée
Maison Maïga
Porte Algasba
Petit Marché
Curio shop
Bâchées for Mopti & Bamako
DIOBORO
KONOFIA
SEYMANI
Le Fleuve
Pama Sinintao (Bogolans)
Bogolan workshop
Port de Seymani
KEY
Permanent open water
Seasonal open water
Port de chantier naval de Seymani
Mission Culturelle, Mopti & Bamako
Ferry, Hôtel Djenné Djenno, Centre Culturel Frédéric Beigbede
Port de Kamansébera

7732 7805

providing a slightly shorter connection between the two towns. Taxis will charge you CFA25,000 for a day's hire in town.

TOURIST INFORMATION The OMATHO office in Djenné (*2142 01 38; m 7620 50 87; 08.00–16.00 Mon–Fri*) is found in a street just behind the market. They can help get you an official guide or any local information. If you arrive and find the door closed, the director is never far away. Call him on his mobile (see listing above). The going rate for a two-hour tour of Djenné is CFA5,000 per person or CFA7,500 for a group of three or more.

WHERE TO STAY Competition in Djenné's hotel business is hotting up with the opening of a couple of 'boutique' style hotels. If you're coming for the Monday market, it is is definitely recommended to reserve accommodation on a Sunday or Monday night.

Upmarket $$$$

Centre Culturel Frédéric Beigbeder (better known as 'the Sandcastle') (4 rooms, 1 suite, 1 Tuareg tent) m 7336 71 64; e info@centreculturelbeigbeder.com; www.malisandcastle.com. On the banks of the river Bani, this is the first sight for visitors entering Djenné by ferry. The imposing building is one of the best examples of Malian mud architecture built by the Dutch writer/filmmaker Ton van der Lee; incidentally they also show African films outdoors on Mon, Tue & Sun nights. Sleep in the 110m² carved-sand loft suite, covering the whole top floor with a canopy bed & balcony; in the garden in a converted Dogon granary mill (b/fast inc); or a traditional Tuareg nomad tent at CFA3,000pp b/fast inc. Rooms have fans – there is no AC thanks to the cool breeze from the river. A romantic 5-course candlelit dinner on the rooftop with wine can be organised on request.

Mid-range $$$

Campement Hotel (48 rooms, 22 with AC) Quartier Sankore; 2142 04 97; e campdjenne@afribone.net.ml. Centrally located with a friendly atmosphere ensuring that it remains very popular with travellers. The rooms certainly have seen better days, but are still all right, if a bit overpriced. Camping costs CFA3,000pp. In recent years, the *campement* has opened the Annexe de Chambres d'Hôtes across the road. The rates are the same, but since the rooms are new, they provide slightly better value with AC or fan with cold-water showers. B/fast extra at CFA1,500.

Hotel Djenné Djenno (12 rooms) Quartier Dotémé Tolo; m 6660 01 17; e hoteldjennedjenno@yahoo.fr; www.hoteldjennedjenno.com. Coming in by bus you can spot the hotel's beautiful traditional mud-brick building on the left just before the river. You can ask the driver to stop but he'll probably ignore you as he won't want to get your luggage off the roof. Never mind; it's only CFA200–500 for someone to carry your bag from the centre of town. Rooms, decorated in both traditional & contemporary designs are good value with AC or fan & hot water. Cocktails (ginger juice with rum, *bissap* with gin (at CFA1,700) are taken daily on the roof whilst watching the sun set over the mosque. Breakfast is fruit, real coffee & homemade guava & mango jams. For a real insight into the life of the Swedish owner Sophie in the ancient town of Djenné, read her wonderful blog: www.djennedjenno.blogspot.com. B/fast extra at CFA2,000.

Hotel Le Maafir (15 rooms) Quartier Kanafa; 2142 05 41; m 6672 32 00; e diawoyesininta@yahoo.fr. Centred on a quiet garden, the small but well-decorated rooms are full of character, perhaps not surprising as it's owned by the ex-Minister of Culture who also has the San Toro Restaurant & the Hotel Djenné in Bamako. All rooms with hot-water interior showers, mosquito nets & AC or fan. 1 dormitory-sized room may be particularly good value for a group of up to 8 people. B/fast inc.

Budget $$

Hotel Tapama (8 rooms) Quartier Kanafa; 2142 05 27; e residencetapama@yahoo.fr. An imposing family residence, converted into a friendly hotel. The courtyard reflects some of the grandeur this household once must have had, but the rooms are rather unpretentious by comparison. As spacious as they are, more beds may be added to reduce the price per person. Camping is allowed for CFA2,500pp. B/fast extra at CFA1,000 & dinner to order CFA3,000.

Shoestring $

Chez Baba (5 rooms) Centre Commercial; ☎ 2142 05 98; m 7614 33 96; e restauranbaba@yahoo.fr. Baba is the friendly, fatherly character who owns & runs this lively guesthouse. Rooms are arranged around a courtyard with simple accommodation in cheap 4–5-bed dormitories. You can take a whole room for the total of the price of all the beds. Cold-water showers. B/fast extra at CFA1,000. *Dorm beds CFA3,500pp or a mattress & mosquito net on the terrace CFA3,000.*

Hotel Kita Kourou Centre Commercial; m 7618 18 11. Staying here feels like living in the middle of a family home – plain but clean rooms (some with a fan) or a mattress on the floor with mosquito nets & communal cold showers. *Dorm bed or a mattress on the terrace CFA2,500.*

WHERE TO EAT The *campement* and all hotels have restaurants, serving hearty meals at reasonable prices, although the food is pretty similar wherever you go. Note that alcohol is not available everywhere.

Mid-range $$$

Hotel Djenné Djenno m 7660 01 17. Non-residents are welcome but should notify the hotel a few hours in advance. All food is freshly bought in the market or grown in the garden. A typical set menu would be something like: smoked fish soup, pepper steak with sweet potato chips & banana crumble with whipped cream (made with fresh milk delivered by the local Fulani tribe). The restaurant is reached by spiral staircase & dining is under the stars lit by gaslight with *balafon* on busy nights such as Sun/Mon.

Cheap and cheerful $$

Campement du Djenné The restaurant on a large terrace not only serves cold beers, but has a choice of spirits too. Food is good with decent-sized portions & traditional musicians in high season.

Hotel Le Maafir Everyone eats in the courtyard. There is a set menu & any other choice of meal must be ordered in advance.

Rock bottom $

Chez Baba Good food in a great atmosphere. Daily menu of meat or fish with either rice, veg or chips. Must get there early or reserve a place to guarantee there's one left. Also sells cold beers. On Sun/Mon some youths will play the *djembe* & sing & dance in the courtyard.

There are several basic restaurants right in the centre of town, just off the square by the mosque. Be warned, the children and guides are never far away and you may get more peace and quiet eating in one of the hotels.

Restaurant des Amies m 7542 01 78. Traditional African dishes served on benches in a small local restaurant; couscous, *riz sauce*, steak & brochettes.

Restaurant Kita Kourou A terrace serving traditional meals including fish & the local dish *tion tion*. Pizza or specialities such as *tarte aux oignons* are available to order.

Restaurant Le Fleuve m 7529 62 14. Basic, rice dishes & cheap meals: *riz sauce, riz tion tion, riz au gras or pigeon*. A nice setting as long as you try not to focus on the open sewer outside.

ENTERTAINMENT AND NIGHTLIFE The **Espace Culturel Tapama** (m *7614 32 51*) managed by the Youth, Sport, Art and Culture Service. Djenné's youth very much needed a place of entertainment like this, since there was virtually nowhere else for them to go. There's a stage for live concerts and a bar/disco where they organise evening events. Abandoned most of the week, this place comes alive on a Saturday night or during holidays such as Tabaski. Give it a try!

Some hotels will organise traditional music on busy nights such as Sundays when lots of tourists are in town for the Monday market. Alternatively musicians can be booked through the local OMATHO office (m *7620 50 87*).

SHOPPING When you go on a guided tour around town, at some point your guide will propose taking you to one of the 'Maisons des Bogolans', where families specialise in this craft. Even if you are not buying, call in and see how *bogolans* are made. The *bogolans* (see page 93) sold by Pama Sinintao have an excellent reputation. Her shop is signposted on the road leading out of town, before you cross the bridge. Also, behind the *marché des moutons* (sheep market) you'll find the Association des Handicapés Physiques, selling *bogolans* and other arts and crafts.

MaliMali is a commercial operation set up in 2007 to promote social and economic progress through trade and provide apprenticeships in sewing, cutting, weaving and the *bogolan* technique. Have a look at their website for more information (*www.malimali.org*).

A visit to a gold- and silversmith's workshop is not a fixed element of a guided tour, but it is worth asking to be taken to one. Alternatively, ask for Ali Kouyaté to come and see you at your hotel with a selection of his work. He can normally be found in Chez Baba (m *7614 32 43*).

The Fondation Beigbeder at the newly opened **Centre Culturel Frédéric Beigbeder** (m *7336 71 64; www.malisandcastle.com*) aims to promote Malian culture, arts and crafts by hosting a wide range of cultural events. The complex includes an art gallery, a restaurant, a concert café, a market hall and a pleasant garden. Every Sunday, Monday and Tuesday at 20.00 a well-known west African praise singer performs at Le Dali Café by the river (*admission €5pp*). There is a weekly Sunday market at 08.00, where you can see the local craftsmen at work and buy their goods. A substantial part of the profit is spent on teaching adults and children to read and write.

OTHER PRACTICALITIES Facilities in Djenné include a post office – which is between the mosque and the Campement du Djenné – and a BIM bank (🕘 *07.30–17.30; Mon–Thu, 07.30–15.30 Fri, 09.00–16.30 Sat*). There's a Western Union and it claims to change euros, US dollars and travellers' cheques. You can make telephone calls at the post office or at one of many *cabines téléphoniques*. There are internet facilities in Djenné at either the *campement*, opposite the OMATHO office or up near the hospital (CFA1,000/hr). The **Mission Culturelle** (✆ *2142 05 35;* e *mcdjenne@afribone.net.ml*) is just before the police checkpoint on the road leading out of town.

WHAT TO SEE

The Djenné Mosque The Djenné Mosque is the largest mud structure in the world; it must also have a claim to be the most beautiful. Standing 18.5m tall, it dominates Djenné's central square and is the town's *pièce de résistance*.

The Djenné Mosque is sometimes called the Konboro Mosque in deference to King Koy Konboro, the 26th ruler of Djenné, who converted to Islam in the 13th century and, intoxicated with new-found devotion, knocked down his royal palace and built a huge mosque in its place. This structure survived until the arrival of the Peul fundamentalist, Sékou Amadou, in the 19th century. As a student at Djenné, Amadou had been shocked by the liberality of the townsfolk and the practice of singing, dancing and drinking millet beer in front of the mosque. Therefore, when he captured the town in 1819, he abandoned the Konboro Mosque – which he considered to be 'contaminated' by evil practices – and let it go to ruin because the Koran forbids the actual destruction of a mosque by a *fidèle* (faithful Muslim). Meanwhile, a new, more sombre mosque was built on a site east of the old one and was inaugurated in 1834.

The present-day mosque dates from 1907, celebrating the centenary in December 2007 – and is constructed on the foundations of Konboro's original structure.

THE MASONS OF DJENNÉ

Building is an art form in Djenné and its builders are revered as great artists – and magicians. Their techniques are simple and have been practised since the foundation of the first caste of masons back in the 15th century. The *bareys*, as they are known, carry no tools, except for an iron trowel to cut and smooth clay walls. The mortar is mixed with the feet, the bricks moulded by hand, and façades as high as those of the Djenné Mosque are erected without the use of a plumb line. To reach this level of skill requires years of preparation. Potential *bareys* – young boys around seven years old – begin their apprenticeship under the guidance of an old mason, who acts not only as a teacher but also as the boy's second father. The apprentice learns about the tools and techniques of the trade – but not its innermost secrets – and by about 18 is skilled enough to graduate as a fully fledged *barey*. However, at this stage he is still only on the second rung of the hierarchical ladder.

Next up are the accomplished younger masons, who are experienced enough to work independently and as foremen on building sites. Then come two categories of *maîtres-maçons*, or master masons: those who are still active and those who have retired. Both know their trade inside-out and the older ones hold the magic secrets handed down from generation to generation of Djenné masons. These magic spells – a mixture of Arabic and indigenous words – are cast to protect the building and its builder from harm and injury. For example, before work is started on a new construction a *maître-maçon* with occult powers recites a text invoking Abrahim or Ibrahim, who, according to the Koran, built the Ka'bah or the House of God at Mecca. This event marked the beginning of masonry and the Ka'bah is considered to be indestructible. Therefore, a spell invoking Abrahim brings bad luck to anyone who tries to destroy or modify the new building without the *barey*'s permission. In this way, customer loyalty is more or less guaranteed.

Amadou's effort was pulled down and a *madrasa* (Muslim college) built in its place. Viewed from the outside, the mosque's architecture is classically Sudanese. The three minarets are each more than 10m high and, along with the rest of the structure, are riddled with bunches of wooden sticks or *toron*. The ends of these bits of wood sticking out of the façade do actually serve a purpose, not only as decoration, but also as scaffolding when repairs become necessary. For example, each year before the start of the rainy season, the people of Djenné volunteer to resurface the mosque with a new layer of *banco* by hand. Huge quantities of *banco* are hauled up to the Djennenké, whose feet seek support on the wooden protrusions. This massive event is known as Crépissage and usually takes place in April (see *Chapter 2*, *Festivals*, page 89).

There are two entrances: the one on the southern side (ie: facing away from the marketplace) is the more ornate, whereas the northern entrance is characterised by six steps leading up to it. The whole mosque is raised 3m above the level of the marketplace, and these six steps symbolise the transition from the profane to the sacred. Inside, the mosque is equally impressive. The prayer area is some 50m by 26m, and 90 pillars hold up the wooden roof. Unfortunately, infidels have not been allowed inside the mosque ever since a French fashion photographer used its interior as a surreal backdrop for his scantily clad models in suggestive poses.

Outside the mosque there will be no shortage of kids offering to take you onto the roof of a nearby house to get a view for photos. It's worth it but you shouldn't pay more than CFA500 per person.

Monday market Djenné may no longer be the commercial powerhouse it once was, but it can still boast one of the most colourful markets in west Africa. Every

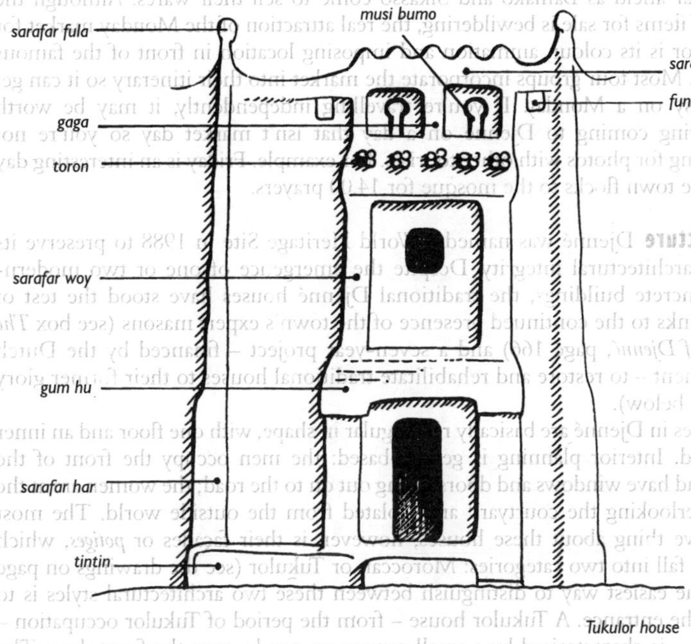

musi bumo
sarafar fula
sarafar idye
funey
gaga
toron
sarafar woy
gum hu
sarafar har
tintin
Tukulor house

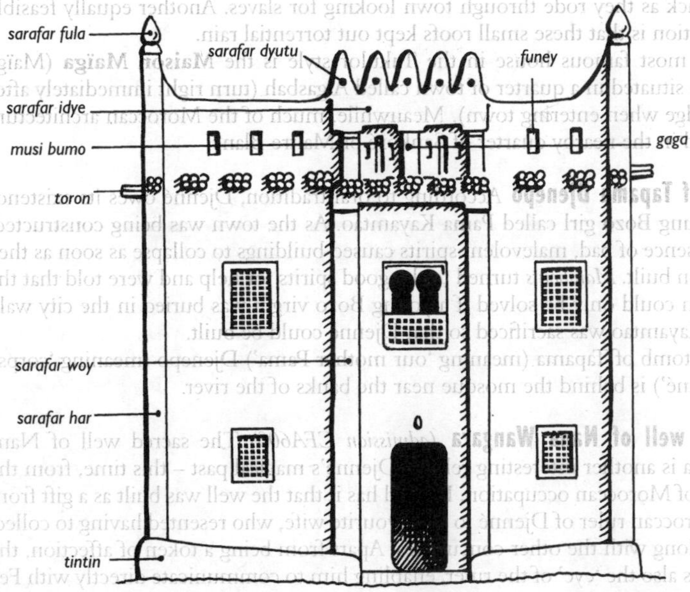

sarafar fula
sarafar dyutu
funey
sarafar idye
musi bumo
gaga
toron
sarafar woy
sarafar har
tintin
Moroccan house

Monday, the town's population roughly triples as people from surrounding villages and as far afield as Bamako and Sikasso come to sell their wares. Although the range of items for sale is bewildering, the real attraction of the Monday market for the visitor is its colour, animation and imposing location in front of the famous mosque. Most tour groups incorporate the market into their itinerary so it can get very busy on a Monday. If you're travelling independently, it may be worth considering coming to Djenné on a day that isn't market day so you're not competing for photos with other tourists. For example, Friday is an interesting day when the town flocks to the mosque for 14.00 prayers.

Architecture Djenné was named a World Heritage Site in 1988 to preserve its unique architectural integrity. Despite the emergence of one or two modern-style concrete buildings, the traditional Djenné houses have stood the test of time thanks to the continued presence of the town's expert masons (see box *The masons of Djenné*, page 166) and a seven-year project – financed by the Dutch government – to restore and rehabilitate traditional houses to their former glory (see box below).

Houses in Djenné are basically rectangular in shape, with one floor and an inner courtyard. Interior planning is gender-based: the men occupy the front of the house and have windows and doors facing out on to the road; the women are at the back overlooking the courtyard and isolated from the outside world. The most distinctive thing about these houses, however, is their façades or *potiges*, which basically fall into two categories: Moroccan or Tukulor (see the drawings on page 167). The easiest way to distinguish between these two architectural styles is to look at the entrance. A Tukulor house – from the period of Tukulor occupation – 1862–93 – is characterised by a small canopy or *gum hu* over the front door. The most common explanation for the presence of the *gum hu* is that it offered protection against the Tukulor cavalry, preventing them from entering houses on horseback as they rode through town looking for slaves. Another equally feasible explanation is that these small roofs kept out torrential rain.

The most famous house in the Tukulor style is the **Maison Maïga** (Maïga House) situated in a quarter of town called Algasbah (turn right immediately after the bridge when entering town). Meanwhile, much of the Moroccan architecture is found in the nearby quarter of Sankoré or Maître Blanc.

Tomb of Tapama Djenepo According to oral tradition, Djenné owes its existence to a young Bozo girl called Pama Kayamtao. As the town was being constructed, the presence of bad, malevolent spirits caused buildings to collapse as soon as they had been built. *Marabouts* turned to the good spirits for help and were told that the problem could only be solved if a young Bozo virgin was buried in the city wall. Pama Kayamtao was sacrificed so that Djenné could be built.

The tomb of Tapama (meaning 'our mother Pama') Djenepo (meaning 'corpse of Djenné') is behind the mosque near the banks of the river.

Sacred well of Nana Wangara (*admission CFA600*) The sacred well of Nana Wangara is another interesting relic of Djenné's magical past – this time, from the period of Moroccan occupation. Legend has it that the well was built as a gift from the Moroccan ruler of Djenné to his favourite wife, who resented having to collect water along with the other concubines. Apart from being a token of affection, the well was also the 'eye' of the ruler, enabling him to communicate directly with Fez and to see into the future. Meanwhile, on Thursdays and Fridays it could apparently cure illnesses. It is hidden in a family courtyard in the old Moroccan quarter, Sankoré or Maître Blanc ('White Master'), not far from the Maïga House.

above **Masked dancers at Tereli** (SP) page 206

below **Tuareg family out on an impromptu performance** (SP) page 249

opposite

top Visit Dogon Country's spectacular cliff villages – this particular mud building is found in Youga Dogorou (SP) page 203

bottom Dust fills the air, but you can still make out the collection of thatch turrets – the granaries – in this Dogon village (SP) page 193

this page

right The neatly drawn boxes and carefully placed nuts within the circle of stones represent a series of questions. When foxes wander through the space at night, their tracks will provide the answers (JA) page 187

below Some of the earliest cloth produced in sub-Saharan Africa can be traced back to communities from Mali's Bandiagara escarpment (SP) page 187

above Piled-high *pinasses* preparing to leave Mopti (SP) page 175

below Aerial view of the vast Niger Inland Delta (CY/TIPS) page 159

above **COMANAV ferry weaving its way through the reeds** (SP) page 174

below left **Collecting cooking water from the ferry deck** (SP)

below right **All aboard!** (SP)

left **Pounding millet – probably for the preparation of millet beer** (JA) page 86

below **Chicken with rice and beans – a local staple** (JA) page 82

bottom **Malian women often bear the brunt of the daily workload, but occupy a position of power in the family unit** (JA) page 29

top Tuareg drinking tea at desert homestead, Timbuktu (AVZ)

above Butcher preparing a cut of meat, Timbuktu (SP)

left Boy copying verses of the Koran on to a prayer board (SP)

above The indigo blue of the Tuaregs' robes is the quintessential Malian image (SP)

below Tuareg rider showing off at a festival (SP)

A MONUMENTAL CHALLENGE

Jolijn Geels

After Djenné was declared a World Heritage Site in 1988, it was time to evaluate the current state of the architecture. There was good news and bad news. The 'good' news was that Djenné as a whole had hardly been affected by modernisation; amenities such as electricity were scarce and most parts of Djenné remained inaccessible to cars – hence there was little associated disfiguration from things like cables, wires, lampposts and cars. The bad news was that many traditional houses were in an appalling state, many had been abandoned, and a shocking number listed as historical monuments had been demolished and replaced.

One of the reasons why houses were either rebuilt or left to crumble was the fact that modern-day Djennenké have different demands for housing compared with the past; the traditional layout simply wasn't considered adequate any longer. At the same time, many Djennenké also wanted a place to live that was low in maintenance. *Banco*, the fermented mixture of mud, chaff and water that is used to plaster the buildings, involves not just a lot of work, but also a lot of mud and water. After two consecutive years of drought – 1984 and 1985 – there just hadn't been enough raw material to keep the *banco* free from serious wear and tear. So families started to give up their traditional homes, building instead houses that better suited their needs – sometimes using modern building materials such as cement and bricks.

The alarm was raised, a plan drawn up, and funds made available to maintain the older houses. In 1996, phase one of the plan was put into effect. It took a while to convince the Djennenké of the importance and the integrity of the programme; there were many more hurdles to overcome and a lot of criticism to be swallowed. Nevertheless, the actual job of rehabilitating and restoring houses began. It took seven years to complete, or perhaps it is more appropriate to say that by then the money had run out and thus this particular project came to a close. Perhaps not all the objectives were met, but what has been achieved is still truly impressive: over 100 houses have had a thorough make-over. The traditional façades have been restored to their former beauty, while the interior layout of the dwellings – invisible from the streets – has often been altered to meet the demands of modern Djennenké families. The project has been a learning process too, and since maintaining the architecture in Djenné is a never-ending story, future programmes to continue this hefty task will be able to lean heavily on past experience and expertise.

More information on the project and guided tours are available from the Mission Culturelle. During the tour you will have the opportunity to visit the interior of some of the restored houses. An excellent book in French, *L'Architecture de Djenné*, about this project is available from the National Museum in Bamako (see *Appendix 2, Further Information*, page 294).

To get there, head north on the street where the OMATHO office is located and it is signposted from there. There's not much to see but it's a nice walk to get there through a maze of winding streets and alleys.

Museums and exhibitions There is a small museum at the **Mission Culturelle** (*2142 05 35; 09.00–17.00 daily (these times are informal); admission CFA500*) with information about Djenné-Djeno and the serious problem of archaeological pillage at the site – scavengers go to Djenné-Djeno at night and steal precious artefacts which are then passed on to dealers and finally sold to collectors. There are also other exhibits and photographs relating to modern-day life in Djenné, and, unlike most museums in Mali, many of the explanations are in English.

The museum is just before the police checkpoint on the road leading out of town.

Just next to the *campement* is an exhibition of photos of Djenné from days gone by (⏲ *08.00–19.00, but only in the high season*).

EXCURSIONS FROM DJENNÉ

A different way to see Djenné is with Max, the horse from the Hotel Djenné Djenno. He can be rented for tours around town, with his brightly coloured carriage (CFA7,000). At night hotel staff will hang gaslights on the outside; a fun way to arrive at a restaurant if you're going out for dinner. He is available for picnics and longer excursions (see *Peul and Bozo villages* below). The Hotel Djenné Djenno also hires bikes (CFA2,000/day).

DJENNÉ-DJENO Djenné-Djeno, or ancient Djenné, is about 3km southeast of the town's modern-day location. Before exploring this historic site, you are strongly advised to visit the museum – which is on the way – to get an idea of what was once there. You may also arrange a guided visit to Djenné-Djeno through the museum.

Although archaeological research continues at Djenné-Djeno today, the most ground-breaking discoveries were made during excavations directed by the American anthropologists, Susan and Roderick McIntosh, in 1977 and 1981. Thanks to radiocarbon dating and a number of important finds – including the foundations of round mud-brick houses, fragments of pottery, statuettes and the remains of the city wall – the McIntoshes were able to prove that Djenné-Djeno flourished many centuries before the Arabs first established trading posts in the Sahara, thus making it the oldest-known city in west Africa. Dating from around 250BC, when it was a small settlement of round mud huts, by about AD800 Djenné-Djeno had grown into an important trading centre with thousands of inhabitants. The city continued to prosper until around AD1400 when it was suddenly and mysteriously abandoned, perhaps to appease the powerful Islamic elite who were offended by a city 'contaminated' by pagan practices.

Whatever the reason for Djenné-Djeno's decline, in its heyday the city reaped the rewards of far-reaching trade – first by river and later by caravan – with the desert town of Timbuktu. Initially, Saharan iron, copper, stone and salt were probably bartered for food; later, salt and gold became the two principal trading commodities.

When you reach the site, you are left to imagine what it must once have looked like. A sign erected by the Mission Culturelle announces your arrival, but there is hardly anything to see. To get there, walk past the police checkpoint and turn right at the arch. Continue across country until you reach a teardrop-shaped mound, about 7m high and 2km in circumference, and see the sign.

BAMBARA VILLAGES Diabolo is a Bambara village that you can visit just 5km from Djenné by road. The architecture and way of life is typical of the Bambara ethnicity, who also perform the dance of the marionettes. There are a couple of old women in Diabolo who make high-quality *bogolan,* as opposed to the tourist tat sold in Djenné.

PEUL AND BOZO VILLAGES Despite the fact that Djenné's hinterland holds much beauty, it is still relatively unknown and unexplored. Depending on the water level, you need a pirogue, a donkey cart or bike – or sturdy hiking boots if you like – a guide (who will cost you CFA6,000 per person), and plenty of time. Scattered all over the Niger Inland Delta are small and picturesque Peul and Bozo villages and settlements, erected from *banco* on muddy mounds. The real hidden pearls are the numerous mosques that sometimes look like melting ice cakes. Enquire at the OMATHO office about guides to accompany you on your explorations.

Two interesting villages within realistic walking – or boating – distance of Djenné are Senossa and Sirimou. The slightly closer one is Senossa, a Peul village of around 6,000 inhabitants some 4km north of Djenné, where women are bare breasted and wear very large earrings. The Peul have always been nomadic people, but drought has forced them to become increasingly sedentary and settle in villages such as Senossa. The other village, Sirimou, is a Bozo settlement about 7km west of Djenné.

Whether or not you can reach the two villages as the crow flies depends on the level of the water and the state of the tracks cutting across the fields – if they have emerged again at all after the river has retreated, that is. If so, ask a local to indicate which is the best way to go, as you may otherwise find yourself stuck in a maze of mud and water (and bear in mind that once outside Djenné very little French – and no English – is spoken).

You can walk around **Senossa** – there are two beautiful mosques and houses in the old architecture. If he's there, you may have to introduce yourself to the village chief, and donate a CFA500 tourist tax or a bag of kola nuts. However, he'll probably then show you around himself, which will keep the hordes of children following you around to a minimum.

There is no easy way across the moat surrounding **Sirimou** most of the year. This Walt Disney-style village is on an island in the middle, with an imposing mosque and a very medieval appearance. You should be able to find a pirogue to take you across the moat. The village's less accessible location keeps visitors down and begging doesn't seem to be such a problem.

When the water level is high, the obvious way to visit the villages is by pirogue. Public pirogues provide a shuttle service and cost very little, and there is always the option to rent a private motorised *pinasse* (CFA30,000) or power-poled pirogue (CFA15,000). It is worth trying to time the pirogue so you're coming back at sunset. Even when the river has dropped tremendously, Sirimou can still be reached by pirogue, following a tributary of the Bani. Senossa, meanwhile, can usually be reached by following the causeway that begins behind the hospital and water tower. This is the first section of the new road that will eventually lead all the way to Ségou, but it is definitely no shortcut to Senossa.

The Hotel Djenné Djenno organises visits to the Peul and Bozo villages with its horse, the aforementioned Max, and trap. A day excursion to Diabolo, Sirimou or Senossa plus an elegant gourmet picnic lunch, bottle of wine, beer and a musical performance by traditional *chasseur* or hunters will set you back CFA20,000 per person with a minimum of two people. A two-and-a-half-hour excursion without the lunch costs CFA15,000 for one or two people, with an additional CFA5,000 for each additional person up to a maximum of six.

Kouakourou Kouakourou is a Bozo village 40km from Djenné with varied architecture representing all the ethnic elements of the village. A highlight is the port when the fishing pirogues are returning with all the different varieties of fish from the Niger Inland Delta. There is also a fish market, and the chance to see the traditional techniques of drying and extracting oil from fish. You can take public transport for CFA1,000 each way.

Sofara Intrepid traveller, John Kupiec, chose to walk the 35km from Djenné to the village of Sofara. In his words: 'the special thing about the walk was the friendliness of the village people because they are not used to seeing tourists. It took just over

24 hours including sleeping and talking to people. It's a nice walk through many villages along the way, where people offer up the same Malian hospitality, food, accommodation and no begging as (they did) in the Mali of days gone by.'

To get there head east to northeast of Djenné, probably 1km short of the main north–south highway that eventually leads to the 'Main de Fatima', Gao, etc. Sofara also has a major yearly celebration when thousands of cattle cross the river (see page 89). It is possible to get a bus from Djenné to Sofara (CFA1,250).

HAMDALLAYE

The ruins of Hamdallaye, the political and intellectual capital of the Peul Empire of Macina, lie between Djenné and Mopti. Created in 1810 when the jihad (religious war) led by the Muslim cleric, Sékou Amadou, defeated the combined forces of the Peul and Bambara Kingdoms in Macina, the Peul Empire was a theocratic Islamic state which at one time exercised control as far away as Timbuktu. Hamdallaye was founded around 1815 and remained the empire's capital until it was overrun by the Tukulor forces of El Hadj Omar in 1862, at which point it became the Tukulor headquarters in Macina.

The modern-day remains of Hamdallaye warrant a visit to the site, although you should not expect spectacular, Athenian-style ruins and fantastic photo opportunities. The walls of what was once Sékou Amadou's palace are most in evidence. Inside, his tomb, along with that of Amadou Sékou, the son who succeeded him in 1844, can be found, while the outline of the site where the mosque once stood is next to the palace. Hamdallaye is about 5km past the picturesque village of **Somadougou** in the direction of Mopti. Stop when you see a hamlet by the side of the road or, if you are coming from Mopti, the sign. The first house on the right of the main path leading through this hamlet belongs to the descendants of Sékou Amadou. Introduce yourself and ask their permission before proceeding to the site, which is about 1km from the main road. It is usually open from around 09.00 to 18.00 and, although there is no entrance fee, you should leave something for the attendant who will be happy to show you around.

MOPTI

Mopti began its transition from small Bozo fishing village to the commercial hub of central Mali and the capital of the country's fifth region at the start of the 19th century. The importance of Djenné had been gradually declining, and Mopti was seen as the ideal replacement – first by the Peul emperor, Sékou Amadou, who was keen to develop the town's potential, then by the French, who transferred the trading functions of Djenné to Mopti in 1893 when they arrived in the region. Initially, the town we now call Mopti was spread over several islands in marshland at the confluence of the rivers Niger and Bani. Over time, these islands were reduced to three interconnected pieces of terra firma by means of dykes and tonnes of landfill. A causeway was then constructed to connect Mopti to the main highway at Sévaré, making it easily accessible by road as well as by river. Since its completion – for this is a town constructed virtually from scratch – Mopti has never looked back. Nowadays, it is by far the most important urban centre in the Niger Inland Delta, performing a role once played by Djenné as a crossroads for trade between the north and south. The official population is made up of mainly Bozos and Peuls – but also includes Dogon, Tuareg, Songhay and Bambara communities – and stands at around 100,000; the itinerant population of travelling merchants, however, may be just as large.

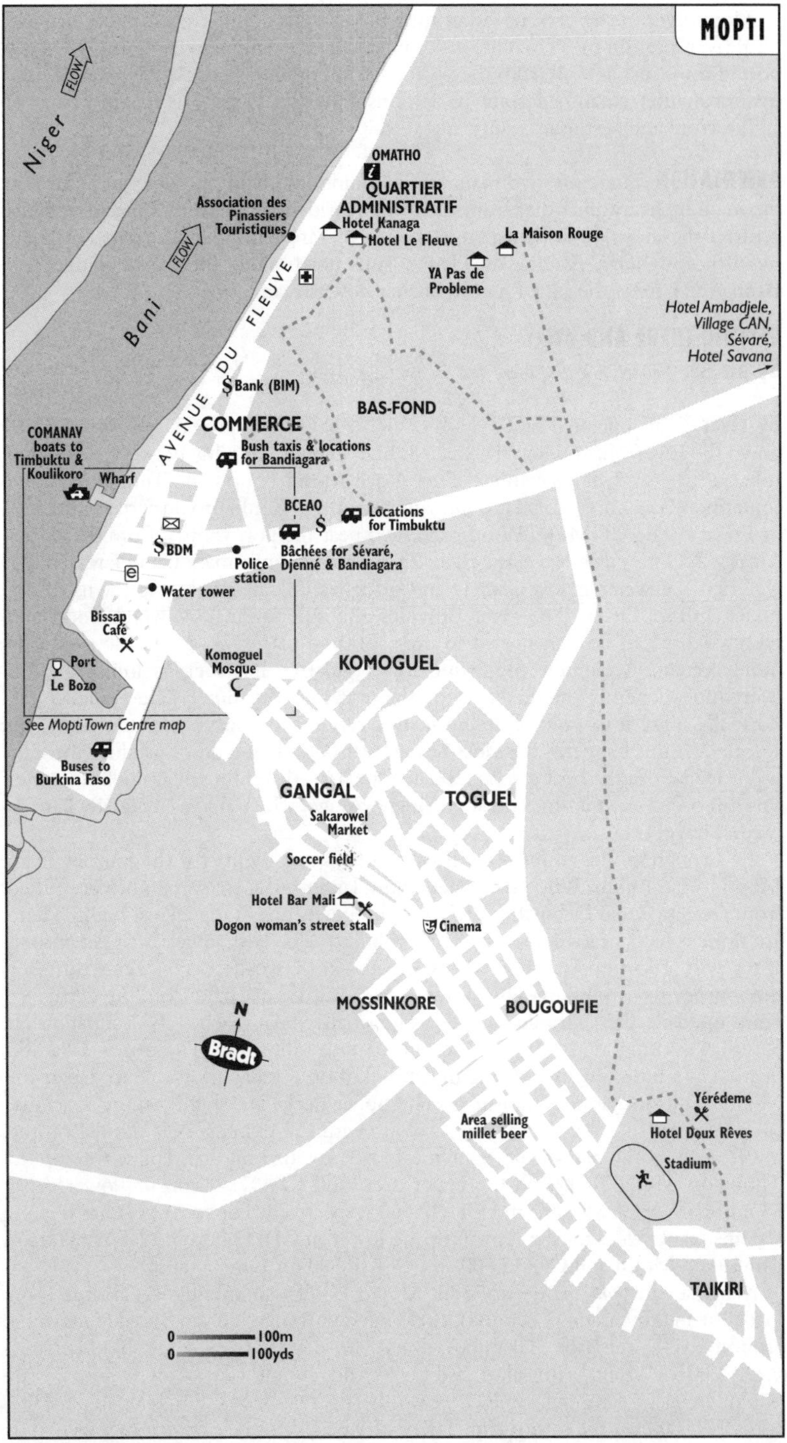
MOPTI
Niger
FLOW
Bani
FLOW
OMATHO
QUARTIER ADMINISTRATIF
Association des Pinassiers Touristiques
Hotel Kanaga
Hotel Le Fleuve
La Maison Rouge
YA Pas de Probleme
AVENUE DU FLEUVE
Hotel Ambadjele, Village CAN, Sévaré, Hotel Savana
Bank (BIM)
BAS-FOND
COMMERCE
COMANAV boats to Timbuktu & Koulikoro
Wharf
Bush taxis & locations for Bandiagara
BCEAO
Locations for Timbuktu
BDM
Police station
Bâchées for Sévaré, Djenné & Bandiagara
Water tower
Bissap Café
Port
Le Bozo
Komoguel Mosque
KOMOGUEL
See Mopti Town Centre map
Buses to Burkina Faso
GANGAL
Sakarowel Market
TOGUEL
Soccer field
Hotel Bar Mali
Dogon woman's street stall
Cinema
MOSSINKORE
BOUGOUFIE
N
Bradt
Yérédeme
Hotel Doux Rêves
Area selling millet beer
Stadium
TAIKIRI
0 100m
0 100yds

Mopti lives in the present rather than the past. Its commercial importance and ideal river location mean that life is dominated by the daily activity around the busy port. This is just as well from the visitor's point of view because Mopti is of little historical interest and, despite its famous mosque, is no Djenné in terms of architecture and aesthetic beauty.

ORIENTATION There are two main roads leading into Mopti: one from Sévaré on the main highway, the other from the town's residential quarters. The commercial centre – the shops, restaurants, bus stations, etc – are centred on the port, while the main thoroughfare, Avenue du Fleuve, runs north along the banks of the river Bani, which joins the Niger a little further downstream.

GETTING THERE AND AWAY

By air See *Sévaré, Getting there and away*, page 180.

By river Boats operated by COMANAV (☎ *2143 00 06*) provide a service up and down the River Niger when the water is high enough, roughly between the end of July and the end of December. They leave Mopti bound for Timbuktu – and sometimes Gao – on Thursdays, and sail upstream to Koulikoro on certain Tuesdays or Fridays. The COMONAV office located near the port is open from 07.30. See *Chapter 2, Getting there and away*, pages 75–6 for more information and fares.

When the water is low, *pinasses* and pirogues link Mopti to the towns of the Niger Inland Delta. The river provides the sole means by which food and merchandise can be transported to these isolated places, so the traffic is usually quite regular. Accurately predicting this regularity, however, is impossible, as everything depends on the level of the water at the time. Large *pinasses* can normally make it to Timbuktu, but if their cargo is too heavy, they can easily run aground. If this happens, the sacks of rice, slabs of salt and other produce must be unloaded before the boat can be refloated, recharged and set sail again. Sometimes this can occur several times during a single voyage, which makes it equally hard to predict travel times.

As a rough guide, count on at least two days and nights for the journey from Mopti to Timbuktu. When the water is low, larger boats are sometimes prevented from crossing Lake Débo after dark by fishing nets put in the lake at night. There are numerous operators departing to Timbuktu. The best advice is to ask around at the port. Tikambo Transport has two boats – both two-deckers – taking turns for the journey to Timbuktu. They leave every Saturday at 16.30 from the departure point opposite the Catholic Mission. The smaller boat reaches its destination on Saturday evening, departing for Mopti on Sunday morning. The bigger Tikambo boat takes a little longer, arriving in Timbuktu on Sunday morning, to depart for Mopti again on Monday morning. The upper decks are slightly more spacious, since most of the freight that travels along with the passengers is stacked on the lower deck. Some drinks and basic meals are provided on board. The full fare to Timbuktu is CFA20,000 on the upper deck, and CFA17,500 on the lower deck. Mopti–Diré is CFA15,000 and CFA12,500 respectively. For some peculiar reason, the upstream prices for the return trip are lower, at CFA15,000 and CFA13,000 for Timbuktu–Mopti and CFA12,500 and CFA10,500 for Diré–Mopti.

Many smaller *pinasses* depart from Mopti; Boulkassoumbougou (Tikambo) on Friday at 14.00; Larabo (Tikambo), Afel Petit and Rougeot every Tuesday morning around 10.00; and Baba (Tikambo), every Saturday at 16.30. They should charge CFA6,000 for Mopti–Timbuktu, and the journey should take about 30 hours, with one night spent camping somewhere on the riverbank, or CFA6,000 Mopti–Diré and CFA5,000 for the return trip. There may be an extra charge for luggage.

If you can, it's best to buy your ticket direct from the boatman and not through a middleman. There have been some reports of people paying for their tickets but when they turn up being told there is no place. Getting the money refunded can be tricky. If you do have any problems, go to the river police, who are normally fairly responsive. It is, of course, best to try and avoid these situations in the first place. In an attempt to regulate operations, the Association des Pinassiers Touristiques in Mopti has set the prices for hiring a *pinasse*. The President, Sine Konta, can normally be found in his office, a bench on the riverbank opposite the Kanaga Hotel (**m** *7639 96 36;* **e** *associationpinassiersmopti@yahoo.fr or kontasine@yahoo.fr*). Every member of the association has an ID card. Hiring a private motor *pinasse* to Timbuktu through them is CFA450,000 (2 nights, 3 days), Djenné CFA200,000 (1 night, 2 days) and Gao or Bamako CFA900,000 (6 nights, 7 days).

A one-hour sightseeing tour around Mopti costs CFA20,000. Though expensive, hiring your own *pinasse* allows you to stop at villages along the way and sunbathe on the roof. Cheaper options include: a pole-powered fishing pirogue, which takes ten days to reach Timbuktu (CFA250,000), or a short sightseeing tour – a *balade* – which costs CFA2,500 per hour. Tour operators in Mopti offer boat-trips as far as Timbuktu (2 nights, 3 days). *Pinasses* are equipped with mattresses and other creature comforts; you camp on the banks of the river and meals are provided. Be warned, it can get extremely cold during the journey, so go prepared.

The other interesting voyage for travellers is along the river Bani to Djenné. Public *pinasses* leave only about once a week – ask around in the port for departure times. Journey time will depend on the number of stops, but allow up to 24 hours.

By road The major bus companies depart from various points around town. Many of these companies – like **Bani Transport** (☎ *2143 01 85*), **Bittar Transport** (☎ *2143 03 48*); **Gana Transport** (☎*21 43 13 75*), **Binke Transport** (☎ *2143 09 55*), etc – are found along Avenue du Fleuve, while Somatra is located opposite the post office. They all have daily services for Bamako, some both in the mornings and afternoons, and the fare is either CFA7,000 or CFA8,000 for Bamako and CFA5,500 for Ségou. Bani Transport leaves daily at 18.00 for Gao,

The departure point for Burkina Faso is by the port. A bus leaves every day at 17.00 for Bobo-Dioulasso (CFA6,500) and Ouagadougou (CFA12,000).

A fair amount of public transport departs from various points not far from the Campement Hotel. At the *gare routière* just past the police station, *bâchées*, minibuses and bush taxis wait for enough passengers to justify journeys to Sevaré (CFA250), Djenné and Bandiagara (CFA1,500), Bankass (CFA2,200) and Koro (CFA3,000). A little further down the road to Sévaré is a place called Bas Fond. It looks like a cross between a deserted market and a junkyard, but nevertheless this is where you should be looking for *locations* (usually Land Rovers) to Timbuktu. For CFA12,500 you must squeeze in the back, while CFA15,000 pays for a shared place on the front seat. Considering the fact that the journey will take at least eight–nine hours, paying the extra CFA2,500 is well worth it.

A ride in a shared taxi within the old or the new part of town should cost no more than CFA250 per person, while a taxi from door to door costs around CFA1,500.

(For more on transport by road, see Sévaré, page 180.)

TOURIST INFORMATION The OMATHO office (☎ *2143 05 06;* **m** *7638 65 40;* **e** *moptitourisme@hotmail.com*), is located two blocks past the Hotel Kanaga. You may also be registered and have your passport stamped here 'for statistics on tourism', but since this is a random procedure it is not clear what these statistics reflect. Staff are friendly though, and willing to give out information on guides and tourist points of interest.

Ashraf Voyages (*2143 02 79; e ashraf@dds.nl*) is run by a Dutch woman and her Malian husband, and is good if you want to visit some of the river villages of the Niger Inland Delta. They are based in the centre of town, two streets north of Pâtisserie Le Dogon, where you can rent mountain bikes for CFA1,000 an hour or CFA6,000 a day.

WHERE TO STAY

Upmarket $$$$

Hotel Kanaga (80 rooms) Ave de L'Indépendance; 2143 05 00; e kanaga@bambara.com. This used to be the best hotel in town, but is now facing serious competition. Large & rather grand with impersonal service though a great location on the banks of the river. The rooms, built around the swimming pool, are a bit on the small side but they're clean & nicely decorated with *bogolans* & other Malian handicrafts. The hotel also has an internet service, AC, TV & telephone. Good for a treat after a trip to the Dogon. B/fast extra at CFA3,000.

La Maison Rouge (14 rooms) 2143 14 02; e lamaisonrouge.hotel@yahoo.fr; www.lesmaisonsdumali.com. Designed by a Parisian architect, this stunning hotel is style junkie heaven. It may not be to everyone's taste, lacking the warmth of some of its African counterparts. Each AC room is individually styled on a different region of Mali & built using traditional processes & local materials – the Dogon room is particularly attractive, as is the bedroom open to the stars. There's a Moroccan salon for relaxing & a swimming pool planned for 2009. B/fast extra at CFA40,000.

Mid-range $$$

Hotel Doux Rêves (16 rooms) 1.2km from the centre of town; 2143 04 90; e douxreves@afribone.net; www.douxreves.com. In a new residential quarter behind the sports stadium, this hotel has superb views from the terrace & a nice atmosphere. From 18.00 to 20.00 Sat, guests are treated to traditional live music in the courtyard. AC or fan rooms. *Sgl CFA11,000, dbl CFA14,000, dorm bed CFA5,000 or sleep on the terrace for CFA4,000.*

Hotel des Roses (14 rooms) 2143 00 87; e thierrycameroun@yahoo.fr. A friendly English-speaking owner & professional staff at this centrally located hotel. Painted in striking pink & silver & of peculiar industrial design, the rooms are no less clinical but they are spacious. There is a *grande salle* serving as a dormitory or camp for CFA3,000pp with a mother parrot & her 5 offspring patrolling the grounds. Satellite TV, AC & bar/restaurant. *Dorm beds CFA5,000.*

YA Pas De Problème (14 rooms, 1 dorm) Quartier Bas Fond, Derrière l'Hôpital; 2143 10 41; e yapasdeproblemehotel@yahoo.fr; www.yapasdeprobleme.com. Although it has the feel of a backpackers' hostel & can be noisy at times, this friendly hotel caters for all budgets from a mattress on the terrace to spotless, tastefully decorated rooms with matching sheets & pillows (in plain colours) & local crafts. Hot water & mosquito nets & a swimming pool. B/fast extra at CFA1,500.

Budget $$

Hotel Campement Rénové (17 rooms) 2143 12 61; m 7631 74 01; e baumannthierno@yahoo.fr; www.hotelcampementmopti.com. Conveniently located near the *gare routière* & the *gendarmerie*, this friendly hotel has some spacious but rather gloomy AC rooms & other smaller ones with a fan. All rooms are en suite & clean & have been recently renovated. A supplementary bed costs CFA2,500 & camping on the terrace CFA2,000pp. Official agent for national airline Air Mali plus a travel agency on site. Cold water only.

Hotel Le Fleuve (13 rooms, 1 dorm) 2143 11 67; m 6672 68 00. The rooms (AC or with fan) are a bit dark & barren, but clean & adequate considering the price. Situated a few streets behind the Kanaga Hotel, with many different price categories in 2 adjacent villas. Mosquito nets & hot water available. *AC rooms CFA20,000; with fan CFA12,500, mattress on terrace CFA2,500.*

Shoestring $

The Mission Catholique 2143 05 45; e germarama@yahoo.fr. The cheapest accommodation in town was closed for renovations at the time of writing, but was scheduled to reopen by May 2009. Simple rooms with internal bathroom.

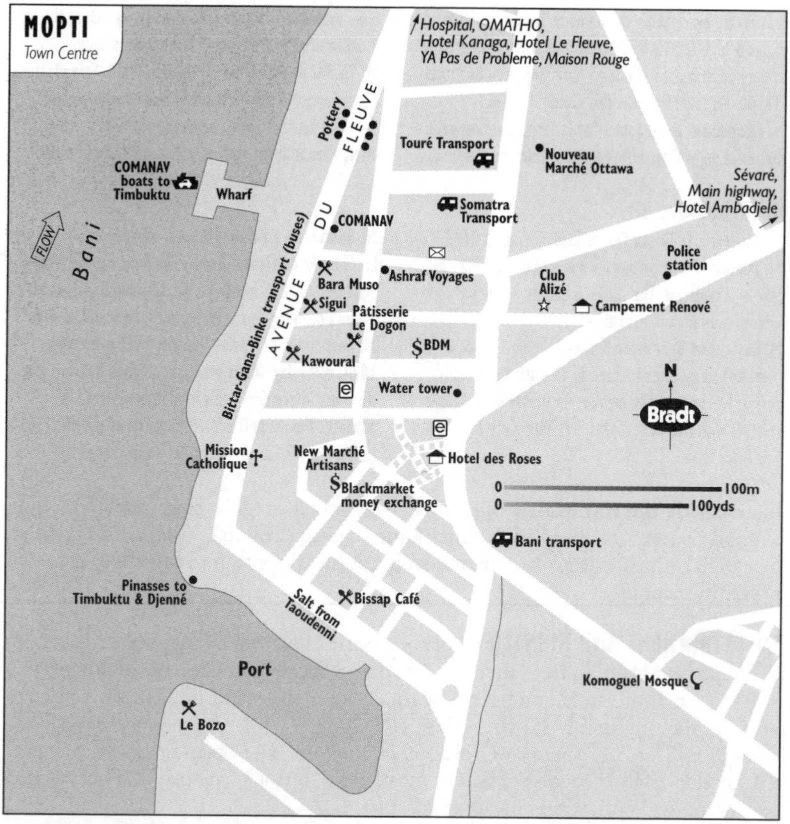

WHERE TO EAT The restaurants at the hotels fall into two categories: good and expensive or moderate and satisfactory.

Above average $$$$

La Maison Rouge 2143 14 02; 12.30–14.00 & 19.30–21.30. The gourmet menu may seem a little over the top in small-town Mopti but amongst the beautiful surroundings of the hotel it works. Marinated smoked fish with pesto, *boeuf bourguignon* with sweet potato & beetroot purée & guava poached in honey with orange mousse are just some examples. Reservation essential.

Mid-range $$$

Hotel Kanaga Restaurant Av de l'Independence; 12.00–22.30. Choice of a 3-course menu or buffet with African specialities such as *fonio*, *tô* or *fakohoye* (a Songhay dish, see *Chapter 2, Eating and drinking*, page 82).

Restaurant Sigui Centre Commercial, opposite Port Fluvial; 2143 06 90. This place is fine but quite expensive, offering standard meat & fish dishes. Guides & hawkers will try & get your attention & they are not easily discouraged.

Cheap and cheerful $$

Bar Restaurant le Bozo 2143 02 46. Justifiably popular, with a prime location overlooking the busy port & good food served in copious quantities. The perfect place to take in the sunset & watch harbour life pass you by. Good *capitaine* brochette. Don't forget the mozzie spray.

Bissap Café Zone Commerciale, in the port; 2143 13 53; e bissapcafe@yahoo.fr; www.bissapcafe.com; from 07.00 everyday. On the north side of the port, in the area where the salt comes in from Taoudenni. A chic café with a nicely decorated ground-floor restaurant

& a terrace overlooking the harbour. Serving wood-fired pizzas & high-quality Western food that is cheaper than in the hotels. A glass of *bissap* juice (see page 86) costs CFA500. No touts frequent this place.

✕ **Campement Hotel** Somewhat lacking in atmosphere (better at night than during the day), but the menu is quite extensive – salads & sandwiches as well as the usual brochette/fillet fare – & the food is tasty.

✕ **YA Pas de Problème** ⌚ 06.30–22.00. Very pleasant AC restaurant & bar on the roof terrace with a good choice of delicious, well-prepared meals. National & international dishes such as *capitaine* & *yassa poulet*.

Rock bottom $

✕ **Pâtisserie Le Dogon** Centre Commercial; ☎ 2143 03 02. Popular with travellers for a cup of tea & a slice of cake or a croissant. The choice & quality of the pastries is bit of a disappointment though.

✕ **Restaurant Bara Muso** Between the post office & the river. Not so much frequented by tourists, but usually busy at lunchtimes. The menu is invariably something-or-other with rice or couscous. Get here early to guarantee food.

✕ **Restaurant Kawoural** Down a corridor by all the buses on Av du Fleuve. Good-value local eaterie serving tasty *capitaine* dishes & the like. Turns into somewhat of a men's drinking den at night, but food is still served.

✕ **Restaurant Yérédeme** Quartier Taikiri; ⌚ from 10.00 every day. Offers good, simple food but note that the more interesting meals have to be ordered in advance. The menu is offered to guests of the Hotel Doux Rêves, just 30m away, which has no restaurant.

Just **outside the Bar Mali**, a big Dogon woman has a regular street stall ($) selling a good variety of fried fish (including *capitaine* fillets), *boulettes* (egg-filled meatballs), chips, salad, plantain and so on. A bit tricky to find but she'll give you a warm welcome.

ENTERTAINMENT AND NIGHTLIFE For some serious nightclubbing, Sévaré has more to offer than Mopti. In fact, since the Tam Tam Africa Night Club burnt down a few years ago, nightlife in Mopti has pretty much come to a standstill. The only place to visit is the nightclub **Club Alizé** (m *7639 77 94;* e *splendidehotelmopti@yahoo.fr;* ⌚ *Thu–Sat; admission CFA2,500 inc 1 drink*). The open-air *paillote* serves as a dancefloor, with a good selection of mostly local music being played.The attached restaurant, La Venis, serves meals and fast food.

Alternatively, if you wander around the *quartier* between Mossinkore and the stadium, you'll find places selling millet beer.

SHOPPING Because of its cosmopolitan population and trading importance, Mopti is a good place to buy souvenirs. You can find almost anything here, either in the side streets north of the port or at the port itself (where there is a new artisans' market under construction). The region of Mopti is well known for its *bogolans*, patterned, woollen blankets (*kassa*), and pottery sold by the wharf where the COMANAV boats dock. Jewellery – especially Peul earrings and bracelets – and various arts and crafts from Dogon country can also be good buys.

Mamdou Guindo (m *6652 81 09*) is located on the road heading east towards Hotel le Fleuve, just south of the Kanaga Hotel. A delightful man with a small shop selling a little of everything, with no pressure to buy, his prices start low yet he's still open to bargaining and even speaks a little English. Next door is the **Centre Artisanat des Femmes**, a workshop/boutique run by women. The **Association des Jeunes Artisans** (e *amadcouciss2003@yahoo.fr*), selling art and jewellery can be found at shop E21 in Sakorowel market. The **Association des Handicapés** (e *associationdeshandicapes@hotmail.com*) next to the YA Pas de Problème Hotel make and sell a variety of handicrafts.

There is an informative website on Mopti arts and crafts created by the Centre Régional de la Promotion de l'Artisanat with a version in English (*www.moptiartisans.com*).

OTHER PRACTICALITIES There are two banks on the one-way street in the commercial centre: Ecobank is in a building called Ousmane Guitteye, whilst the BCIM bank is oppsite the Pharmacie Diall. Ecobank has a Visa cashpoint with 24-hour cash withdrawal and Visa cash advances, as does the BDM bank, in the centre of town, next to Pâtisserie Le Dogon (🕘 *08.30–14.00 Mon–Sat*).

There is a BCEAO bank at the entrance to Mopti, near the taxi rank for Sévaré and Djenné, past the police station where you can exchange cash euros only between 08.00 and 11.00. A fifth bank (BIM/Western Union, also for exchanging cash euros and Visa withdrawals), is between the Hotel Kanaga and the town centre, as is the town's hospital. There is a safe and reliable black-market money exchanger in the centre of Mopti, operating out of a little grocery shop opposite the entrance to the new Marché Artisane. The shop has a glass-doored fridge on the right as you go in. He will change US dollars, euros and pounds sterling at reasonable rates and with the minimum of fuss.

It is not really necessary to have your passport stamped at Mopti. As far as your own safety is concerned, it is certainly less important than in the desert towns of Gao and Timbuktu; on the other hand, it might be worth the hassle so as not to fall foul of Malian bureaucracy. Anyway, having your passport stamped is free of charge and takes little time. The police station is located next to the Campement Hotel du Mopti, and you need to bring a photograph. Incidentally, this is probably also the best place to get a visa extension, should you need one (🕘 *07.30–17.00 Mon–Fri*). Whereas it takes at least a day in Bamako, having your visa extended in Mopti takes about five minutes and is done with a smile. Bring two photographs and make sure your passport has an empty page. Each month's extension costs CFA5,000 up to a maximum of one year (CFA60,000). You must extend while your visa is still valid or you will have a problem.

One internet café is just next to Mali Voyages, two more cybercafés are located in shops not far from the water tower, while a fourth is opposite Pâtisserie Le Dogon (CFA750 for one hour, CFA500 for half an hour).

WHAT TO SEE Although there is a weekly market on Thursdays, it is somewhat overshadowed by the continually busy **port** – the essence of Mopti. The main local industry is fishing and one side of the port is awash with dried and smoked fish – which is also exported. One of the other principal commodities is salt, which is brought down the river in huge tablets from Timbuktu and the mines at Taoudenni. Salt comes in three categories: the top-grade stuff has a smooth, layered texture, while the other two varieties are rougher, the second quality being whiter than the third. Wandering around the port, you might also see dried onions from Dogon country, along with the millet and assorted spices typical of all west African trading centres. Next to the Restaurant Le Bozo on the southern side of the port there are **pirogue-builders**, some of whom might be constructing the large *pinasses* which fan out around the harbour and can carry up to 150 tonnes of cargo. These are just some of the highlights of Mopti's port; there are plenty of others.

The small settlements on the other side of the river are **Bozo fishing villages**. There are two not far from Mopti – Djenné Daga and Kakolodaga – that are particularly interesting architecturally. They can be reached by pirogue from the port or various points along the Mopti side of the river. Remember to introduce yourself to the village chief before wandering about.

In the same way that Mopti inherited Djenné's trading functions, it also tried to emulate its neighbour's beautiful architecture. These attempts are best viewed in the quarter of **Komoguel**, which has retained many of the traditional *banco* houses typical of Djenné. The town's main mosque is also in Komoguel. It was built in 1935 in the same style as the mosque at Djenné and, although certainly not ugly, in this respect at least the new kid on the block has failed to surpass its elder sister.

BETWEEN MOPTI AND SÉVARÉ

Only seven minutes from Mopti, just off the main road, you'll find the **Ambedjele**, a beautiful *hôtel de charme*. (*24 rooms; ☎ 2142 10 31; e ambedjelehotel@ambedjelehotel.com; www.ambedjelehotel.com;* $$$$). Built in 2005 by a group of Spanish friends, particular attention was paid to using local materials and respecting the native environment. The resulting hotel was modelled on a traditional Dogon village with rooms shaped like granaries, dispersed over a hectare of land. Owing to the architecture, the rooms are fairly small but the stylish air-conditioned interiors have hand-dyed curtains and bed covers, soft pillows and locally carved doors and windows. There's hot water in the en-suite bathrooms and a free bottle of mineral water is placed in the room every day. The lush garden houses an inviting natural pool by a shaded bar serving margaritas and pina coladas. Free Wi-Fi is provided. The restaurant serves European cuisine, and breakfast is extra at CFA3,500.

SÉVARÉ

Sévaré is a small but important town on the main highway between Bamako and Gao, through which all traffic to Mopti and Bandiagara must pass. This position at the major crossroads in the centre of Mali, along with its close proximity to Mopti airport, has made Sévaré a popular base for several of the largest NGOs operating in Mali. Amongst others, Save the Children UK, Plan International and the Peace Corps have offices here.

There is not a great deal to see in Sévaré. However, the accommodation and restaurants are plentiful and there is none of the tourist-related hassle for which Mopti is renowned. The distance between the two towns is only 12km and public transport is regular and inexpensive. Taking these factors into account, you might consider basing yourself in Sévaré instead of Mopti.

GETTING THERE AND AWAY

By air Mopti airport (Aéroport Ambadéjo) (*☎ 2142 01 08*) is less than 1km from the main highway, from where *bâchées* and bush taxis leave for Mopti and Bandiagara, passing through Sévaré *en route*. Apart from a small waiting-lounge and bar, the airport has no facilities. From the end of October to March, Point Afrique (*☎ 2143 09 55; e pointafrique.mopti@afribone.net.ml*) has one weekly flight from Paris to Mopti/Sévaré on Sunday, returning to Paris on Monday. MAE (*☎ 2143 02 73; m 7614 63 15*) has flights from Mopti/Sévaré to Timbuktu on Tuesday and Saturday, while flights to Bamako leave on Wednesday and Sunday. Air Mali/CAM (*www.camaero.com*) also flies from Mopti to Timbuktu on Wednesday and Saturday and to Bamako on Thursday, Friday and Sunday. Tickets cost CFA60,000 one-way and can be bought at the Campement Hotel in Mopti. (See *Chapter 2, Getting around*.)

By road The crossroads at Sévaré is one of the busiest in the country. The enormous *gare routière* is 1km out of town on the road to Bandiagara. Since all the major bus companies are represented here, it is easy to shop around for a bus that suits your itinerary best. Names of the companies, their destinations and fares are clearly marked near the respective ticket offices. Departure times are to be taken with a pinch of salt, since many buses come from a distance and may have run into all sorts of delay. On the other hand, you as a passenger should always be on time, of course. Even if a bus is not due to leave within hours, a *vendeur des billets* is never too far away, but you may need to wake him up to have your ticket written out for you.

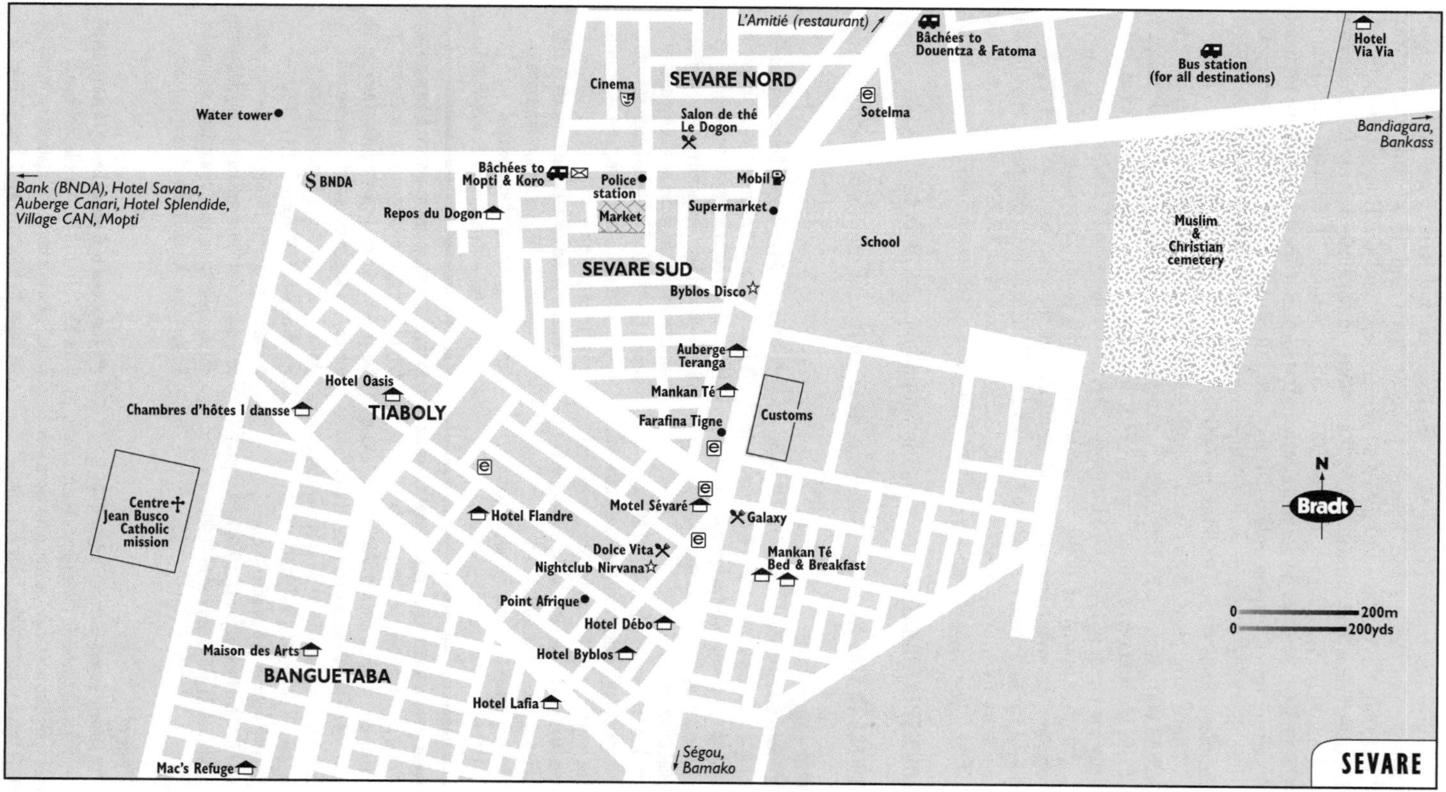
SEVARE
L'Amitié (restaurant)
Bâchées to Douentza & Fatoma
Bus station (for all destinations)
Hotel Via Via
Cinema
SEVARE NORD
Water tower
Salon de thé Le Dogon
Sotelma
Bandiagara, Bankass
Bank (BNDA), Hotel Savana, Auberge Canari, Hotel Splendide, Village CAN, Mopti
BNDA
Bâchées to Mopti & Koro
Police station
Mobil
Supermarket
Repos du Dogon
Market
School
Muslim & Christian cemetery
SEVARE SUD
Byblos Disco
Auberge Teranga
Mankan Té
Hotel Oasis
Chambres d'hôtes I dansse
TIABOLY
Customs
Farafina Tigne
Centre Jean Busco Catholic mission
Hotel Flandre
Motel Sévaré
Galaxy
N
Bradt
Dolce Vita
Nightclub Nirvana
Mankan Té Bed & Breakfast
Point Afrique
Hotel Débo
0 200m
0 200yds
Maison des Arts
Hotel Byblos
BANGUETABA
Hotel Lafia
Mac's Refuge
Ségou, Bamako

To give just a few indications of destinations and fares: buses for Carrefour Djenné, San, Ségou and Bamako leave at 06.00 and 15.00 daily (CFA2,000, CFA3,000, CFA5,000 and CFA7,000 respectively) and for Koutiala at 14.00 on Tuesday, Friday and Sunday (CFA5,000). Somatra has buses leaving for Douentza (CFA3,000), Bandiagara (CFA1,500–2,000), Fatoma (CFA600) and Konna (CFA3,500). You should get there early in the morning but the buses have no fixed departure times, leaving only when they are full. Buses for Sikasso leave every day from the Bani bus stop at the Mopti roundabout (CFA5,500) and for Bobo-Dioulasso at 07.00 and 08.00 (CFA7,000).

There are also *bâchées* and small buses leaving for Bandiagara, Sangha (CFA3,000), Koro (CFA3,500) and Bankass (CFA2,500), from just outside the gate of the bus station, Yacouba Traoré (YT), amongst others, has departures at 18.00 daily for Gossi (CFA5,000) Hombori (CFA5,500) and Gao (CFA7,000).

Another departure point for *bâchées* and small buses to nearby destinations is between the main crossroads and Sotelma, on the road to Gao. Look here for transport to Fatoma Kona and Douentza. Walk towards the Shell station for transport to Mopti, which costs CFA250 for a 4x4, CFA225 for a *bâchée* and CFA4,000 for a taxi one-way. To hire a motorbike, ask in any hotel or *campement*.

TOURIST INFORMATION See listings in Mopti on page 175 for help.

WHERE TO STAY Many hotels are located on – or just off – the main road to Bamako.

Mid-range $$$

Hotel Debo (14 rooms) 2142 01 24. All rooms are AC & self-contained. An adequate & convenient hotel although they need to fix the mosquito nets on the windows or hang them in the rooms. Wi-Fi is coming soon. B/fast inc.

Hotel Flandre (25 rooms) 2142 08 29; e hotelflandre@hotmail.com; www.hotelflandre.com. Less centrally located & somewhat lacking in style but with large, clean rooms. There is also a garden with swimming & a restaurant/bar. AC & TV.

Mac's Refuge (10 rooms) Banguetaba *quartier*; 2142 06 21; e malimacs@yahoo.com; www.geocities.com/malimacs/MacsRefuge.html. All rooms are named after Malian ethnic groups & decorated accordingly. Original in style & very friendly & informative – they can help with Dogon guides. Camping CFA4,000 (with your own gear) or CFA5,000 (gear included). Non-guests may use the small swimming pool hidden in a corner (CFA1,500). Massage & kineseotherapy are also on offer. Bike hire CFA1,000/day. Menu du jour CFA5,000. Serves a great b/fast for CFA1,800. *Dorm bed CFA7,000.*

Maison des Arts (10 rooms) Banguetaba *quartier*; 2142 08 53; www.maisondesarts.co.uk. Of free-style *banco* design & run by a sympathetic mixed British–Dogon couple. Immaculate rooms – note the soft pillows! A peaceful garden to relax or eat dinner in. *Rooms CFA18–20,000, 4-person dorm bed with mosquito net CFA8,000, camping (out of the rainy season) CFA4,000pp.*

Mankan Te Bed and Breakfast (6 rooms) 2142 01 93; e info@mankan-te.de; www.mankan-te.de. German-run guesthouse offering peaceful accommodation in 2 villas just off the main road. The fan or AC rooms are simple with natural & tasteful furnishings. Mosquito nets on windows & hot water in fully functioning internal or communal bathrooms. There's even a pet tortoise in the garden. Check out the website – all sorts of useful local info & over 600 photos. B/fast inc with fruit & homemade jam.

Motel Sévaré (40 rooms) 2142 00 82; e sibyhotel@yahoo.fr. Friendly & popular with groups on organised tours, so in high season it might be worth making a reservation. Could do with some maintenance & a good clean. Rooms AC, though some with fans.

Budget $$

Auberge Teranga (6 rooms) 2142 07 06; e hoteranga@yahoo.fr. Though primarily a restaurant, this Senegalese-run guesthouse rents a few rooms with large beds & shared facilities. Fan or AC rooms.

Campement Le Repos du Dogon (16 rooms) Sévaré, II Rue 23; 2142 10 93; e hotelreposdogon@yahoo.fr. A simple *campement* catering for visitors to the Dogon. No frills, but it works. 5 outside toilets &

showers shared amongst the rooms with mosquito nets & fans. There is a laundry service & cold water, but they will heat it up for you if you ask. Camping CFA3,000 or you can park your car in the yard. Restaurant with set menu at CFA5,000 – the chef used to cook for the governor. B/fast extra at CFA1,500.

Chambres d'Hotes I Dansse (13 rooms) 2142 07 51; m 7605 27 48; e asalfon@yahoo.fr; www.idansse.com. Opened in 2006 by a friendly Malian family who spent 15 years living in Tuscany. With a tranquil courtyard with shady corners to sit & relax, this is a clean & comfortable place to stay. Organic fruit is grown in the garden; guavas, papayas & banana all feature on the Tuscan menu. Look out for the wild birds. All rooms have fan & 2 have internal bathrooms. Camping on the terrace CFA5,000. Safety is insured, thanks to the friendly guard dog, Scooby Doo.

Hotel Oasis (6 rooms) 2142 04 98. A bit tatty & rather sober but super clean – no discerning mosquito would dare enter with the amount of spray applied. Camping or a mattress on the rooftop CFA2,500. AC or fan & a restaurant serving meals.

Hotel Via Via (10 rooms) 2142 12 64; e mopti.mali@viaviacafe.com; www.viaviacafé.com. Given its location next to the bus station, it may well serve those travellers who find themselves stranded there. Open 24hrs with comfortable & clean rooms. Food is served in the restaurant including the speciality of the house, *capitaine viavia*. A shady bar under a palm-leaf roof. B/fast not inc.

Shoestring $

Mission Catholique Centre Jean Busco Closed 12.30–15.00 & if you arrive outside the opening hours, you won't be allowed in. A peaceful location if you aren't too disturbed by the sound of barking dogs. Basic accommodation; some rooms have bathrooms inside. Cold water. *Dorm bed CFA2,000.*

Village CAN (just outside Sévaré, towards Mopti) was built to house the athletes during the Africa Nations Cup in 2002 & is more of an extension to Sévaré than anything else, hence its inclusion in this section.

Village CAN

Mid-range $$$

Auberge Canari (17 rooms) 2142 11 37; m 7611 68 39; e auberge_canari@yahoo.fr; www.auberge-canari.com. A hotel set up 3 years ago in the actual accommodation buildings built for CAN participants. A cute hotel with lovely AC rooms, tastefully decorated & very clean. Bright blue-, white- & yellow-painted walls around the swimming pool. The owner, Martine, is by all accounts, a wonderful cook producing dishes such as lemon guinea fowl, *capitaine* curry & *poulet yassa*. Homemade fruit juices & yoghurt for b/fast which is extra at CFA3,000.

Hotel Savana (8 rooms) m 6678 11 82. Run by a helpful & energetic French lady Madame Jacqueline, who has been in Mali for 20 years. She has just opened a new hotel in Youwarou on the road to Timbuktu (m *7625 00 72*). Accommodation is in villas, which can be rented in their entirety by groups. Rooms are spotless & nicely furnished. Set menu CFA5,000. AC rooms & TV.

Hotel Splendide (13 rooms) 2142 13 42; e splendidehotelmopti@yahoo.fr; www.splendidehotelmopti.jimdo.com. Newly built in 2007, this hotel is clean with very bright AC rooms though the mirrored cupboards, plastic flowers & clashing bed linen are a little harsh on the eye. There is a swimming pool, satellite TV, hot water & Wi-Fi. Restaurant with set menu CFA6,500.

WHERE TO EAT All of the hotels in Sévaré have restaurants.

Mid-range $$$

Motel Sévaré The restaurant serves standard African fare on the terrace or in the large garden.

Cheap and cheerful $$

Hotel Débo The chef here is the son of Madame Cat at the Bol de Jade in Bamako (see page 123). Highly regarded Vietnamese food.

Restaurant Mankan Te 2142 11 21; 11.30–23.00, closed 15.00–19.00. As well as the famous smoked *capitaine*, there are many interesting millet dishes such as millet with spinach (in layers with a white sauce) or millet with vegetables & meat sauce. There's also a selection of 10 vegetarian dishes. All served in the garden shaded by *paillotes*.

Rock bottom $

✕ **Galaxy** Opposite Motel Sévaré; ☏ 2142 12 06. Their meat brochettes for CFA1,000 have a good reputation around town as do those sold in the restaurant belonging to Oumou Dicko, opposite Farafinge Tigne.

✕ **Salon de thé Le Dogon** Has a good choice of pastries.

✕ **Teranga Bar Restaurant** Generally has excellent food, including 1 or 2 dishes from Senegal plus other national dishes. Eat on the terrace under the stars.

There is a large supermarket run by the ubiquitous Lebanese next to the Mobile service station at the crossroads.

Entertainment and nightlife Sévaré now has a few places to keep you entertained after dinner – otherwise most hotels will be able to organise traditional musicians with guitar and *kora*.

☆ **Discothèque Byblos** m 7608 43 37; ⌚ from 22.00 Sat/Sun & other days during holidays; admission CFA1,500 or CFA2,000, except on ladies' nights (Thu), when accompanied ladies get in for free. Apart from loud music, it features a billiard table, flipper games & video games.

☆ **Restaurant Dolce Vita** ☏ 2142 08 11; ⌚ every night. This place comes alive during the evenings. A musical restaurant with performing local artists, serving an expensive menu (CFA3,000–6,500) & along with the meal comes traditional music (such as *kora, balafon, djembe*; see page 31). There is an attached nightclub, the **Nightclub Nirvana** m *6639 77 94;* e splendidehotelmopti@yahoo.fr; ⌚ from 21.30 Thu–Sun; admission CFA2,500 inc 1 drink. This *boîte de nuit* plays mostly African but some international music with Fri reserved for salsa.

☆ **Restaurant Mankan Te** The *paillote* doubles as a dancefloor with live music on Fri–Sun & Dogon dance or music on Thu during the high season.

SHOPPING Next to the Restaurant Mankanté is Farafina Tigne (☏ *2142 04 49*) – sometimes spelt 'Farafina Tiyen' – a shop-cum-museum specialising in beads and necklaces. Their downstairs collection is truly impressive, but do not forget to visit the upstairs exhibition too. Good prices and they ship as well. You may get a discount if you spend over CFA30,000.

If you find you're in Sévaré on a Wednesday, you can wander around the market which sells mainly vegetables.

OTHER PRACTICALITIES There is an Ecobank for Western Union transfers, Visa withdrawals and changing travellers' cheques. It is situated just at the crossroads on the road to Gao, opposite the Gendarmerie Mixte de Sévaré. Otherwise, the only place in the area to change travellers' cheques is at the BNDA bank on the road to Mopti. Note that the bank closes at 11.00 on Fridays but is open from 08.30 to 11.30 on Saturdays. There are four internet facilities, as well as in some hotels, charging CFA1,000 for an hour. The fastest connection is found one block south of Motel Sévaré. A police station and post office are along the road to Mopti, opposite the Salon de Thé Dogon.

ELSEWHERE IN THE NIGER INLAND DELTA

The floodplain of the River Niger extends almost as far as the fringes of the Sahara. Sailing north from Mopti, sooner or later you will arrive at **Lake Débo**, the best known of the several seasonal lakes in the Inland Delta region. Although some 30km in diameter, Débo is shallow and, therefore, difficult for larger vessels to cross, especially on the numerous days and nights when it is windy. On the other hand, this is a popular spot for much of Mali's migratory birdlife, which comes to the Niger floodplain to spend the winter. The best time to see various species of heron, ibis and other Palaearctic waterfowl is around February, when the birds are concentrated on the remaining patches of water.

Continuing downstream, you reach **Niafounké**, the home of the late great African bluesman, Ali Farka Touré (see page 34), and the venue for the Ali Farka Touré International Festival, held in his honour in November (*www.fondationalifarkatoure.org*). His nephew, Afel Bocoum, a successful musician in his own right, still lives here. *Pinasses* and the COMONAV boat stop here on their way to and from Timbuktu and I would definitely recommend a stop in this quaint, laid-back riverside town; preferably on a Thursday when there is an interesting market to wander around. If you're lucky, you may see the mythical crocodile that has been spotted by the Bozo but luckily has never eaten anyone.

There are two reasonable hotels to choose from. The **Hotel Ali Farka Touré** (15 rooms; $$) is a small, nice, clean and very cosy hotel, set up in the house belonging to Ali and his Dutch wife, it's right on the river with water lapping up to the terrace. Two of the rooms are air conditioned (CFA20,500), and three have interior toilets. The rest are with fans. A bar and restaurant are available.

The **Hotel Campement Niafunké** (8 rooms; $$) is again very cosy with a nice atmosphere and Ali Farka Touré memorabilia everywhere. There is a bar and restaurant and performance space for local artists. Rooms have either air conditioning or fans.

Lake Débo and Niafounké are the two main stops for boats travelling downstream across the Inland Delta. By the time you reach **Diré**, the next major town after Niafounké, the floodplain has given way to the fringes of the Sahara. Diré has a basic and rather derelict *campement* with rooms and a terrace for camping. There are, of course, many smaller towns and fishing villages throughout the Niger Inland Delta, which are almost always picturesque and which often have their own 'matchbox' versions of the Djenné Mosque. Some tour operators offer river excursions to fishing villages, the lakes and other places of interest (see *Chapter 2, Tour operators in Mali*, page 46). Otherwise, getting to these riverine locations will involve renting a pirogue and a decent guide, or travelling by *pinasse publique*, which will cut the cost tremendously (see *Chapter 2, Getting there and away*, page 51).

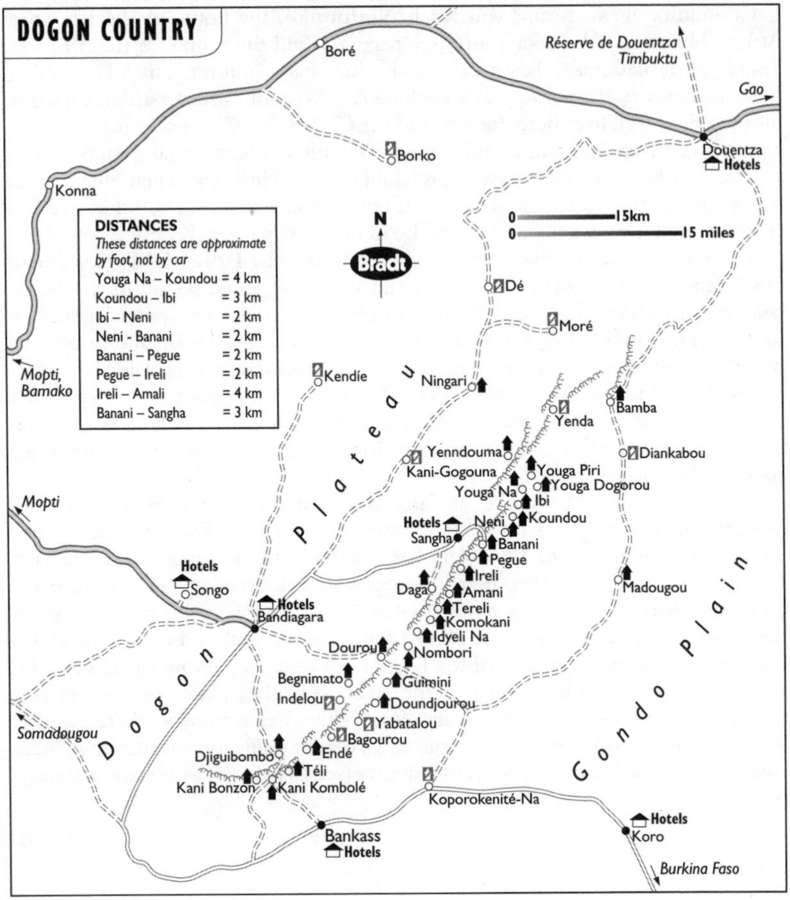
DOGON COUNTRY
DISTANCES
These distances are approximate by foot, not by car
Youga Na – Koundou = 4 km
Koundou – Ibi = 3 km
Ibi – Neni = 2 km
Neni - Banani = 2 km
Banani – Pegue = 2 km
Pegue – Ireli = 2 km
Ireli – Amali = 4 km
Banani – Sangha = 3 km
Boré
Réserve de Douentza
Timbuktu
Gao
Douentza
Hotels
Borko
Konna
N
Bradt
0 15km
0 15 miles
Dé
Moré
Mopti, Bamako
Kendíe
Ningari
Yenda
Bamba
Yenndouma
Diankabou
Kani-Gogouna
Youga Piri
Youga Na
Youga Dogorou
Ibi
Mopti
Hotels
Neni
Koundou
Sangha
Banani
Pegue
Hotels
Songo
Ireli
Daga
Amani
Madougou
Hotels
Bandiagara
Tereli
Komokani
Idyeli Na
Dourou
Nombori
Begnimato
Guimini
Indelou
Doundjourou
Yabatalou
Somadougou
Bagourou
Djiguibombo
Endé
Téli
Kani Bonzon
Kani Kombolé
Koporokenité-Na
Hotels
Koro
Bankass
Hotels
Burkina Faso
Dogon Plateau
Gondo Plain

6

Dogon Country

Tour operators, tourist offices and, indeed, guidebook writers have adopted the term 'Dogon country' (or *pays Dogon* in French) to neatly describe the most visited area in Mali. In the interests of convenience, I have followed suit, but at the same time I am embarrassed by the overgeneralisation of the term. There are about 350,000 Dogon people living on the plateau, cliffs and plain of an area in the south of the administrative region of Mopti. However, apart from a certain geographical bond and cultural similarities, the Dogon in Dogon country are diverse and different. It is not possible to talk about 'a typical Dogon village', 'a typical Dogon dance' or – worst of all – 'a living museum', where all things are apparently obvious to the visitor's eye and generally understood. On the contrary, this is a place full of surprises. Few things are as they seem and there is always something new to discover. I have an example of my own. It was dusk and I was walking back to Sangha with my guide after a visit to the cliff village of Banani. We had scaled the escarpment and were now on the flat ground of the plateau. In the half-light I saw two old men crouched in the sand with sticks in their hands. I thought that they were simply relaxing and cooling off after another hot day, doodling in the sand to while away the time and to compensate for the lack of conversation between them. Unprompted, my guide explained what they were really doing. Their doodling was not quite as aimless as I had thought, for as we drew nearer I saw that they had been drawing boxes, each with a slightly different design, into which nuts had been placed. The boxes each represented different questions; and when the foxes came to scavenge the nuts at night, their tracks would provide their answers.

HISTORY

The history of the Dogon is based on oral tradition and, as such, is rather muddled. One thing, however, seems clear enough: the Dogon were not the original inhabitants of the Bandiagara Escarpment. Their predecessors were known as the Tellem, mysterious people who built houses on the rocks of the cliff face, buried their dead in caves high above these houses, and made some of the earliest cloth and wooden objects found in sub-Saharan Africa. These are the concrete facts. Ask the Dogon, however, and they will tell you about the magical powers of these pygmies: how they could fly or transform themselves into giants and climb up to their caves in a single step. The Tellem were probably hunters; the Dogon, on the other hand, were cultivators. When the latter arrived in Tellem country they may have cleared the forest, which at that time covered the plain, so that they could farm the land. The Tellem, thus deprived of their traditional means of survival, deserted the cliffs, never to be seen again. Another version of events has the Dogon driving the peaceful Tellem away by force.

Opinions differ as to why the Dogon came to the Bandiagara Escarpment in the first place. Some argue that it was to escape drought and the invading Almoravids

THE DOGON AND THE DOG STAR

Philip Briggs

In the late 1930s, a quartet of venerable chiefs and priests divulged the most intimate Dogon traditions to the French anthropologist Marcel Griaule. Surprisingly, it emerged that these isolated animists were familiar with several cosmic objects invisible to the naked eye: for instance Saturn's rings and four of Jupiter's moons. More intriguing still were the traditions and beliefs relating to Sirius (aka the Dog Star), the brightest star as seen from Earth, and the most venerated celestial object in Dogon culture.

Sirius, the priests explained, is not one star but three, with the bright main star being orbited by two other stars that are invisible from earth – the bright white Pa Tolo (Seed Star) and duller Emme Ya (Sorghum female). Pa Tolo, though relatively small, is the heaviest object in the heavens, and it rotates on its own axis following an elliptical 60-year orbit around Sirius (mirrored in the cycle of the once-in-a-lifetime Sigi Festival).

The odd thing about this was that the existence of Pa Tolo – or Sirius B – had gone unsuspected by Europeans prior to the 1840s, when irregularities consistent with a binary star were noted in Sirius's movements. The corresponding star was seen faintly through a telescope in 1862, but it wasn't until the 1920s that scientists recognised its exceptionally dense nature and classified it as a 'white dwarf', the first such entity known to Western science. So how was it that this remote African tribe had known about the existence of Sirius B centuries earlier?

The traditions recorded by Griaule were initially aired quietly in a rather arcane anthropological journal, but they went into broader circulation in 1977 following the publication of Robert Temple's controversial book, *The Sirius Mystery*. Temple postulated that the only credible explanation for the Dogon's knowledge of Sirius B is that the amphibious deity they know as Nommo was in fact a group of spacemen from Sirius who visited earth and passed on information about their home solar system to the Dogon. Temple reckons that the Ancient Egyptians (who also associated Sirius with a deity) were visited by the same extraterrestrials, and that the event occurred about 5,000 years ago, which is when Egypt adopted a new annual calendar that started on the same day that Sirius appeared back in the spring night sky after a three-month winter absence.

The biggest chink in Temple's hypothesis is that it rests so heavily on his assumption that the Dogon possessed ancient knowledge of Sirius's binary nature. And this assumption is itself based solely on Griaule's research. If Griaule got the wrong end of the stick, then Temple's theories amount to groundless speculation. And as it transpires, Griaule's information has yet to be corroborated by any subsequent research. Furthermore, the existence of Sirius B had been confirmed a full 80 years before Griaule collected his information, while other details about the nature of Pa Tolo as supplied by Griaule's informants had been established by astronomers in the 1920s.

in the lands of the old Ghana Empire (see page 15). Others maintain that the Dogon were forced to seek refuge in the cliffs in order to avoid being taken as slaves by either the forces of the Songhay ruler, Sonni Ali (see page 16), or bands of Mossi cavalry. Another popular opinion is that the Dogon were once serfs of the Keita dynasty of the Mali Empire (see page 15). They were freed during Mali's decline and, deprived of royal protection, needed a safe place to live.

Depending on the theory, the Dogon reached the Bandiagara Escarpment around the 14th or 15th century. Most agree that four families – the Dyon, Arou, Ono and Domno – were the first to arrive at Kani Bonzon, led there, apparently, by a dog. These families exist to this day and descendants of the forefathers are dispersed in different villages throughout Dogon country.

After the departure of the Tellem, the Dogon's main enemy were the fiercely Islamic Peul, who frequently attacked them on horseback from the Peul heartland

Could it be, then, that the ancient knowledge of Sirius B communicated to Griaule was actually information acquired more recently through contact with Europeans and grafted onto existing Dogon legends surrounding Sirius? Well, one tellingly devilish detail is the Dogon assertion that Pa Tolo is the heaviest star in the galaxy – coincidentally, the 'white dwarf' Sirius B was the heaviest celestial body known to Europeans at that time, yet any civilisation sophisticated enough to travel in space would surely have been aware of the many thousands of similar stars subsequently discovered by, um, earthlings! Likewise, the Dogon's supposedly ancient knowledge of the solar system – which omits features such as smaller moons and rings around Jupiter, or of any planets further from the sun than Saturn – is more consistent with European knowledge c1930 than information gleaned from extraterrestrials.

Temple and his supporters argue that Dogon Country c1930 was too isolated to have learned about Sirius B from Europeans, yet mission schools were established in the area as early as 1910, and it would also have been visited by French colonial administrators and other outsiders. Proponents of the spacemen theory also characterise as absurd the suggestion that an early European visitor would have banged on about the binary nature of Sirius to his Dogon hosts, yet this seems quite plausible considering how important Sirius is in Dogon cosmology.

A criticism more worthy of consideration is whether it's realistic for information gleaned from European visitors to have been grafted onto the ancient traditions regarding Sirius in such a short space of time. But surely this scenario – or even one in which Griaule inadvertently conspired with his informants by asking them leading questions – has to rank a notch or two higher on the scale of probability than one in which a bunch of amphibious spacemen appeared on the scene in 3200BC?

And what of Emme Ya, the third member of the celestial Dogon trinity? Well, it scarcely entered the debate until 1995, when Benest and Duvent's paper entitled 'Is Sirius A Triple Star?' (published in *Astronomy & Astrophysics*) made a persuasive case for the existence of Sirius C based on orbital quirks recorded over the previous 100 years. Soon after, Temple published a revised edition of *The Sirius Mystery*, citing the latter-day emergence of a star that conformed to the Dogon's prescient Emme Ya as proof of the theories he'd expounded first time around. But the notion that Sirius is a trinary star actually predates Benest and Duvent's paper by several decades – it had been quite a talking point in the 1920s when a few astronomers claimed to have glimpsed a third member of the Sirius system.

For further information about *The Sirius Mystery*, visit www.robert-temple.com. Two excellent critiques of Temple's theories are *The Sirius Mystery* by James Oberg (*www.debunker.com/texts/dogon.html*), and *Investigating the Sirius 'Mystery'*, by Ian Ridpath, published in the *Skeptical Enquirer* in autumn 1978 (*www.csicop.org/si/7809/sirius.html*).

on the plain. The former managed to keep control of the *falaise* (escarpment) and the plateau, but only started to spread out on to the plain after the French had conquered the region and pacified the people – both Peul and Dogon – in 1921. By 1937, almost half of the Dogon had left the cliffs to live on the plain where water was more plentiful and the land easier to cultivate.

ECONOMY

The Dogon survive by farming small plots of land on the plateau, plain and wherever else water can be found. Some of what is produced is for personal consumption, while the rest is sold at the market. The main crops are millet, rice, sorghum and onions, which are a common sight – and smell – in Dogon country. When the onions ripen they are pounded into a paste, which is then rolled into balls and dried in the sun. Formerly used as currency, these onion balls are still traded as far away as Bamako and Côte d'Ivoire. Another common sight at the market is millet beer, which is made by the women, lugged up the *falaise* by the women, sold by the women – but drunk by the men. Profits made from the sale of the beer, however, are for the women to keep and dispose of as they see fit. Apart from the one at Bandiagara, there are five main markets in Dogon country – one for each day of the Dogon week, which has only five days. The most important is held on the first day of the week at Sangha. The others follow on consecutive days: Ireli, Ibi and Tireli, Banani and Nombori and finally Dourou and Yendouma, before starting again in Sangha.

The Dogon raise animals – cattle, goats, sheep, chickens, donkeys, etc – for food, sacrifice or work; and small-scale hunting with flintlock rifles made by their own blacksmiths also takes place, although the wild game is minimal and hunters usually have to make do with monkeys, hares, rats, birds and snakes. The other mainstay of the Dogon economy is the revenue derived from tourism: the sale of arts and crafts, village taxes, guides, accommodation, etc.

BELIEFS

Although many of the Dogon have now converted to Islam or Christianity, the remainder are still largely animist, a word defined by the *Oxford English Dictionary* as 'one who attributes a living soul to natural objects and phenomena'. This is a useful definition to keep in mind during your stay in Dogon country, for in this world almost everything is infused with meaning and significance. The French ethnologist, Marcel Griaule, was the first European to investigate and discover some of the meanings and ideas behind the complexities of Dogon symbolism and cosmology, and he wrote about them in *Dieu d'eau (Conversations avec Ogotemmêli)* and *Le Renard Pâle*, the two classics about Dogon literature (see *Appendix 2, Further Information,* page 294). Read them and the numerous other books on the Dogon for a proper introduction to what these people believe.

IN THE BEGINNING... The master of the Dogon universe is Amma. Having created the sun, moon and stars, he threw a ball of clay which transformed into Earth – his intended mate. Earth had both male and female organs, the first represented by an anthill and the second by a termite hill. When Amma tried to mate with Earth, access to the termite hill was barred by the masculinity of the female (the clitoris), which he was obliged to cut off before he could copulate. The god's original intention had been to produce twins – the ideal unity of a being is formed by a couple – but the result of this first, disordered attempt was a single birth in the form of the Jackal (or fox). Amma and Earth tried again and this time were successful in producing twins, the Nommo, who would gradually replace Amma as the arbiter of human affairs. The essence of the Nommo was in water, the source of all life, and they had the torsos of men, the tails of snakes, green skin, red, human eyes and forked tongues. Their first task was to dress Earth, which they did with a grass skirt. The Jackal, meanwhile, wanted to possess Earth and committed incest with his mother. The grass skirt was stained with blood – the origins of women's menstrual blood – and Amma rejected Earth who was now impure. He threw another ball of clay to create the first human couple, who in turn procreated and produced twins. However, after the coming of these two beings, the birth of twins became a rare exception. The Nommo, in order to reduce the impact of this situation – for twins are ideal – took to drawing silhouettes of the male and female souls on the ground. The newborn, once laid on these shadows, absorbs both their male and female souls. If the child is a boy, his female principal will lie in the foreskin; if it is a girl, the male principal will be placed in the clitoris.

The first human couple produced eight ancestors, four being predominantly male and four predominantly female, but each possessing a male and female soul. These eight ancestors each started their own family – their mortal descendants – and descended from the celestial world to earth one-by-one in order of seniority. The first ancestor, the Blacksmith, arrived in an ark containing all that was necessary for man to survive, and he began to teach the eight families how to make tools and plant the seeds which he had brought with him. The remaining ancestors descended in their hierarchical order, each one bringing his or her own particular tools and knowledge. However, the sequence was upset when the eighth ancestor descended before the seventh, the Master of the Word. Incensed, the seventh took the form of a snake and sneaked into the granary to steal the grain brought by the Blacksmith. The Blacksmith advised the humans (the eight families) to kill the snake, which they did, eating the body and giving the head to the Blacksmith who buried it under his forge.

However, humans had not yet learnt the word, and the only one who could give it to them, the Master of the Word, was dead. The oldest man in the world, Lébé, belonged to the family of the eighth ancestor, who represented the Word itself. Therefore, Lébé was the only human who could be taught the Word, and to be able to learn it he had to die and pass into the same world as the seventh ancestor. (At this point, it must be noted that neither Lébé nor the Master of the Word had *actually* died: for humans, death had not been invented yet, and the seventh ancestor was, in any case, immortal.) Lébé's remains were placed in a field not far from the Blacksmith's forge, his head pointing north towards the interred serpent's head.

As the Blacksmith worked, the noise of his anvil and bellows transformed the seventh ancestor into a Nommo, with the trunk of a human and the tail of a serpent. He crawled over to Lébé's corpse, swallowed and regenerated it, vomiting everything up in a torrent of water, the one missing ingredient for human survival.

This is an imperfect précis of what a blind hunter called Ogotemmêli told Marcel Griaule when the latter spoke to him in 1948. The complete interview is recorded in *Dieu d'eau (Conversations avec Ogotemmêli)*.

RITUALS

Cults Dogon rituals are, naturally, linked to their mythical beliefs, and most are performed in the context of one of the four principal cults. All men – but absolutely no women – are instructed in the cult of the masks or the *awa*, and a select few are chosen to be the keepers of the traditions of the masks or the *oloubarou*. Masks play a major role in Dogon culture and members of the *awa* will dance at ritual ceremonies wearing masks representing various people (old men, young girls, hunters, blacksmiths and thieves, for example); animals (including black-and-white monkeys, crocodiles and antelopes); and the most famous mask of them all, the Kanaga Mask, which relates to the creation myth.

The cult of *lébé* is associated with several agrarian ceremonies dedicated to the glory and resurrection of the Nommo. There is an altar of *lébé* in the public place of each village and ceremonies are presided over by the high priest or *hogon*, the spiritual leader and the oldest direct descendant of the original ancestors.

The cult of *binou* is pseudo-totemic. Dogon families are linked to one of the eight ancestral groups and the *binou*, which is often in the form of an animal, is taken to represent the ancestor. Each village or clan has its own totem and sacrifices are laid before the *binou* to encourage the immortal ancestors to look favourably on the living.

The cult of the ancestors is similar to that of *binou*, the essential difference being that the former relates to individual families. The aim of the cult is to maintain

A DOGON BONJOUR

Greetings are important all over Africa and Dogon country is no exception. Learn the following exchange and work on getting it up to speed. When two Dogon meet, even if they are simply crossing each other in the road, the oldest begins by saying *aga po* (hello) followed by *séo* (*ça va* or how are you?), to which the other replies *séo* (*ça va*). The first then continues with *oumana séo* (how is the family?), *ounou séo* (how are the children?) and *yahana go séo* (how is the wife?). The latter responds each time with *séo*. When the first has completed his enquiries, the roles are reversed and the second poses the same questions. A shorter version exists whereby *po séo* is replied simply with *ho* and that's all, but it is rarely used. Although a little cumbersome and unusual for the untrained novice, this greeting should eventually sound more like a duet than a verbal exchange, and the words should be sung as much as spoken.

good relations between the living and the dead. Each family household or *ginna* has an altar dedicated to an ancestor and the head of the family or the *ginna bana* presides over sacrifices and other rituals.

The Sigi Of all the Dogon rituals, the Sigi (pronounced with a hard 'g') is the most important. Originating at Youga (see page 207) and held every 60 years – the next one should be in 2027 – the Sigi is a ceremony of atonement and initiation. It is held to demand pardon for the death of an ancestor after the folly and forgetfulness of some young men at – so the story goes – the village of Youga Dogorou. The grass skirt covered with blood after the incest between the Jackal and Earth had fallen into the possession of a woman, and then of a group of young men who had been frightened by the powers assumed by the woman when she wore the skirt. All of this should have been reported to the oldest man, the guardian of tradition, but was not. As a result, he was transformed into a Nommo and remained on earth in the form of a snake. One day he met the young men and began to scold them for not telling him about the skirt. However, in his anger he spoke to them in Dogon, thus breaking the rule which forbids the Nommo to communicate directly with humans in their own language. He was thus impure and died.

At each Sigi ceremony a brand-new Great Mask, carved out of a tree trunk in the form of a serpent and sometimes 10m high, is made and initiated along with a selection of 'impure men' or *oloubarou*, who have the lifelong responsibility of preserving the tradition of the masks.

The signal for the commencement of the Sigi is the appearance of a glimmer of red light in the east, leading many observers to link the Sigi with the cycle of a star called Sirius B. Until 1970, when it was photographed by the United States Naval Observatory, astronomers had only suspected the existence of Sirius B. The Dogon seem to have a profound insight into some of Sirius's specific properties, causing wild speculations about the origins of this knowledge. One popular theory, based on Marcel Griaule's published works, is now subject to heavy criticism (see box *The Dogon and the Dog Star*, pages 188–9).

Death rituals When a Dogon dies, the soul leaves the body and remains in the village. Before it can leave and proceed to the spiritual world of the ancestors, three separate funeral rites must be performed. The first is the burial itself, performed immediately after the death. In many cliff villages the corpse is hoisted by ropes made from the fibres of the baobab tree to its final resting place in the ancient burial caves of the Tellem.

However, the soul of the dead person remains in the family house. Therefore, after a delay of between six months and a year – to allow time for the period of mourning and to give the family of the deceased an opportunity to collect all that is needed for the second ceremony (huge quantities of millet beer, for example) – the death rites continue with a celebration lasting three days and three nights, during which the soul of the deceased is invited to leave the family home. This, however, is not the end of the matter; the soul may have left the house, but it remains in the village. The *dama* takes place five years after the death to ensure that the soul leaves the village for good. Members of the *awa* perform mask dances and follow the soul out of the village and into the bush, from where it continues on its journey to the land of the ancestors.

Circumcision and excision In the beginning, the rule of procreation was the production of twins and everything was done to provide an individual with two souls, or *kindu kindu*, to compensate for the failure to produce actual twins. Therefore, a newborn child is composed of two spiritual twins, a male and a female, and neither wins over the other until circumcision or excision. By removing the foreskin or clitoris – the material expressions of the opposite sex or other soul – an individual becomes definitely male or definitely female and thus gains his or her urge to procreate. However, the rejected half of the *kindu kindu* is not destroyed. The clitoris turns into a scorpion, while the foreskin turns into a *nay* or a kind of lizard. In this way, the male and female souls of individuals live on in animal twins.

THE DOGON VILLAGE

The layout of a Dogon village is rarely haphazard. Even though the style of the village can vary depending on whether you are along the *falaise*, on the plateau or on the plain, urban planning is always indelibly linked to Dogon spiritual beliefs and symbolism.

Villages are usually divided into several, often quite autonomous quarters, each made up of a grouping of family households or *ginna*. The layout of each *ginna*, which comprises the house of the head of the family, the *ginna bana*, as well as other habitations for his wives and children, storerooms and stables, is considered to represent a man lying on his side in the act of procreation, while the habitations themselves often symbolise a human body.

The **granaries** are one of the most distinctive features of a Dogon village. These mud pillboxes with thatched roofs like witches' hats are used to store millet and other worldly possessions: clothes, pottery, jewellery, food for the family, etc, depending on whether the granary belongs to a woman or a man. In the centre of each village, or quarter, there is a *togu na*, a shelter reserved for men, where the elders hold meetings, councils and pronounce judgements. Eight posts – symbolising the original ancestors – support a thick, millet-stalk roof which is only 1.2m off the ground. This provides maximum shade – for this is also a place of rest and relaxation – and prevents standing up whilst in the *togu na*. The only circular buildings to be found in Dogon country are the *maisons des femmes* or **menstruation houses**. For reasons already mentioned (see page 190), women are considered to be impure during their period and are banished to these hovels, many of which are decorated with mud carvings of men and women with huge genitals and real pubic hair, until they have finished menstruating.

The ***binou* shrine** (part of the *binou* cult) is a decorated, single-chambered building. As a spiritual leader of the *binou* clan, the *binou* priest is responsible for maintaining a harmonious relationship between the clan-members and the

RESPONSIBLE TOURISM IN DOGON COUNTRY

One day I was in a Dogon village happily taking photographs of the houses and granaries when something grabbed my attention. I turned my camera on the object of my curiosity – a mound of clay splashed with what looked like white paint – and prepared to take its picture. 'Stop,' cried my guide 'that's an altar. It's sacred. No photo.' I had not even stopped to think; it looked far too ordinary to be sacred.

In a world littered with taboos, fetishes, sacred objects and forbidden areas, using your common sense and good intentions as a responsible tourist will only get you so far before you inadvertently break the rules. For this reason, you should not tramp across Dogon country without the company of a good guide. Follow him at all times, don't touch anything and ask before you take photographs (the general rule is that you can take pictures of the houses and granaries, but not the people and sacred places – unless you pay).

It stands to reason that the best guides will normally be Dogon themselves. Try to avoid the numerous *petits guides* touting for business in Mali's tourist towns, who profess expertise in all matters Dogon but, in fact, know very little indeed. On one infamous occasion, an enthusiastic youth employed by a group of travellers eager to 'discover' Dogon country was asked why the women go around bare-breasted. 'Because they can't afford to buy clothes,' he answered, with as much confidence as ignorance.

Many other potential tourist blunders can be avoided with a little thought, common sense and respect. For example, you don't have to be a genius to work out that water is in chronically short supply in Dogon country and that, as a result, daily ablutions should be quick and economical. Giving sweets or the ubiquitous *bics* (pens) to children is a thorny issue. I sought the advice of the Mission Culturelle in Bandiagara and a number of senior guides, and the general consensus seemed to be that *bics* should be given to the village school rather than to individual children and that sweets were no good because they caused cavities and the Dogon could not afford to go to the dentist – which all seemed to make sense to me. Another thing often overlooked by visitors is their choice of dress when trekking through Dogon country. Despite the scorching heat on the Bandiagara Escarpment, figure-hugging shorts and skimpy vests (or worse) which would turn heads on the Côte d'Azur are obviously not appropriate in Dogon country, where contact with the outside world has been so limited and the people are more easily shocked than in more open societies.

While the Mission Culturelle are keen to re-educate scantily clad backpackers and shutter-happy tourists, their main task is to stop the theft of Dogon and Tellem artefacts. At one end of the scale, professional grave robbers routinely plunder Tellem burial objects from the caves high above the villages on the escarpment and sell them for a small fortune to western collectors. Meanwhile, tourists walk through Dogon villages, take a fancy to intricately carved doors of millet granaries, masks and statues, offer an irresistible number of dollars for the object of their desire, and walk away with yet another piece of Mali's cultural heritage. To combat the problem, the Mission Culturelle are trying to encourage the creation of village museums, where each family donates an exhibit – pots, pans, Dogon underwear – it hardly matters what – instead of selling them to tourists. The money generated by these museums will go back into the village, hopefully creating jobs and the beginning of an infrastructure to support a new way of life – in other words, the tourist boom.

supernatural world. Libations of millet gruel on the façades of the shrine are an indispensable part of the *binou* cult. The millet leaves clear white marks on the façade. The **house of the *hogon*** is associated with the Lébé cult. The *hogon* and the *binou* priest may be considered as complementary counterparts, as they both serve as spiritual leaders. When a *hogon* dies, he is succeeded through election by one of the village elders. After a period of initiation the new *hogon* has to live by strict rules and taboos. One of these forbids him from leaving his compound and he is not to be touched by anyone – not even his wife and family.

ORIENTATION

Although most people come to visit the cliff villages built on the rocks of the Bandiagara Escarpment, otherwise known as the *falaise*, which cuts a 200km swathe through central Mali, Dogon country actually covers an area of some 4,000km^2, with hundreds of settlements on the plateau and the vast Gondo Plain, which stretches south from the cliffs into Burkina Faso. The land of the Dogon is divided into four *cercles*: Bandiagara and Douentza on the plateau, Bankass and Koro on the plain. These, in turn, are split into several *arrondissements*.

Bandiagara is the largest town on the plateau and the main base for trekking in Dogon country. Bankass, on the Gondo Plain, is closer to the escarpment, but facilities for visitors here are inferior to those at Bandiagara.

Along the escarpment, the most popular tourist route is between the villages of Banani in the northeast and Kani Kombolé in the southwest. Access to the cliff villages along this route is possible by vehicle from Sangha (for Banani) and Djiguibombo (for Kani Kombolé). Although there is something resembling a road leading down from Dourou to Nombori, this option should be considered only by those with a 4x4 and no fear of soft sand. However, since Dourou is roughly halfway between Sangha and Djiguibombo, and accessible by vehicle from Bandiagara, for many visitors it marks the beginning or end of a hiking trip in Dogon country.

Both Djiguibombo and Dourou have *campements* with prices ranging from CFA1,000 to CFA2,000 per person, while Sangha has better tourist facilities, including some comfortable hotels.

GETTING AROUND Trekking in Dogon country involves, by definition, a lot of walking; indeed, the villages along the *falaise* are only accessible by foot. You don't have to be a great climber or super fit, and any guide worth his salt will be quick to evaluate how much you can do in a day. Trust his judgement! Porters are also available at about CFA3,000 a day to carry your bags. It is now possible to stop for a drink and even stay the night at most of the cliff villages, allowing travellers to spend several days exploring Dogon country at a relaxed pace. The distances between the cliff villages are relatively short and easily covered on foot. However, you can also drive along the Gondo Plain – 4x4, motorbikes, and cart and donkey are the preferred means of transport – stopping to visit any village that takes your fancy.

Vehicles are more necessary for tours of the more spaced-out villages on the plateau and for travel between the principal towns in Dogon country – Bandiagara, Sangha, and Bankass (see the *Getting there and away* sections for these towns).

WHERE TO STAY AND TO EAT While there are hotels and restaurants in Bandiagara, Bankass, Koro and Sangha, board and lodging in the villages along the *falaise* and on the plateau is predictably rustic. Pretty much all villages now have at least one *campement*. These should not be compared with others across Mali, for in Dogon country creature comforts are minimal. You must wash with buckets of water, taking great care not to use too much of this precious commodity, and sleep on lumpy mattresses in box-like rooms, on the roof, or pitch a tent. The majority of *campements* have some form of toilet, and a select few possess a fridge. Bottled drinks are usually available, along with spaghetti, macaroni, rice, couscous and the

Dogon favourite, *tô* with gumbo sauce (see page 82). The cost of spending the night at one of these *campements* varies depending on the facilities available and the popularity of the village. Expect to pay between CFA1,000 and CFA2,000 for camping or to sleep on the roof and between CFA2,000 and CFA15,000 for a room, the most expensive with internal cold-water shower. Food and drink is more expensive than elsewhere in Mali (bar perhaps Timbuktu during the Festival in the Desert). Food is between CFA2,000 and CFA4,000 for a main dish and expect to pay CFA1,250 for bottled mineral water and CFA1,350 for a big beer.

Several of the tour operators prefer to camp on the Gondo Plain rather than lodge their clients in the villages themselves. There are areas of soft sand not far from the *falaise*, which serve as good campsites, although you should be aware of snakes and scorpions! In case you end the day in a village with no *campement*, ask for the *chef du village*. He will find you a place to spend the night, most likely in or near his family compound. A tourist tax is payable and as a general rule, charges are as follows: Djiguibombo to Dourou, known as Zone A, CFA500; Dourou heading north along the *falaise*, known as Zone B, CFA1,000.

GUIDES Guides all over the country purport to have an intimate knowledge of Dogon country. If they are not actually Dogon themselves, they will invariably boast some impressive link to Mali's most popular tourist attraction. Be suspicious of guides who approach you in towns such as Bamako and Mopti offering to take you there. Of course, your suitor might be 100% genuine: knowledgeable, friendly and hard-working. Unfortunately, there is an equally good chance that he will know next to nothing. The general rule is to look for your guide in Dogon country itself. There is no shortage of them in Bandiagara, while at Sangha the Bureau des Guides is reliable and respected (see page 199). If you find your guide in Bandiagara, visit the Mission Culturelle to check out his credentials (see page 197).

It cannot be stressed enough that a guide can make or break your experience in Dogon country, so before making up your mind about a guide, take some time to get to know him a bit. See whether he will be able to give you the kind of information you are looking for and whether his knowledge of French or English suits you. One way to find a good guide is by recommendations from other travellers. A word of warning: some guides are wise to this and will say they're the guide you're asking for, even though they're not, just to get the business. One way to avoid this is to ask the guide to see letters of recommendation from previous clients and then ask to see his *carte professionnelle* (see page 45) to verify that he is the same guide that the letters are talking about. One English-speaking guide whose name keeps coming up in recommendations from travellers and who 'knows the Dogon country and its people very well' is Abdramane Guindo (**e** *draguindo@hotmail com*). Try and find him if you want 'a unique experience and a good insight into the country'.

You should also try and get a clear picture of what is – and what isn't – included in the price. If meals are included, make sure you know what type of food you are talking about. Some tourists end up living on huge servings of couscous or spaghetti and tomato sauce, but little else. Also check the flexibility of your prospective guide, as certain guides will decide on their own what is best for you, regardless of your expectations and wishes. The fee for a guide should be roughly CFA10,000 per day; food, accommodation, *taxes touristiques*, etc are not included. Expect to pay between CFA15,000 and CFA20,000 with food and accommodation or CFA30,000 per day with transport as well. If that sounds like a lot of wages, good guides generally will accept no less than that. A porter charges between CFA2,000 and CFA2,500 per day. Some popular excursions have fixed rates with most expenses (but not drinks) included.

Having packed this section – and others in the book concerning guides – with warnings and precautions, I should add that I have heard of more good experiences with guides in Dogon country than bad. A lot depends on the relationship you strike up with your prospective guide. If you warm to a particular person and have a good feeling about him, the chances are that he will not disappoint. Bear the precautions I have mentioned in mind, but also trust your instinct.

Finally, you are not obliged to be with a guide when you trek through Dogon country. However, there is so much to discover in this land, and so many forbidden areas and other traditions to respect, that I strongly advise you to take one (see box *Responsible tourism in Dogon country*, page 194).

FESTIVAL OF THE DANSES DES MASQUES If you are planning to visit Dogon country towards the end of December or the beginning of January, ask around if the Festival des Danses des Masques is about to take place. This gathering of groups of dancers is staged in a different village every year, and offers a spectacular opportunity to see a whole variety of costumes, masks and dances. It is visited by the Dogon as well as an international public. The entrance fee is CFA4,000 per person, which also buys you the right to take pictures. (See also page 90.)

BANDIAGARA

Bandiagara is 'base camp' for any visit to Dogon country. Whether you intend to access the cliffs via Sangha or Djiguibombo, or want to see some of the villages on the plateau, Bandiagara is hard to avoid. For this reason, there are several hotels and restaurants, and plenty of guides – but no bank.

You will be disappointed if you come to Bandiagara expecting a picture-postcard Dogon village. Instead, this is a reasonably sized town which, by Dogon standards at least, is cosmopolitan and busy. The largest market on the plateau takes place here on Mondays, while the smaller *marché des femmes* takes place on Fridays. A picturesque river, the Nyamé, runs along the eastern edge of town. Otherwise, Bandiagara is of limited interest to the sightseer. It is, if you like, a point of transition – a link between the private, spiritual world of the Dogon on the escarpment and the remote plateau, and the rat race 75km away.

GETTING THERE AND AWAY Getting to Bandiagara is simple enough in principle: *bâchées* leave from Mopti and Sévaré and take approximately one hour to cover the smoothly tarred 75km across the Dogon Plateau to Bandiagara. However, if the demand is light – as it tends to be in the afternoons – you might spend hours waiting for your *bâchée* to fill up. With this in mind, ask how many tickets remain to be sold before you hand over your CFA1,500. If there are plenty, it might be quicker to hitchhike. The same is true when you want to leave Bandiagara. On market days (Mondays and Fridays) there is a steady flow of *bâchées* and bush taxis to Mopti, and even a direct (and very slow) bus to Bamako (CFA8,000). On other days, however, the extent of the traffic is hard to predict. You can get to Sangha by public transport (1½ hours; CFA1,500), but try to travel on a market day which, in Sangha's case, is every five days. Alternatively, you might be able to find an *occasion* by going to the Restaurant Petit Coin. A ride to Djiguibombo on the back of a mobylette (a small motorbike) will cost around CFA5,000, while a small car will take you there for CFA11,000.

TOURIST INFORMATION The **Mission Culturelle** (✆ *2144 22 63*) in Bandiagara is responsible for preserving and promoting the cultural heritage of the Dogon.

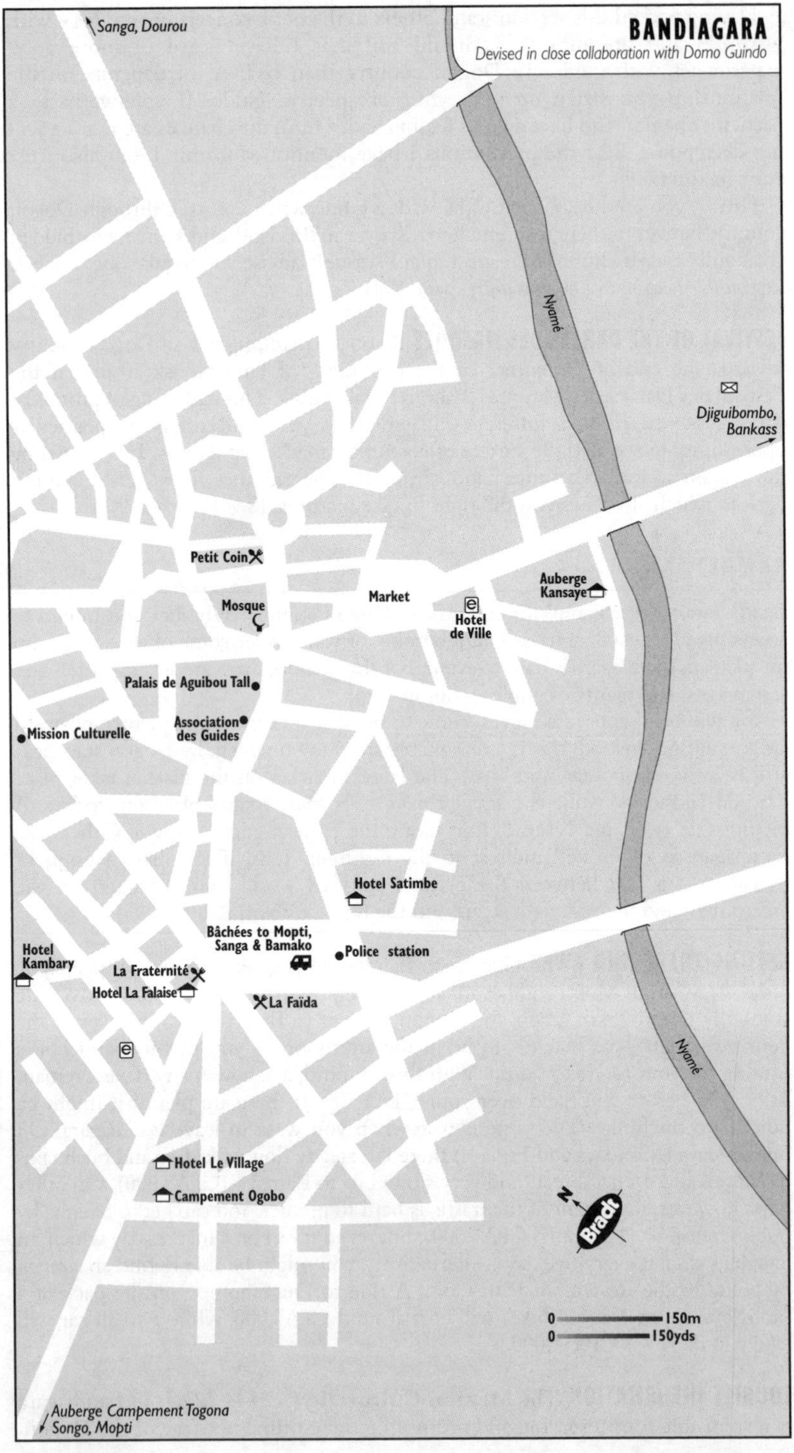
BANDIAGARA
Devised in close collaboration with Domo Guindo
Sanga, Dourou
Nyamé
Djiguibombo, Bankass
Petit Coin
Market
Auberge Kansaye
Mosque
Hotel de Ville
Palais de Aguibou Tall
Association des Guides
Mission Culturelle
Hotel Satimbe
Bâchées to Mopti, Sanga & Bamako
Police station
Hotel Kambary
La Fraternité
Hotel La Falaise
La Faïda
Nyamé
Hotel Le Village
Campement Ogobo
N
Bradt
0
150m
0
150yds
Auberge Campement Togona
Songo, Mopti

Although this is not a tourist office – and should not be treated like one – the staff are friendly, approachable and experts in their field. You could ask them to recommend guides for treks in Dogon country, which at least guarantees someone who knows what he is talking about – people recommended by the Mission Culturelle have normally taken lessons with them before becoming guides. The guides have now organised themselves, and their **Association des Guides et Accompagnateurs Touristiques au Pays Dogon** (*2144 29 05*) has its office not far from the mosque. The **Association des Groupements Villageois Féminins** is located just next to the La Fraternité restaurant (see page 200).

WHERE TO STAY

Mid-range $$$

Hotel Kambary (also known as Le Cheval Blanc) (16 rooms) 2144 23 88; e chevalblancmali@yahoo.fr; www.kambary.com. This Swiss-owned hotel, designed by an architect flown in from Italy, is a little different from the norm. A cluster of futuristic, domed buildings built on an arid piece of land near the road to Mopti look more like an extraterrestrial colony in the *Star Wars* prequel than the most luxurious & expensive hotel in Dogon country. There is minigolf & a small but attractive pool lying well hidden behind the spacious & sparsely furnished rooms. TV & AC with en-suite shower. A good base for exploring the Dogon.

Hotel La Falaise (18 rooms) 2144 21 28; e napopapa2003@yahoo.fr; www.hotel-lafalaise-mali.com. This new, well-managed hotel is proving very popular. Built in traditional style, the rooms are organised around a central courtyard & whilst quite basic & small have AC, TV & en suite with shower. *Dorm bed CFA4,500pp.*

Shoestring $

Auberge Camping Togona (19 rooms) Several kilometres before Bandiagara, if you're coming from Mopti; 2144 21 59. The whole setting is pleasant & spacious, as are the rooms with open-air showers. The friendly management have recently spruced it up & it is now good value. Camping CFA2,000pp & there is also a restaurant recommended by readers.

Auberge Kansaye (8 rooms) m 7322 99 92/6684 24 56; e kansayebouba@yahoo.fr. On the banks of the river, the atmosphere in this popular *auberge* manages to be both upbeat & laid back, with reggae music & a gregarious Rastafarian manager. It's a bit shabby & nothing really works properly. The rooms, by all accounts, get extremely hot & you pay extra for a fan. A cooler option may be to sleep on the roof with a mosquito net provided for CFA3,000.

Hotel Le Village (7 rooms) 2144 23 31. Cheaper & friendlier than the nearby Hotel Kambary (also known as the Cheval Blanc). Rooms are decent with fans & comfortable bamboo beds & you can pitch a tent in the peaceful garden for CFA2,000. You share washing facilities – note that the water pressure is sometimes very low – & there is a clothes-line in the garden. They will also store luggage while you go trekking along the *falaise*.

Hotel Satimbe (5 rooms) Behind the bus yard; 2144 23 78; m 7686 76 45. Slightly more basic than Le Village, but no less friendly. A bed comes with a mosquito net & fan. It might be possible to sleep on the roof & the small *jardin de repos* is, as its name suggests, a peaceful garden in which to relax. B/fast inc.

WHERE TO EAT AND DRINK

Cheap and cheerful $$

Auberge Kansaye m 7322 99 92; 07.00–midnight. A large terrace serves a selection of food from CFA1,000 to CFA4,000. You'll probably need an early night to prepare for a trek in the Dogon or recover if you've just returned but if you do want some night-time entertainment, the manager of the Kansaye organises dancing nights in the bar, separate to the hotel.

Restaurant Bar Le Cheval Blanc 2144 23 88; 11.00–22.00. This is the official name of the restaurant at the Hotel Kambary. You eat here for the ambience rather than the great quality of the food. Swiss diners will be disappointed by the 1 or 2 Swiss dishes on the menu, while the rest might end up wishing that they had stuck to drinking an aperitif on the cool & pleasant terrace.

Restaurant Bar La Falaise 2144 21 28; 24hrs Mon–Sun. There is a nice terrace restaurant upstairs serving good, reasonably priced African & European specialties. A buffet-concert with traditional music & local artists almost nightly Nov–Feb.

Rock bottom $

Hotel Le Village Meals are taken in a pleasant garden. The servings are not stingy here, but you must order in advance if you want anything out of the ordinary, which effectively means something other than spaghetti. At breakfast, once again taken in the garden, the papaya, guava & other types of jam are homemade & delicious. The same rule applies at the restaurants of the other hotels in town: order in advance.

La Fraternité At the roundabout to Mopti/Burkina Faso; e moussajoel@yahoo.fr. Thanks to Moses, the English-speaking owner from Cameroon & his wife Promise from Nigeria, this restaurant has become a bit of a meeting place for Anglophones. The new owners are helpful & the food plentiful. Moses does the cooking & though it takes a while to prepare, it's worth it. Steak, couscous, *capitaine* & salads; good-quality ingredients make for a tasty experience. Superb value for money & some say the best food in the whole of west Africa!

Restaurant Pâtisserie La Faïda Near the *gare routière* with a small terrace around the back, for a limited choice of meals but no pastries.

Restaurant Petit Coin Near the market; 2144 25 79. This place has gained a reputation as *the* travellers' hangout in Bandiagara. As such, guides & hassle are part of the fixtures, but the food is good – especially the *sauce arachide* – & reasonably priced. This can also be a good place to find people to go trekking with in Dogon country or to hitch a lift to Sangha, as many groups stop here for lunch *en route* to the *falaise*.

If you are in Bandiagara on a market day, ask directions to – or stumble across – a *cabaret* or ad hoc bar where men gulp *tchapulo* (millet beer) from calabashes as quickly as the women can make it. It's only CFA125 a litre, so spirits are usually quite high, and rumour has it that *tchapulo* often washes down mouthfuls of the Islamic forbidden fruit – pork.

OTHER PRACTICALITIES The post office is on the other side of the river just past the bridge near the road to Djiguibombo. The police station is next to the bus yard. There is one internet café in Bandiagara, Café Clic, located in the Hotel de Ville. The Palais de Aguibou Tall has several rooms displaying old photos and one original door. There is also a mausoleum in the grounds (*Sun morning only; admission CFA1,000*).

BANKASS

Bankass, with its distinctive red *banco* houses, is another base for visits to Dogon country. Situated on the Gondo Plain at the southeastern end of the *falaise*, it is conveniently located for visits to the villages on the 'Kani Kombolé circuit' (see page 203). So is Bandiagara, however, where facilities are more comfortable and numerous. Therefore, unless you are arriving in Dogon country from Burkina Faso – in which case Bankass is the logical stopping point – choose Bandiagara as your main base.

GETTING THERE AND AWAY Most visitors to Bankass are at either the beginning or the end of their stay in Dogon country. The majority of tourist traffic, therefore, is either to the main highway in Mali or to Burkina Faso. During the dry season, the occasional vehicle linking Bankass to any Malian town other than Bandiagara, Mopti or Sévaré may opt for the shorter route via Somadougou. However, until the section between Somadougou and Wo is significantly upgraded, most traffic to Bankass will go by way of Sévaré (2 hours; CFA3,000) and Bandiagara (CFA1,000). Here you will find *bâchées* and small buses leaving for Bankass, but other than on market day (Tuesday) they could take a very long time to fill up. From the *gare routière* in Bankass, look for the occasional vehicle leaving directly for Bamako (CFA6,000) or Sikasso (CFA6,000), again especially on Tuesday. For Burkina Faso, take a *bâchée* from Bankass to Koro (1–2 hours; CFA1,000), from where an excellent daily SOGABAF bus leaves at 15.00 for Ouagadougou (about 6 hours) via Ouahigouya (3–4 hours).

Bankass is about 10km from Kani Kombolé on the *falaise*. The walk across the sandy Gondo Plain is not the easiest – or the most scenic – but it might be your only option. On market day in Bankass (Tuesday) hitching a lift from Kani Kombolé is a possibility; otherwise, renting a cart and donkey is the best bet for those who would rather not walk (around CFA4,000–5,000).

WHERE TO STAY

Hotel Les Arbres (10 rooms) 2128 66 42. Check if the water is running before handing over your money; there have been serious problems with the water supply in the past. Camping in the garden costs around CFA2,500. The only hotel in town & pricey for what's on offer. $$

Campement Hogon (11 rooms) Situated at the entrance to town, all rooms have a fan & mosquito nets. Otherwise a mattress on the terrace costs CFA2,500pp. This is the best of the budget options. $

Seno Camping (7 rooms) Next to the water tower. Camping only at CFA5,000pp. $

WHERE TO EAT

Hotel Les Arbres The restaurant is overpriced, but it does have the best selection of food in town. $$

Campement Hogon One of the few alternatives, where unadventurous chicken & spaghetti dishes must be ordered in advance. $

OTHER PRACTICALITIES The post office is opposite Hotel Les Arbres. One *cabine téléphonique* (2144 30 02) is the only available telephone, serving the whole of Bankass.

KORO

Most travellers going this way are in transit between Mali and Burkina Faso.

WHERE TO STAY

Hotel Campement l'Aventure (4 rooms) 2144 10 40; m 6553 16 52; e contact@afrikhorizons.com; www.aventure-dogon.com. A recommended place to stay. Rooms are in a pleasant traditional setting built in Sudanese style. Camping CFA4,500pp. If you are planning to go to Dogon country, this is a good place to enquire & even book a trip. Quad-bike trips & 4x4 for hire at €75/day. $$

SANGHA

Sangha is the village made famous by the French ethnologist Marcel Griaule, who spent much of his time here researching Dogon traditions and beliefs. Compared with other villages along the *falaise*, Sangha is better described as a town; it comprises ten villages or quarters which sprawl across the plateau and lie only a couple of kilometres from the escarpment. It is this convenient location – the cliff village of Banani is within easy walking distance – rather than any intrinsic beauty which has made Sangha so popular with tourists. As a result, some hotels and other tourist facilities have emerged, making Sangha the most convenient of the three 'bases' – Bandiagara and Bankass being the others – for direct access to the *falaise*.

GETTING THERE AND AWAY The only time when *bâchées* are sure to leave for Bandiagara is on market day in Sangha, which is every five days, or once a Dogon week. At other times, departures are entirely dependent on demand. If you're lucky enough to find a place in a car, they will normally charge CFA1,500. But if you charter a lift, expect to pay CFA15,000. You can sometimes find someone willing with a moped. Offer to pay for petrol there and back – about CFA5,000.The market takes place behind Campement Sangha near the entrance to town. During high season, 4x4s are always parked outside Campement Sangha, so it might be possible to hitch a lift back to Bandiagara – and perhaps beyond – with returning tour groups.

WHERE TO STAY AND EAT All hotels and *campements* have their own restaurants, although often you have to pre-order food.

Mid-range $$$

Campement Hotel Sangha (also known as 'La Guina') (35 rooms) 2144 20 28; e hotelsangha@yahoo.fr. This hotel had an illustrious past: it used to be the Campement Administratif, then Sangha's first school & the home of Marcel Griaule. Nowadays, it caters for the needs of Sangha's tourists. Rooms are en-suite sgls/dbls/trpls with AC or fan. Budget travellers have the option to stay in a *paillote* for CFA6,000, to camp for CFA4,000, or to sleep on the terrace (overlooking the plateau) for CFA2,500pp. Many of the organised groups stay here, which is why it is overpriced & often full. Food is uninspiring with main dishes at CFA3,500. This is where you'll find the main Bureau des Guides. B/fast extra at CFA2,000.

Budget $$

Auberge Le Grand Castor (12 rooms); 2144 20 04; e grandcastordogon@yahoo.fr. A nice atmosphere & a nice owner. Beautifully decorated rooms using local materials. Some have internal shower & toilet; all have fans. A dorm bed costs CFA5,000 or sleep on the terrace for CFA2,500. There's a large courtyard across the road where you can pitch a tent for CFA2,500. The restaurant is under the stars in the garden; menu du jour CFA3,000. There's a well-stocked bar selling big beer for CFA1,100 & Guinness CFA1,100 & a small souvenir shop opposite.

Hotel Gir-Yam (has a number of different spellings) (8 rooms) 2144 20 14; e hotelguiruyam@yahoo.fr. Reasonable rooms but with a bit of a bleak atmosphere; 5 are luxury with toilet & cold-water shower inside. All have fans & mosquito nets. They're clean, especially the new rooms & everything appears to work. Camping or sleeping on the terrace CFA2,500. There is also a Bureau des Guides. The restaurant serves rice & spaghetti with meat, chicken & beef for CFA2,500.

Hotel Les Deux Caïmans (8 rooms) 2144 20 21. Little imagination was used when this hotel was built, yet the rooms are decent with big beds. The passable showers & toilets are communal but there are plans to make them en suite. Sleep on the terrace for CFA2,000. Meals to order: CFA2,000 for macaroni, couscous with meat or steak. B/fast extra at CFA1,000.

Shoestring $

Gîte de la Femme Dogon (18 rooms) 2144 20 13. Independent travellers tend to like it here in the Protestant mission, which means it's busy. The rooms are basic & vary, so have a look at a few. There are no fans but very clean toilets, if you can reach the toilet roll, which is attached to the roof. CFA2,500pp allows you to sleep on the terrace. It also has a Bureau des Guides, 4x4 rental & a laundry service. Meals to order from the restaurant with basic meals such as rice, spaghetti, couscous or chicken for CFA2,500. B/fast extra at CFA1,000.

OTHER PRACTICALITIES One of the conspicuously new concrete boxes in the middle of town is the post office; another is Sotelma.

Guides are available for hire at Campement Sangha, Gir Yam and Femme Dogon. The **Bureau des Guides** (*2144 20 32*) at Campement Sangha is the oldest guide office in all of the Dogon. It used to be run by the state but when it was privatised, the old workers took it over. It has some of the best guides in the country and is recommended by the Mission Culturelle. You can choose from several suggested itineraries or arrange your own tour. The *chef des guides*, Sékou Dolo (e *hotelsangha@yahoo.fr*) will be happy to discuss options with you. He has been guiding since 1975 and was the one who welcomed ex-French president Chirac during his visit to the Dogon. He is even a published author (*La Mère des Masques; un dogon raconte; www.seuil.com*). He doesn't guide himself during high season as he's running the office but can in low season.

Campement Hotel Sangha has a small permanent exhibition of Dogon artefacts and pictures. Most of the material has been offered by the Dutch architect Joop van

Stigt, who is a frequent visitor to the hotel, which serves as a base for his many activities in Dogon country (see box *Foreign aid: every little helps*, page 99 and *Chapter 2, Local charities and NGOs*, page 100).

CLIFF VILLAGES *Revised by Jolijn Geels*

The villages along the *falaise* between Banani in the northeast near Sangha and Kani Kombolé in the southwest receive the most tourist visitors. Here you will find the picture-postcard Tellem architecture, the ancient burial caves, villages built precariously on the rocks of the cliff face and other quintessentially Dogon attractions. The distance between Banani and Kani Kombolé is about 45km and, of course, it is quite feasible to trek from one to the other, eating and sleeping at village *campements en route*. However, the more popular choice – and the one offered by most guides and tour operators – is to visit either the group of villages in proximity to Banani or those near Kani Kombolé. Although it is not impossible to cover the full stretch on foot in a matter of days, it is far more rewarding to cover smaller distances, allowing time to explore the many points of interest and enjoy a siesta during the hottest midday hours. In fact, slowing down is a first requirement to fully appreciate the Dogon pace of life. To walk the full distance between Djiguibombo and Sangha, allow at least a week to ten days. Walking in this direction means having the sun behind you, which is always preferable.

KANI KOMBOLÉ The descent from the plateau at **Djiguibombo** to Kani Kombolé is about 3km if you walk down the *falaise*, but nearer 5km if you take the paved road – which is now suitable for most types of vehicles all year around. On clear days you can see Bankass in the distance. Kani Kombolé is not built on the *falaise* itself, but nestles in a shady corner of the plain. However, the lack of cliff-face architecture is made up for by an attractive mosque, built in the traditional Sudanese style and evidence of the increasing number of Dogon who have converted to Islam.

KANI BONZON At 4km to the southwest, along the *falaise*, and well worth the return trip, Kani Bonzon is the place where the migrating Dogon couples first arrived on the *falaise*. The original settlement is halfway up the cliff, where the remains of a former *hogon* house mark the place where the first four couples chose to stay (see box *Animism along the* falaise, page 208).

TELÍ At 4km from Kani Kombolé is Telí, a picturesque village with former Tellem dwellings – now sometimes used for food storage or as burial sites – Dogon granaries and a well-preserved abandoned village. As in many other villages, the Dogon formerly lived sheltered in the cliffs for security reasons, as they feared both predators (hyenas and lions) that used to roam the plains, and human aggressors. Some 60 years ago, when the French cavalry no longer posed a threat to the Dogon, people started moving to the site of the present village below the cliff. The last families moved out as recently as ten–15 years ago. The abandoned village has since been restored by the villagers and can be visited on payment of a small fee. The view from up above is well worth the climb. Note the new and strikingly ugly church with its corrugated-iron roof, which is used by around ten Christian families in and around Telí. The lovely mud-built mosque is testimony to the predominance of Islam. Add to this the few animist families that reside here, and Telí stands out as an example of one of the many Dogon villages that are religiously highly eclectic and tolerant.

ENDÉ Past **Walia** (2km from Telí) is Endé (another 2km), which is similar to Telí but considerably larger. The granaries here are even more impressive, but the remains of the old cliff dwellings have seen better days. It is no longer considered safe to climb up to the highest level of the granaries, but you may be taken to visit the *hogon* who resides well above the village. The old man is one of the few living *hogons*, the spiritual leaders of the animists. When you visit the *hogon*, remember that he is not to be touched by anyone, nor should you touch his seat, which also serves as an altar for sacrifices. Bring some money and kola nuts, and leave those in the calabash or clay pot at his feet.

Endé is divided into four quarters, all of which seem to be thriving on tourism. A museum opened at the end of 2004 (*admission CFA500*). There are several workshops where woodcarvings are being produced and sold, but *bogolans* or mud cloths are what the quarter just below the cliff is about. Observe the different laborious stages of production, from the spinning and weaving of cotton, to the process of decorating the blankets, before you start haggling over prices.

Though Endé has several good *campements*, the one in Endé Toro merits a mention. Whether just for a drink or for an overnight stay, **Campement Alakala** is worth a visit. So far nine rooms are ready, all of them traditionally built and representing various examples of Dogon architecture (the House of Amma, a *ginna*, etc). The owner will gladly give some explanation, so if this is where your trip ends and you haven't come across any similar buildings yet, this is your chance. The tastefully decorated rooms are by far the most comfortable ones along the *falaise*, and all come with a washbasin and private bucket shower. Toilets are outside, but who wants an en-suite long drop anyway? On busy evenings the *campement* is generator-powered.

On leaving Endé in the direction of Bagourou, you will pass below the *pierre unique d'Endé*, locally known as Endé Touserelé – with *tou* meaning 'rock', and Serelé being the name of a girl who lived in the area some 300 years ago. One day, the 12-year-old Serelé scrambled up the rocks towards a huge baobab tree to collect firewood. After having chopped off the branches she felt tired, and so she turned away from the tree to quench her thirst from the water-filled calabash she carried. Then she took a little sleep in the shade of the tree. Refreshed and rested, she turned back to the baobab, only to find that it had transformed into solid rock. Scared and bewildered she ran down to the village, where she barely managed to explain what had happened. Nobody could calm the girl; no treatment would ease her anxiety. Serelé died 60 years later, never having regained her sanity.

BAGOUROU Bagourou (3km from Endé) lies on the plain, with no counterpart along the cliff. In fact, the cliff opposite Bagourou is reserved as a burial place for all the *hogon* in Dogon country, as well as for the *femmes sacrées* – the very few elected women who are allowed to see the sacred masks – some important blacksmiths and *griots* (see *Chapter 1, Traditional music*, page 31). The bodies are hoisted up with ropes and placed in niches. Obviously, this part of the cliff is sacred, but so are many other sites and objects around the village. Bagourou houses an important family of blacksmiths, and their workshop can be visited.

DOUNDJOUROU Following the track along the base of the *falaise* will take you past **Yabatalou** to Doundjourou. With the exception of one Muslim family, this village is entirely animist, but is not entitled to have a *hogon*. Although it is possible to continue walking – and even driving if you like – along the cliff, the track becomes extremely sandy, which makes the going very tough. It is therefore preferable to scramble up the escarpment, gradually reaching the higher levels of the rocky plateau. As a reward, you will get to enjoy stunning views of the Gondo Plain, and see the other type of Dogon villages, built on top of solid rock.

INDELOU From Yabatalou a steep track winds its way upwards, eventually leading to beautiful Indelou. Much of the traditional architecture here is largely intact, as is the deep belief in animism. When visiting Indelou, it is essential to be accompanied by a local guide who is familiar with what might be going on while you are there. Some guides may actually refuse to go anywhere near the village of Indelou, such is the respect for and fear of the power of the animists in this village. Many sites are sacred and certain walls are not to be touched; when fetishists are at work, they should be left to do whatever they do in silence, and care should be taken where blood and millet stains mark the spots where sacrifices have been made not too long ago. Never walk alone, and do not take pictures unless your guide has given clear permission. However, the woman who makes the traditional *dolo* or millet beer will happily put a smile on her face while you taste her brew and take her picture. Life in Indelou is not all about fear.

BEGNIMATO A somewhat easier way up the *falaise* starts at Doundjourou and takes you to Begnimato (a further 3km), a village very much geared towards tourism and one of the locations where the *danses des masques* regularly take place for tourists' eyes only. Traditionally, the masks were solely meant for ceremonial purposes, and some of the masks still are. These are kept in a place outside the village, and they are for no-one to see. However, CFA40,000 will bring out some equally impressive masks and costumed dancers, accompanied by drums, to give a dazzling performance that will stir the dust.

INDELI On your way to Indeli you will pass (and smell!) the typically checquered onion plots that are repeatedly watered from calabashes filled from streams, ponds or deep wells. The track is sometimes wedged in between huge boulders, but then it opens up totally to offer expansive views of the Gondo Plain. Note the pink and orange sand dunes at the bottom of the *falaise*. Hidden somewhere down there lies Guimmini.

GUIMMINI Once upon a time, when this village was much smaller and home to only a handful of families, it was located between Endé and Bagourou. These two villages were caught up in a serious and violent conflict over land ownership. Guimmini was caught in the middle, receiving many attacks from both sides. The families eventually decided they'd had enough, and they chose to move to their present-day location.

DOUROU Another hour or so past Indeli is Dourou (7km from Begni Mato), which can be reached from Bandiagara by car. Many trips either start or end here for obvious reasons, but Dourou isn't the friendliest of places. It seems noisier than elsewhere in Dogon country, and both children and adults alike can come across as rather aggressive. Having said that, it is one of the best places to buy indigo blankets and watch the women as they prepare and dye the cotton cloth. On market days (once every five days) there is a lot of activity, since this is where most of the onions and other produce from a wide area are marketed.

NOMBORI After Dourou, the track leads down again, to the base of the escarpment and Nombori (4km from Dourou). On arriving there, it is hard to miss the museum (*admission CFA500*). Inaugurated in December 2002, this was the first museum to be created as part of a programme by the Mission Culturelle to promote sustainable tourism in Dogon country. Its purpose is not only to cater for passing tourists, but also to encourage the local people to conserve, protect and promote their cultural heritage. The locals were heavily involved in the development of the idea and the construction of the museum, and now they enjoy the benefit of the income generated by the museum. It should be open during the daytime, but if it isn't ask any villager to find the museum warden. The exhibition shows numerous artefacts that have been handed in by the people from Nombori, along with some interesting explanations – currently in French only. This is where to find out about the procedure used in Nombori to install a *hogon*, which involves a year of preparation before the identity of the new *hogon* is revealed, followed by a period of initiation and finally the actual installation. Nombori boasts not one, but two *hogons*. In Nombori there are different groups of dancers who will perform the *danses des masques* on request. Enquire at one of the *campements* and expect to pay CFA40,000 or more, depending on the number of dancers.

Numerous lush gardens spreading out along a dry riverbed lead to Idyeli Na (2km further on).

IDYELI NA According to local legend, the founder of the village discovered a waterfall and pond with a big fish in it. After ten days the fish still refused to be caught, so instead the man found an onion not far from the water. On the 11th day he found a tomato, and on the following days more edible greens appeared. Thereafter, the man took to planting and harvesting, thus becoming the first farmer of a community of farmers. Pass a few small hamlets before reaching Komokani (after 3km).

KOMOKANI Before walking around the village, make sure to pay your respects to the village elder. Bring some kola nuts, and expect to pay CFA500 if you want to take pictures of the impressive *togu na*.

TERELI Tereli (3km from Komokani) must be one of the most spectacular Dogon villages, with the picture-postcard pointed thatched roofs crawling upwards along the escarpment. Not surprisingly, many tour operators visit Tereli, often driving all the way from Sangha and dropping off clients for a short visit, including a performance of the *danses des masques*. Indeed, the section between Tereli and Sangha probably receives more visitors than anywhere else in Dogon country, but given the beauty of these villages this is understandable. Tereli is known for its pottery, though you are not likely to see the potters at work as most of the work centres on the hottest months of April and May, just before the rainy season. The dried clay pots are then placed and fired in huge pits.

AMANI Just before entering Amani (3km from Tereli), a small pond on the plain harbours sacred crocodiles (locally known as *caïmans*). A visit to the pond costs CFA500, and for CFA1,000 you are allowed to take pictures. Don't expect to see much activity unless they are being fed, and don't expect the animals to be of an impressive size. Amani is of great importance to the Dogon, since near Amani is where the sacred masks that are used exclusively for the Sigi Festival are kept. As you leave Amani, you will pass the local school, which has been designed, financed and built by the Dutch architect Joop van Stigt and his foundation (see box *Foreign aid: every little helps*, page 99 and *Chapter 2, Local charities and NGOs*, page 100).

IRELI Ireli (3km from Amani) looks different in scale from most other villages along the escarpment. The cliff looks higher and steeper, and the old Tellem dwellings are spread over an impressively wide section of the *falaise*. Here it is even harder to imagine how the Tellem managed to find their way up, but many Dogon believe they could fly. Some actually believe the descendants of the Tellem are still alive today, and moreover that they occasionally return to their ancestral sites for offerings and sacrifices. When they do, it is believed they come 'as the wind does', and nobody ever sees them. Traces of blood and millet on their altars and shrines high up the escarpment, however, are considered visible evidence that the Tellem have once again returned.

BANANI Banani (4km beyond Ireli) is made up of four rather distinct quarters, and it has a little bit of everything: Tellem architecture, burial caves, plenty of granaries, *togu nas*, *binous* (see *The Dogon village*, page 193) and a selection of *campements*. This, combined with its proximity to Sangha/Sanga, makes Banani a good place to visit if you are short of time and want only a 'taste' of Dogon country. When Banani marks the end of a long trek in Dogon country, though, it will probably strike you as overwhelmingly touristy and commercial. In the busy season, you may see cars winding their way along the narrow road to Sangha. When you are trekking the final 3km stretch to Sangha, follow the steep but stunningly beautiful footpath rather than the road.

OTHER VILLAGES ALONG THE *FALAISE* About 12km northeast of Banani and accessible by 4x4 along the plain, the Youga group of villages – **Youga Dogorou**, **Youga Piri** and **Youga Na** are actually built on a small hill opposite the *falaise*. Apart from being where the Sigi is supposed to have originated (see page 192), there is also some well-preserved Tellem architecture at Dogorou and Piri, as well as fine views of the plain – the most panoramic being at Dogorou. Finally, a village further north called **Yenda** is also worth mentioning as the place where, according to legend, the sacred crocodiles in Dogon country go to die.

PLATEAU VILLAGES

In all honesty, the average tourist does not come to Dogon country to visit the villages on the plateau. The hardcore Dogon fanatic, however, will find much of interest away from the *falaise*, even if the villages themselves are not quite as photogenic as their cliff-side counterparts. There is another, practical reason why the plateau is not as popular as the *falaise*. The distances between villages tend to be greater and trudging across the plateau is not as interesting as walking along the plain. There are also fewer village *campements* and other places to eat and sleep than there are along the *falaise*. For these reasons, hiring a vehicle might be worth considering – which, of course, is expensive and hardly an incentive to spend a great deal of time exploring the plateau.

Having said this, **Songo**, a village 11km from Bandiagara on – or rather 4km off – the road to Sévaré, is well established on the tourist circuit. It is famous for its grottoes and rock paintings representing different clans of the region; and, although Songo is now almost entirely Islamic, elaborate circumcision rites are held here every three years. This village, more than any other, is held up as an example of how tourism should be developed in Dogon country. The villagers themselves have taken a real interest in – and have directly benefited from – Songo's popularity with visitors. For example, they have built an excellent *campement* which is not privately owned, but belongs to the whole community, and anyone showing you around Songo must come from the village itself, thereby ensuring that tourist dollars are used for local projects. The *taxe touristique* is triple that of most other villages in Dogon country (CFA1,500), but it is put to good use, such as the installation of solar panels, or maintenance of the school and the sandy track leading to the village.

ANIMISM ALONG THE *FALAISE*

Jolijn Geels

With many Dogon converting to Islam and Christianity, animism seems to be on the decline in many villages in Dogon country. Indeed, only a few villages now have a *hogon* (a spiritual leader of the animists); villagers may seek the spiritual advice of a *marabout* (a Muslim religious leader) rather than consulting a fetishist (a potent animist leader, who performs rituals and sacrifices), and a mud-built mosque may be more prominently present than the traditional places of sacrifice.

One could easily believe that in some parts of Dogon country, animism is all but dead. Officially, the converted consider animism to be an inferior belief, and they may even claim that animism will gradually lose ground altogether. However, just below the thin crust of Islam and Christianity, animist beliefs lie deeply embedded in the minds and hearts of the Dogon people.

During my visit to Kani Bonzon – the cradle of the Dogon presence along the *falaise* – an old Muslim testified that the big mosque in the new quarter on the Gondo Plain had been there for as long as he could remember, and that to this day the mosque serves as many as 40 villages and hamlets on special Muslim days. Although the whole area looked quiet and serene, during those occasions the mosque must be buzzing with religious activity and prayer.

While smoking his pipe, the old man said that he must have been about eight years old when many villagers abandoned their cliff dwellings to move down to the plain and construct the new quarter around the mosque. By then, most of the people had embraced Islam as their religion, creating the predominantly Muslim environment in which he grew up. Around half a century ago, when the last *hogon* in Kani Bonzon died, nobody took his place and the house of the *hogon* was left to crumble to a ruinous state. However, at the same time, while the inhabitants of Kani Bonzon would claim to be purely Muslim, and while the outside world had little reason to refute this claim, legendary places continued to be respectfully treated as sacred, and, moreover, many animist traditions were still being practised indoors. As part of the cultural heritage that nobody would question or deny, certain customs were simply continued on a smaller scale, and without much fuss.

The generations of the old man's sons and grandsons started to reflect on the meaning of these traditions within their Dogon culture and the Muslim religion. They openly showed a deep interest in animist practices and even requested the elders to pass on their knowledge before it was lost. And they wondered: would life not be much better with the old beliefs restored? Would it not keep the youngest generation from leaving their home villages and straying from their culture? Would harvests not stop failing when the appropriate traditional sacrifices were made? So, while animism seems to be losing ground, Kani Bonzon has had a new *hogon* (dwelling) installed not far from the original one in the village halfway up the cliff. He seems a respectable and sociable man, who has given up his present life amongst the villagers in favour of a rather isolated life serving the restoration of animism. To the people of Kani Bonzon, their choice is considered a matter of progress, rather than going back in time.

Though the story of Kani Bonzon may be an extreme example of how animism lived on in hiding through the generations, it is by no means exceptional. All along the *falaise*, from Kani Bonzon to Banani, I met Dogon – animists, Muslims and Christians alike – who were willing to share some thoughts on sacrifices, magic spells and *gris-gris*, totem animals, sacred and potent places, genies and taboos. I suppose I was lucky, for I walked the *falaise* with a wonderful – Muslim – guide who lifted the veil of animism in a most respectful way. Once again this stresses the importance of choosing a guide carefully. You may always enjoy the beauty of the Dogon country, but you could still miss out on what lies beneath the surface.

Most of the other villages of special interest on the plateau lie between Bandiagara and Douentza. The following are just a few examples

TABITONGO Known for its eclectic religious mix – animism, Islam, Catholicism and Protestantism are all tolerated – and for having one of the most beautiful menstruation houses in Dogon country.

NINGARI An Islamic village and one of the largest between Bandiagara and Douentza, where each family owns a snake belonging to a species particular to the region, which represents the original ancestors.

ONDOUGOU The village chief was working as an ebonist in Côte d'Ivoire when his father died and he was obliged to return to Ondougou and take up his hereditary responsibilities. This village is also known for the house built by a woman who had taken the unprecedented action of rejecting her husband and living alone until she died.

MORÉ Home to a massive grotto – allegedly large enough for the entire population of the village to fit inside.

DÉ Made famous during the war between the Tukulor Empire and the French when the nephew of the Tukulor emperor arrived here looking for reinforcements to help his uncle. Relics and manuscripts still remain in the village.

BORKO This village is located approximately 50km from Douentza, and around one hour off the tarred road. A guide is needed to find the *piste* leading to Borko. Since the valley is rich in water, the area is surprisingly lush with palm trees and gardens. Borko is well known for its dozens of sacred crocodiles, with which the villagers seem to happily coexist. Of course it helps that they are being fed almost daily. The downside of a visit to Borko is that tourists are expected to pay extravagant amounts of money to see these crocodiles being fed morsels of chicken. A friendly atmosphere can turn sour rather quickly when you are not prepared to hand over the proposed figure.

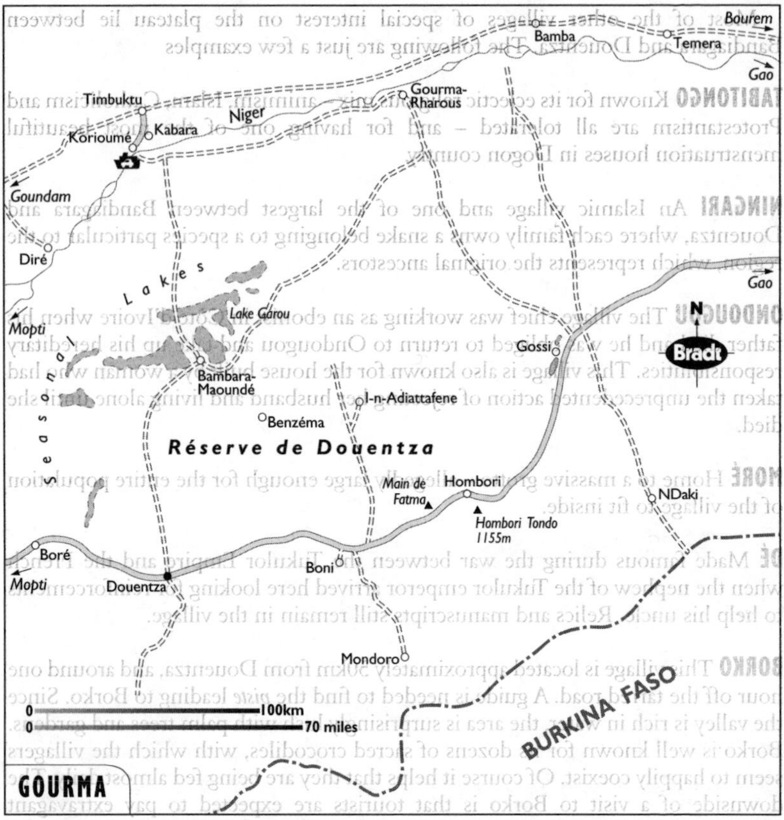
Bourem
Bamba
Temera
Gao
Gourma-Rharous
Timbuktu
Niger
Kabara
Korioumé
Goundam
Diré
Seasonal Lakes
Lake Garou
Gao
N
Bradt
Mopti
Gossi
Bambara-Maoundé
I-n-Adiattafene
Benzéma
Réserve de Douentza
Main de Fatma
Hombori
NDaki
Hombori Tondo
1155m
Boré
Mopti
Douentza
Boni
Mondoro
0
100km
0
70 miles
BURKINA FASO
GOURMA

Gourma

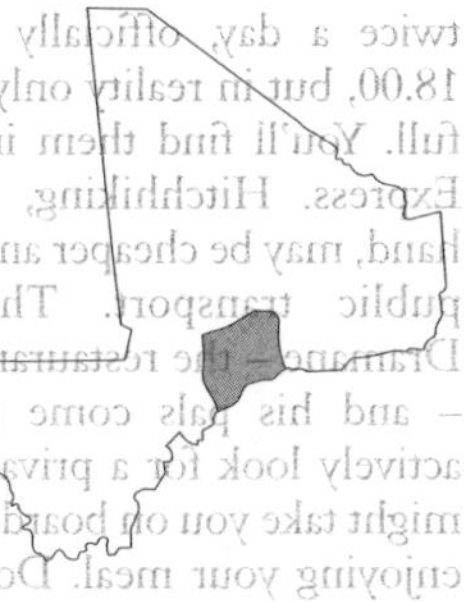

Gourma is not one of the country's eight official regions. Strictly speaking, it covers the *cercles* of Gourma-Rharous and parts of Ansongo, Gao and Bourem. However, for the purposes of this guide it is the land south of the Niger Bend (Boucle du Niger) in the centre of Mali – in parts Sahelian, in others mountainous, with lakes, ponds and, at the right time of year, elephants – which is made up of parts of the regions of Mopti, Timbuktu and Gao. Much of Gourma is taken up by the Réserve de Douentza, which is home to herds of elephants for several months of the year. The other main feature of this part of the country is the craggy Hombori mountain range, where the Main de Fatma (Fatma's Hand) is the most famous and challenging of several climbable rock formations. However, elephant-spotters and rock-climbers apart, Gourma is not one of Mali's most visited areas and even its larger and more accessible towns, such as Douentza, Hombori and Gossi, have limited facilities for the visitor.

DOUENTZA

Beyond Mopti, the main highway to Gao continues northeast until it reaches Konna, where it gradually veers eastwards, passing Boré before reaching Douentza. Officially the *chef-lieu* (main town) of one of the four *cercles* of Dogon country, Douentza can also be considered the principal town of the Gourma area. This, however, is not saying much. Douentza is a rather bleak town, with maybe three reasons to detain you for a while. First of all, if you want to see the elephants, it might be worth stopping at Douentza for advice on where best to spot them. Secondly, you might want to pay a visit to the nearby attractive Dogon village of Fombori. Lastly, this is the place where many independent travellers look for transport. Looking at a map it may not be that obvious, but Douentza is actually a kind of crossroads. The upgraded dirt road going north is the most commonly used *piste* towards Timbuktu, while two other unpaved roads lead to less explored parts of Dogon country. Starting a journey towards the *falaise* from Douentza is becoming increasingly popular, but the bad state of the roads will ensure that it is for serious hikers only, and not so much for day trippers.

GETTING THERE AND AWAY Traffic on the highway to Gao dwindles considerably after Mopti. In Douentza, the best place by far to look for transport is the Restaurant Express. This is the official bus stop for Bani Transport, Binke Transport, etc, serving the routes between Bamako/Mopti and Gao. A representative for these companies should be around somewhere. Tickets cost CFA4,000 for Gossi, CFA5,000 for Gao, CFA3,000 for Mopti and Sévaré, and CFA10,000 for Bamako, but bear in mind that buses are often full and places are not guaranteed.

A ticket for public transport – by 4x4 – to Timbuktu costs CFA12,500 for a seat in front and CFA10,000 for a seat behind. There are two organised Toyotas, leaving twice a day, officially at 06.00 and 18.00, but in reality only when they're full. You'll find them in front of the Express. Hitchhiking, on the other hand, may be cheaper and quicker than public transport. That is where Dramane – the restaurant owner's son – and his pals come in. They will actively look for a private vehicle that might take you on board, while you are enjoying your meal. Don't expect the ride to be free of charge and the fee will most likely include some kind of commission. It is well worth it though, because these young men work very efficiently.

To hitch a ride into Dogon country from here would be pot luck. However, *bâchées* for Bamba or Dé and Moré leave when full from the *gare routière* near the market, mostly on Saturdays and Sundays (Sunday being market day in Douentza). Occasionally there are also 4x4 vehicles for Dé and Bandiagara.

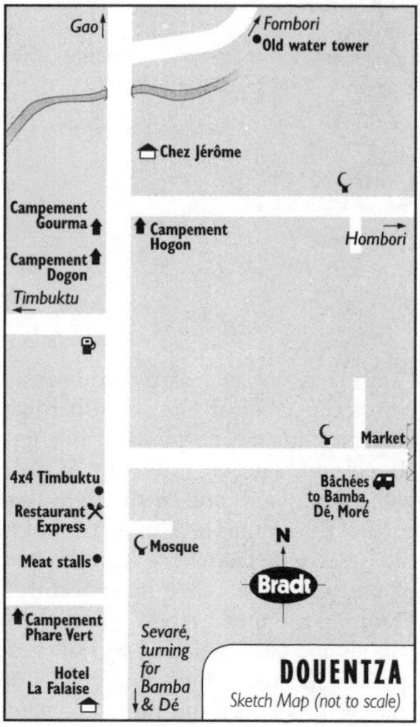

TOURIST INFORMATION For many, the most useful address will be that of the **Service de la Conservation de la Nature** (*2145 20 29*). Run by one of Mali's pre-eminent elephant experts, Mamadou Baga Samaké, this is the place to come for information about the elephants of Gourma. Samaké will tell you exactly where to find them at any given time, and can also recommend guides. You will probably not escape the charms of the 'faux guides' trying their luck in Douentza, so always ask to see their *carte professionnelle*. The **Bureau des Guides** at the Campement Gourma provides guides for Dogon country, Fombori, and quests for elephants. It is possible to rent 4x4 vehicles from here, as well as camels for an increasingly popular way to search for elephants. Guides' fees range from CFA10,000 up to CFA25,000, so clearly there is room for negotiation.

WHERE TO STAY

Mid-range $$$

Campement Dogon (6 rooms) Just down from the Campement Gourma. Not to be confused with the Campement Hogon opposite. Has a couple of expensive AC rooms & 4 cheaper ones with fan surrounding a leafy courtyard hung with *bogolans*. Fully booked when I visited, with the rooms locked – presumably a good sign. Camping on terrace CFA2,500.

Budget $$

Campement Hogon (6 rooms) Located off the main highway, opposite Campement Gourma & Campement Dogon; m 7521 77 58/7943 31 04. This *campement* has recently moved &, at the time of writing, the creative, hardworking owner was busy adding new elements, such as a traditional hut with fan. He had already built a great little bar & Dogon ladder leading up to a terrace restaurant. The kitchen specialises in local dishes, such as *tô*, *fouton* (mashed yam) & *sauce arachide* (peanut sauce).

Hotel Restaurant La Falaise (10 rooms) 2145 20 95. This used to be the most upmarket place to stay but now it has seen better days. The large rooms are dark & depressing but have mosquito nets & are adequate to get your head down for 1 night. The majority are AC with communal bathrooms; 2 are self-contained & 2 have fans. A mattress on the terrace costs CFA3,000pp. Cold water but they can heat it for you. Though it's overpriced for what's on offer, it's often full. No restaurant.

Shoestring $

Campement Gourma (6 rooms) 2145 20 54; e ongoibahama@yahoo.fr. Simple rooms with *lits Dogon* (wooden or bamboo frames & thin mattresses) & fans. Camping CFA3,000pp. Meals are filling & satisfactory. The Bureau des Guides is based here.

Chez Jérôme (tents for 60 people) 2145 20 50. A very original set-up where accommodation consists of huge airy tents with up to 8 mattresses & mosquito nets each. Caters mostly for groups, but has a friendly bar & restaurant serving meals for CFA4,000. Closed during the rainy season.

La Phare Vert (4 rooms) A stone's throw from the Restaurant Express; m 7316 21 93. Rooms are very basic with portable fans. They can get extremely hot, so you may be best sleeping on the terrace for CFA2,000. There is a restaurant serving meals. B/fast extra at CFA1,000.

Mission Catholique Off the main highway. As with a lot of missions in smaller non-touristy towns, there is no charge for staying or eating in this family-run establishment. Whether you stay or not, you can buy wine & warm beer & drink & chat to the priest in the courtyard.

WHERE TO EAT

Restaurant Express m 7316 21 93. This roadside restaurant is designed to cater for travellers who do not want to waste their time waiting for some food to be prepared. Usually you can choose between several basic meals such as *riz gras*, *riz sauce* & *couscous* with vegetables, which are tasty, filling & inexpensive. $

Many local travellers plan a stop in Douentza to pick up some of the tasty, roasted goat or mutton baked in clay ovens and sold by street vendors at the side of the road. The seasoned morsels wrapped in sacking are a good accompaniment on the long road north.

Several grocery stores have sundry items.

WHAT TO SEE If you have a few hours to spare, or if a visit to Dogon country is not on your travel agenda, consider a visit to the village of **Fombori**. The location, not far from a rocky cliff, is scenic, the village itself could be described as a characteristic Dogon village, and the villagers are hospitable and friendly. Apart from the *banco* houses, the granaries and the labyrinth-like maze of alleys, there is a small mud-built mosque that you may or not be able to visit. It's hit or miss in Mali, depending on who you ask at any given time. The **Musée Dogon de Fombori** (*admission CFA1,000*) is open daily, which in real terms means that someone will open the door for you once the key has been collected. The exhibition is a wonderful hotchpotch of artefacts belonging to local people, who receive some money in return for allowing their items to be displayed. Bring a torch to fully appreciate the museum, since there is a distinct lack of light. The torch will also be useful if you visit the cliff, where a short scramble will lead to **Tellem tombs** with human bones and skulls, and fragments of pottery. It is recommended to take a guide, either from Douentza or from Fombori, though it may be hard to find a villager who speaks good French – not to mention English.

To get to Fombori (4km from Douentza), follow the main highway in the direction of Gao until you cross a bridge. Turn right towards a derelict water tower, and continue on this track, keeping the marshy area to your right. The right turning for Fombori is signposted.

HOMBORI

WHERE TO STAY There are no fewer than three *campements* in Hombori, all within shouting distance of each other but all with a distinctive character.

Budget $

Auberge Le Tondanko Located off the road behind the Campement Hotel; 2145 10 02. Offers similar accommodation in a more serene atmosphere, with the additional option of traditional huts. The restaurant serves a range of dishes – rice & *sauce arachide* as well as the usual chicken/brochettes; chilled beer & juices are available. The owner, known as Dourcy, can give you good itineraries for rock-climbing & lighter hiking possibilities, & can also arrange guides or *charrette* (donkey & cart) and bike hire.

Campement Hotel (13 rooms) On the main highway. I met a South African chap in Hombori who had spent the past several years constructing wells in Mali. For much of that time he had been in Gourma, so I felt that he was well qualified to give me his opinion of Hombori & the Campement Hotel. 'This place is Las Vegas, man!' he beamed, a bottle of Castel beer in one hand & a scraggy chicken leg in the other. Slot machines & showgirls may not yet have arrived at the Campement Hotel, but, even so, it is a lively place. The rooms are reasonably clean or you can sleep on the terrace. The restaurant serves well-prepared tourist fare including excellent brochettes.

Campement Kaga Tondo On the main road, 200m from the Campement Hotel; m 7635 13 01; e maoulouddaou@yahoo.fr; blog: http//lelele.skyblog.com. This is the new kid on the block with a friendly, chaotic family atmosphere. Accommodation ranges from mattresses on the pretty terrace to simple rooms & huts. Lelele, the owner, is a Songhay *griot* with an extensive knowledge of local history. He also gives lessons in African cuisine – dishes such as *fakohoye*, *gombo* or *sauce arachide* – & can organise trips.

Located right at the beginning of the trail that leads around the Main de Fatima, just off the main road, you'll find a *campement* offering beds for the night ($). Around the same area is a small hamlet of huts and houses and amongst them is a second *campement*. Accommodation is in grass huts or on the terrace. Note they are closed in the rainy season.

ACTIVITIES Hombori has a number of gentle walks for those who haven't come for the rocks. If you arrive in the evening, take a wander to the low-rising dunes behind the *campements* for a beautiful view of the sun setting behind the mountains. Hombori itself is not an unattractive town, so another option is to wander up into the old village to survey the views. You will be surrounded on all sides by the Hombori Mountains, the highest range in Mali and a major challenge for serious rock-climbers. Note the word 'serious'. None of the rock formations here is easy to climb, and there is no infrastructure in the area for this type of adventure tourism; in case of emergency, the nearest hospital is 255km away in Gao. Rock-climbers who come to Hombori bring their own equipment and know more or less what they are doing. Beginners beware!

The highest peak in Mali is **Hombori Tondo** (1,155m), the sandstone mesa to the left of the road coming from Gao. This is one of the easier mountains to climb. It takes about four hours to reach the top: two hours walking and two hours climbing. The flat summit covers an area of about 2km and is inhabited by monkeys and other typical forest mammals and birds. There are also remains of old pottery and such like, which should be neither touched nor removed. The most famous rock formation in the Hombori Mountains is Gami Tondo or the **Main de Fatima** (Fatima's Hand). Coming from Douentza, the Main de Fatima is the distinctive rock formation looming into view some 10km before you reach Hombori, which, at certain angles, looks like a human hand. Living in the hamlet next to the rock is a Spaniard, Salvador, who is famous in these parts and well worth consulting before you attempt to climb Fatima – a considerably more challenging proposition than Hombori Tondo.

Other activities are beginning to arrive in Hombori. For instance, if you fancy a go at dune-skiing, contact Oumar Meinanga (aka Demba) (m *7625 11 20*), a local climbing guide who has all the gear.

GOSSI

Gossi is the last town of any note along the main highway before it reaches Gao. Gossi market is one of the most important cattle markets in the region. Hundreds of camels, cows, goats, sheep, bulls and donkeys are sold to customers who have come from as far afield as Burkina Faso and Niger.

GETTING THERE AND AWAY Buses cost CFA2,500 for the 156km journey to Gao and stop on the main road – the town itself does not border the highway. Buses to Hombori cost CFA1,000. As at Douentza and Hombori, finding a place on one of these buses is very much a question of luck. If you are travelling to Hombori only, Monday evening and Tuesday morning are your best options; 4x4 trucks with merchandise, vendors and passengers then leave Gossi to meet the Tuesday market in Hombori. More 4x4 vehicles leave for Gourma-Rharous on Wednesday evenings, this time to meet the market on Thursday. In Gossi Sunday is market day, and the options for transport should also work the other way around.

Buses stop at the main road near a cluster of houses and small shops that catch the passing trade; Gossi village itself is 1km or so off the road.

WHERE TO STAY AND EAT Facilities for tourists used to be very thin on the ground here, but a Peace Corps volunteer has been hard at work and there's a new **Campement Touristique** with an **Association des Guides Touristiques** to match (see page 217). Both of these are run by brothers Ali and Ibadas Dicko (m *7610 93 72 & m 7537 46 58 respectively*). They run a drinks and snacks stall by the bus stop, so ask around for them and they will take you to the *campement*, which lies off the road towards Hombori close to the **Mare de Gossi**. This is translated as 'Gossi Pond', but more comparable in size to a lake. It is home to several species of waterbirds and is a popular drinking spot for the elephants, which are probably the main reason for coming to Gossi in the first place. The *campement*, built in *banco*, has an air of Sahel tranquillity; it has five two-bed rooms (one bed is double) at CFA5,000 per room and clean showers. Meals are prepared on request. As well as trips to see the elephants, the Association offers half-day pirogue trips on the pond (CFA15,000), camel trips (CFA5,000 per person) and overnight trips into the bush.

Should you want to kip down closer to the bus stop, there is also the **Hotel Restaurant Bohanta** some 200m from the main road, near the signpost for Handicap International. CFA2,000 per person buys you a mattress in a clean and simple room. If you're interested in seeing the village itself, a donkey cart will take you and your luggage for CFA500–1,000, but there's not much to it unless you coincide with the market; the town *campement*, which offers delapidated accommodation at CFA1,500 a night, has seen much better days.

WHAT TO DO With Gossi being such a small place, you are bound to meet – or at least hear about – **Sister Anne-Marie Saloman** before too long (see *Chapter 2, Local charities and NGOs*, page 100). Anne-Marie runs the local hospital – many of whose patients are Tuareg nomads – which is on the other side of the Gossi Pond.

THE ELEPHANTS OF GOURMA

Mention of Mali hardly conjures up images of herds of migrating elephants. Yet, for several months of the year, Gourma is home to hundreds of them – apparently the largest elephant species in the world – as they mill around the numerous ponds and waterholes of the **Réserve de Douentza** (Gourma means 'place of the well').

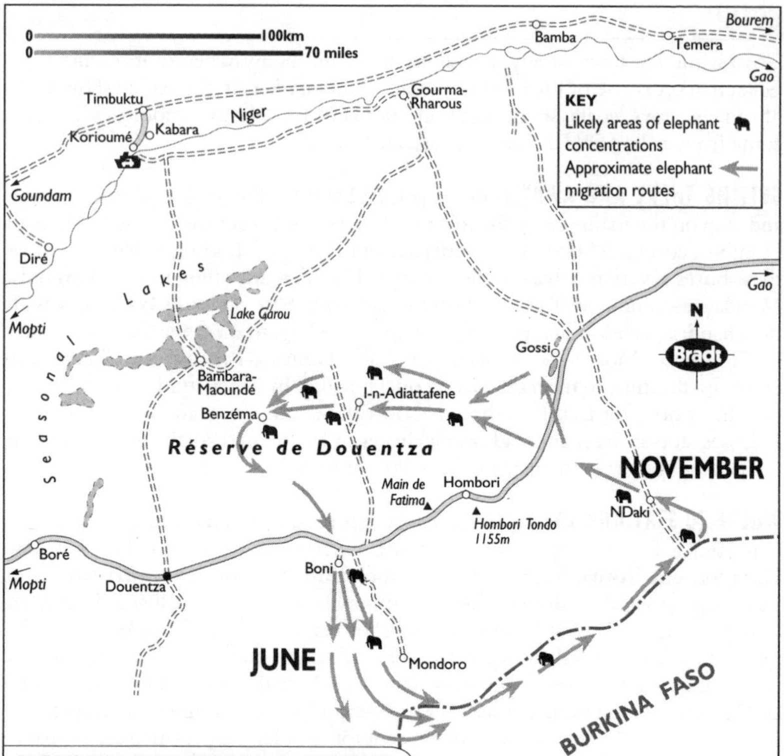

ELEPHANT MOVEMENTS IN GOURMA

Devised in close collaboration with Mamadou Baga Samaké

These elephants are something of a contradiction in a country where the wildlife has been hunted so mercilessly. Cohabitation with the human population has been the key to their survival – and, indeed, their popularity. The elephants play an important role in the daily struggle for survival in this harsh Sahelian environment: they trample down vegetation, clearing paths for local herders and their cattle, in exchange for which they're spared the hunters' rifles. However, this balance between man and nature is precarious. As bulldozers, the elephants are welcome; but when they start to destroy gardens and eat food intended for human consumption, questions – and rifles – are raised. In short, the future of the elephants of Gourma is uncertain.

WHERE AND WHEN TO SEE THEM Like any safari, seeing the elephants is a question of good timing and luck. However, it is not always necessary to travel hundreds of kilometres into the reserve to catch a glimpse of them. Their relatively harmonious relationship with humans means that they are not afraid to install themselves at favourite drinking spots, even if these are quite close to towns and villages.

The elephants of Gourma follow the longest migratory circuit of any elephants in the world. Around November they start to walk north from Burkina Faso to the area south of the Niger Bend in central Mali in search of water. During the dry season, they drink at the ponds and waterholes of the Gourma region – mainly north of the main highway – before returning south towards Burkina after the first rains in June.

Therefore, the best time for travellers to see the elephants is roughly between February and May. During this period, large numbers are often seen around I-n-Adiattafene and other places in the middle of the reserve. The world elephant 'experts' always go to the reserve in April as this is the easiest time to see them (it hasn't rained for a long time and so there is little foliage). They can usually be found in and around Benzéma, as there is a small lake there, where they drink. However, you might also be able to catch up with the elephants near the main highway not far from towns such as Boni (late May/early June) and Gossi (February/March).

TOURIST INFORMATION The new **Association des Guides Touristiques** (m *7610 93 72*/*7537 46 58*; see page 215) in Gossi has been set up in association with the somewhat weightily named Projet de Conservation et de Valorisation de la Biodiversité du Gourma et des Éléphants (PCVBGE), a Malian government project funded by the World Bank. The Peace Corps volunteer working on the project has produced a number of information sheets about the elephants and their habits, as well as fixed rates for trips to see them. There is apparently a small group of elephants that spends an extended period of time around the Gossi ponds – possibly between November and March – though of course this can't be guaranteed. A half-day 4x4 trip to see them costs CFA25,000.

Other than this, excursions into the Réserve de Douentza require a couple of days. The cost varies according to the quality of your guide and your own powers of persuasion, but you should budget on at least CFA50,000 a day for the 4x4 vehicle plus petrol and up to CFA25,000 for the guide. An increasingly popular alternative is to hire camels. You should at least feel comfortable watching the world from a camel's back, but you don't have to be an experienced rider; the guides will keep you at a safe distance from the elephants. Rates are around CFA50,000 to CFA125,000 for a guide and camels for one to five clients, though prices obviously drop the nearer the elephants are to your point of departure. A good person to speak to about organising excursions, worthwhile guides and the elephants in general is Mamadou Baga Samaké, the Director of the Service de la Conservation de la Nature in Douentza (*2145 20 29*).

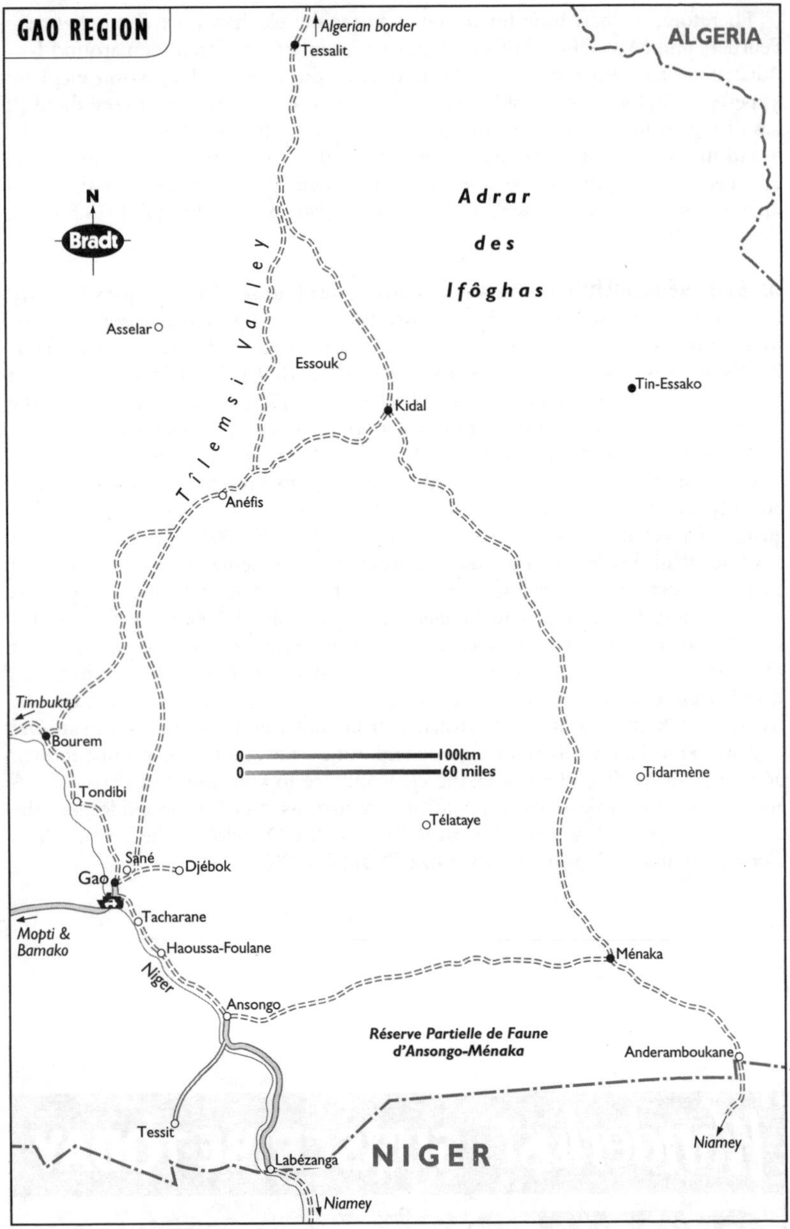
GAO REGION
Algerian border
Tessalit
ALGERIA
N
Bradt
Adrar
des
Ifôghas
Asselar
Essouk
Tilemsi Valley
Kidal
Tin-Essako
Anéfis
Timbuktu
Bourem
0 100km
0 60 miles
Tidarmène
Tondibi
Télataye
Sané
Djébok
Gao
Tacharane
Mopti & Bamako
Haoussa-Foulane
Niger
Ménaka
Ansongo
Réserve Partielle de Faune d'Ansongo-Ménaka
Anderamboukane
Tessit
Niamey
Labézanga
NIGER
Niamey

8

Gao

At one time, the region of Gao occupied well over half of the surface area of Mali. Nowadays, three regions – Gao, Kidal and Timbuktu – divide the desert between them, although for the purposes of this chapter, Gao and Kidal will be treated together – indeed, until 1991, Kidal was a cercle of Gao. Most of this area of Mali is desert; and even the regional metropolis, Gao, is caught between the banks of the River Niger and a vast blanket of sand. The great droughts of 1970–74 and 1984–85 (see page 23) exacted a heavy toll in this region, and survival – particularly in undeveloped Kidal – is a constant struggle against the elements. The greenest area is in the south, where the Réserve Partielle de Faune d'Ansongo-Ménaka used to have significant giraffe and ostrich populations before the hunters moved in.

Independent travellers will spend most – if not all – of their time in Gao, which is well linked to the rest of the country by road and river. Most other areas are off the beaten track and require time, patience and stamina to explore. There is also the limited but tangible threat of Tuareg banditry in this part of the country and clashes between Tuareg rebels and the Malian army (see page 64). For just these reasons, the best way to explore the Sahara is through a tour operator who is familiar with this region. Organised adventure tourism in the regions of Gao, Kidal and Timbuktu is developing and several tour operators – most of them based in Gao – offer tailor-made excursions to the more interesting and out-of-the-way places such as Kidal and the Adrar des Ifôghas.

GAO TOWN

It does not take long for the visitor to realise that this place was not built with aesthetics in mind: if the architecture is not ugly, it is unspectacular; the layout of the town is slapdash and sprawling; and, apart from the peculiar Tombeau des Askia, antiquity has left Gao only a modest legacy. However, this place can be beautiful and attractive in spite of itself. I particularly like the contrasts: the blinding yellow of the sand under the midday sun and the soothing blue waters of the river, for instance, or the commotion at the port during the day and the dead quiet at night. These qualities alone are not enough to make Gao a highlight of a trip to Mali, but they might persuade you to stop for a while should you be passing through. Not many people, however, are just 'passing through'. Throughout history, Gao has benefited from its strategic location, and what limited prosperity it has today is owing to its position as the eastern terminus of Mali's main highway and its downstream river traffic.

For many travellers, therefore, Gao was the end of the line and the result is a town full of a mixture of different cultures.

HISTORY Although it was destined to become the nerve centre of the Songhay Empire (see page 16), Gao was of secondary importance when it was founded by

REBELLION FLARE UPS

The rebellion in 1990 started in the area around Gao, when Tuareg rebels, recently returned from Gaddafi's military training camps in Libya, attacked government buildings. Following the signing of the peace treaty in 1995, Gao and the small town of Kidal slowly recovered from the damage and the inhabitants rebuilt their lives. Gao's international airport started to receive direct flights from France and by the early 2000s fast-developing Kidal was enjoying a local boom. This could in part be credited to the raised awareness of this part of the northern desert through the international success of local Tuareg guitarists, Tinariwen, and through festivals in the area such as Saharan Nights in Essouk attracting tourists to town. The government was overwhelmed by applications from desert areas, hoping to ride the wave and set up their own lucrative festivals. However, in 2006, trouble flared up again, with renewed fighting between one rebel group who had refused to sign and the Malian army, thus isolating the area and sending thousands of nomads fleeing to neighbouring Burkina Faso.

By September 2008, a new peace agreement had been signed and the situation seemed to have calmed down. But the damage had been done. Although Gao, the 'gateway to the desert', was never at any risk, the insecurity further north, coupled with a short two-month tourist season, has forced many businesses to close down. All festivals have been cancelled in the area for the time being. Hopefully, the differences have been resolved this time and the desert inhabitants can once again begin rebuilding their lives. Travel north and east of Gao is not recommended at the present time. For more information see *Chapter 2, Safety*, page 64, and to keep up to date with the current situation consult www.africa.reuters.com/nbc/ML.

Sorko fishermen around AD650. At this time, Koukia, a settlement to the south between the present-day town of Ansongo and the Niger border, was the Songhay capital. For some reason – perhaps to please the Berber merchants upon whom the Songhay depended for their trade – Dia Kossoï, the 14th king of the ruling Dia dynasty, converted to Islam in 1009, an event which was to prove the making of Gao. The king and his court moved upstream shortly after embracing Islam, and for the next three centuries Gao rivalled Timbuktu and Djenné as the Sudan's commercial and cultural centre *par excellence*.

With its excellent strategic location on the banks of the River Niger and the edge of the Sahara, the town was coveted by the Mali Empire and the Tuareg alike – indeed, it was abandoned from 1374 to 1377 while these two forces fought for control of it, until the great dynasties of Sonni and Askia established Songhay dominance in the western Sudan and Gao became the centre of this empire. Ironically, at this time Gao also started to decline, relinquishing its trading functions to Timbuktu which had been captured by Sonni Ali Ber in 1468. The defeat of the Songhay Empire by the Moroccans in 1591 marked the end of Gao's golden age, the *Arma* of the Moroccan occupation preferring Timbuktu as a base from which to rule.

During its heyday, Gao had a population of nearly 70,000 – double what it is today.

ORIENTATION The River Niger marks the western boundary of Gao. To the north, south and east, however, there is nothing but desert, and the town has sprawled into it like a large stain on a carpet. In terms of surface area, then, Gao is one of Mali's largest towns – a fact which you will appreciate when looking for accommodation, most of which is found in neighbourhoods some distance from the town centre. In this respect, Gao is Mali's Los Angeles.

The main highway linking Bamako to Gao comes to an end on the eastern bank of the river. A new 30m bridge connects Gao to the rest of Mali. Before the bridge was built a ferry, or *bac*, used to transport vehicles to the other side of the river, with the last one leaving at around 17.30. Trucks, buses and cars all had to wait until morning to cross, and often people ended up spending the night waiting in the cold desert.

The main road into town ends in Gao's central square, Place de l'Indépendance. This is also where buses from Bamako and Mopti terminate. North of the town centre there is a crossroads called Place des Martyrs: continue straight ahead for Bourem and Timbuktu; turn right for Kidal and the Algerian border. Gao's streets are paved wth sand and laid out in a simple grid system. The town centre is dominated by the port and various markets. The Hotel Atlantide, meanwhile, is a large hotel at or near which most of Gao's tourist facilities can be found (post office, banks, guides, etc).

GETTING THERE AND AWAY

By air The airport is about 7km east of town. From December to March, **Point Afrique** operates flights between Lyon and Gao (t/f *2182 02 24;* e *pointafrique.gao@afribone.net.ml*). Depending on when you travel, fares can be very attractive.

By river The COMANAV building (t *2182 04 66*) is between the Hotel Atlantide and the river. When the boats are running, for two out of three weeks they should arrive in Gao at the end of their voyage downstream on Sunday evening or Monday morning. They return upstream on Monday evening at around 20.00. See *Chapter 2, Getting there and away* for more information and fares.

At times when the water is too low for the COMANAV boats, you should be able to get to Timbuktu on a *pinasse*. The Coopérative de Transport Fluviale at the port will have all the latest information. Note, however, that the traffic of goods between Gao and Timbuktu is much lighter than between Mopti and Timbuktu, so be prepared to wait some time for a boat. Sailings further downstream to Ansongo, however, are more common. As a rough guide, expect to pay about CFA10,000 on a public *pinasse* to Timbuktu and CFA7,500 to Ansongo. If you have the money, tour operators such as Point Afrique operate their own river trips to Timbuktu. The all-inclusive fare for a four-day trip from Gao to Timbuktu by *pinasse* is from CFA75,000 to around CFA225,000 per person, depending on the number of people travelling.

By road Gao is about 1,200km from Bamako along the longest stretch of good tar road in the country. There are a number of bus companies travelling between Gao and Bamako as well as between Gao and Niger. Gana Transport, Bani (t *2182 04 24*), Binké (t *2182 05 58*), Maiga (m *7610 16 36*), and SONEF (t *2182 03 91;* e *sonef_mali@yahoo.fr*). All have regular, well-run services using reliable vehicles. Other bus companies may be less reliable with unpredictable schedules, taking substantially longer to complete the journey. Most companies charge CFA2,500 for Gossi, Hombori (CFA4,000), Douentza (CFA6,000), Sévaré (CFA7,500), Carrefour du Djenné (CFA9,000), San (CFA10,000), Ségou (CFA13,000) and Bamako (CFA15,000), though SONEF claim to have the edge by charging only CFA13,000 for Bamako.

Bani Transport has departures for Bamako every day at 05.00 except Monday when it leaves at 11.00. Gana Transport also leaves every day at 10.00, Maiga Transport at 14.30 (though this is a less reliable departure time), while SONEF and Binké have two daily services leaving at 05.00 and 12.00 (13.00 on Friday) and 02.00 and 12.00 (13.00 on Friday) respectively. The journey to Bamako takes approximately 18 hours.

Bani Transport has buses to Sikasso (18 hours; CFA13,000) on Tuesday and Friday at 07.00 via Sévaré and Koutiala, whilst Maiga has a direct service leaving every day at 14.00. SONEF and SNTV (☎ *2182 03 95*) have daily services to Niamey at 06.00 (8 hours; CFA8,500). Note that during holiday times, buses run less frequently.

Buses leave from different bus stations in town. Binké's depot is just along from the Place des Martyrs. SONEF is situated in three different places: Dioulabougou opposite the Direction Régionale de Santé, near the mosque and Washington market; at Sanèye near the Hotel Bon Séjour Annexe and IGM; the third is a couple of blocks from the back of the hospital. Bani Transport is just along Place de l'Indépendance, while Gana Transport (well signposted) is nearby, a couple of blocks down a side road. SNTV leaves from Sosso Koira, on the road taking you to the Algerian Consulate. As well as these big companies, there are numerous 17 – 25-seater minibuses serving the villages that leave on the demand of clientele.

There are currently no buses between Gao and Kidal. Travel is generally in converted Land Rovers with about 16 places, or 4x4 pick-ups which leave from next to the monument at Place des Martyrs, usually at 08.00 (CFA10,000). *Camions* frequently go from here to Bourem, 95km north of Gao on the road to Timbuktu, although you can get to Timbuktu directly – most often with Arab merchants on their way to Mauritania. The fare depends on the degree of discomfort you're willing to put up with. In the open back, on top of the luggage is cheapest at CFA10,000 to Kidal or Timbuktu, while the best place is the shared seat in the cabin at CFA15,000. The journey will take at least ten hours, and add another ten hours to continue to Bassikounou in Mauritania (CFA20,000–30,000). The night will be spent camping wherever it suits. More transport for Kidal, Tessalit and the Algerian border leaves from the *autogare*. Rather than approach each *camion* individually, ask the Coopérative des Transports Routiers de Gao at the *autogare* for details of who is going where. It is then up to you to fix a price with the driver.

At the eastern end of the Place de l'Indépendance, Land Rovers leave when full for Ansongo, 100km southeast of Gao (3 hours; CFA2,500). From Ansongo, you can continue on to Ménaka in the eastern corner of Mali or to Niger, crossing the border at Andéramboukane. Alternatively, you can travel directly from Gao to Niamey, the capital of Niger, going via Ansongo and crossing the border at Labézanga. One company, the Société Nationale des Transports Nigeriens, leaves at 07.00 on Wednesdays for Niamey (CFA8,000) from Sosso-Koïra. Other companies leave on Tuesdays, Wednesdays and Fridays for Niger from the *autogare*. Look for *camions* from Erfo-Gaz, Askia Transport and Bahiya Transport.

TOURIST INFORMATION The Gao representation of the OMATHO (☎ *2182 20 36;* **m** *7605 15 59;* **e** *omathogao@yahoo.fr;* ⏲ *08.00–17.00 Mon–Fri or by appointment any day, any time)* is located in the middle of town, just off the Place de l'Indépendance roundabout, next to the bus station. Here you can get information about guides and sites around Gao and book taxis. A Peace Corps volunteer was given the task of launching a website for the OMATHO during her time in Gao. The finished results, posted in 2006, are impressive with lots of useful information in English (*www.visitgaomali.com*). If you have an interest in history and archaeology, enquire about the archaeological site in Gao. In 1325, on his return from Mecca to his Manding Empire, King Kankou Moussa stopped over in Gao and decided to build a mosque and a palace here. The remains of his palace were discovered as recently as December 2003. Excavations may still be in progress. **Guides** in Gao should be

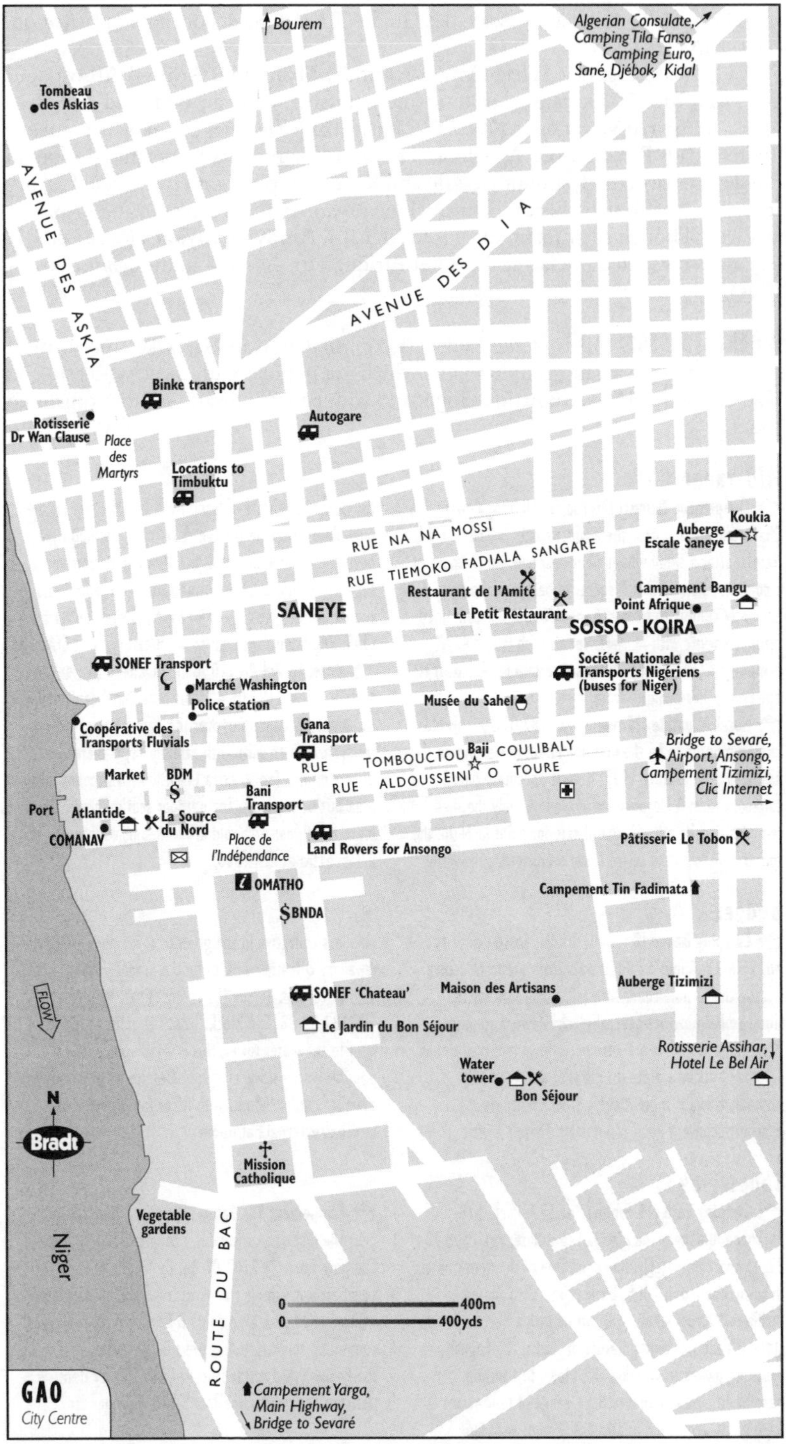

Bourem
Algerian Consulate, Camping Tila Fanso, Camping Euro, Sané, Djébok, Kidal
Tombeau des Askias
AVENUE DES ASKIA
AVENUE DES DIA
Binke transport
Rotisserie Dr Wan Clause
Place des Martyrs
Autogare
Locations to Timbuktu
RUE NA NA MOSSI
RUE TIEMOKO FADIALA SANGARE
Koukia
Auberge Escale Saneye
Restaurant de l'Amité
Le Petit Restaurant
Campement Bangu
Point Afrique
SANEYE
SOSSO - KOIRA
SONEF Transport
Marché Washington
Police station
Société Nationale des Transports Nigériens (buses for Niger)
Musée du Sahel
Coopérative des Transports Fluvials
Gana Transport
Baji
RUE TOMBOUCTOU COULIBALY
RUE ALDOUSSEINI O TOURE
Bridge to Sevaré, Airport, Ansongo, Campement Tizimizi, Clic Internet
Market
BDM
Port
Atlantide
La Source du Nord
Bani Transport
COMANAV
Place de l'Indépendance
Land Rovers for Ansongo
Pâtisserie Le Tobon
OMATHO
BNDA
Campement Tin Fadimata
FLOW
SONEF 'Chateau'
Maison des Artisans
Auberge Tizimizi
Le Jardin du Bon Séjour
Rotisserie Assihar, Hotel Le Bel Air
Water tower
Bon Séjour
N
Bradt
Mission Catholique
Vegetable gardens
Niger
ROUTE DU BAC
0 400m
0 400yds
GAO
City Centre
Campement Yarga, Main Highway, Bridge to Sevaré

members of the Association Askia des Guides Touristiques. For more information, see OMATHO.

A Gao-based agency, Echagil Voyages, run by **Mohamed Anmed Alhousseni** (m *7619 78 86*), specialises in 'tourisme equitable' and can be found in Sosso-Koïra. **Timitrin Voyages** (m *7603 23 25; www.mali-tour.com*) is run by the amiable Tuareg, Badi Faradje from Aguelhok. He can tailor-make well-organised tours in the desert, particularly around Tessalit and Kidal, complete with unexpected luxury items such as french cheese. Point Afrique organises many trips through Amawal Voyages. Though their main office is in Ménaka, **Amawal Voyages** (*223 603 17 96*) are represented in Gao at the Point Afrique office, found in the *quartier* Sosso-Koïra.

WHERE TO STAY Much of the budget accommodation in Gao takes the form of *campements* – cheap and simple rooms which are popular with those who arrive in Gao on the weekly Point Afrique flight and with people on various other organised tours.

Mid-range $$$

Campement Tizimizi (20 rooms, 10 bungalows) Chateau Secteur II near the airport road; 2182 01 94. Named after a small village near Ansongo, this is more of a complex than a hotel & seems to be ever-expanding. It currently comprises simple 'bungalows', 2 self-contained *appartements* with AC & TV, rooms with fan or AC, & camping at CFA3,500pp. There's a restaurant & bar. It is, however, a fair distance from town.

Hotel Atlantide (27 rooms) 2182 01 30. This old lady, rumoured to be the first hotel built in west Africa, has been around since 1932. It must once have oozed colonial charm & elegance but nowadays, only the shell remains: despite a fresh coat of exterior paint in 2006, the rooms have lost their lustre & are overpriced, considering the ramshackle state of furniture & facilities. Yet it's the only place to stay in the centre of town, situated right next to the lively market & just 100m or so from the Niger, so it should be in business for a few more years to come. Also the sales agent for Air Mali. Place on terrace CFA3,000. Rooms with fan or AC. B/fast extra at CFA1,500.

Hotel Le Bel Air (20 rooms) Chateau (water tower) Secteur IV; 2182 05 40. This hotel has been steadily expanding & upgrading over the past few years. AC rooms are all en suite with satellite TV, & there's an *appartement* for an extra CFA5,000 (this means lounge area but no kitchen). The outdoor seating area is a great place for dinner or a cold drink. Rooms with fan or AC. B/fast extra at CFA1,000.

Budget $$

Camping Bangu (8 rooms, 3 huts) Sosso-Koïra; m 7619 76 75. About a 20min walk from the town centre – take the airport road, turn left at the sign for the Hotel Le Bel Air & it's several blocks down. Camping Bangu's basic rooms are with or without fan; traditional Songhay huts or a place on the roof are justifiably popular. Hawa is a great cook & her *capitaine* brochettes have a good reputation. There's a little women's collective in the grounds too, selling well-priced jewellery & leatherwork to fund a kindergarten.

Hotel Bon Séjour (13 rooms) Chateau Secteur I; 2182 03 38. Two blocks from the artisans market & next to the water tower, this is a cosy place that is popular with visiting charities. Despite its proximity to town it is quiet. Rooms with AC or fan & choice of internal/external bathroom.

Shoestring $

Camping Euro (15 rooms) Rue 527, Porte 570, Alijanabandia, near the Algerian consulate; m 7608 78 27; e shaolumese@yahoo.com. One of the newer hotels in town, opened in 2005. Basic rooms with shared facilities & a roof where you can sit with a beer under the stars. It's the welcoming nature of Shaka, the English-speaking owner that makes this place. In addition, they have hired a new cook offering a range of sandwiches & fresh pizza, if ordered in advance. Rooms with fans.

Campement Tila Fanso (10 rooms) Alijanabandia, near the Algerian consulate, a couple of blocks from Camping Euro; 2182 08 88. By far the neatest *campement*. Simple rooms with fan are immaculately whitewashed with blue doors & line a pretty courtyard; communal showers/toilets are tiled & spotless. There's a shady courtyard restaurant. At CFA8,500 for *demi-pension*, it's good value too. B/fast & dinner inc.

Campement Touristique Tin Fadimata (10 tents, 4 huts) Chateau Secteur I; ☎ 2182 02 34. Accommodation in Tuareg/Mauritanian tents, sleeping 8 to 12 people or traditional Songrai huts for up to 6 people.

Camping Yarga (8 rooms) Boulgoundjé; m 7624 20 47. A long walk from the centre along Route du Bac. Founded in 1951, this was the first of all *campements* in Gao, & old Yarga himself still offers an informal kind of hospitality. If you are just passing through & would like to take a shower & freshen up, you can do so here for CFA1,000. Basic *banco* rooms are arranged around a shady courtyard; sleeping on the roof is CFA1,500.

WHERE TO EAT Establishments are listed in descending price order.

Restaurant Bon Séjour The most exotic menu is probably at this French-run restaurant next to the water tower, where you can choose from items such as pork sausages or veal escalopes. $$$

Hotel Le Bel Air The restaurant here is also not bad. $$$

Restaurant de l'Amitié A few blocks along from the Musée du Sahel. This is one of the larger restaurants in town, serving international food as well as traditional rice & sauce. It livens up later in the day – there's a dancefloor with big mirrors, & sometimes live music. $$$

Case Mystérieuse Located in the Dioulabougou *quartier*, near the police station; m 7601 18 79. Open only for dinner & offering a selection of dishes including chicken, fish, fried plantains & an excellent hors-d'oeuvre platter. $$–$$$

Pâtisserie Le Tobon On the road to the airport. Open for lunch & dinner, this new eatery has a variety of pastries as well as a full menu of European & African dishes, including cheeseburgers, pizzas & rôtisserie chicken. $–$$

Le Petit Restaurant A few blocks down from Camping Bangu. With a cheerful Algerian owner, Oumar (of Berber descent), this simple restaurant is a favourite with expats & Tuaregs alike. The food is always ready, & always tasty. Drinks are ice cold. $$

Restaurant Source du Nord Near the market; ☎ 2182 03 55. Different traditional dishes prepared every day of the week, in addition to crispy salads & sometimes fresh fruit juices. You can also get regional specialities like *wigila* if you order in advance. $$

Rôtisserie Assihar Château Secteur II. Gao has more than its fair share of rôtisseries, but this one's famous for its succulent mutton, smoked for hours in huge cookers & served in basic surroundings to locals. If you go on a football night, they'll all be glued to the TV. The friendly owner, Moha Yattara, will be glad you stopped by. $

Rotisserie Dr Wan Clause At the end of Askia Blvd. Specialties such as sheep meat & sheep head (CFA1,500) and an array of sausages & *Mechoui*, a favourite amongst locals & tourists alike. You can buy the meat in any quantity of CFA500. $

ENTERTAINMENT AND NIGHTLIFE

☆ **Auberge Escale Saneye** Sosso Koira; ☎ 2182 09 76/ 6337646. A functioning bar with traditional music on Fri & Sat evenings, at a reasonable cover charge.

☆ **The Casa Bar** Not far from Bani & Gana Transport, is a local nightclub with 3 slot machines!

☆ **Nightclub Baji** Near the hospital, this place has a laid-back atmosphere & provocative dancing girls who should be regarded as prostitutes unless you see any evidence to the contrary. Also serves inexpensive, light meals including brochettes & *nems*, the Malian equivalent of spring rolls.

☆ **Restaurant de l'Amitié** Quartier Sosso-Koïra, At night, this restaurant becomes a bar with cold drinks & live music & often hosts dance parties. Food is served late.

SHOPPING Although Gao is on the edge of the desert and the amount of produce grown locally is limited, the paved highway from the fruit- and vegetable-producing areas of Bamako and Sikasso ensures that the market has a good supply of fresh produce – unlike Mali's other main desert town, Timbuktu.

OTHER PRACTICALITIES The post office and one of the BNDA banks are just off opposite sides of the Place de l'Indépendance. This bank changes cash and travellers' cheques and allows cash withdrawals with an international Visa card. The other bank (BDM) is not far from the Hotel l'Atlantide and has a Western Union office. Additionally, Ecobank and BIMSA offer these services. It is strongly advised that you change CFA before arrriving in Gao but if really necessary, arrive when the banks open, usually around 07.00, and expect to wait in a 'queue' for anywhere between 30 minutes and two hours. The police, meanwhile, are a little further down the road.

Owing to long-standing insecurity in the desert regions in Mali, you should still get your passport stamped by the police as soon as you arrive in town. This is a simple procedure, costs nothing – but you need two photographs – and is intended for your safety. Moreover, passports are sometimes checked when leaving town, and tourists have been sent back because their Gao stamp was missing. There are internet facilities at the EU-funded Télécentre Mulitmédia Communautaire 'Bon Feeray' (air-conditioned and very fast connection) on Route de l'Aéroport, near the Maisons des Artisans, and nightclub Baji (for CFA750 per hour). CLIC of Gao (🕘 *08.00–12.00 & 15.00–17.00 Mon–Fri & Sat; CFA1,000/hr*), located in L'institute de Formation des Maîtres, also on Route de l'Aéroport, offers a more reliable service.

WHAT TO SEE Given the relatively small amount of urban traffic and the endless, sandy streets of this sprawling town, Gao is a good place to explore on foot. Indeed, much of your time will be spent wandering about with no fixed destination in mind, because there are only one or two established 'sights' in Gao itself. The most famous is the World Heritage Site, the **Tombeau des Askias** (Tomb of the Askias), which is in the north of town on Avenue des Askia. This strange building might have been inspired by the Egyptian pyramids, as its shape is roughly that of a truncated pyramid, albeit ill-defined and riddled with branches – something resembling a sandcastle, in fact. The mud-brick tomb was built in 1495 by the first Askia emperor, Mohamed (see page 16), who is interred inside. Guides will be loitering around outside the tomb – which is surrounded by a wall – and you will have to pay CFA1,500 to be shown around.

The **Musée du Sahel** (🕘 *08.00–12.00 & 15.00–18.00 Tue–Fri & Sun; admission CFA2,000*) is three blocks behind the hospital. Despite being small it has some interesting exhibits, particularly about the day-to-day lives of the Tuareg and Songhay people, with most descriptions written in French but some in English.

Vegetable gardens are a common feature along the banks of the River Niger as it winds through Mali. Ironically, some of the most lush and fertile are to be found in the desert town of Gao. One of the largest and greenest is opposite the Mission Catholique on Route du Bac, where a surprising variety of vegetables, fruit, flowers and other plants grow around ponds and a channel branching off from the river.

Elsewhere, the **port** – the main downstream terminus for river traffic in Mali – is usually quite lively and worth exploring.

EXCURSIONS FROM GAO

LA DUNE ROSE From the roof of the Hotel l'Atlantide you can see a huge sand dune some 60m high on the eastern bank of the river, which at sunset glows through several shades of orange and pink before night descends. This is the *dune rose* (pink dune), where, according to legend, sorcerers used to gather to consult their magic and hold conferences. However, it is the peace, tranquillity and great views from the top which make this one of the most worthwhile excursions from Gao.

It is easy enough to arrange a pirogue to take you over to the dune, but try to find other people to share the cost. Bagna Touré at the Association Askia des Guides Touristiques will quote you a fair price. It is also possible to negotiate directly with one of the *piroguiers* in the port, and the owner of Camping Yarga (see page 225) offers very competitive rates also. The dune is best visited at sunset, which means setting off from Gao an hour or so before the sun goes down.

CATTLE MARKET AT DJÉBOK For six days of the week, Djébok is a nondescript desert village about 45km east of Gao. On Monday mornings, however, it is a nondescript desert village with one of the most important cattle markets in the region, with plenty of camels and, therefore, plenty of photo opportunities.

Public transport to Djébok departs early on Monday mornings from the *autogare* in Gao and costs CFA1,500. Prepare yourself for an early start and a bumpy ride, and be careful not to miss the vehicles returning to Gao after the market – unless you fancy a week in sunny Djébok!

WABARIA Tuesday is camel-market day in this village, found 12km south of Gao, just before crossing the new bridge. If you are interested in buying a camel, start negotiating at CFA150,000 for a baby and up to CFA1,000,000 for a racing camel. Don't forget to check their teeth! To get there, take public transport, leaving in the morning from behind Gao market. Cross the river over the new bridge or pay a small fee of CFA100 to ride across in a small pirogue. The livestock market is a fenced-in area across from the police checkpoint. Climb the hill behind town to arrive there. If in doubt, follow the camels. If you're feeling energetic, there are bikes to hire in Gao from Douma Maiga right behind Bani Transport (*2182 11 78;* m *7610 33 84; CFA1,500/day*). Try to give one to two days' notice.

SANÉ About 5km along the road to Algeria in the same direction as Djébok, the archaeological site of Sané or ancient Gao is the original location of the town when it was founded in the 7th century. Arguably the most important findings at the site were several tombstones of Spanish marble with Arabic engravings commemorating some of the first Songhay kings of the Dia dynasty, who migrated to Gao in the early 11th century.

As with many archaeological sites (Djenné-Djeno springs to mind), there is not much to see – let alone recognise – at Sané. There is, however, a reasonable explanation of ancient Gao at the Musée du Sahel (see page 226).

HIPPOS Your best chance of seeing some hippos near Gao – and they are quite common along this stretch of the River Niger – is downstream towards Ansongo. The village of **Tacharane** will be your closest vantage point, although the hippos tend to prefer the water around **Haoussa-Foulane**, at a rocky site in the middle of the river which is aptly named Île des Hippopotames, or Hippo Island.

Pinasses to Ansongo pass both of these towns. This is probably the cheapest way to go hippo-spotting, although it is not ideal if you want to return to Gao on the same day, as *pinasses* will continue downstream all the way to Ansongo (CFA5,000). The alternative, therefore, is to rent a boat for the day. Most guides will charge around CFA60,000 – including lunch – for a trip that will last until early afternoon. However, making arrangements through Camping Yarga (see page 225) may more than halve these rates.

ANSONGO AND THE SOUTHEAST

One of the region's largest towns is Ansongo, 100km downstream of Gao. The *cercle* of the same name is famed for its hippos and at one time was famed for its giraffes and ostriches, which used to cross the stretch of road between Tacharane and Ansongo to drink from the River Niger. Poaching has seen off most of the ostriches, and local experts say that only two giraffes still remain in the area. Your best chances of seeing some wildlife will be within the confines of Mali's second national game reserve, the **Réserve Partielle de Faune d'Ansongo-Ménaka**, which lies between Ansongo, the town of Ménaka and the Niger border. Although you should not count on meeting the pair of giraffes, you might see some antelopes, warthogs, herons and white flamingoes. As with the country's other game reserve, the Parc National de la Boucle du Baoulé (see page 285), the appearance of interesting and exotic fauna is the exception rather than the rule. Mali is not, after all, known for its great safari parks. You will need your own 4x4 transport and a good guide to explore the Réserve Partielle de Faune d'Ansongo-Ménaka.

Getting to the town of Ansongo, on the other hand, is simple enough by public transport (see *Getting there and away*, page 221). In fact, most travellers pass through the town – and sometimes stay overnight – on their way to or from Niger, whose border is a further 115km south of Ansongo at Labézanga.

KIDAL AND THE DESERT

The region of Kidal was created in 1991 as a concession to the Tuareg after the end of their rebellion. Unlike the seven other regions of Mali, Kidal enjoys a good deal of autonomy and the mainly Tuareg population exercises a significant amount of local control. After the beginning of the first rebellion in 1962, and before the end of the second, a large contingent of the Malian army was based in Kidal, which was also a popular place to send political prisoners. It was – and still is – the most isolated and inhospitable corner of Mali; a vast expanse of desert in the extreme northeast, where hardly anything grows and hardly anyone goes. It is, however, 'home' for the bulk of the country's Tuareg and Maure populations. A visit here promises a more authentic view of Tuareg culture than, say, Timbuktu. There are plenty of friendly Tuareg who are more than happy to talk about their culture, history and way of life. Do be aware that tradition and religion are far less influenced by external forces in Kidal so girls don't be surprised if men don't greet you or shake your hand. And boys, if women hide their faces or refuse to sit next to you in shared transport, it will be for the same reason.

From 1997, the Kidal region hosted **Takoubelt**, a festival celebrating the Tuareg culture. The yearly three-day celebration of music and culture, aimed largely at a local audience of nomads, took place in the beginning of January, somewhere in the vast region of Kidal inadvertently competing with other festivals for the title of the 'most remote festival in the world'. In 2004, it moved permanently to Essouk, 60km from Kidal, where it became known as Les Nuits Sahariennes d'Essouk, or Saharan Nights of Essouk. The people there were hoping it would remain an annual event: the last one held in 2006 had the town of Kidal buzzing as 1,000 or so nomads came and went, amongst them around 100 tourists. But then trouble flared up again in the northern desert area and for the time being the festival – along with all others in the northern desert region – has been cancelled. A great shame.

If, however, the situation does remain calm and the festival starts up again, unless you join an organised tour or have your own 4x4, finding transport to the location may not be easy. The safest option is to contact the organisation well beforehand, and they will try and find you a seat in any vehicle going to the festival. Travelling to Kidal – or any other town nearest to the chosen location – and hoping to hitch a ride may also work. On the first day you can probably catch a ride from one of the hundreds of cars milling around. You can maximise your chances by travelling to the nearest town several days before the festival, since plenty of service vehicles will be going there at some point. Even with your own vehicle, bear in mind that the location will be somewhere deep into the desert and barely – or not at all – signposted. Driving in a convoy is highly recommended. The festival is based on the humbling Tuareg hospitality, and food and shelter can be provided. It is wise, though, to bring some supplies, as on the festival grounds you will not be able to buy much: biscuits, very sweet fizzy drinks and mineral water are available while stocks last.

KIDAL

The region's largest town is Kidal, which lies about 350km northeast of Gao, almost 1,500km north of Bamako, and has a population of around 2,000. The first impression may be that of a dusty, dormant desert town, but on second sight it is actually a pleasant place to be. People are very friendly and – as Kidal does not receive that many visitors – curious to know who you are. Although the first couple of questions will sound all too familiar, a hidden agenda – to lure you into buying something for instance – is very unlikely. On the contrary: in Kidal you may encounter the heart-warming hospitality of the Tuareg, and this is only a taster of what lies ahead further north, deeper into the desert.

If you are planning to venture out there but still need to organise your trip, an excellent, Kidal-based travel agency is **Affala Voyages** (see page 232 for contact details). It is best to try and contact them before coming to Kidal, but this may prove difficult. Other agencies include **Touareg Tours** (see page 115 for contact details).

Even outside the professional circuit you should be able to find all you need for a journey into the desert. However, as you are not going for a Sunday picnic, make sure you are teaming up with the right people: get to know them a little, check that the language barrier does not cause misunderstandings, draw up a contract with all the expenses specified, and talk about the kind of food you will be having – as desert food is usually little else than gritty rice, bread and sometimes meat. If you are travelling independently, consider registering at the police station, and do not hesitate to check your prospective guide's credentials, for example at the **OMATHO** or the **Mission Culturelle** (see page 222). Most local people have never heard of the OMATHO (m *7608 48 70*) run by Sidi Mohamed ag Idal – or the Mission Culturelle – temporarily run by Jean Pierre Tita – so you'll have to ask around to find either of these men who are passionate about the Tuareg culture, the archaeological treasures of the Adrar des Ifôghas, and the potential for tourism in the Kidal region.

In Kidal, you can visit the **fort** and **prison**. These buildings of historical importance were constructed in 1929 by the French. The prison was in use until 1997, and now there are plans to convert the fort and prison into a museum. The **town gardens** provide a surprisingly green haven in this barren landscape. All kinds of vegetables are cultivated here, and they look their best between November and March. They are sold in the market which is best to visit in the morning before the midday heat. In the marketplace, you'll also find the Maison Artisans selling all sorts of traditional Tuareg stuff such as jewellery, brightly coloured leather cushions, camel saddles and carved leather boxes. Prices however are not cheap.

GETTING THERE AND AWAY Travelling to Kidal by public transport is possible by *camion* from Gao (see *Getting there and away*, page 221). Plenty of trucks or lorries travel up towards the Algerian border so if you're looking for transport to Tessalit, it shouldn't be a problem. It should normally cost around CFA7,500. To get back to Gao, ask around in the main square or go and wait at the police checkpoint on the way out of town. They can normally help you get a lift with someone who is leaving.

WHERE TO STAY AND EAT Accommodation is limited to a few comfortable, if not luxurious, places.

Motel Krutel 2185 00 90. En-suite rooms with a fan or AC. Meals are very good & taste even better when having them on the terrace overlooking the *wadi* at sunset with a beer! Food comes up in a refrigerated van once a week, so depending on what time of the week it is, there may be nothing left. It's best to make a lunch or dinner order in the morning. $$

THE DESERTED MARKETPLACE OF ESSOUK

Jolijn Geels, with thanks to Jean Pierre Tita for his valuable information

One could describe the Adrar des Ifôghas as a desolate landscape of epic beauty. Or as a barren region where any living creature has to struggle for survival. Or maybe as a place where the Tuareg have so little in terms of wordly possessions, while their lives are imbued with a rich history and refined culture. So to describe the Adrar as 'one big marketplace' may sound a bit odd at first, but historically that is just what it was.

Let us step back in time, to about 100BC. It was still a fairly green environment and there were many – mainly Tuareg – settlements scattered all over the Adrar. The horse had already been introduced to the area, but now a sweeping development took place: the camel appeared on the scene. It marked the beginning of the prosperous era of the trans-Saharan caravans, trading salt, slaves, gold and ivory. Because water was plentiful and the location was favourable, the Adrar became a crossroads of trading routes and a meeting point for caravans. News and merchandise were exchanged, the local population was thriving, and the Adrar des Ifôghas became a huge marketplace.

By the 9th century, a particularly popular settlement of at least 3,000 inhabitants was one of those meeting points for caravans. Whereas traders profanely referred to the abundant life that awaited them after the hardships of travelling, chroniclers described it as the most beautiful place of the Adrar. As the route through the settlement was also used by Muslims bound for a pilgrimage to Mecca, one day two pilgrims on their way to the holy city reached this place. It exceeded their expectations and they thought it the most beautiful place in Africa! They stayed to rest and stayed some more, and eventually they nearly forgot they were actually pilgrims.

'What about Mecca?' asked one of them one day.

'*Tada Mekkat!* (This is Mecca!)' was the other man's reply. That is how the settlement acquired the legendary name of Tadamakat.

Trade flourished over the next centuries, and at its peak it was not unheard of for one caravan to consist of 12,000 camels. Every morning Tadamakat would receive at least 200 camels, each of them laden with four bars of salt from the mines in Taoudenni. Before the sun set, all of that salt had been sold. The valuable bars still had a long way to go: to Europe or to the Middle East. It was said that by the end of the day not one grain of salt was left for the *marmite*, or cooking pot. Nor was there any water left in any of the 383 wells in Tadamakat. Replenished every morning, they would be emptied completely by thirsty traders, camel drivers and camels.

But the hospitality seemed without limits; the local women – who were said to be the most beautiful women of the Adrar – always went part of the way to meet and welcome

Chez Cathérine A friendly place run by a French lady. Travellers have recommended both food & accommodation here. $

Hotel Campement Les Dattiers ☎ 2185 00 36. Offers rooms with a fan & shared facilities, & en-suite rooms with AC. $

Maison du Luxembourg *Dorm beds CFA2,000.* $

ENTERTAINMENT AND NIGHTLIFE Nightlife in Kidal is fairly limited. However, you'll normally find performances some weekends, either by Tinariwen, if they're in town, or one of their many young protégés, such as the emerging Tamikrist.

These take place at either the youth centre, Maison du Luxembourg, which has a performance area and sells soft drinks or Radio Tisdas (☎ *2185 00 66*), the local radio station and location for the recording of Tinariwen's first album, *Radio Tisdas Sessions*. On a concert night, pretty much the whole town will turn out, dressed up in their best clothes, the men proud in their puffed-up indigo turbans and the woman and girls, beautiful with heavy kohl eyes and shimmering shawls. It really is a sight to be seen.

the caravans. They provided the weary travellers with water, food and shelter and everything else they could wish for. Really, this was the place to feel at home after an arduous journey! Moreover, it was a place of tremendous religious tolerance, as in two of the three different quarters of the town, Jews, Christians and Muslims alike would live happily together. Just one quarter was reserved for Muslims alone, but still they all coexisted in Essouk, as Tadamakat eventually became known later on.

So what went wrong? Why did Essouk – the Arab word meaning 'market' – perish, almost without a trace? What happened to the 'big marketplace' as a whole? Probably more than one factor contributed to the decline of Essouk and just about all of the other trading places in the Adrar des Ifôghas. One reason must be the shift in importance of the trans-Saharan routes, as traders from Europe established ports along the coast of west Africa. As a result, slaves were traded and shipped from the coastal towns rather than from the inland Adrar. The region of the Adrar des Ifôghas was faced with more difficulties that affected the towns directly. Natural disaster was creeping in, as the desert advanced and the wells no longer provided enough water for all.

Still, while there were profits to be made, greed got the upper hand of many merchants. Sapping the society from within, tolerance became overshadowed by fratricide, when even kinsmen stood up against each other. Maybe the towns and settlements in the Adrar des Ifôghas would have stood a chance of survival, had the overall situation of the ruling empires been more favourable. However, by the end of the 14th century, the Mali Empire started to decline as a result of internal power conflicts. The same fate would befall the Songhay Empire two centuries later, once again resulting in increased vulnerability and insecurity for the whole region.

Once upon a time the Adrar des Ifôghas was a thriving trading place, with Essouk being the most magnificent town of all. Then it was abandoned, forgotten almost. The remnants have been scavenged for gold, beads and other treasures. Even the rocks and stones with which the ancient town was built were removed and used to build wells and other constructions. In fact, one could now walk past the ruined remains of the three quarters of Essouk and barely notice them, leaving the valley oblivious of all the rock engravings that are testimony to the rich history and the famed eclectical tolerance of the area. Only trained eyes or vivid storytelling can make the site come alive. Then, with some imagination, one can even hear voices and footsteps, the thuds of salt slabs being off-loaded, and the unmistakable growling of camels bickering over water by the well.

Both of these venues can make you cassettes or CDs of local performances and they sell them for CFA1,500.

Le Grotto, located on the road to Gao just before the Motel Krutel, has beer and dancing 'til late.

OTHER PRACTICALITIES Kidal has a post office and a BMS bank where you can change cash euros and US dollars. Most of the time, telephone lines are down, but theoretically you could make phone calls in one of the *cabines téléphoniques*. You can go to Sotelma – follow the big red antenna – who may let you use their phone. They also have several computers for checking emails (CFA1,000 per hour). There is another internet café at Maison de Luxembourg. Orange has mobile network coverage in Kidal so if you have a local SIM card or international roaming on your mobile, you can use it here. It's best to stock up on top-up cards befrore getting there as supplies can run low.

THE DESERT You will need your own 4x4 vehicle and someone who knows the territory to explore the rest of the region effectively and safely. Alternatively, one or two tour operators specialise in desert adventures and excursions (see *Chapter 2, Tour operators in Mali*, page 46).

Two tour guide companies operating out of Kidal are **Affala Voyages** (☎ *2185 00 92;* **f** *2185 00 90;* **m** *7608 32 94;* **e** *cheikh@affala.com; www.affala.com*) and **Touareg Tours** (**m** *7645 44 18;* **e** *info@touaregtours.com; www.touaregtours.com*).

One possible trip is to the **Adrar des Ifôghas**, an eroded sandstone plateau which forms part of the Hoggar mountain system of the Sahara. Rising to a height of approximately 500m, the Adrar has a diverse ecosystem which, despite the debilitating effects of drought in the 1970s and 1980s, still includes a wide variety of fauna and desert vegetation. There are species of gazelle and antelope, hyenas, jackals and several varieties of snakes and lizards. The vegetation includes acadia trees and *cram-cram* grass. This is also an area rich in archaeological remains – notably rock paintings depicting men hunting, farming and cattle-rearing. These drawings, along with the fossil of a man discovered to the west of the Adrar at **Asselar**, have been dated back to the Neolithic period (see *Chapter 1, History*, page 13) and suggest that the Sahara was once densely populated and relatively rich and fertile. Indeed, the fossilised bed of the river which once irrigated the Sahara, the **Tîlemsi Valley**, stretches along the western flank of the Adrar des Ifôghas.

Essouk, which hosted the Takoubelt festival in 2004 (see page 91), is a site of great prehistorical and historical importance. The hills surrounding the ruined remains of the once prosperous town are scattered with rock engravings, depicting animals and various types of script. One rocky slab shows Hebrew, Roman and Arab script alongside each other. This is regarded as testimony to the extreme degree of tolerance between the Jews, Christians and Muslims, all of whom coexisted peacefully in the town of Essouk.

Elsewhere in the region, travellers *en route* to Kidal might stop at **Anéfis**, a picturesque village in the first foothills of the Adrar, or **Tessalit**, famous for its ancient salt mines and the border post for the trickle of traffic continuing on to Algeria. It's a laid-back town; home to Ibrahim ag Alhabibe, the equally laid-back lead singer of Tinariwen. The village also has great vegetable gardens. If you find yourself in Tessalit for a night, you can stay at the Centre d'Accueil, located next to the school (though there's no sign on the building) for CFA1,500. They also serve food. The Restaurant Benkadi serves food in the morning.

Just over 300km east of Gao is the small desert town of **Menaka**, credited for where the June 1990 rebellion started, with an attack on the military post there by young Tuareg, who had recently returned from Gaddafi's camps in Libya. It's difficult to find public transport in or out of the town, despite a newly paved road between Menaka and Ansongo. The only options are to rent a 4x4 or hitch a ride on the back of a date truck. The town itself is small, laid back and very pleasant.

At 100km from Menaka, on the Malian side of the Malian–Niger border is the tiny settlement of **Anderamboukane**, which plays host to a biennial festival, known traditionally as Tamadacht. This has to be one of the most authentic, and also well-organised, traditional festivals with local musical performances, camel racing and sand hockey.

Timbuktu

As well as being one of the most famous places in the world, Timbuktu is also the name of Mali's sixth region, created in 1977 by clumping together former *cercles* of the Gao region. This effectively makes Timbuktu the country's largest region, stretching from the Niger Bend to the northern frontiers of the Malian Sahara. Virtually all of the human activity takes place in the vicinity of the River Niger, where Timbuktu, Goundam, Diré and Gourma-Rharous are the main towns. The desert hotel at Araouane, 270km north of Timbuktu, is now derelict; and the only other permanent settlement is a further 400km across vast plains, dunes and shifting 'sand seas' known as *ergs* – at the Taoudenni salt mines.

TIMBUKTU TOWN

…Wide Afric, doth thy Sun
Lighten, thy hills enfold a City as fair
As those which starr'd the night o' the elder World?
Or is the rumour of thy Timbuctoo
A dream as frail as those of ancient Time?

Alfred Tennyson, Timbuctoo, *1829*

A year before this poem was published, René Caillié became the first European to visit Timbuktu and live to tell the tale. Previously, this fabled city of gold had been no more than a 'frail dream' in European minds: Mungo Park arrived at the port of Kabara in 1805, but was not allowed up the channel to Timbuktu; and Gordon Laing, the first European to reach the city in 1826, was slaughtered by the Tuareg as he tried to leave. Timbuktu in those days hardly needed a tourist brochure: like a lady playing hard to get, she had men falling over themselves to see her.

In this respect, not much has changed today, and the very name – choose between Timbuktu, Timbuctoo or Tombouctou – still intrigues modern-day travellers. In reality, it may no longer be the most isolated and inaccessible place in the world – nowadays, there is even internet access – but Timbuktu continues to enjoy the *reputation* of being somewhere out of the ordinary. Without this it would be, in René Caillié's words, no more than 'a mass of ill-looking houses, built of earth' – a disappointment, in fact. However, you should not visit Timbuktu expecting it actually to live up to its reputation. The very fact that you are in a place which was once the nerve centre of trade and learning in the western Sudan, a place men devoted their whole lives to discovering, should be enough to justify a visit.

Three impressive mosques and the houses of explorers, scholars and other VIPs are generally well preserved and protected as World and National Heritage Sites. The other main attraction, of course, is the Sahara. Timbuktu is built in a slight depression or hollow – the Songhay word for which is 'Tombouctou' – and as such the desert surrounds it on all sides. The River Niger, meanwhile, is about 10km to the south.

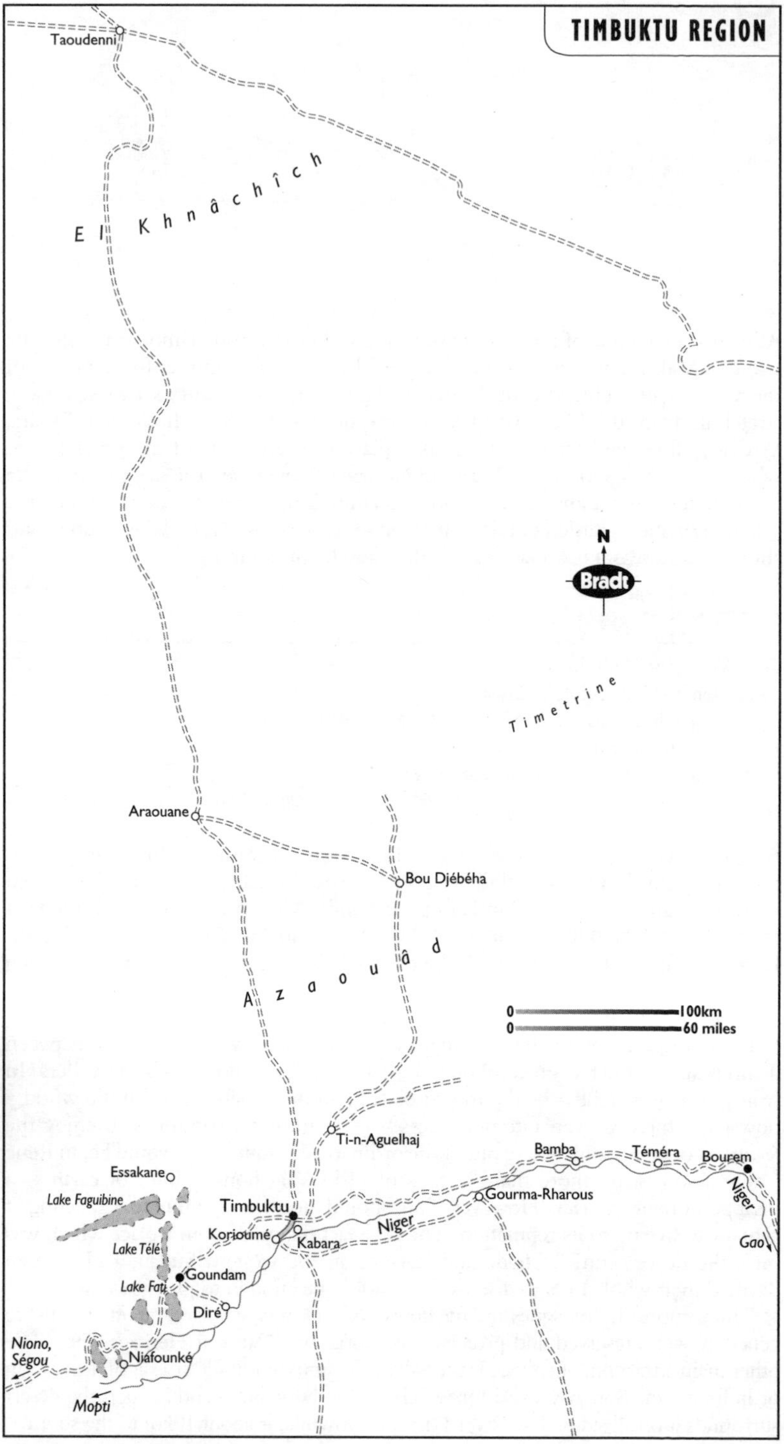

TIMBUKTU REGION
Taoudenni
El Khnâchîch
N
Bradt
Timetrine
Araouane
Bou Djébéha
Azaouâd
0
100km
0
60 miles
Ti-n-Aguelhaj
Bamba
Téméra
Bourem
Essakane
Lake Faguibine
Timbuktu
Gourma-Rharous
Niger
Koriоumé
Kabara
Niger
Gao
Lake Télé
Goundam
Lake Fati
Diré
Niono,
Ségou
Niafounké
Mopti

HISTORY Timbuktu was founded at the beginning of the 12th century by Tuareg nomads, who probably used it as a storage centre for their property and grain while they were in the desert. Not much is known of the town's early history, except that it was brought into the Mali Empire around 1275 and was visited by Kankan Moussa on his way back from Mecca in 1325.

At this time, Timbuktu was no more than an oasis for travellers crossing the desert: strategically important, of great potential, but not yet the great trading post it was destined to become. Instead, this role was played by desert towns further west such as Walata and Awdaghust, where gold from the fields of Bambouk and Buré was traded for salt from the mines of Téghaza.

However, towards the end of the 14th century, gold started to come from the Akan Forest east of Bambouk and Buré to satisfy the increasing demand in Europe. Suddenly, Walata and Awdaghust were rather out of the way for traders bringing gold from the Akan Forest, and their landlocked positions meant that travel was slow and expensive. Timbuktu, on the other hand, was on the edge of the desert and therefore accessible to caravans bringing salt from Téghaza, as well as being less than 10km from the River Niger, down which gold from the south could be transported quickly and easily via Djenné.

But trans-Saharan trade was not restricted to gold and salt; by 1468, when Sonni Ali Ber captured Timbuktu for the Songhay, the market at Timbuktu did a brisk trade in gold, kola nuts, ivory, ostrich feathers and slaves from the south, and salt, copper, tin, cloth and horses from the north.

Timbuktu enjoyed its golden years under the Askia dynasty, which ruled the Songhay Empire from 1493 to 1591. Although Sonni Ali was nominally a Muslim, he cared little for religion, and under his rule many Islamic clerics and scholars fled the town in order to escape persecution. On the other hand, his successor, Mohamed Askia, encouraged the return of the exiles and the development of Timbuktu as a centre of Islamic learning.

In the mid 16th century, there were approximately 150 Islamic schools in Timbuktu and students came from as far afield as north Africa and the Middle East, drawn by an academic reputation second to none in the western Sudan. Ahmed Baba was arguably the most famous – and surely the most prolific – of Timbuktu's scholars, producing some 56 works dealing mainly with theological subjects and jurisprudence. Other notable thinkers of the period were Mohamed Kati II, author of the *Tarikh el Fettach*, a chronicle of the western Sudan up to 1599; and Abderrahman Es-Sadi, writer of another important chronicle of the region, the *Tarikh es Sudan*.

Timbuktu slipped into decline when the Moroccans took over in 1591 and established the town as their headquarters. Religious leaders and scholars, including Ahmed Baba, were either arrested or forced into exile, and the town's population – around 25,000 during the Askia period – dwindled due to drought and famine. Under Mali and Songhay rule, the region had prospered through stable and peaceful government; Moroccan control, however, was less effective, and the *pashas* and their descendants, the Arma, were unable to protect Timbuktu from Bambara, Peul and Tuareg raids.

Eventually, in 1737, the Tuareg had a decisive victory over the Arma and became the dominant power in Timbuktu. In 1863, the marauding forces of El Hadj Omar Tall conquered Timbuktu and brought it within the Tukulor Empire, which is where it remained until the French arrived in 1893. The town was in a bad way and the French set about rebuilding some of its depleted infrastructure. However, as with Djenné, Timbuktu had lost its great trading importance and no special effort, such as a railway or a tarmac road linking the town to the south of the country, was expended to restore its past glories. Timbuktu has had its day and, although salt caravans occasionally arrive from the mines at Taoudenni, the town now relies more on tourism than trade to keep the wolves from the door.

Every January since 2003, more than 10,000 visitors descend on Timbuktu, for three days of music and festivities. The Festival in the Desert, which takes place 60km from Timbuktu, was created in the aftermath of the signing of the peace treaty to end the 1990s' Tuareg rebellion. It was a Tuareg initiative, based on a traditional annual gathering. The idea of the festival was to open up the whole idea of this gathering to other Malians and people from around the world, not only as a celebration of peace, but also to show who the Tuareg were and what their problems were, living in the inhospitable desert. It has become an important event for the Malian government and a showcase for Mali's talents, launching the international careers of local Tuareg musicians such as Tinariwen and Tartit, who have helped put Tuareg culture firmly on the map (see page 38 for more details).

In 2006, a search was launched by British photographer Stuart Redler to find a British town to twin with Timbuktu. In February 2007, Hay-on-Wye beat off 52 other British towns and villages, including York and Glastonbury, to become Timbuktu's official twin. Both towns are closely associated with books and learning; Timbuktu through its ancient collections of Islamic manuscripts, Hay for its world-famous secondhand bookshops and annual literature festival.

ORIENTATION Timbuktu is, quite literally, on the edge of the desert – walk to the western or northern edges of town, for example, and you can sit on sand dunes with the feeling of being in the middle of nowhere. Although the town itself is not large, getting around can be slow going due to the heat and sandy streets. However, although these sandy streets were for us, perhaps romantic, the town is progressing

FONDO KATI

Jolijn Geels

During the 15th century, religious intolerance in Spain was the cause of turmoil and violence. People were persecuted and even killed for their convictions, and therefore many preferred to flee the country and live in exile. The Muslim Kati family from Toledo were amongst the fugitives; taking with them the family library, they fled in 1468 to settle eventually in Gumbu in the area of the Niger Bend. Not long after, the Kati family became related to the family of Emperor Askia Mohamed through marriage. This happy conjunction had significant implications for the library, as imperial manuscripts trickled into the collection. Through the generations, the collection expanded and eventually consisted of several thousands of manuscripts. Unfortunately, though, after 1648 they got dispersed as the heirs of Mohamed Kati II claimed their share, taking valuable manuscripts with them to their respective places of residence. Some descendants of the Kati family struggled to bring the collection together again, but this proved a difficult task. The final blow was dealt by Peul kings from Macina, as they took the partly rebuilt library into their possession at the beginning of the 19th century, and dispersed it once more. It took until 1999 before another descendant of the Kati family stepped forward to salvage whatever might be left of the manuscripts. The family, by now very much dispersed along the River Niger, started handing in what they had; sometimes the manuscripts had been cherished and pampered, sometimes they could only be retrieved after a thorough search – as the long-forgotten specimens were stacked in a long-forgotten corner.

Only a few years later, over 3,000 manuscripts have been recovered, which is a truly impressive achievement. With funding from different institutions in Andalucía (Spain), a house in Timbuktu has been restored and is dedicated entirely to storing, preserving, cataloguing and studying the manuscripts. Evidently, another objective is to salvage the remainder of the missing manuscripts, and thus to reunite more of the 7,026 known

and tarred roads are gradually moving in. From the roundabout at the Place de l'Indépendance, past the Djingareiber Mosque and around to the Monument des Martyrs; around the Centre de Santé Référence and down the main street to the hospital; from the roundabout just before the Monument des Martyrs down Rue de la Paix and ending at the Flamme de la Paix; they're all covered. The old town, where most of your time will probably be spent, is a maze of disjointed streets and alleys, littered with famous places and with the marketplace, or *grand marché*, as its nucleus. The other market, the *petit marché*, is at the northern end of the town's main thoroughfare, Boulevard Askia Mohamed. Many of Timbuktu's tourist facilities (restaurants, post office, banks, etc) are on Route de Kabara – the main road into town.

GETTING THERE AND AWAY

By air The airport at Timbuktu is no more elaborate than other regional airports, although it seems to function well enough. It is located 4km from the town centre just off Route de Kabara. **MAE** (☎ 2192 11 21 ; **e** *sae@cefib.com*) operates two weekly flights from Bamako to Timbuktu, on Tuesdays and Saturdays, returning to Bamako on Wednesdays and Sundays. **Air Mali/CAM** (☎ *2192 13 45;* **m** *7602 35 48;* **e** *tomcam@cam-mali.org*), who also fly three times a week from Mopti and Bamako, can be found in the Quartier Badjindé, behind the governor of Timbuktu.

By river Although flying to Timbuktu is quick and practical, it is also slightly sacrilegious. After all, this place has become synonymous with isolation and inaccessibility and it seems only right to spend days of slow and uncomfortable

specimens that were once part of the private library. Sadly, many of them have been destroyed or severely damaged, especially the ones that were written on paper. A truly magnificent and well-preserved specimen, however, is a Koran written on the delicate and hairless skins of unborn lambs. Only a few similar manuscripts exist in the whole world.

Dating from the 12th to the 19th centuries, the present collection covers a whole array of subjects, including Islam, theology and law, philosophy and logic, medical science and mathematics, and philology and grammar.

Obviously the manuscripts are an invaluable source of information on all these subjects, but perhaps surprisingly a lot of time is spent deciphering and studying the many thousands of notes and comments that have been jotted down in the margins. These notes usually originate from members of the Kati family, and the majority of them can be traced back to Alfa Kati Mohamed and some of his descendants. Many notes have undoubtedly played a crucial role in the forming of the famous chronicle, the *Tarikh el Fettach* (see page 235), written by Mohamed Kati II.

Two parallel studies are now taking place in order to understand the full scope and significance of the library: the subject of the manuscript, and the many historical, scientific and (auto)biographical notes. Ismaël Diadié Haïdara – descendant of the Kati family, and founder and director of the Fondo Kati – is dedicating his life to the study, digitalisation and conservation of the library. While the two studies are already in progress, conservation is seriously lagging behind owing to lack of funds. Although the manuscripts are kept in a secure room and handled as little as possible, many of them are in desperate need of restoration. Visitors to the library and anyone with a heart for the story of this family library are invited to adopt a manuscript and salvage it for future generations.

For more information, check out www.fondo-kati.com, or **e** fondokati@yahoo.fr.

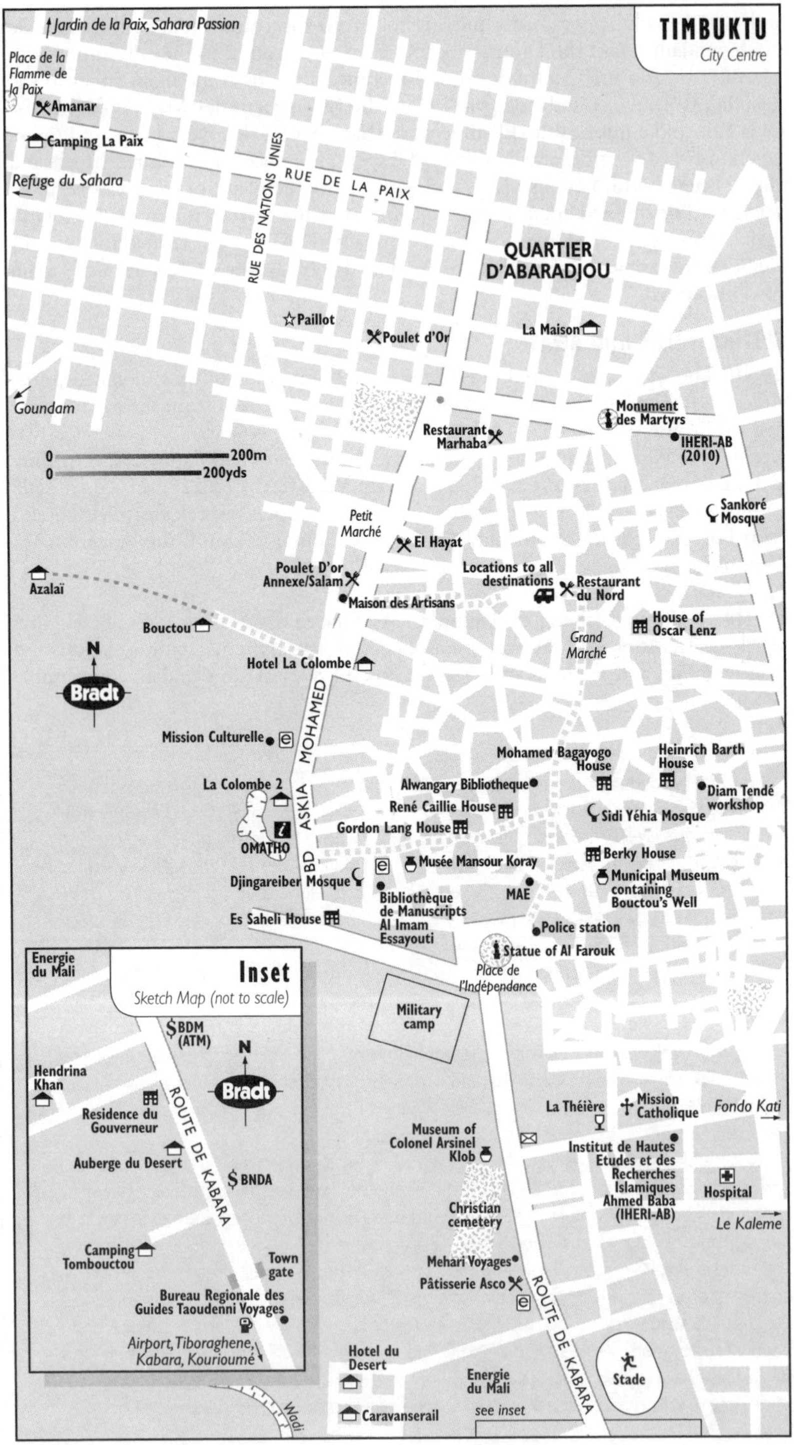

TIMBUKTU
City Centre
Jardin de la Paix, Sahara Passion
Place de la Flamme de la Paix
Amanar
Camping La Paix
Refuge du Sahara
RUE DES NATIONS UNIES
RUE DE LA PAIX
QUARTIER D'ABARADJOU
Paillot
Poulet d'Or
La Maison
Goundam
Monument des Martyrs
Restaurant Marhaba
IHERI-AB (2010)
0 200m
0 200yds
Sankoré Mosque
Petit Marché
El Hayat
Poulet D'or Annexe/Salam
Locations to all destinations
Restaurant du Nord
Azalaï
Maison des Artisans
Bouctou
House of Oscar Lenz
Grand Marché
Hotel La Colombe
N
Bradt
BD ASKIA MOHAMED
Mission Culturelle
Mohamed Bagayogo House
Heinrich Barth House
La Colombe 2
Alwangary Bibliotheque
Diam Tendé workshop
René Caillie House
Sidi Yéhia Mosque
Gordon Lang House
OMATHO
Musée Mansour Koray
Berky House
Djingareiber Mosque
MAE
Municipal Museum containing Bouctou's Well
Bibliothèque de Manuscripts Al Imam Essayouti
Es Saheli House
Police station
Statue of Al Farouk
Place de l'Indépendance
Energie du Mali
Inset
Sketch Map (not to scale)
BDM (ATM)
Military camp
Hendrina Khan
Residence du Gouverneur
ROUTE DE KABARA
Auberge du Desert
BNDA
La Théière
Mission Catholique
Fondo Kati
Museum of Colonel Arsinel Klob
Institut de Hautes Etudes et des Recherches Islamiques Ahmed Baba (IHERI-AB)
Hospital
Christian cemetery
Le Kaleme
Camping Tombouctou
Town gate
Mehari Voyages
Bureau Regionale des Guides Taoudenni Voyages
Pâtisserie Asco
Airport, Tiboraghene, Kabara, Kourioumé
Hotel du Desert
Energie du Mali
Stade
Wadi
Caravanserail
see inset

travel getting there. Getting to Timbuktu by river, therefore, is the romantic – if not always the sensible – option.

Timbuktu itself is a few kilometres from the River Niger. For the big boats the main COMANAV office (☎ 2192 12 06) is in Kabara. You must go there or to the boat when it's in port to buy your tickets. A smaller office is in Korioumé – some 19km from Timbuktu and a CFA500 taxi ride along a paved road. This is where boats are diverted to when the water level is low and the channel to Kabara is not navigable, normally between September and December. However, after 13 years of absence, most COMANAV boats once again dock at Kabara (see *Kabara*, page 249). Here you can buy tickets to go upstream towards Koulikoro (leaving on certain Sundays and Wednesdays) or downstream to Gao (leaving on certain Saturdays). (See *Chapter 2*, *Getting there and away* for more information and fares.)

For travel by *pinasse* and pirogue, see *Getting there and away*, page 174; a variety of *pinasses* and pirogues service the river and the cost increases or decreases with the level of comfort. Private tourist *pinasses* are pricey but a good investment if you want control over your trip or have enough people to share the cost. *Pinasses* to Gao sail all year, but much less frequently than upstream to Mopti. On the other hand, it is a lot easier to arrange a boat in Mopti – where you can deal directly with the owners at the harbour – than it would be in Timbuktu. There appears to be a regular *pinasse* on Friday afternoons from Korioumé, so people can get to the Sunday market in the village of Tonka but to negotiate for a river trip directly, you would have to go to Korioumé or Kabara first. The cost of a ticket to Mopti should be around CFA25,000 including food, though this can probably be negotiated down.

The alternative – dealing with boat owners through an intermediary – may prove disappointing: though many guides in Timbuktu are wonderful people, there are also a number of unreliable characters who may well let you down. Several forms of swindle to be on the alert for include: paying for a private *pinasse*, only to find you are travelling on a heavily laden public *pinasse*; paying for the Friday boat to Mopti but once you reach Tonka, finding it's not continuing; and being told food is included but then finding out it's not. Of course, by now your middleman is nowhere to be seen.

By road For those travellers with their own 4x4 vehicle, driving to Timbuktu has become much more straightforward than it was before the *piste* between Douentza and Korioumé was significantly upgraded. Only a few years ago, the *piste* was sometimes distinct, sometimes rather faint, and all too often consisted of numerous tracks fanning out in all directions, with no signposts telling you which way to go. With little oncoming traffic and only a handful of villages along the way, losing the track altogether posed a serious risk. Those days have gone, however, and even though the surface of the *piste ameliorée* can by no means be described as 'smooth', its outlines are distinguishable from Douentza all the way to Korioumé. At least the present *piste* seems to be going somewhere, rather than to be just heading out into the desert (there are rumours that it will be paved before long). For some reason, neither the old nor the new *piste* appear on the IGN and ITMB maps. The map on page 234 roughly shows the route: heading north from Douentza, skimming the desert town of Bambara-Maoundé, cutting between the seasonal lakes and fording Lac Garou, then turning left where the *piste* meets the River Niger, towards a causeway and landing place for the ferry. This Korioumé *bac* runs from 06.00 to 18.00 and the CFA20,000 fee gets split between the drivers of vehicles. So, if there are four vehicles it will be CFA5,000 each but if you're the only one, you pay it all. Foot passengers travel for free.

Travel by road to and from Timbuktu is difficult during the rainy season when much of the Niger Inland Delta is flooded. When the river is high it can take up to an hour to cross, but when it's low, around 15 minutes. During the dry season, on the other hand, the section between Douentza and Korioumé now takes only four to five hours. The stretch to Gao can be covered in a day, though most drivers prefer to camp somewhere *en route*.

A GDF bus leaves from in front of the Al Hayat Restaurant in Timbuktu for Bamako (via Douentza) every Thursday and Sunday (CFA15,000). You can buy tickets from the owner there or else go to the *gare routière*. The journey takes 24 hours if there are no breakdowns, with only brief stops for toilet, prayer, police and meals in Douentza, Sévaré, Bla, San and Ségou. Another GDF bus goes to Bamako via Goundam, Tonka, Diré, Niafounké, Léré and Ségou. It takes three days and normally leaves on Monday (CFA15,000).

Public transport comes in the form of *locations*: Land Rovers or other 4x4 vehicles with space in the back – in theory, at least – for about 16 people. The office where you go to reserve a seat or ask about departures is in the east corner of the *gare routière*, across from the *grand marché*. Bourema is the head honcho for all drivers operating legitimate public transport. His service is quite reliable and going to him can cut through a lot of the hassle. In fact, Timbuktu is probably the only place in Mali, even in west Africa, where transport leaves on time, if not earlier than the scheduled time.

Locations leave daily, very early, and you take your chances if you want a later departure. Prices are fixed at CFA15,000 for Mopti and CFA12,500 for Douentza, in the front cabin and CFA2,500 less for seats in the back. The journey can take between five and eight hours depending on the season. If you take the early car, you can be in Douentza by 11.00, although nothing, of course is guaranteed. Land Rovers to Gourma-Rharous, Bourem and Gao depart less frequently, and cost CFA5,000/6,000 for Gourma and CFA12,500/15,000 for Gao depending on the location of your seat. *Camions* leaving for Gao charge CFA7,500, while those trucks leaving in the opposite direction charge CFA2,000 for a journey to Goundam. From December/January to June, Tikambo Transport offers an interesting weekly option for travellers with stamina: a *camion* to Bamako, via Goundam, Diré, Niafounké, Léré, Niono and Ségou. Departure is scheduled for Mondays around 13.00, and the boldly estimated time of arrival in Bamako is Wednesdays around noon. Note that although the truck stops at regular intervals, it does not halt for a good night's sleep. Be prepared for two rough and bumpy nights on board. The fare is CFA2,500 for Goundam and Diré, CFA12,500 for Niono and CFA15,000 for Bamako. For transport to Essakane ask around at the *gare routière* or go to the road heading out of town and try flagging down a vehicle . Expect to pay CFA7,500 in the cabin or CFA5,000 in the back.

Hitching a ride is possible, although not very regular, and should only be attempted by people with enough time on their hands. For Douentza/Mopti, take a *bâchée* from the market to Korioumé (CFA500) and approach drivers while waiting for the ferry. Public transport, tourist vehicles going back empty or private vehicles may pick you up, but you should always expect to pay. Some ONGs and wealthy people pick up travellers for free but it is not very common (ONG is the French version of NGO, or non-governmental organisation). ONGs often have rules that they cannot transport non-employees and road checks are fairly strict. If a passenger is not on the paperwork, there could be difficulties. For Goundam, stop at the police checkpoint just outside Timbuktu, and police officers will help you to find a vehicle. For Gao, ask around at the marketplace or approach drivers individually.

TOURIST INFORMATION If you are heading out to the desert, you are advised to register and get your passport stamped at the police station at the Place de l'Indépendance. Given the history of dubious security in the desert regions, this is still considered a logical – but not compulsory – safety procedure. Bring one photograph; it shouldn't take very long and it is free of charge. Many tourists like to have a stamp in their passport just to prove that they have been to Timbuktu. If the stamp is what you are after, the new **OMATHO** office (☎ *2192 17 79*) which doubles as a tourist office (Direction Régionale du Tourisme) issues a stamp at no cost in a minute. Other than a few outdated leaflets, there is little information to be found here, though the director Sane Chirrfi Alpha and his staff are helpful and enthusiastic (e *sanechirfi@yahoo.fr*) and that may improve over time. The better place to contact is the **Mission Culturelle** (☎ *2192 10 77*), which is responsible for protecting, preserving and promoting Timbuktu's cultural attractions. Any information about Timbuktu and its environs can be gleaned from the knowledgable, English-speaking director, Ali Ould Sidy (m *7602 39 41*).

Tourism has greatly increased in recent years, yet the season is very short. Locals rely on just three months to earn enough money to survive for the rest of the year. In spite of this, Timbuktu has more than its fair share of hawkers and false guides. There are 70 official guides in Timbuktu – 59 local and 11 national. If you want to employ the services of a guide, always ask to see their professional badge; then if something goes wrong, you have the backup of the OMATHO. The most reliable sources of guides are through the OMATHO office or one of the hotels such as the Auberge du Desert, Refuge du Desert or Sahara Passion (where you'll find Shindouk, the president of the local association of guides and camel drivers (m *7631 91 45;* e *shindouk@yahoo.fr*).

TOUR OPERATORS

Tafouk Voyages BP 130, Quartier Abaradjou; ☎ 2192 23 46; e alhous.t@nomade.fr; www.tafouk.com. Quite the mover & shaker of Timbuktu, this tour guide is responsible for the catering at the Festival in the Desert.

Taoudeni Voyages m 7942 6947, 7631 9145; e taoudenivoyage@yahoo.fr. Offer tailor-made off-the-beaten-track desert trips. They're based in Timbuktu but go up into Mauritania, Algeria & Niger, avoiding the routes that have become off-limits.

WHERE TO STAY Thanks to the increase in visitors to Timbuktu during the Festival in the Desert, hotels have improved in both quality and quantity. There are even a couple of 'boutique' hotels amongst them.

Upmarket $$$$

La Maison (9 rooms) Near the PMI (Centre de Santé de Référence), Quartier d'Abaradjou; ☎ 2192 21 79; e lamaison.hotel@gmail.com; www.lesmaisonsdumali.com. A new 'boutique' style hotel run by Awa & her mother, with tasteful, minimalist AC rooms & a shaded area with plenty of cushions to laze around on. Partnered with the Maison Rouge in Mopti, it is considered to be the best hotel in Timbuktu. B/fast extra at CFA3,500.

Mid-range $$$

Campement Hotel Bouctou (29 rooms) Between the Azalaï & Bd Askia Mohamed; ☎ 2192 10 12. An attractive traditional building in a good location with a terrace overlooking the dunes. Rooms are cheap & aimed at a broad cross-section of travellers. Consequently, guides & Tuareg salesmen keep a constant vigil outside the hotel. AC or fan with choice of internal/external bathroom, though the upstairs shared bathrooms are generally cleaner. You can pitch a tent in the sandy courtyard for CFA6,000 pp with b/fast. In high season, when the whole of Timbuktu is fully booked, they may still have a mattress on the floor in their basic but adequate annex.

Camping La Paix Rue de la Paix; m 7602 36 47/7604 19 07; e bll_css@yahoo.fr. On the former site of the Sahara Passion (which has moved, though you may be told otherwise; see below), just before the Flamme de la Paix & across the street from the Restaurant Amanar. These basic rooms with either fan or AC are a bit dirty & overpriced. There's a restaurant but no beer. *Dorm beds CFA4,000.*

Caravansérail (10 rooms) m 7541 43 02; www.tombouctoucaravanserail.com. This French-owned *hôtel du charme* was opened in 2007 & created as a meeting place for travellers. Rustic rooms are decorated with interesting items, picked up in the local market, from as far afield as Pakistan. There's a pet monkey, a plunge pool to cool your toes & a bar made from slabs of salt. Caters for all budgets: rooms with a fan, a mattress on the terrace, or nomad tent facing the desert for CFA6,000. Henna, massage & hair braiding available. Hot water & AC. B/fast not inc.

Hotel Azalaï 2192 21 06. Currently closed for renovation but should reopen in 2010. On a sandy hillock at the western edge of town, the Libyans (group Azalaï) are investing large amounts of money to create a channel, allowing you to arrive at the door by *pinasse*.

Hotel du Désert (12 rooms) 2192 11 99; e hoteldudesert@hotmail.com. Another new hotel at the entrance to town, tucked away down a quiet side street. Friendly with clean, if rather unimaginative rooms. AC or fan with TV & telephone & choice of internal or communal hot-water bathrooms. There's a small garden & roof terrace & the restaurant serves standard African fare; *yassa poulet* or couscous for CFA3,000. B/fast inc.

Hotel Hendrina Khan (24 rooms) 2192 16 81; e hotelhendrina@yahoo.fr; www.tomboctou.com. A Malian-owned hotel with basic, clean rooms. All are en suite with AC, hot water, minibar & TV. The main drawback is the non-central location, near the entrance to Timbuktu; a good 25min walk into town. However, a courtesy van is available for transfers. The hotel has internet for guests.

Hotel La Colombe I (50 rooms) & the nearby annex, referred to as **La Colombe 2** (37 rooms); 2192 14 35; e hotelcolombe@afribonemali.net. Centrally located & close to the main sites, this is one of the longest-running establishments in Timbuktu. However, they will have to pull their socks up with all the new competition in town. Rooms are shabby & overpriced with unpredictable service. Try to get a room in the newer **La Colombe 2**, where they are also building a pool. Very expensive laundry service. AC & hot water. B/fast not incl.

L'Auberge du Désert (5 rooms) 2km from the airport, just after the BNDA bank, Quartier Sanfil; m 7602 34 14; e alhous.t@nomade.fr; www.tafouk.com. A simple *auberge* owned by Alous of Tafouk Voyages (see page 241). The en-suite rooms with AC or fan are practical & clean. But the real advantage here is Alous's expertise. He can organise any type of excursion into the desert. Hot water & a bar serving alcohol. B/fast not inc.

Budget $$

Hotel Camping Tombouctou Near the entrance of town; 2192 14 33. Simple but uninspiring budget accommodation with functional AC or fan rooms. Sleeping on the roof costs CFA2,500/3,500 (with or without mattress).

Refuge du Sahara (5 rooms) m 7602 36 47; e elmoctar@yahoo.com. A laid-back little place with a great atmosphere & owned by Khalis, one of Timbuktu's English-speaking guides. He can organise excursions into the desert, to the salt mines of Taoudenni or to his camp 10km away. The rooms have different prices, depending on whether you use the AC or not. Tuareg dishes such as *alabadja* or *fakohoye* (the traditional sauce of Timbuktu) are served, CFA3,500. Camping available, CFA5,000. Hot-water showers. B/fast inc.

Sahara Passion (2 rooms, 1 dorm) 150m north from the Flamme de la Paix; m 7631 91 45; e megdodd@yahoo.com; www.hotelsaharapassion.com. A community of thatched huts is all that stands between the guesthouse & the open desert & during the season you can watch the salt caravans arriving from the Taoudenni mines. Quiet & away from the crowds, thanks to a strict policy of keeping guides & hawkers off the hotel grounds. That said, beware disgruntled guides who may try & tell you it's closed down. Thick walls made from traditional *banco* keep the rooms cool during the day & solar panels provide electricity. Camping in the yard or on the terrace CFA3,000. Local meals to order.

Shoestring $

Mission Catholique Across the street from IHER-AB, this family-run establishment with no priest accommodation is in small rooms or for CFA1,000 you can sleep on the terrace.

Restaurant Poulet d'Or Travellers with scant regard for creature comforts might be attracted by the basic *banco* rooms & 'African' showers. It is a welcoming place.

WHERE TO EAT All hotels have restaurants or at least the option to order a meal.

Above average $$$$

La Maison 2192 21 79; lunch (orders only), dinner reservations should be made before 18.30. A fixed menu, served in a small rooftop restaurant, combining French, Italian & Moroccan cuisine with personal inspiration; cheese soufflé with green salad, tagine of *capitaine* with lemon, olive oil & coriander seasoning or tornedos of beef with a confit of sun-dried tomatoes & balsamic onions & pear tart with chocolate ganache for dessert. Non-residents can eat but must book in advance (see above).

Mid-range $$$

Caravansérail m 7629 45 88. Dine by torchlight on the terrace facing the open desert. Traditional Timbuktu casseroles with a European twist or sheep, 'hamburger au désert' & brochettes from the barbecue. Sorbets for dessert. All meals made to order. There's only 20 covers so it's best to reserve.

Hotel La Colombe 2192 14 35. The terrace on the 1st floor is certainly attractive, but meals may take a while to be prepared. Standard set menu; salad, mutton with rice & sauce & watermelon.

Restaurant Hendrina Khan 2192 16 81. The most sophisticated & expensive menu of all the other hotels. Good food but no gastronomic surprises.

Cheap and cheerful $$

Pâtisserie Asco Opposite the post office on Route de Kabara; 2192 11 68. Traditional Songhay & Tuareg dishes can be prepared for groups of at least 4 people if you order in advance. Otherwise there's a limited choice such as chicken & chips, spaghetti or omelette. The *pâtisserie* is a disappointment, with only croissants, *pains au chocolat* & meat patties available on a regular basis. Occasionally, the *pâtisserie* organises *soirées gala*, where a CFA5,000 cover charge buys you a soft drink & a set menu accompanied by live traditional music.

Restaurant Amanar Opposite the Flamme de la Paix; m 6677 62 66; 10.00–14.00 & 17.00–midnight (closed in the rainy season). Excellent & inexpensive meals in a fantastic setting on the edge of the dunes. Choice of several dishes including grilled meats & seasonal fish. Serves beer & in high season there can be live entertainment.

Restaurant Poulet d'Or Very friendly though the regular menu is quite plain & service is slow. The chips are reputedly the crispiest in town, though the chicken a little frazzled. Excellent brochettes. Talk about food to the owner Dédéou Maïga, & he may propose something out of the ordinary, like an entire sheep from the clay oven in his courtyard, accompanied by various sauces & side dishes. They'll light a fire on cold winter nights.

Rock bottom $

Restaurant El Hayat Opposite Centre Artisanal; m 7903 84 57; 06.00–22.00. Dinners are on the 2nd-floor terrace with a good view. It tends to fill up rather quickly, so despite the fact that the service is highly efficient you may have to wait before finding a seat. Open early for a filling b/fast; meat with sauce, liver with bread or heart omelette. Lunch a choice of traditional dishes; rice with peanut sauce, *saga-saga* or *fakohoye*.

Restaurant Marhaba m 7887 49 46. On the man paved road going north past the Maison Artisans, turn right at the roundabout toward the Monument des Martyrs. If you get to a pharmacy you have gone too far. Opened in Aug 2008 by Lella Mariam, serving a variety of locally available cuisine including rice & sauce, pasta & couscous, kebabs & grilled chicken. The downstairs dining room has satellite TV or there's a terrace.

Restaurant du Nord In the *grand marché. Riz gras* (fried rice) & *riz sauce* (rice with sauce) available at most times, but for more exotic dishes such as omelette & chips, you must order in advance. Good helpings for little money.

Restaurant Salam (also known as or Poulet d'Or Annex) In the Maisons Artisans; m 7614 58 50; 08.00–22.00. Opened by Dédéou Maïga's apprentice & serving dishes like couscous or rice with meat & sauce, which are served on long benches. Conveniently central & good enough to fill the gap especially after visiting the artisans.

ENTERTAINMENT AND NIGHTLIFE If you're staying at the southern end of town and fancy a beer, the **Café La Théière** (m *7524 08 57*), to the left of the Mission Catholique, is a French/Timbuktu-owned bar with regular concerts by the same traditional musicians who perform at Caravanserail. It is also a *salon de thé*, *pâtisserie* and restaurant rolled into one. Also down this end of town is the **Pâtisserie Asco** (*admission CFA2,000– 3,000*), which sometimes has concerts at weekends: a sight to be seen when one of the local bands play and the Tuareg come out, dressed up to the nines in glistening indigo. Seats are set up in the courtyard and beer and spirits are served. Next to the Pâtisserie Asco is a '*buvette*' bar which, out of season,

THE FESTIVAL IN THE DESERT, ESSAKANE

Suzanne Porter

The Festival au Desert is based on an ancient traditional gathering of the nomadic Tuareg (or *Tamasheq*, as they'd rather be known) in the deserts of Mali, Niger and Algeria. Every year at the end of the nomadic season, the Tuareg would congregate for three days of music, dancing and feasting whilst exchanging information and settling disputes.

The festival was created in the aftermath of the signing of the peace treaty to end the 1990s' Tuareg rebellion. It was a Tuareg initiative, created by Manny Ansar and the association of Efes whose objectives were to promote the Tuareg culture and show the world who they really were and the problems they were facing, living in the desert. They revived the festival and opened it up to other Malians and people all over the world.

The first festival was held in Tin Essako in 2001. The original aim was to keep it nomadic but with the festival expanding and financial constraints, a concrete stage was constructed and since 2003 the festival has stayed permanently in Essakane, 60km from Timbuktu.

Each year sees headlining performances from musicians from Mali and other African countries. Tinariwen, Vieux Farka Touré (son of Ali) and Ticken Jah Fakoly performed in 2008; Ali Farka Touré, Habib Koité, Amadou and Mariam (with Manu Chao) and Oumou Sangaré are amongst others who have made it there in the past. The programme isn't confirmed until almost the day of the festival and even then is subject to last-minute change. Some Malian artists, finding fame and fortune, become either too busy or expensive to turn up. Visiting stars such as Robert Plant or Damon Albarn are rare, therefore the festival is largely limited to those willing to play for free and pay their own transport.

But it's not the music that should bring you to the festival. It's the getting there and being there that's important. It's the meeting and exchanging and drinking tea; the soft feel of white sand in your toes and the inquisitive camels coming up to say hello; the chaos, the freedom, the stars in the sky. It's the acceptance of everyone, no matter where you're from.

Daytime can be spent wandering the dunes and catching impromptu performances of traditional musicians or wannabe Tinariwens jamming with battery-powered amps. There are discussions on Tuareg culture and haggling over jewellery in the lively artisan market. The descent of the sun is marked by the traditional Tindé drum. Everyone gathers to watch the camel racing where riders take great pleasure in mowing down innocent spectators.

Once the sun disappears, the music starts on the main stage, built in a natural hollow surrounded by dunes. The sound system and lights rival any Western festival stage but the most memorable collaborations are normally around the campfires.

Minister, musician, nomad or tourist: everyone at the festival sleeps in a tent. Agencies set up camps, often with private showers, toilets, and camp beds. They cook for the group and employ security so you don't have to worry about your belongings.

is livelier and cheaper than anywhere else. A bit further South is **Caravansérail**. Once a week at 21.00, the rugs and cushions are rolled out, to show African films. Aperitifs and cocktails are served from the salt-slab bar and every weekend at 23.00 traditional musicians perform.

At the other end of town, the **Amanar Restaurant** sometimes has concerts. They're normally announced at the last minute on the radio but unless you understand *Tamasheq* (the Tuareg language) you will be none the wiser. It's best to ask around town or at the local OMATHO office.

Next door to the restaurant is the **Amanar Club** (m *7629 45 88;* ⌚ *from 22.30 Fri/Sat until the last person leaves; admission CFA3,000pp or CFA5,000 for a couple*). The best nightclub in town. Look out for special nights during Christmas and holidays

Entrance to the festival is around €120. Tickets can be bought as part of a full-board package for €270 or you can turn up with your own camping equipment and eat at one of the many restaurants, temporarily relocated from Timbuktu.

If this seems a bit expensive, an alternative for getting there is as a volunteer. It's hard work but a great way to see behind the scenes. Send your CV to e festivalaudesert@yahoo.fr.

Though the festival is a magical experience, there are a few things to bear in mind for the inhabitants who are left behind afterwards. You'll find endless artisans and cameleers hawking their wares and although the continuous stream can be annoying, remember that they have just three days to maybe earn enough money to feed their families for the rest of the year.

In the absence of rain, consumption of water at the festival can leave local wells empty, driving away pastoralists who were just about making a living. Use water sparingly and try not to complain when it runs out in the makeshift showers.

Despite what Tuaregs try to tell you, plastic is not biodegradable and cannot be broken down by the harsh desert climate. The festival has increased pollution in the area and goats are eating plastic bottles left behind. This enters their milk cycle, which as milk is sacred, isn't going down too well.

Other nomads are moving away as they don't want their children influenced by Western behaviour such as drinking alcohol and lack of appropriate clothing. Although it is a festival, with the emphasis on enjoyment and having fun, try to observe the local customs (see *Chapter 2, What to wear*, page 97).

The Festival in the Desert is sponsored by the charity UNICEF. For more details of their work and to find out ways you can help, contact the local office (*2020 44 01;* e *bamako@unicef.org; www.unicef.org.uk*).

A FEW FACTS AND FIGURES

- The Inuit musicians, Artcirq, caught 26 flights from their home in the Arctic Circle to be able to perform in the desert.
- It took eight days to get the sound system to the site, including three days stuck in sand.
- More than 50 volunteers and visiting technicians helped the local organisation get everything in place.

People often ask me if the festival has changed since the first one I went to in 2002 and if it has lost its appeal now that it's so well known. It's true more tourists can get there as it's more accessible than before. In 2008, 10,000 people made it; 1,200 were tourists and amongst them 130 accredited journalists. But then, it's achieving its aims: showing the world of the Tuareg and their culture, in a celebration of peace. The setting and their hospitality still makes it an experience definitely worth travelling for.

For more information, see the festival website www.festival-au-desert.org.

such as Tabaski. **Paillote** is Timbuktu's second nightclub and can be found 500m from Amanar, next to the original Poulet d'Or and north of the *petit marché*. The **Kaleme**, a few blocks behind the hospital east of the Baptist church, has dancing every night and live music Saturday and Sunday.

Other than that there's not much else, unless you stumble on a local celebration. The night of Mouloud (Muhammad's birthday) and New Year's Eve are both heavily celebrated and you can find a lot of interesting things going on.

OTHER PRACTICALITIES The post office and three banks (BDM, BNDA and BHM) are on Route de Kabara. BDM – with a Western Union office – does Visa cash advances and changes travellers' cheques in euros and US dollars, but not cash.

There is a Visa-only cash-dispensing machine in the entrance that you can get to anytime. BDM changes euros and American Express US dollar travellers' cheques and you must have a copy of the purchase receipt. BNDA is the only bank that changes US dollars cash. They also have a Moneygram office for money transfers. BHM does not deal with foreign currency.

Télécentre Communautaire Polyvalent – or TCP for short – next to the Pâtisserie Asco provides internet access (🕘 *until 22.00 daily; CFA1,000/hr*). There is another internet café at the Bibliothèque Essayouti facing the main entrance of the Djingareiber Mosque (🕘 *08.00–22.00 daily; CFA1,000/hr*).

WHAT TO SEE In 1992, the old town of Timbuktu, with its mosques, houses of famous explorers and scholars, ancient university and other places of historical interest, was declared a National Heritage Site. You should consult the map on page 234 to help you locate the sights, all of which can be seen quite easily in a day. Next to the Djingareiber Mosque there is a sign, erected by the Mission Culturelle, with an overview of the main places of interest in the old town.

Mosques There are three mosques classified as World Heritage Sites. The **Djingareiber Mosque** is the oldest, arguably the most interesting and probably the landmark most closely associated with Timbuktu. Built in 1325 by an Andalucian architect and poet, Es Saheli, on the orders of Kankan Moussa, who had just returned from his pilgrimage to Mecca full of religious zeal, the Djingareiber Mosque is shaped like a pyramid at its base and has conical towers. There is a platform at the top with good views of the city and upon which René Caillié apparently made some of his notes. However, entrance is currently closed to the public. This is for two reasons: first, renovations, and secondly, as in Djenné, infidels. Still it's a sight not to be missed, particularly on a Friday when 15,000 people flock to the mosque to pray.

The other two mosques were built some time during the 15th century and are not open to tourists. The **Sankoré Mosque** is small and simple, which adds some credence to the story that it was built by a Berber woman to resemble the Ka'bah or the house of God at Mecca. During the 15th and 16th centuries, Timbuktu's famous **University of Sankoré** was also based here. The 15th-century **Sidi Yéhia Mosque**, meanwhile, is the least attractive of the three, although there is a wrought-iron door which is as good an example of this feature of the town's architecture as you'll find. Again, entry to the mosque is forbidden.

Houses of explorers, scholars, etc In 1512, a fire destroyed much of Timbuktu. Its subsequent reconstruction followed Arab and north African traditions, with rectilinear, flat-roofed houses, often two or more storeys in height and built of sun-dried mud, becoming the dominant form of architecture.

A plaque, courtesy of the Mission Culturelle, identifies the house of virtually every famous person who ever spent time in Timbuktu. Many of these houses were used by explorers, such as Gordon Laing, René Caillié, Heinrich Barth, Oscar Lenz and Berky. The adventures of the first three of these men have been well documented and are elaborated on in the box *Discovering Mali*, pages 20–1. Oscar Lenz was an Austrian explorer who followed Heinrich Barth (in July 1880) as the next European to visit Timbuktu (his plaque is mounted on the house opposite his original dwelling which now no longer exists); and Berky was the first American to reach the city, which he did in 1913.

Most of these houses are now the homes of local inhabitants and should be respected as such, except Gordon Laing's house, which has now been turned into a free museum (**m** *7605 11 06;* **e** *sidiki_najim@yahoo.fr;* 🕘 *08.00–18.00*). Inside you'll find Mr Boubacar Sadeck, who has an exhibition of ancient and Arabic manuscripts from the 11th and 12th centuries and the traditional materials used to make them. He is a copier and makes reproductions of 16th-century manuscripts, which he offers for sale as well. Donations are requested. Heinrich Barth's house has a small museum (*admission CFA1,000*) with captions in English, French and German and is run by the lady who now lives there. The former dwellings of several other Timbuktu notables are dotted around the old town. There is that of Ahmed Baba, for example, perhaps the city's most famous scholar; Mohamed Bagayogo, a former *imam* and professor at the University of Sankoré; the architect of the Djingareiber Mosque, Es Saheli, and other important figures during Timbuktu's cultural heyday.

Museums and libraries

Municipal museum containing Bouctou's well (m *7619 77 42;* ⌚ *08.00–13.00 & 15.00–18.00 daily; admission CFA2,500 which you have to pay even if you want to see the well only*) The origins of the name Tombouctou (French spelling) are a contentious issue. However, most go along with the scholar Es-Sadi, who claims in his *Tarikh es Sudan* (1655) that the town owes its name to a distortion of the Targui (Tuareg) word 'tin' and 'Bouctou'. According to legend, a woman called Bouctou watched over the Tuareg well or *tin* while the nomads were in the desert. Timbuktu, therefore, means **Bouctou's Well**, the original site of which is supposed to be in the old town, housed within the courtyard of the new Municipal Museum. This interesting museum contains lots of traditional Tuareg bits and pieces. There's a tent, utensils, bowls, drums, shoes, jewellery, slabs of salt, and several other pieces, all with written explanations.

Other museums and libraries There are two places to visit near the Djingareiber Mosque. The **Museum Mansour Koray** (*admission CFA1,500*), one block east, along the cobbled walk, is a traditional family home made from limestone and *banco* in the Timubktu style with rooms filled with artefacts from everyday life. The **Bibliothèque de Manuscripts Al Imam Essayouti** (☎ *2192 12 61; admission CFA1,000*), just opposite the mosque, contains ancient manuscripts.

In the southern part of town there's a new museum, named after a **Colonel Arsinel Klob**. It's attached to the Christian cemetery, across from the post office just north of Chez Asco, and retraces the history of colonisation.

Opposite the Mission Catholique, also in the south, is the **Institut des Hautes Études et de Recherche Islamique Ahmed Baba (or IHERI-AB)**, formerly known as the Centre de Documentation et de Recherches Historiques Ahmed Baba (or CEDRAB). The CEDRAB was inaugurated in 1973 to systematically collect, conserve and exploit the 20,000–30,000 rare and precious manuscripts which are estimated to be at large in northern Mali. These goals still prevail, but since July 2000 – under the new umbrella of the IHERI-AB – the structure of the institute has changed. Not only will the manuscripts be read and listed, they will increasingly be made available for studies in the field of Islamology, history, anthroposociology, Arab–African literature and medicine. The Institute already receives many PhD students from abroad. In addition to all this, the extremely laborious process of rescuing and restoring the manuscripts – well over 20,000 by now, the oldest one being from AD1204 – is finally in progress.

The main reason for a tourist to visit the IHERI-AB (*admission CFA1,000; guides available*) is to see some of the manuscripts on display and to admire the minute work and the prudent handling of manuscripts in the *atelier de restauration*. If your interest is more than average, make an appointment to see one of the many experts in the field. In 2010, the centre will move to a new building constructed by the South African government, near the Sankoré Mosque.

Not far from the IHERI-AB are a few private libraries, such as **Fondo Kati** (☎ *2192 13 95*), open to the public since September 2003. The family are passionate about their collection and will show you the library and an interesting exhibition of facsimiles. For more information, see box *Fondo Kati*, pages 236–7.

Other sights in the old town The quarter of Badjinde is in the heart of the old town. All that remains today of its glorious past as Timbuktu's bustling trading centre is the ***grand marché***, which was rebuilt in Sudanese style in 2003, and where there is a brisk trade in rotting tomatoes, sour oranges and lumps of salt – for lack of anything more appealing.

The workshop of **Diam Tendé**, whose craftsmen are reputed to be descendants of Es Saheli's companions, still produces traditional doors, windows and other furniture with wood from Côte d'Ivoire – the door of the restaurant at the Kanaga Hotel in Mopti, for example, is one of theirs. The workshop opens on to the road, so you can usually see the carpenters and other craftsmen at work. Doors can be made to order, normally taking one month and starting at CFA200,000.

As you're walking around town, you will no doubt stumble across a dome-shaped traditional bread oven, found in every *quartier*. Although fascinating to watch the women baking flat round bread for the community in the early morning, if you want to take photographs, you will be expected to pay.

If you're interested in arts and crafts, then the **Maisons des Artisans**, next to the Petit Marché, is an interesting place to go. Downstairs is a hive of activity with all the artisans in the middle busy at work with shops selling their wares around the outside. Alternatively retire to the peaceful tearoom upstairs, where the friendly artisan, Mohammed Almahmoud, will offer you a cup of sweet, bitter Tuareg tea and if you're interested, show you his wares in a relaxed environment with no pressure to buy (*www.bijoux-touaregs-tombouctou.com*).

The statue in the middle of Place de l'Indépendance is of **Al-Farouk**, a legendary figure dressed all in white and mounted on a pure white horse who, according to tradition, was sentenced to 700 years' imprisonment in the waters of the river Bani at Djenné, having been found guilty of misconduct towards the Ulémas of Sankoré.

The Flame of Peace Few places in the world have as much symbolic value as Timbuktu. It was appropriate, therefore, that the symbolic ceremony marking the end of the Tuareg rebellion (see page 24) took place here on 27 March 1996. On this day in an open square in the northern quarter of Abaradjou, 10,000 people watched as 3,000 weapons belonging to the Tuareg rebels and Malian army were burnt in what was dubbed the Flamme de la Paix (Flame of Peace). Before these weapons were set alight, a certificate was handed to the former Malian president Alpha Oumar Konaré by a representative of the United Nations confirming: 'We have of course checked, Mr President, before laying them on the bonfire, that none of these weapons contain any ammunition and that they can be burned without danger, to make a true "Flame of Peace".'

A **monument** commemorating the event has since been constructed in the middle of the Place de la Flamme de la Paix. Its already crumbling marble-tiled arches look rather disproportionate, but on closer inspection the metal, skeleton-like remains of the burnt weapons – embedded in cement – do leave an impression. As a whole, the monument is much appreciated by the inhabitants of Timbuktu, for both its appearance and significance and is a popular meeting place at sunset as the camel caravans are heading out of town.

About 400m behind the Place de la Flamme de la Paix, the **Jardin de la Paix** (Garden of Peace) contains young trees planted by some of the major players in the rebellion and its resolution, including the former president Konaré himself and the United Nations' resident representative in Mali, Tore Rose.

EXCURSIONS FROM TIMBUKTU

TUAREG CAMPS AND THE SURROUNDING DESERT Sand dunes surround Timbuktu and it never takes very long to walk out to them. The best time for this is at sunset when it is cooler and the desert is at its most beautiful. Apart from the odd camel returning to a Tuareg camp, any wildlife is normally restricted to desert beetles scurrying across the dunes. It is a good idea to bring a torch with you for the walk back to Timbuktu after the sun has gone down.

Many of the salesmen milling around the Hotel Bouctou will try to sell you camel rides into the desert and visits to Tuareg camps. On the face of it, the idea is romantic, attractive and, when you look out over the dunes from the hotel's terrace as the sun is setting, almost irresistible – which is why the sales pitch is often at its most frantic during the sunset hours! You can choose between trips lasting a few hours or the whole day and night. The former usually involves stopping at a nomad camp for the obligatory cup of tea, while the latter includes dinner, traditional music, staged sword fights and night-time rides in the desert. Prices range from CFA5,000 to CFA30,000, depending on the length of the trip and the number in the party. Although many enjoy this type of excursion, you should realise that they are designed for tourists and not for those who want to visit the Tuareg in their true element. However, it can be a good way of seeing something of the desert, and riding a camel is always an experience!

For those with more time, stamina and a sense for adventure, it is also possible to organise an expedition by camel or 4x4 to more remote desert destinations such as Lac Faguibine, Araouane and the Taoudenni salt mines (see *Elsewhere in the region* on page 250).

Before making all the necessary preparations, you first of all need an experienced and reliable guide. In this respect, a word of warning is called for, since there have been reports of guides who have seemed all too genuine at first, but who have vanished into thin air after a hefty down payment has been made. Do not hesitate to check the identity and credentials of your prospective guide. One place to do this would be at the Mission Culturelle. Since a lot of money may be involved, it is also advisable to draw up a contract, with a clear specification of all the expenses included.

A local agency specialising in desert excursions is **Tafouk Voyages** (for contact details, see page 241) and for camel expeditions only, Alphady Oumar Askofaré at **Mehari Voyages** (☎ *2192 11 68*), next to the Pâtisserie Asco, is your man. They offer various *circuits*, lasting from five days (*Circuit des Lacs*, CFA120,000-420,000 for one to four persons, all but mineral water included) to 30 days (*Circuit du Sel*, starting from €1,000 for one person). It could also be worth enquiring at the **Sahara Passion** (see page 242), which runs a travel agency as well. Their representative, Shindouk, is the president of the local association of cameleers (*www.shindouk.org*). They are reliable, charge fair rates and can arrange day trips or long expeditions.

KORIOUMÉ If all the sand is becoming a bit much you could always head to Koriouméand hire a pirogue for a couple of hours around the Bourem Inlay. There's a good chance you'll spot hippopotamuses.

KABARA Kabara used to be a lively port and the docking place for most freight and passenger boats, including the COMANAV diesel boats. Then natural disaster struck, and the canal – linking the river port of Koriouméé (9km upstream) to Kabara – was blocked with sand. Kabara became a deserted town; in fact, for years it was not far from being a ghost town. The town's new lifeline became land rather than river and the population survived on rice cultivated on the surrounding plains. Then, finally, action was taken: the canal was dug out and deepened. Imagine the joy of the inhabitants when on 1 October 2002, after an absence of 13 years, the first COMANAV boat reached the port of Kabara! Nowadays life has been pretty much rehabilitated, with most of the activities in town centred on the port. *Bâchées* to Kabara leave occasionally from the marketplace in Timbuktu; or squeeze in a *bâchée* for Korioumé and walk the last 1km after the junction. They will try to get CFA1,000 from you for the journey but the real price for a place is CFA400–500. It is also feasible to walk the 19km during the cooler parts of the day.

ELSEWHERE IN THE REGION

TIBORAGHENE Tiboraghene is a small village on the south side of the River Niger, 50km from Timbuktu and 30km from the landing place for the ferry. Coming from Douentza, it's the very last settlement – last house, last well – you pass before continuing towards the ferry. The village of 1,263 inhabitants is not mentioned on any map.

Where to stay

Campement Tenéré m 7602 36 17; e campementtenere@gmail.com. Simple accommodation in a rural setting; there's space for 38 people in traditional tents, sleeping up to 6 people; CFA4,000pp or CFA12,500 if you take a small tent for 2. If you can't stay the night, it's a good place to stop off for food on the way to (or from) the bac or ferry for Timbuktu. Substantial Tuareg meals are served from CFA3,000. The campement forms part of the Eco Tuareg Museum, showing all aspects of traditional Tuareg life, such as pulling water from a well, with explanations written in English, German & French (see Responsible Tourism, page 95). $$

GOUNDAM Goundam was a thriving town during the period of Songhay domination and many of the salt caravans from the mines further north terminated here – as well as at Timbuktu. The town fell to the Moroccan invaders in 1591, and periods of Peul and Tuareg rule were to follow before the French arrived in 1894. Nowadays, the *cercle* of Goundam – which stretches across the desert to the Mauritanian border – is populated mainly by Tuareg and Maure nomads, some of whom have settled along the shores of the largest lake in west Africa, **Lake Faguibine**, which lies north of the town. At a stone's throw from Lake Faguibine is **Essakane**, the oasis which is the location of the **Festival in the Desert** (see box *The Festival in the Desert, Essakane*, pages 244–5, and also page 90).

There are various options to get to Essakane. Joining an organised tour – by camel or 4x4 – is obviously easiest but comes at a price. Book well in advance, since the demand is very high. If you have your own 4x4 you can join up with service vehicles towards the beginning of the festival, or join the convoy leaving from Timbuktu the first morning of the festival. The convoy is hard to miss, as dozens of cars will be circulating in Timbuktu before heading for the meeting point. Do note that the *piste* involves a lot of soft sand. Getting away from Essakane involves a lot of asking around. Do not worry; you will not be left out there, but prices will go up while the quality of vehicles may plummet. If you wait at the collection point after the last concert has finished, you should find something; otherwise you may have to wait for the second round of service vehicles.

Goundam is just under 100km southwest of Timbuktu and is not an unattractive town. It's built on a slight elevation, with more hills about 10km north and two lakes, **Lake Télé** and **Lake Fati**, nearby. Add to this a French-run *campement* (which has a fridge), and Goundam might be worth a visit. Roadworks

INSECURITY IN THE DESERT

There are often incidents of insecurity in the desert north of Timbuktu. If you're hoping to travel there, take advice from either the locals or the OMATHO. According to security experts in the United States, an Algerian group, calling themselves al-Qaeda in the Maghreb, have crossed the border and are running training camps for Islamic militants from other north African countries. There's also the threat of banditry (in January 2008 four Italians were robbed at gunpoint in Araouane). However, incidents like this are rare and the risk should not be exaggerated. (See *Chapter 2*, page 64, for more details.)

to upgrade the *piste* linking the town to **Niafounké** (see page 185) and to the nearest river port at **Diré** started a few years ago. Like Diré, **Gourma-Rharous** is important as the centre of its *cercle*, but has little to detain the tourist for too long. Those travelling to Gourma-Rharous are usually just in transit between the Réserve de Douentza or Gossi and Timbuktu. Gourma-Rharous has its own ferry to cross to the northern shore of the Niger, but it is not functional throughout the year. Alternatively, there is a *piste* – heading west from Gourma-Rharous towards the ferry at Korioumé – which is always in a bad condition but even more so during the rainy season. Consequently, it depends on the season and the water level of the Niger whether you should follow the northern or the southern bank. Public transport in this region is erratic, but it does exist (see *Gossi*, page 215 and *Getting there and away*, page 237).

ARAOUANE The Sahara dominates the remainder of the region of Timbuktu. Apart from the occasional Tuareg camp, there are three permanent settlements in the northern desert region of Mali: Araouane, Boû Djébéha and Taoudenni. There is a vivid description of Taoudenni in Richard Trench's *Forbidden Sands: A Search in the Sahara* (see *Appendix 2*, *Further Information*), a book which inspired Ernst Aebi to visit the area and discover Araouane, 270km north of Timbuktu.

When Aebi, a loft-renovator from New York, first passed through Araouane, he discovered a settlement of 125 people living on locusts and waiting for rains which never came: 'Hell on earth', was his immediate reaction. When he returned to Araouane in 1988 – for the loft-renovator had decided to 'save' the town – he brought with him a truckful of tomatoes, beets, figs and anything else which might stand a chance of growing in the desert. He spent the next three years transforming Araouane into a true oasis in the middle of the desert, with vegetable gardens and even a hotel to accommodate the tourists who had heard about Aebi's social experiment and wanted to see its results. Araouane's good fortune, however, was short-lived. Aebi left to write up his book, *Seasons in the Sand*, and the town was overrun and destroyed during the Tuareg rebellion.

Today, the gardens have disappeared and locusts are back on the menu. Tourists occasionally visit Araouane on organised excursions and camp in the derelict hotel, though rumour has it that the hotel will be restored to some inhabitable state. Local people will provide a roof over the heads of smaller parties. By 4x4, it takes at least six hours from Timbuktu to get to Araouane – by camel, about seven days.

TAOUDENNI The further north you go, the more dramatic the scenery becomes. Only sand dunes and *ergs*, or shifting 'seas' of sand, disturb the awesome flatness of vast plains such as the Tanezrouft, which spreads across northern Mali and continues into Algeria. In this setting, Taoudenni, some 700km north of Timbuktu, is the remotest human settlement in Mali.

Taoudenni was discovered in the 16th century by the Moroccans as a replacement for the salt fields further north at Téghaza. Salt is still mined at Taoudenni today in large, tombstone-shaped slabs, although the huge caravans or Azalaïs, which in their heyday comprised as many as 400 camels and took one month to carry salt to Timbuktu, are now rarely seen. According to Trench (see *Appendix 2*), Taoudenni's 1970s' workforce consisted mainly of political prisoners, common criminals, debtors and other people who were not there by choice. Nowadays miners are paid for their work.

10

Sikasso

The southern region of Sikasso is Mali's 'bread basket'. Nowhere in the country is greener and, although there is no great river to irrigate the land, the higher rainfall and humidity brought about by a rather more tropical than Sahelian latitude means that the land is rich and fertile. Cotton is a major crop in the *cercle* of Koutiala; tea in Sikasso; and *fonio*, millet and corn grow in abundance almost everywhere else. The region is also something of a 'melting-pot'.

The Sénoufo are the indigenous ethnic majority, although Bambara, Peul, Bobo, Minianka, Dioula and Wassalunké groups are also present. However, for all its richness – both agricultural and ethnic – Sikasso is not overrun with tourists and is seldom treated as more than an area of transit between Côte d'Ivoire, Burkina Faso and the better-known regions of Mali.

HISTORY

THE KÉNÉDOUGOU KINGDOM Just as the Bambara kingdom dominates the history books of Ségou, the Kénédougou kingdom is at the heart of Sikasso's history.

Founded by the Dioula people in the 17th century, Kénédougou began life as a small, disparate kingdom, only developing into an organised state in the mid 18th century under the leadership of the Traoré dynasty. Massa Daoula Traoré (r1840–77) is generally credited with being the first of the Kénédougou kings to expand the kingdom, defeating, amongst others, the Ouattara of Kong (in northern Côte d'Ivoire) and Bobo-Dioulasso. However, his successor, Tieba Traoré (r1877–93), was the greatest, presiding over the kingdom while it was at its apogee. Under Tieba, the Sénoufo – the ethnic majority – conquered the Minianka and famously defended the town of Sikasso for 15 months when it was attacked by the forces of Samory Touré (see page 255) in 1887. However, in order to repel Samory's forces, Tieba was obliged to seek French military assistance. The price was a treaty, signed in 1890, which effectively made Kénédougou a French protectorate. Tieba's successor, Babemba Traoré, was bound by the conditions agreed upon by his elder brother and the French, but nonetheless continued to expand the kingdom's borders, and by 1898 the Kénédougou lands stretched into modern-day Côte d'Ivoire and Burkina Faso.

Meanwhile, the French were looking for an excuse to invade and take full control of the region, and the proud Babemba, resentful of the French interference brought about by the 1890 treaty, was only too happy to provide it. Early in 1598, the Kénédougou king suddenly refused to send the annual tax of 80 head of cattle to the French commandant at Ségou, and then antagonised the colonialists further by expelling the French military ambassador from Sikasso. The French response was predictable enough. On 15 April 1898, they attacked Sikasso, breached the tata (city wall) which had successfully repelled Samory ten years earlier, and took the town on 1 May. Babemba decided to shoot himself rather than surrender.

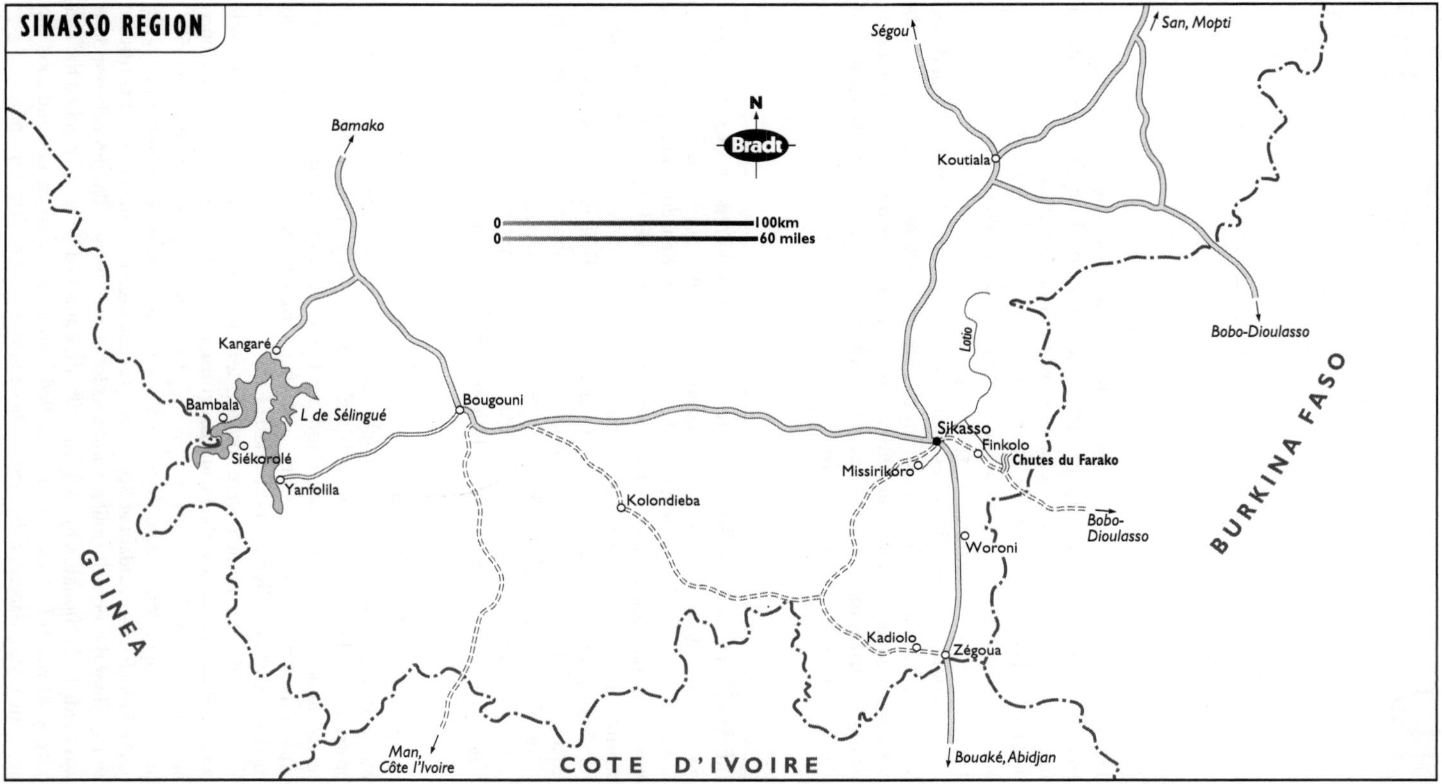
SIKASSO REGION
Bamako
Ségou
San, Mopti
Koutiala
Bobo-Dioulasso
BURKINA FASO
0 100km
0 60 miles
Bradt
N
Kangaré
Bambala
L de Sélingué
Siékorolé
Yanfolila
Bougouni
Kolondieba
Latio
Sikasso
Finkolo
Chutes du Farako
Missirikoro
Bobo-Dioulasso
Woroni
Kadiolo
Zégoua
Bouaké, Abidjan
Man, Côte l'Ivoire
COTE D'IVOIRE
GUINEA

SAMORY TOURÉ The other major player in the south of Mali – at least during the second half of the 19th century – was Samory Touré, a Muslim imam warrior who established a loosely knit state across lands in what is now Guinea, Mali, Côte d'Ivoire and Burkina Faso. Samory spent most of the 1880s fighting the French on the left bank of the River Niger, until the Treaty of Bissandougou in 1887 marked a break in hostilities, leaving Samory free to attack Tieba Traoré's Kénédougou kingdom. His attempt to take the town of Sikasso failed when the French came to Tieba's assistance, and in 1889, he revoked the Treaty of Bissandougou and moved his armies south as far as present-day Ghana and Sierra Leone. Finally, in 1898, he was captured by the French and exiled to Gabon, where he died in 1900.

SIKASSO TOWN

Many travellers would describe themselves as being 'stuck' in Sikasso rather than being there out of choice. Since it is situated only 100km from Côte d'Ivoire and 40km from Burkina Faso, and is linked to Bamako, Ségou and Mopti by excellent paved roads, travellers might indeed have cause to be passing through only en route to Mali's more interesting towns.

However, dismiss Sikasso at your peril! It may not be the most attractive and exciting place in the world, but it does represent a slightly different side of life in Mali. For a start, things grow here. The climate is more humid and with an average annual temperature of 27°C the countryside is certainly greener than the dust bowls in the Sahel: if you're there in mango season you'll see.

Despite the strong Islamic implantation, the residents of Sikasso have stayed very attached to their traditions. The richness of their diverse culture can be observed in the masked dance, balafon and the musical style of the Wassoulou, celebrated at numerous ceremonies and traditional rituals. Oumou Sangaré is probably the most famous artist from the region.

You should also take advantage of the fact that few tourists stop in Sikasso. There are few guides and the people are ready to speak to you normally – that is to say, in the humorous, curious, respectful and gentle Malian way. In this respect, a visit to Sikasso might be worth ten Djenné mosques. But hurry, news must be getting out. In 2002, just 5,000 tourists visited Sikasso whereas in 2007, 15,000 found their way there.

Little is known about Sikasso before Tieba Traoré made it the capital of the Kénédougou kingdom in 1878. The village was probably founded at the beginning of the 19th century on a site in the forest where elephants were abundant – hence the original Sénoufo name, Solo-Khan or 'village of elephants'. The old city wall, the remains of which are still visible today, played an important part in the two defining moments of Sikasso's relatively short history: in 1887–88, it withstood a 15-month siege by the forces of Samory Touré, but ten years later, in 1898, it was to be breached with relative ease by the French army. Other than the city wall, there is a hillock in the middle of town and one or two tombs of Kénédougou kings to visit.

ORIENTATION Sikasso lies 370km from Bamako along a newly upgraded road. If you arrive by bus, you will be driven through the downtown part of Sikasso before stopping at the bus station, which is a couple of kilometres from the town centre, on the road to Côte d'Ivoire and Burkina Faso. Therefore, if you're staying at one of the hotels on the way into town, ask the bus driver to drop you off soon after you have passed the arch welcoming you to Sikasso if you want to avoid the walk back into town. Remain on the bus if you intend to stay at one of the hotels near the bus station.

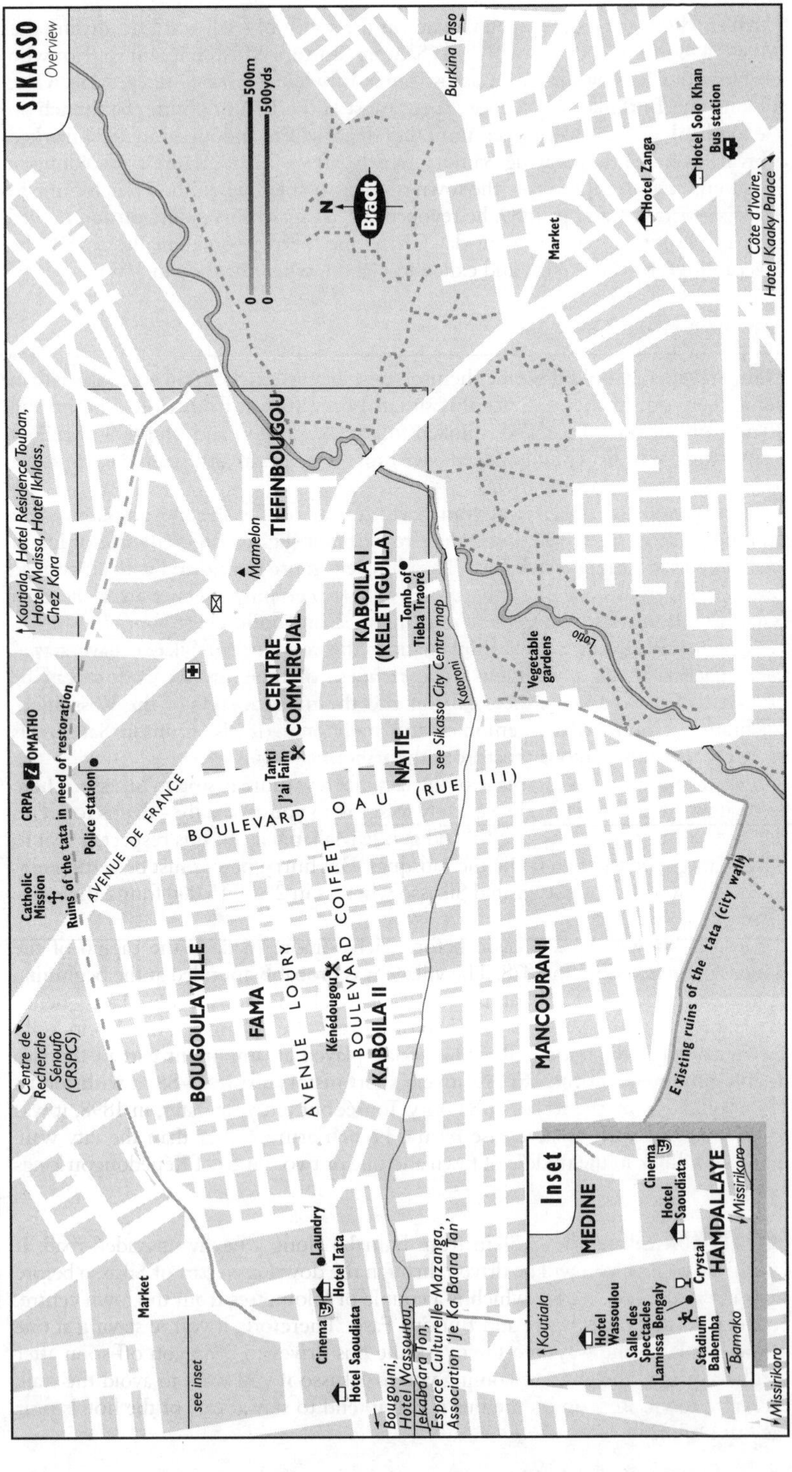
SIKASSO
Overview
500m
500yds
Bradt
N
Burkina Faso
Koutiala, Hotel Résidence Touban, Hotel Maïssa, Hotel Ikhlass, Chez Kora
CRPA
OMATHO
Catholic Mission
Ruins of the tata in need of restoration
Police station
Centre de Recherche Sénoufo (CRSPCS)
AVENUE DE FRANCE
BOULEVARD OAU (RUE 111)
BOULEVARD COIFFET
AVENUE LOURY
BOUGOULAVILLE
FAMA
KABOILA II
Kénédougou
Tanti J'ai Faim
CENTRE COMMERCIAL
NATIE
TIEFINBOUGOU
Mamelon
KABOILA I (KELETIGUILA)
Tomb of Tieba Traoré
see Sikasso City Centre map
Kotoroni
Vegetable gardens
Lotio
MANCOURANI
Existing ruins of the tata (city wall)
Market
Hotel Zanga
Hotel Solo Khan
Bus station
Côte d'Ivoire, Hotel Kaaky Palace
Market
see inset
Cinema
Hotel Saoudiata
Hotel Tata
Laundry
Bougouni, Hotel Wassoulou, Jekabaara Ton, Espace Culturelle Mazanga, Association 'Je Ka Baara Tan'
Inset
MEDINE
HAMDALLAYE
Koutiala
Hotel Wassoulou
Salle des Spectacles Lamissa Bengaly
Crystal
Stadium Babemba
Bamako
Hotel Saoudiata
Cinema
Missirikoro
Missirikoro

The Mamelon – the sacred hillock in the centre of town – is a good point of reference. The market and much of the town's other activities are close to the roundabout at the foot of this hill. As the main highway passes through Sikasso it splits in two: one road crosses town to the north of the market, the other crosses to the south. These are the two main roads in Sikasso, either side of which are the town's residential neighbourhoods.

GETTING THERE AND AWAY Before the violent crisis in Côte d'Ivoire started, a great deal of traffic passed through Sikasso, since this was, economically speaking, the most important town linking Bamako to its closest port, Abidjan. Even though virtually all traffic to Abidjan was suspended, Sikasso never lost its importance as a crossroads town in the proximity of both Burkina Faso and Côte d'Ivoire. Now the route is open again, with buses travelling between the two countries, the majority of tourists tend to be going through the town on their way to and even through Burkina Faso, and a handful of travellers still find their way to Bouaké, the second-largest town in Côte d'Ivoire.

Various bus companies have services to Bobo-Dioulasso (CFA3,500) and Ouagadougou (CFA10,000). Kénédougou Voyages (☎ *2162 07 19*), Kénédougou Transport (☎ *2162 08 27*) and Sangarela (m *7629 61 51*), all have an early daily departure at 07.00, whilst Wassa Magny leaves at 08.30 and Kénédougou Transport has a second departure at 15.00. Bani Transport (m *6699 38 14*) has direct services all the way to Lomé (CFA22,500), Niamey (CFA22,500) and Cotonou (CFA25,000). Kénédougou Voyages has departures for Bouaké at 10.30 and 16.00 (CFA8,000).

For Bamako, companies such as Folona, Diarra (m *7645 42 19*), Bittar Transport (m *6679 18 57*), Diominé and Bani Transport leave at almost hourly intervals throughout the day (9 hours; CFA5,500). YT (☎ *2162 08 27*) have an overnight service leaving at 23.00. Note that some companies travel via Koutiala (CFA3,000) and Ségou (CFA4,500), while others travel via Bougouni (8 hours; CFA3,000). Bani, Maiga (m *6672 80 22*) and Kenedougou Voyages have daily departures for Mopti at 13.00, 19.00 and 22.00 (CFA5,000) and Bani Transport has two weekly buses leaving for Gao on Thursdays and Sundays at 13.00 (CFA11,000).

All these companies leave from the Gare Routière de Sikasso in Sanabougou. For nearby destinations, look for minibuses and *bâchées* leaving from the centre of Sikasso, especially where the market peters out in Avenue Loury and Avenue de France. A shared taxi between Sanabougou and the town centre should cost no more than CFA200.

TOURIST INFORMATION OMATHO (☎ *2162 18 05*) on the premises of the Haute Commisariat at the end of Rue Fôh Traoré. Thanks to the services of an enthusiastic Peace Corps volunteer, the information centre here is well organised and informative. There is a noticeboard with photos of Sikasso's seven official guides (including one woman), with information in both French and English including languages spoken and contact details. A guided day tour in and around town costs CFA6,000 for up to ten people and CFA500 for each extra person after that. This rises to CFA12,000 if you venture out of town and CFA20,000 per day for another region, which includes accommodation and food.

WHERE TO STAY Prior to the Africa Nations Cup (CAN) in 2002, there was only one private hotel, the Hotel Tata; the Mamelon and Lotio were both state-run. During the CAN, the government encouraged people to invest and build hotels and as a result there are now a number of decent options to choose from.

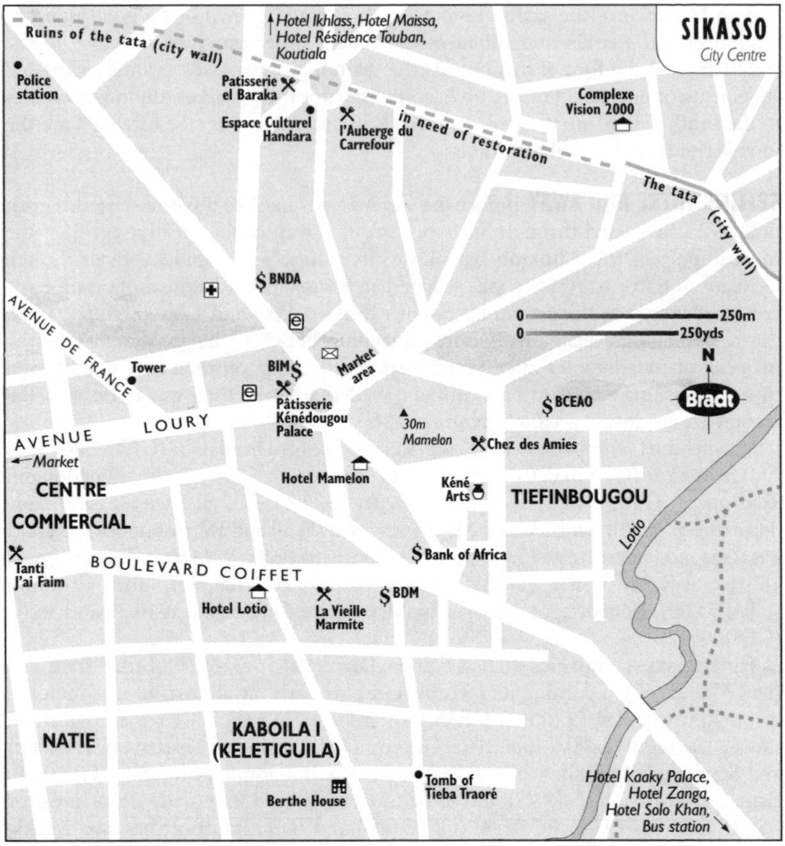

Mid-range $$$

Hotel Ikhlass (10 rooms) 2162 19 49. A nice new hotel with simple, good-sized rooms & comfortable beds. Satellite TV with a choice of 6 channels & there's a bar, but it doesn't serve alcohol. There's no restaurant as such but they can cook meals to order.

Hotel Kaaky Palace (45 rooms) Sanoubougou; 2162 10 34; e kaakypalace@kenedougou.com. You'll know you've come to the right place when you see the giant elephant at the entrance. The smartest hotel in town is found behind customs on the road to Côte d'Ivoire. The rooms are clean & new with bright clashing furnishings & lots of plastic fruit. There are some rooms with a fan, otherwise all have AC with their own balconies. Table tennis, restaurant, bar & an *espace culturelle* for night-time entertainment. A taxi into town costs CFA500–1,000. B/fast inc.

Hotel Maissa (50 rooms) Wayèrema II; 2162 15 60; e hotelmaissa2000@yahoo.fr. A pleasant new hotel with AC rooms & all the luxuries you could wish for including swimming pool, gym & massage to order in your room. If you're feeling flush, try the Presidential Suite (CFA100,000) with a jacuzzi. There's also a restaurant & bar, internet & giant-screen TV.

Hotel Mamelon (12 rooms) Centre Commercial; 2162 00 44; e fagmonik99@yahoo.fr. In the heart of town at the foot of the Mamelon, this hotel is the best you can find location-wise. All rooms have AC & TV but are a bit shabby for the price, except the CFA30,000 room, which is rather nice. Wi-Fi available.

Hotel Tata (37 rooms) Route de Bamako, Médine; 2162 04 11. Next to the entrance to town, you can ask the driver to drop you at the door. Rooms are OK – though the toilets could do with some seats – & it's within reasonable walking distance from the centre. There's a restaurant serving good food. TV & AC. B/fast not inc.

Hotel Résidence Touban (26 rooms) Wayèrema II; 2162 05 34; e panierkone@cefib.com. This hotel, on the old road to Koutiala, whilst both homely & quite upmarket, has a bit of an air of abandonment about it as the owner concentrates on his new hotel, the Maissa. The considerable distance from the centre of town makes it less convenient unless you have your own transport. Rooms with fan or AC. TV, restaurant & bar.

Hotel Zanga (41 rooms) Sanoubougou; ☎ 2162 04 31. Around 1km out of town, towards the bus station, the AC rooms are bright & kept spotlessly clean. There is also a good *pâtisserie* on the premises & a newly built restaurant with AC & reasonably priced food. Other facilities include a swimming pool.

Budget $$

Hotel Lotio (9 rooms) Kaboila I; ☎ 2162 10 01. This hotel, on the main thoroughfare in the centre of town, has singles/doubles with a fan which are generally rented out by the hour (CFA2,000) to working girls from Côte d'Ivoire. You could also use that time to have a rest & a shower. They were all occupied when I went to see them so not sure what state they're in.

Hotel Saoudiata Médine; ☎ 2162 19 48. On a par with the Tata but with toilet seats & a little terrace. AC. Rooms have fans & some have TVs. There's a garden with thatched *paillotte* to sit under & a restaurant/bar serving beer & reasonably priced meals. B/fast extra at CFA1,000.

Hotel Wassoulou (14 rooms) Route de Koutiala; ☎ 2162 04 24. Arguably the most comfortable hotel in Sikasso, the AC double rooms in cute thatched bungalows are clean, bright & functioning. Mosquito nets, TV, real flowers & little bedside chandeliers all come as standard. They've kept the prices the same for the last 5 years so it now offers great value. There's an enormous turtle in the garden. Bar/restaurant.

Shoestring $

Hotel Solo Khan ☎ 2162 05 64. Near the bus station & patronised mainly by transit passengers on their way through. Very cheap & basic with en-suite bucket showers.

WHERE TO EAT The OMATHO are clamping down on restaurants operating without the correct papers, so you may well find that some of the smaller places have been closed down.

Cheap and cheerful $$

Hotel Mamelon ☎ 2162 00 44. Set in a nice garden, the atmosphere here is very agreeable. A huge selection of meat dishes, eg: heart, chicken, lamb chops, but also some dishes for vegetarians such as salads, sandwiches or omelettes. Serves alcohol – a big beer CFA800 – & a popular meeting place at night.

Hotel Tata ☎ 2162 04 11. Reasonable food with friendly service though the restaurant interior is a tad uninspiring. Chicken, fish or meat with the usual choice of garniture: peas, chips or *aloco* (fried plantain).

Hotel Zanga ☎ 2162 04 31. The best of the hotel restaurants. Its excellent *pâtisserie* selling croissants, pastries & cakes is an ideal place for b/fast or a snack – perhaps while waiting for a bus at the nearby station.

Rock bottom $

Chez des Amis Wayèrema II; m 6637 70 29. Situated at the base of the foot of the Mamelon. Well-portioned & well-priced African dishes such as fish & chicken. Also open at night & a bit of a locals' hangout.

Restaurant l'Auberge du Carrefour Just behind L'Éspace Culturelle Handara. A bar/restaurant serving the usual roast chicken, brochette, steak, couscous & spaghetti, amongst other things. Well cooked & reasonably priced, in a relaxed & friendly atmosphere.

Restaurant Jekabaara Ton Médine; m 7629 60 12. A spotlessly clean, traditional restaurant serving *riz sauce*, whole guinea fowl & chicken at very reasonable prices.

Restaurant Kénédougou Bd Coiffet; ☎ 2126 08 71. Offers African specialties & Malian food.

Restaurant La Vieille Marmite Bd Coiffet, the main thoroughfare, almost opposite the Shell station; m 7943 01 17. This small & very popular place has been run by the same family for over 40 years. Try the delicious *pintade* (guinea fowl) & sauce!

Tanti J'ai Faim Kaboila II; m 7948 16 40. Traditional fare is produced in huge bubbling cauldrons on wood fires & served to the population of Sikasso who come to the market. *Toh, riz au gras, fornio* & *viande de vache* are eaten on long trestle tables to the sound of blasting Malian tunes.

There are a couple of *pâtisseries* in town:

✕ **Pâtisserie el Baraka** Opposite L'Éspace Culturelle Handara; m 7317 10 23; ⏲ 06.00–02.00. Tunisian-run, serving cake, ice cream, *pâtisseries* & pizza, but no alcohol.

✕ **Pâtisserie Kénédougou Palace** Near the Mamelon hill & overlooking the market. It's hard to miss &, though the décor isn't all that great, the wide choice of pastries, fast food & yoghurt attracts many clients. The *pâtisserie* is open all week, but note that the kitchen (for pizzas & such) is closed on Sun.

ENTERTAINMENT AND NIGHTLIFE At Complexe Tata (which also includes the Hotel Tata), a large cinema shows Hindu films. However, as DVDs and TVs have taken away business it is only open during the Christmas and Tabaski holidays. Tickets cost a mere CFA200.

Éspace Culturelle Handara (*Wayèrema I;* m *7413 73 62;* ⏲ *22.00; admission CFA2,000–2,500, CFA5,000 for a couple*) This nightclub certainly fills a niche in Sikasso's nightlife. A *boîte de nuit*, or just a place to hang out for a drink and some brochettes. Maybe live performances on the weekends. Check it out!

Salle des Spectacles Lamissa Bengaly (*On the road to Bamako;* m *6678 85 86;* e *marico_bourama@yahoo.fr; tickets CFA2,500*) A 1,700-seater concert hall opened by the president in May 2005. If any of the big musicians are in town, this is where they'll play. This can be once a week or once a month, depending on the programme of events. Artists who have previously performed include Néba Solo (*balafon*), Cheche Drame (*griot*) and Abdoulaye Diabaté. The programme can change from one minute to the next so it's best to phone to check. Refreshments available.

Éspace Culturelle Mazanga (*Also on the road to Bamako in Hamdallaye;* m *6672 76 21;* ⏲ *from 17.00 until the last person leaves*) Live music every night.

Other venues The **Hotel Maïssa** generally has live acts every Saturday with soft traditional music playing on other nights. The **Hotel Mamelon** and the **Hotel Wassoulou** both have popular bars. At the Mamelon you can sit outside and listen to *bafalon.* It closes when there's no-one left which is normally around 02.00. For the real night owls, **Escale** at the Hotel Lotio is open 24 hours and if you're staying at the **Hotel Touban**, then try the Ivoirian-run bar 300m away. The hotel should be able to give you directions.

Le Crystal (*on the route de Bamako in Médine quartier;* ☎ *2162 05 35*) is a bar which by all accounts rocks, with dancing and drinking until all hours. **Chez Kora** in the *quartier* of Wayèrema and close to the Hotel Ikhlass, is run by a woman with a *maison de passe*.

SHOPPING The biggest supermarket in Sikasso is at the **Hotel Résidence Touban**.

You should try one or two of the region's very large and very tasty **mangoes** while in Sikasso. March/April is drying season and you can pick up a plastic-bagful for a few hundred cents to save them rotting in the streets. Otherwise, although much of the country's fruit and vegetables come from this region, the market is not overflowing with fresh produce.

Kéné Arts (*behind the Bank of Africa at the bottom of the Mamelon hill;* ☎ *2162 05 23;* ⏲ *08.00–16.00 Mon–Sat*). There's not a lot inside but you may find some good-quality *objets d'art* if you're interested in doing some souvenir shopping. Soyelman Kone, a jeweller who has travelled in Europe to international fairs, can be found here.

There are many local artisans in Sikasso who you can visit, if you can find them. To make things easier, the newly established **Centre regional de la promotion de l'artisanat** (CRPA) situated next to the OMATHO, can organise a half-day tour that would include some of the following.

Closest to the office, just 200m from the OMATHO, leather workers make and sell bags and belts (m *7614 79 05*). Women making *bogolan* cloth can be visited in their houses. A donation is normally expected.

If it's indigo you're after, **Aminata Konté** (m *6681 64 48*) is an indigo dyer who is happy to receive tourists.

Le Centre de Couture offers three-year *haute couture* training courses for apprentices. The centre produces articles which you can buy or it will demonstrate how to properly wear traditional African clothes.

Alternatively **La Coopérative Multi-fonctionnelle des Artisans des Femmes**, run by Fatima (m *6679 21 14*), makes very pretty bags to put foodstuffs such as dried coconut and mangoes in, whilst the **Association 'Je Ka Baara Ton'** in Médine has a dyeing and tanning operation, selling small leather bags. There's a restaurant of the same name here.

Finally, if you're interested in hair braiding, the office can organise a visit to one of the many local salons, if you notify them in advance

To arrange a tour, see Mamadou, the director, or give him a call (*2162 23 59;* m *7614 79 05*).

OTHER PRACTICALITIES There are five banks in Sikasso. BIM and BDM both have a Western Union office. These banks do not deal with foreign currency, though BDM does Visa cash advances. BCEAO (which is like a fortress), BOA and BNDA (both open on Sundays) change cash euros only.

There are two internet cafés – Sicanet next to Pâtisserie Kénédougou, and another one next to Sotelma.

Several of Sikasso's public services can be found near the roundabout at the foot of the Mamelon: these include the post office, Sotelma and the hospital. Sikasso boasts numerous well-stocked pharamacies in town, but if you're suffering from haemorrhoids, general fatigue or sexual impotence, you may want to give Mr Abou Traoré a call, a traditional medicine practitioner who can be found in Wayèrema I (m *7612 57 85*).

It is not possible to get visa extensions in Sikasso. These can only be obtained in Bamako or Mopti.

WHAT TO SEE Although none of the sights in Sikasso will exactly take your breath away, they do reverberate with historical resonance and, with a little imagination, are worth visiting.

The highlight is **Le Mamelon**, a small hill of about 30m in the centre of town. When the Kénédougou kings ruled Sikasso in the 19th century, the top of the Mamelon was covered with lush vegetation – a sacred wood where a *bon génie* (good spirit) looked over the town and protected it. King Tieba Traoré built a two-storeyed house here where he received royal guests; and a sacred serpent would dispense advice from a well, the opening of which can still be seen today. When the French took Sikasso on 1 May 1898, they planted the *tricouleur* on top of the Mamelon – symbolic, perhaps, of the hill's importance. Later, in 1945, they built a tower which served as the town's tribunal and library.

In more recent times, water towers and antennae have graced the summit, which is one of the best places for views of Sikasso. You shouldn't have to pay to come up here but the men that keep it clean will often try their luck. Another good place for uninterrupted views is the tower – with ladders and platforms – in the market area.

Sunday is the best day to visit the *grand marché*, whereas Saturday's the day for the Marché de Médine. On other days, you will find little more than fruit.

Like other towns in this region of Mali, Sikasso was protected from attacks – first by rival kingdoms, then French colonialists – by the ***tata*** or city wall. Because of their strategic and commercial importance, three *tatas* were constructed before Sikasso eventually fell to the French. An outer wall built in three months in 1885 was the largest and most recent. It had a perimeter of nearly 9km, an average height of 5m and five *portes* (gates) situated at strategic points around the town. Inside the outer wall, a smaller *tata* protected the merchants, soldiers and nobility. Finally, the smallest and oldest wall encircled the *dionfoutou*, where the king and his family lived.

Nowadays, the only part of the *tata* which is being properly conserved skirts around the quarter of Mancourani.

The **tomb of Tieba Traoré**, arguably the greatest Kénédougou king, is in the quarter of Kabiola also known as Keletiguila. Look for an inconspicuous white building covered in graffiti which looks like a transformer kiosk, in the vicinity of a striking *banco* house. King Tieba Traoré had many enemies, including members of his own family, and he feared that after his death his body might be mutilated and body parts used for sorcery. He therefore asked for his body to be buried in the protective vicinity of the house of his most trusted warrior, Keletigui Berthe. Up to this day, the oldest living member of the Berthe family, who also happens to be the *chef du quartier*, is the keeper of the key to the tomb. Before disturbing the old man and having the tomb opened up for you, bear in mind that, in all frankness, the interior reveals nothing whatsoever that reminds you of the presence of royalty. More impressive is the nearby *banco* house, which still belongs to the descendants of Keletigui Berthe.

The **tomb of Lieutenant Loury**, who led the French into Sikasso in 1898, is next to a patch of ground which served as a *fosse commune* (communal grave) during the French occupation. Apparently, it is one of many.

If you are craving to see some lush green for a change, walk from the Hotel Lotio towards the *banco* house and the king's tomb, and continue onwards until you stumble upon the town's gardens. There is always a lot of activity going on here, as the carrots, beetroots, onions, etc need daily watering from the sparse waters of the rivers Lotio and Kotoroni.

Follow the Lotio in a southeasterly direction, until you come across a paved road. This road will take you back into town, past a ruined part of the old *tata*.

Le centre de recherché pour la promotion et la sauvegarde de la culture Sénoufo (*Quartier Résidentiel, Rue 209, Wayèrema I;* ☎ *2162 18 16;* e *info@Sénoufo.com; www.Sénoufo.com*) A fascinating research centre, opened in 2005 by Spanish priest, Father Emilio Escudero, who works passionately to promote the Sénoufo culture and language. There's a cupboardful of more than 450 logged audio and videotapes documenting subjects as varied as marriage, work, birth, puberty, hairstyles, basket ware and the making of *shea*. Everything that is talked about in cassettes has photographs in a file. In another room a researcher laboriously works on rewriting the oral tradition using a *balafon*. Tourists can visit and there's hope in the future to sell videos and open a museum. The building and gardens are interesting in themselves containing the work of the Sénoufo sculptor, Madou Traoré.

Cotton There are two cotton factories in Sikasso and it may be possible to visit all stages of the cotton process from the field to the factory. Contact the director for rural development at CDMT (☎ *2162 02 24;* m *7617 99 45*).

Festival 'Triangle du Balafon' Held every year in Sikasso, anytime between April and November, *balafon* players from Mali and the bordering African countries perform during four days of exhibitions, plays and competitions. (See *Chapter 2, Festivals*, page 92 for more details.)

EXCURSIONS FROM SIKASSO

THE TOMB OF MASSA DAOULA TRAORÉ If Tieba Traoré is widely considered to be the greatest of the Kénédougou kings, then his father, Massa Daoula Traoré, is generally credited with being the person who established the kingdom as a real force in the region. Before Tieba moved it to Sikasso, the capital of the kingdom was at **Bougoula**, 6km east of Sikasso. This is where Massa Daoula, several members of his family, and an assortment of the king's weapons and fetishes are buried. Introduce yourself to the chief when you arrive at the village. The upkeep of the tombs is the responsibility of a family of Coulibalys who were once slaves of Massa Daoula but who were set free before the king died.

THE STONE MOSQUE The village of **Missirikoro**, 12km southwest of Sikasso, owes its name to the nearby grotto, Fara Missiri (Stone Mosque). This natural grotto, complete with stalactites and stalagmites, reaches a height of 50–80m and has traditionally been used as a place of worship and sacrifice for both Muslims and animists. A staircase made of cobbles leads to the main entrance of the 'mosque'. *Génies* (guardian spirits) were thought to inhabit the cave and were always consulted by the Kénédougou kings before any expedition or military exercise. According to another legend, the genies also prepared food and drink for passing travellers until they were spotted by an old woman curious to know the source of the meals.

Nowadays the most obvious presence is that of an old cave-dweller who seems to have lived there forever, sharing his grotto with a noisy colony of bats.

There are two other entrances leading into the rocky outcrop. Animist sacrifices take place at the eastern entrance. This corridor is clearly connected to the main grotto as from inside the 'mosque', when peeping into the right pit, the light and the pile of stones and skulls are visible. On the western side, inside a deep crevasse, Muslim worshippers retreat for months and even years of seclusion. Unless the crevasse is covered with a curtain, you are allowed in. Remember to take off your shoes, and do not disturb the Muslims while they are involved in any sort of religious activity – which is most of the time. A couple of metres inside to the right, there is a small niche which is sometimes used for a period of seclusion pushed to extremes.

Around the bend you will find ladders and chains, to help you find your way up the rocky hillock for a magnificent view. Beware of snakes around this area.

There is no easy and obvious way of getting to Missirikoro. Unless you fancy walking the 12km, you will probably have to arrange private transportation. A taxi there and back costs CFA7,500 or you can try and find someone willing with a motorbike.

ALONG THE ROAD TO BOBO-DIOULASSO The most direct road from Sikasso to Bobo-Dioulasso in Burkina Faso is a track which passes through some of the region's tea plantations. There are one or two places of interest along this road, although you will probably need your own transport to get to them – the buses to Bobo-Dioulasso take the paved road via Koutiala.

About 18km from Sikasso just before you reach the village of **Finkolo** – the capital of the Kénédougou kingdom before Massa Daoula Traoré moved it to Bougoula – there is a picturesque spot in a wooded area at the confluence of two rivers, the Tchintchinko (river of sand) and the Farako (river of stone), known as the **Kofilaben**. Mixing the water from these two rivers in the same container is forbidden, except in extreme cases of drought when it is permitted to encourage rainfall. However, if the first drops of rain hit the person who mixes this water, he will die. Not surprisingly, this is another spot frequented by genies!

A further 10km or so down the road, the **Chutes de Farako** tip into the 'river of stone' – so called because of its limestone bed. This waterfall drops in several tiers, the highest being a modest 3m. Naturally, the best time to see the falls is during the rainy season when the river is at its highest. The site is a popular weekend getaway for Sikasso's youth. It's possible to swim and camping is permitted anywhere in the forest. Buses leave from the *gare routière* or if you don't have a private vehicle, you can commission a taxi for CFA7,500 return (this will go up if you want to stay the whole day).

Near the falls and very close to the Burkina border, you can visit the **tea plantations** of Farako. The Sogetem factory (*2162 02 22; Mon–Fri but phone first*) produces 100–150 tons per year from several hectares of tea planted beneath the mango trees. Visits are allowed at the processing factory where you can see

COTTON WOOL AND SOAP

Mali remains vulnerable to fluctuations in the world market value of cotton, its principal export product (43%).

In 2003–04 Mali was Africa's premier cotton producer (1,050,000 bales) and the tenth largest producer in the world. (*Source: www.nationmaster.com/graph/agr_cot_pro-agriculture-cotton-production*).

These clinical statistics mean that many Malians must work in the cotton industry. What is it that they do there – apart from growing cotton? A visit to a *usine d'égrenage* (cotton ginnery) in Bougouni and a group of soap-making women in Koutiala reveal a fragment of the human factor.

COTTON WOOL One could almost think the whirling cloud of white fluff consisted of snowflakes, and that the men had covered their heads and mouths to keep out the cold. However, we are in a huge factory building with a tin roof and soaring temperatures; snow would melt and evaporate before reaching the ground. I also cover my mouth to keep out the dust and the cotton fibres, while the foreman shows me around, shouting through the noise of the giant installations: 'This is where the trucks dump their load. Look and touch the raw cotton. Do you feel the seeds and the grit? It is therefore cleaned in steps. First to remove the coarse bits, like small stones and even twigs. Then once more to remove smaller particles.'

He opens a hatch and sticks his hand in, catching some of the cotton wool that is blown through the pipes.

'The seed is still in there, so the cotton passes through the carding engine. See? The blades are so little apart, that the seeds are removed while the cotton is carded. Feel the difference.'

I do, and wonder if the foreman can feel the sweat trickling down his back as I can feel the sweat trickling down mine. Yet my mouth is dry.

'Then the cotton is blown through this pipe to the furnace, where it passes the...well, the drycleaners, one could say. Now feel this fluffy cotton wool! Then it passes through here and into this machine, where the cotton is pressed into these bales, each weighing around 230kg. We process appoximately 50,000 tons each year.'

This is where more human labour comes in, with four young men in sweat-sodden shirts preparing the press with iron wires to hold each bale together, handling the heavy blocks of fluff, taking samples of each bale to be tested for quality in a lab, sewing the

people at work and receive an explanation of the procedure from harvesting to arriving in your cup. Depending on the processing stage, there might not be anybody available to show you around. The black tea can be bought in little 25g sachets for CFA60.

At 65km from Sikasso and 3km from the small Sénoufo village of Woroni, you'll find the **Chutes de Woroni**. Twin falls, 15–20m high, surrounded by a natural pool and pristine ecosystem, they far outshine the Chutes de Farako. There's a 1km walk through the forest to get there, passing wild kola and orange trees, lots of plants used for traditional medicines and 15 species of birds. You can swim in the water, which is so clean you can drink it – though I wouldn't recommend it. To get there, take the public bus leaving Sikasso for Zégoua or Kadiolo and ask to be dropped off at Woroni. From there, if you want a guide, the village can provide one to show you the way. A new camp is under construction, so soon there will be somewhere to stay overnight. The price should be no more than CFA5,000 per person.

At the end of the forest and the beginning of the savanna, there's a natural door-like rock formation called the Portes du Soudan. Colonialists so named this area as

wrapping by hand and jotting down all the details – date, farmer, truckload and so on – on the wrapping with a marker. Then the bales are wheeled outside, and I follow my guide into the blinding sunlight. The scorching sun feels refreshing after spending an hour in that furnace. As I dust down my hair and clothes, I seek solace in mathematics in an attempt to make sense of all this labour. It has the reverse effect: 50,000 tons makes 217,391 bales of 230kg. The process of ginning lasts six months or 180 days of non-stop labour in three shifts a day, so that makes 1,208 bales per day, 403 per shift or 50 bales per hour. The ginning campaign lasts through the hottest months of the year, which have not even begun yet.

As I take my place on the back of a motorbike, I realise that by the time I get back to the *campement* to replenish fluids and take a shower, these men will have finished another 15 bales, with 200 more to go before the end of their shift.

SOAP The cotton seeds are pressed into oil, most of which is sent to Koulikoro to be refined and processed into long bars of soap. Neat and shiny, sometimes even perfumed, they're for many purposes. They can be bought all over the country at every market and in many shops. The plant where the seeds are pressed produces a foul and oily waste water. Behind the plant, outside the fence in the open air, women collect the waste water in dozens of rusty oildrums. After a couple of days, the unrefined oil is scooped from the surface, collected in containers, and carried to the soap-makers – all women – around the corner. At first glance it looks like a busy market square, but there are striking differences: the soil is black and slippery, the women's garments are smothered in various shades of brown, grey and black. Instead of a pleasant odour of spices and fruit, the air is filled with a fatty fragrance. The heat from dozens of fires is everywhere, while thick smoke and fumes hover over the site like a blanket. Who would have thought that a poor man's soap is made in hell? Here comes the recipe:

Pour the oil into huge cauldrons and mix with a potassium solution. Bring to the boil. With wooden spoons the size of paddles, stir and stir the thick grub for hours until it becomes a sort of smooth, creamy brown sludge. Leave to cool, stirring firmly without stopping. Transfer the slippery substance to smaller containers. Wrap your hands in plastic bags. Scoop a handful out of the bowl or bucket and turn into balls. Think of big meatballs. Dozens of them. Leave to dry in the sun. Sell at CFA50 up to CFA150 apiece, depending on size and quality. Ignore the smell; these brown soap balls are meant for cleaning only. They perform miracles on heavily stained clothes, though. They honestly do.

it marked the start of French Sudan when coming from Burkina Faso in the south with the chain of mountains forming the natural border. If you go there today you will see a sacred cave with people's offerings. The Portes du Soudan are found a further 4km from the village of Woroni.

ELSEWHERE IN THE REGION

SÉLINGUÉ Sélingué is situated at an almost equal distance between Sikasso and Bamako. If you're coming from the capital, after about 85km on a paved road, there is a turning for Kangaré and a dam at Sélingué. Before the completion of the Manantali project (see page 281), the hydro-electric plant at Sélingué was the largest of its kind in Mali, with a capacity of 44.8MW – although when the volume of water flow is low, it is sometimes unable to produce any electricity at all. The artificial lake created by the dam has been promoted as a tourist attraction, with *pinasse* rides, traditional dances, several species of waterbirds and places to stay at Kangaré, Sélingué and Yanifolila. You can get a bus to Sélingué/Kangaré from the BCEAO bank in Bamako. The journey takes roughly three hours and costs about CFA2,000. *Bâchées* leave for Kangaré (CFA1,500) – more widely referred to as Sélingué – from near the Gare Routière de Sogoninko, beside the main road opposite the yard from where buses leave for Sikasso; Air Sélingué also has a bus leaving daily from Sogoninko bus station around 15.00, arriving at 16.00 (CFA3,000), and returning to Bamako around 06.00. Alternatively, take a bus in the direction of Bougouni, get off at the turning to Sélingué, and look for onward transport from there.

There are plenty of fishing villages around the lake and the best way to explore is by pirogue. Find your way to the village of Carrière – 3km south of Kangaré – first. Pirogues leave from the market, which lies right on the shore of the lake. One option is to take a pirogue to Bambala on the west coast, take a ferry across to Siékorolé, and then take the road to Yanifolila and onwards to Bougouni. In 2003, John Kupiec chose the other option: for CFA2,000, a pirogue took him almost directly to the shore nearest to Yanifolila. From there he walked a pleasant 15km to Yanifolila.

Where to stay and eat

Mid-range $$$

Hotel Club Sélingué (23 villas) m 6671 41 83; e info@hotelclubselingue.net; www.hotelclubselingue.net. Approx 3km away & just off the main road in town. Although there's a lot of potential in the villas, their general appearance is rather rundown. The Olympic-size swimming pool, though much bigger than that at Woloni, is rarely clean. An injection of money is badly needed to spruce up this place, but since it's largely government-owned, it's not expected any time soon.

Hotel Woloni (10 huts) m 6689 66 78. Without doubt, this is the best place to stay. It takes about 1½–2hrs to get there from Bamako & is worth a special journey. Situated on the banks of the lake, not only is the location calm & relaxing but the round, AC huts are new & stylishly decorated. Water surrounds the restaurant serving French cuisine during the rainy season so you can dive straight in. Alternatively there's a well-maintained swimming pool. B/fast extra at CFA1,500.

Yaala Campement Based in the village of Kangaré; m 7409 51 00; e contact@yaalacampement.com; www.yaalacampement.com. A good budget option with basic but comfortable huts kitted out with fan & mosquito nets. Situated in a shady courtyard. Simple Malian meals are available. Sgl CFA7,000, dbl CFA 9,000, dorm beds CFA2,500.

BOUGOUNI Bougouni is the first major town after Bamako, 160km from the capital and roughly at the halfway point of a bus journey to Sikasso. This is a factory town – economically important, but of little interest to the tourist. Having said that, migrating elephants have been seen in this area. If you're lucky you might see one, but it's unlikely. Or if it's cotton factories you're after, you should be able to organise a visit. There are places to stay should you wish to break your journey here, but note that they cater for business rather than tourist clientele. Another point to bear in mind is the fact that none of the hotels has a restaurant. Finding a filling meal for little money in one of the small local restaurants, however, should not be a problem.

Campement les Moulins, usually simply referred to as **Le Campement** (*2165 11 15; $$ b/fast inc*), to avoid confusion, is just before the turning to Sikasso to the left of the road. Continuing on the same road, ignoring the turning to Sikasso, you'll see another hotel. Coming from Bamako, to the right of the paved thoroughfare is the **Hotel Piedmont** (*2165 13 73*).

When arriving by bus from Bamako or Sikasso, ask to be dropped off at one of the hotels, since the bus station is around 1km off the road and you would have to walk back.

KOUTIALA Koutiala is 140km on the other side of Sikasso – that is to say, on the road to Ségou and Mopti. Like Bougouni, it is a factory town, although larger and more important. In fact, the *cercle* of Koutiala is one of the most economically productive areas of Mali and a principal cotton-growing region.

Getting there and away For travellers, Koutiala is important as a crossroads for traffic to Bamako, Sikasso, Ségou, Mopti and Bobo-Dioulasso. Buses to all of these destinations can be found at the **bus station** on the road to Sikasso. Between Bani Transport, Bittar Transport, Binke Transport and Somatra, you can choose from at least eight daily departures for Ségou (2–3 hours; CFA3,000) and Bamako (CFA4,000), and four daily departures for Bobo-Dioulasso (CFA4,000). Ask around to find out which company is leaving next before purchasing your ticket and if you're staying overnight, it's best to buy your ticket the night before to guarantee a place on your bus of choice.

Comfortable TSR Escales buses leave daily for Bobo-Dioulasso, Ouagadougou (CFA9,000), Cotonou (CFA22,500) and Lomé (CFA22,500). However, buses to Sikasso (CFA2,000) or to San (CFA2,000), Mopti (CFA4,000) and Gao (CFA10,000) depart less frequently. Minibuses and *bâchées* to Sikasso, Bla and San leave when full from the departure point opposite the BDM bank.

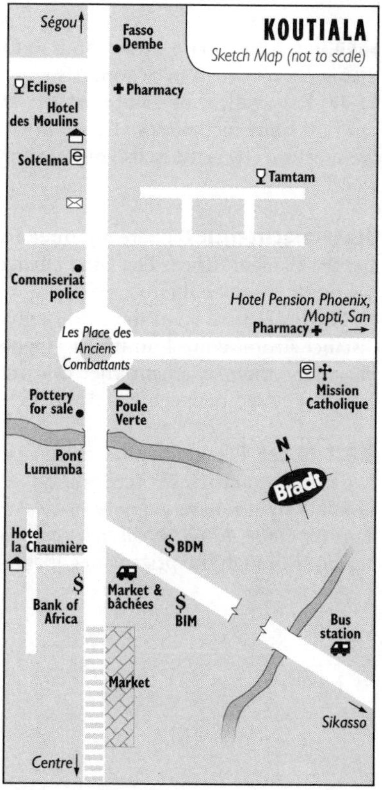

Where to stay and eat Koutiala has a fair selection of reasonable hotels.

Budget $$

Hotel La Chaumière 2164 02 20. This hotel comes highly recommended, with large, clean AC rooms. Some rooms are available with a fan. The restaurant serves excellent food, though you may have to wait a while.

Hotel des Moulins m 7622 51 46. This quiet hotel is similar in price & standard to Hotel La Chaumière. There's no restaurant though. B/fast only.

Hotel Pension Phoenix 2164 09 16. Affordable, quiet & on the road to San, about 1km from the roundabout in the centre of town. It's not marked so it's hard to find. Rooms with AC or a fan are bright & spotlessly clean. There's hot water & a beer garden serving cold beer.

Poule Verte 2164 02 38. For budget travellers who are hard of hearing, this centrally located hotel could be a good choice. It is a drinking place, where loud music blasts from speakers on the terrace until late. It is also a place where 1 wing is reserved for prostitutes, but travellers who want to spend the night get the better rooms & clean sheets. A choice between rooms with AC or fan, or camping in the garden, which can hardly be recommended. Meals, like tasty, tender chicken with sauce, are quite good.

Entertainment and nightlife If you do find yourself with a night in Koutiala, there are several places to try.

The Poule Verte serves beer on a large terrace and is a popular hangout with the locals. The Tam Tam Garden (*every night; admission free*) has live music on Fri/Sat; Dabo Diarra plays saxophone with his band in a mix of traditional and modern music. A big beer costs CFA800. Just off the road to Ségou is Bar Eclipse (*2164 05 58; 07.00–03.00 daily; nightclub from 22.00 Fri/Sat; admission CFA1,000–2,000*), with a beer garden. Food is also served; a whole roast chicken or pigeon will set you back CFA1,000. There's a nightclub on the same premises, playing a mix of African and European music.

Shopping At the main roundabout in town, you'll find a selection of black pottery that is cheaper than in Ségou. Also on the road to Ségou, Fasso Dembe (m *7616 91 44*) has a gallery of traditional arts. It's a bit cluttered but if you rummage, you can find some nice pieces at good prices, certainly cheaper than you would pay in the Dogon. The artist is also quite happy for you to sit and watch him sculpting in wood.

Other practicalities There are three banks in Koutiala: the BDM bank, the BIM and the Bank of Africa. The latter changes euros, US dollars and travellers' cheques if you can produce the receipt.

The post office is on the throroughfare to Ségou and Bamako, within walking distance from Pont Lumumba. Opposite a large and extremely well-stocked pharmacy, there is an internet café in the grounds of the Mission Catholique, which is closed between 12.00 and 15.00.

What to see During the day there is an interesting **market** to wander around or two **cotton factories** where you can try to organise a visit. If you have some time to kill, why not have a *djembe* or *balafon* lesson with Dabou Diarra from the Tam Tam (m *7504 46 68;* e *daboudiarra@yahoo.fr*). He charges CFA12,500 per person per hour though the price is negotiable if you want longer than an hour.

11

Kayes

Most tourists see the western region of Kayes from the window of a train as they travel between Dakar and Bamako. If they do set foot in this part of the country, it is more often than not in the old colonial town of Kayes. Kita also receives the odd visitor thanks to its rail-side location, but otherwise the region is rarely explored. One of the main reasons for this used to be the paucity of good roads in the west of Mali. The Dakar–Bamako railway line has long been seen as a replacement for a sophisticated road network, and as a result access to most of the region used to be difficult and time consuming. To a great extent, this still applies. However, the recent construction of a tarred road linking Bamako to Kayes has opened up a previously inaccessible region of Mali, giving both the town and the inhabitants a boost. Now, only a few isolated pockets remain in Mali, which receive no more than a handful of tenacious travellers. The Parc National de la Boucle du Baoulé is one of these.

HISTORY

The history of the present-day region of Kayes is not as clear-cut as those of other areas, where one great kingdom or empire has usually stamped its mark and influence. In this part of west Africa regional dominance has always been up for grabs: the French, the Tukulor and the Bambara kingdom of Ségou have all controlled certain parts of it at certain times, while the two indigenous power blocks – the state of Khasso and the kingdoms of Kaarta – have struggled against outside influences.

KHASSO Khasso was originally a Malinké state running along both sides of the River Senegal and extending from present-day Senegal in the west to the Kaarta kingdom in the east. When Mungo Park passed through here in 1796, the Peul were in charge and the capital was at Koniakari.

By the middle of the 19th century, civil wars had divided the state into two important and rival groups. The hereditary ruler, Dyoukou Sambala, had moved the capital from Koniakari to Médine on the right bank of the River Senegal, where he and his followers had established themselves, while a few kilometres upstream at Sabousséré on the left bank a group called the Logo opposed him. Meanwhile, the French and the Tukulor had recently arrived in the region and were jostling for power. El Hadj Omar had taken advantage of the state of civil war, and by 1855 the Tukulor had conquered most of the Khasso chiefdoms – including Koniakari – on the right bank of the river. This prompted Sambala to ally himself with the French, who built a fortress at Médine in 1855 ostensibly to protect their own commercial interests in the area. In 1857, this fortress passed its first – and arguably its sternest – test when it successfully repelled a siege by Omar's forces.

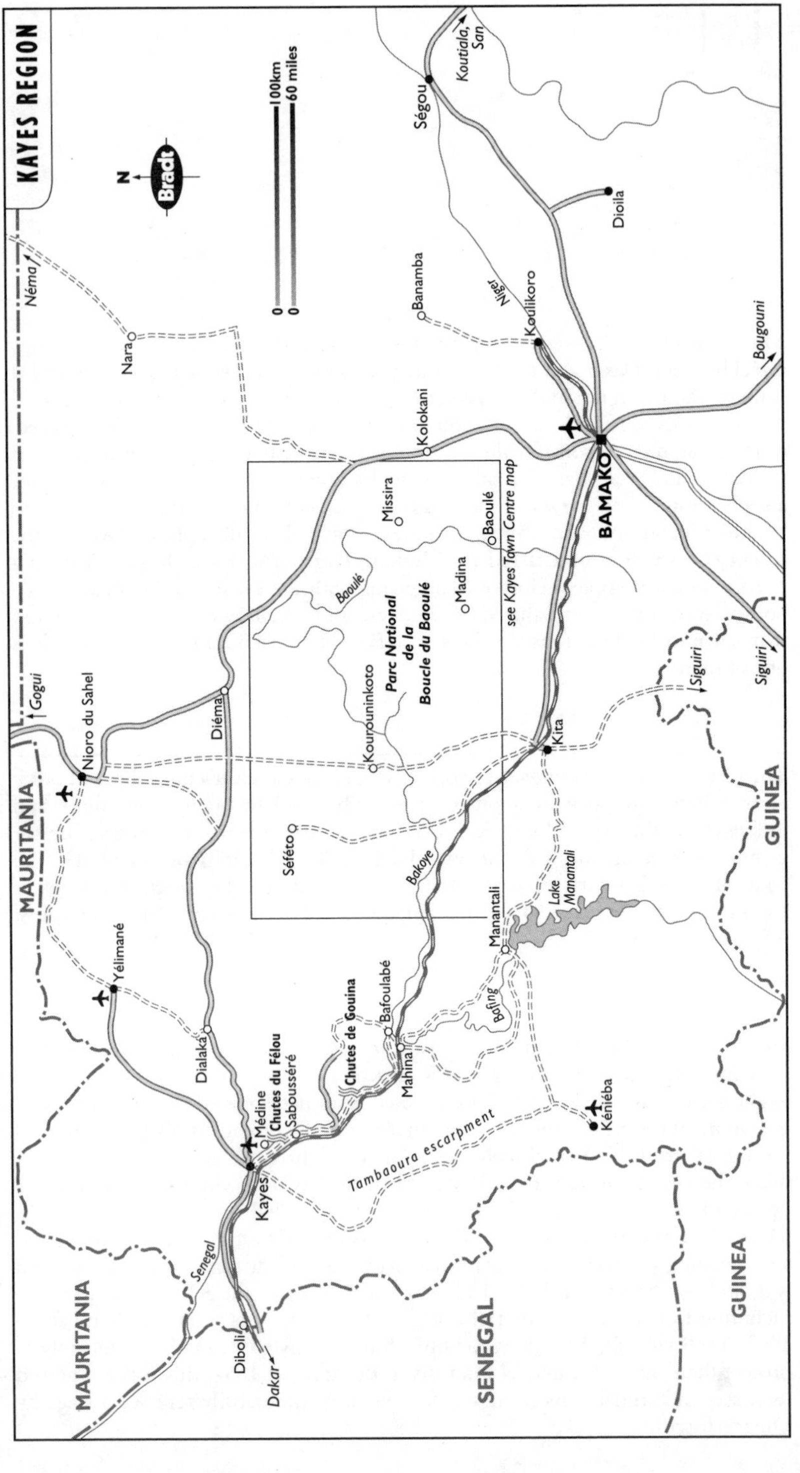
KAYES REGION
N
Bradt
0 100km
0 60 miles
MAURITANIA
MAURITANIA
SENEGAL
GUINEA
GUINEA
Néma
Nara
Gogui
Nioro du Sahel
Diéma
Yélimané
Dialaka
Kolokani
Banamba
Koulikoro
Niger
Ségou
Koutiala, San
Dioila
BAMAKO
Bougouni
Siguiri
Siguiri
Kita
Missira
Baoulé
Baoulé
Madina
see Kayes Town Centre map
Parc National de la Boucle du Baoulé
Kourouninkoto
Séféto
Bakoye
Manantali
Lake Manantali
Bafing
Bafoulabé
Mahina
Chutes de Gouina
Chutes du Félou
Sabousséré
Médine
Kayes
Kéniéba
Tambaoura escarpment
Senegal
Diboli
Dakar

The French, however, had no desire to be in a constant state of war with the Tukulor, as it disrupted the profitable trade engaged in by the colonialists along the River Senegal. For this reason, the French preferred to remain neutral as the Tukulor fought to maintain their authority in conquered lands. However, when the Logo, led by Niamody, allied themselves with the Tukulor, thus becoming a direct threat on the left bank of the river where the French had their sphere of influence, something had to be done. Sambala was encouraged by Brière de l'Isle, the French governor of Senegal, to invade his old enemy in November 1877; but when the Logo, helped by the Tukulor, were on the verge of victory the French themselves intervened, defeating Niamody and destroying his capital at Saboussére in September 1878. French commercial interests were secured, and in 1892, the town of Kayes became the capital of Upper Senegal and Niger.

KAARTA The traditional lands of the Bambara kingdoms of Kaarta – not to be confused with the Bambara kingdom of Ségou (see page 141) – lie north of the river Baoulé. There were, in fact, two Kaarta kingdoms. The first was ruled by the Massassi dynasty and dates from 1650. The Ségou ruler, Biton Coulibaly, was a major thorn in the side of the various Massassi rulers, and in 1753, he finally succeeded in conquering them after several previous attempts. Coulibaly's success spawned the creation of a second Bambara kingdom of Kaarta in 1754 by Sey Bamana Coulibaly, which was to become, unlike its predecessor, an organised political state in the second half of the 18th century. Although battles continued to be lost against Ségou, Kaarta enjoyed military victories over Khasso and reached its apogee under Bodian Moriba (ruled 1818–32), whose first capital was at Yélimané, before being moved to Nioro.

The development of Kaarta as a powerful political state was cut short by El Hadj Omar, who brought Nioro under Tukulor control in 1854.

KAYES TOWN

Kayes is reputed to be the hottest town in Africa. Temperatures in April and May can sometimes reach 50°C and the very slight breeze coming off the River Senegal is about as soothing as a fan heater. One explanation for the heat is that the town is surrounded by hills which contain a lot of iron. As the sun beats down on these hills it warms up the iron and turns Kayes into an oven – or rather a bun in an oven. However, the temperature during the cooler months is more tolerable and certainly not too high to put you off visiting this attractive and busy town.

Kayes was – and still is – an important commercial centre. Founded in 1880 when it was a small and irrelevant Khassonké village, it replaced Médine as the capital of the Upper Senegal and Niger colony 12 years later and, thanks largely to the railway, became a major trading centre for gum arabic (a gum produced by certain acacia trees and used in the manufacture of ink, food thickeners, pills, emulsifiers, etc). Kayes continued as the undisputed centre of French commercial interests in the region until the railway eventually reached Bamako in 1908. However, although Kayes lost out to Bamako – especially after 1923 when the railway reached Dakar and the Atlantic coast – it remains to this day one of Mali's most important economic centres. In fact, Kayes claims to be the region with the greatest number of Malians living abroad. One goes over, does some business, makes some money and sends for his brother. The population remains optimistic for their future, especially regarding tourism.

Tourists who are not continuing on to Senegal will ask themselves whether or not it is worth the 1,200km round trip from Bamako to visit the town of Kayes. My answer is an unreserved 'yes'. This place is, at the same time, relaxed and busy, attractive and jaded. It has some of the finest colonial architecture in Mali and also gives visitors the chance to see west Africa's other great river, the Senegal.

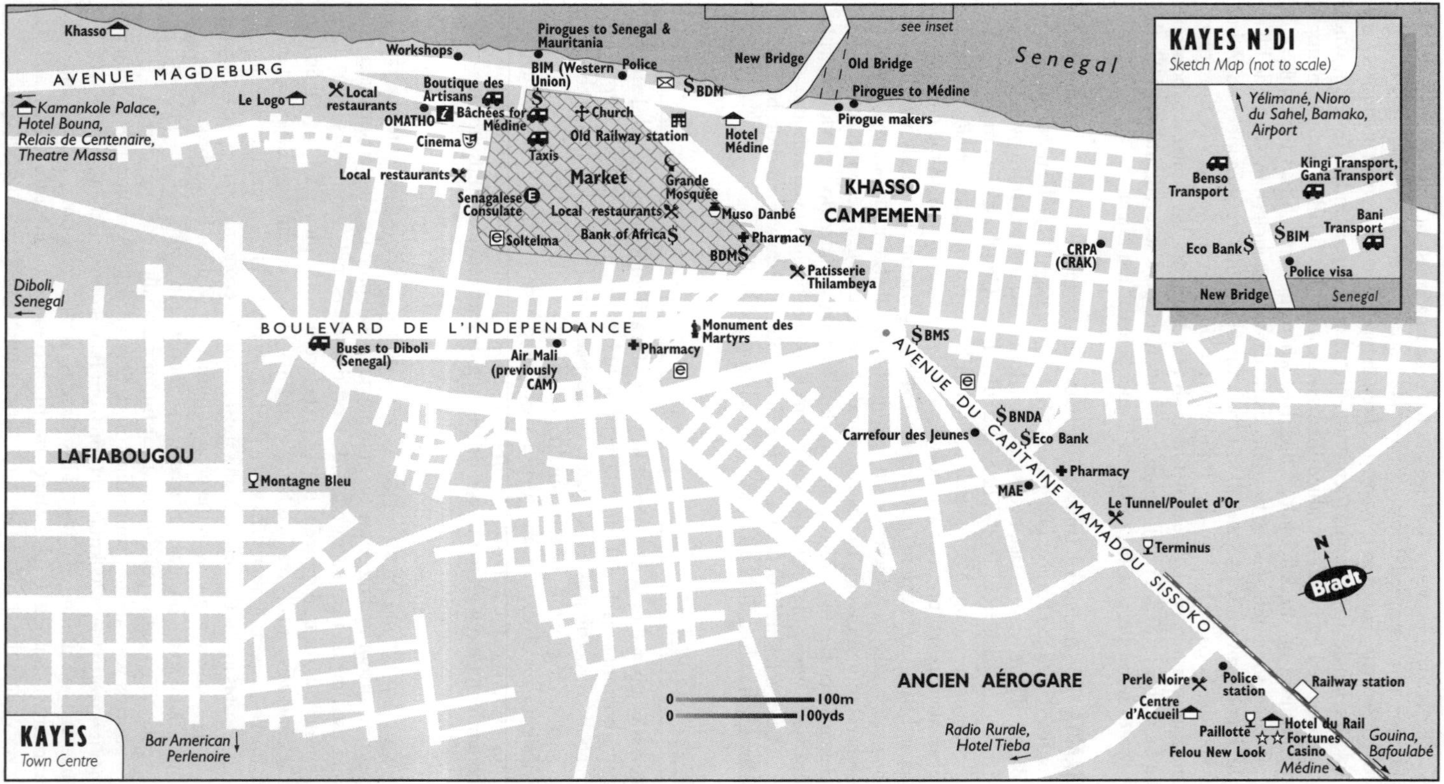
KAYES
Town Centre
KAYES N'DI
Sketch Map (not to scale)
Yélimané, Nioro du Sahel, Bamako, Airport
Benso Transport
Kingi Transport, Gana Transport
Bani Transport
Eco Bank
BIM
Police visa
New Bridge
Senegal
Senegal
see inset
Khasso
AVENUE MAGDEBURG
Kamankole Palace, Hotel Bouna, Relais de Centenaire, Theatre Massa
Le Logo
Local restaurants
Workshops
Boutique des Artisans
OMATHO
Bâchées for Médine
Cinema
Local restaurants
Pirogues to Senegal & Mauritania
BIM (Western Union)
Police
Church
Old Railway station
Taxis
Market
Senagalese Consulate
Local restaurants
Bank of Africa
Soltelma
BDM
New Bridge
Old Bridge
Pirogues to Médine
Pirogue makers
Hotel Médine
Grande Mosquée
Muso Danbé
Pharmacy
BDM
KHASSO
CAMPEMENT
CRPA (CRAK)
Patisserie Thilambeya
Diboli, Senegal
BOULEVARD DE L'INDEPENDANCE
Buses to Diboli (Senegal)
Air Mali (previously CAM)
Pharmacy
Monument des Martyrs
BMS
AVENUE DU CAPITAINE MAMADOU SISSOKO
BNDA
Eco Bank
Carrefour des Jeunes
Pharmacy
MAE
Le Tunnel/Poulet d'Or
Terminus
N
Bradt
LAFIABOUGOU
Montagne Bleu
ANCIEN AÉROGARE
0 100m
0 100yds
Bar American Perlenoire
Radio Rurale, Hotel Tieba
Perle Noire
Police station
Railway station
Centre d'Accueil
Paillotte
Hotel du Rail
Fortunes Casino
Felou New Look
Médine
Gouina, Bafoulabé

ORIENTATION When you arrive by train, you will be about 2km from the town centre. This part of town is dominated by the railway, which in its heyday in the early 1900s used to terminate near the banks of the River Senegal. Nowadays, the station is in the southeastern part of town on the road to Médine. This road, along with Boulevard de l'Indépendance (the road to Diboli on the Senegalese border) and Avenue Macdeoura (the road running parallel to the river), are the main arteries in a town which is relatively simple to figure out. A new bridge across the River Senegal was opened in 2001, after holes in the old one made it impassable, with cars being swept away by the current. The bridge links the various quarters of old Kayes to Kayes N'Di or Small Kayes, a large, residential quarter built – and still being built – on the right bank of the river, where the roads to Nioro du Sahel and Yélimané begin. This area of town is expanding fast and it's from here that you'll find transport leaving for other parts of the country.

GETTING THERE AND AWAY

By air The new airport of Kayes, Dacdac, named after a nearby village, is located north of the River Senegal, 15km from Kayes . Both MAE and Air Mali operate flights between Bamako and Kayes. MAE (*2152 15 82;* **m** *6672 93 96*) has an office along the Avenue du Capitaine Mamadou Sissoko and flights both arrive and depart on Monday, Tuesday, Thursday and Saturday. Air Mali (**m** *7615 36 00;* **e** *kyscam@cam-mali.org*) by the Harlem roundabout, offers the same service on Monday, Thursday and Sunday. Tickets are CFA60,000–70,000 one-way. The planes servicing the Bamako to Kayes route are small so it is worth making reservations well in advance and bear in mind that the schedule is subject to change (see *Chapter 2, Getting there and away*). A taxi from the airport into town should be no more than CFA5,000.

By river Travelling down the River Senegal – which passes through Kayes and continues west along the border between Senegal and Mauritania before emptying into the Atlantic Ocean at the Senegalese town of Saint-Louis – is an original and adventurous way to travel to or from Kayes. The best place to ask about pirogues is on the bank of the river, roughly halfway between the bridge and the Hotel Khasso. Pirogues also leave daily for Médine from just right of the bridge (see *Excursions from Kayes*, page 279).

By train Kayes is roughly halfway between Dakar and Bamako on the railway linking the two capital cities. Huge delays are commonplace and therefore the train is very unlikely to arrive in Kayes as scheduled, but roughly speaking the Bamako–Dakar express train arrives on Thursday morning from Bamako, and returns on Sunday, at lunchtime from Dakar. Three more trains run between Bamako and Kayes. A new train was put into service in 2008, supposedly more comfortable and rapid. For more details on fares and departure times, see *Chapter 2, Getting around*. All local trains have been suspended.

By road For travellers, a most useful land route is the 92km pot-holed track leading to Diboli on the Senegalese border, from where you can travel to Dakar. Buses and *bâchées* leave every day from opposite the Sad Oil Service station on Boulevard de l'Indépendance (3 hours; CFA3,000). Every now and then – try Saturdays at 17.00 – there is a direct bus to Dakar (at least 15 hours; CFA14,000).

Until recently, travelling by road to Bamako was not an option. Now big buses leave for the capital every morning – to reach their destination late in the afternoon or early in the evening – from the Gare Routière Kayes N'Di across the bridge.

THE BUTCHER OF KAYES

There is a small kiosk opposite the Hotel Le Khasso in Kayes selling cigarettes, bottled water, biscuits and various other sundry items. I had got into the habit of purchasing an after-dinner snack at this shop and then whiling away the warm evenings in conversation with its gregarious owner. On one such evening we were installed in our usual chairs solving the problems of the world, shrouded in an atmospheric half-light provided by a lantern which hung on one side of the kiosk. All around us it was pitch-black. During a lull in the conversation, a gentle rattling sound punctuated by heavy scuffs on the ground could be heard in the darkness. We remained silent, obviously more intrigued by the approaching sound than the subject of our suspended conversation. A few seconds later a bicycle crept into our canopy of light and stopped in front of the kiosk. Its rider slipped off the crooked saddle and held the bicycle between his legs as he fumbled in his pocket for some change. In his other hand he held a machete, gleaming like a bar of gold as it caught the light of the lantern. I tried to see his face, but dark shadows obliterated his head and shoulders and they merged effortlessly into the night sky. The stranger purchased one cigarette, slipped it behind what I presume was his ear and rode off into the darkness.

I had just met one of the most important men in Kayes: the butcher. Every night he passes the kiosk on his way to the slaughterhouse, where he spends the night hacking, sawing and slicing so that there can be meat in the market the next day. He works alone and saves his cigarette for breakfast.

There are four companies with bus stations: Gana Transport (☎ *2152 39 07*) has 'express' buses, some with air conditioning, leaving at 05.00 (arriving at 14.00) or at 06.00 (arriving at 16.00 or 17.00). They have the biggest fleet and the most reliable buses. In the likely event of a breakdown, they can send a replacement, which is not possible with the smaller companies who may leave you stranded. Benso (☎ *2152 16 38*) on the other hand have the most comfortable buses leaving at 06.00, 08.00 and 09.00 and Bani Transport's buses depart at 06.00 and 08.00. All three companies have air conditioning and tickets cost CFA10,000. Kingui meanwhile charges CFA8,000 for non air-conditioned buses leaving at 06.00 and 14.00. The fare matches that of a second-class train ticket, but many Malians consider travelling by bus as being far more comfortable than a full day in a second-class train wagon. The road, which does not show on commercially available maps yet, heads east from Kayes to Sandaré (CFA5,000), then to Diema and Kolokani before reaching Bamako.

Buses from Bamako also stop here on the way to Dakar. Passengers are left overnight before continuing in the morning. You can sleep on a mat at the bus station or go to a hotel as long as you're back for the departure in the morning. It's best to reserve tickets, which you can normally do by telephone two–three days in advance. This allows you to turn up one hour before the bus leaves. If you leave it less than 24 hours before departure, then you have to go to the ticket office to buy a ticket.

Yélimané is also linked to Kayes by tar. Buses leave daily from the same bus station (CFA3,500). However, although most maps show a connection by road between Yélimané and Nioro du Sahel, this section of road is in an appalling state. Only *camions* travel between Kayes and Nioro du Sahel, bypassing Yélimané and the impassable section by cutting from the new road to Bamako straight to Nioro du Sahel. The least uncomfortable option is a converted truck which carries passengers only. The alternative is a truck carrying goods and as many passengers as possible on top of the freight. Look for Diema Transport which has daily departures, and expect to pay CFA5,000 for a long and bumpy ride to Nioro. If you are lucky, take a shared cabin seat for CFA7,500. 4x4 vehicles to Nioro are CFA7,500 in the back, while a front seat is CFA10,000.

Small buses and *bâchées* bring people and their merchandise from villages to the market every day, returning in the afternoon around 15.00. The departure point for vehicles to Yélimané is near the cinema, while from between Hotel le Logo and the Senegalese consulate, vehicles for Médine depart when full.

Kayes is one of the few towns with some kind of public transport service between quarters. The green minibuses, like the *sotramas* in Bamako, costs as little as CFA100 for an average ride.

TOURIST INFORMATION The OMATHO (*2152 35 98;* m *7605 51 64*) (see also page 44) has to be the best OMATHO office in the country with the extremely enthusiastic and helpful director, Aliou Diarra (e *bamana@yahoo.fr*). So keen is he to promote Kayes as a tourist destination, any questions you have he will do everything he can to help, including finding a guide or organising tours. Kayes has four certified guides available for visits to sites, one of whom speaks English; Bréhima Sissoko (e *bsissoko62@yahoo.fr*).

WHERE TO STAY When there is a conference in town – which happens quite frequently during the cooler months – the accommodation in Kayes fills up very quickly. The train from Bamako often arrives in the early hours of the morning, so consider making a reservation, at least for the first night.

Upmarket $$$$

Hotel Kamankole Palace (55 rooms) Village CAN2002; 2152 62 42. A friendly 4-star hotel set in 5ha of gardens with large clean rooms & a swimming pool surrounded by round huts for meditation. Guests can use the gym & there's a tennis court planned for next year & a golf course, sometime in the future. B/fast inc.

Mid-range $$$

Hotel Bouna (27 rooms) 3.5km out of town; 2152 35 60; e bounahotel@yahoo.fr. Opened in Dec 2007, this new hotel is bright & modern, though the AC rooms leading off soulless corridors are a bit dark. There are internet facilities & a doctor on site, should you need one. The restaurant serves international dishes such as pizza & *capitaine*.

Hotel Le Khasso (14 rooms) 2153 16 66; m 6679 65 83. This hotel has a very African feel. The service is laid back & during the hot season, the slight yet significant breeze blows around the little thatched bungalows set on the banks of the River Senegal. AC with hot running water, TV & phone.

Hotel Médine (14 rooms with 8 more under construction) Between the bridge & the post office; 2153 11 09. Well-kept rooms with AC, hot water & TV (which only seems to show football). There's a garden in the back with a bar for live music & entertainment & a nice terrace in the front, to sit & watch the world go by, except when the dust-laden hepatitis blows (see page 6). Laundry service. B/fast inc.

Hotel du Rail (20 rooms) Opposite the railway station; 2152 12 33. A charming colonial building full of history & character. The rooms are clean but rather tatty compared with the immaculate bungalows at the Khasso & even the copious amounts of plastic flowers can't brighten up the dim corridors. The hot water only comes on in the evening.

Hotel Tieba (22 rooms) 2152 60 52; e hoteltieba@yahoo.fr. Clean, simple AC rooms all with small balconies, TV & en-suite, hot-water showers. There's a laundry service & guests have free use of the internet. Some cheaper rooms are available with fan. In the evening *brochettes de boeuf* are served in the bar or garden for CFA250 each. B/fast inc.

Budget $$

Le Logo Hotel (5 rooms) Next to the prison; 2152 13 81; e leloghotel@yahoo.fr. They were in the middle of renovating at the time of visiting but if the white paint & the hotel under the same ownership, the Bouna, are anything to go by, it should be simple & bright. The budget options in Kayes are limited so this is relatively good value & worth a try.

Radio Rurale (9 rooms with 6 more under construction) 2153 14 76/2152 37 55; e bathiss2003@yahoo.fr. A rustic & charming guesthouse in a converted house, inhabited by the French army during colonial times. The AC or fan rooms with mosquito nets are large & above a radio station where you can watch them broadcasting. Calm & tranquil, this place is surrounded by nature. The telecentre opposite has telephone & internet. Meals are cooked to order: fish, chips, chicken ragout, couscous for CFA3,000–3,500. Cold water only. B/fast not inc.

Relais de Centenaire (21 rooms, inc 2 dorms) About 200m west of the Hotel Khasso as the road turns away from the river; 2152 18 97. Part of the Mission Catholique in Kayes. The distance from the centre of town is a slight disadvantage, but is more than made up for by the good-value accommodation. There are some en-suite AC rooms, otherwise a room with fan or tidy dorms with mosquito net are available. There is no hot water though you can get it heated up & there's a kitchen for guests to use & a TV in the salon. Pétanque or bowling in the garden. B/fast not inc. *Dorm bed CFA2,500.*

Shoestring $

Centre d'Accueil (8 rooms) Behind the Commissariat de Police; m 7606 16 24. Very basic accommodation with fans. It appears maintenance or cleaning are not their priority but even though it's scarily dirty, it fills up just like the smarter hotels at busy times. You can take a mattress & sleep on the terrace, or camp for CFA2,000. Smelly communal toilets & cold-water showers.

WHERE TO EAT Although this is one of Mali's largest towns, no-one will claim that it is one of its most gastronomic. But even in the hotels, you will find that it's much cheaper than other major towns.

Mid-range $$$

Hotel Kamankole Palace The restaurant serves plenty of fish, either African, Malian or French style. There's a bar with cocktails, billiard table & French wines.

Cheap and cheerful $$

Hotel Khasso This is arguably the most popular restaurant in town. The food is OK, even if the ambience is a little depressing. Sheep, guinea fowl, duck & rabbit are all on the menu. A better choice might be to order brochettes & eat them in the garden by the river.

Hotel Médine A good little restaurant. Not much atmosphere but serving tasty European & African dishes such as half a chicken or *capitaine*. Also serves alcohol.

Hotel du Rail The restaurant is rather kitsch & funky with lots of bright plastic flowers that must be left over from the hotel. Normal fare: steak, chicken & fish with garniture. A 3-course *menu du jour* is available for CFA6,000 including tea or coffee.

Rock bottom $

Le Logo Hotel Again closed for renovation, so not sure what the décor will be like but serves cheap meals; steak, brochette, *capitaine* & beer (CFA600 for a small one).

Pâtisserie Thilambeya They have a great selection of cakes, sticky buns & ice cream as well as serving dishes such as liver with onion, hamburgers & spring rolls.

Restaurant Perle Noire Within the Carrefour des Jeunes in Plateau; m 6673 74 79; 08.00–midnight. A pleasant garden with outside dining, serving international & national dishes & entertainment from local praise singers. There's not much for vegetarians – choose from whole chicken, wild pig, beef tongue or fish served with plantain. The locals really dress up at the w/end when it doesn't close until the last person leaves.

Restaurant Senegalé m 7608 95 64. Situated behind the cinema, serving simple Malian meals such as *riz à la sauce arachide* (*tigadege*) & *ougnon djabai* (rice with beef & tomato sauce & onion).

Restaurant le Tunnel/Poulet Doré Along Av du Capitaine Mamadou Sissoko, Kayes Khasso; m 6639 54 30. It's all right, as long as you do not expect anything other than the usual fish, chicken & brochettes.

Albarka and **Sigui FM** next to the mosque – you'll have to ask directions, as it's a maze (m *7622 65 85;* $). These are the two local restaurants, found in the market, which are the cleanest and serve mineral water. Rice and fish and *riz au gras* are on the menu; CFA250 for drinks.

For other options, look around the market where a mound of rice ladled with *sauce arachide* should not be too hard to find.

ENTERTAINMENT AND NIGHTLIFE Kayes prides itself on its night-time entertainment and with many musicians hailing from the region, Bouboucar Traoré probably being the most famous, it's not surprising there are lots of spots to catch some music.

☆ **Carrefour des Jeunes** Drama & sport are on offer here, where dance troupes rehearse & where judo & karate are practised in the evenings.

☆ **Centre d'Accueil** Has a bar next door of the same name which is sometimes full of people & has a bit of an ambience.

☆ **Hotel Khasso** The garden is the nicest place for a drink in the early evening, under the individual thatched huts right on the river. A real locals' hangout with a fun atmosphere, before heading to Le Mamery Nightclub next door.

☆ **Le Mamery** ⌚ Fri–Sun except during holiday time when it's open for longer; admission free for hotel guests, otherwise CFA3,000–7,500pp, depending on the day and occasion. The busiest night is Sat but the most interesting is the Sun Senegalese night. People come dressed in their best outfits & practise their moves to the Senegalese beats. A great atmosphere.

☆ **The Paillote** Hotel du Rail; admission CFA3,000–7,500 depending on the occasion. A pleasant open-air place for a drink & brochettes. Laid back & local with a stage for entertainment; at the weekend musicians or the audience gets up to sing. Every night is busy & animated. The hotel's nightclub, **Felou New Look**, plays a variety of music as well as hosting special nights. Alternatively try your hand at Fortunes Casino next door. Mostly CFA50 & CFA100 slot machines with a few poker machines & helpful young men to help get change & trade in your winnings.

🍸 **Perle Noir American Bar** m 6676 08 91; ⌚ from 09.00 daily until the last person leaves. A chilled-out, cosy bar within the President of the association of hotels & restaurant's home. Well-stocked & nicely decorated with traditional artefacts & AC in the summer.

🍸 **La Montagne Bleue** Lafiabougou; m 6672 95 10; ⌚ 09.00–05.00 daily. An open-air bar with a great atmosphere serving *phaco* (wild pig).

🍸 **Terminus Bar** m 6672 93 84. Another open-air bar where you can really hang out with the locals.

🎭 **Théâtre Massa Mankan Diabaté** This used to occasionally play host to some of Mali's best musicians until it burnt down. It should have been rebuilt by now.

Not far from the market is a cinema, showing violent films for CFA250–500. The soccer stadium is behind the airport.

SHOPPING

Boutique des Artisans de Kayes (*Next to the OMATHO; m 6661 87 73/7615 13 05*) Opened by an American Peace Corps volunteer, the idea was to gather the work of all the artisans of Kayes in one place so tourists didn't have to trek around everywhere. The artisans bring their products to the shop and if it sells they get a percentage.

Centre Muso Danbé (*In the market in a small street behind the pharmacy; m 6639 35 62*) A sewing and textile-dyeing training centre for young women. You can go and see them in action or you can arrange to take part and learn some traditional skills yourself. There's a shop to buy their creations; a set of seven embroidered place mats will set you back CFA30,000 whilst a fruit basket made from recycled plastic bags is a mere CFA2,000. They also sell *bogolan* and an indigo unique to the region of Kayes.

CRAK (coordination régionale des artisans de Kayes) (*Kayes Khasso; ☎ 2152 24 45*) They have a list of all the artisans in Kayes. If you have any special requests (and can speak French), you can call and they'll try to sort it out. **CRPA** – the regional centre in charge of the promotion of artisans (☎ *252 18 98*) – can also be found here.

OTHER PRACTICALITIES The post office, Sotelma and a bank (BIM) with a Western Union office are all a stone's throw from each other on Avenue Macdeoura, the road running parallel to the river. BIM (*closed on Fri*) and BHM banks change euros, while the BDM-SA is the only bank in Kayes that does Visa cash advances. The BNDA bank changes cash euros and US dollars, as well as travellers' cheques. BDM and BNDA are also open on Saturday mornings and the Bank of Africa can be found in the Immeuble Alou Kouma.

Kayes seems to have more than its fair share of smart, well-stocked pharmacies. There is a hospital (*2152 12 32*) and polyclinic – Yonki Yaha (*2152 26 29*).

The police station (*2152 11 81*) is near the post office by the river. The police dealing with visas are north of the river by the bus stations. If you get a visa at the border, you can extend it here.

There is also a Senegalese consulate (*2152 11 15*) between the market and the Hotel le Logo.

Internet facilities can be found along the Avenue Capitaine Mamadou Sissoko, at the internet centre of Soltema (*08.00–20.00*) and Cybercafé Diata Net in Plateau for CFA500 per hour. If you're staying at Radio Rural, there's a telecentre there (*08.00–13.00 & 15.00–19.00, 14.00–18.00 Mon only*), but the guardian will open it up for guests at any time of the day or night.

The **church** in the market is closed every day except Sunday.

WHAT TO SEE It is not difficult to tell that Kayes was once the French capital of Upper Senegal and Niger and a major colonial trading centre. These days, the **colonial architecture** remains largely intact and is frequently used to house government ministries, police *commissariats* and other public offices. In other cases – the old railway station in the centre of town, for example – these buildings have become children's playgrounds and good places to get out of the sun. Either way, the colonial legacy lives on in Kayes. The most impressive buildings can be found along the river and around the new railway station. Indeed, traditional Sudanese architecture is not at its most striking and beautiful in Kayes. The ***grande mosquée***, for instance, is a conventional, white, concrete structure in the market area.

Walk past the post office westwards along Avenue Magdeburg to find **artisans** selling their work between the road and the riverbank: calabashes, urns and pestles used for pounding millet; look for blacksmiths recycling old car parts and metal trunks made out of old oildrums. Every day is market day in Kayes (except Sunday when it is kept at a minimum for cleaning). A buzzing hub of a place selling vegetables, spices, beads, pots, old shoes, massive fish and smouldering cauldrons of local food. Although not a major problem, it's prudent to keep an eye on your pockets and carry bags in front of you.

The heat and dryness of Kayes make the **River Senegal** a favourite spot for man and beast alike. Walk down to the causeway to see people bathing, washing clothes, animals and cars, or simply sitting under the shade of one of the giant pillars of the new bridge.

The people of Kayes are friendly and open and always ready for a chat. It won't be long before someone has engaged you in a conversation; it may always be the same questions but it never seems boring! The pirogue workshops down by the old bridge are a particularly pleasant place to spend a morning either watching them skilfully craft boats from huge bits of wood or unloading boats laden down with bananas from Médine or watermelons from Félou.

Though the River Senegal is very beautiful, it's not recommended to swim in it. Cases are rare but there is bilharzia present.

Across the river and on the right bank in the new quarter of Kayes N'Di there is a **sheep and goat market** at sunset.

EXCURSIONS FROM KAYES

MÉDINE Today, Médine is more or less how it started out: a small, quiet Khassonké village surrounded by mango groves on the banks of the River Senegal. The only difference between now and when it was founded in 1826 is the presence of a **fortress** by the French in 1855 to protect important commercial interests in the area. For at this time Médine was the capital of Sambala's Khasso state (see page 269) and one of El Hadj Omar's early military targets as he began his march east from the Fouta Djallon. The fortress proved its worth in 1857, when it withstood a siege by Omar, and later in 1878, it served as a base for French troops as they launched a decisive offensive against the Khasso allies of the Tukulor.

The fortress has recently been restored, along with several cannons and various other peripheral buildings related to Médine's colonial past – the old railway station and courthouse, for example. A guide is compulsory in Médine and although the village is sparsely populated and few people venture out during the hottest parts of the day, they have a habit of appearing from nowhere when the scent of tourists is in the air. Expect to pay CFA10,000–15,000 per day.

Getting there Médine is about 12km from Kayes. Walking is an option, but only during the day; hyenas come out after dusk and are known to attack humans. A taxi from Kayes will cost CFA10,000. An alternative is to travel by donkey and cart. The journey takes one to two hours and costs around CFA10,000–15,000 return or CFA1,000 if you hitch a ride in someone else's vehicle. The most pleasant way to get there is by pirogue. It's a two-hour journey, but they tend to leave in the early afternoon from Kayes and return the next morning when most people come in for the market. The fare is approximately CFA500 or you can charter your own for around CFA30,000. The only other alternative is a dusty and crowded *bâchée* ride. Once again, they leave in the afternoons from the marketplace in Kayes and return the following morning (CFA1,000 each way). The problem with public transport to Médine is self-evident: it is difficult to do the round trip on the same day.

Where to stay Due to the lack of public transport, you might consider an overnight stay. Bréhima Sissoko (**m** *6699 31 55;* **e** *bsissoko62@yahoo.fr*), the English-speaking official guide, lives in Médine and offers accommodation in his own home. Mattresses and mosquito nets are provided and you can choose between fish, pigeon or duck for dinner. He doesn't charge for his hospitality but a 'gift' of at least CFA5,000 would be recommended.

There are some lovely spots along the river, so camping for the night is also an option. If you do, watch out for waders and small riverbank rodents. Travellers with their own transport often have the same idea, so you may be able to hitch a lift and borrow some water – but don't count on it.

A good time to visit is during the Kayes Cultural Festival in February every year. One day is dedicated to Médine with traditional site visits and performances of music and dance (see *Chapter 2, Festivals*, page 91).

WATERFALLS One of the most popular spots for camping is by the **Chutes du Félou**, a small waterfall created by a hydro-electric project 3km past Médine. The *bâchée* from Kayes passes Félou and continues on to Lontou. Much more impressive, however, are 'Mali's Niagara Falls', the **Chutes de Gouina**, known as 'the waterfalls that sing', which are about 80km from Kayes. However, until the local train resumes its service, allowing travellers to get off at Bagoukou – some 6km from Gouina – there is no easy way to get to the falls unless you have your own reliable 4x4. In that case, follow the track, which runs roughly parallel to the railway track. After a while, the sandy track becomes a pot-holed tarred road, and where the tar diverts from the river, Gouina (and Mahina and Bafoulabé) is soberly signposted to the right. The track is in a dilapidated state, but word has it that at some point even this stretch will be upgraded. Without a vehicle, you need plenty of time, energy and determination to get to Gouina. If hitching a ride doesn't work – try waiting where the sandy road starts, to the left of the railway track, and keep your hopes up – your only options may be to rent a donkey cart or walk. In either case you should be fully self-supporting. The Festival de Gouina, is held at the waterfalls in February every year, a three-day celebration of dancing and feasting (see *Chapter 2*, *Festivals*, page 92 for more details).

BETWEEN KAYES AND KITA

Not too long ago, the only feasible way to travel to Bamako by road was via Mahina, Manantali and Kita. It was considered an expedition rather than an ordinary journey. The Kita to Manantali stretch is being upgraded and should have been finished by early 2009 but the section between Kayes and Manantali must be considered a bottleneck, which can only be tackled by 4x4 with high clearance. With more comfortable options between Kayes and Bamako to choose from, this route – which still takes up to two days – need no longer be considered an unavoidable obstacle. As things stand, however, you could now opt for this road simply because there is a lot to be seen along the way, not least the chimpanzees who are thinly distributed over the catchment area of the Manantali Dam.

BAFOULABÉ One of the principal agglomerations between Kayes and Kita is Bafoulabé. The name of this town ('where two rivers meet') reflects exactly where it is located: at the confluence of the rivers Bafing and Bakoye. The murky waters of the former ('Black River') mix with the clearer waters of the latter ('White River') to produce the grey waters of the Senegal, Mali's second great waterway. Apart from this claim to fame, Bafoulabé is also noted for its large hippopotamus population.

There is a new tarred road programmed to Bafoulabé, which has been financed, but work hasn't started yet. So for now, to get to Bafoulabé, choose between the signposted sandy track mentioned above or stick to the pot-holed tar, which is only marginally better. This road eventually leads to a ferry across the Bakoye. The fare per vehicle is around CFA2,500–5,000, depending on the number of vehicles, as the total fare is shared. After 18.00, when the ferry service has stopped, expect to pay at least CFA1,000 to have the ferryman – who lives at the other side of the river – fetched, and another CFA12,000–15,000 to persuade him to take you across.

Where to stay The **Campement le Loisir** is located at the other end of Bafoulabé, and has basic but adequate rooms at CFA4,000 (single) or CFA6,000 (double). Camping costs CFA2,000 per person. There is an ample supply of chilled beers and soft drinks, but meals have to be ordered in advance. As the *campement* is located on the banks of the river Bafing, the real attraction of this place must be the hippopotamuses that are regularly spotted just behind the premises. They are creatures of habit, so look out for them around 06.00 and 17.00.

MAHINA The two roads coming from Kayes merge in Mahina, which is always a lively town, but even more so on market day (Monday). There are three hotels to choose from: the **Hotel Wayowananko**, **Hotel Bafing** and **Hotel Djeneba**. **Bar Dancing Montana**, its entrance hidden between market stalls, also has one room at CFA2,000.

The easiest option to proceed to Manantali is to cross the bridge, which happens to be the railway bridge. Get permission from the *chef de gare* first, as he knows more or less when the next train is due to cross the bridge and you will be using the same single track. He has developed the habit of expecting some money or a gift in return, but officially there is no fee to be paid.

MANANTALI Before the completion of the dam in 1988, Manantali was a small village of about 200 people. Nowadays, its population has swelled to around 15,000 and there is a lake here as big as the one at Geneva. Work on the dam was started in 1982 on the river Bafing as part of a wider development plan for the River Senegal. The aim was to provide much of the electricity for Mali, Senegal and Mauritania and, provided that the water is high enough, the hydro-electric plant at Manantali has a capacity of 800MW – which, in layman's terms, is very, very big!

The lake used to be renowned for its hippopotamus population. However, in recent years the animals have not been spotted anywhere near the dam. Although the water may look very appealling for swimming, note that it is very likely to be infected with bilharzia (see page 59).

Getting around It is possible to explore the lake by *pinasse*. In October 2003, John Kupiec travelled in this region and has supplied a lot of the following information. He took a *pinasse* which was equipped with ice chests for fish. For CFA5,000 the *pinassier* took him to the southern end of the lake in about three hours, only to continue pootling about at that far end for another 15 hours. During this time the *pinasse* halted repeatedly to buy and sell merchandise – mainly fish. Since the journey continued throughout the night, falling asleep and waking up by the light of torches, with people wading or paddling around the *pinasse*, created a 'dreamy, mysterious aura' which John Kupiec describes as the best part of this trip. He ended up staying at a family home for a night, and returned to Manantali with the same *pinasse* the following day, at no extra charge.

As a sign of its contemporary importance, a new road linking Manantali to Kita was completed in 1998, making it one of the first places in the region to be accessible to something other than a train (see *Getting there and away*, page 273).

Where to stay There are two places to stay in Manatali. **Bar Restaurant Bougouba Sewese** offers basic rooms with a fan at CFA6,000, or a mattress on the floor at CFA5,000. The restaurant serves tender steak and other tasty meals, but they may take a while to be prepared. On Fridays and Saturdays, the nightclub opens its doors and plays disco and African music. The **Mission Catholique** also has some rooms available.

Other practicalities The only bank is a BDM bank with a Western Union office. Manantali has a post office and a police station.

KOUNDIAN AND THE RÉSERVE DU PARC NATIONAL DU BAFING Although there is some sort of public transport from Manantali to Koundian, John Kupiec decided to walk.

The first part of this walk was composed of many small hamlets/villages each having water. On two occasions I encountered lines of women working in the fields. There was wonderful hootin' hollerin' singing. I stayed on the road until somebody took me to them. I was met with warmth and hospitality along this stretch. Getting closer to Koundian the road curves around and downhill to a tropical setting. I surprised a bunch of brown monkeys who traversed an escarpment. I slept just off the road here (there are two big sandy clearings large enough for vehicles to camp). I heard the screeching and murmuring of the monkeys all night long, along with the sound of fruit dropping to the ground with a thud.

From Koundian, the road goes to **Makandougou**, passing by the villages of Foret and Kofe. There are sections with tricky deviations, which can result in a lot of asking directions and backtracking. From Makandougou it is another 25km to the **Réserve du Parc National du Bafing**, where a ranger may take you in search of chimpanzees. (Although John spotted some chimpanzees near Foret, his quest into the reserve with a ranger was unsuccessful in this respect.) From here continue to **Nanifara** and **Kéniéba**. There is no obvious means of public transport along this route.

For more information on the Réserve du Parc National du Bafing, enquire at the Ministère de l'Environnement (☎ *2122 24 98*), opposite the National Museum in Bamako.

KÉNIÉBA The *cercle* of Kéniéba in the extreme southwestern part of the region is known for its picturesque scenery, mesas, mountains and lions, which have been known to venture into the town of Kéniéba itself. This is where Mali's other major chain of cliffs, the **Tambaoura Escarpment**, is to be found.

To the west the famous Bambouk gold fields stretch into Senegal. Gold mining still takes place at **Sadiola**, a town on the track linking Kayes and Kéniéba. Public transport from Kéniéba to Kayes usually comes in the form of *camions*. To join the crowd in the back costs CFA5,000, while a shared seat-with-a-view in the cabin costs CFA7,500. The fare for the journey to Bamako – also by truck – is CFA12,000.

KITA

Kita, 185km from Bamako, is a good place to break the train journey between the capital and Kayes. The *cercle* of Kita is of considerable economic importance and consequently its main town is second only to Kayes in terms of the quality of its infrastructure and facilities for visitors. However, Kita offers more than just a comfortable bed for the night – although this alone is an adequate draw after an arduous day on a train!

For one of Mali's main towns, Kita is remarkably calm and guides are conspicuous by their absence. This is also one of the richer and more fertile areas of the region, where the Guinean forests still hold sway over the encroaching sands of the desert.

GETTING THERE AND AWAY

By train Kita is the main stop between Bamako and Kayes. Nearer to the capital (the journey takes about five hours) than Kayes (at least seven hours from Kita), there are four trains passing in either direction every week. The Bamako–Dakar express arrives on Wednesdays from Bamako, and returns from Dakar on Sundays. (For more information, the departure schedule and fares, see *Chapter 2, Getting around*.)

By road Thanks to a new road completed by the Germans in 1998, it takes *bâchées* about four hours to cover the 150km to the famous dam at Manantali. They leave when full from two departure points near the town hall and near the railway station, and cost CFA3,500. The journey to Kéniéba takes at least ten hours by 4x4 and costs CFA12,500 for a seat in the back and CFA15,000 for a shared front seat. Minibuses and even big *camion* buses (Simbo Voyages) leave at least three times a day for Bamako (5–6 hours; CFA2,500). Simbo Voyages also has some departures

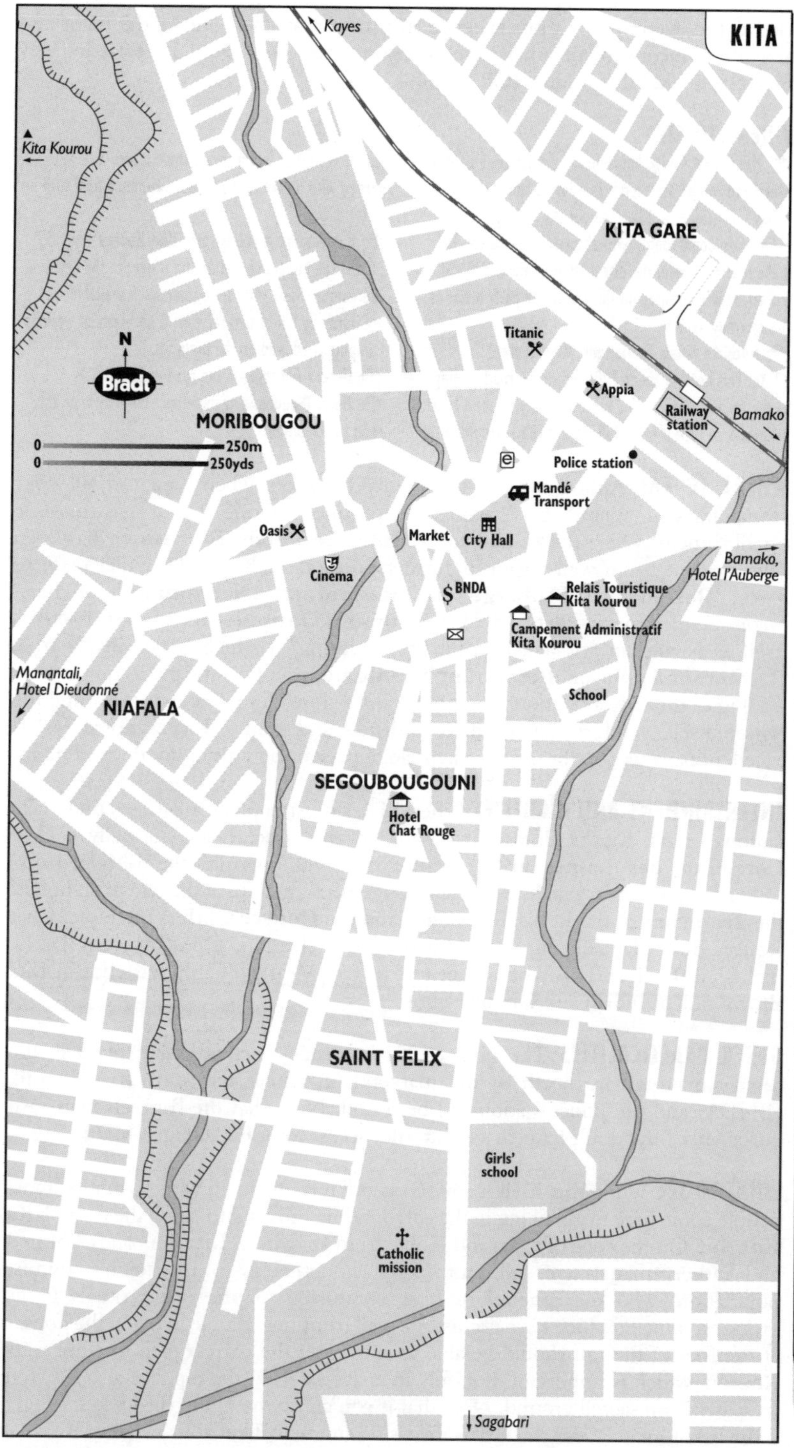

KITA
Kayes
Kita Kourou
KITA GARE
N
Bradt
MORIBOUGOU
0 250m
0 250yds
Titanic
Appia
Railway station
Bamako
Police station
Mandé Transport
Oasis
Market
City Hall
Cinema
BNDA
Relais Touristique Kita Kourou
Bamako, Hotel l'Auberge
Campement Administratif Kita Kourou
Manantali, Hotel Dieudonné
NIAFALA
School
SEGOUBOUGOUNI
Hotel Chat Rouge
SAINT FELIX
Girls' school
Catholic mission
Sagabari

late in the evening, for those who do not mind travelling during the night and arriving at inconvenient times. Gana transport has buses every day for a journey they claim takes three hours (CFA2,500).

WHERE TO STAY

Hotel Chat Rouge This hotel – the establishment to which you will be escorted if there is no room at the Relais Touristique – charges about the same priceas Le Relais for gloomy rooms with absolutely no appeal. To make matters worse, the discothèque in the courtyard will virtually guarantee no sleep until the early hours of the morning. $$

Hotel Le Relais Touristique 'Kita Kourou' 2157 32 46. This hotel is about 200m down the road leading to the railway station. This is quite clearly the best hotel in town & as such is often full. Rooms come with AC or a fan, TV & cans of insect spray. There is also a large garden with plenty of shade, & a swimming pool with no water in it. $$

Campement Administratif 'Kita Kourou' 2157 30 46. The budget option in Kita is next to the Relais Touristique. Basic rooms are sometimes available, but are normally full of civil servants & government workers. Camping is allowed on the premises. $

Hotel l'Auberge On the road to Bamako. $

Hotel Dieudonné At the other end of Kita, on the road to Manantali. $

WHERE TO EAT Although there are plenty of places where you can fill your stomach, you would be wasting your time looking for a gastronomic establishment. Once the restaurant at **Hotel Le Relais Touristique** has been renovated, it could well regain its former position as the most popular place in town. **Restaurant l'Auberge** and **Restaurant Dieudonné** have been recommended by travellers, while **Restaurant l'Oasis** near the market describes itself as having *un peu de tout* (a bit of everything) – which is not always true. **Restaurant Appia** and **Restaurant Titanic** are two of several places on the road leading to the railway station where you can sit down for a bite to eat. Around the station itself, vendors sell bread, cold drinks and fruit – Kita is noted for its excellent papayas – to the captive clientele of passengers waiting for delayed trains.

ENTERTAINMENT AND NIGHTLIFE When Mali's most popular musicians undertake national tours, Kita is almost always visited and concerts are normally held at **Carrefour des Jeunes** in the centre of town opposite the BNDA bank. Otherwise, the town's nightlife is centred on the nightclubs at the two main hotels: the **Tropicana** at the Relais Touristique and the **Denver Club** at the Hotel Chat Rouge. Both play African music and the cover charge is CFA2,000. On 'ladies' nights' at the Tropicana women get in for free. Meanwhile, the **cinema** in Kita shows violent Indian and Oriental films.

OTHER PRACTICALITIES The bulk of Kita's business activity takes place in the town's main square north of the marketplace, where the post office, a bank (BNDA) and the police station can be found. Note that the bank changes cash euros only. Sirandou Net provides internet access for CFA2,000 per hour.

WHAT TO SEE While Kita itself is a pleasant and relaxing town with no guides, most people come here to go hiking in the surrounding hills and to climb the 617m **Kita Kourou**. On the edge of town and visible from anywhere, Kita Kourou is a rugged and rather unattractive hill, but sacred nonetheless to the town's animist population, who for generations have conducted sacrifices and rituals in its grottoes, some of which have prehistoric wall paintings. People living in the houses at the foot of the hill should be able to show you the correct path to climb Kita Kourou, which is important, not only to arrive safely at the top, but also to avoid trespassing on sacred ground. Note that if you climb the hill in the early morning – the best time to avoid the heat – the rising sun will affect your views of Kita.

ELSEWHERE IN THE REGION

PARC NATIONAL DE LA BOUCLE DU BAOULÉ The Parc National de la Boucle du Baoulé (Baoulé Bend National Park), which is situated northeast of Kita and overlaps the administrative regions of Kayes and Koulikoro, is Mali's largest **game reserve**. However, before wildlife enthusiasts get too excited, much of the fauna which once roamed around the well-watered forests in the bend of the river Baoulé has disappeared, largely as a result of indiscriminate hunting, particularly by the military during the Traoré regime. Of the animals still remaining, monkeys are probably easiest to see. Baboons apparently also exist, hippos are found at various spots along the river, and gazelles, hyenas, buffaloes and the occasional lion might also be present. Elephants, giraffes and sadly even chimpanzees have not been spotted in years. In any case, look for wildlife in one of the three reserves within the boundaries of the national park: Kongosambougou, Fina and Badinko; but don't expect an east African-style safari.

In fact, the Parc National de la Boucle du Baoulé is better known these days for its abundance of **archaeological remains**. Although the area is sparsely populated today, over 200 archaeological sites ranging from the Stone Age to the colonial period prove that it was once densely populated. There are rock paintings and cave dwellings of hunter-gatherers from the Neolithic era (see *Chapter 1, Early times*, page 13), as well as ancient tombs, burial grounds and colonial forts. The map on page 270 indicates the zones where many of these archaeological remains are situated.

Practicalities Please note that at the time of writing, no updated map to the national park was available. However, a new map with more detailed information on the *pistes*, *campements* and the different sections of the national park was made available a few years ago. To get this map, go to the Ministère de l'Environnement (☎ *2122 24 98*) which is located opposite the National Museum in Bamako. When not available from stock, it will be printed out for you to be picked up the following day. Expect the charge to be around CFA17,500. If you are planning to go to the Parc National de la Boucle du Baoulé, this is the place to go anyway for general information and suggestions on itineraries, as within the boundaries of the national park you'll find next to nothing in terms of general information.

Most visitors enter the national park via **Faladié**, but there are other tracks leading into the park where you will have to report at the Poste de Contrôle. This is where you must register and pick up a guide; either a local farmer who should know the area inside-out (CFA7,500/day) or an *agent des eaux et forêts* or ranger (CFA4,000/day). The latter has the right to carry a weapon, and this will allow you more freedom: with an armed guide you may roam more deeply into the park, and even camp outside the villages or *campements*. **Campement Baoulé** is only 50km from Bamako, and is located in the zone known as Koundou, where there is a French fort and the largest rock dwelling in the national park. Rooms cost CFA5,000, while camping is free of charge. Other *campements* are in **Madina**, **Missira** and **Kourouninkoto**, but access is more difficult. This is not to say that access to any part of the park is easy, and you will need to have or hire your own 4x4 vehicle.

Well away from the *campements*, villagers will put you up for the night at a nominal charge. Unless you are happy to eat what they are having, you should bring your own supplies. On leaving the park, you must pay a hefty entrance fee (CFA7,500/day). The reason why you you do not have to pay in advance is to allow you to make up your mind about the itinerary and the length of your stay. By the same token, you are not obliged to exit the park where you entered.

PARC NATIONAL DE LA BOUCLE DU BAOULE

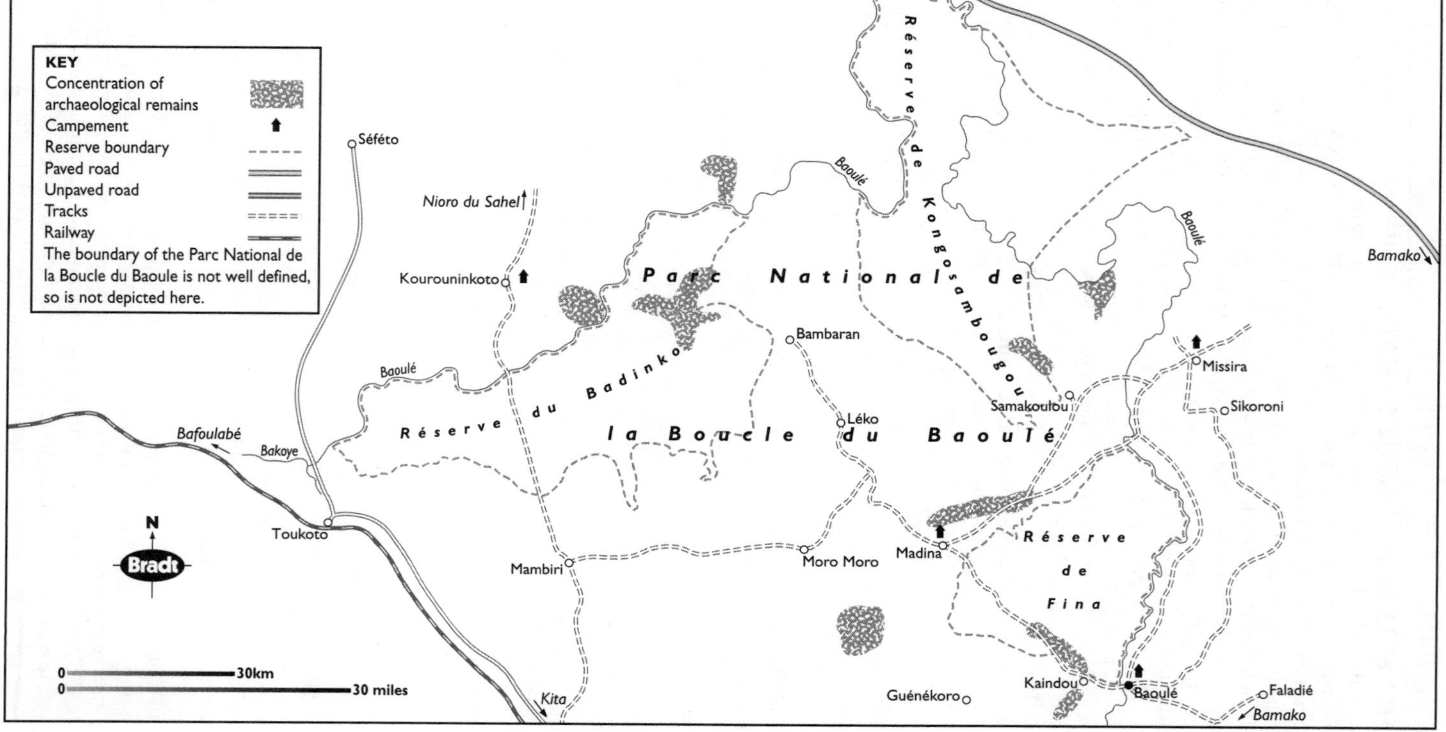
KEY
Concentration of archaeological remains
Campement
Reserve boundary
Paved road
Unpaved road
Tracks
Railway
The boundary of the Parc National de la Boucle du Baoule is not well defined, so is not depicted here.
Diema
Bamako
Réserve de Kongosambougou
Parc National de la Boucle du Baoulé
Réserve du Badinko
Réserve de Fina
Baoulé
Bakoye
Séféto
Nioro du Sahel
Kourouninkoto
Bambaran
Léko
Samakoulou
Missira
Sikoroni
Bafoulabé
Toukoto
Mambiri
Moro Moro
Madina
Guénékoro
Kaindou
Faladié
Kita
N
Bradt
0
30km
0
30 miles

YÉLIMANÉ AND NIORO DU SAHEL Two towns northeast of Kayes, Yélimané and Nioro du Sahel, were both former capitals of the Bambara kingdom of Kaarta (see page 271). Nowadays, they are dusty Sahelian towns kept going by livestock raising and subsistence farming. Although geographically these towns are twinned by remoteness, they could hardly be more isolated from each other. While the roads linking Yélimané and Nioro du Sahel to bigger towns – like Kayes and Diéma – have been upgraded, certain sections between the two towns have been left to deteriorate to such a degree that even walking between them has become problematic.

Practicalities To get to Yélimané (CFA12,500), look for Diema Transport at the Gare Routière du Nouveau Marché Médine in Bamako. There are two weekly departures (Mondays and Thursdays). Trucks (CFA6,500) and buses or converted trucks (CFA10,000) for Nioro du Sahel leave from the same bus station. Look for Diema Transport and Mandé Transport for departures on Mondays, Thursdays and Saturdays. To travel to both towns from Kayes, see *Getting there and away*, page 273. **MAE** (☎ *2152 22 62; www.malipages.com/mae*) flies to Nioro du Sahel and Yélimané.

Contributor John Kupiec travelled in this region in 2003 and provided the following information. About 10km before reaching Yélimané, John got off where the road intersects a marshy area, in the village of Diongoulani. He made a complete circuit of the lake (and recommends it for birdwatching), visiting the mud village of Fonga on the way. **Yélimané**, another good place for birdwatching, is past the mosque and the cemetery, where there is a marshy area with trees. You can stay at the Maison de l'Amitié, which has rooms at CFA3,000 (with private shower) and CFA1,500 (without shower). Bar Nightclub le Bambeau is not far from the Mission Catholique, while Buvette Lafia serves chilled beer and not much else.

From Yélimané, John tried to travel to Nioro du Sahel directly: 'There does seem to be a daily vehicle to Kirane, but then it's another 75km to Nioro. This may not even be walkable'; and so he backtracked to Kayes to find transport to **Nioro du Sahel**. This desert town has a mosque, and though you may catch a glimpse of the interior by peering over the wall, it is not open to non-Muslims. There are two *campements*: Restaurant Bar Tamare, with a defunct restaurant but rooms at CFA2,000, and the Complexe Culturelle Jamana, which is frequented by prostitutes. It is located out of the centre on the road to Kayes. NB Please bear in mind that this information is now six years old and may have changed.

EXPERIENCE
Feel the adventure
There's a whole world of extraordinary experiences just waiting to be discovered in our incredible collection of adventurous tours. Choose from over 500 trips to more than 130 countries – each led by well-travelled tour leaders with a passion for out-of-the-ordinary travel.
Order any of the following brochures
■ Worldwide ■ Family Adventures
■ Cycle
■ Short Breaks ■ Beyond
■ History Tours ■ Eclipse
■ School Adventures ■ Volunteer
0844 499 0901
EXPLORE.CO.UK
EXPLORE!
AITO
THE ASSOCIATION OF INDEPENDENT TOUR OPERATORS
Ref. BRADT

Appendix I

LANGUAGE

BAMBARA Bambara is one of several Manding or Mande languages spoken in varying degrees in 11 west African countries. In Mali it is the lingua franca of trade and administration, although travellers should note that it is not understood all over the country. In this respect, a working knowledge of French might be more useful than proficiency in Bambara. A smattering of the local language, however, demonstrates respect for your hosts and can be fun to practise on unsuspecting Bambaraphones.

Pronunciation The Bambara alphabet is a mixture of the French alphabet and the International Phonetic Alphabet conceived by Paul Dassy and Daniel Jones between 1886 and 1900. As far as pronunciation is concerned, the following letters might need clarifying:

c	**tch**é
é	closed (like f**é**e in French)
è	open (like f**ai**t in French)
g	**gué**
j	**di**é
ò	closed (like s**au**t in French)
u	c**ou** in French

Essentials

Welcome	*i ni sè*	Please	*a ke to*
Hello	*i ni sògòma/i ni ce*	No, thank you	*akain*
Good evening	*i ni wula*	Yes, please	*awò o be dja njè*
Good night	*i ni su*	Maybe	*a ma don*
Goodbye	*kambufo* (to a person leaving)	Why?	*mun ka ma?*
		When?	*uma ju mè?*
Goodbye	*kambè* (when you are leaving)	Tonight	*bi wula/bi su*
		This morning	*bi sògòma*
How are you?	*i ka kènè wa?*	Today	*bi*
I am fine/all is well	*toorò té*	Tomorrow	*sini*
All is very well	*toorò si té*	Yesterday	*kunu*
Thank you	*i ni ce*	Next week	*dogo kunwèrè*
yes	*òwò*	What is your name?	*i togo?*
no	*ayi*	My name is…	*n'togo…*
OK	*a njé na*		

I am British (American)	*ne ye anglais (américain) ye*
I am French (Dutch)	*ne ye français (hollandi) ye*
I am…	*m'bi… /n'bè…*
Do you speak English?	*i bi angèlèkan men wa?*

What time is it?	*leer jumen be yên?/heure jumé be?*
When is the car/bus leaving?	*mobili be taa heure jumé?*
We are leaving	*a be taa*
I am going to…	*n'be taa…*
I arrived from…	*n'be bò…*
Where is…? …	*bè min?*
Where is the road to…?	*…sira bè min?*
Where is the bus station?	*mobili sera bè min?*
Where is the train station?	*train gare bè min?*
Where is the bank (toilet)?	*banki (njekèn) bè min?*
There is no water	*ji tè*
Do you have…?	*…bi yan wa?*
How much?	*joli? joli don?*
I don't have any change	*waarime sen tè*
It is too expensive	*a sogo ka cha*
Do you have rice?	*malo be i bolo wa?*
Do you have milk?	*nono be i bolo wa?*
(Do you have) sugar?	*sukara (be i bolo wa)?*
…fruit? …hot water?	*yiri de…? ji kalan…?*
…drinks? …water? …beer?	*boisson…? ji…? dolo…?*
Do you have mineral water?	*tubabu ji b'i bolo wa?*
I don't eat meat/fish	*n'e tè sogo/djègè dun*
I am feeling ill	*n'man kènè*
I have a stomach ache	*n'kònò bè dimi*
I have toothache	*n'da be dimi*
I am looking for a doctor	*n'be taa docteur so la*
Where is the dentist?	*njigilana be mi?*
Where is the pharmacy?	*pharmacie be mi?*

Numbers

1	*kelen*	11	*tan ni kélén*
2	*fla*	12	*tan ni fla*
3	*saba*	20	*mugan*
4	*naani*	30	*mugan ni tan* or *bi saba*
5	*duurun*	40	*bi naani*
6	*wooro*	50	*bi duurun*
7	*wolonfla*	100	*keme*
8	*seegin*	500	*keme duurun*
9	*kononto*	1,000	*ba kelen*
10	*tan*		

FRENCH In terms of getting by and getting things done with your foreign language skills, French will be more useful than Bambara. Moreover, the fact that it is taught in most Western schools should make it easier to master – or at least mimic! – than a completely alien African language.

Pronunciation The key to pronouncing French is knowing which letters not to pronounce. Otherwise, a selection of the more important general rules of pronunciation is as follows:

a	c**a**t
c	**s** before e, i and y; **k** before a, o and u
ç	**s**
ch	**sh**oe

é	long **a**
è	short **e**
g	vi**s**ion before e, i and y; **g**un before a, o and u
h	silent
i	m**ee**t
j	vi**s**ion
o	r**o**t
ou	Timbukt**oo**
qu	**k**
r	a mix between an **r** and a **ch** in loch
s	**z** between vowels; silent at the end of words
th	**t**
u	like an English **e** said with pursed lips
w	usually **w**; occasionally **v** (eg 'wagon')
x	**ks** before most consonants; **gz** before most vowels; silent at the end of words

Essentials

Hello	*Bonjour (day); bonsoir (evening)*
How are you?	*Comment allez-vous?*
Please	*S'il vous plaît*
Thank you	*Merci*
Goodbye	*Au revoir*
My name is…	*Je m'appelle…*
I am…	*Je suis…*
Where is…?	*Où est…?*
Do you have…?	*Est-ce-que vous avez…?*
Can you…?	*Est-ce-que vous pouvez…?*
Can I…?	*Est-ce-que je peux…?*
I would like…	*Je voudrais…*
I need…	*J'ai besoin de…*
How much?	*C'est combien?*
What time is it?	*Quelle heure est-il?*
Do you speak English?	*Parlez-vous anglais?*

Numbers

0	*zéro*	17	*dix-sept*
1	*un/une*	18	*dix-huit*
2	*deux*	19	*dix-neuf*
3	*trois*	20	*vingt*
4	*quatre*	21	*vingt-et-un*
5	*cinq*	22	*vingt-deux*
6	*six*	30	*trente*
7	*sept*	40	*quarante*
8	*huit*	50	*cinquante*
9	*neuf*	60	*soixante*
10	*dix*	70	*soixante-dix*
11	*onze*	80	*quatre-vingt*
12	*douze*	90	*quatre-vingt-dix*
13	*treize*	100	*cent*
14	*quatorze*	500	*cinq cents*
15	*quinze*	1,000	*mille*
16	*seize*		

Days

Monday	*lundi*	Friday	*vendredi*
Tuesday	*mardi*	Saturday	*samedi*
Wednesday	*mercredi*	Sunday	*dimanche*
Thursday	*jeudi*		

Months

January	*janvier*	July	*juillet*
February	*février*	August	*août*
March	*mars*	September	*septembre*
April	*avril*	October	*octobre*
May	*mai*	November	*novembre*
June	*juin*	December	*décembre*

Other useful words

afternoon	*après-midi*	morning	*matin*
bed	*lit*	passport	*passport*
bread	*pain*	post office	*bureau de poste*
breakfast	*petit déjeuner*	rice	*riz*
bus station	*gare routière*	river	*fleuve*
cheap	*bon marché*	room	*chambre*
chicken	*poulet*	street	*rue*
day	*jour*	thing	*chose*
diarrhoea	*diarrhée*	today	*aujourd'hui*
early	*tôt*	tomorrow	*demain*
eat	*manger*	town	*ville*
egg	*œuf*	United States	*États-Unis*
English	*anglais*	very	*très*
expensive	*cher*	water	*eau*
fish	*poisson*	what?	*quoi?*
go	*aller*	when?	*quand?*
good	*bon*	where?	*où?*
how	*comment*	which?	*quel?*
hungry	*faim*	who?	*qui?*
late	*tard*	with	*avec*
man	*homme*	woman	*femme*
money	*argent*		

TAMASHEQ Tamasheq is a Berber language or family of closely related languages spoken by the nomadic Tuareg in the desert regions of Mali, Niger, Algeria, Libya and Burkina Faso. The traditional writing is the indigenous Tifinagh; the second-oldest African alphabet, after Amharic in Ethiopia.

I wasn't able to find an official research on pronunciation of Tamasheq – it's a little-studied language. But any effort you make to try and speak the language in the desert, especially at the desert festival, will be greatly appreciated and met with much delighted surprise.

It sounds pretty much as it reads. The only advice I can offer is that a 'g' is pronounced as a throaty 'r' and 'kh' as a guttural 'h'.

Essentials

Hello	*Taglassad*
How are you?	*Ma Idjane? Ou Madar tolahad (masculine)/ Madar tolaham? (plural)*
I am fine	*Alkher ghass*

yes	*Iyya*
no	*Kala*
OK	*Ikna*
Please	*Anchahid*
Thank you	*Elkher adjene*
Goodbye	*Inamadaradagh*
My name is	*Issimine Suzanne*
I am	*Nak*
Where is?	*Indeke dil la?*
I would like	*Arhegh*
How much?	*Manikétt?*
I am lost	*Aba-hi*
I feel ill	*Ofrayagh ou Idiarawahi haratt*

Numbers

0	*wala*	20	*sanatatt tam-marwene*
1	*diyane*	30	*karadatt tam-marwene*
2	*dissine*	40	*akozatt tam-marwene*
3	*karad*	50	*samossatt tam-marwene*
4	*akoz*	60	*sadissatt Tam-marwene*
5	*samoss*	70	*assayatt tam-marwene*
6	*sadiss*	80	*attamatt tam-marwene*
7	*ass-ssa*	90	*taz zayyatt tam-marwene*
8	*at-tam*	100	*temedde*
9	*taz-za*	500	*samossatt tammadd*
10	*maraw*	1,000	*effadd*

Days

Monday	*Litni*	Friday	*Aljoumkatt*
Tuesday	*Altanata*	Saturday	*Issibitt*
Wednesday	*Allarba*	Sunday	*Alhadd*
Thursday	*Akkamiss*		

Months

January	*Younayar*	July	*Youl-Youl*
February	*Febrayar*	August	*Gouchatt*
March	*Mariss*	September	*Choutambar*
April	*Ibril*	October	*Ouktoubar*
May	*Maaya*	November	*Nouvambar*
June	*Youn-Youn*	December	*Doujambar*

Other useful words and phrases

breakfast	*tadjoumdjemt*	I'm hungry	*Idjlakagh ou Issigassassagh*
bus or car	*torraft*		
camel	*amniss*	room	*tagachammt*
chicken	*ekkaz*	today	*achili*
English	*Anglezi (masculine), Tanglesitt (feminine)*	tomorrow	*achik-ka*
		USA	*Amrik*
goat	*taghatt*	water	*aman*

Appendix 2

FURTHER INFORMATION

BOOKS

Background

Bovill, E W *The Golden Trade of the Moors* Oxford Paperbacks, 2nd edition, 1970. A standard history of west Africa.

Griaule, Marcel *Conversations With Ogotemmêli: An Introduction to Dogon Religious Ideas* Oxford University Press, 1977. A seminal work about the Dogon.

Griaule, Marcel *The Pale Fox* Continuum Foundation, 1986. Another seminal work about the Dogon.

Imperato, Pascal James *Mali: A Search for Direction* Westview Press, 1989. Everything you ever wanted to know about Mali.

Imperato, Pascal James *Historical Dictionary of Mali* Scarecrow Press, 1996. Contains a comprehensive bibliography.

Levtzion, Nehemia and Spaulding, Jay *Medieval West Africa: Views from Arab Scholars and Merchants* Markus Wiener, 2002. Writings of geographers and chroniclers in the Muslim world between the 8th and 15th centuries.

Niané, Djibril Tamsir *Sundiata: An Epic of Old Mali* Longman, 1965. An English translation of a description of Soundiata Keita by a Malian author (see *Chapter 1, the Mali Empire*, page 15).

Pateaux, Agnes *Dogon: People of the Cliffs (Imago Mundi)* Five Continents, 1999. Beautiful photographs capturing the essence of the Dogon people of Mali.

Riesman, Paul *Freedom in Fulani Social Life: An Introspective Ethnography* University of Chicago Press; New edition 1998. Well-written and insightful account of Fulani life.

Van Beek, W E A *Dogon: Africa's People of the Cliffs* Harry N. Abrams Inc, 2001. A photographic book by photojournalist Stephenie Hollyman and anthropologist van Beek demonstrating how geography has protected and dictated the culture of the intensely spiritual Dogon.

Books in French

Andriamirado, Sennen *Le Mali Aujourd'hui* Les éditions j a, 1985. Not really for practical travel in Mali, but with good pictures and background information on all of the country's regions.

Bedaux, R et al *L'Architecture de Djenné* Rijksmuseum voor Volkenkunde Leiden, 2003. Apart from an overview about the architecture of Djenné, this is a revealing report on the restoration project that took place between 1997 and 2004.

Benoist, Joseph-Roger de *Le Mali* Editions L'Harmattan, 1998

Clark, Dr Bill *Mammifères – Reptiles et Oiseaux du Mali* IFAW 2004 An informative book with pictures and explanations of all Mali's mammals and birds. For further information or to order copies **e** amepane@yahoo.fr.

Gardi, Bernard et al *Djenné, il y a cent ans* KIT Publications, 1994. A photograph album with some of the first pictures and postcards of Djenné from its colonial period.

Gaudio, Attilio *Le Mali* Editions Karthala, 1988
Guide des Arts du Mali Has information on all Mali's artists and musicians. Recommended by the OMATHO. Order from e seydonimali@afribone.net.ml.
Sissoko, Fily Dabo, *La Savane Rouge* Presses Universelles, 1962. Memoirs of the writer and politician, imprisoned and condemned to hard labour by the Malian president Modibo Keita before dying in jail in 1964.

Health

Wilson-Howarth, Dr Jane, and Ellis, Dr Matthew *Your Child Abroad: A Travel Health Guide* Bradt Travel Guides, 2005
Wilson-Howarth, Dr Jane *Bugs, Bites & Bowels* Cadogan, 2006

Literature

Condé, Maryse *Segu* Viking Penguin, 1987. A fictionalised history of the 18th and19th centuries.
de Villiers, Marq and Sheila Hirtle *Timbuktu: The Sahara's Fabled City of Gold* Walker & Company, 2007. A portrait of Timbuktu that brings the city back to life.
Ouologuem, Yambo *Bound to Violence* Harcourt Brace Jovanovich, 1971
Sembene, Ousmane *God's Bits of Wood* Presses Pockets, 1960
The above are four of the best-known contemporary Malian novels translated into English.
Kryza, Frank T *The Race for Timbuktu: In Search of Africa's City of Gold* Ecco, 2006. Kryza recreates the journeys of early 19th-century British explorers Alexander Gordon Laing and Hugh Clapperton.
Sattin, Anthony *The Gates of Africa: Death, Discovery, and the Search for Timbuktu.* St Martin's Press, 2005

Music

Eyre, Banning *In Griot Time: An American Guitarist in Mali* Serpent's Tail; New edition, 2001. An American guitarist chronicles the lives of musicians in Mali during seven months, living and studying with Djelimady.
Mande Music: Traditional and Modern Music of the Maninka and Mandinka of Western Africa Chicago University Press, 2000

Natural history

Borrow, Nik and Demey, Ron *Birds of Western Africa* Helm Identification Guide, 2001
Kingdon, Jonathan *The Kingdon Guide to African Mammals* Academic Press, 2001
Hutchinson, J and Dalziel, J M *Flora of West Tropical Africa* Volume 1, Part 2 and Volume 3, Part 1

Travel

Aebi, Ernst *Seasons of Sand* Simon & Schuster, 1993. The story of how a loft-renovator from New York transformed the remote desert settlement of Araouane into a reasonably pleasant place to live – for a while!
Barth, Heinrich *Travels and Discoveries in North and Central Africa* Frank Cass, 1965
Benanav, Michael *Men of Salt: Crossing the Sahara on the Caravan of White Gold* The Lyons Press, 2006. 40 harrowing days crossing some of the world's most unforgiving desert.
Caillié, Réné *Travels Through Central Africa to Timbuctoo* Frank Cass, 1968
Dunn, Richard E *The Adventures of Ibn Batuta: A Muslim Traveller of the 14th Century* University of California Press, 1986
Fremantle, Tom *The Road to Timbuktu* Robinson Publishing, 2005. The author, inspired by Mungo Park, makes his own journey down the River Niger.
Holloway, Kris *Monique And the Mango Rains: Two Years With a Midwife in Mali* Waveland Pr Inc, 2006. Memoir recalling the two years spent as an impressionable Peace Corps volunteer in the remote village of Nampossela in Mali.

Joris, Lieve *Mali Blues: Traveling to an African Beat* Lonely Planet Publications, 1998. The Belgian-born writer travels through Senegal, Mauritania and Mali.

Park, Mungo *Travels into the Interior of Africa* Eland Books, 2003

Trench, Richard *Forbidden Sands: A Search in the Sahara* Chicago Academy Limited, 1978. A British journalist describes his journey across the Sahara in the 1970s, with a vivid account of the salt mines at Taoudenni. Influenced Aebi when he wrote *Seasons of Sand*.

Salak, Kira *The Cruelest Journey: 600 Miles by Canoe to the Legendary City of Timbuktu* Bantam Books, 2006. The first person to successfully canoe 600 miles down the River Niger.

FILMS

With the Nomads A 120-minute documentary by Julian Richards. An intimate but unromantic portrait of Tuareg herders in the Sahara Desert (*www.julian-richards.co.uk*).

Dolce Vita Africana A 60-minute documentary directed by Cosima Spender for BBC Storyville. A portrait of the African photographer Malick Sidibe, and a journey through Malian history inspired by his iconic images.

From Hay to Timbuktu A film documenting Rosanna Westwood's, and Anne Brichto's, first trip to Mali to make the case for Hay to be twinned with Timbuktu (*www.fromhaytotimbuktu.com*).

WEBSITES

Archaeology

www.archaeology.org Go into search; article index.

Arts and culture

www.bamako-culture.org Magazine on Bamako's arts and culture (in French).

www.friendsofmali-uk.org This British organisation promotes Mali and the Malian culture through information and activities.

www.euronet.nl/users/edotter Puppetry and music anthropology, with photos, music and video.

www.moptiartisans.com An informative website on Mopti arts and crafts created by the Centre Régional de la Promotion de l'Artisanat (in English).

Development

www.usaid.gov/regions/afr/leland/malindex.htm With many links to issues concerning development.

www.irinnews.org/Africa-Country.aspx?Country=ML Humanitarian news and analysis.

www.uk.oneworld.net/guides/mali/development Exploring the issues relevant to narrowing the divide between rich and poor countries.

Facts and figures

www.cia.gov/library/publications/the-world-factbook/geos/ml.html

General information

www.afribone.com A little bit of everything, including newspaper articles, bank rates, nightlife in Bamako and much more (in French).

www.lemali.fr A detailed website on everything you need to know on politics, economy, the arts and culture, etc (in French).

www.malikounda.com News, arts and culture (in French).

Gao

www.visitgaomali.com Set up by a Peace Corps volunteer. Lots of useful information (in English).

Kidal

www.kidal.info Information on the region of Kidal.

Malian Ministry of Tourism

www.malitourisme.com Ministry of artisan and tourism's website, with agenda of events, festivals and other useful stuff. Also links to other governmental institutions (in French).

Music

www.mali-music.com K7 site with good biographies and some downloadable music.
www.djembe.com All you ever wanted to know about west Africa's most famous drum, *the djembe* (in French).

News

www.allafrica.com A pan-African news agency.
www.essor.gov.ml Daily news from Mali (in French).
www.maliweb.net News (in French).
www.africa.reuters.com/nbc/ML News agency Reuters website (in English).
www.afrol.com/countries/mali/news News (in English).

OMATHO

www.le-mali.com/omatho/index.htm Information about this office aimed at promoting and developing tourism (in French).

Overlanding

www.horizonsunlimited.com/hubb/sahara-travel-forum Good website forum with all you need to know regarding trans-Saharan travelling by bike.
www.the153club.org Club for Sahara Desert travellers, taking its name from the old Michelin 153 map of NW Africa.

Photographs

www.foto8.com/issue08/djenne01.html Photos of Crépissage by Christien Jaspars.
www.maliphotos.de/e/e_default.html Over 600 photos and lots of useful information on the region of Mopti.

River Niger

www.nationalgeographic.com/adventure/0301/photo_1.html Story and pictures about a river trip to Timbuktu.

Rock-climbing

www.reeladventure.net/mali_story.htm Story and pictures about the climbing of the Main de Fatima near Hombori.

Ségou

www.tourisme-segou.com A useful website with practical information on Ségou.

Tessalitt

www.tessalit.info Information on Tessalit (in French).

Timbuktu

www.exploretimbuktu.com Practical and cultural information on Timbuktu, set up by Miranda at Sahara Passion (in English).

Train

www.seat61.com/Senegal.htm How to travel by train in Senegal and Mali.

Tuareg issues

www.temoust.org (in French).
www.tuaregcultureandnews.blogspot.com Highlights (in English).

Yellow pages

www.malipages.com In French, but with a link to the English site.

WIN £100 CASH!

READER QUESTIONNAIRE

Send in your completed questionnaire for the chance to win £100 cash in our regular draw

All respondents may order a Bradt guide at half the UK retail price – please complete the order form overleaf.

(Entries may be posted or faxed to us, or scanned and emailed.)

We are interested in getting feedback from our readers to help us plan future Bradt guides. Please answer ALL the questions below and return the form to us in order to qualify for an entry in our regular draw.

Have you used any other Bradt guides? If so, which titles? ....

....

What other publishers' travel guides do you use regularly? ....

....

Where did you buy this guidebook? ....

What was the main purpose of your trip to Mali (or for what other reason did you read our guide)? eg: holiday/business/charity etc. ....

....

What other destinations would you like to see covered by a Bradt guide?

....

Would you like to receive our catalogue/newsletters?

YES / NO (If yes, please complete details on reverse)

If yes – by post or email? ....

Age (circle relevant category) 16–25 26–45 46–60 60+

Male/Female (delete as appropriate)

Home country ....

Please send us any comments about our guide to Mali or other Bradt Travel Guides. ....

....

....

....

Bradt Travel Guides

23 High Street, Chalfont St Peter, Bucks SL9 9QE, UK

t +44 (0)1753 893444 f +44 (0)1753 892333

e info@bradtguides.com

www.bradtguides.com

CLAIM YOUR HALF-PRICE BRADT GUIDE!

Order Form

To order your half-price copy of a Bradt guide, and to enter our prize draw to win £100 (see overleaf), please fill in the order form below, complete the questionnaire overleaf, and send it to Bradt Travel Guides by post, fax or email.

Please send me one copy of the following guide at half the UK retail price

Title	*Retail price*	*Half price*
... .	....	....

Please send the following additional guides at full UK retail price

No	*Title*	*Retail price*	*Total*
...	....	....	....
...	....	....	....
...	....	....	....

Sub total ....

Post & packing ....

(£2 per book UK; £4 per book Europe; £6 per book rest of world)

Total ....

Name ....

Address...

Tel .... Email ....

☐ I enclose a cheque for £. . . . . . . made payable to Bradt Travel Guides Ltd

☐ I would like to pay by credit card. Number: ....

Expiry date: . . . / . . . 3-digit security code (on reverse of card) . . . . .

Issue no (debit cards only) . . . . .

☐ Please add my name to your catalogue mailing list.

☐ I would be happy for you to use my name and comments in Bradt marketing material.

Send your order on this form, with the completed questionnaire, to:

Bradt Travel Guides MALI3
23 High Street, Chalfont St Peter, Bucks SL9 9QE
☎ +44 (0)1753 893444 f +44 (0)1753 892333
e info@bradtguides.com www.bradtguides.com

Bradt Travel Guides

www.bradtguides.com

Africa

Africa Overland	£15.99
Algeria	£15.99
Benin	£14.99
Botswana: Okavango, Chobe, Northern Kalahari	£15.99
Burkina Faso	£14.99
Cameroon	£15.99
Cape Verde Islands	£14.99
Congo	£15.99
Eritrea	£15.99
Ethiopia	£15.99
Gambia, The	£13.99
Ghana	£15.99
Johannesburg	£6.99
Madagascar	£15.99
Malawi	£13.99
Mali	£13.95
Mauritius, Rodrigues & Réunion	£13.99
Mozambique	£13.99
Namibia	£15.99
Niger	£14.99
Nigeria	£17.99
North Africa: Roman Coast	£15.99
Rwanda	£14.99
São Tomé & Principe	£14.99
Seychelles	£14.99
Sierra Leone	£16.99
Sudan	£13.95
Tanzania, Northern	£13.99
Tanzania	£16.99
Uganda	£15.99
Zambia	£17.99
Zanzibar	£14.99

Britain and Europe

Albania	£15.99
Armenia, Nagorno Karabagh	£14.99
Azores	£13.99
Baltic Cities	£14.99
Belarus	£14.99
Belgrade	£6.99
Bosnia & Herzegovina	£13.99
Bratislava	£9.99
Budapest	£9.99
Bulgaria	£13.99
Cork	£6.99
Croatia	£13.99
Cyprus see North Cyprus	
Czech Republic	£13.99
Dresden	£7.99
Dubrovnik	£6.99
Estonia	£13.99
Faroe Islands	£15.99
Georgia	£14.99
Helsinki	£7.99
Hungary	£14.99
Iceland	£14.99
Kosovo	£14.99
Lapland	£13.99
Latvia	£13.99
Lille	£6.99
Lithuania	£14.99
Ljubljana	£7.99
Luxembourg	£13.99
Macedonia	£14.99
Montenegro	£14.99
North Cyprus	£12.99
Paris, Lille & Brussels	£11.95
Riga	£6.99
Serbia	£14.99
Slovakia	£14.99
Slovenia	£13.99
Spitsbergen	£14.99
Switzerland Without a Car	£14.99
Tallinn	£6.99
Transylvania	£14.99
Ukraine	£14.99
Vilnius	£6.99
Zagreb	£6.99

Middle East, Asia and Australasia

China: Yunnan Province	£13.99
Great Wall of China	£13.99
Iran	£14.99
Iraq: Then & Now	£15.99
Israel	£15.99
Kazakhstan	£15.99
Kyrgyzstan	£15.99
Maldives	£15.99
Mongolia	£16.99
North Korea	£14.99
Oman	£13.99
Shangri-La: A Travel Guide to the Himalayan Dream	£14.99
Sri Lanka	£15.99
Syria	£14.99
Tibet	£13.99
Turkmenistan	£14.99
Yemen	£14.99

The Americas and the Caribbean

Amazon, The	£14.99
Argentina	£15.99
Bolivia	£14.99
Cayman Islands	£14.99
Chile	£16.95
Colombia	£16.99
Costa Rica	£13.99
Dominica	£14.99
Falkland Islands	£13.95
Grenada, Carriacou & Petite Martinique	£14.99
Guyana	£14.99
Panama	£13.95
Peru & Bolivia: The Bradt Trekking Guide	£12.95
St Helena	£14.99
Turks & Caicos Islands	£14.99
USA by Rail	£14.99

Wildlife

100 Animals to See Before They Die	£16.99
Antarctica: Guide to the Wildlife	£15.99
Arctic: Guide to the Wildlife	£15.99
Central & Eastern European Wildlife	£15.99
Chinese Wildlife	£16.99
East African Wildlife	£19.99
Galápagos Wildlife	£15.99
Madagascar Wildlife	£16.99
New Zealand Wildlife	£14.99
North Atlantic Wildlife	£16.99
Peruvian Wildlife	£15.99
Southern African Wildlife	£18.95
Sri Lankan Wildlife	£15.99
Wildlife and Conservation Volunteering: The Complete Guide	£13.99

Eccentric Guides

Eccentric Australia	£12.99
Eccentric Britain	£13.99
Eccentric California	£13.99
Eccentric Cambridge	£6.99
Eccentric Edinburgh	£5.95
Eccentric France	£12.95
Eccentric London	£13.99

Others

Your Child Abroad: A Travel Health Guide	£10.95
Something Different for the Weekend	£9.99
Britain from the Rails	£17.99

NOTES

NOTES

NOTES

NOTES

NOTES

NOTES

Index

Page numbers in **bold** indicate major entries; those in *italic* indicate maps